Industrial Internet of Things and Cyber-Physical Systems:

Transforming the Conventional to Digital

Pardeep Kumar
Quaid-e-Awam University of Engineering, Science, and Technology, Pakistan

Vasaki Ponnusamy
Universiti Tunku Abdul Rahman, Malaysia

Vishal Jain
Bharati Vidyapeeth's Institute of Computer Applications and Management (BVICAM), India

A volume in the Advances in Computer and
Electrical Engineering (ACEE) Book Series

Published in the United States of America by
    IGI Global
    Engineering Science Reference (an imprint of IGI Global)
    701 E. Chocolate Avenue
    Hershey PA, USA 17033
    Tel: 717-533-8845
    Fax: 717-533-8661
    E-mail: cust@igi-global.com
    Web site: http://www.igi-global.com

Library of Congress Cataloging-in-Publication Data

Names: Kumar, Pardeep, 1977- editor. | Ponnusamy, Vasaki, 1974- editor. |
  Jain, Vishal, 1983- editor.
Title: Industrial internet of things and cyber-physical systems :
  transforming the conventional to digital / Pardeep Kumar, Vasaki
  Ponnusamy, and Vishal Jain, editors.
Description: Hershey, PA : Engineering Science Reference, an imprint of IGI
  Global, 2020. | Includes bibliographical references and index. |
  Summary: "This book explores recent advances in the development,
  implementation, and business impact of IoT technologies on sustainable
  societal development and improved life quality"-- Provided by publisher.

Identifiers: LCCN 2019046118 (print) | LCCN 2019046119 (ebook) | ISBN
  9781799828037 (hardcover) | ISBN 9781799828044 (paperback) | ISBN
  9781799828051 (ebook)
Subjects: LCSH: Internet of things--Industrial applications. | Cooperating
  objects (Computer systems)
Classification: LCC TK5105.8857 .I48 2020 (print) | LCC TK5105.8857
  (ebook) | DDC 004.67/8--dc23
LC record available at https://lccn.loc.gov/2019046118
LC ebook record available at https://lccn.loc.gov/2019046119

This book is published in the IGI Global book series Advances in Computer and Electrical Engineering (ACEE) (ISSN: 2327-039X; eISSN: 2327-0403)

British Cataloguing in Publication Data
A Cataloguing in Publication record for this book is available from the British Library.

All work contributed to this book is new, previously-unpublished material. The views expressed in this book are those of the authors, but not necessarily of the publisher.

For electronic access to this publication, please contact: eresources@igi-global.com.

Advances in Computer and Electrical Engineering (ACEE) Book Series

Srikanta Patnaik
SOA University, India

ISSN:2327-039X
EISSN:2327-0403

MISSION

The fields of computer engineering and electrical engineering encompass a broad range of interdisciplinary topics allowing for expansive research developments across multiple fields. Research in these areas continues to develop and become increasingly important as computer and electrical systems have become an integral part of everyday life.

The **Advances in Computer and Electrical Engineering (ACEE) Book Series** aims to publish research on diverse topics pertaining to computer engineering and electrical engineering. **ACEE** encourages scholarly discourse on the latest applications, tools, and methodologies being implemented in the field for the design and development of computer and electrical systems.

COVERAGE

- Applied Electromagnetics
- Programming
- Algorithms
- Circuit Analysis
- Computer Architecture
- Optical Electronics
- Analog Electronics
- VLSI Fabrication
- Microprocessor Design
- Electrical Power Conversion

IGI Global is currently accepting manuscripts for publication within this series. To submit a proposal for a volume in this series, please contact our Acquisition Editors at Acquisitions@igi-global.com or visit: http://www.igi-global.com/publish/.

Titles in this Series

For a list of additional titles in this series, please visit:
http://www.igi-global.com/book-series/advances-computer-electrical-engineering/73675

Computational Methodologies for Electrical and Electronics Engineers
Rajiv Singh (G.B. Pant University of Agriculture, India) and Ashutosh Kumar Singh (Indian Institute of Information Technology Allahabad, India)
Engineering Science Reference • © 2020 • 300pp • H/C (ISBN: 9781799833277) • US $225.00

Research Advancements in Smart Technology, Optimization, and Renewable Energy
Pandian Vasant (Universiti Teknologi PETRONAS, Malaysia) Gerhard Weber (Poznan University of Technology, Poland) and Wonsiri Punurai (Mahidol University, Thailand)
Engineering Science Reference • © 2020 • 330pp • H/C (ISBN: 9781799839705) • US $225.00

Machine Learning and Deep Learning in Real-Time Applications
Mehul Mahrishi (Swami Keshvanand Institute of Technology, India) Kamal Kant Hiran (Aalborg University, Denmark) Gaurav Meena (Central University of Rajasthan, India) and Paawan Sharma (Pandit Deendayal Petroleum University, India)
Engineering Science Reference • © 2020 • 300pp • H/C (ISBN: 9781799830955) • US $245.00

Advanced Applications of Fractional Differential Operators to Science and Technology
Ahmed Ezzat Matouk (Majmaah University, Saudi Arabia)
Engineering Science Reference • © 2020 • 401pp • H/C (ISBN: 9781799831228) • US $245.00

MatConvNet Deep Learning and iOS Mobile App Design for Pattern Recognition Emerging Research and Opportunities
Jiann-Ming Wu (National Dong Hwa University, Taiwan) and Chao-Yuan Tien (National Dong Hwa University, Taiwan)
Engineering Science Reference • © 2020 • 181pp • H/C (ISBN: 9781799815549) • US $175.00

Handbook of Research on Engineering Innovations and Technology Management in Organizations
Loveleen Gaur (Amity University, India) Arun Solanki (Gautam Buddha University, India) Vishal Jain (Bharati Vidyapeeth's Institute of Computer Applications and Management (BVICAM), New Delhi, India) and Deepak Khazanchi (University of Nebraska at Omaha, USA)
Engineering Science Reference • © 2020 • 500pp • H/C (ISBN: 9781799827726) • US $325.00

Open Source Software for Statistical Analysis of Big Data Emerging Research and Opportunities
Richard S. Segall (Arkansas State University, USA) and Gao Niu (Bryant University, USA)
Engineering Science Reference • © 2020 • 237pp • H/C (ISBN: 9781799827689) • US $225.00

701 East Chocolate Avenue, Hershey, PA 17033, USA
Tel: 717-533-8845 x100 • Fax: 717-533-8661
E-Mail: cust@igi-global.com • www.igi-global.com

The editors dedicate this book to their families.

Editorial Advisory Board

Table of Contents

Detailed Table of Contents

Chapter 1

Vasaki Ponnusamy, Universiti Tunku Abdul Rahman, Malaysia
Naveena Devi Regunathan, Universiti Tunku Abdul Rahman, Malaysia
Pardeep Kumar, Quaid-e-Awam University of Engineering, Science, and Technology,
*   Pakistan*
Robithoh Annur, Universiti Tunku Abdul Rahman, Malaysia
Khalid Rafique, AJK Information Technology Board, Pakistan

The internet usage for commercial and public services has significantly increased over these decades to where security of information is becoming a more important issue to society. At the same time, the number of network attacks in IoT is increasing. These include distributed denial of service (DDOS) attack, phishing, trojan, and others that will cause the network information to not be secure. With the revolution in Industry 4.0 and IoT being the main asset in the Fourth Industrial Revolution, many companies spend thousands or millions to protect their networks and servers. Unfortunately, the success rate to prevent network attack is still not welcoming. The attacks on physical layers, such as jamming, node tampering; link layer, such as collision, unfairness, battery exhaustion; network layer, such as spoofing, hello flood, Sybil attack, wormhole, DOS, DDOS; transport layer, such as flooding, de-synchronization; application layer, such as flooding, are alarming. This chapter reviews attacks and countermeasures.

Chapter 2

Sandeep Mathur, Amity Insitute of Information Technology, Amity University, Noida, India
Ankita Arora, Amity Insitute of Information Technology, Amity University, Noida, India

The internet of things (IoT) is described as the arrangement of physical articles—contraptions, automobiles, structures, and various things—fixed with equipment, programming, devices, and framework accessibility that engages these things to accumulate and exchange data. Practically paying little mind to industry, IoT is anticipated to be the absolute most significant factor affecting basic business rationale in the coming decades. PKI is the best alternative for arrangement suppliers to secure information and associated gadgets. When effectively executed, PKI can fabricate and bolster security and trust in IoT biological systems. PKI's job in IoT gives solid personality validation and makes the establishment of trust that frameworks, gadgets, applications, and clients need to securely connect and trade delicate information. PKI and the brought forth trust networks spread the basic security necessities IoT tasks need, giving the encryption, confirmation, and information respectability that make the establishment of trust. This chapter explores PKI-based security architecture.

Chapter 3

Muhammad Suleman Memon, University of Sindh Jamshoro, Dadu Campus, Pakistan
Pardeep Kumar, Quaid-e-Awam University of Engineering, Science, and Technology, Pakistan
Azeem Ayaz Mirani, Department of Information Technology, Shaheed Benazir Bhutto University, Pakistan
Mumtaz Qabulio, Institute of Information and Communication Technology, University of Sindh, Jamshoro, Pakistan
Irum Naz Sodhar, Department of Information Technology, Shaheed Benazir Bhutto University, Pakistan

The agriculture sector plays a big part in the overall economy of any country. The population of the world is increasing day by day, which is also increasing the overall demand of the food. Due to various diseases and nature of the soil, it is difficult to meet the overall demand of the food. The agronomists and farmers also face many problems in the agriculture sector such as disease identification, knowing nature of the soil, pesticide management, etc. The old methods of managing crop do not help in an effective way in meeting the increasing demand for food. The modern methods such IOT, machine, deep learning, and image processing help to identify the crop health and to predict crop yield. This chapter generally discusses various state-of-the-art technologies and methods for predicting crop yield and disease identification.

Chapter 4

Rejo Rajan Mathew, Mukesh Patel School of Technology, Management, and Engineering, NMIMS University, India
Vikram Kulkarni, Mukesh Patel School of Technology, Management, and Engineering, NMIMS University, India

Green building (GB) is a game changer as the world is moving towards conserving its resources. Green building management systems available nowadays are too expensive and cannot cater to small or medium-sized buildings. Internet of things-based systems use simple, low-cost sensors, signal processing, and high-level learning methods. Studies on building occupancy and human activities help improve design and push the energy conservation levels. With huge amounts of data and improved learning systems, the impetus is to capture the information and use it well to improve design and justify the green building concept. Cloud-based architecture helps to monitor, capture, and process the data, which acts as input to intelligent learning systems, which in turn help to improve the design and performance of current green building management systems. This chapter discusses role of cloud-based internet of things architecture in improving design and performance of current building management systems.

Chapter 5

Aun Yichiet, Universiti Tunku Abdul Rahman, Malaysia

Jasmina Khaw Yen Min, Universiti Tunku Abdul Rahman, Malaysia

Gan Ming Lee, Universiti Tunku Abdul Rahman, Malaysia

One of the core features of IoT is global device discovery, allowing people to control and manage their connected devices anywhere across the internet. In pervasive IoT, device management becomes seamless and automated using AI for device pairing, content discovery, actions signaling, and command scheduling based on contextual information in a self-managed device paradigm. This chapter presents a novel handoff technique for smart speakers to ensure playback continuity when the users move around in a smart space consisting of multiple discoverable speakers. Current implementations include Spotify Connect, which is service specific, thus lacking in discovery robustness. The proposed handoff discovers at the device level instead of service level to improve device visibility and interoperability through a self-learning topology discovery (SLTD) method. For timely handoff, a rapid preemptive handoff method (RPF) is designed to optimize the TCP handshake mechanism and a content pre-caching technique is used to minimize playback gaps during the soft handoff.

Chapter 6
Khuda Bux Jalbani, Riphah Institute of Systems Engineering, Riphah International
    University, Islamabad, Pakistan

Akhtar Hussain Jalbani, Department of Information Technology, Quaid-e-Awam University
    of Engineering, Science, and Technology, Pakistan

Saima Siraj Soomro, Department of Information Technology, Quaid-e-Awam University of
    Engineering, Science, and Technology, Pakistan

The usage of the internet of things (IoT) devices is growing for the ease of life. From smart homes to smart cars, from smart transportation to smart cities, from smart hospitals to smart highways, these IoT devices send and receive highly sensitive data regarding the privacy of users or other information regarding the movement of users from one location to another location. The timing traces users when present at home and out of the home. But how does one secure this information from the attacker? There is a need for IoT devices security. As there are three layers of IoT devices—the application layer, network layer, and perception layer—three layers to be secure. IoT devices are heterogeneous and constrain energy consumption. The proposed solution in this chapter is three-way authentication of IoT devices by generating tokens from the device serial number and from the few configuration devices at the network layer. For high availability of IoT device services, the protection against distributed denial of service attack is implemented at the network layer.

Chapter 7
Vasaki Ponnusamy, Universiti Tunku Abdul Rahman, Malaysia

Said Bakhshad, Universiti Tunku Abdul Rahman, Malaysia

Bobby Sharma, Don Bosco University, Assam, Malaysia

Robithoh Annur, Universiti Tunku Abdul Rahman, Malaysia

Teh Boon Seong, Universiti Tunku Abdul Rahman, Malaysia

An intrusion detection system (IDS) works as an alarm mechanism for computer systems. It detects any malicious activity that happened to the computer system and it alerts an alarm message to notify the user there is malicious activity. There are IDS that are able to take action when malicious or anomalous networks are detected, which include suspending the traffic sent from suspicious IP addresses. The problem statement for this project is to find out the most accurate machine learning algorithm and the types of IDS with different placement strategies. When it comes to the deployment of a wireless network, IDS is not as easy a task as deploying a traditional network IDS. There are many unexpected complexities of the problem of reliable intrusion detection in a wireless network. The motivation of this research is to find the most suitable classification techniques that are able to increase the accuracy of an IDS. Machine learning is useful for the upcoming trend; it provides better accuracy in the detection of malicious traffic.

Chapter 8

    Ali Raza, Quaid-e-Awam University of Engineering, Science, and Technology, Pakistan
    Pardeep Kumar, Quaid-e-Awam University of Engineering, Science, and Technology, Pakistan
    Adnan Ahmed, Quaid-e-Awam University of Engineering, Science, and Technology, Pakistan
    Umair Ali Khan, Quaid-e-Awam University of Engineering, Science, and Technology, Pakistan

Wireless body area networks (WBANs) are one of the applications of IoT that deal with the remote transmission of patient data. The health-related data is of highly sensitive nature. The loss of critical data packets might lead a patient to an embarrassing position. Therefore, WBANs require a secure and efficient data transmission mechanism. However, wireless transmission traditionally remains vulnerable to many security attacks such as node misbehavior attack. Routing protocols play a key role in the extended network lifetime. However, efficient data routing in WBAN is a challenging task. In addition, sensor nodes due to wireless communication produce electromagnetic radiation that is absorbed by the human body and results in temperature rise. Therefore, routing protocols along with security issues must consider temperature rise to ensure safe wireless transmission. In this chapter, the authors present a comprehensive review of most relevant security and privacy concerns and relevant routing protocols addressing the aforementioned routing issues.

Chapter 9

    Saima Sultana, Hamdard University, Pakistan
    Shamim Akhtar, Majmaah University, Saudi Arabia
    Sadia Nazim, Hamdard University, Pakistan
    Pardeep Kumar, Quaid-e-Awam University of Engineering, Science, and Technology, Pakistan
    Manzoor Ahmed Hashmani, University Technology PETRONAS, Malaysia
    Syed Sajjad Hussain Rizvi, Hamdard University, Pakistan

During the recent decade, wireless body area network (WBAN) was developed and prioritized. This gives reliability, energy efficiency, and guaranteed results. Moreover, internet of medical things (IoMT) also enhances the significance of WBAN networks. To achieve high throughput, performance, and efficiency, WBAN deserves a new protocol definition as compared to general wireless sensor network along with a more enhanced framework. The standard 802.15.6 with PHY and MAC layers follow the standardization of WBAN. The wireless nature of the network and various varieties of sensors in the presence of IoMT made it possible to develop new, effective, innovative, and demand-driven solutions for health improvement and quality of service. In the recent literature, the researchers have proposed an IoMT-based secure framework for WBAN. In this chapter, an in-depth and comprehensive depiction of the security issues of IoMT-based framework of the wireless network is highlighted that incorporates security measures in different levels of the WBAN network.

Chapter 10

Shahzadi Tayyaba, Department of Computer Engineering, University of Lahore, Pakistan
Salman Ayub Khan, Department of Computer Engineering, University of Lahore, Pakistan
Muhammad Tariq, Superior University, Lahore, Pakistan
Muhammad Waseem Ashraf, Department of Physics (Electronics), GC University, Lahore, Pakistan

Information security is the most critical component of the information system. It is also a challenge of the organizations to build a secure network. Every organization that developed its organizational network has faced security attacks, security risks, and vulnerabilities. Internet of things (IoT) is based on smart devices that connect with each other to formulate a complex network. Therefore, in order to build a secure traditional network and IoT network, understanding the basics of the network layers, network security, and different types of network attacks is essential for network security beginners who are interested in working in the field of information security. In this chapter, the authors reviewed the essential and most important concepts of information security, IoT, and explained these topics in an easy-to-understand way. Furthermore, the chapter discussed the basic level of information security challenges to familiarize the undergraduates and postgraduate students and IoT information security practitioners about it.

Chapter 11

Mumtaz Qabulio, Institute of Information and Communication Technology, University of Sindh, Jamshoro, Pakistan
Yasir Arfat Malkani, Institute of Mathematics and Computer Science, University of Sindh, Jamshoro, Pakistan
Muhammad S. Memon, Department of Information Technology, University of Sindh, Dadu Campus, Pakistan
Ayaz Keerio, Institute of Mathematics and Computer Science, University of Sindh, Jamshoro, Pakistan

Wireless sensor networks (WSNs) are comprised of large collections of small devices having low operating power, low memory space, and limited processing capabilities referred to as sensor nodes. The nodes in WSNs are capable of sensing, recording, and monitoring environmental conditions. Nowadays, a variety of WSNs applications can be found in many areas such as in healthcare, agriculture, industries, military, homes, offices, hospitals, smart transportation, and smart buildings. Though WSNs offer many useful applications, they suffer from many deployment issues. The security issue is one of them. The security of WSNs is considerable because of the use of unguided medium and their deployment in harsh, physically unprotected, and unattended environments. This chapter aims to discuss various security objectives and security attacks on WSNs and summarizes the discussed attacks according to their categories. The chapter also discusses different security protocols presented to prevent, detect, and recover the WSNs from various security attacks.

Chapter 12

An enterprise has a challenge in keeping pace with the quickly evolving technology. The biggest challenge comes in terms of legacy application migration to technologies like cloud. Legacy application migration should be well thought out at the very start (i.e., pre-migration and supported by migration framework). In this chapter, the author proposes a legacy application migration framework with a focus on pre-migration area. A robust technical and business analysis of existing/legacy applications, based on the enterprise's focus parameters, during pre-migration sets the migration path for subsequent area of framework. The proposed pre-migration mathematical assessment helps an enterprise to understand a legacy application's current state and also helps in unearthing the information with respect to candidate application and helps in taking well-informed decisions like GO or NO-GO w.r.t legacy application migration. Considering application migration a journey, it is important that it reaches its destination, so pre-migration is an important area of the migration journey.

Chapter 13

This chapter discusses the relevant effects of li-fi technology in data transfer. The chapter should enable the reader to identify and relate to evolving data transmission technology. The chapter gives details of the basic components of li-fi. This chapter also discusses data transmission through light. The chapter should enable the reader to identify the difference between VLC and li-fi communication. The chapter also discusses the important properties, misconceptions, and limitations of this emerging technique. Furthermore, how various modulation techniques used in li-fi and its advantages over wi-fi technology has been mentioned in this chapter. The authors elucidate the major challenges and application areas of li-fi.

Chapter 14

Due to the growing volume of multimedia data generated these days, it has become extremely difficult to manually analyze the data and extract useful information from it. Especially the analysis of videos pertaining to different fields such as surveillance, videos, social media, education, etc. cannot be done efficiently by manual methods. This requires automatic analysis algorithms that can intelligently analyze videos and derive salient information from them. This information can be useful in a number of tasks such as video segmentation, incident detection, anomaly detection, query-based video retrieval, and content censorship. This chapter provides a detailed review of the techniques proposed for video analysis to provide a compact set of video tags. This chapter considers it a joint tag-segmentation problem and critically analyzes the relevant literature to highlight their respective pros and cons. At the end, potential research areas in this domain and suggestions for improvement are discussed.

Chapter 15

Renu Jangra, Kurukshetra University, India
Ramesh Kait, Kurukshetra University, India
Sarvesh Kumar, Poornima University, Jaipur, India

Wireless sensor networks (WSN) offer great expertise that club the sensing, execution, communication, and network technology along with microelectronics and micro-mechanical devices together to study the environment. It is a new concept and a consequence of few steps in the communication field. If the original prospect of this new network works according to the planned concept, it will recover the examining and control systems used these days in the environment for consumer, medical, industries, and military sectors. The wireless technology gives the advantage of decrease in cost that cabling operation has in recent systems and also makes it possible to perform measurements in unreachable places. Many applications can work on the concept of this technology.

Chapter 16

Soobia Saeed, Department of Software Engineering, Universiti Teknologi Malaysia,
*   Malaysia*
N. Z. Jhanjhi, School of Computing and IT (SoCIT), Taylor's University, Malaysia
Mehmood Naqvi, Faculty of Electrical and Computer Engineering Technology, Mohawk
*   College of Applied Arts and Technology, Canada*
Vasaki Ponnusamy, Universiti Tunku Abdul Rahman, Malaysia
Mamoona Humayun, College of Computer and Information Sciences, Jouf University, Saudi
*   Arabia*

Weather forecasting is a significant meteorological task and has arisen in the last century from a rational and revolutionary point of view among the most difficult problems. The authors are researching the use of information mining techniques in this survey to measure maximum temperature, precipitation, dissipation, and wind speed. This was done using vector help profiles, decision tree, and weather data obtained in Pakistan in 2015 and 2019. For the planning of workbook accounts, an information system for meteorological information was used. The presentations of these calculations considered using standard implementing steps as well as the estimate that gave the best results for generating disposal rules for intermediate environment variables. Likewise, a prophetic network model for the climate outlook program, contradictory results, and true climate information for the projected periods have been created. The results show that with sufficient information on cases, data mining strategies can be used to estimate the climate and environmental change that it focuses on.

Chapter 17

Sindhu P. Menon, Jain College of Engineering and Technology, India

In the last couple of years, artificial neural networks have gained considerable momentum. Their results could be enhanced if the number of layers could be made deeper. Of late, a lot of data has been generated, which has led to big data. This comes along with many challenges like quality, which is one of the most important ones. Deep learning models can improve the quality of data. In this chapter, an attempt has been made to review deep supervised and deep unsupervised learning algorithms and the various activation functions used. Challenges in deep learning have also been discussed.

Chapter 18
    Soobia Saeed, Department of Software Engineering, Universiti Teknologi Malaysia,
       Malaysia
    N. Z. Jhanjhi, Taylor's University, Malaysia
    Mehmood Naqvi, Faculty of Electrical and Computer Engineering Technology, Mohawk
       College of Applied Arts and Technology, Canada
    Mamoona Humayun, College of Computer and Information Sciences, Jouf University, Saudi
       Arabia
    Vasaki Ponnusamy, Universiti Tunku Abdul Rahman, Malaysia

Human beings have a knack for errors. Counter-effective actions rendered to specify and rectify such errors in a minimum period of time are required when effectiveness and swift advancement depends on the capability of acknowledging the faults and errors and repair quickly. The software as audit module application in IT complaint is in review in this commentary as is another significant instrument created in the field of data analysis that digs deep into quickly and successfully assessing the imprecisions or grievances identified by the users in a certain company. The target of this study is to evaluate the statistical significance in relationship between client reporting attitude and client reliability and to evaluate the impact of strong responsiveness on client reliability, to measure the statistically noteworthy effect of client grievance conduct on service quality, and to test the impact of service quality on client dedication.

Foreword

The IoT is an enormous network of connected devices, objects and machines having built-in sensing, computing and communicating facilities. It integrates data collected from those devices to the existing internet and applies intelligence and analytics to make most of that data. Thus IoT generates an opportunity for effective, efficient and contextualized interactions among objects resulting in improved quality production and services whilst saving us time, money and efforts. IoT possesses great potential to offer significant changes for industrial and business processes, medical, surveillance, safety, education, transport, environment, governance and many other domains.

This book addresses the major aspects of IoT especially relevant to industry revolution and cyber physical systems, which is indeed a need of time. The authors of the different chapters in this book present diversified applications and implementations of IoT in these domains.

Summarizing, the ultimate objective of this volume is to provide academic, industrial and local government communities with recent advances in development and implementation of IoT based cyber-physical systems and Industry 4.0 processes, which are destined to effectively cope up with the demand of ever increasing population and future economies.

Bhawani S. Chowdhry
Mehran University of Engineering and Technology, Jamshoro, Pakistan

Preface

The term 'Internet of Things (IoT)' was first coined by Kevin Ashton in 1999, however it is being felt and experienced today more than ever since. Researchers, academicians, industrialists, practitioners, government agencies and other stakeholders around the world are all working towards methods to interconnect different physical objects and devices, as per the vision of IoT, so that our world can effectively and efficiently be transferred to the digital one. This also makes IoT an integral part of the 'future Internet' that aims at multiplying the number of connected hosts, users and services of the current Internet. Subsequently, IoT is bound to address a variety of applications, services, systems, protocols, architectures and technologies to achieve its main goal.

With the hype in Industry 4.0 and realization of Cyber-Physical Systems (CPS), IoT is paving the way for an entire industrial transformation from conventional business processes to the digital one. With the help of artificial intelligence, machine learning and big data analytics, IoT is helping in creating a "smart and automated industry" where machines, processes and humans communicate with each other in order to coordinate and monitor progress right from manufacturing to ordering to delivery to maintenance and so on. This results into the rapid designing, more and cheap manufacturing and effective customization of products as per the consumer preferences in order to seamlessly satisfy the steep supply-demand requirements of ever-growing world population.

This book is an attempt to collect and publish innovative ideas, emerging trends, implementation experience and use-cases pertaining to different enabling technologies for IoT in general and their usage in industry 4.0 in particular for the purpose of serving the mankind and societies in a better way. Hence, this volume presents recent advances in development, implementation and business impact of IoT technologies on the sustainable societal development and improved life quality.

Overall, this book is a collection of ideas and experience mainly focusing on the digital transformation approaches towards the realization of IoT based cyber-physical systems and Industry 4.0, which is destined to revolutionize the economies and businesses of today's and tomorrow's world.

THE ORGANIZATION OF THE BOOK

Chapter 1: A Review of Attacks and Countermeasures in Internet of Things and Cyber Physical Systems

In this modern era, the Internet usage for commercial and public services have significantly increased over these decades where security of information is becoming more important issues to the society. At the same time, number of network attack in IoT is increasing over the years such as Distributed Denial of Service (DDOS) attack, Phishing, Trojan and other which will cause the network information not secure. With the revolution in Industry 4.0 and IoT being the main asset in Fourth Industrial Revolution, many companies spend thousands or millions of money to protect their network and server. But unfortunately, the success rate to prevent network attack is still not welcoming. The attacks on physical layer such as jamming, node tampering, link layer such as collision, unfairness, battery exhaustion, network layer such as spoofing, hello flood, Sybil attack, wormhole, DOS, DDOS transport layer such as flooding, de-synchronization, application layer such as flooding are alarming.

Chapter 2: Deep Learning and IOT – The Enabling Technologies Towards Smart Farming

Agriculture sector plays a big part in overall economy of any country. The population of the world is increasing day by day which is also increasing the overall demand of the food. Due to various diseases, and nature of the soil, it is difficult to meet the overall demand of the food. The agronomists, farmers also face many problems in agriculture sector such as disease identification, knowing nature of the soil, pesticide management etc. The old methods of managing crop do not help in effective way to meet the increasing demand of the food. The modern methods such IOT, Machine, Deep Learning and Image Processing helps to identify the crop health, to predict crop yield. This chapter generally discusses various state-of-the art technologies for predicting crop yield and disease identification.

Chapter 3: Cloud-Based IoT Architecture for Green Buildings

Green Building (GB) concept is a game changer as the world is moving towards conserving its resources. Green building management systems available nowadays are too expensive and cannot cater to small or medium sized buildings. Internet of Things based systems use simple low cost sensors, signal processing and high level learning methods. Studies on building occupancy, human activities help improve design and pushes the energy conservation levels far more. With huge amounts of data and improved learning systems the impetus is to capture the information and use it well to improve design and justify green building concept. Cloud based Architecture helps to monitor, capture and process the data which acts as input to intelligent learning systems which in turn helps to improve design and performance of current green building management systems. This chapter discusses role of Cloud Based Internet of Things Architecture in improving design and performance of current building management systems.

Chapter 4: Pervasive Internet of Things (IoT) for Smart Speakers Discovery and Playback Continuity

One of the core features of IoT is global device discovery; allowing people to control and manage their connected devices anywhere across the Internet. In pervasive IoT, device management becomes seamless and automated using A.I. for device pairing, content discovery, actions signalling and command scheduling based on contextual information in a self-managed devices paradigm. This chapter presents a novel Handoff Technique for Smart Speakers to ensure playback continuity when the users move around in a smart space consisting of multiple discoverable speakers. Current implementations like Spotify Connect is service specific, thus lacking in discovery robustness. The proposed handoff discover at the device level instead of service level to improve device visibility and interoperability through a self-learning topology discovery (SLTD) method. For timely handoff, a rapid preemptive handoff method (RPF) is designed to optimize the TCP handshake mechanism and a content pre-caching technique is used to minimize playback gaps during the soft handoff.

Chapter 5: IoT Security – To Secure IoT Devices With Two-Factor Authentication by Using a Secure Protocol

As the usage of the Internet of Things (IoT) devices growing for the ease of life. From smart homes to smart cars, from smart transportation to smart cities, from smart hospitals to smart highways. These IoT devices send and receive highly sensitive data regarding the privacy of users or other information regarding the movement of users from one location to another location. The timing traces of user when is present at home and out of the home. How to secure this information from the attacker there is a need for IoT devices security? As there are three layers of IoT devices the application layer, network layer, and perception layer these all three layers need to be secure. The IoT devices are heterogeneous and constrain of energy consumption. The proposed solution in this chapter is three-way authentication of IoT devices by generating tokens from the device serial number and from the few numbers from configuration device at the network layer. For high availability of IoT device services the protection against Distributed Denial of Service attack is implemented at the network layer. proposed by the body of knowledge. The paper then presents how some countries have adopted this secured online voting systems and giving an avenue to secured digital electoral governance.

Chapter 6: Internet of Things (IoT) and PKI-Based Security Architecture

The Internet of Things (IoT), is described as the arrangement of physical articles—contraptions, automobiles, structures and various things—fixed with equipment, programming, devices, and framework accessibility that engages these things to accumulate and exchange data. Practically paying little mind to industry, IoT is anticipated to be the absolute most significant factor affecting basic business rationale in the coming decades.PKI is the best alternative for arrangement suppliers to secure information and associated gadgets. When effectively executed, PKI can fabricate and bolster security and trust in IoT biological systems. PKI's job in IoT gives solid personality validation and makes the establishment of trust that frameworks, gadgets, applications, and clients need to securely connect and trade delicate information. PKI and the brought forth trust networks spread the basic security necessities IoT tasks need, giving the encryption, confirmation, and information respectability that make the establishment of trust.

Chapter 7: A Survey on Intrusion Detection in Wired and Wireless Network for Future IoT Deployment

Intrusion detection system (IDS) works as an alarm mechanism for computer system. it detects any malicious activity happened to the computer system and it alerts an alarm message to notify user there are malicious activity. There are IDS that are able to take action when malicious or anomalous network was detected, which include suspend the traffic sent from suspicious IP address. The problem statement for this project is to find out the most accurate machine learning algorithm and the types of IDS with different placement strategy. When it comes to the deployment of a wireless network IDS is not an easy task as deploying a traditional network IDS. There are many unexpected complexity of the problem of reliable intrusion detection in a wireless network. The motivation of this research is to find out the most suitable classification technique that are able to increase the accuracy of an IDS. Machine learning is useful for the upcoming trend; it provides a better accuracy in detection malicious traffic.

Chapter 8: Comprehensive Survey of Routing Protocols for Wireless Body Area Networks (WBANs)

Wireless Body Area Networks (WBANs) is one of the applications of IoT that deals with the remote transmission of patient data. The health-related data is of highly sensitive nature, the loss of critical data packets might lead a patient to an embarrassing position. Therefore, WBANs require a secure and efficient data transmission mechanism. However, wireless transmission traditionally remains vulnerable to many security attacks such as node misbehavior attack. Routing protocols play a key role in the extended network lifetime. However, efficient data routing in WBAN is a challenging task. In addition, sensor nodes due to wireless communication produce electromagnetic radiations which are absorbed by the human body and results in temperature rise. Therefore, routing protocols along with security issues must consider temperature rise to ensure safe wireless transmission. We in this chapter, present a comprehensive review of most relevant security and privacy concerns and relevant routing protocols addressing the aforementioned routing issues.

Chapter 9: A Critical Study on Internet of Medical Things for Secure WBAN

During the recent decade, WBAN wireless body area network developed and prioritized. This givens, reliability, energy efficiency and guaranteed result. Moreover, IoMT Internet of Medical Things also enhances the significance of WBAN networks. To achieve high throughput, performance and efficiency WBAN deserves a new protocol definition as compared to general Wireless Sensor Network along with a more enhanced framework. The standard 802.15.6 with PHY and MAC layers follow the standardization of WBAN. The wireless nature of the network and various numerous varieties of sensors in the presence of IoMT made it possible to develop various new, effective, innovative and demand-driven solutions for health improvement and quality of service. In the recent literature the researchers have proposed an IoMT based secure framework for WBAN. In this paper a n in-depth and comprehensive depiction of the security issues of IoMT based framework of the wireless network is highlighted which incorporates security measures in different levels of the WBAN network

Chapter 10: Network Security and Internet of Things

Information Security is the most critical component of the information system and also a challenge of the organizations to build a secure network. Every organization that developed its organizational network faced security attacks, has security risks and vulnerabilities. Internet of Things (IoT) is based on smart devices that connected with each other to formulate a complex network. Therefore, in order to build a secure traditional network and IoT network, understanding with the basics of the network layers, network security, and different types of network attacks is essential for network security beginners who are interested to work in the field of information security. In this chapter, the authors reviewed the essential and most important concepts of information security, IoT, and explained these topics in an easy way to understand manners. Furthermore, the book chapter discussed the basic level of information security challenges to familiarize the undergraduates and postgraduate students about it as well as an IoT information security practitioner.

Chapter 11: Security of Wireless Sensor Networks – The Current Trends and Issues

The Wireless Sensor Networks (WSNs) are comprised of large collection of small devices having, low operating power, low memory space and limited processing capabilities referred sensor nodes. The Nodes in WSNs are capable of sensing, recording and monitoring environmental conditions. Nowadays, variety of WSNs applications can be found in many areas such as in health care, agriculture, industries, military homes, offices, hospitals, smart transportation, and smart buildings. Though WSNs offers many useful applications, but it suffers from many deployment issues; Security issue is one of them. The security of WSNs is considerable because of the use of unguided medium and their deployment in harsh, physically unprotected and unattended environments. This chapter aims to discuss various security objectives and security attacks on WSNs and summarizes the discussed attacks according to their categories. The chapter also discusses different security protocols presented to prevent, detect, and recover the WSNs from various security attacks.

Chapter 12: A Process Framework to Migrate Legacy Application to Cloud – LAMP2C

An enterprise has challenge in keeping pace with the fast evolving technology. Biggest challenge come in term of legacy application migration to technology like cloud. Legacy application migration should be a well thought at the very start i.e. pre-migration and supported by migration framework. In this chapter author proposes a legacy application migration framework with a focus on pre-migration area. A robust technical and business analyses of existing/legacy application, based on enterprise's focus parameters, during pre-migration area sets the migration path for subsequent area of framework. Proposed pre-migration mathematical assessment helps an enterprise to understand legacy application's current state, also helps in unearthing the information with respect candidate application and helps in taking well-informed decision like GO or NO-GO w.r.t legacy application migration Considering application migration a journey, it is important that it reaches its destination, so it makes pre-migration an important area of migration journey.

Chapter 13: Light Fidelity – Data Through Illumination

This chapter discusses the relevant effects of Li-Fi Technology in data transfer. The chapter should enable the reader to identify and relate to evolving data transmission technology. The chapter gives details of the basic components of Li-Fi. This chapter also discusses data transmission through light. The chapter should enable the reader to identify the difference between VLC and Li-Fi communication. The chapter also discusses the important properties, misconceptions, and limitations of this emerging technique. Furthermore, how various modulation techniques used in Li-Fi and its advantages over Wi-Fi technology has mentioned in this chapter. The authors elucidate the major challenges and application areas of Li-Fi.

Chapter 14: Semantic Analysis of Videos for Tags Prediction and Segmentation

Due to the growing volumes of multimedia data generated these days, it has become extremely difficult to manually analyze the data and extract useful information from it. Especially, the analysis of videos pertaining to different fields such as surveillance, videos, social media, education, etc cannot be done efficiently by manual methods. This requires automatic analysis algorithms which can intelligently analyze videos and derive salient information from them. This information can be useful in a number of tasks such as video segmentation, incident detection, anomaly detection, query-based video retrieval, and content censorship, etc. This chapter provides a detailed review of the techniques proposed for video analysis to provide compact set of video tags. This chapter considers it as a joint tag-segmentation problem and critically analyzes the relevant literature to highlight their respective pros and cons. At the end, potential research areas in this domain and suggestions for improvement are discussed

Chapter 15: ACO-Based Algorithms in Wireless Sensor Network

Wireless Sensor Network (WSN) offers a great expertise that clubs the sensing, execution, communication and network technology along with microelectronics and micro mechanical devices and together to study the environment. It is a new concept and a consequence of few steps in the communication field. If the original prospect of this new network works according to the planned concept, it will recover the examining and control systems used these days in the environment, for consumer, medical, industries and military sectors. The wireless technology gives the advantage of decrease in cost that cabling operation has in recent systems and also makes it possible to perform measurements in unreachable places. Many applications can work on the concept of this technology.

Chapter 16: Analysis of Climate Prediction and Climate Change in Pakistan Using Data Mining Techniques

Weather forecasting is a significant meteorological task and has arisen in the last century from a rational and revolutionary point of view among the most difficult problems. We are researching the use of information mining techniques in this survey to measure maximum temperature, precipitation, dissipation, and wind speed. This was done using Vector help profiles, Decision Tree and weather data obtained in Pakistan in 2015 and 2019. For the planning of workbook accounts, an information system for meteorological information was used. The presentations of these calculations considered using standard implementing steps, as well as the estimate that gave the best results for generating disposal rules for intermediate environment variables. Likewise, a prophetic network model for the Climate Outlook Program, contradictory results, and true climate information for the projected periods have been created. The results show that with sufficient information on cases, data mining strategies can be used to estimate the climate and environmental change that it focuses on..

Chapter 17: A Survey on Algorithms in Deep Learning

In the last couple of years, artificial neural networks have gained considerable momentum. Their results could be enhanced if the number of layers could be made deeper. Of late, a lot of data is generated which has led to term Big Data. This comes along with many challenges like quality which is one of the most important ones. Deep Learning models can improve the quality of data. In this article, an attempt has been made to review deep supervised and deep unsupervised learning algorithms and the various activation functions used. Challenges in deep learning has also been discussed.

Chapter 18: Analyzing the Performance and Efficiency of IT-Compliant Audit Module in Using Clustering Methods

Human beings have a knack for errors since it's in our mold. Counter-effective actions rendered to specify and rectify such errors in minimum period of time is the ability required to be possessed in these days when effectiveness and swift advancement immensely depends on the capability of acknowledging the faults and errors and repair quickly. The software as audit module application in IT complaint is in review in this commentary is another significant instrument created in the field of data analysis that digs deep into quickly and successfully assessing the imprecisions or grievances identified by the users in a certain company. The target of this study is to evaluate the statistical significance in relationship between client reporting attitude and client reliability and evaluate the impact of strong responsiveness on client reliability; measure the statistically noteworthy effect of client grievance conduct on service quality and to test the impact of service quality on client dedication.

Pardeep Kumar
Quaid-e-Awam University of Engineering, Science, and Technology, Pakistan

Vasaki Ponnusamy
Universiti Tunku Abdul Rahman, Malaysia

Vishal Jain
Bharati Vidyapeeth's Institute of Computer Applications and Management (BVICAM), India

Acknowledgment

We would like to express our great appreciation to all of those with whom we have had the pleasure to work during this project. The completion of this project could not have been accomplished without the support of them.

First, the editors would like to express deep and sincere gratitude to all the authors who shared their ideas, expertise and experience by submitting chapters to this book and adhered to its timeline.

Second, the editors wish to acknowledge the extra ordinary contributions of the reviewers for their valuable and constructive suggestions and recommendations to improve quality, coherence and content presentation of chapters. Most of the authors also served as referees. Their willingness to give time so generously is highly appreciated.

Finally, our heartfelt gratitude go to our family members and friends for their love, prayers, caring and sacrifices in completing this project well in time.

Pardeep Kumar
Quaid-e-Awam University of Engineering, Science, and Technology, Pakistan

Vasaki Ponnusamy
Universiti Tunku Abdul Rahman, Malaysia

Vishal Jain
Bharati Vidyapeeth's Institute of Computer Applications and Management (BVICAM), India

Chapter 1

A Review of Attacks and Countermeasures in Internet of Things and Cyber Physical Systems

Vasaki Ponnusamy
Universiti Tunku Abdul Rahman, Malaysia

Naveena Devi Regunathan
Universiti Tunku Abdul Rahman, Malaysia

Pardeep Kumar
 https://orcid.org/0000-0002-8624-9020
Quaid-e-Awam University of Engineering, Science, and Technology, Pakistan

Robithoh Annur
Universiti Tunku Abdul Rahman, Malaysia

Khalid Rafique
AJK Information Technology Board, Pakistan

ABSTRACT

The internet usage for commercial and public services has significantly increased over these decades to where security of information is becoming a more important issue to society. At the same time, the number of network attacks in IoT is increasing. These include distributed denial of service (DDOS) attack, phishing, trojan, and others that will cause the network information to not be secure. With the revolution in Industry 4.0 and IoT being the main asset in the Fourth Industrial Revolution, many companies spend thousands or millions to protect their networks and servers. Unfortunately, the success rate to prevent network attack is still not welcoming. The attacks on physical layers, such as jamming, node tampering;

DOI: 10.4018/978-1-7998-2803-7.ch001

link layer, such as collision, unfairness, battery exhaustion; network layer, such as spoofing, hello flood, Sybil attack, wormhole, DOS, DDOS; transport layer, such as flooding, de-synchronization; application layer, such as flooding, are alarming. This chapter reviews attacks and countermeasures.

INTRODUCTION

Technologies have been evolving from the day it was founded. We are currently transitioning from the Industry 3.0 to Industry 4.0 which is a whole new addition to technology. Industry 3.0 deals with computers, automation, last-mile/kilometre access and digital sales and purchase while the Industry 4.0 is solely focused on Automated Physical Systems, Smart Cities, Internet of Things(IoT), Robotics, Artificial Intelligence (AI) and Blockchain. This change defines the change in work culture around the world almost in all industries. This era is said to be a combination of a cyber-physical system, where Industry 4.0 is made possible by IoT and the Internet of Systems and also it made the smart factories into reality.

With every good thing, there is always a flaw or a problem. The same goes for Industry 4.0 as it is closely associated with cybersecurity. A good cybersecuritry governance and secured systems is needed in this case. This survey work is an extension to the previous published works (Ponnusamy. V et al. 2020) on cybersecurity governance and secured systems. The cases of the attacks are increasing rapidly day by day and it is stressing the need to strengthen cyber resilience. In those days before IoT existed, the cyber experts were only dealing with attacks over the wired network and now they have to deal with attacks over a wireless network where it can be attacked from the physical layer, the network layer, processing layer and the application layer. These are the attacks that can be done in the physical layer which are Jamming in Wireless Network Sensors (WSN), Node Tampering, Physical Damage, and Social Engineering. For the network layer, the attacks are Traffic Analysis Attack, RFID Cloning, Man In The Middle Attack, Sleep Deprivation Attack, RFID Spoofing and Malicious Code Attack. On the other hand, the processing layer the attacks can be done by Unauthorized Access, Malicious Insider, Data Security, Virtualization Threats, and Application Security. Last but not the least, for the application layer; the attacks are Phishing attacks, Sleep Deprivation Attack Viruses and Trojan horse attacks, Malicious Scripts, Encryption Attacks, Side-Channel Attack and Distributed Denial of Service. Once the hackers use one of these methods to bypass the security in any layer, the victim's money or personal information can be stolen or tampered. The hackers will use all the information they gather to either blackmail the victim or even impersonate them. They can also use the victim's personal information to commit fraud or even endanger the victim's life. This can also disrupt the IoT services if hacked by a hacker. For example, an IoT printer where documents are being printed, a hacker can hack the devices and view all the important documents like Financial Reports and Personal Banking information.

What Is Internet of Things (IoT) and Industrial Internet of Things?

The Internet of Things (Figure 1), or IoT, is billions of physical devices connected to the internet throughout the world. They are all transmitting, receiving and sharing data. It is possible to turn anything to

Figure 1. Components of Internet of Things (IoT)

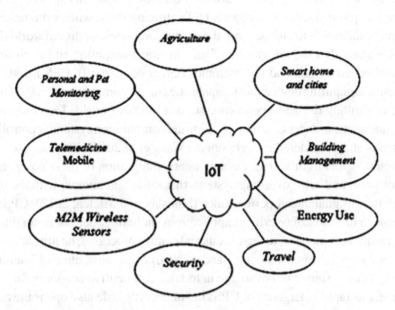

become IoT. For example, a self-driving car is part of IoT. IoT is the merging of the physical and digital world and it adds the level of intelligence to the devices enabling them to communicate real-time without a human present. The industrial internet of things (IIoT) is the use of smart sensors and actuators to enhance manufacturing and industrial processes. Also known as the industrial internet or Industry 4.0, IIoT leverages the power of smart machines and real-time analytics to take advantage of the data that dumb machines have produced in industrial settings for years. The driving philosophy behind IIoT is that smart machines are not only better than humans at capturing and analyzing data in real time, they are better at communicating important information that can be used to drive business decisions faster and more accurately.

What Is Cyber Physical Systems (CPS)?

Cyber-Physical Systems (CPSs) are large-scale heterogeneous networks that destine to bring unfathomed technological changes by integrating the physical world with cyber ecosystem. Like IoT, CPS has got several application domains; the US government's Networking Information Technology Research and Development (NITRD) program has highlighted nine of such distinct sectors namely agriculture, industry, health care, manufacturing, transportation, buildings, defense, energy and emergency response. Nonetheless, large scalability and heterogeneity encounter numerous crosscutting challenges for CPS that include, but not limited to, integration, interoperability, scalability, reliability, energy efficiency, cybersecurity, safety, big data management, social and economic related aspects etc. These issues need to be properly tackled in order to get most of these innovative systems. This section discusses some of the cybersecurity vulnerabilities of CPS, history and statistics of such attacks and proposes some possible countermeasures against these attacks.

Helen Gill coined the term Cyber Physical System in 2006, whereas the term Internet of Things was first used by Kevin Ashton in 1999. Both of these terms have different backgrounds, although their definitions intersect with each other and have various similarities. Generally speaking, both CPS and IoT enhance capabilities of physical devices / objects by facilitating them with communication and digital computation that make them able to interact with the digital component or digital world (Burg et al.2017). The concept of CPS arose after the integration of information, computing and engineering technology with the field of embedded system and mechatronics (Greer et al. 2019). CPS is hybrid in nature and provides integration of computing devices with capabilities of the communication system for the purpose of monitoring and controlling the heterogeneous system of physical world. The components of the CPS include sensors, actuators, transducers, communication and computation systems, controlled elements and occasionally human is also considered as component (Wang et al.2015). The mechanical and electrical systems are interacted by means of software components. Integration of these components results in a novel generation of smart and self-governing systems that sense and interact with the physical world to collect real-time data with guaranteed performance (Sanislay and Miclea, 2012). CPSs are destined to play a very vital role in diverse safety-critical applications including, but not limited to, infrastructure, logistics, manufacturing, automobiles, diverse industrial control processes, health care, building controls, smart grid, smart cities, etc. (Mosterman and Zander, 2016) Sabaliauskaite and Mathur, 2013). Hence CPSs and IoT are a decisive source of advantage in today's competitive economy for any country.

At the same time, this rapid emergence of CPSs in our everyday life also opens the challenging doors of different types of cybersecurity risks and cyberattacks that could have discomforting impact on human lives and the environment. These attacks are of different types, severity, scale and impact and need to be dealt with proactive, coordinated and smart efforts. This section of the chapter firstly presents the overview of security challenges and vulnerabilities of CPS and then discusses different cyberattacks on the CPS, their categories and some related statistics. Lastly, some countermeasures against these cyberattacks are proposed.

Attacks and Countermeasures in Internet of Things (IoT)

In these few years, the usage of Internet has increased significantly, more and more people access to the internet to boost the development in this industry. However, the amount of attacks have also increased and these attacks have become more sophisticated and advanced. As shown in Figure 2, IoT attacks have increased drastically from year 2017 to year 2018. Security have become an important issue as it brings a lot of consequences to the users. For example, the Avast smart home report 2019 have shown that they have scanned sixteen million network of smart home across the world and 40.8% of the digital household, two out of five digital household are vulnerable and easily targeted by attacker. For a user, it may result in being private information disclosed to the public, financial loss or loss of important data. What if a popular e-commerce server has been attacked and shut down, how much loss will the company have to face? All the personal data of their user and all the financial data being accessed and revealed by the attackers.

There are a few risks in the privacy and security in IoT. The confidentially of IoT is often threatening because of a lack of security architecture by the service provider and lack of awareness from the user. The next one is the insecure transmission of data where the technology depends on the physical devices to transmit and collect data. All the data can be compromised with just one vulnerability in the devices. The application risk is another security issue that needs to be worried about IoT. The application is just another surface for attacks to be performed by the hackers and due to its weakness, it can be exploited by hackers.

Figure 2. IoT Attacks in Year 2017 and 2018
(2019 Cyber Threat Report)

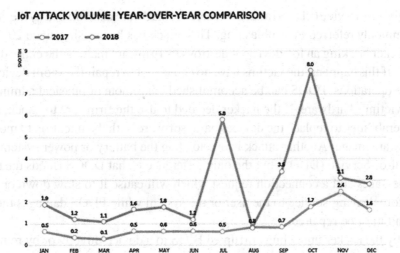

Denial-of-Service (DOS)

See Figure 3.

Figure 3. Illustration of Denial-of-Service (DOS)
(Rashid, 2016)

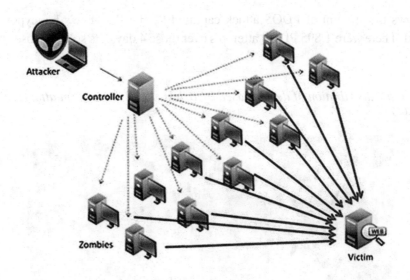

Permanent Denial-of-Service (PDOS)

A Permanent Denial-of-Service (PDOS) attack is where the hardware is sabotaged by the denial of service. This attack is commonly referred to as phlashing. This attack has been rising since 2017. The attack is performed by a hacker bricking an IoT device or destroys its firmware making the entire device or system useless (Figure 3). If this happens, the victims have no choice but to repair the spoilt device or replace the devices to resume operations. PDOS can be accomplished via remote or physical administration on the interfaces of the victim's hardware. If the hacker decided to use the firmware to attack, then the hacker may find for vulnerabilities to replace the devices basic software with the intention to modify, corrupt or to defect the firmware image. Another attack is overloading the battery or power system. It is similar to Distributed Denial-of-Service (DDOS) but the only difference is that DDOS floods the targeted system with incoming messages and a connection request which will cause it to slow down or even crash and shut down, therefore denying service to the user or the system while PDOS damages the device until it cannot be used and must be repaired.

PDOS works by the hacker uploading corrupted BIOS to a device directly or by remote administration of the management interface. PDOS attacks can be done physically, for instance, using a USB stick. There was an article called USB Killer 2.0 released by the helpnetsecurity.com where research goes by the name of Dark Purple have created a USB where it draws power from the device itself (Zorz, 2015). With the assistance of a voltage converter, the device's capacitors are charged to 220V, and it discharges a negative electric flood into the USB port. The first flood "fries" the USB port but the process can be repeated until no power is drawn from the device. This will make the device not useable so the device must be replaced so that its services can be used again. This USB Killer 2.0 is not only limited to computers but any devices that has a USB port. There is a growing concern where if the ability of malware or bots to overheat the devices remotely is very high, then devices can end up being damaged or even catching on fire.

Figure 4 shows the amount of PDOS attack captured by the Radware's honeypot over four days around the world. There were 1,895 PDOS attempts over those 4 days. Its sole purposes were to damage

Figure 4. Geographic distribution of devices used by BrickerBot.2 to perform attacks. (Securityradware, 2017)

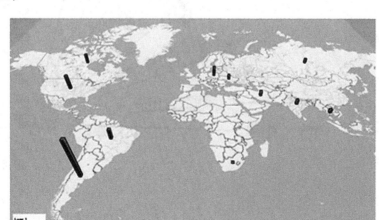

and compromise the storage and IoT devices. Figure 5 shows the bot count during the first 12 hours of those days. There are severe consequences for the PDOS attack. Firstly, if the attack is on an organization there will be revenue loss because all of the systems will be in offline mode. The next is the loss in productivity as nothing can be accessed and done as the attack is carried out. Furthermore, the reputation of an organization can be damaged because there could be a data breach or the organization websites cannot be accessed by the users. The next consequence is an organization has to spend tons of money to repair all their damaged devices and if the devices are on 24 hours a day they might risk arson due to the overheating of devices. Last but not the least, there could be stolen funds; intellectual property and customer personal data like for example credit card number, phone number or even email addresses.

Figure 5. Bot growth timeline over a 12 hour period.
(Securityradware, 2017)

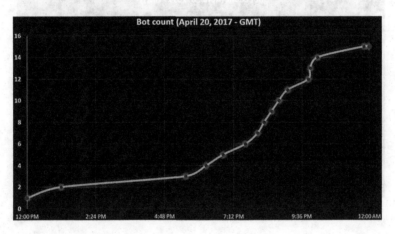

An example of the PDOS attack is a case which happens on the 20th March of 2017 where the first attack of the BrickerBot 1.0 happened and on the same day, BrickerBot 2.0 happened after the first one stopped. The next incident is exactly after a month where BrickerBot 3.0 happened. It was called the vengeance of the BrickerBot. The BrickerBot use the commands called busybox to attack the IoT devices from around the world. Busybox is based on a Linux device which has Telnet uncovered publically and has manufacturing plant default accreditations unaltered are a potential victim. It is similar to the Mirai botnet attack.

Brickerbot

BrickerBot is malware that targets Linux-based IoT devices running the BusyBox toolkit that have their Telnet ports open and publicly exposed. It conducts brute force attacks against the devices by using a list of known default credentials. This is similar to the attack vector conducted by the Mirai botnet. Once BrickerBot gains access to a vulnerable device, it conducts a Permanent Denial-of-Service (PDoS) attack by deploying a set of Linux commands designed to corrupt storage, disrupt internet connectivity, and delete all of the device's files. It writes random bits to the storage drives, rendering the device's flash storage unusable, disables TCP timestamps which hampers internet connectivity, stops all kernel operations, and then reboots the device. Within seconds of becoming infected, the targeted device will stop working, leaving the victim with only two options: reinstall the firmware or replace the device. Figure 6 shows the popularity of Brickerbot attack in 2016. Cybersecurity firm, Radware, discovered Brickerbot when 1,895 PDoS attempts were made on the firm's honeypot over a four-day period starting on March 20, 2017. Radware noted two BrickerBot variants - BrickerBot.1 and BrickerBot2. Attacks from BrickerBot.1 originate from IP addresses all across the globe and they appear to be assigned to Ubiquiti network devices running an older version of the Dropbear SSH server. BrickerBot.2 is a more advanced version of the malware. It executes additional commands and the source of the attacks are difficult to trace as the traffic is masked by Tor exit nodes.

Figure 6. Brickerbot being the most popular IoT attack in 2016 Q3.

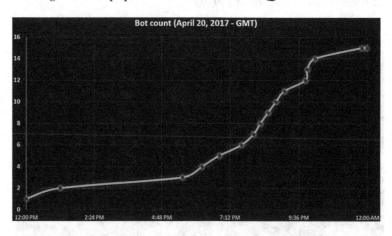

The most effective countermeasure against BrickerBot is to change and strengthen the device's default credentials to lessen their susceptibility to unauthorized access. Disabling components like remote administration features such as Telnet—which BrickerBot is known to leverage—should also be considered. Apart from these, enterprises and end users can prevent BrickerBot from bricking their IoT devices by keeping the device and its firmware updated to patch vulnerabilities that can be used as entry points into the device. Deploying intrusion prevention systems in the gateway can also provide an additional layer of security by detecting and blocking intrusions in the gateway. IT administrators and information security professionals should also be proactive in spotting suspicious or malicious activity within their organization's network.

Mirai Botnet

A botnet is a collection of internet-connected devices that an attacker has compromised. Botnets act as a force multiplier for individual attackers, cyber-criminal groups and nation-states looking to disrupt or break into their targets' systems. Commonly used in distributed denial of service (DDoS) attacks, botnets can also take advantage of their collective computing power to send large volumes of spam, steal credentials at scale, or spy on people and organizations (Korolov, 2019). Mirai had infected over 380,000 devices and Figure 7 shows the effect on Mirai attack by geographic distribution.

In an effort to counter Mirai attacks, a honeypot is a system left open to intentionally let an attacker penetrate and infect it. This makes it possible for security researchers to study its behavior. Cymmetria, a security firm that specializes in the technique, published an open-source honeypot designed for the Mirai botnet on Github. We spoke with Cymmetria after it flagged a doxxing service on the dark web. The Internet Storm Center will be using the honeypot to look out for Mirai, including future iterations (Dale, B., & Dale, B. 2018).

The countermeasure to prevent the PDOS attack is to develop a reasonable comprehension of the distinctive firmware adaptations, parallels, chip-level programming (like ASICs and FPGA) and innovation that is being used in the organization environment. The next countermeasure is to make the battery, power, and fan system vulnerabilities are taken into consideration. Furthermore, to prevent a physical

Figure 7. Mirai infected devices by geographic distribution

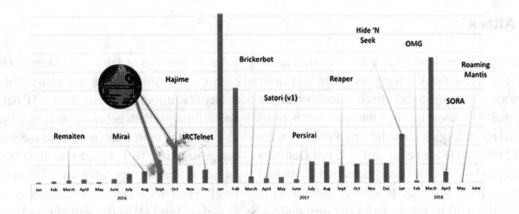

Figure 8. DOS attack in 2018 from Kaspersky

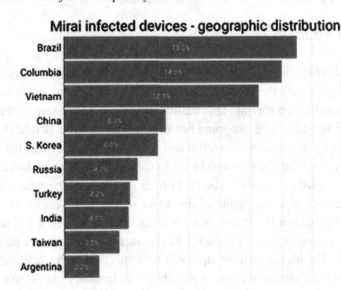

attack, make sure the device is not accessible to an outsider or have a clearance level to who can use the devices. Besides, the telnet should be disabled across the devices.

Deauhentication Attack

The deauthentication attack is a type of denial of service attack (DOS) to deauthenticate the IoT access to the access point, for example when this attack is performed at the smart industry, the IoT devices will be deauthenticated by the access point and unable to transmit the data to the network for further analysis (Noman et al. 2015). The intruder would forge a deauthentication frame and transmit it either to the IoT or to the access point to cause a disconnection state in WLAN networks. For a smart industry, IoT devices disconnecting from the network may cause the entire industry working processes to be down or the devices do not follow the instructions causing some unexpected damages.

From Figure 8, the percentage of DOS attack in 2017 are stable in 100% in every session. In 2018, as we can see in Q1 session, there is 83.30%, Q2 session has decreased to 75.50%, and Q3 session has increased to 132.40%, but most important is in Q3 session, the percentage has increased to 500%.

Sybil Attack

Sybil attack can be done by attackers through identity stolen or creation of fabricated identity (Rajan et al. 2017). Sybil attack is triggered when IOT devices cannot differentiate the unique identity of each of the nodes. Through Sybil attack, attacker can use fake identity to join the network of IOT devices. Sybil attack will affect the data integrity in a network by performing selfish behavior such as dropping some packets or forging some fake packets. For mitigation, one of the most famous defense mechanism is Sybil Defender (Rajan et al. 2017). Sybil Defender is categorized into two parts, Sybil identification algorithm and Sybil community detection algorithm. Sybil identification algorithm will flag nodes of IOT devices as honest node or suspect node. After detecting a Sybil node, the Sybil community detection algorithm will be run to detect the surrounding Sybil nodes. Sybil Defender will always take into consideration on two rules. Firstly, the linking of honest nodes and Sybil nodes are limited. Next, the size of honest community is always larger than Sybil community.

Man-In-The-Middle Attack

A man-in-the-middle (MITM) attack (Figure 9) is the interception of a third party or an outside entity in a 2-way communication among the victims. This can happen to anyone or on any platform like for instance emails, social media, web surfing, applications, IoT devices or even Wi-Fi Eavesdropping. A MITM attack is not only used for eavesdropping but to steal the victim's personal information. To illustrate it, a hacker is sitting in between the victim and a social media website that they are visiting to intercept and capture any data that the victim submits to the site such as password and username.

There are a few types of MITM attacks. The first one is email hijacking where the hackers use this tactic to target email accounts of large organizations. Once they gain access to all the important email accounts, the hackers will monitor the transaction to make their attack more impactful. The next one is WI-FI Eavesdropping where the hacker uses WI-FI connections preferably a public network like in airports and coffee shops. The hackers will set up a WIFI-Connection with a believable sounding name. Then they wait for a potential victim to connect and they will instantly access to a connected device.

The next one is the session hijacking where the victim will log in to the website and a connection is established between the computer and the website. The hacker will hijack the session with that website by stealing the victim's browser cookies. A cookie is where small pieces of information are stored making web browsing easier. It can be pre-fill forms, online activity and in some cases, the victim's location.

Another type of attack is using the Secure Socket Layer (SSL) or Transport Layer Security (TLS) to create secure channels over an insecure network. The attacks begin by using SSL over HTTP which is also known as HTTPS as it is the most common SSL .The hacker intercepts the traffic between the cli-

Figure 9. An example of the MITM attack.
(Cekerevac, 2017)

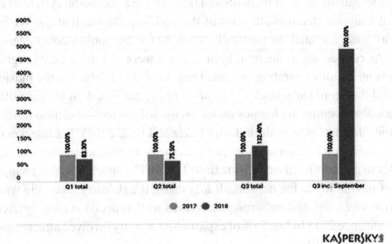

Figure 10. Types of MITM Attacks

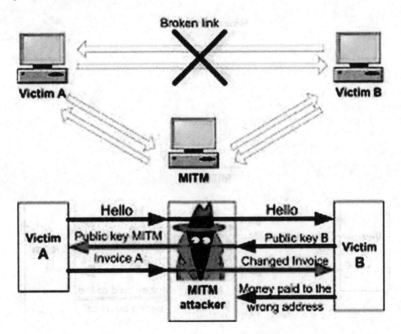

ent and the web server. When the HTTPS URL is found, the sslstrip replaces it with an HTTP link and keeps a mapping of the changes. The machine which is attacking supplies certificates to the web server and impersonates the client and traffic is received back from the secure website and back to the client.

From Figure 10, from the year 2016 two types of MITM attacks which are the vulnerability of the browser (36%) and SSL (11%). For the year 2017, there is only one attack which is the vulnerability of the browser (20%). As we can see the browser is getting less vulnerable. The consequences of the MITM attack is all the personal information of the victims can be read by the hacker and which might harm the victim in any way possible. Another consequence is the data which is being sent out or receiving may be altered by the hacker.

There was a case which happened in July 2015 where two hackers took over a Jeep Cherokee due to its defective security safeguard. Both of them hacked through the multimedia system of the Jeep through Wi-Fi connection of Chrysler (the manufacturer of the car). It turns out that the Wi-Fi wasn't hacked because the password was generated automatically when the car and multimedia system is turned on for the very first time. As connecting to the unit, both of them were able to hack through the multimedia computer which runs on a Linux operating system. They were able to control, the music player, the settings on the radio and they could also track the location of the car based on the car GPS.

The MiTM attack also become the famous attack on the IoT network, because this attack allows the intruder to collect the information from the industry (Aziz abd Haq, 2018). The attacker does not need to actually appear on the location of a network, he just uses the communication protocol of IoT to interfere the two sensor nodes to get the classified information. The MiTM attack also can change the data value while the data pass from the IoT to the network. It may cause the Industry receiving wrong information or data from the IoT devices and making wrong analysis as well as decision making. According to IBM X-Force's threat intelligence 2018 Index, 35% of exploitation activity involved attacker attempting MiTm attacks (Figure 11) (Dobran, 2019).

Figure 11. Types of exploiting targeting inadvertent weaknesses from IBM threat Index

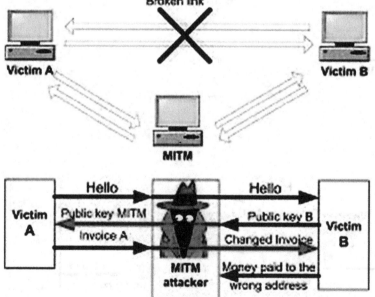

The countermeasure to prevent MITM attack in IoT is to ensure to use Digital Certificate for VPNs where the communication between two or more devices are encrypted whether the information coming in or going out. The VPN will require a Digital Certificate and after that, every one of the devices it speaks with will require certification with a public and private key. During correspondence, required keys are swapped in a handshake and all information remains encrypted until it achieves its last destination. The next countermeasure is to use a strong encryption like Advanced Encryption Standard (AES) to encrypt the data transmit from IoT to the network by allowing the server to authenticate the client and then validating the client's digital certificate. After the validation is successful, then only the client and server can establish a connection. The manufactures of the IoT devices must identity and authentication in mind when designing and manufacturing the devices before selling them to the market. Besides that, intrusion detection system can be used to monitor, analyze the traffic patterns to identify unusual behavior.

Universal Asynchronous Receiver/Transmitter (UART) Access Attack

Universal Asynchronous Receiver/Transmitter also known as UART is a serial communication protocol. In Figure 12, the red circle shows a sample of UART pins in the device. It is a physical layer attack. Since UART is asynchronous, it does not utilize a clock for correspondence with another device. While it is transferring packets, extra care should be given to prevent packet loss. UART can be used by the attacker to physically to access and alter the IoT device to bypass the normal authentication using a serial cable connection. UART interfaces will in general grant root access, far surpassing the authorizations of normal clients.

Figure 12. Universal Asynchronous Receiver/Transmitter (UART)

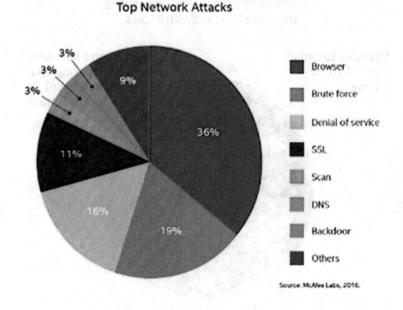

Top Network Attacks

Source: McAfee Labs, 2016.

UART is used for "jailbreaking" or "rooting" devices. This can lead to some vulnerability which can lead to attacks. IoT devices like the UART will show evidence if it is being tampered with or if it has been altered. The initial step the hacker takes when attempting to access a UART console is to find the three connections on the circuit board which are RX, TX and GND. After finding the three connections, equipment is attached to the header pins. The next part is where the hacker uses a logic analyzer such as a Saleae product. It uses a decoding protocol to analyze an asynchronous serial. Once the UART connection is activated and identified, can connect to the interface of the targeted device from the desktop operating system of the hacker.

Figure 13 shows the statistics from the year 2017 and physical tampering shows 7% of the type of breach related to IoT. This is the statistics of 2 years. There was a case in 2016 where Wi-Fi baby heart monitor have been compromised due to the UART access attack (Garlati, 2016). The device had sensors in the baby socks to monitors the baby's heartbeat and relays the data wirelessly to the nearby hub. If there was something wrong with the baby's heartbeat, a message will be sent to the baby's parents. The consequences of UART access are it can be used as a debugging interface on the devices to view serial logs and it will be possible for the attacker to gain shell or root shell access to the device. Once the attacker has access to the root shell, the attacker can reverse engineer the firmware and retrieve the sensitive information. They can also get the API key stored and identify the communication protocol of the targeted devices. This will enable them to target other devices or an organization. The code of the device did not have a software update mechanism to fix the issue. It was very vulnerable and it can be hacked by attackers. The countermeasures of UART access are enabling password to protect the device

Figure 13. IoT breaches in 2015-2017.
(IIOT, 2017).

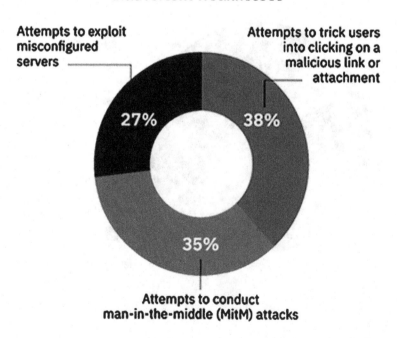

**Types of exploitation targeting
inadvertent weaknesses**

Attempts to exploit
misconfigured
servers

Attempts to trick users
into clicking on a
malicious link or
attachment

27%

38%

35%

Attempts to conduct
man-in-the-middle (MitM) attacks

from being hacked. The next countermeasure is to block the UART access with another chip so that the hacker will not take advantage of the device.

Stuxnet

Stuxnet is an extremely sophisticated computer worm that exploits multiple previously unknown Windows zero-day vulnerabilities to infect computers and spread. Its purpose was not just to infect PCs but to cause real-world physical effects. Specifically, it targets centrifuges used to produce the enriched uranium that powers nuclear weapons and reactors. Stuxnet was first identified by the infosec community in 2010 after the attack as shown in Figure 14, but development on it probably began in 2005. Despite its unparalleled ability to spread and its widespread infection rate, Stuxnet does little or no harm to computers not involved in uranium enrichment. When it infects a computer, it checks to see if that computer is connected to specific models of programmable logic controllers (PLCs) manufactured by Siemens. PLCs are how computers interact with and control industrial machinery like uranium centrifuges. The worm then alters the PLCs' programming, resulting in the centrifuges being spun too quickly and for too long, damaging or destroying the delicate equipment in the process. While this is happening, the PLCs tell the controller computer that everything is working fine, making it difficult to detect or diagnose what is going wrong until it is too late (Fruhlinger, J. 2017)

Figure 14. Stuxnet infected hosts by country in 2010.

To prevent Stuxnet attacks, logging of events should not be performed on the same device which generates the logs but should write identical logs to a separate device for pre- and post-event analysis. This also helps minimizing the possibility of an attacker "hiding their tracks" and altering system logs. Security Information and Event Management (SIEM) systems are designed for precisely this purpose and will securely maintain audit trails regardless of attacks against other systems on the control system network (Joel Langill, 2010).

Worm Attack

Worms are similar to viruses, they replicate themselves and can cause the same types of damages to the devices or to the system (Edwards and Profetis, 2016). The intruder scans through the network to see which ports are open in the industrial IoT devices. The intruder can easily spread worms to the industrial IoT device because IoT devices do not have the security layer to prevent or detect the network attacks. When the particular worm successfully enters into the IoT system, it may damage the entire IoT devices as well as wiping the firmware out.

Figure 15 shows the types of network attacks. As we can see there are many network attacks, Browser attack, Denial of services as well as Worm attack. The worm attack has 13% over 100% in 8 types of network attacks. Basically to prevent from being attacked by worm, it is best to update the anti-virus software so that the software has the latest worm behavior in order to eliminate the worm from the system. Besides that, users should prevent from using the company computer in order to open some spam e-mail or browsers. (Deogirikar and Vidhate, 2017).

Figure 15. The top network attacks in Q2 2017 from McAfree lab

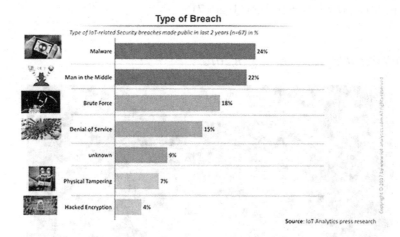

Black Hole Attack

The first attack is Black Hole Attack or also known as Sinkhole Attack (Ali et al., 2018). As shown in Figure 16, the attacker will try to create a malicious node near the victim's network. Then the malicious node advertises wrong information to other nodes. The malicious node would try to attract other nodes to send data through him. The malicious node would declare itself as the shortest path to be taken to reach the destination. The nodes would then send all the packets to the malicious node. The malicious node will then drop those packets instead of redirecting them.

Black Hole attack is being categorized into two categories such as Single Black Hole Attack or Collaborative Black Hole Attack (Ali et al., 2018). Single Black Hole Attack is performed by using only one malicious node to attack the victim. While Collaborative Black Hole attack is performed by using more than one malicious node to perform the black hole attack. Collaborative Black Hole Attack is much

Figure 16. Black Hole Attack
(Alattas, 2016)

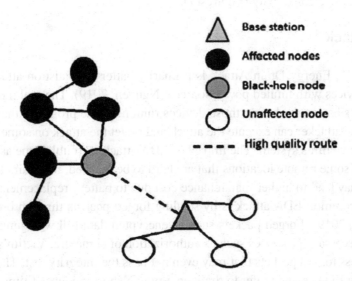

more dangerous than Single Black Hole Attack because the network throughput and the node's energy will be greatly affected than using only a single node.

Alattas 2016 proposed a scheme against Black Hole Attack by using multiple base stations and check agents to detect Black Hole Attack. A table of neighbor nodes is maintained in every node in the system. Check agents, special nodes in the network are also added into the network. The check agents will try to monitor the incoming and outgoing packets of those nodes. Once a node with zero incoming and outgoing traffic is detected, the node is flagged as suspicious node. Then, the algorithm of the multiple base stations will be executed. Packets or route request will be sent to those suspicious nodes. If the suspicious node does not reply within a limited amount of time, the node will be flagged as malicious. The

Figure 17. Message Complexity vs No. of Nodes
(Alattas, 2016)

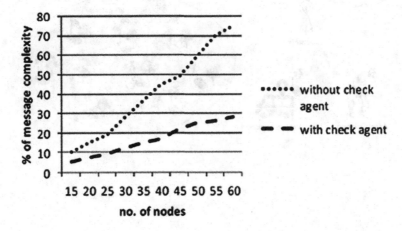

malicious node will then be kicked out from the system. The outcome with check agent shows promising results in terms of message complexity (Figure 17).

Energy Drain Attack

As shown in Figure 18, Energy Drain Attack is primarily battery exhaustion attack that are targeted onto those mobile devices with limited power sources (Nguyen, 2019). The real motive od EDA attack is to drain the victim's battery by letting those devices running some programs that consume the most energy repeatedly. The attacker can execute the attack and target the attack on some sensors that handle important roles in the victim's system. The impact of EDA attack is troublesome as those sensor nodes are usually placed on some remote locations that are hard to be reached, for example in the forest or on the mountain. This may lead to higher maintenance cost due to battery replacement.

One of the most common EDA attack is by sending forged packets through broadcasts to the victim's nodes (Nguyen, 2019). Forged packets such as encrypted data full with junk may let the victim to perform some unnecessary processes such as authorization of signature. Victim's nodes will waste a lot of energy to process forged packets that may even not pass the integrity test. The attacker may have a different strategy on EDA, some prefer to drain energy in a short amount of time. Some are going to drain the victim's battery slowly to avoid being detected.

The most efficient way to mitigate EDA is by having firmware or software update of the devices (Nguyen, 2019). Once the latest version of firmware is being deployed, firmware is to be updated to prevent EDA Attacks. Moreover, securing the frame header of the IOT devices is also one of the best ways to mitigate EDA. This may help to prevent exploitation of sending encrypted junk packets for signature verification, which may then drain the battery for those unnecessary verification tasks.

Figure 18. Energy Drain Attack
(Nguyen, 2019).

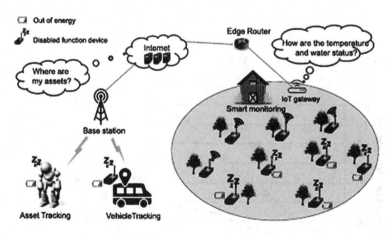

Attacks and Countermeasures in Cyber Physical Systems (CPS)

Along with several issues such as integration, heterogeneity, interoperability, scalability, reliability, complexity, resource sharing, distributed management and control, power consumption, big data management, etc., CPS face several security and privacy related challenges [6 - 10]. Some of these challenges include:

- Physical security due to large-sized, distributed and geographically dispersed CPS
- Authentication & strong encryption
- Unauthorized access to resources
- Compromised or hotspot nodes
- Multitenancy due to large scale CPS such as grid being shared, accessed and managed by multiple operators
- Unknown perimeters and multiple points of attack
- Unspecified or badly-defined information-, control- and access-flow mechanism
- Service interruption or discontinuation
- Exploitation of software bugs

It is important to protect the various types of devices from unauthorized access, so that they can function properly. By using strong security mechanisms we can protect services, communication paths, storage resources, computing components other hardware systems [10]. The reliability of CPs can be addressed by autonomous and smart control methods that could handle the compromised or hotspot nodes and prevent any conspiracy to interrupt the CPS functionality. An energy-efficient and sovereign Intruder Detection System (IDS) may help in collecting facts and figures concerning such conspiracies and suspicions and in analyzing the collected information (Sadeghi et al., 2015)(Giraldo et al. 2018). Examples of collected information are log files of local nodes or of whole network and recording of communicated data among devices. The data analysis mechanism audits the gathered information efficiently and generates the meaning reports or patterns for any future corresponding (Mitchell and Chen, 2014).

Cyberattacks on CPSs

In general, network attacks are categorized in active and passive attacks. In active attacks intruders attack on the data directly and alter it, whereas in passive attack intruders monitor the data or user behavior and do not immediately alter the data. However, most of the passive attacks turn into active attacks by the time. The network based attacks include spying, data alteration, replay, deceiving, denial-of-service, sniffer, application layer attacks, etc. (Mitchell and Chen, 2014).

- **Cryptographic attacks:** In cryptographic attacks, attacker identifies the weakness in the security system i.e. in the cipher, key management design, cryptographic protocol, OS or security algorithm. The cryptographic attacks are selected plaintext, crypto locker, selected cipher text and key, brute force attacks, identified plaintext and cipher text, etc. (Giraldo et al.,2018).
- **Cyber threat:** A cyber threat is also famous as a malicious attack. In this type of attack, attackers try to find the weakness of the protected scheme in cyber physical system with the ill intention to disrupt the integration of a system. There exist various categories of cyber-attacks. They can be

initiated from key sources like earthquakes, faults in line, hardware failure, floods, interference and leakage of electromagnetic (Singh and Jain, 2018).

- **Malicious software:** In this attack, intruder can steal the information of the network and avoid the access control of the CPS. The core purpose of this attack is to destroy the host system. Examples of this attack include adware, spyware, phishing, bots, Trojan horses, viruses, hackers and worms, etc.(Beek et al., 2017).
- **Deception (Fraud):** The attackers can fraud with the system by making the changes in the working nature or behavior of the data collecting devices. These attacks are also known as false data injection, stealthy deception and covert attacks (Abomhara, 2015).
- **Denial of service:** Denial of service attacks may play with the channel of the communication system by jamming it, the result is inaccessibility of resources (Mitchell and Chen, 2014).
- **Replay attack:** In this attack, intruder captures and records the collected data of network and then repeatedly sends the same data intentionally (Singh and Jain, 2018).
- **Resilient control issues:** This attack is based on the involvement of the human. In this attack adversary can corrupt the control packets generated by the network for the communication purpose (Giraldo et al., 2018).

Vulnerability Identification in CPS

The weakness in the security policy, rules, system organization, strategy or any other issue with either hardware or software could result in vulnerabilities for the CPS. This weakness of CPS opens the doors for attackers to intrude the system and compromise its efficiency. The vulnerabilities of the CPS system vary based on different factors such as hardware, platform, network, software and management vulnerabilities (Singh and Jain, 2018). There are various differences between CPS and ICT for detecting the cyber-attacks in the network. In an ICT, monitoring activities are based on the host / network level activities, user triggered, non-zero-day attacks, having no deal of legacy components & user/machine activities. CPS activities are based on behavior of devices, time driven, zero-day attacks & legacy technology (Albright et al., 2014).

There are basically two detection techniques used in CPS for the identification of cyber-attacks based on the knowledge and behavior. Some researchers also define behavior specification based techniques as sub part of behavior based technique. The knowledge based technique looks for matching particular predefined pattern. However, this technique is not suitable to detect new types of cyberattacks. The behavior based techniques does not look for specific pattern, so it has more chance of detecting new types of cyber-attacks but vulnerability to false positives also exist (Abomhara,2015). Nowadays, due to the increasing rate of cyberattacks, security and privacy develop the important concern between consumers and businesses. There are various research groups that focus on providing the acceptable privacy for all stakeholders of the CPS (Mitchell and Chen, 2014).

Countermeasures for the CPS Cyberattacks

There is an ever-increasing need of designing cyber security measures, mechanisms, processes and protocols to protect the CPS system, network, data, physical & communication resources and to get avoided from unauthorized access of system components. Some layer based security measures are discussed below (Singh and Jain, 2018).

Cyber Security Measures for the Physical Layer

In the physical layer, main concerns for cyber physical system is physical security of different devices i.e sensor, actuators and Radio Frequency Identification devices. The administrator/user must consider the following suggested instructions for the security of CPS against cyber-attacks i.e backup system of data & recovery plans, user awareness, analysis & monitoring the traffic regularly, control access, disaster protection, tracking malicious activities and restrict native administrative rights etc. (Huang et al., 2015).

Cyber Security Measures for the Transport Layer

The purpose of this layer is to defend the communication traffic and the system. The point to point encryption guarantees the protection of data. End to end confidentiality information is gain through the End-To-End mechanisms. The mechanisms of security include key management, security protocols, firewall and authentication. (Giraldo et al., 2018).

Cyber Security Measures for the Application Layer

The main purpose of this layer is to perform decision on cyber physical system. This layer has effects on the security of CPS because there are many applications having their own threats. The followings are some of security measures for this layer of CPS included: updated access control policies, deployment of detection and authentication process, secure payment protocols and secure HTTP (Singh and Jain, 2018).

CONCLUSION

IoT and CPS have become a hot topic in last few years. IoT and CPS are the main assets in industry 4.0 so lots of company still try to protect their network and server although the result is not welcomes. In a nutshell, IoT has a lot of security flaws which needs to be addressed soon In this paper, we introduced IoT, IIoT and CPS along with their attacks which can bring consequence to user and the industry. For example, DNS flood, spear phishing, SQL injection, Ransomware, ARP spoofing, Permanent Denial-of-Service (PDOS), Man-In-The-Middle Attack, UART Access attack and backdoor attack. Statistic are provided to prove the appearance and the importance of these attacks. The possible countermeasure and policies also discussed to mitigate or prevent these attacks. The consequences of these attacks are very harmful to the victim. Some attacks can even ruin the reputation of an individual or an organization. If one has the knowledge to do these of attacks, they should never abuse it and should practice ethically.

REFERENCES

Abomhara, M. (2015). Cyber security and the internet of things: Vulnerabilities, threats, intruders and attacks. *Journal of Cyber Security and Mobility*, *4*(1), 65–88. doi:10.13052/jcsm2245-1439.414

Alattas, R. (2016). Detecting black-hole attacks in WSNs using multiple base stations and check agents. In 2016 Future Technologies Conference (FTC) (pp. 1020-1024). IEEE. doi:10.1109/FTC.2016.7821728

Albright, D., Brannan, P., & Walrond, C. (2010). *Did Stuxnet take out 1,000 centrifuges at the Natanz enrichment plant?* Institute for Science and International Security.

Ali, S., Khan, M. A., Ahmad, J., & Malik, A. W., & ur Rehman, A. (2018). Detection and prevention of Black Hole Attacks in IOT & WSN. In *2018 Third International Conference on Fog and Mobile Edge Computing (FMEC)* (pp. 217-226). IEEE. 10.1109/FMEC.2018.8364068

Avast smart home security report. (2019). Avast.

Beek, C., Frosst, D., Greve, P., Gund, Y., Moreno, F., Peterson, E., & Tiwari, R. (2017). *Mcafee labs threats report. McAfee*. Santa Clara, CA: Tech. Rep.

BrickerBot Malware Emerges. (n.d.). *Permanently Bricks IoT Devices*. Retrieved from https://www.trend-micro.com/vinfo/us/security/news/internet-of-things/brickerbot-malware-permanently-bricks-iot-devices

Burg, A., Chattopadhyay, A., & Lam, K. Y. (2017). Wireless communication and security issues for cyber–physical systems and the Internet-of-Things. *Proceedings of the IEEE*, *106*(1), 38–60. doi:10.1109/JPROC.2017.2780172

Cekerevac, Z., Dvorak, Z., Prigoda, L., & Cekerevac, P. (2017). *Internet of Things and The Man-In the-Middle Attacks – Security and Economic Risks*. MEST Journal. doi:10.12709/mest.05.05.02.03

Dale, B., & Dale, B. (2018, January 22). *Three Whitehat Countermeasures to the Botnet Threat*. Retrieved from https://observer.com/2016/11/mirai-bestbuy-popopret-imperva-cymmetria-virgil-security-spiffy/

Deogirikar, J., & Vidhate, A. (2017, February). Security attacks in IoT: A survey. In *2017 International Conference on I-SMAC (IoT in Social, Mobile, Analytics and Cloud)(I-SMAC)* (pp. 32-37). IEEE. 10.1109/I-SMAC.2017.8058363

Dobran, B. (2019). *The Ultimate Guide to Man in the Middle Attacks: Prevention is Key*. Retrieved from https://phenixnap.com/man-in-the-middle-attacks-prevention

Edwards, S., & Profetis, I. (2016). Hajime: Analysis of a decentralized internet worm for IoT devices. *Rapidity Networks, 16*.

Fruhlinger, J. (2017). *What is Stuxnet, who created it and how does it work?* Retrieved from https://www.csoonline.com/article/3218104/what-is-stuxnet-who-created-it-and-how-does-it-work.html

Garlati, Z. (2016). *Owlet Baby Wi-Fi Monitor "Worst IoT Security of 2016"*. Retrieved from: https://www.informationsecuritybuzz.com/expert-comments/owlet-baby-wi-fi-monitor-worst-iot-security-2016/

Giraldo, J., Urbina, D., Cardenas, A., Valente, J., Faisal, M., Ruths, J., ... Candell, R. (2018). A survey of physics-based attack detection in cyber-physical systems. *ACM Computing Surveys*, *51*(4), 76. doi:10.1145/3203245 PMID:31092968

Greer, C., Burns, M., Wollman, D., & Griffor, E. (1900). Cyber-Physical Systems & the Internet of Things. *NIST Special Publication*, *202*, 2019.

Huang, S., Zhou, C. J., Yang, S. H., & Qin, Y. Q. (2015). Cyber-physical system security for networked Industrial processes. *International Journal of Automation and Computing*, *12*(6), 567–578. doi:10.100711633-015-0923-9

IIOT. (2017). *An overview of the IoT Security Market Report 2017-2022*. Retrieved from: https://iiot-world.com/reports/an-overview-of-the-iot-security-market-report-2017-2022/

Korolov, M. (2019). *What is a botnet? When armies of infected IoT devices attack*. Retrieved from https://www.csoonline.com/article/3240364/what-is-a-botnet.html

Langill, J., & Mitigation, S. (2010, November 17). *Defense in Depth Needed*. Retrieved from https://isssource.com/stuxnet-mitigation-defense-in-depth-needed/

Letsoalo, E., & Ojo, S. (2017). Session hijacking attacks in wireless networks: A review of existing mitigation techniques. In 2017 IST-Africa Week Conference (IST-Africa) (pp. 1-9). IEEE. doi:10.23919/ISTAFRICA.2017.8102284

Mitchell, R., & Chen, I. R. (2014). A survey of intrusion detection techniques for cyber-physical systems. *ACM Computing Surveys*, *46*(4), 55. doi:10.1145/2542049

Mosterman, P. J., & Zander, J. (2016). Industry 4.0 as a cyber-physical system study. *Software & Systems Modeling*, *15*(1), 17–29. doi:10.100710270-015-0493-x

Nguyen, V. L., Lin, P. C., & Hwang, R. H. (2019). Energy Depletion Attacks in Low Power Wireless Networks. *IEEE Access: Practical Innovations, Open Solutions*, *7*, 51915–51932. doi:10.1109/ACCESS.2019.2911424

Noman, H. A., Abdullah, S. M., & Mohammed, H. I. (2015). An Automated Approach to Detect De-authentication and Disassociation Dos Attacks on Wireless 802.11 Networks. *International Journal of Computer Science Issues*, *12*(4), 107.

Pasqualetti, F., Dörfler, F., & Bullo, F. (2013). Attack detection and identification in cyber-physical systems. *IEEE Transactions on Automatic Control*, *58*(11), 2715–2729. doi:10.1109/TAC.2013.2266831

Ponnusamy, V., Jhanjhi, N. Z., & Humayun, M. (2020). Fostering Public-Private Partnership: Between Governments and Technologists in Developing National Cybersecurity Framework. In *Employing Recent Technologies for Improved Digital Governance* (pp. 237–255). IGI Global. doi:10.4018/978-1-7998-1851-9.ch012

Ponnusamy, V., Selvam, L. M. P., & Rafique, K. (2020). Cybersecurity Governance on Social Engineering Awareness. In *Employing Recent Technologies for Improved Digital Governance* (pp. 210–236). IGI Global. doi:10.4018/978-1-7998-1851-9.ch011

Rajan, A., Jithish, J., & Sankaran, S. (2017). Sybil attack in IOT: Modelling and defenses. In *2017 International Conference on Advances in Computing, Communications and Informatics (ICACCI)* (pp. 2323-2327). IEEE. 10.1109/ICACCI.2017.8126193

Rao, T. A. (2018). Security challenges facing IoT layers and its protective measures. *International Journal of Computers and Applications*, *975*, 8887.

Rashid, F. Y. (2016). *NTP fixes denial-of-service flaws*. Retrieved from: https://www.infoworld.com/article/3144471/security/ntp-fixes-denial-of-service-flaws.html

Sabaliauskaite, G., & Mathur, A. P. (2013). Intelligent checkers to improve attack detection in cyber physical systems. In *2013 International Conference on Cyber-Enabled Distributed Computing and Knowledge Discovery* (pp. 27-30). IEEE. 10.1109/CyberC.2013.14

Sadeghi, A. R., Wachsmann, C., & Waidner, M. (2015). Security and privacy challenges in industrial internet of things. In *2015 52nd ACM/EDAC/IEEE Design Automation Conference (DAC)* (pp. 1-6). IEEE. 10.1145/2744769.2747942

Sanislav, T., & Miclea, L. (2012). Cyber-physical systems-concept, challenges and research areas. *Journal of Control Engineering and Applied Informatics*, *14*(2), 28–33.

Securityradware. (2017). *BrickerBot PDoS Attack: Back with A Vengeance*. Retrieved from: https://security.radware.com/ddos-threats-attacks/brickerbot-pdos-back-with-vengeance/

Selvam, L. M. P., Ponnusamy, V., & Rafique, K. (2020). Democratic Governance: A Review of Secured Digital Electoral Service Infrastructure. In *Employing Recent Technologies for Improved Digital Governance* (pp. 256–272). IGI Global. doi:10.4018/978-1-7998-1851-9.ch013

Singh, A., & Jain, A. (2018). Study of cyber attacks on cyber-physical system. In *Proceedings of 3rd International Conference on Internet of Things and Connected Technologies (ICIoTCT)* (pp. 26-27). 10.2139srn.3170288

Wang, L., Törngren, M., & Onori, M. (2015). Current status and advancement of cyber-physical systems in manufacturing. *Journal of Manufacturing Systems*, *37*, 517–527. doi:10.1016/j.jmsy.2015.04.008

Yampolskiy, M., Horvath, P., Koutsoukos, X. D., Xue, Y., & Sztipanovits, J. (2012). Systematic analysis of cyber-attacks on CPS-evaluating applicability of DFD-based approach. In *2012 5th International Symposium on Resilient Control Systems* (pp. 55-62). IEEE. 10.1109/ISRCS.2012.6309293

Zorz, Z. (2015). *USB Killer 2.0: A harmless-looking USB stick that destroys computers*. Retrieved from: https://www.helpnetsecurity.com/2015/10/15/usb-killer-20-a-harmless-looking-usb-stick-that-destroys-computers/

Chapter 2
Internet of Things (IoT) and PKI–Based Security Architecture

Sandeep Mathur

Amity Insitute of Information Technology, Amity University, Noida, India

Ankita Arora

Amity Insitute of Information Technology, Amity University, Noida, India

ABSTRACT

The internet of things (IoT) is described as the arrangement of physical articles—contraptions, automobiles, structures, and various things—fixed with equipment, programming, devices, and framework accessibility that engages these things to accumulate and exchange data. Practically paying little mind to industry, IoT is anticipated to be the absolute most significant factor affecting basic business rationale in the coming decades. PKI is the best alternative for arrangement suppliers to secure information and associated gadgets. When effectively executed, PKI can fabricate and bolster security and trust in IoT biological systems. PKI's job in IoT gives solid personality validation and makes the establishment of trust that frameworks, gadgets, applications, and clients need to securely connect and trade delicate information. PKI and the brought forth trust networks spread the basic security necessities IoT tasks need, giving the encryption, confirmation, and information respectability that make the establishment of trust. This chapter explores PKI-based security architecture.

INTRODUCTION

The Internet of Things (IoT), is described as the arrangement of physical articles gadgets, automobiles, structures and various things fixed with equipment, programming devices, and framework accessibility that engages these things to accumulate and exchange data. Practically paying little mind to industry, IoT is anticipated to be the absolute most significant factor affecting basic business rationale in the coming decades. The net of factors, or IoT, is a widget of interconnected processing widgets, mechanical and virtual technologies, items, creatures or people which are furnished through exact attribute besides the capacity for allocation of information over a framework deprived of expecting homo-to-homo or homo-

DOI: 10.4018/978-1-7998-2803-7.ch002

to-system interplay. It can be a particular one with a heart screen fixed, a farm animal with a microchip electrical device, an automobile that has operated in devices to alert the manner of thinking power, thing that can be doled out an IP address with and can switch records over a system. Gradually, organizations in a dissemination of businesses are the utilization of IoT to perform more noteworthy viably, higher catch customers to supply predominant client care, improve determination making and development the cost of the endeavour. Kevin Ashton, setting up the "Auto-ID centre" at Massachusetts Institute of Technology, initially suggested the snare of components that are in a relationship which was completed with Procter and Gamble (P&G) in 1999. Expecting to pass on wireless repetition id to the idea of P&G's elder society, Web of Things is the new presentation and the name given by the Ashton to join the cool new example: the net in 1999. Massachusetts Institute of Technology coach Neil Gershenfeld's book, "when things start to think", additionally performing in 1999, fail to use the definite term but anyway gave an ideal vision in which IoT become directed technology. IoT consumes as the association of wi-fi headways, microelectromechanical structures (mems), micro-services and the net. Despite the situation that changed into the essential announcement of the network of components, the knowledge of associated strategies has remained grounded since the 1970s, underneath monikers installed net and inescapable registering. The principal wireless routers, for instance, transformed into a first IoT device at Carnegie Mellon college inside middle of 1980's. It can be invented since "machine-to-machine (M2M)" dispatch, that is, technologies interfacing by respectively other through an agenda deprived of human cooperate Machine-to-Machine infers companion a contraption towards the cloud, directing it besides societal event estimations. Enchanting it to the going with degree, Internet of Things is a device planning of many of the clever gadgets that link individuals, organizations and different claims to accumulate and rate bits of knowledge. The network of variables is moreover an augmentation of Supervisory Control and Data Acquisition, a class of software design program computer database for framework deal with the public event of records in real time from faraway areas to oversee device and circumstances.

Figure 1 and 2 shows the possible of the IoT environment, which may include all possible gadgets used in today's world.

Figure 1. Internet of Things
(http://www.techsmartglobe.com/IoT-wearables/, n.d.)

Figure 2. An IoT System
(IoT explained: What is the internet of things?, n.d.)

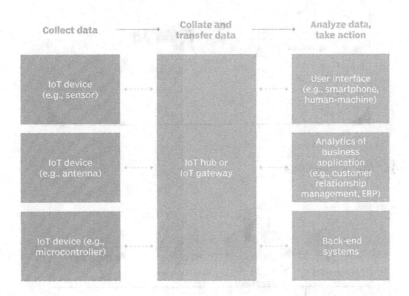

EXECUTION OF IOT

An IoT air fuses net-engaged insightful gadgets which are used for embedded workstations, instruments and verbal exchange equipment to store up, guide also survey for proceeding their valuations and they gather it from the atmosphere. IoT devices extent the device realities they accumulate by associating with an IoT portal or diverse side gadget where information is also showed in the direction of the cloud near be dissected locally. Here and there, those gadgets exchange with supplementary interrelated gadgets and act at the realities they get from an individual. The devices ensure limit of the artistic creations deprived of human mediation, certain circumstance that individuals can connect with the gadgets - for example, to established them, give them guidelines otherwise contact the records. The availability, agendas body and report show cast-off with those web-engaged devices, all things considered, hang on the extraordinary IoT projects conveyed.

IoT Standards and Frameworks

6LOWOWAN (IPv6 over low - control remote individual region organizes), an open general characterized with the guide of the web designing team (IETF). The 6LOWPAN across the board permits any low-power radio to converse with the net, which incorporate 804.15.4, Bluetooth low vitality and z-wave (for local mechanization). ZIGBEE0, a low-quality, uninformed rate remote system utilized especially in business settings. ZIGBEE depends on basically built the IEEE 802.15. four commanders. The ZIGBEE coalition made Dot, the prevalent verbal for IoT that grants cunning things to artworks safely on in the least system and perceive each other. LiteOS, a Unix-like working device for wi-fi device systems. LiteOS

Figure 3. Working of Internet of Things
(CA Hierarchies (Sun Directory Server Enterprise Edition 7.0 Reference), n.d.)

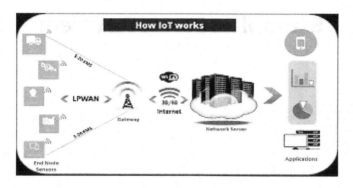

Figure 4. Three-layer IoT Architecture
(Hern et al., 2016)

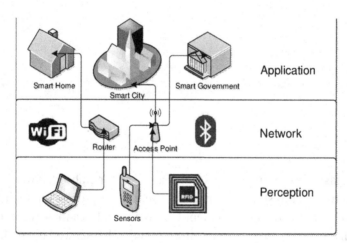

helps cell phones, reasonable creation bundles, wearables, shrewd houses and web of vehicles (IOV). The working machine furthermore fills in as a keen gadget advancement stage. OneM2M, a framework to-machine supplier sheet that can be implanted in programming system and equipment to associate gadgets. The worldwide institutionalization outline, oneM2M, become made to increment reusable pre-requisites to allow IoT bundles crosswise over unmistakable verticals to talk. Data Distribution Service (DDS) changed into cutting edge by method for the Object Management Group (OMG) and is an IoT favoured for continuous, versatile and exorbitant execution gadget to-framework discussion. Advanced Message Queuing Protocol (AMQP), an undeveloped stock posted well known for offbeat informing through twine. AMQP empowers scrambled and interoperable informing among administrations and projects. The convention is used in client/server informing and in IoT apparatus the executives. Constrained Application Protocol (CoAP), a convention planned through the IETF that determines in what manner low-control process constrained contraptions can work in the web of variables. Long Range wide Area Network, a show for inclusive region sorts out, it's planned to support tremendous frameworks, nearby canny metropolises, with an enormous quantity of low-control contraptions. IoT frameworks consist of:

AWS IoT, a cloud stage for IoT propelled with the guide of amazon. This framework is planned to engage smart gadgets to effectively interface and securely have coordinated effort with the AWS cloud and various related devices. ARM Mbed IoT, a stage to increment applications for the IoT essentially dependent on arm microcontrollers. The point is that the support of Mbed IoT stage is to offer a versatile, related and quiet condition intended for IoT contraptions by incorporating Mbed gear and administrations. Microsoft's purplish blue IoT group, a stage that comprises of an immovable of administrations that empowers clients to draw in through and get measurements of the IoT gadgets notwithstanding perform differing tasks over certainties, together with multidimensional investigation, change and total, and imagine those activities in a way that is fitting for corporate venture. Google's Brillo/weave, a stage for the expedient usage of IoT bundles. The stage comprises of overwhelming spines: Brillo, an android-based working gadget for the improvement of installed low-quality contraptions; and pile, IoT-situated verbal trade convention that serves since the discussion language among the gadget and the cloud. Calvin, an undeveloped stock of IoT stage that can be discharged through Ericsson intended for structure and overseeing dispensed projects that grant gadgets converse with one another. Calvin comprises of an improvement structure for utility designers notwithstanding a runtime surroundings for adapting to the walking software.

Applications of IoT

IoT applications certification to take enormous motivating force into our survives. With increasingly current remote frameworks, predominant sensors and dynamic enlisting limits, the Internet of Things might be the accompanying wild in the contest meant for a great deal of the case.

Figure 5. Applications of Internet of Things
(Upasana, 2018)

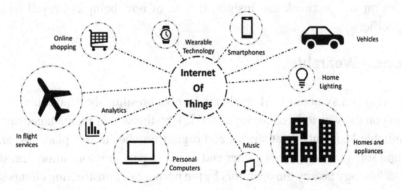

Imagine a keen contraption, for instance, a circulation camera. The camera can screen the roads for road circulation blockage, mishaps, climate circumstances, besides impart of this information toward a typical door. This section in like manner gets information as of further such cameras then moves of the evidence added to a city-wide circulation checking structure. Presently, gross for example, the Public Firm chooses to fix a specific street. This may cause a queue blockage while in transit to a countrywide thruway. This knowledge is delivered to the megalopolis-broad queue checking framework. Presently, seeing this is a savvy traffic framework, it rapidly absorbs and anticipate designs in rush hour gridlock, using AI. The savvy framework can, break down these circumstances, anticipate its effect and transfer the data to different urban communities that interface with a similar roadway through their own individual shrewd frameworks. The Traffic Management System can examine information obtained and determine courses around the undertaking to stay away from bottlenecks. The structure could moreover pass on live headings to motorists through splendid devices and wireless stations. In the meantime, the metropolitan institutes and workplaces near the endeavour could in like manner be called to change their timetables.

Figure 6. Model the Applications of Internet of Things
(Upasana, 2018)

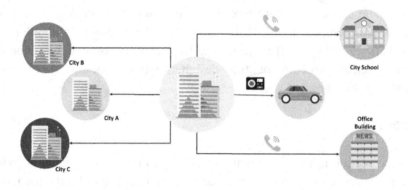

IoT is basically a stage where implanted gadgets are associated with the web, so they can gather and trade information with one another. It empowers gadgets to connect, work together and, gain from one another's encounters simply like people do. IoT applications are relied upon to prepare abundance of ordinary articles through network and insight. It is as of now being conveyed widely, in different domains, to be specific:

IoT Applications – Wearables

It is the modernization is a symbol of IoT applications also presumably is possibly the furthermost on time manufacturing on the way to have conveyed the IoT by the side of its management. These days we usually realize Suitable Moments, beat shades and digital watches at any place. Wearable appliances through devices and software design can gather and examine person information, transfer communications to different technology nearby the operators by the purpose of constructing clients survives simpler and further secured. Wearable gadgets are used to aimed at community safety -- for instance, enhancing initial responders' reaction instances for the duration of crises by using improving developments to an area otherwise through monitoring production employees' or firefighters' important symptoms at existence-threatening web sites. Figure 6 and 7 represents IoT real life commonly used applications.

The lesser-acknowledged wearables fuse the Protector glucose inspection device. The device is made for helping peoples to encounter diabetes. Glucose sensor is a device which recognizes glucose points in our body using a little cathode. It put beneath the skin and moves the information by methods for Wireless Occurrence to a watching contraption.

Figure 7. Application of IoT-Wearables
(Pasluosta et al., 2015)

IoT Applications – Smart Home Applications

Once we exchange conversations about IoT Applications, they are likely the primary concern that we consider. At whatever point we consider IoT structures, the main basic and effective operation that stands isolated is the keen household, arranging the most raised IoT operations on overall the stations. The measure of individuals sifting for cunning homes develops each month by around 60,000 individuals. Extra enamoring object is that record of savvy households aimed at IoT assessment combines 256 affiliations and new associations. More affiliations are correct presently reasonably attracted with sharp homes, correspondingly as close to applications in the field. The assessed extent of financing for sharp home new associations beats $2.5 billion and making at a speedy rate. The once-over of new organizations consolidates indisputable innovative commercial names, for instance, Alert Me or Nest, similarly as different worldwide associations, like Philips, Haier, or Belkin.

Figure 8. Application of IoT- Smart Home Appliances
(Alavi et al.,2018)

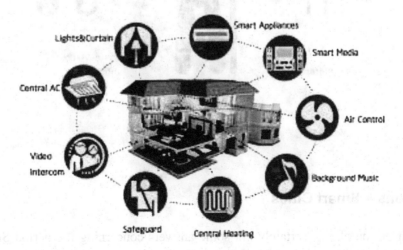

IoT Applications – Health Care

In healthcare, IoT gives many advantages, inclusive of the capability to display sufferers greater carefully to use the facts it truly is generated and analyse it. IoT executes transformation responsive restorative based building addicted to positive health-built frameworks. The rewards that rhythmic movement helpful examination practices, want essential real info. It used for the furthermost portion customs remaining information, measured conditions, and helpers for therapeutic evaluation. IoT releases customs to deal with an aquatic of noteworthy information over examination, steady ground information, and testing. Hospitals frequently use IoT structures to complete obligations which includes stock management, for both prescription drugs and medical units. The Internet of Things furthermore recovers the present contraptions in control, accuracy, and openness. IPT bases on making structures In IoT, separately sheet is characterized by its capacities and the contraptions that are utilized in that sheet relatively than simply gear. Figure 9 represents IoT collaboration with other technology domains such as Human computer Interaction in Medical and health care domain.

Figure 9. Application of IoT- Healthcare System
(The Importance of UX in IoT | HCL Blogs, n.d.)

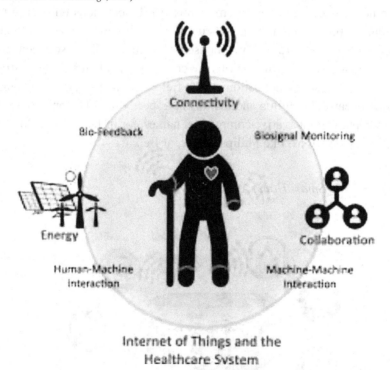

IoT Applications – Smart Cities

An enormous bit of you almost certainly got some answers concerning the period Smart City. The hypothesis of the propelled queue structure. I assigned previously that the one of the various points of view that set up in a splendid city. The item close by the awe-inspiring city thought is that it's extremely certain to a city. The problems glanced in Mumbai are completely not equivalent to those in Delhi. The problems in Hong Kong are not proportional to New York. Undoubtedly, unfluctuating overall the problems, as constrained hygienic consumption liquid, self-destructing air superiority also the growing city thickness, happen in dissimilar powers transversely over urban territories. Along these lines, they impact each city in an unforeseen manner.

The Administration and architects can operate IoT to pause the commonly mind-boggling essentials of city placing plain to every city. The operation of IoT tenders can support in regions such as aqua the board, misuse power, also the disasters. Palo Alto is a real case of smart city. It is the principal town of its sort, that adopted an entirely different strategy towards traffic. They understood, most vehicles in the city go around and round a similar square, looking for parking spaces. That is the fundamental explanation behind traffic blockage in the city. In all the parking spaces in the city an instrument was introduced. These gadgets permit the inhabitance position to each advertisement of the cloud. A little figure of customs could be using the information. It can control the motorists over the most restricted course to an undeveloped point. This game-plan here joins the utilization of gadget packs supporting posterior towards their ideas which indicates the information and customs for different manners of thinking.

IoT Applications – Agriculture

In Agriculture, IoT - on a very basic level made harsh creating frameworks can help screen, as an occasion, smooth, persistence and soil-soaked quality of yield grounds operating related devices. IoT is similarly useful in robotizing water system structures. Bits of knowledge check the normally creating complete masses to touch base at very nearly 10 billion always 2050. To sustain few types of a monstrous people in which one of them wants to marry agribusiness to advancement and achieve finest results. There are different potential results in this field. Such as the Smart Greenhouse. A plant sales outlet developing framework improves the crop of harvests via monitoring biological limitations. In any case, manual dealing with results in progress incident, essentialness hardship, and labour fee, manufacture the techniques in few incredible. A plant sales outlet is introduced for makes it less difficult to be situated just by means of to switch the climate privileged. Instruments show the amount of different limitations as per shown thru the plants essential then refer that towards the cloud. It, by then, frames the data and applies a control movement.

Figure 10. Applications of IoT-Agriculture
(Citing Images and Tables Found Online | UNSW Current Students, 2019)

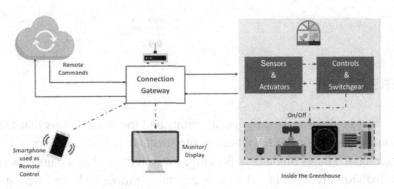

IoT Applications – Industrial Automation

This is an individual ground where all the speedier redesigns, comparatively as per the possibility of things stay a crucial part meant for a vast amount of Arrival on Invests. Through the Applications of IoT, individual might uniform re-engineer things also their pushing in the direction of passing the good act in mutually outlay and consumer skill. At this point IoT can display in the direction of down shifting by answers used for all the going with zones in its munitions store.

- Processing plant Digitalization
- Item stream Monitoring
- Stock Management
- Wellbeing and Reliability
- Survey
- Bundling streamlining
- Coordination and Source linked Optimization

Only in 1-year web related strategies departed since 5 million to billions. Commercial Insider Intellectual watches that 24 billion IoT gadgets would be announced always 2020, making a result further than 300 billion. IoT focuses on, progresses and continues building. Its systems don't show up pre-amassed, they make after a while. The Internet of Things (IoT) has joined gear then programming on the way to the web in the direction of making an increasingly clever creation. It has been creating next to a basic step also suggestions an immense many chance used for administration and commercial. In all honesty, the measure of beginnings for IoT specialists is next to a perfect top.

Figure 11. Applications of IoT- Industrial Automation
(Citing Images and Tables Found Online | UNSW Current Students, 2019)

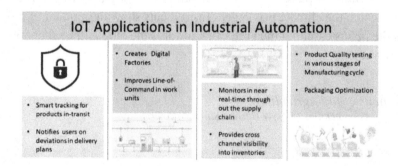

ARCHITECTURE OF IOT

In IoT, separately sheet is characterized by its capacities and the contraptions that are utilized in that sheet. There are lots of conclusions as to figure out the sheets in IoT. Regardless, giving to various investigators, the Internet of Things fundamentally chips away at three sheets named as Awareness, Web, and Claim sheets. Individually sheet of IoT has innate safety problems linked with it. Below displays the elementary three-sheet auxiliary arrangement of IoT with admiration on the way to the gadgets and advancements that join separately sheet.

Discernment Layer

The discern layer is generally called the "Instruments" coat in IoT. The determination behind this coat is to get the information as of the condition through the benefits of instruments and actuators. This sheet recognizes, accumulates, and methodology information and a short time later transmits it to the framework layer. This layer in like manner plays out the IoT center point joint exertion in close by and short-go frameworks.

System Layer

The framework coat of IoT assists the limit of information coordinating what's more, broadcast to un-like IoT focus focuses and contraptions concluded the Web. At this layer, conveyed figuring stages, Internet entries, trading, also directing gadgets, etc work by via a segment of the amazingly continuous advances, for instance, Wi-Fi, LTE, Bluetooth, 3G, Zigbee, etc. The framework openings fill in in place of the center individual for many IoTs centers by gathering, isolating, likewise, conveying information towards different devices.

Application Layer

Its assurances the validity, decency, furthermore, order of the information. At this deposit, the explanation behind IoT or then again, the arrangement of a sharp area is cultivated.

IMPORTANCE OF INTERNET OF THINGS

The web of variables encourages individuals remain and artworks more brilliant just as advantage whole power over their lives. Notwithstanding providing savvy gadgets to robotize houses, IoT is fundamental to commercial undertaking. IoT bears associations with a continuous look in what way the associations' structures really masterful manifestations, giving over encounters into all from the introduction of technologies to pass on chain and coordination errands. IoT authorize associations to systematize forms and reduce efforts charges. It furthermore removes squander and upgrade bearer transport, better significantly less costly to manufacture and pass on items notwithstanding offering straightforwardness into customer trades. IoT associates each factory, alongside human facilities, currency, trade and gathering. Keen town groups support occupants lessen unused and quality admission and linked devices are uniform utilized in cultivating to support show harvest and ranch creatures yields and expect increment styles. All things considered, IoT is one of the most significant advances of standard ways of life and it will protect to pick up steam as more prominent organizations perceive the limit of related gadgets to keep them aggressive.

Figure 12. Importance of IoT
(Lee & Lee, 2015)

CURRENT CHALLENGES OF INTERNET OF THINGS

It is another perspective like it can enable assembling and exchanging data that have never been reachable already. It prepared to pass on and report customer's information in an undeniably secure manner. The reports of Cisco specialists check that the IoT will have more than 50 billion of splendid sensors and other splendid devices or contraptions, all partner and passing on continuous data on the web by 2020. This will give further bits of learning data assessment using the IoT perspective to develop new business, improve proficiency and adequacy, and make creative pay streams. Besides, the IoT configuration may unite features and advances proposed by various methods. Since, this building is organized where the progressed and real universes are joining and partner constantly, various headways are consolidated to shape IoT, for instance, distinguishing headways, unpreventable figuring, unavoidable handling, web shows, astute articles, embedded parts, etc. Exactly when a standard device uses sharp administrators, it transforms into a smart article. Along these lines, it isn't simply used to gather the earth information or on the other hand interface with the physical world, yet more than that, it must be interconnected with various framework devices to exchange additionally, grant data over the web. Accordingly, the gigantic extent of open data which is conveyed by the epic number of interconnected contraptions will offer opportunities to make information that will pass on critical points of interest to the economy. The improvement of computational things and things have been outfitted with correspondence and canny capacities of embedded knowledge. This improvement induces over the span of the fast headway of the IoT field. Around the rising IoT perspective, a worldwide amazing framework will interface everything and anything by confining virtual linkage of joined and addressable devices.

Henceforward, the outcome will bolster customers to develop novel responses for be a strong and weighty key structure to the around the globe. In this way, the examples of IoT space have been discussed in this paper in the perspective of different research areas, for instance, structure, data getting ready, security and insurance. Finally, we have analysed the essential IOT nuts and bolts close by the execution challenges what's progressively, future course of its requirements.

SECURITY ON "INTERNET OF THINGS"

The reliability has demonstrated clear inadequacies, in addition, isn't near the security of existing PC structures. While the Internet of Things have grown quickly in the course of the maximum current couple of years, the core interest on safety has not kept up. The Internet of Things presents a plenty of new imperatives and difficulties that expects security to be engaged on in another manner than is normal in existing information frameworks. While the present frameworks use measures that are anything but difficult to execute and works for most types of correspondence and capacity, there is no such standard arrangement that will take a shot at each gadget inside the Internet of Things, because of the changed impediments between different contraptions, realizing game plans inside the Internet of Things. This theory establishes the framework on how security ought to be taken care of inside the Internet of Things, both in present and future frameworks. Existing gadgets inside various spaces and with various innovations, have been broke down to make an unmistakable, substantial image of the difficulties and arrangements that exists in the Internet of Things today. The three principle limitations in the Internet of Things, calculation, data transmission and vitality, are portrayed and used to make the establishment for the difficulties that are exhibited. Various potential fates for the Internet of Things, and what difficulties that will involve, are likewise depicted. The answers for the difficulties will attentive between what assets are accessible, so an inside and out introduction of potential arrangements dependent on accessible assets are clarified. To build the attention among designers on significant inquiries with respect to security, complete rules are displayed sequentially from start to finish of structure, improvement and support of gadgets in the Internet of Things, directed towards engineers both with and without inside and out learning of data security. Potential arrangements, furthermore, options are exhibited, just as key inquiries that will make engineers consider the outcomes of the decisions they make during the procedure. Security in the present Internet of Things isn't as great at it should be. This proposition demonstrates some glaring defects in existing items, which is frequently made because of oversight from the designers, as the imperatives existing in IoT requires a more careful point of view than is typical in work area registering. Because of constrained power, data transfer capacity and preparing power, everything requirements to get stripped down to the absolute minimum, while yet keeping up great security properties.

Security is an oversight in numerous undertakings. Utilizing models from past research, what's more, leading exceptional investigation on existing items, it is demonstrated that numerous designers pretty much disregards everything identified with security (BMW, Home Easy, Sonos), or makes their own cryptographic calculations with clear blemishes (Eye-Fi, OSGP smart grid). To guarantee that the eventual fate of IoT is secure, this proposition intends to make engineers consider the confinements that exists and give answers for the issues that will happen when planning a gadget for the Internet of Things (IoT). Verifying the Internet of Things is fundamental to buyer. Through past inquire about it is demonstrated precisely how obliterating not concentrating on the security of IoT gadgets can be, with most of buyers (62%) "feeling totally abused what's more, very irate to the point where I would make a

Figure 13. IoT in Security
(seouser, 2017)

move.". Near half (48%) of all customers would consider the maker dependable if an imperfection was to be found in the framework, demonstrating the undeniable efficient dangers taken by not verifying a gadget appropriately. A portion of the themes of difficulties introduced are basic in information security, in any case, presents new difficulties due to the remarkable requirements. Verifying an IT framework requires classification, respectability, and authorization. Where this typically is dealt with by libraries like OpenSSL and utilizing TLS int work stations, settling on an encryption, confirmation and mark calculation isn't as simple as calling an alternate strategy. The constrained power, data transfer capacity and preparing abilities will require a careful manner of thinking to choose how to both proficiently, and adequately secure a gadget. Different difficulties are progressively explicit to the Internet of Things. In standard work area processing, a propelled UI is generally accessible, and physical misfortune of a gadget during use is generally unprecedented. IoT gadgets will then again normally have a truly restricted UIs, and will regularly be put in uncovered regions also, utilized in circumstances with high physical pressure. Security ought to be a thought through the entire venture. Sometime before the first model PCB-plan is sent to the processing plant, key choices on security ought to have been chosen. These incorporate how keys ought to be circulated to every gadget, if equipment speeding up ought to be utilized, how updates can be taken care of, if PKI is a reasonable answer for the gadget, what sort of cryptographic calculations ought to be utilized, and so forth. The Internet of Things any place will create billions of contraptions, individuals and associations to interrelate and trade information and pleasing information. As IoT buildings will be comprehensive and unescapable, diverse wellbeing and affirmation problems will rise. In the daily basis, the IoT vision, current safety perils, and exposed troubles in the region of IoT are inspected. The back and forth movement public of investigation on IoT safety necessities is debated besides upcoming investigation orientation concerning IoT safety and coverage are shown. The Internet of Things is a one of a kind overall framework establishment with self-organizing limits subject to standard and interoperable correspondence shows. Physical and practical things consume characters, bodily traits, and computer-generated characters, use canny edges that are perfectly combined addicted to the data form. The idea of IoT is to enable individuals also effects to be associated at whatever point, wherever, with everything and anybody, in a perfect creation by techniques in the least method/system and association. Distinguishing proof advances, for example, RFID and related instruments will be the foundation of the forthcoming Internet of Things. Shrewd parts are anticipated to be equipped for executing various arrangements of activities, as per the environment and errands they are intended for. There will be no restriction to the activities and tasks these savvy things can perform; for example, gadgets will most likely coordinate their exchange, adjust to their particular surroundings, self-arrange, self-keep up, self-fix, and in the long run even assume a working occupation in their individual special exchange. The IoT make it conceivable to build up various applications either intently or legitimately appropriate to our present living, for example, individual and general areas, versatility and conveying spaces, venture and industry spaces just as administration and utility checking spaces. So as to make IoT administrations accessible with an enormous number of gadgets speaking with one another, there are numerous difficulties to survive. The safety showdowns identified with safety administrations have been examined, for example, validation, protection, dependability, and start to finish safety. In synopsis, it is inferred that to understand the IoT, more grounded safety representations are necessitated that utilize setting linked security, which consequently will enable residents to assemble trust and trust in these novel advances as opposed to build fears toward complete observation situations. The central target of this paper was to give an express review for the furthermost critical pieces of IoT with explicit attention scheduled the idea also safety troubles connected with the Internet of Things. The idea of IoT will empower individuals and belongings to be related at whatever point, with everything and everyone, if possible, consuming any way/mastermind and any organizations. Even though Wireless Occurrence Proof of identity procedures and the associated advancements get the idea of IoT attainable, there are a few conceivable application territories for savvy objects. The major IoT targets incorporate making brilliant conditions and unsure/self-sufficient gadgets, e.g., keen vehicle, savvy things, shrewd urban communities, savvy wellbeing, savvy living, etc. Different issues and inflames correlated to IoT are consequently faraway life gone up

Figure 14. Smart Home Appliances

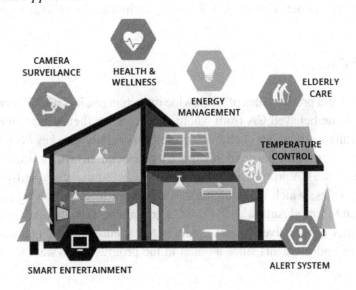

against. Difficulties alike confirming interoperability, accomplishing a ready strategy in which a colossal number of articles can be interrelated through an agenda, also safety and declaration tasks, used for occurrence approval and authorization of materials are displayed. In the following years, tending to these difficulties will continually be the concentration and essential assignment of systems administration and correspondence examine in both modern and scholastic research centres.

PUBLIC LEY INFRASTRUCTURE (PKI)

"A public key infrastructure (PKI) permits clients of the Internet and other open systems to participate in secure correspondence, information trade and cash trade".

Public Key Infrastructure (PKI) to ensure the open key while yet enabling its source to be followed. Each PKI regularly includes at least one CA which make and issue advanced authentications. Each endorsement contains the open key of the private key holder, the name of the private key holder, a sequential number, the name of the accreditation power and other picked and huge focal points. The testaments are carefully set apart by the CA to ensure their protection and decency. There are a few layers of security PKIs are both extremely secure and dependable. The methodology consolidates a couple of layers of security, including the choice to check the sign of the affirmation power incorporated into the confirmation. When affirmed, the beneficiary concentrates the open key and interprets the information. PKI systems are that they are costly and confused, require great arranging and can be difficult to keep up establishment and organization. The usage method can be reached out for IT staff people, considering PKI systems oblige individual submitted hardware and servers to work to their most extreme limit. Customers will battle generally with the entangled system to build up wellbeing. Security mindfulness preparing ought to be obliged to smooth out any customer request or concerns and assurance that the structure is being used appropriately. Such preparing ought to teach customers on the most ideal approach to guarantee their private keys through a couple of security best practices, for instance, secure limit, offsite versatile workstation insurance, hostile to malware frameworks and how to pick a solid login secret word. PKIs can similarly be used as a sort of two-factor confirmation. The advancement will fill in as one with other confirmation gadgets and higher security then a solitary technique for validation would.

HIERARCHY OF CA

With immense systems and prerequisites of worldwide interchanges, it is for all intents and purposes not attainable to have just one believed CA from whom all clients get their declarations. In such case, the various levelled accreditation model is of enthusiasm since it enables open key declarations to be utilized in conditions where two conveying parties don't have trust associations with a similar CA. The origin CA is at the highest point of the CA progression and the root CA's testament is a self-marked endorsement. The Certificate Authorities, which are straightforwardly subordinate to the origin CA (For instance, Central Authority 1 and Central Authority 2) have CA testaments that are marked by the origin CA.

Declaration authority progressive systems are reflected in authentication chains. An authentication chain follows a way of endorsements since a outlet in the progressive system to the foundation of the

Figure 15. Heirarchy of Certificate Authorities
(Public Key Infrastructure – Tutorials point, n.d.)

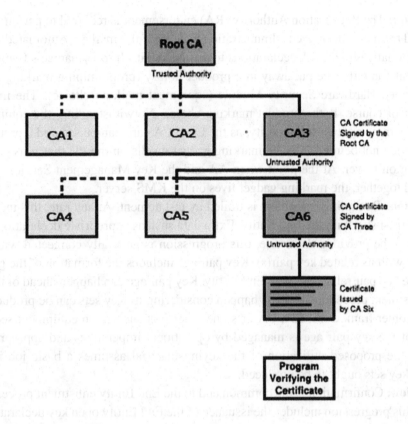

pecking order. The accompanying outline display a CA pecking order with an endorsement chain driving from an element authentication through two subordinate CA declarations (CA6 and CA3) to the CA testament for the origin of Central Authority.

Confirming an authentication chain is the way toward guaranteeing that a testament chain is legitimate, effectively marked, and dependable. The accompanying strategy confirms an endorsement chain, starting with the testament that is displayed for verification –

- A customer whose legitimacy is being checked supplies his authentication, by and large alongside the chain of endorsements active to the Origin of Central Authority.
- The Authenticate receipts the authentication and approves via utilizing open significant of backer. The guarantor's open key is found in the backer's endorsement which is in the chain by customer's declaration.
- Nowadays, progressive CA who has noticeable the sponsor's authorization, is important by the verifier, crisscross is operative and breaks here.
- Otherwise, the guarantor's testament is checked likewise as accomplished for customer in above advances. This procedure proceeds till either believed Central Authority is originate in the middle of or otherwise it yields till origin Central Authority.

PKI MANAGEMENT FUNCTIONS

- **Registration:** The Registration Authority (RA) endorsement is required to permit all information transmitted from the Automated administration to be carefully marked. Automated Administration (AA) additionally utilizes RA declarations to distinguish itself to Symantec's Issuing Centre. The endorsement can either be put away in a product library (programming marking alternative), or on an affirmed Hardware Security Module (equipment marking choice). The marking gadget, as a matter of course, is the product marking choice. Notwithstanding, the equipment marking choice gives more noteworthy security, as the Luna CA card can be secured a protected stockpiling zone when not being used. The marking gadget dwells on the PC that runs your Automated Administration server. At the point when AA and the Key Management Service (KMS) choices are utilized together, the marking gadget lives on the KMS server.

- **Initialization:** Beginning enlistment is trailed by instatement. At any rate, this includes instating the related trust stay with the End Entity. Extra data such as appropriate declaration arrangements may likewise be provided. Likewise, this progression is generally connected with instating the End Entity with its related key pair(s). Key pair age includes the formation of the general population/private key pair related with an End Entity. Key pair age can happen ahead of time of the End Entity enlistment procedure or it can happen considering it. Key sets can be produced by the End Entity customer framework, RA, CA or some other part such as an equipment security module. The area of the key pair age is managed by operational imperatives and appropriate strategies. Regularly, the proposed utilization of the keying material assumes a basic job in figuring out where the key sets ought to be produced.

- **Certification:** Confirmation is the common end to the End Entity enlistment process. As its name suggests, this progression includes the issuance of the End Entity open key declaration by the CA. On the off chance that the key pair is produced outside to the CA, the open key segment must be

Figure 16. Certificate Authority
(Housley, 2001)

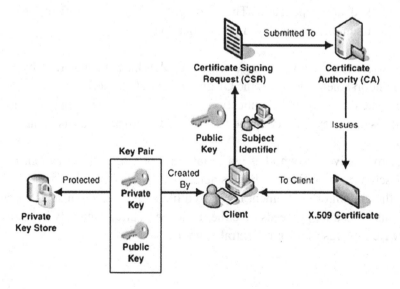

passed on to the CA in a safe way. Once produced, the endorsement is come back to the End Entity or potentially distributed to an authentication archive. Much though we have exhibited enlistment, instatement and accreditation as independent the executive's capacities, note that at least two of these can be consolidated into a solitary convention activity. For instance, this is the situation with the PKIX Certificate Management Protocols.

- **Key Pair Recovery:** Key sets can be utilized to help computerized signature creation and check, encryption and unscrambling, or both. At the point when a key pair is utilized for encryption/ decoding, it is essential to give a system to recuperate the vital unscrambling keys when "typical" access to the keying material is never again conceivable, else it won't be conceivable to recuperate the scrambled data.4 Normal access to the decoding key can result from overlooked passwords/ PINs, undermined plate drives, harm to equipment tokens, and so on. Key pair recuperation permits End Entities to re-establish their encryption/ unscrambling key pair from an approved key fortification office (normally, the CA that given the End Entity's testament). It is additionally conceivable that an End Entity's relationship with an association can change (for instance, on account of worker renunciation, rejection, or individual damage), and the association has a genuine need to recuperate information that has been scrambled by that End Entity. It is additionally conceivable that entrance to the keying material might be required in relationship with genuine law implementation necessities. Key pair recuperation can be utilized to help both necessities also.

- **Key Pair update:** Testaments are given with fixed lifetimes (alluded to as the "legitimacy period" of the endorsement). While these fixed lifetimes can be liberal (express two to five years or somewhere in the vicinity), the testament will in the end lapse. Key pair update may likewise be required ever since of testament denial as examined in Section 3.2.6. Key pair update includes age of another key pair, and the issuance of another open key certificate5 Key pair update can happen ahead of time of a given key pair's lapse. This will help to guarantee that the End Entity is consistently possessing an authentic key pair. Although the PKIX working gathering prescribes against the utilization of this element on the Web, it is conceivable to build up various legitimacy periods for the private and open keys that are utilized to carefully sign and check. This would compel a key pair update before the related open key really lapses. It likewise gives a window of time where the non-lapsed open key endorsement can be used to check computerized marks that were made with the now lapsed private key. This will limit insignificant admonition messages that would some way or another be shown to the End Entity.

- **Cross- Verification:** cross-affirmation happens between Central Authorities. A cross-declaration is an open key authentication that is given by one CA to alternative CA. At the end of the day, a cross-testament is an open key authentication that holds the open vital of a CA that takes carefully marked by another CA. Many translate cross-affirmation to signify "between space" cross-accreditation. Notwithstanding, "intra-area" cross-accreditation is likewise conceivable. This can be shown by utilizing the Government of Canada (GOC) PKI for instance. Significant divisions inside the GOC PKI cross-affirm with the Canadian Central Facility, which goes about as a connect CA between these divisions. As these offices all "have a place" to the GOC PKI, this is "intra-area" cross-confirmation. The Canadian Central Facility is likewise liable for cross-affirmation with outer PKI spaces, for example, the US Government Bridge CA. This is "between area" cross-confirmation. It ought to likewise be noticed that cross-confirmation can be bi-directional or unidirectional. Bi-directional cross-affirmation ordinarily happens between peer CAs as portrayed in the past section. Unidirectional cross-confirmation commonly happens in a progressive trust model where better CAs issue cross-declarations than subordinate CAs, yet the switch isn't valid.

FUTURE ASPECTS OF INTERNET OF THINGS

As indicated in figure 17 the world is pushing ahead at a quick pace, and the credit goes to consistently developing innovation. One such idea is IoT with which mechanization is never again a computer-generated experience. IoT associates different non-living articles through the web and empowers them to impart data to their locale system to computerize forms for people and makes their lives simpler. The paper introduces what's to come difficulties of IoT, for example, the specialized (network, similarity and life span, principles, astute investigation and activities, security), business (venture, unassuming income model and so on), cultural (evolving requests, new gadgets, cost, client certainty and so forth) and law-ful difficulties (laws, guidelines, methods, approaches and so forth). An area additionally talks about the different fantasies that may hamper the advancement of IoT, security of information being the most basic factor of all. A hopeful way to deal with individuals in receiving the unfurling changes brought by IoT will likewise help in its development. While utilizing information gathered from gadgets carefully, reliance of IoT on versatile systems, significance of the information made from various contraptions, vitality of systems close by datacentres, necessity of an affirmed association structure with disengaged controller determinations, movement of interoperability measures, heterogeneity and straightforward-ness are a touch of the issues that should be kept an eye out for, wellbeing and protection of information will play a basic occupation how the image of Internet of Things will look like in the coming decades flexible frameworks, importance of the data delivered from different devices, hugeness of frameworks close by datacentres, need of a confirmed organization system with remote control choices, progression of interoperability checks, heterogeneity and straightforwardness are a part of the issues that ought to be watched out for, security and insurance of data will show a vital activity in how the picture of IoT will look similar as the approaching years.. Parallel to it additionally comes the difficulties looked by this innovation that represent a danger to its prosperity. The most critical difficulties of things to come of IoT is associate a few gadgets, this correspondence will wind up opposing the at present existing structure

Figure 17. Future of Internet of Things
(Zhang et al., 2014)

furthermore, the advancements related with it. Directly, a concentrated, server/customer engineering is being used to validate, approve and associate a few terminals in a system. Each angle including innovation, business, society and law oppose the achievement pace of IoT. Acknowledgment of innovation by individuals is additionally fundamental and ought to be mulled over during its advancement as individuals who are not partial to utilizing devices, savvy gadgets and don't feel good managing innovation will have a troublesome time working with the intricacy usefulness IOT will lock in them with. Ample opportunity has already past to manage the variables that may fundamentally cut down the strong eventual fate of IoT.

REFERENCES

Abomhara, M., & Køien, G. M. (2014, May). Security and privacy in the Internet of Things: Current status and open issues. In *2014 international conference on privacy and security in mobile systems (PRISMS)* (pp. 1-8). IEEE.

Alavi, A. H., Jiao, P., Buttlar, W. G., & Lajnef, N. (2018). Internet of Things-enabled smart cities: State-of-the-art and future trends. *Measurement, 129,* 589–606. doi:10.1016/j.measurement.2018.07.067

Atzori, L., Iera, A., Morabito, G., & Nitti, M. (2012). The social internet of things (siot)–when social networks meet the internet of things: Concept, architecture and network characterization. *Computer Networks, 56*(16), 3594–3608. doi:10.1016/j.comnet.2012.07.010

Chen, S., Xu, H., Liu, D., Hu, B., & Wang, H. (2014). A vision of IoT: Applications, challenges, and opportunities with china perspective. *IEEE Internet of Things Journal, 1*(4), 349-359.

Citing Images and Tables Found Online | UNSW Current Students. (2019). https://student.unsw.edu.au/citing-images-and-tables-found-online https://dzone.com/articles/the-internet-of-thingsgateways-and-next-generation

Conoscenti, M., Vetro, A., & De Martin, J. C. (2016, November). Blockchain for the Internet of Things: A systematic literature review. In *2016 IEEE/ACS 13th International Conference of Computer Systems and Applications (AICCSA)* (pp. 1-6). IEEE. 10.1109/AICCSA.2016.7945805

Hern, C. (2016, October 23). *IoT Smart City – What is a Smart City?* http://www.infiniteinformation-technology.com/IoT-smart-city-what-is-smart-home

Hierarchies, C. A. (Sun Directory Server Enterprise Edition 7.0 Reference). (n.d.). https://docs.oracle.com/cd/E19424-01/820-4811/gdzdp/index.html

Housley, R., & Polk, T. (2001). *Planning for PKI: best practices guide for deploying public key infrastructure.* John Wiley & Sons, Inc.

IoT explained: What is the internet of things? (n.d.). *IoT Agenda.* Retrieved February 23, 2020, from https://internetofthingsagenda.techtarget.com/feature/Explained-What-is-the-Internet-of-Things

Khan, M. A., & Salah, K. (2018). IoT security: Review, blockchain solutions, and open challenges. *Future Generation Computer Systems, 82,* 395–411. doi:10.1016/j.future.2017.11.022

Khan, R., Khan, S. U., Zaheer, R., & Khan, S. (2012). Future internet: the internet of things architecture, possible applications and key challenges. In *2012 10th international conference on frontiers of information technology*, (pp. 257-260). IEEE. 10.1109/FIT.2012.53

Lee, I., & Lee, K. (2015). The Internet of Things (IoT): Applications, investments, and challenges for enterprises. *Business Horizons*, *58*(4), 431–440. doi:10.1016/j.bushor.2015.03.008

Leo, M., Battisti, F., Carli, M., & Neri, A. (2014, November). A federated architecture approach for Internet of Things security. In *2014 Euro Med Telco Conference (EMTC)* (pp. 1-5). IEEE. 10.1109/EMTC.2014.6996632

Madakam, S., Lake, V., Lake, V., & Lake, V. (2015). Internet of Things (IoT): A literature review. *Journal of Computer and Communications*, *3*(05), 164–173. doi:10.4236/jcc.2015.35021

Mahmoud, R., Yousuf, T., Aloul, F., & Zualkernan, I. (2015, December). Internet of things (IoT) security: Current status, challenges and prospective measures. In *2015 10th International Conference for Internet Technology and Secured Transactions (ICITST)* (pp. 336-341). IEEE.

Pasluosta, C. F., Gassner, H., Winkler, J., Klucken, J., & Eskofier, B. M. (2015). An emerging era in the management of Parkinson's disease: Wearable technologies and the internet of things. *IEEE Journal of Biomedical and Health Informatics*, *19*(6), 1873–1881. doi:10.1109/JBHI.2015.2461555 PMID:26241979

Public Key Infrastructure – Tutorials point. (n.d.). Www.Tutorialspoint.Com. https://www.tutorialspoint.com/cryptography/public_key_infrastructure.htm

Seouser. (2017, October 10). IoT Security: Understanding PKI's Role in Securing Internet of Things. *About SSL Certificates*. https://cheapsslsecurity.com/blog/iot-security-understanding-pki-role-in-securing-internet-of-things/

Team, D. (2018, June 16). *Top 10 Interesting Facts About Future of IoT*. https://data-flair.training/blogs/future-of-IoT

The Importance of UX in IoT | HCL Blogs. (n.d.). *Importance of UC in IOT*. https://www.hcltech.com/blogs/importance-ux-IoT

Tuen, C. D. (2015). *Security in Internet of Things Systems* (Master's thesis). NTNU.

Upasana. (2018, September 20). Real World IoT Applications in Different Domains. *Edureka*. https://internetofthingsagenda.techtarget.com/definition/Internet-of-Things-IoT

Zhang, Z. K., Cho, M. C. Y., Wang, C. W., Hsu, C. W., Chen, C. K., & Shieh, S. (2014, November). IoT security: ongoing challenges and research opportunities. In *2014 IEEE 7th international conference on service-oriented computing and applications* (pp. 230-234). IEEE. 10.1109/SOCA.2014.58

Zhao, K., & Ge, L. (2013, December). A survey on the internet of things security. In *2013 Ninth international conference on computational intelligence and security* (pp. 663-667). IEEE. 10.1109/CIS.2013.145

Chapter 3
Deep Learning and IoT:
The Enabling Technologies Towards Smart Farming

Muhammad Suleman Memon
https://orcid.org/0000-0002-0418-0681
University of Sindh Jamshoro, Dadu Campus, Pakistan

Pardeep Kumar
https://orcid.org/0000-0002-8624-9020
Quaid-e-Awam University of Engineering, Science, and Technology, Pakistan

Azeem Ayaz Mirani
https://orcid.org/0000-0003-2083-9391
Department of Information Technology, Shaheed Benazir Bhutto University, Pakistan

Mumtaz Qabulio
https://orcid.org/0000-0002-9294-2657
Institute of Information and Communication Technology, University of Sindh, Jamshoro, Pakistan

Irum Naz Sodhar
https://orcid.org/0000-0001-9082-4924
Department of Information Technology, Shaheed Benazir Bhutto University, Pakistan

ABSTRACT

The agriculture sector plays a big part in the overall economy of any country. The population of the world is increasing day by day, which is also increasing the overall demand of the food. Due to various diseases and nature of the soil, it is difficult to meet the overall demand of the food. The agronomists and farmers also face many problems in the agriculture sector such as disease identification, knowing nature of the soil, pesticide management, etc. The old methods of managing crop do not help in an effective way in meeting the increasing demand for food. The modern methods such IOT, machine, deep learning, and image processing help to identify the crop health and to predict crop yield. This chapter generally discusses various state-of-the-art technologies and methods for predicting crop yield and disease identification.

DOI: 10.4018/978-1-7998-2803-7.ch003

INTRODUCTION

The population of the world is growing rapidly, and the demand of the food is increasing. The world is using modern techniques of smart farming to increase the crop productivity with the help of IOT, cloud computing, machine learning and deep learning. Deep learning is the sub field of AI and machine learning. In order to meet large increasing demand of food the food security and crop yield prediction is important. This can be achieved by using the technologies such as deep learning. Crop diseases cause huge damage to the crop. The disease affects different areas such as leaf, flower, stem etc. The disease identification at an early stage is difficult, time consuming and costly. Due to multiple diseases in the crop, the crop does not give enough production and does not meet the over all demand of the food. The crop disease identification with manual methods such hiring experts to visit the land physically is a very difficult job to visit whole land and identify the infected areas. As human can overlook and leave the infected areas unattended. This does not help to asses the crop correctly. Therefore, the technology can help in this area to assess the disease early when it first appears. The correct and timely disease identification helps farmers and agronomists to protect the crop from the loss, to increase the crop production and to meet the food demand. The deep learning is a new field of AI which helps a lot to identify the crop diseases timely and effectively. The correct disease identification (Kamilaris and Prenafeta-Boldú, 2018) is a difficult job. First step in disease identification is to capture image through mobile camera, drone camera or through different sensing devices such employing different camera sensors, then analyzing and classifying the images according to diseases they contain. The sensing methods are used to acquire images remotely includes satellite, multispectral, hyperspectral, near infrared and many more. There are many popular techniques available to process digital image and classify image according to the infected parts of the leaf, fruit or stem. The commonly used techniques for analyzing and classifying images includes machine learning, K-Means algorithm and SVM. DL is like ANN. These all mentioned techniques are good at some point but when we it is required to know deep inside then the Deep Learning is more powerful technique to solve this type of problem.

Deep Learning

Artificial Intelligence is a broad field and has been for long time. The deep learning is the sub field of Artificial Intelligence. The human brain contains almost 86 billion neurons. The activity of human spinal card and other things are carried out by neurons in the brain. The Natural Neuron contains a very complex structure. The Artificial Neural Networks mimics the Natural Neuron. The artificial neurons work same as natural neurons where one neuron carries information and passes to another neuron. The deep learning deals with neural networks with more than two layers. Deep learning methods (LeCun, Bengio, and Hinton, 2015) are also called representation learning methods. They give multiple level of representation. We take an example of image as we know image comprised of pixel values and represented in the form of array. The first layer typically represents the presence or absence of edges at some location in the image. The second layer detects motifs. The third layer assembles motifs into large combinations that form a close relationship with known parts of objects and later all are combined. The deep learning models (Pamina and Raja, 2019) should at least contain three layers . Every layer in deep learning receives data from the previous layer and sends it to the next layer. The deep learning models works very well with huge volume of data than the lesser data. Image classification provides a great opportunity to extend research in the field of agriculture.

Figure 1. AI and Deep Learning

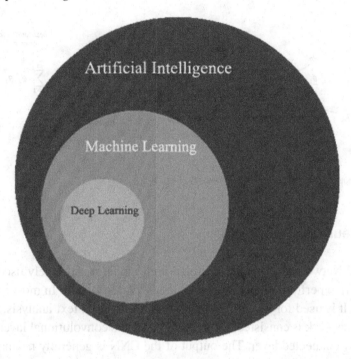

Figure 2 shows the function of deep learning. The model is trained to identify the input. The example illustrated in figure 2 is a model of identifying a Car. The network contains number of hidden layers.

Figure 2. Deep Learning function

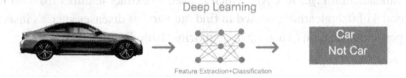

Deep Neural Network

The perceptron is the fundamental building block of deep learning which is a single neuron on a neural network. The figure 3 shows the working mechanism of neural network. The network has n inputs each multiplied by a weight. The weighted combination of n inputs is then summed up. Deep Neural Network contains multiple hidden layers.

Figure 3. Neural Network Architecture
(Pamina and Raja 2019)

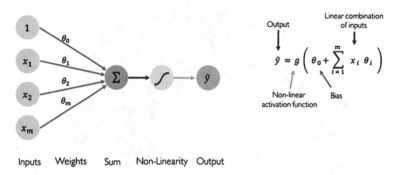

Convolutional Neural Network

Convolutional Neural Network [4-5] is the deep learning model most widely used for large scale images (Xiao et al. 2018) to perform object detection, image classification. In most cases CNN is applied to image processing. It is used for image recognition, classification, text analysis, video labeling. The convolutional neural network is consisted of three layers, first is convolutional layers, second is pooling layer and third is fully connected layer. The output of the CNN is generally normalized with SoftMax activation function. The convolutional neural network is most widely used due its great results in image recognition and classification. The deep learning model CNN (Yamashita et al. 2018) processes data that has grid patterns and adapts automatically to learn from hierarchies from low to high level patterns. The CNN model contains convolution which is used to process 2D image, since the image is in array form and contains pixel values. The CNN is used to extract features from an image as the nature of an image it can contain the feature at any location, so the CNN is a best model to extract features from an image. The performance of CNN model is measured through loss function. The convolution layer (Yamashita et al. 2018) is a fundamental layer in CNN which is used to extract features from an image. In recent years the CNN model of deep learning is used to find out various diseases such as insect identification, weed detection, pest classification (Thenmozhi and Srinivasulu Reddy, 2019).

Figure 4. Typical CNN Architecture

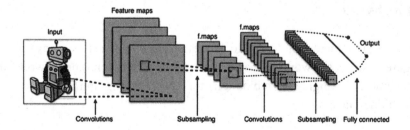

Convolution Neural Network Architectures

- GoogleNet
- AlextNet
- ResNet
- CifarNet

Figure 5. Emotion Detection using CNN

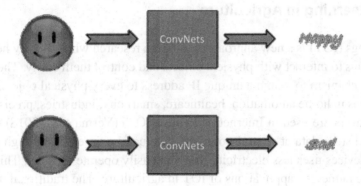

Deep Convolutional Neural Network

Deep Convolutional Neural Network is gaining lot of attention due to its power for providing accuracy in image classification.

Recurrent Neural Network

The recurrent neural network (Zhang et al. 2018) is a sequential learning model. The model learns from previous input data to predict the next input. For input units the model includes (x0,x1,.....xt,xt+1,.....), for hidden units {s0,s1,.....st,st+1,.....} and for output units it includes {y0,y1,.......yt+1,.....}.

Transfer Learning

Transfer learning (Bosilj et al. 2019, 2019; Coulibaly et al. 2019; Kaya et al. 2019; Mehdipour Ghazi, Yanikoglu, and Aptoula 2017) uses pre trained models such as ResNet, VGG, GoogleNet, AlexNet. Transfer learning allows to learn from previously trained data. For example, in transfer learning applied to recognize apples may help to recognize pears (Pan and Yang, 2010). Transfer learning techniques are categorized in three ways, what to transfer, how to transfer and when to transfer. The technique helps solve problems through utilizing previously knowledge.

Applications of Deep Learning

- Pattern analysis
- classification
- Speech recognition
- Audio Processing
- Natural Language Processing (NLP)
- Computer Vision

IOT and Deep Learning in Agriculture

The Internet of Things (IOT) is a new approach in modern research which is very helpful for providing a great help to humans to interact with physical objects and control them easily. The Internet of Things (IOT) provides a mechanism to assign a unique IP address to every physical object. Internet of Things has many applications in home automation, healthcare, smart city, industries, precision agriculture and many more. The sensors are used in Internet of Things (IOT) (Verma et al. 2018) to gather data from the environment and store data at central point and data can be accessed through internet for further analysis. The IOT devices uses less electricity they can easily operate on solar. This also saves cost of electricity. There are numerous applications of IOT in agriculture. The traditional methods are applied monitoring crop health, measuring the Ph level, measuring the nature of the soil etc. Manual methods are inaccurate, time consuming, and human reliant. The IOT plays an important role in precision agriculture. The use of IOT in agriculture (Puranik et al. 2019) helps in automation of agriculture such as minimizing human effort, providing quick access to crop and soil health, remotely monitoring crop etc. Different sensors such as Ph sensor, DHT sensor, soil sensor etc are deployed in the agriculture field to gather data of the crop periodically. In figure 6 shows the drone is deployed in the field to gather series of images of the crop and are stored in the central database. The farmer can access the field images in a real time. This is quite helpful for farmers to know the nature of crop. Timely and accurately gathering data from the crop helps in making timely decisions in farm management. Since last many years the research on Unmanned Ground Vehicles (UGVs) and Unmanned Aerial Vehicles (UAVs) (Bacco et al. 2018) is going. The UAVs utilizing tiny sensors in drones make it small and light weight. The UAVs are commercially utilized in agriculture industry. The drones are utilized at various places in the agriculture field to monitor the health of plants. The UGVs are used more due to less human threat. As compared to UAVs the UGVs are more secure. The UAVs may cause damage such as flight collision with other objects or on the ground.

The deep learning is helpful once data is collected. The Back propagation neural network (Abouzahir et al. 2017) works like human brain. The network solves various problems of segmentation. K-means clustering algorithm perform image segmentation in combining similar pixel values of images. Only deploying sensors such as soil sensor will not give clear idea. Deep learning can be applied once the data is collected about the nature of the soil. Deep learning (Aruul Mozhi Varman et al. 2017) will predict which crop will be suitable according to the nature of the soil.

Figure 6. Smart Agriculture using IOT
(Abouzahir, Sadik, and Sabir 2017)

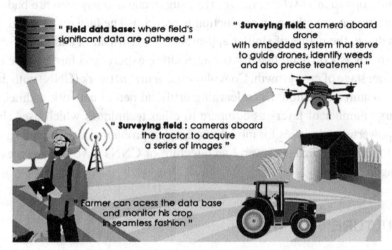

Deep Learning in Agriculture for Identifying Crop Health

Crop disease is the major problem in agriculture. The damage in the crops caused by diseases result in a major economic loss (Kamilaris and Prenafeta-Boldú, 2018). It is important to diagnose the disease in crop at an early stage to stop it from further spreading. The traditional methods of identifying crop diseases is dependent on human and it is time-consuming job. In recent years the technology has improved a lot. Computer vision and machine learning in the past played an important role in crop disease identification. But recent approaches such as deep learning (Thenmozhi and Srinivasulu Reddy, 2019)

Figure 7. UAV Based Unmanned Aerial Weed Classification
(Lottes et al. 2017)

helps identify crop diseases, classify fruits, identify weed and identify crop pests more accurately. The growth of different crops such as wheat, maize, rice, sugarcane and soybean are badly affected due to attack of various pests therefore the crop production is reduced. The farmers find it difficult to classify the infected crops due to the nature of similar appearance. Classification and identification of all types of crop insects correctly is a difficult task for the agriculture experts and farmers due to the similar appearance in the earlier stage of crop growth. Convolutional neural network (CNN) with deep architectures helps in automatic feature extraction. Deep learning artificial neural network architecture (Ferentinos, 2018) contains large number of layers as compare to other techniques which uses shallow approach. CNNs uses most powerful techniques for modeling complex problems such as pattern recognition from images. In order to recognize images several architecture of CNNs have been successfully applied to very complex images.

IoT IN AGRICULTURE

Precision agriculture has been greater influence on cultural, social and economic growth of human civilization. Due to its importance of agriculture in human life, this field has grown more historical skills and economical management. Most of the country's economy relying on agriculture due to fertile soil and good weather conditions. Precision agriculture depends on many critical attributes such as topography, air, rapid weather changes, soil properties, nitrogen and fertilizer management, proper irrigation control and management. These attributes comprise on many sub-attributes of each having very sensitive impacts on agricultural crops yield. IoT technology introduced effective way to measure these parameters by deploying very small devices called sensors and actuators for action activities in PA (Dlodlo and Kalezhi, 2015). Satellite and airborne, scanning, videos capturing, photo capturing made more advanced management of PA. IoT digital devices make more effective way of PA sensitive parameter monitoring time by time. Below fig: represents overview of application of IoT in PA.

World is switching from traditional crop cultivation methods to more advanced digital farming to help monitoring and improving crop yield. Growing interest in remote sensing technology brought revolutionary changes in PA and used in different crop species such as cotton, wheat, maize, sugarcane and fruit framing. Few of important applications of IoT in PA are discussed in detail below:

Smart Irrigation and Water Management

Water management directly impacts on hydrological, climatological and agronomical balance. Plant growth and effective crop yield production is dependent on proper water pouring in soil. Secrecy of water in soil is critical for plants during seasonal crop cultivation. In whole world water conservation and water requirement management is important issue in these days. Efficient irrigation supply management in agricultural fields usually achieved by different channels and canals. However traditional method of water control is time consuming and also causes water wastage (Kirby et al. 2017). Methods of irrigation varies region wise and water supply is important factor for proper feeding and nutrition. Irregular and unpredictable drought conditions and floods can cause of greater damage of plant growth. Hydrological effects are important to manage water requirements in agricultural field. Number of factors can impact on crop yield which is important to consider in account. Soil evapotranspiration is important way of measuring effects of water requirement in agricultural land. Soil moisture content (MC) utilized ecological parameters with soil effective requirements for agriculture land requirements. Water management in agriculture land is important application of WSN and IoT in research and development (Goap et al. 2018). However, an efficient and uniform distribution of water in dense areas considering several factors such as environment, soil and water data. Efficient monitoring environmental parameters can improve irrigation management. IoT intruded environmental and soil monitoring digital methods by deploying sensors connected with small micro controller for monitoring and collecting real time data. Water requirement resides on some factors such as quality of Soil, water level and proper water arrival in all regions. Ecological change in environment can cause increase in water needs in the field. Fluctuations in environmental factors also leave impact on water sustainability in soil. Evaporation such as minimum air temperature (*Tmin*), maximum air temperature, Solar radiation (SR), mean relative humidity (RH), wind speed (WP) are needed to control and estimate water requirement are important climate factors. Whereas different nature of soil has different properties and capacity to absorb water which arise different water requirement to maintain required crop water level in crop land. This can be achieved by deploying IoT and WSN smart framework to control and co-ordinate water irrigation activities on the basis of sensed data from agriculture land. IoT and WSN devices can further be connected by i-e WiFi and 4G LTE to process recorded data over cloud for online monitoring. Real time monitoring (Shah and Yaqoob, 2016) makes easy to maintain agriculture water requirement for better improvement of crop yield. It is important especially for those crops which are water sensitive and not having capacity to survive in hot and dry conditions. Different devices for efficient irrigation management are used to overcome issues for efficient water utilization. Optimization techniques are introduced for example called conjugated gradient BFGS Quasi-Network based on neural network algorithms (Mohapatra and Lenka, 2016). These techniques are used to optimize by applying different machine learning techniques for better management of water management and wastage control. Micro-controller based small devices are used to record real time input data for further data analysis. These microcontroller-based technologies are very smart and well-developed modules are also available to implement real time monitoring. Microcontroller-boards such as Adriano Uno, MeGA (Canales-Ide, Zubelzu, and Rodríguez-Sinobas, 2019), Raspberry Pi and Adriano Ultra are important for collecting real time and accurate data for decision making. Bulletin kits i-e Raspberry Pi Module is also available with number of sensors to fix desired region for real time monitoring of water irrigation.

Crop Yield Prediction

Crop yield prediction is to predict growth rate of crop yield. However, it has been very crucial and difficult task by applying traditional methods. Smart agriculture methods with computer intelligence made easy to predict crop yield. IoT enabled digital devices deployed in agricultural field are used to monitor critical parameters. The crop parameters such as soil, air and water directly affect crop production. Collected data from sensors is important part for crop yield prediction (Gandhi, Petkar, and Armstrong, 2016). Machine learning supervised models like classification and regression, unsupervised approaches such as clustering, associations and semi supervised models are used for different levels of data classification and data regression. Different methods such as supervised and unsupervised computational methods such as SVM, RF and CNN are introduced to deal with efficient and reliable prediction of data. However, data is analyzed by applying machine learning approach. The fast and rapid data collection methods and equipment's have brought computational approaches easier and more efficient for predicting crop yield.

Smart Farming and Ware House Monitoring

Smart farming is important application of IoT in agriculture industry. IoT digital devices involve number of sensors and actuators to perform monitoring tasks automatically. IoT devices can control agricultural activities automatically like spraying, weeding and watering and soil monitoring. Smart farming involves several new trends like vertical farming, autonomous farming control and timely monitoring parameters can help framers. Agriculture ware house monitoring is also very effective area of research in IoT. Monitoring gaseous control in warehouse, detecting threat and object detection for avoidance of farm theft are important to make aware of warehouse premises status (Kamilaris and Prenafeta-Boldú, 2018). Most important is to make sure warehouse activities are being effectively monitored. All activates in warehouse can be controlled by smart sensor technology. Deployment of sensors in warehouse premises ensure security and privacy. Digital alarm system is important application of IoT for threat detection which can make aware of any unwanted activities in warehouse.

Crop Soil Monitoring

Science of soil comprises on many crucial factors of soil. Agricultural soil has heterogonous natural resource with several complex management process. Its properties can vary from region to region as temperature and soil contents may increase or decrease. Fertility of soil keeps greater importance for plant growth. Several soil mapping factors can affect plant growth and properties are directly dependent on sufficient soil constraint requirements and their efficient management. Important parameters of soil like soil pH level, electrical conductivity, solar radiation, salinity of soil and other important factors can leave deep impact on crop yield (Reshma and Pillai, 2016). Deficiencies in soil parameters can cause diseases in plant leaves, stem, roots and plant flowering process. IoT introduced a method of soil mapping called Digital soil mapping (DSM). DSM has been greater part in PA since last decade. In present days DSM is easier and fast way of recording soil constraints digitally. As contrast traditional method is very risky and time consuming because it works human guesses and prediction. The human guess can overlook and misjudge resulting in poor management. Data processing power of computer, data mining tools, geographical information system are important tools and techniques of modern computer world for evaluation of obtained statistical data. Statistical data analyses can arise many new questions for analyzing critical factors which may help to avoid from critical situation. Soil mapping can be more accurate and rapid by applying IoT soil mapping digital sensors (Ananthi et al. 2017). Soil parameters such as soil organic carbon (SOC), Calcium Carbonate equivalent and content of clay are important applications of digital soil mapping. Soil moisture monitors by deploying tension-meter and volumetric sensors in soil layer. Gypsum block is used to measure soil water tension and time domain reflectometry technology is used to measure actual soil water content. Electrical conductivity of soil is used to measure efficiency of soil conductivity. Applying classification and regression methods of machine learning on statistical data of obtained from soil will help predict soil and water content status for future. Linear, non – linear models and multiple linear regression algorithms helps investigate soil properties and make efficient utilization of fertilizer, water and other important parameters of soil.

Environmental Air Monitoring

Agriculture crop product is main objective of crop cultivation which depends on several in and outside filed. Environmental factors are fundamental aspects for agricultural plants which can cause environmental pollution in air. Damaging and negative impacts on crop plants can easily detect and monitor by applying IoT and emerging technology. IoT increase profitability and fulfill market demands in these very fast. This adoption made several new opportunities for researchers to invent new trends and techniques for more advanced and accurate monitoring in agriculture industry. As pollution in environment is increasing day by day due to smoke and poisonous gases in environment are cause of human health damage and more important plant health damage. Environment parameters such as temperature, humidity, wind speed and poisonous gases monitoring is important to measure for plant effective growth (Talavera et al. 2017). Furthermore IoT provide solution to solve problem of effective parameters by deploying small Nano-technology devices called "Sensors". These sensors have different characteristic to measures different parameters such relative humidity (SHT15) and for temperature (DHT11). These parameters are also important for plant health assessment and identify influencing factors on plant growth. However it is difficult to make aware former about environmental factors by traditional methods. IoT and its supporting technologies made easy to monitor and improve accurate measurement of environment. Currently data collection is important phase of research which is evaluated for decision making by applying machine learning models for accurate prediction and analysis. IoT helps for monitoring and recording environmental parameters for data collection with cloud connectivity is used to send data over cloud. Machine learning models such as Supervised and unsupervised learning models (SVM, RFM, CNN) can be further experimented for future prediction of crop status, growth ratio and efficient crop yield prediction and recommendations. Popular Equipment's and Sensors in Agricultural Environment and Field Monitoring

CONCLUSION

In this chapter various methods and techniques have been discussed for managing agriculture crop using Machine, Deep Learning and IOT. The detailed techniques discussed so far provided an insight in implementing technologies such as IOT, Machine Learning and Deep Learning for monitoring crop, identifying crop health such leaf disease, predicting crop production. The chapter highlights the applications and importance of different techniques such CNN, SVM, RFM etc in agriculture.

REFERENCES

Abouzahir, S., Sadik, M., & Sabir, E. (2017). IoT-Empowered Smart Agriculture: A Real-Time Light-Weight Embedded Segmentation System. In Ubiquitous Networking. Cham: Springer International Publishing. doi:10.1007/978-3-319-68179-5_28

Ananthi, N., Divya, J., Divya, M., & Janani, V. (2017). IoT Based Smart Soil Monitoring System for Agricultural Production. In 2017 IEEE Technological Innovations in ICT for Agriculture and Rural Development (TIAR). Chennai: IEEE. doi:10.1109/TIAR.2017.8273717

Aruul Mozhi Varman, S., & Arvind Ram Baskaran, S. (2017). Deep Learning and IoT for Smart Agriculture Using WSN. In *2017 IEEE International Conference on Computational Intelligence and Computing Research (ICCIC)*. Coimbatore: IEEE. 10.1109/ICCIC.2017.8524140

Bacco, M., Berton, A., Ferro, E., Gennaro, C., Gotta, A., Matteoli, S., . . . Zanella, A. (2018). Smart Farming: Opportunities, Challenges and Technology Enablers. In 2018 IoT Vertical and Topical Summit on Agriculture - Tuscany (IOT Tuscany). Tuscany: IEEE.

Bosilj, Aptoula, Duckett, & Cielniak. (2019). Transfer Learning between Crop Types for Semantic Segmentation of Crops versus Weeds in Precision Agriculture. *Journal of Field Robotics*.

Canales-Ide, F., Zubelzu, S., & Rodríguez-Sinobas, L. (2019). Irrigation Systems in Smart Cities Coping with Water Scarcity: The Case of Valdebebas, Madrid (Spain). *Journal of Environmental Management*, *247*, 187–195. doi:10.1016/j.jenvman.2019.06.062 PMID:31252223

Coulibaly, S., Kamsu-Foguem, B., Kamissoko, D., & Traore, D. (2019). Deep Neural Networks with Transfer Learning in Millet Crop Images. *Computers in Industry*, *108*, 115–120. doi:10.1016/j.compind.2019.02.003

Dlodlo, N., & Kalezhi, J. (2015). The Internet of Things in Agriculture for Sustainable Rural Development. In *2015 International Conference on Emerging Trends in Networks and Computer Communications (ETNCC)*. Windhoek, Namibia: IEEE. 10.1109/ETNCC.2015.7184801

Ferentinos, K. P. (2018). Deep Learning Models for Plant Disease Detection and Diagnosis. *Computers and Electronics in Agriculture*, *145*, 311–318. doi:10.1016/j.compag.2018.01.009

Gandhi, N., Petkar, O., & Armstrong, L. J. (2016). Rice Crop Yield Prediction Using Artificial Neural Networks. In 2016 IEEE Technological Innovations in ICT for Agriculture and Rural Development (TIAR). Chennai, India: IEEE. doi:10.1109/TIAR.2016.7801222

Ghazi, M., Mostafa, B. Y., & Aptoula, E. (2017). Plant Identification Using Deep Neural Networks via Optimization of Transfer Learning Parameters. *Neurocomputing*, *235*, 228–235. doi:10.1016/j.neucom.2017.01.018

Goap, A., Sharma, D., Shukla, A. K., & Rama Krishna, C. (2018). An IoT Based Smart Irrigation Management System Using Machine Learning and Open Source Technologies. *Computers and Electronics in Agriculture*, *155*(September), 41–49. doi:10.1016/j.compag.2018.09.040

Kamilaris, A., & Prenafeta-Boldú, F. X. (2018). Deep Learning in Agriculture: A Survey. *Computers and Electronics in Agriculture, 147*, 70–90. doi:10.1016/j.compag.2018.02.016

Kaya, A., Keceli, A. S., Catal, C., Yalic, H. Y., Temucin, H., & Tekinerdogan, B. (2019). Analysis of Transfer Learning for Deep Neural Network Based Plant Classification Models. *Computers and Electronics in Agriculture, 158*, 20–29. doi:10.1016/j.compag.2019.01.041

Kirby, Ahmad, Mainuddin, Khaliq, & Cheema. (2017). Agricultural Production, Water Use and Food Availability in Pakistan: Historical Trends, and Projections to 2050. *Agricultural Water Management, 179*, 34–46.

LeCun, Y., Bengio, Y., & Hinton, G. (2015). Deep Learning. *Nature, 521*(7553), 436–444. doi:10.1038/nature14539 PMID:26017442

Lottes, P., Khanna, R., Pfeifer, J., Siegwart, R., & Stachniss, C. (2017). UAV-Based Crop and Weed Classification for Smart Farming. In *2017 IEEE International Conference on Robotics and Automation (ICRA)*. Singapore: IEEE. 10.1109/ICRA.2017.7989347

Mohapatra, A. G., & Lenka, S. K. (2016). Neural Network Pattern Classification and Weather Dependent Fuzzy Logic Model for Irrigation Control in WSN Based Precision Agriculture. *Procedia Computer Science, 78*, 499–506. doi:10.1016/j.procs.2016.02.094

Pamina, J., & Beschi Raja, J. (2019). *Survey on deep learning algorithms*. Academic Press.

Pan, S. J., & Yang, Q. (2010). A Survey on Transfer Learning. *IEEE Transactions on Knowledge and Data Engineering, 22*(10), 1345–1359. doi:10.1109/TKDE.2009.191

Puranik, V., Sharmila, A. R., & Kumari, A. (2019). Automation in Agriculture and IoT. In *2019 4th International Conference on Internet of Things: Smart Innovation and Usages (IoT-SIU)*. Ghaziabad, India: IEEE. 10.1109/IoT-SIU.2019.8777619

Qin, Z., Yu, F., Liu, C., & Chen, X. (2018). *How Convolutional Neural Network See the World - A Survey of Convolutional Neural Network Visualization Methods*. ArXiv:1804.11191 [Cs]

Reshma, Juhi, & Pillai. (2016). Impact of Machine Learning and Internet of Things in Agriculture: State of the Art. In *International Conference on Soft Computing and Pattern Recognition*. Springer.

Shah, S. H., & Yaqoob, I. (2016). A Survey: Internet of Things (IOT) Technologies, Applications and Challenges. In 2016 IEEE Smart Energy Grid Engineering (SEGE). Oshawa, Canada: IEEE.

Talavera, J. M., Tobón, L. E., Gómez, J. A., Culman, M. A., Aranda, J. M., Parra, D. T., ... Garreta, L. E. (2017). Review of IoT Applications in Agro-Industrial and Environmental Fields. *Computers and Electronics in Agriculture, 142*, 283–297. doi:10.1016/j.compag.2017.09.015

Thenmozhi, K., & Srinivasulu Reddy, U. (2019). Crop Pest Classification Based on Deep Convolutional Neural Network and Transfer Learning. *Computers and Electronics in Agriculture, 164*, 104906. doi:10.1016/j.compag.2019.104906

Verma, S., & Gala, R. (2018). An Internet of Things (IoT) Architecture for Smart Agriculture. In *2018 Fourth International Conference on Computing Communication Control and Automation (ICCUBEA)*. Pune, India: IEEE. 10.1109/ICCUBEA.2018.8697707

Xiao, Q., Li, G., Xie, L., & Chen, Q. (2018). Real-World Plant Species Identification Based on Deep Convolutional Neural Networks and Visual Attention. *Ecological Informatics*, *48*, 117–124. doi:10.1016/j.ecoinf.2018.09.001

Yamashita, R., Nishio, M., Richard, K. G. D., & Togashi, K. (2018). Convolutional Neural Networks: An Overview and Application in Radiology. *Insights Into Imaging*, *9*(4), 611–629. doi:10.100713244-018-0639-9 PMID:29934920

Zhang, Q., Yang, L. T., Chen, Z., & Li, P. (2018). A Survey on Deep Learning for Big Data. *Information Fusion*, *42*, 146–157. doi:10.1016/j.inffus.2017.10.006

Chapter 4
Cloud–Based IoT Architecture for Green Buildings

Rejo Rajan Mathew

https://orcid.org/0000-0002-0549-2695

Mukesh Patel School of Technology, Management, and Engineering, NMIMS University, India

Vikram Kulkarni

Mukesh Patel School of Technology, Management, and Engineering, NMIMS University, India

ABSTRACT

Green building (GB) is a game changer as the world is moving towards conserving its resources. Green building management systems available nowadays are too expensive and cannot cater to small or medium-sized buildings. Internet of things-based systems use simple, low-cost sensors, signal processing, and high-level learning methods. Studies on building occupancy and human activities help improve design and push the energy conservation levels. With huge amounts of data and improved learning systems, the impetus is to capture the information and use it well to improve design and justify the green building concept. Cloud-based architecture helps to monitor, capture, and process the data, which acts as input to intelligent learning systems, which in turn help to improve the design and performance of current green building management systems. This chapter discusses role of cloud-based internet of things architecture in improving design and performance of current building management systems.

INTRODUCTION

Basic Principles of Sustainable Green Buildings

The Green Building (GB) concept is a going to define the relationship between the indoor environment and natural environment (B. Campbell et al., 2016). In the recent times the GB plan is becoming very important and creating awareness by adapting efficient building material, equipment to improve energy efficiency etc. The building has positive and negative impacts on both the natural environment and inhabitants who live every day (Latif Onur Uğur, 2018). GB main aim is to decrease the negative

DOI: 10.4018/978-1-7998-2803-7.ch004

influence on environment by initiating the decreased use of water, power and decreased emission of radiation are some expectations (Ziwen Liu, 2017). The modern home automation technologies have created many opportunities and have proposed many intelligent solutions for the problems identified by the GB's society. Among the intelligent solutions necessary for modern home automation based GB's, many research groups have identified the Internet of Things (IoT) is most suitable and is going to address all the requirements needed. (Yujie Lu et al., 2017).

IoT is an advanced system which is embedded with technologies like modern instrumentation (smart sensors and smart actuators), information and data-communication and cloud computing (S. D. T. Kelly et al. 2013), (Georgios Lilis et al. 2014) . The modern GB's is thus becoming the data-hub generating huge data (Andreas P et al. 2018). Rapid advancements of GB technology have created a lot of new opportunities in the areas like Energy Management (Smart Grid) (S. Sofana Reka et al., 2018), Advanced Health-Care for overcoming the challenges faced (Ana Reyna et al. 2018) [10]. The progress in IT technology and data analytics have found increased relevance in the way GBs are transforming themselves to the "Connected Hub-of-Buildings" (Dragos Mocrii et al. 2018).

The Hub-of-Buildings generate huge volumes of the data in terms of Energy usage, Data identification for Security reasons, Smart cities, Health care, Control and Automation and integration of Renewable energy. The huge volumes of data needs proper recognition and must be made use of, to take appropriate decisions hence that leads to Big-data solutions (D. E. Boubiche et al. 2018).

IoT combined with ubiquitous computing provides enormous data and information about building (M. W. Condry et al. 2016). These relationships enable GB to forecast, predict, and optimize its operations and needs. This ability of Green Building to be self-aware, self-regulated and optimized transforms it into "Sustainable Green Building." IoT generating Big-Data in correlation with GB's is at primary stage. This union of different technologies is influencing the industry of GB's. The mechanisms of Green Buildings is shown in Figure 1.

Figure 1. Mechanisms for Green Buildings

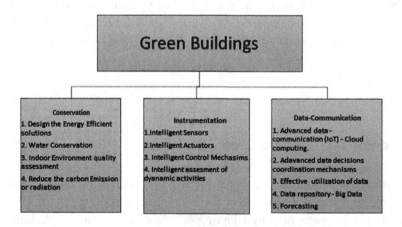

Site and Structure Design Efficiency

Location of building, cost effective design without compromising on performance defines efficiency. Construction industry is not streamlined and varies from one building to the other. Complexity increases as the variables are too many. Even a variation in a single variable impacts the overall calculations. Low energy homes have solar design so as to balance the overall feasibility. Planning and development phase is most crucial phase as all the future decisions are made based on initial design. Overall cost saving and green impact depends on all factors considered during initial phase. Factors to be taken into account for the first phase includes topology, alignment and orientation, materials, chemical composition, exterior and interior design, heating/cooling systems, height above sea level, climate conditions throughout the year, residential or commercial space, number of occupants, energy resources used, power backup systems, waste management systems.

Energy Efficiency

Energy costs are increasing daily affecting daily budget of all consumers. Maximum usage of natural light helps avoid cost escalation. For daylighting window positioning, building alignment and orientation, shading of roofs and walls, proper selection of material used in buildings. Usage of natural resources like solar, hydro, thermal, biomass to produce energy for building consumption reduces need for artificial resources. Ultra-modern waste management system helps reduce impact as well supplements energy production for local use. Buildings are designed so that in summers the heat can be stored and reused later and in during cold seasons maximum solar energy inside homes. Minimum use of lights, cooling/heating systems, lifts, water sprinklers is promoted and consumers are constantly advised to make optimum use and avoid any wastage.

Water Efficiency

Water conservation and ensuring pure and potable water availability to everyone are focus points in a building. More the people more the water needed for daily consumption. Especially during summers, the consumption increases and leads to water scarcity in many parts of the country. Lot of money and energy is needed to reach to all such areas which it causes monopoly and black-marketing of water. Ground water table is going down so water reuse is prime focus. Use of non-sewage and greywater helps reduce it to some extent. Most buildings are deploying low flush toilets and low flow shower to minimize excessive usage of water. Water sanitization, chlorination, de-salinization, treatment and heating impacts energy, cost and water conservation tremendously. Dual piping used by many companies help to keep same water in circulation.

Materials Efficiency

Use of eco-friendly polyurethane blocks reduces cost, increases speed, is compatible and durable. Reducing carbon footprint by using environment friendly products is must. Materials used on site should be manufactured off site as it helps in reducing waste and pollution, focusing on using environment friendly top quality products, improved OHS management. The EPA (Environmental Protection Agency) guidelines focus on recycled and redeveloped good like debris, sand, combustible materials in projects.

Indoor Air Quality

Focus is to reduce air pollution and enhance air quality providing clear and fresh air to all the occupants. Microbes, bacteria, pollen particles, virus and volatile chemical compounds contaminate the air. Isolation of drying area, kitchen area, washing area, work area and providing proper ventilation to each area is primary key factor. Many substances that are used have harmful chemical compositions so preference should be given to eco-friendly products. Especially paints, glass, finished products contain chemicals and emit toxic gas. These are detrimental to all beings in the vicinity hampering the climate around. A well designed HVAC system based on buildings position, orientation, ventilation will help provide maximum natural light in the building. Natural light and clean air will help improve quality of living as well. Green buildings lead to clean and green cities thereby impacting and reducing effects of global warming. Vertical gardens being developed and used across countries to save space and cost and contributing to green globe. Vertical gardens are natural air cleaning systems to improve breathing conditions and promote healthy lifestyle. They help reduce noise pollution which provides a calm serene and peaceful atmosphere for employees to relax and focus on their work. Our world is suffering from rising temperatures due to global warming, poor air quality standards due to pollution, fatal ultraviolet radiations, inconsistent rains. Exterior vertical gardens do evapotranspiration in summer which helps cool the air and protect against all of these.

Operations and Maintenance Optimization

Not just initial investment but constant upgrade and maintenance of green buildings is a challenge. One way is to involve all the team members to be part of project from initial decision making and all process itself. Initial planning will help O&M personnel later to look at various means to successfully sustain green buildings across various domains. New green technologies need to be studied and implemented. Recycling and processing have to be worked upon. Areas like waste management, air purification, water and energy conservation etc. will be primary focus for them.

Reduction of Waste Materials

Due to increase in number of constructions the landfills areas are increasing and landfills are coming up in humongous quantity. One objective should be to minimize the waste which impact the landfills and indirectly pollute the environment. Buildings with proper design help minimize the output waste and also provide solutions for onsite treatment of waste so that nothing is left to be sent to landfills. "Greywater", wastewater from sources is used for irrigation or non-potable activities e.g. washing and cleaning. Rainwater gutters and reservoirs are popular and even sponsored by local government bodies. Contemporary wastewater treatment systems are costly and consume lot of energy. Using it as biowaste avoids these costs and shows other benefits. Use techniques to remove carbon dioxide and control greenhouse emissions

Cost

Investing in green computing now is investing in future of country and upcoming generations. The upcoming generations will be left with no resources left looking at the current depletion rate of resources.

Companies find it tough to balance initial cost versus life-long cost. Savings on initial cost becomes priority with the investment in green computing taking the hit. Nowadays companies have studies to suggest the long term impact of green computing on human and other resources which gives overall benefit to company as well as mother earth. Other costs can be covered by improving worker performance, cost cutting and other services costs. Better living standards, hygiene, lower mortality rate have given an impetus to the idea of green computing. The idea where everyone contributes to save nature and build future generations is gaining momentum worldwide.

ARCHITECTURE

Recent surveys and research studies show that 60% of energy consumption is due to buildings (W. Tushar, C. Yuen, W.-T. Li, D. Smith, T. Saha, & K. L. Wood, 2018). Therefore, there is lot of research going on to effectively manage the consumption and make green buildings efficient and cost effective. Internet of Things uses various low cost sensors to collect data and provide it to learning systems so as to modify the current expensive design and improve efficiency to acceptable and justifiable costs. The Figure 2 shows the Cloud Based Internet of Things Architecture for Green Building Management Systems. It consists of following components

Figure 2. Cloud Based IOT for Green Buildings

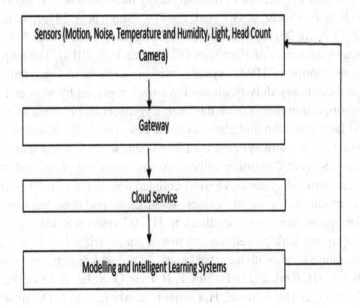

Sensors

Different Internet of Things sensors, smart meters and actuators which can be integrated with current management systems to monitor the following

1. **Lighting**: the focus is to attain desired illumination with low energy consumption. Daylighting and Daylight harvesting use natural resources (Daylighting: Whole Building Design Guide)and reduce usage and wastage of artificial resources(Sandhyalaxmi G. Navada, Chandrashekara S. Adiga, and Savitha G. Kini, 2013). Studies on smart building design, use of proper material etc are covered by many researchers (IzzetYüksek &TülayTikansakKaradayi, 2017). Studies on smart lighting and control systems are done for best prediction based on occupancy. The methods focus on reducing power requirements by capturing occupancy data and calculation minimum light conditions to cater to all. Efficient sensor technology alongwith fast response signal techniques help achieve optimized results (Z. Cheng, Q. Zhao, F. Wang, Y. Jiang, L. Xia, & J. Ding, 2016) (S. Jain & V. Garg, 2018) (A. Pandharipande & D. Caicedo, 2015) (X. Guo, D. Tiller, G. Henze & C. Waters, 2010)

2. **Flexible Loads**: This looks after loads including geysers, refrigerators, television, washing machines, dishwashers, energy storage systems. With improvement in living standards across all countries the use of electronic systems and power consumption has increased tremendously. Human control and intervention have lots of limiting in controlling this load. A non-intrusive load monitoring in each building with built-in automation gives best results. Load requirements are calculated by combining behavior and usage patterns, occupancy, demand variations. This data is stored in memory systems which are later fed to learning management systems which predict and forecast future requirements for the building. Automated controllers limit the input to these load consuming giants and regular logs maintained on these servers act as reporting tools to people managing these systems as well as load calculation systems. Using natural resources for most devices help reducing costs as well as green computing. Ongoing studies emphasize on monitoring the usage pattern and control their operation for effective energy management. (A. Belmonte-Hernandez, G. Hernandez-Penaloza, F.Alvarez, & G. Conti, 2017)S. (Singh & A. Majumdar, 2017)(D. Zhang, S. Li, M. Sun, & Z. O'Neill, 2016)(W. Kong, Z. Y. Dong, D. J. Hill, F. Luo& Y. Xu, 2017)

3. **HVAC:** It is a major consumer of electricity (W. Tusharet. al, 2018). The major focus has been to reduce power consumption of HVAC systems without compromising comfort levels. Most mechanical and electrical heavy duty machines have been replaced by high end electronic systems. With more automation introduced there has been a considerable amount of saving of energy and costs. Advanced fault detection and alarm systems have raised the standards of HVAC systems. Building far more fault tolerant systems with intelligent sensors, controllers and actuators are in progress. Actuator, Sensor, Controller information is stored on cloud and web hosted services which is integrated with IoT systems. Thereby collated data is fed to IoT based systems for granular level analysis which makes use of business intelligence and deep learning algorithms to form accurate decisions providing instant feedback to HVAC systems using signals. Ongoing studies emphasize on improving fault prevention and use of nature friendly power resources. Studies for controlling temperature levels with increased focus on reducing electricity consumption of HVAC systems. (S. Ali & D.-H. Kim, 2013)(B. Sun, P. B. Luh, Q. S. Jia, Z. O'Neill& F. Song, 2014)(A. Mirakhorli & B. Dong, 2016)(A. Javed, H. Larijani, A. Ahmadinia & D. Gibson, 2017)(A. Al-Ali, I. A. Zualkernan, M. Rashid, R. Gupta& M. Ali Karar, 2017)(M. Aftab, C. Chen, C.-K. Chau& T. Rahwan, 2017)

4. **Occupancy Detection:** Different machine learning algorithms are used to detect human occupancy and also classify their activities. Modern camera and sensor technology like face recognition tagging, head counting alongwith different thermal imaging mechanisms assist human tracking and detection. Advanced motion sensors technology using infrared in sync with parametric and non-

parametric algorithms have led to accuracy. Background subtraction model and other machine learning algorithms are being tried to predict, track and classify occupant activities. Sound sensors are also being used in many cases these days. Earlier methods had lot of false positives and lead to erroneous results and incorrect prediction. That has been overcome over the period of time and far better results have been obtained. Researchers do lot of normalizing, sampling and testing before finalizing the results. Low light conditions camera is used these days to work in all conditions. Supervised learning methods where pre-set data is used to train the real time data. (J. Salamon& J. P. Bello, 2015) (A. Tyndall, R.Cardell-Oliver, and A. Keating, 2016)(Y. P. Raykov, E. Ozer, G. Dasika, A. Boukouvalas, and M. A. Little, 2016)(W. Li, Y. Lu, J. Sun, Q. Chen, T. Dong, L. Zhou, Q. Zhang, and L. Wei, 2017)

5. **Diagnostics and Prognostics:** Fault detection and maintenance of electric systems have become cumbersome. To reduce load there have been different tools used over period of time. But to monitor these individual tools and reporting discrepancies are far more tedious. Lack of standardization and non-compatibility has made things more complex. IoT has helped collect all the data from different sources and input for processing in one standard format which has help reduce the complex tasks. Data-driven fault prevention has taken it to next level. Integration of all energy management systems in tandem with deep analysis has reduced manual intervention and optimized efficiency without overshooting the budget. Internet of Things provides advanced data driven applications for detecting faults, predict maintenance issues and periodic diagnostics of the HVAC system. (B. Sun, P. B. Luh, Q. S. Jia, Z. O'Neill& F. Song, 2014)

6. **Role of IoT in Designing of Energy Efficient Solutions:** The conservation of natural resources is very important for the extended life on the earth. The consumption of natural resources like coal and petroleum products for the power generation is not supportable as that leads to scarcity for future generations (Kumar et al. 2014). The Governments and Utility companies should think seriously of the using non-conventional energy resources to meet the power demand (Myers T et al. 2017). For achieving the 100 percent generation from the alternate energy sources there should be a systematic policy to be adapted (Y. Liu et al. 2018). In the modern days the Utilities are utilizing all the efficient ways to conserve the generation and utilize the generated power wisely. The utilities are employing the IoT based cloud computing technologies for the energy conservation. Companies like Siemens are exclusively designing software's for both the utility and consumer for effective controlling of electronic devices that regulate power usage efficiently. There is a proverb in electrical engineering industry is "A unit energy saved a unit energy utilized." Based on the data generated from the IoT devices about the electrical usage the end user or utility can control the power wastage. Rexel is one among the many companies that are maintaining its generation, transmission, distribution and utilization system efficiently with IoT based could computing technology. With the efficient transmission of the energy data to utility center, cloud-based IoT operating system which connects devices, applications, plants, systems, and machines and makes it possible to integrate all these entities to use the massive amounts of data from the Internet of Things in comprehensive analyses. There by this data can be precisely used to analyze and can develop recommendations for action (S. Pérez et al. 2018) (Ankit Singh et al. 2018).

The recent standards used for energy provide all information to customers like billing, variation in usage, events, pre and post payment methods ZigBee Smart Energy 1.x, Smart Energy Profile 2.0 / IEEE

2030.5-2013, Green Button / Energy Services Provider Interface (ESPI) / NAESB REQ 21 (NAESB) (Smart Energy Consumer Standards)

The different platform offered by IoT these days for retailers consist of three parts mainly sensing, controlling and metering. Data collection, pre-processing and monitoring is done by different sensors to detect humidity, heat, pressure, noise, movements, light, objects. Controllers are used to control the environment based on inputs from the sensors which include switches, actuators, smart plugs and thermostats. Metering is to measure the information precisely to keep track of consumption and changes in energy requirements. This includes electric meter, water meter etc.

Current trends show usage of Internet of Things devices such as battery less energy harvesting switches and sensors (Cherry, EnOcean, ZF KNX modules), low-cost Wi-Fi controller (Particle, Ayla Networks, Exosite, relayr, FogHorn, Plat.One, RilHeva, LoneStar, SAP, xPico, Microchip) (microcontrollers are preferred as it provides simplicity, security, cost), Nest by Google, ecoBee, NETATMO, SimpliSafe, TenDril, Canary, Quby, iSmartAlarm and many others. The idea is to ensure features like adaptability, flexibility, compatibility, low latency, interoperability, scalability, feasibility using IoT based systems (S. K. Viswanath, C. Yuen, W. Tushar, W.-T. Li, C.-K. Wen, K. Hu, C. Chen, and X. Liu, 2016)

Gateway

It performs data conversion from device specific data to cloud specific data. Data from different sensors are connected via adapters that provide connectivity and compatibility on both sides. It ensures that data received in various formats (Wi-Fi, ZigBee, Bluetooth, LWPAN) are converted into standard format. For e.g. transforms 6LoWPAN messaged to IPv4 formats to be stored and processed further. Sensors/devices send data to gateways which then backhaul the data to cloud via high speed connection.

This allows sensors to talk within short distances thus boosting battery life which is critical for most application which in turn enhances life of each sensor/device. Sometimes the amount of data captured is huge and it becomes very difficult at later stage to segregate the data.

Nowadays lot of filtering and preprocessing is done prior to pushing data to cloud which helps in reducing overload and time. It also helps minimize overall requirements and save on storage costs as well. This is fruitful for lag free operations for real time applications. Overall performance will increase.

An efficient back-end sharing design of device to gateway communication system is shown in Figure 3 it gathers data from individual Internet of Things device for analysis. Such active actual back-end information sharing designs provide users the flexibility to switch between Internet of Things services, overcoming traditional model of information storage systems.

Cloud Service

Cloud Service mainly consists of cloud service brokers that assimilate information from gateway or other devices and does pre-processing before storing them in local databases in a specific format. Data analyzed can be displayed so as to monitor and check for errors in any device. Event Managers makes rules and trigger alerts if faults are detected or in case of emergency. For e.g. based on data from temperature sensor it will check if the threshold level set is crossed to trigger an alert and process it further. Control module will monitor the health of devices and display current status via mobile or web application. It identifies and monitors essential energy variables to calculate the heating and energy requirements to keep the building healthy and smartly assess the subsystems behavior.

Figure 3. Device to Gateway to Cloud Service Communication

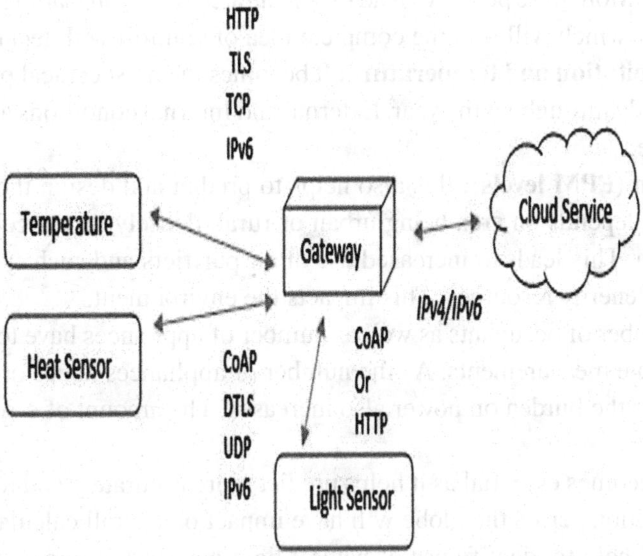

An integrated cloud enabled Internet of Things system has an open architecture which allows the building manager to look at all parameters of the building. The input parameters will be collected from electric meters, water sensors, thermal sensors, noise sensors, motion sensors. Data about occupants and their movement will be traced by respective sensors. Overall energy consumption past and present records will be measured. This data will be given as input to the intelligent systems which will analyze and predict the output. Once the analysis is done based on designed rules and potential the controllers are put into action. Actuators play the important role of execution. Thermostats, controllers and switches help utilize the feedback from the smart systems.

Modelling and Intelligent Learning Systems

It takes as input the energy usage information from cloud model and helps in condition monitoring, predictive maintenance, smart energy control, fault detection and maintenance of Internet of Things systems. Major focus area is on HVAC where dataset is huge and complex. Most studies apply machine learning along with human control. Unsupervised learning methods have been used by many researchers but the end result being human interpretation and intervention is needed. (L. P. L. Billy, N. Wijerathne, B. K. K. Ng, and C. Yuen, 2017) (Fernanda Cruz Rios, Kristen Parrish, Wai K Chong, 2016)

Detailed Modeling – Based On Parameters

Consider parameters like occupancy, humidity, temperature, precipitation, PPM levels, appliances, positioning, ventilation and other energy variables to design new models that optimize resource utilization and reduce overall costs in green buildings. These parameters are crucial to design and optimize.

1. **Occupancy:** Prediction of occupants and their activity at different time intervals are essential to model the system. More false positives lead to inaccurate prediction leading to giving wrong signals to control systems which will ruin the complete idea of comfort with technology.

2. **Humidity, precipitation and temperature:** It becomes the most critical parameter due to climate changing constantly throughout the year. External and Internal conditions alongwith moisture ratio have to be precise.

3. **Parts per million (PPM levels):** this also helps to predict and design the system. Parts per million (PPM level) depends on area being urban or rural, densely or scarcely populated, industrial or residential area. This leads to increased use of air purifiers and such systems leading to rise in cost and usage of energy resources. This impacts the environment.

4. **Appliances:** Number of occupants as well as number of appliances have to be considered and calculated for accurate measurements. As the number of appliances keeps on increasing as standard of living improves the burden on power also increases. The amount of e-waste generated has also added to the list.

5. **Positioning:** It becomes essential as it helps predict more accurately and topology is fixed parameter. Also the position across the globe will have impact on overall calculation.

6. **Ventilation:** Will help to identify use of natural light and daylighting so that artificial resources are not utilized much.

Split the data available on cloud and create new algorithms/methods to ease load on artificial resources and focus on renewable energy. Real-time data forecasting with timely feedback to Internet of Things devices will enhance the monitoring and control giving instant results. It will lead to proper scheduling of systems and mitigate man made errors.

Lots of learning algorithms have been tested and applied on extensive data collected. Machine Learning as well as deep learning algorithms have been tried and tested by experts individually as well as in various combinations. From most of these papers it can be concluded that best known models like Support Vector Machine as well as Neural Networks (Giovanni Tardioli, Ruth Kerrigan, Mike Oates, James O'Donnell, Donal Finn, 2015) fail to work for long term and large predictions. Accuracy is least even in detailed building profiling. (Lai Wei, Wei Tian, Elisabete A Silva, Ruchi Choudhary, QingXinMeng & Song Yang, 2015) (Kadir Amasyali & Nora El-Gohary, 2016). Few researches show that deep extreme learning machine (DELM) are accurate and better than other neural networks for hourly and weekly energy consumption prediction. (Muhammad Fayaz and DoHyeun Kim, 2018). It is also seen that deep auto-encoder performs better compared to a principal component analysis (Hinton, G.E.; Salakhutdinov, R.R, 2006). These researches are most challenging and depend on so many factors that their results cannot be considered uniform and effective. Also the datasets used for time series predictions in these algorithms have less data than other researches in that domain. Trial and error prediction mechanisms prove effective only in small or controlled environments rather than open and large commercial spaces.

Anomaly Detection for Predictive Maintenance

From pre-processed data machine learning can detect anomaly or fault in system or process. This would help to locate and find out root cause of problems causing failures or affecting performance of systems. It will help scan all resources which could have integrated and cost effective solutions. It can help predict retrofit candidates which will help cut costs. (Daniel E Marasco, Constantine E. Kontokosta, 2016)

Complex to Simple

Breakdown complex data sets and apply machine learning to analyze the data from all devices. Qualitative and Quantitative analysis will help build an intelligent learning system. Results of analysis would help make the system intelligent to control the environment effectively. Learn and adjust as we call the process. For example, indoor air quality depends on heating/cooling, ventilation and positioning of building. Creation of intelligent buildings based on different parameters (Szilagyi& P. Wira, 2018) (M. Manic, D. Wijayasekara, K. Amarasinghe and J. J. Rodriguez-Andina, 2016) (M. Manic, K. Amarasinghe, J. J. Rodriguez-Andina& C. Rieger, 2016)

Companies like Singapore Technologies Electronics Limited, Allied Digital Services limited, NG Bailey Group, Schneider Electric SE, Delta Electronics, Inc., Siemsatec Ltd., Pacific Control Systems, Larsen & Toubro Limited, T-Systems International GmbH and Advanced Control Corporation etc. have already created effective design solutions by integrating intelligent Internet of Things solutions with cloud architecture. Major features are customized integrated solution with single front-end interface, reduced energy consumption with less operating cost and low carbon footprint, auditing is digitized with no manual interference so compliance is regulated, Elevators, fire/ flood, life safety and security systems are prompt and reporting is excellent. (Enertiv – Smart Building Solutions) (M. Manic, K. Amarasinghe, J. J. Rodriguez-Andina& C. Rieger, 2016).

REFERENCES

Advanced Control Corp. (n.d.). Retrieved from https://advancedcontrolcorp.com

Aftab, M., Chen, C., Chau, C.-K., & Rahwan, T. (2017). Automatic HVAC control with real-time occupancy recognition and simulation-guided model predictive control in low-cost embedded system. *Energy and Building, 154,* 141–156. doi:10.1016/j.enbuild.2017.07.077

Al-Ali, A., Zualkernan, I. A., Rashid, M., Gupta, R., & Alikarar, M. (2017). A smart home energy management system using Internet of Things and big data analytics approach. *IEEE Transactions on Consumer Electronics, 63*(4), 426–434. doi:10.1109/TCE.2017.015014

Ali, S., & Kim, D.-H. (2013). Effective and comfortable power control model using Kalman filter for building energy management. *Wireless Personal Communications, 73*(4), 1439–1453. doi:10.100711277-013-1259-9

Amasyali & El-Gohary. (2016). Building Lighting energy consumption prediction for supporting energy data analytics. *Procedia Engineering, 145,* 511-517.

Andreas, P. (2018). Efficient IoT-based sensor BIG Data collection–processing and analysis in smart buildings. *Future Generation Computer Systems, 82,* 349–357. doi:10.1016/j.future.2017.09.082

Belmonte-Hernandez, A., Hernandez-Penaloza, G., Alvarez, F., & Conti, G. (2017). Adaptive fingerprinting in multi-sensor fusion for accurate indoor tracking. *IEEE Sensors Journal, 17*(15), 4983–4998. doi:10.1109/JSEN.2017.2715978

Billy, Wijerathne, Ng, & Yuen. (2017). Sensor fusion for public space utilization monitoring in a smart city. *IEEE Internet of Things Journal.*

Boubiche, D. E., Pathan, A.-S. K., Lloret, J., Zhou, H., Hong, S., Amin, S. O., & Feki, M. A. (2018). Advanced Industrial Wireless Sensor Networks and Intelligent IoT. *IEEE Communications Magazine*, *56*(2), 14–15. doi:10.1109/MCOM.2018.8291108

Campbell, B., Clark, M., DeBruin, S., Ghena, B., Jackson, N., Kuo, Y.-S., & Dutta, P. (2016). Perpetual Sensing for the Built Environment. *IEEE Pervasive Computing*, *15*(4), 45–55. doi:10.1109/MPRV.2016.66

Cheng, Z., Zhao, Q., Wang, F., Jiang, Y., Xia, L., & Ding, J. (2016). Satisfaction based Q-learning for integrated lighting and blind control. *Energy and Building*, *127*, 43–55. doi:10.1016/j.enbuild.2016.05.067

Condry, M. W., & Nelson, C. B. (2016). Using Smart Edge IoT Devices for Safer. Rapid Response With Industry IoT Control Operations. *Proceedings of the IEEE*, *104*(5), 938-946. 10.1109/JPROC.2015.2513672

Daylighting: Whole Building Design Guide. (n.d.). Retrieved from https://www.wbdg.org/resources/daylighting

Enertiv – Smart Building Soultions. (n.d.). Retrieved from https://www.enertiv.com

Fayaz & Kim. (2018). *A Prediction Methodology of Energy Consumption Based on Deep Extreme Learning Machine and Comparative Analysis in Residential Buildings*. Academic Press.

Gebreslassie, B., Zayegh, A., & Kalam, A. (2017). Design, modeling of an intelligent green building using, actuator sensor interface network protocol. *Australasian Universities Power Engineering Conference (AUPEC)*, 1-6. 10.1109/AUPEC.2017.8282492

Guo, X., Tiller, D., Henze, G., & Waters, C. (2010). The performance of occupancy-based lighting control systems: A review. *Lighting Research & Technology*, *42*(4), 415–431. doi:10.1177/1477153510376225

Hinton, G. E., & Salakhutdinov, R. R. (2006). Reducing the dimensionality of data with neural networks. *Science*, *2006*(313), 504–507. doi:10.1126cience.1127647 PMID:16873662

Jain, S., & Garg, V. (2018). A review of open loop control strategies for shades, blinds and integrated lighting by use of real-time daylight prediction methods. *Building and Environment*, *135*, 352–364. doi:10.1016/j.buildenv.2018.03.018

Javed, A., Larijani, H., Ahmadinia, A., & Gibson, D. (2017). Smart Random Neural Network Controller for HVAC Using Cloud Computing Technology. *IEEE Transactions on Industrial Informatics*, *13*(1), 351–360. doi:10.1109/TII.2016.2597746

Kelly, S. D. T., Suryadevara, N. K., & Mukhopadhyay, S. C. (2013). Towards the Implementation of IoT for Environmental Condition Monitoring in Homes. *IEEE Sensors Journal*, *13*(10), 3846–3853. doi:10.1109/JSEN.2013.2263379

Kong, W., Dong, Z. Y., Hill, D. J., Luo, F., & Xu, Y. (2017). *Short-term residential load forecasting based on resident behavior learning, IEEE Transactions on Power Systems*. Pre-print. doi:10.1109/TPWRS.2017.2688178

Kumar, A., & Hancke, G. P. (2014). An Energy-Efficient Smart Comfort Sensing System Based on the IEEE 1451 Standard for Green Buildings. *IEEE Sensors Journal, 14*(12), 4245–4252. doi:10.1109/JSEN.2014.2356651

Li, W., Lu, Y., Sun, J., Chen, Q., Dong, T., Zhou, L., . . . Wei, L. (2017). People counting based on improved gauss process regression. *Proc. of International Conference on Security, Pattern Analysis, and Cybernetics (SPAC)*, 603–608.

Lilis, G., Conus, G., Asadi, N., & Kayal, M. (2017). Towards the next generation of intelligent building: An assessment study of current automation and future IoT based systems with a proposal for transitional design. *Sustainable Cities and Society, 28*, 473–481. doi:10.1016/j.scs.2016.08.019

Liu, Y., Akram Hassan, K., Karlsson, M., Weister, O., & Gong, S. (2018). Active Plant Wall for Green Indoor Climate Based on Cloud and Internet of Things. *IEEE Access: Practical Innovations, Open Solutions, 6*, 33631–33644. doi:10.1109/ACCESS.2018.2847440

Liu, Z., Chen, D. K., Peh, D. L., & Tan, D. K. W. (2017). A feasibility study of Building Information Modeling for Green Mark New Non-Residential Building (NRB): 2015 analysis. *Energy Procedia, 143*, 80–87. doi:10.1016/j.egypro.2017.12.651

Lu, Y., Wu, Z., Chang, R., & Li, Y. (2017). Building Information Modeling (BIM) for green buildings: A critical review and future directions. *Automation in Construction, 83*, 134–148. doi:10.1016/j.autcon.2017.08.024

Manic, M., Amarasinghe, K., Rodriguez-Andina, J. J., & Rieger, C. (2016). Intelligent Buildings of the Future: Cyberaware, Deep Learning Powered, and Human Interacting. *IEEE Industrial Electronics Magazine, 10*(4), 32–49. doi:10.1109/MIE.2016.2615575

Manic, M., Wijayasekara, D., Amarasinghe, K., & Rodriguez-Andina, J. J. (2016). Building Energy Management Systems: The Age of Intelligent and Adaptive Buildings. *IEEE Industrial Electronics Magazine, 10*(1), 25–39. doi:10.1109/MIE.2015.2513749

Marasco & Kontokosta. (2016). Applications of machine learning methods to identifying and predicting building retrofit opportunities. *Energy and Buildings,* 431-441.

Mirakhorli, A., & Dong, B. (2016). Occupancy behavior based model predictive control for building indoor climate - A critical review. *Energy and Building, 129*, 499–513. doi:10.1016/j.enbuild.2016.07.036

Mocrii, D., Chen, Y., & Musilek, P. (2018). IoT-based smart homes: A review of system architecture, software, communications, privacy and security. *Internet of Things, 1–2*, 81–98. doi:10.1016/j.iot.2018.08.009

Myers, T., Mohring, K., & Andersen, T. (2017). Semantic IoT: Intelligent Water Management for Efficient Urban Outdoor Water Conservation. *Lecture Notes in Computer Science,* 10675.

Navada, Adiga, & Kini. (2013). A Study on Daylight Integration with Thermal Comfort for Energy Conservation in a General Office. *IJOEE,* 18-22.

Pandharipande, A., & Caicedo, D. (2015). Smart indoor lighting systems with luminaire-based sensing: A review of lighting control approaches. *Energy and Building, 104*, 369–377. doi:10.1016/j.enbuild.2015.07.035

Pérez, S., Hernandez-Ramos, J. L., Matheu-Garcia, S. N., Rotondi, D., Skarmeta, A. F., Straniero, L., & Pedone, D. (2018). A Lightweight and Flexible Encryption Scheme to Protect Sensitive Data in Smart Building Scenarios. *IEEE Access: Practical Innovations, Open Solutions, 6*, 11738–11750. doi:10.1109/ACCESS.2018.2801383

Raykov, Y. P., Ozer, E., Dasika, G., Boukouvalas, A., & Little, M. A. (2016). Predicting room occupancy with a single passive infrared (PIR) sensor through behavior extraction. *Proceedings of ACM International Joint Conference on Pervasive and Ubiquitous Computing*, 1016–1027. 10.1145/2971648.2971746

Reka, S. S., & Dragicevic, T. (2018). Future effectual role of energy delivery: A comprehensive review of Internet of Things and smart grid. *Renewable & Sustainable Energy Reviews, 91*, 90–108. doi:10.1016/j.rser.2018.03.089

Reyna, A., Martín, C., Chen, J., Soler, E., & Díaz, M. (2018). On blockchain and its integration with IoT. Challenges and opportunities. *Future Generation Computer Systems, 88*, 173–190. doi:10.1016/j.future.2018.05.046

Rios, F. C., Parrish, K., & Chong, W. K. (2016). Low-investment energy retrofit framework for small and medium office buildings. *Procedia Engineering, 145*, 172–179. doi:10.1016/j.proeng.2016.04.057

Salamon, J., & Bello, J. P. (2015). Unsupervised feature learning for urban sound classification. *Proceedings of IEEE International Conference on Acoustics, Speech and Signal Processing (ICASSP)*, 171–175. 10.1109/ICASSP.2015.7177954

Singh, A., Kumar, D., & Hötzel, J. (2018). IoT Based information and communication system for enhancing underground mines safety and productivity: Genesis, taxonomy and open issues. *Ad Hoc Networks, 78*, 115–129. doi:10.1016/j.adhoc.2018.06.008

Singh, S., & Majumdar, A. (2017). Deep sparse coding for non-intrusive load monitoring. *IEEE Transactions on Smart Grid*.

Suh, C., & Ko, Y. (2008). Design and implementation of intelligent home control systems based on active sensor networks. *IEEE Transactions on Consumer Electronics, 54*(3), 1177–1184. doi:10.1109/TCE.2008.4637604

Sun, B., Luh, P. B., Jia, Q. S., O'Neill, Z., & Song, F. (2014). Building energy doctors: An SPC and Kalman filter-based method for systemlevel fault detection in HVAC systems. *IEEE Transactions on Automation Science and Engineering, 11*(1), 215–229. doi:10.1109/TASE.2012.2226155

Szilagyi & Wira. (2018). *An intelligent system for smart buildings using machine learning and semantic technologies: A hybrid data-knowledge approach. In IEEE Industrial Cyber-Physical Systems* (pp. 20–25). St. Petersburg: ICPS.

Tardioli, G., Kerrigan, R., Oates, M., O'Donnell, J., & Finn, D. (2015). Data driven approaches for prediction of building energy consumption at urban level. *Published in Energy Procedia, 78*, 3378–3383. doi:10.1016/j.egypro.2015.11.754

Tushar, W., Yuen, C., Li, W.-T., Smith, D., Saha, T., & Wood, K. L. (2018). Motivational psychology driven AC management scheme: A responsive design approach. *IEEE Transactions on Computational Social Systems*, *5*(1), 289–301. doi:10.1109/TCSS.2017.2788922

Tyndall, A., Cardell-Oliver, R., & Keating, A. (2016). Occupancy estimation using a low-pixel count thermal imager. *IEEE Sensors Journal*, *16*(10), 3784–3791. doi:10.1109/JSEN.2016.2530824

Uğur, L. O., & Leblebici, N. (2018). An examination of the LEED green building certification system in terms of construction costs. *Renewable & Sustainable Energy Reviews*, *81*(Part 1), 1476–1483. doi:10.1016/j.rser.2017.05.210

Viswanath, S. K., Yuen, C., Tushar, W., Li, W.-T., Wen, C.-K., Hu, K., ... Liu, X. (2016). System design of the internet of things for residential smart grid. *IEEE Wireless Communications*, *23*(5), 90–98. doi:10.1109/MWC.2016.7721747

Wei, Tian, Silva, Choudhary, Meng, & Yang. (2015). Comparative Study on Machine Learning for Urban Building Energy Analysis. *Procedia Engineering*, (121), 285-292.

Yüksek & Karadayi. (2017). Energy-Efficient Building Design in the Context of Building Life Cycle. In Energy Efficient Buildings. IGI.

Zhang, D., Li, S., Sun, M., & O'Neill, Z. (2016). An optimal and learning-based demand response and home energy management system. *IEEE Transactions on Smart Grid*, *7*(4), 1790–1801. doi:10.1109/TSG.2016.2552169

Chapter 5
Pervasive Internet of Things (IoT) for Smart Speakers Discovery and Playback Continuity

Aun Yichiet
Universiti Tunku Abdul Rahman, Malaysia

Jasmina Khaw Yen Min
Universiti Tunku Abdul Rahman, Malaysia

Gan Ming Lee
https://orcid.org/0000-0002-0993-1130
Universiti Tunku Abdul Rahman, Malaysia

ABSTRACT

One of the core features of IoT is global device discovery, allowing people to control and manage their connected devices anywhere across the internet. In pervasive IoT, device management becomes seamless and automated using AI for device pairing, content discovery, actions signaling, and command scheduling based on contextual information in a self-managed device paradigm. This chapter presents a novel handoff technique for smart speakers to ensure playback continuity when the users move around in a smart space consisting of multiple discoverable speakers. Current implementations include Spotify Connect, which is service specific, thus lacking in discovery robustness. The proposed handoff discovers at the device level instead of service level to improve device visibility and interoperability through a self-learning topology discovery (SLTD) method. For timely handoff, a rapid preemptive handoff method (RPF) is designed to optimize the TCP handshake mechanism and a content pre-caching technique is used to minimize playback gaps during the soft handoff.

DOI: 10.4018/978-1-7998-2803-7.ch005

INTRODUCTION

Towards cloud and edge computing, devices discoverability is becoming more prevalent as ever for active device participation and network formation (Tianfield, 2018; Hong, 2017). In the early days, *Digital Living Network Alliance* (DLNA) is the go-to protocol for detecting the presence of devices but it has limited device support thus lacking in robustness. SNMPv3, a modern discovery protocol can identify devices up to sensors level, but the knowledge is local to the device's attributes without global awareness of surrounding networks (Yin, 2012). The inception of IoT further enhances the reachability of connected devices riding on popular application protocols like *XMPP, CoAP, MQTT* and some proprietary platforms like *Apple Home, Google Home,* and *Amazon Alexa* (Luzuriaga, 2015). Today, the vast connectivity among devices allows modern applications to take advantage of the device to device interoperability to enhance user experiences, like seamless connectivity for services continuity (Kang, 2013; N. Fathima, 2017; Barnaghi, 2016).

In the next-generation IoT, devices-to-devices communication is gradually replacing human-to-device communication towards A.I. driven IoT networks (Dawod, Georgakopoulos, Jayaraman, & Nirmalathas, 2019). User commands, which is traditionally invoked using *IFTTT* and *Siri* shortcuts (Vongchumyen, 2019) can now be delegated to A.I. for command prediction through probabilistic reasoning (Këpuska, 2018; Pham, 2018). One naïve example is the transition from user turning on a connected air purifier through *MQTT* publishing message is now automated by a PM2.5 sensor detecting bad air quality, then turning on the air purifier (Luzuriaga, 2015). The PM2.5 readings; called ambient data is used as a cue for reasoning; they can be extrapolated into the multi-dimensional aware system when cues like location, proximity, user identity, activity information are incorporated (Vishwakarma, 2019; Fortunato, 2019). Context-aware systems have taken great strides courtesy of modern IoT devices that are becoming more sensor-laden (Valarmathi, 2016). IoT devices can now benefit from ambient intelligence that unshackles them from limited locale constraints to seamlessly works and synchronise among IoT devices for more complex and coordinated tasks.

This chapter presents a novel technique for smart speakers' handoff through user location tracking in indoor space. For the acoustic community, two of the most common challenges for desirable audio experience are; (1) audio fidelity and (2) area of coverage; which can now be addressed using location-aware speakers. Traditionally, music is streamed to a connected speaker talking to a nearby Access-Point (AP) in a smart space consisting of multiple independent speaker units. Currently, services like *Spotify* provides API for the discovery of all possible playback capable nodes; then, users can manually select the main speaker based on individual preferences. This chapter presents an automatic speaker selection technique to delegate the playback device selection to A.I. reasoning to fulfil the spatial requirement of balanced audio playback. The intuition here is music should be playback on the speaker that is closest to the listener in a smart space with multiple speakers connected in a near-mesh topology. Using spatial awareness, the music can be continuously played across a set of speakers by tracking user movements and changes in indoor positions. For example, among a speaker set $S_s = \{S_1, S_2, S_3...S_n\}$; the algorithm chooses one active speaker (S_a) based on distance (d) between the user (U_x) and the speaker node (S_i) at a discrete-time, t_i. The handoff method ensures audio playback continuity towards an associated tracklet through speaker selection and hopping.

Ad-Hoc Devices Handoff for Services Continuity

IoT brings devices discovery to a new playing field. Through MQTT, devices that traditionally confined to proprietary protocol now become visible to any authorized connected devices (Lu, 2009). This paves the way for unprecedented kind of continuity in services like device-to-device synchronization, device hopping, and cross-platforms device automation. One prominent feature is observed in continuity; where IoT devices can smartly handoff their roles to a set of the potential device when certain contexts or states of operations, devices, or ambient has changed; depending on the classification of the device (Bashah, 2011; Sharma, 2018; Marbukh, 2019). The intuition is given the vast availability of connected devices; the challenge in pervasive IoT is to identify the most fitting candidate to serve certain user requests autonomously. The concept of handoff has been used for many years in the domain of telecommunications; where mobile phones are constantly connecting to different base stations during transit (Hashem, 2000; Dutta, 2006). Similarly, the capability to transfer services from one IoT device to another can have a profound impact on user experiences.

Handoff Techniques

Handoff can be defined as transferring active user requests or sessions from one or many 'current' devices to some 'next' devices. The next devices can be from the same classification in device taxonomy, or some other class when the service context changed. Handoff is often implemented through handshake transfer algorithms and can be customized into device-to-device or controller-to-device communication topology to fit IoT requirements (Sharma, 2018; Klems, 2010). This section discusses some commonly used handoff techniques.

1. Periodic handoff – service request transfers from device A to device B when certain time constraints are met. Periodic deals with temporal triggers; which can be some threshold defined during device or protocol design, or from user-specified preferences. The concept of periodic handoff is to rotate between devices among same classes; for many reasons, such as (1) to load balance user requests across time, (2) to prevent some devices from hogging resources, (3) to address hardware constraints (cooling, compute load) and (4) occasionally to promote service diversity (Kaur, 2018; Nishad, Kumar, & Bola, 2016). There are several strategies but they mostly revolve around threshold; which can be preset in seconds or milliseconds. Some common handoff pattern includes round-robin, least weighted and custom scheduling. For example, A transfer the active role to B after threshold x, says $x_1=10$ms are met; and B transfer to C after the next $x_2=10$ms. Periodic handoff is often seen in IoT lighting; where different light source takes turns to lit up to conserve energy. Another use case is seen in recent Olympic Games where Intel demonstrated a drone light show; in which each drone is temporally controlled to light up to form certain unique formation.

2. Positional handoff – is a location-aware handoff technique that considers device positioning in a smart space. Smart space is an area with a collection of smart devices that are visible to each other. For simplicity, consider a standard layout house with 3 rooms and a hall. Four individuals but connected speakers are installed in each of the rooms (Weirathmueller, 2007; Morhart, 2009; Dong, 2016). The goal of positional handoff is to choose the ideal speaker for music playback; that in itself is a selection problem. There are two important components; that involves a tracking mechanism and a selection strategy. Tracking here refers to user tracking, such that a person of inter-

est (POI) movement can be measured across the smart space. There are many tracking techniques which will be discussed in great length in the next section. IoT use cases for indoor scenarios often render GPS triangulation ineffective; however, the consensus is that there is certain leeway for the accuracy given the spatial allowance between IoT devices (Hashem, 2000; Gu, 2009). For device selection, the main intuition is to constantly transfer service request from a chain of IoT devices depending on the user to device distance to preserve service continuity. Most selection strategies are derivates of distance approximation, but optimized for different constraints. Duplicative selection deals with choosing one out of many similar devices in a saturated space; intention-aware selection evaluates user needs and wants on top of algorithmic reasoning, and machine-learning-based technique augments the device selection based on user behaviors. For example, the music playback can be a handoff from speaker A->B->C in sync with user movement. The downside of positioning handoff is the lack of intention awareness; such that when a user in room A intended to stay here; who move to room B for a short period to pick up a glass of water before moving back to A. despite that, positioning based handoff is gaining traction given its general purposes, similar to those proximity sensor-enabled lighting which is popular in the early 20s.

3. Profile-based handoff – is a device selection technique for continuity based on device roles and functions. Modern IoT devices are embedded with rich metadata describing device information; one important entry is on the device 'types'. Similar to UPnP; devices advertised their role on the network; such as 'smart TV', 'hue light', air purifier, etc (Lu, 2009). There is also active discovery, be it protocol-specific like Apple Bonjour service or echo enabled devices (Yin, 2012; Vongchumyen, 2019). For universal use, many researches look into device fingerprinting to unfold device roles and functionality. The difference for IoT handoff is on how this information is used to enrich user experience. The main strategy for this kind of handoff is to select fitting device based on the compatibility index; such as device A is best fitted to perform certain service. For example, a smart TV is most likely to be the first choice for movie playback (although sound is also a major factor); but not for music playback; meanwhile, a dedicated speaker is more ideal for audio fidelity. The idea is that there is no one size fit all device to meet a diverse range of user requests, but there exists one for each job. The handoff can happen in sequential mode, where A pass to B, B pass to C when the different stages of tasks are executed; or in composite mode; where {A, B, C} work collectively to address one service request. Profile-based handoff can be effective if device roles are highly visible and discoverable; to prevent dominance of one IoT device and to delegate services among IoT nodes with different expert capability.

The abundant availability of visible smart speakers has added to the complexity in device selections (Huang, 1997; Venkataram, 2000). In a smart space where speakers coverage zones overlap, there is a need for selection criteria to choose the 'best fitting' device to fulfil user requests. The problem is formulated as given a set of IoT device, $S = \{D_A, D_{b...}, D_i\}$; f(s) is designed to select optimal device D_x based on contexts and constraints. Unlike traditional selection designed for load balancing, IoT continuity requires understanding of device roles, functions and also service requests semantics (Wong, 2008). This section shows some additional considerations for smart speaker continuity.

1. Hold out – is a timing delay that is added prior to some anticipated handoff. This prevents immediate handoff whenever applicable to accommodate handoff that are short lived; for example, user moving from node A to node B momentarily but going back to node A shortly after. Hold out attempts to

add delay to the at the onset of device to device handshake; thus, the name hold out (Moon, 2018). One common implementation is to add *x* milliseconds delay to each imminent handoff; and if the next handoff is perceptible; then *x* is reduced for the next handoff; or incremented otherwise.

2. Spatial awareness – is used to evaluates structural cues for device selection. Though only useful for acoustic devices; it is especially important for smart speakers' selection for a smart space with many physical obstacles. The technique works using spatial engine; speaker emit sound waves (omnidirectional) and sense the echo return timing to guess surrounding objects. The selection is then modelled as choosing the speaker that has fewer obstacles towards the source. Consider a case where a user is closer to speaker A than B; but there is a wall separating user from speaker B. Traditional handoff favors B (smaller distance is better). Spatial-aware selection considers physical and acoustic properties; and choose speaker A knowing that acoustic signal decline dramatically when penetrating through rigid structures (Chu, 2012; Wright, 1995; Evers, 2016).

3. Predictive techniques – leveraging on machine learning; Ai is used to model the behavior of speaker handoff patterns (from manual handoff in Spotify connect or Airplay) for guessing the potential next hop speaker if a handoff is imminent. Handoff patterns are often deterministic; since user sequential actions are repetitive; and the routing in smart space (the way user moves) is rather limited. Using trajectory dataset, user-specific machine learning models can be trained using kNN, SVM, or RNN coupled with activity and time information. The selection problem is thus defined as given set S = {$D_A, D_b... D_i$}; the next node D_i is the most probable visited node such that $D_i = f(D -> D_{i-1} -> D_{i-2})$; inferring on RNN trajectory models. This selection method is apparently more important in acoustic domain, as preemptive handoff allows for smooth audio transition rather to reduce playback gap between devices (Weirathmueller, 2007; Evers, 2016).

4. Fairness and Queuing Theory – round-robin is a turn based naïve selection technique that delegate user requests. In round robin, each speaker take turns for music playback if user is in close proximity to multiple speakers (Datta, 2016; Kaur, 2018; Joshi, 2018). It is a quick selection scheme, without context awareness; but useful for general purpose handoff. There are two derivatives; (1) narrow network and (2) wide network. In (1). localization is considered; the selection algorithm chooses an optimal node among a set of adjacent nodes with overlapping coverage (Wright, 1995). In (2), selection happen across a global view of IoT nodes without proximity cues. One popular implementation is through speaker tokenization, where each speaker passes the token to next adjacent speaker (requires speaker forming a prior synchronization network). A multicast network hosting these speakers' memberships is elastic; as speaker can join or leave the group anytime depending on network discovery status. This method is more beneficial to the speaker (in terms of task delegation and resources management) rather than for improved user experience. Weighted RR is a customised version in which speaker technical specifications are crawled from device metadata (such as acoustic ratings) as additional selection rules.

Overview of Indoor Tracking Mechanism

One deciding element for seamless playback is determined by the accuracy of positional handoff. Tracking is commonly classified into outdoor and indoor tracking; however, they are not used interchangeably. Outdoor tracking is dominated by GPS triangulation, but GPS signals deteriorate 3.0 greatly when penetrating indoor premises. Meanwhile, indoor tracking exploits sensors' spatial positional cues to approximate location information. Some useful indoor tracking is as follows:

- Round Trip Time approximation (RTTA) – attempts to estimate a device's distance to an access point. For this to works, the location of the AP must be defined either using global coordinate or relative annotated indoor points. This method uses the time for a probe packet takes to travel from the device to the AP back to the device (a round trip) as an indicator of the distance between these devices. The distance is approximated, relative to all participating nodes but not discrete (Morhart, 2009). The intuition is that if a device is located near to the AP, the packet traversing the medium towards the destination is shorter than a packet originating from a distanced device. In a single AP scenario, the device location is only approximated to be x unit nearby to the AP; x is measured in meter(s). In this case, device Da may appear to be 10 meters away from the target AP, but in any direction within the AP coverage area. For improved pinpoint, the average RTT towards multiple carefully positioned AP(s) is used for triangulation. RTTA method is comparatively less reliable, due to inevitable noise that distorts RTT readings from device interferences and router processing delay (Alessandretti, 2018). Figure 1 shows RTT increases as two nodes are further apart.

Figure 1. The relative distance of Node A to B is 2(2x) milliseconds while Node A to C is 2(3x) milliseconds for a roundtrip time in Echo Request/Reply

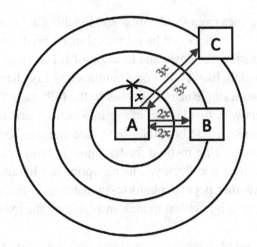

- Radio Signal Strength (RSS) Indicator – guess device location based on RSS values between two nodes. RSS is a measure of how strong the signal between sender-receiver gain to destination-receiver gain. Theoretically, the RSS value is higher when two devices are close to each other (Lee, 2016). Thus, increasing RSS indicates the increasing distance between nodes. similar to RTT, RSS is subject to interference noise and becomes less reliable in saturated smart spaces using the same radio frequency and Wi-Fi channels. RSS, however, is not sensitive to other types of delay; like processing delay and transmission delay. Comparing to RTT, RSS can be implemented more easily as there is no need for establishing network sessions. The advantage of RSS becomes more apparent in ad-hoc mode; measuring the RSS between the tracker and tracked devices means there is no master-slave architecture unlike the use of AP (controller) in RTTA that can easily be congested (Karakuşak, 2016).

Figure 2. The changes in RSS value when the distance between two nodes increases; measured in –dBM format (-100 to 0). Theoretical RSS value from B to A is stronger than C to A due to the shorter distance, and C to A is stronger than D to A due to interferences from obstacles

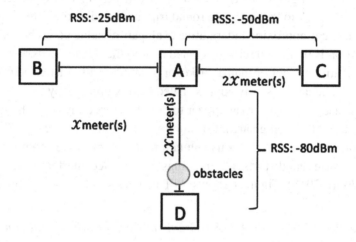

- Visual Mapping – taking cues from localization and mapping algorithms found in robot vacuum; the location of user and IoT devices can be estimated using predictive models (Dong, 2016; Xu, 2017). Using computer vision, the types and location of IoT devices in a smart space can be recognized using object models like YOLO or Simultaneous Localization and Mapping (SLAM) (Evers, 2016). YOLO uses a single neural network to the full image for object detection based on a global context. This network divides the image into regions and predicts bounding boxes and probabilities for each region. These bounding boxes are weighted by the predicted probabilities. YOLO also has a built-in tracking method for fast-moving objects to support target mobility. A custom model can be trained and deployed using optimized libraries leveraging on YOLO for real-time recognition. Another popular platform-agnostic approach uses multiple containers (or Kubernetes) leveraging on public vision models available on the hybrid cloud like Google Cloud ML or AWS Sagemaker.
- Spatial sensing – is a subset of mapping method that uses acoustic sensing to approximate device to device distance (Wright, 1995). Using biosonar and sound localization, device location can be determined by evaluating very small-time differences between the outgoing signal and the echo return (similar to beamforming). The method is more meta-psychic than algorithmic; thus, there is no pre-requisite like protocols or special sensor support on IoT devices (Chu, 2012; Martin, 2015). Interestingly, in the context of speaker continuity; the speakers themselves are the source node that emits the sonar signal towards the target user. These speakers then join a multicast group to elect a speaker with the closest proximity after aggregating distance information. The effectiveness of spatial sensing can be a mixed bag and greatly depends on the structural design in the smart space. In open space with fewer obstacles, spatial sensing can accurately determine the location of the pinged target; but suffers in a congested environment. Another downside is the lack of multi-user supports as spatial cues do not discriminate between objects in physical space, the only distance towards the objects (Weirathmueller, 2007). Spatial sensing is immune to processing delay but is highly sensitive to transmission and propagation delay. Figure 3 shows the U1 chip emitting ultra-

wideband radio signal to a spatial aware device; on collision with an object the signal bounce back with distance and device ID information.

Figure 3. Omni-directional ultrawideband signal broadcast; in anticipation of a collision to determine the object to object distance

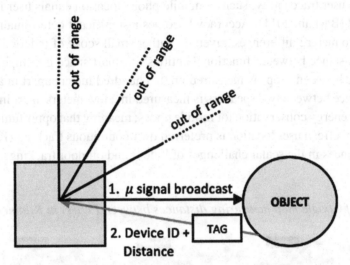

- Zoning technique – this method approximate user location based on the technical specifications of Bluetooth, infrared, and 802.11x protocol coverage limit. The intuition is user location can be guessed based on their respective discoverability; and their corresponding signal strength to these connections. For example, a smart space can be divided into distinct zones where each zone is covered by one AP. In the area where AP(s) coverage overlaps; user proximity is guessed based on the signal strength of the user (mobile phone WIFI signal) towards the AP sets. In the case where 2 AP(s) are discovered and if gain A is higher than gain B; then the user is deduced to be closer to APA. Similar to RTTA, the zoning technique is prone to the fluctuation of WIFI Signal due to interference. The zoning technique addresses the problem where there exist multiple AP in each zone. The coverage overlapping is what made the improved approximation when more AP(s) spatial cues are used for triangulation (Kho, 2015).

Challenges in IoT Continuity

The concept of continuity has been greatly explored; evidently in mobile base station handoff, cross-device continuity in Apple iOS ecosystem and many other screen sharing protocols like Airplay. Similar to these services, the goal of general-purpose continuity is to transfer active roles from device to device depending on contexts like location, user intention and types of services. This section discusses certain challenges exclusive to IoT device continuity; ranging from pervasive tracking and device selections.

On User Tracking Method

Pervasive continuity is user and location-aware. Unlike manual handoff, the continuity is unsupervised; carefully evaluating user real-time position; and reasoned with other contexts like distance, ambient cues, and intention to make an educated decision in device handoff. Traditional tracking method like GPS is erratic for indoor uses; many alternatives are proposed as discussed in previous sections. There are many assumptions to user traceability; such as mobile phone location equals user live location; or user has wearable on 24/7 (Bashah, 2011). Accuracy becomes a significant determinant; such that tracking must be accurate up to meter2 differences, given the rather small scope of indoor space of interest. The rationale is that the distance between 'functional entities' in smart space is comparatively smaller. For example, the distance between shops is measured up to a hundred meters apart in an outdoor scenario; meanwhile, the distance between two speakers is measured in a few meters apart in an indoor scenario. Then there is need for energy conservation for mobile nodes; meaning that opportunistic tracking method like knowing when to refresh user location is preferred over continuous tracking (Klems, 2010). Figure 4 compare the differences in the scalar challenges of indoor and outdoor tracking.

Figure 4. A snippet of Google map measuring distances between POI(s) in Kilometer(s)

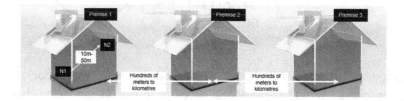

On Protocol Support

There is a distinct difference between device hopping and device continuity. In device hopping, service requests can be a handoff from Node A to Node B without true continuation. For example, music playback from A can be paused before transfer over to B if A and B do not have overlapping coverage. Meanwhile, device continuity requires the playback to be a handoff to B without interruption; which is called soft handoff. For guaranteed continuity, the protocol supports become an important factor for both device discovery (visibility) and the actual handoff. Consider two cases with similar nodes specification 5 speakers, each positioned 10 meters apart linearly but in case (1) with multiple protocols supports, and in case (2) with homogenous protocol support. Assume that each speaker coverage overlaps the speaker adjacent to it (Barnaghi, 2016). In case (1), a condensed network; the handoff is more fine-grain such that if the user moves from speaker A to E; each speaker takes turns for playback in sequential order. As for case (2), a sparse network, the handoff happens on speaker n+1 hop away as the next adjacent speaker does not share the same IoT protocols despite sitting in the same LAN. Some common workarounds are to use a middle layer for discovery and handoff, or to embed popular IoT platforms (Alexa, Apple Homekit, and Google Home) support into the devices. Figure 5 shows an example of a physically condense network but logically sparse network (due to lack of interoperability). Figure 6 shows an IoT network with full interoperability.

On Device Discovery and Selection

Figure 5. Sparse network has less discoverable nodes and homogenous nodes are saturated apart

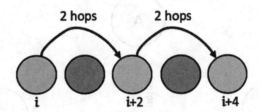

Figure 6. Condense network is a rich collection of heterogeneous IoT nodes

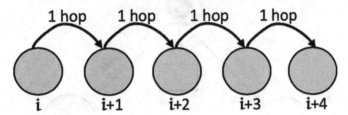

Distance-based device selection has been used in many smart devices; for example, smart TV using a proximity sensor to track user eye movement to automatically pause playback. Tracking using primitive sensors like proximity, gyro-meter, and light sensors works well for a single device to user relationship; but they lack global device-to-device visibility. Handoff deals with a set of devices to user relationships, and IoT provides the required device visibility through network discovery for subsequent selection use. Proximity sensing only addresses discovery but not synchronization. For example, consider 5 speakers equipped with the same proximity sensors positioned in a sphere layout. Intuitively, the speaker closer to the user (proximity distance) become the active speaker. This method assumes that the next nearby speaker is not detecting the user; else the speakers will playback concurrently since there is no controller to delegate these user requests. Now, consider the case where the user moves into the middle point of the sphere; here, all 5 speakers will playback concurrently due to proximity among all nodes. Figure 7 shows a possible scenario of equal distance handoff (Wong, 2008; Venkataram, 2000).

Besides, the synergy of discovery protocols towards actual hand-off is still in the infancy stage. General-purpose protocols like UPnP works well to discover neighboring devices, but lack handoff implementation (Kang, 2013). Meanwhile, platform-specific protocols like Airplay and Alexa have a seamless handoff technique but have limited cross-platform device visibility. In the best-case scenario (full visibility and no handoff constraints), IoT merely provides an operational platform with vanilla device selection rules (smaller distance is better). Trivial issues like having two equal distance nodes, devices with homogenous roles but heterogenous specifications should be addressed using machine-learning reasonings.

Figure 7. Device selection algorithm choose next node x ={A,B,C,D,E} if distance d(x.u) is the smallest. In equal distance node, the handoff is paused until new d(x,u) is detected. In many cases, speakers are sync for surround playback as in Dolby Atmos technology

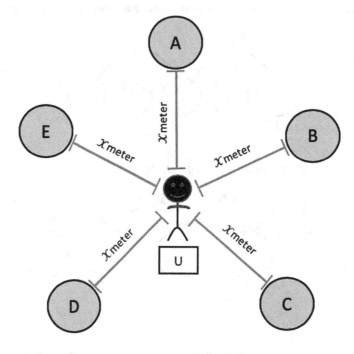

Smart Speakers Handoff based on User's Positioning

Music playback continuity is enabled through pervasive handoff by automatic selection of smart speaker in a smart space based on user positioning. Figure 8 visualize the overview of a holistic speaker handoff from discovery to handshake and finally the handoff process itself.

In the first stage, the AP (acting as the controller) is modified with beam-forming antenna sends out multiple discovery signals to 360 angles for **device discovery**. IoT capable speaker sends a *hello signal* continuously until a full convergence, which all speakers node can be identified through spatial mapping. The second stage deals with **device positioning**; which is pivotal for spatial awareness using a technique called round trip time (RTT) to router traversal delay for approximation. The distance among {router-speaker} is triangulated using beam-forming signals for exact positioning in smart space. At the core, an occlusion aware pathfinding algorithm is designed to identify the closest neighbor (speaker) towards a movement free target (user). Instead of mapping a physical environment manually, a collision detection and avoidance technique are designed based on *Air Obstacle Avoidance* technique used in many commercial drones for walls detection; which is important for an indoor setting, since acoustic signal does not penetrate hard wall effectively. Meanwhile, user trajectory tracking can be pinpointed using a triangulation of wearables positional data, mobile phones or through image processing using camera sensing. For pervasiveness, the algorithm constantly monitors for user movement using sensor-specific cues; like increase heart rate on a smartwatch, or the changes of RSS on a mobile phone. For added robustness, the algorithm periodically checks for location changes using continuous RTT monitoring. In a single-user use case, the common trajectory can be modeled for subsequent early detection. A.I. driven IoT speak-

Figure 8. Components in Pervasive Smart Speakers Handoff

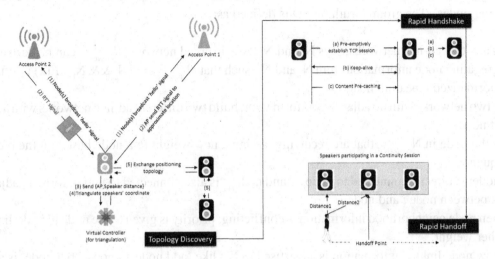

ers can now see similar classified devices as one, instead of isolated entities that can now synchronize to selectively take turns to play music by proximity to a user based on a shared responsibility model. Some popular music streaming apps like Spotify that support multiple devices streaming is inherited for implementation. Based on devices discovered by Spotify, the proposed algorithm automatically selects preferred playback devices based on proximity.

Topology Discovery and Rapid Handoff Pipeline

Comprehensive node discovery and fast handoff remain the de-factor challenges for pervasive computing. This chapter proposed a self-learning topology discovery (SLTD) method implemented using some techniques discussed in section 3 to maps neighboring nodes. Then, a rapid preemptive handoff (RPF) module is designed to optimize the TCP handshake mechanism on top of a precaching module for improved continuity. The next section discusses these components in detail.

Self-learning Topology Discovery (SLTD)

SLTD leverages on any types of sensors that provide spatial cues. There are two types of implementations: (1) using U1 (ultra-wideband) chips; ultra-wideband is a low-energy, short-range radio technology primarily used for wireless data transmission. The distance between two ultra-wideband-equipped devices can be measured much more precisely by calculating the time that it takes for a radio wave to pass between the two devices (2) using a customized RTT triangulation for existing IoT devices with 802.11x chips. RTT smoothing is used to minimize the noise coming from processing delay and propagation delay; like using a less busy radio channel and using preferential QoS treatment for discovering packets. In a volatile network, a fast convergence technique like aggregated discovery (AD) is useful to detect fast turn over in members joining and leaving the network. AD is a topology sharing method; the intuition is 'for every two ad-hoc networks with 1 common node; these networks can be converged into a bigger network that eventually forms a full mesh network consisting of global knowledge of all neighboring nodes'. The ground truth of AD is defined as:

1. For any two ad-hoc networks, says N_a and N_b. A converged network, $N_{converged}$ can be derived from aggregating node information from N_a and N_b; such that $N_{converged} = f(N_a$ && $N_b)$. $F(x)$ is a function of normalized repeating nodes.

2. For two networks with no adjacency information; build two different ad-hoc networks with a unique root node.

3. For the node in $N_{converged}$ that are recurring, assign a new weight to a node based on the recurring frequency

4. If node$i$ is directly connected to node$_{i+1}$; and node$_{i+1}$ is also connected to node$j$; form an adjacency link between node i and node j.

5. When node neighborhood information is conflicting; priority is given to the node to node-link with higher weight.

6. If new node linking information is advertised to N_a; like 'add node$_i$ to node$_k$' but node$_k$ is already visible in N_a; discard this link. These rules give precedence to local link information over advertised information. The local network does not learn local node information from a foreign network.

7. Repeat node discovery to find new adjacency link until all root nodes are connected to a new adjacent link not found in the original local topology; to form a full mesh network.

Rapid Preemptive Handoff (RPF)

Rapid preemptive handoff is a predictive handoff technique to reduce the handoff gap during devices hopping for large-scale IoT mesh network. RPF is a holistic approach to tweaks existing handoff methods. There are two components, including (1) pre-synchronization using rapid-handshake and (2) content pre-caching.

In the pre-sync stage, RPF establishes sessions among neighboring nodes even before actual data transfer takes place. The early connection allows for immediate handoff; even if a node just recently joins a network. Another implication is reduced latency; which is measured from the time needed for the last byte of data in the current node to be sent to the (1st byte of data) in the next adjacent node. This approach is a departure of standard TCP/IP practice; where nodes only establish sessions on-demand through a 3-ways handshake. Pre-sync is an extension to discovery protocol; existing discovery only makes device visible but no subsequent control traffic flows among nodes. With pre-sync, devices attempt to communicate after discovery and place sessions on hold in anticipation of any handoff transmission.

Rapid-handshake is a lightweight handshake for IoT nodes to establish a session to implement pre-sync. Similar to MQTT replacing HTTP; the goal of rapid-handshake is to reduce overhead during sessions creation in large-scale mesh networks. In rapid-handshake, the total handshake is reduced from three to two; the first and the third handshakes are combined into SYN (to destination) and ACK (to destination). This means there is no need for the sender to explicitly acknowledge a connection request from the destination; which is a response to the initial connection request. One major change in the second handshake is the support of PSH and RST flags on top of the standard SYN+ACK. This allows for immediate data transfer (thus handoff) after discovery, and assumes that if the neighboring node is visible then they are authorized. Some extra security measures can be imposed by upper layers protocol and access can be revoked in response to incidents and illegitimate access. The rapid handshake in this chapter is implemented on a custom TCP/IP stack.

Figure 9. The handshake mechanism proposed in rapid-handshake

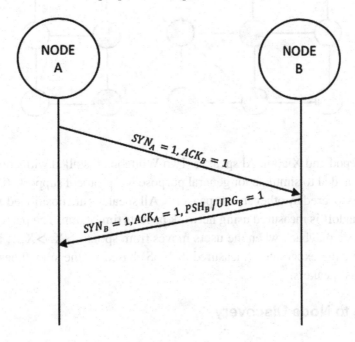

A content pre-caching module is designed for selective pre-emptive handoff. Similar to caching in the content delivery network; pre-caching here refers to pre-storing data on potential next node in a mesh network. Cached data means faster data access; thus, when node$_a$ handoff to node$_b$; it is only dealing with control traffic whereas a subset of user traffic has been stored locally in node$_b$. The amount of pre-cached data and the degree of neighbor (s) to participate in pre-caching depends on the application contexts. The complexity of caching increased depending on network density; caching one data byte k in a 2-degree network requires 2n data overhead. Instead of flooding; a set of potential next adjacent candidates is determined using a polynomial regression model on progressive device to user spatial distance or received signal power (RSP) values. Figure 10 visualizes node selection for pre-caching when a user moves linearly from left to right in a full mesh topology.

PERFORMANCE COMPARISON

This section evaluates some key performance metrics using SLTD-RPF comparing to existing handoff methods. The first experiment evaluates the latency in global node discovery. The second experiment evaluates the latency in node to node handoff. A smart space consisting of 12 smart speakers are setup as shown in Figure 10 that are programmed with custom firmware (to support SLTD-RPF). To test discovery robustness; 5 different speakers are used; two units each of Amazon Echo (Alexa), LG soundbar, Sonos

Figure 10. Content being pre-cached at all neighboring nodes with degree of n=1 (next hop); neighbors are discovered using SLTD (orange nodes indicated next hop cache)

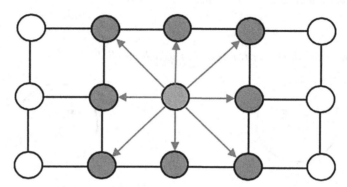

speaker, Apple Homepod and Xiaomi AI speaker. Two Whitebox installed with common IoT protocols like MQTT, CoAP is added to simulate for general purpose IoT protocol supports (these are not used to discover but can be discovered by other smart speakers). All speakers are positioned 10 meters away. The speaker to speaker handoff is measured using network packets timestamp. The perception test measures the experience of music playback when the users moves from spot x_1->X_2->X_3... in a U-shaped path. Users are asked to rate the experience (measured in MoS) based on the smoothness and timeliness of audio transition across speakers.

Latency in Node to Node Discovery

The latency for neighborhood discovery indicate the reliability of the discovery protocols. This is measured in (1) the number of nodes discovered and (2) the time used for detecting these neighbors. For (1), the higher number which indicate a more general-purpose discovery is favored; and for (2) shorter time which indicate faster discovery is better. Table 1 summarize the discovery latency for some popular IoT protocols. The third column, 'completeness' indicate how many nodes are discovered among all available nodes; expressed as:

Figure 11. The topology design for Smart Speaker Positioning layout

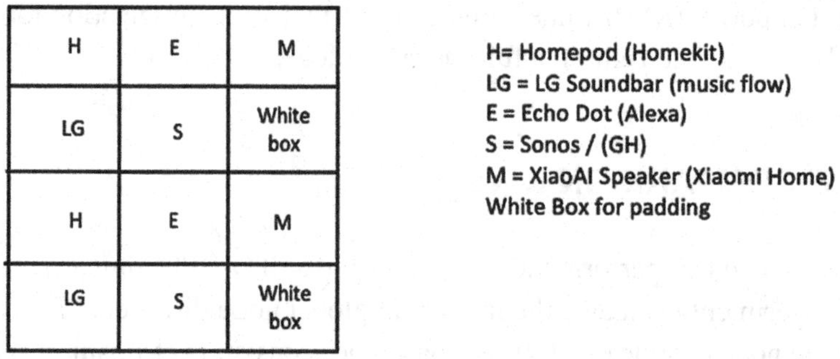

H	E	M
LG	S	White box
H	E	M
LG	S	White box

H= Homepod (Homekit)
LG = LG Soundbar (music flow)
E = Echo Dot (Alexa)
S = Sonos / (GH)
M = XiaoAI Speaker (Xiaomi Home)
White Box for padding

Table 1. Performance Evaluation on Discovery Latency of Popular IoT Protocols/Platforms

Protocols	Number of Nodes Discovered	Average Discovery Latency (seconds)	Completeness [n=12]
Apple Homekit	4	5.36	0.33
Alexa (Echo)	10	12.08	0.83
LG Musicflow	2	23.17	0.17
Google Home (Sonos)	6	11.98	0.50
Xiaomi Home	2	15.2	0.17
Whitebox (custom IoT)	-	-	-

C = number of discovered nodes/total number of nodes in topology

The experimental results showed that Alexa has the highest number of supported devices; followed by Google Home, Apple Homekit, LG musicflow and Xiaomi Home. Note that speaker manufacturer often designs own IoT protocol; and while some protocols like Alexa is accessible through API calls; not all protocols are supported by most speakers. The findings consolidate that the adaption rate of IoT protocol is important to ensure complete discovery coverage; evidently from the mass integration of Alexa in smart speakers by the industry. Using Proprietary protocol like LG and Xiaomi results in only 2 visible devices; meaning IoT devices are only harmony to manufacturer specific protocol. In modern IoT, locking devices to specific protocol limit the size of discovered network; unless one specific vendor is used for entire network design. Meanwhile, Apple homekit clocks in the shortest latency; probably due to the optimized software and hardware integration by Apple. Google home rank in 2nd with 11.98, followed closely by Alexa in 3rd place with 12.08. The minimal differences could be disregard since Alexa has more participating devices; also, network delays are not factored in during the evaluation. The finding showed that the three IoT platforms with most consumer adoption has fast convergence in discovering available devices. In terms of topology discovery, Alexa remained the go-to option given the mass adoption of Alexa ecosystem; noting that any protocol can easily be made available in any smart speakers through firmware updates. Figure 12 visualize the device's visibility of respective protocols after full discovery.

Latency in Node-to-Node Handoff

The transition time measures the gap (in seconds) for the session to be carry over to the next hop node. A speaker network consisting of 10 similar speaker units is built. The experiment is repeated for LG music flow, Google Home and SLTD-RPF on same setup using speakers with different protocol supports. At the time of testing, Homekit, Xiaomi Home and Alexa do not support native handoff. Experiment is conducted after full topology convergence.

Theoretically, the latency encompasses the handshake period, processing delay (speaker A to router to speaker A+1), and propagation delay depending on network environment. For simplicity, the experiment measures the timestamp differences; for the last packet in node A and the first packet in Node A+1 indicate the transition time; which is expressed as handoff latency. In context of smart speakers, shorter handoff means less pause (reduced judder perception) in between music playback from node A to node

Figure 12.

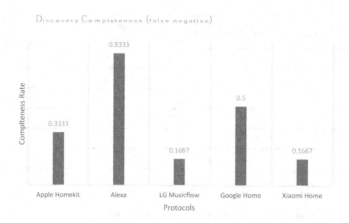

A+1. Table 2 summarized the average handoff of the studied IoT protocols; whenever applicable. Second column shows number of successful handoff measures if the next hop smart speaker is triggered when user proximity changes. The rest of the columns shows latency from hop n_i to n_i+1.

Figure 13. Performance evaluation for device discovery completeness (number of available devices vs. number of visible devices based on topology in Figure 10)

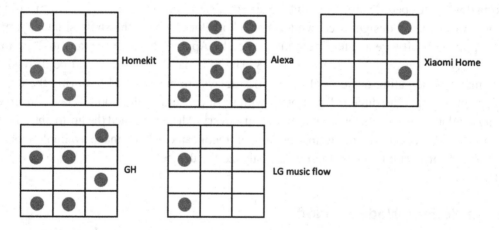

Note that despite the RSS is somewhat similar in both cases; actual handoff happens earlier in SLTD-RPF, reacting in 2.12 and 1.96 seconds respectively. Meanwhile, Musicflow only reacts after 5.12 seconds in hop1-hop2 and 8.33 in hop2-hop3. The reduced handoff is a composite product of pre-emptive handoff and rapid handshake mechanism used in SLTD-RPF handoff method. Figure 14 shows the actual speaker node selected by Musicflow, Google, and SLTD-RPF respectively. The finding show that handoff protocol can be currently follows a path of most 'RSS'; they can be somewhat more sensitive to way users are being tracked, thus, resulting in non-deterministic node selection during handoff. The accuracy of node selection is addressed with accurate tracking; which is beyond the scope of this chapter.

Table 2. Comparing the numbers of successful handoff and handoff timeliness

Protocols	Number of Successful Handoff [n=10]	Hop 1-Hop 2 (seconds)	Hop2-Hop3 (seconds)
Apple Homekit	-	-	-
Alexa	-	-	-
LG Musicflow	4	5.12	8.33
Google Home	3	6.27	5.39
Xiaomi Home	-	-	-
SLTD-RPF	4	2.12	1.96

Perception Test

The perception test is carried out on 50 diverse listeners to listen on mixed genres music in the smart space during speaker to speaker handoff based on Median of Score (MoS). The MoS value is averaged

Figure 14. Visualizing selected speakers by Google Home, LG Musicflow and SLTD-RPF

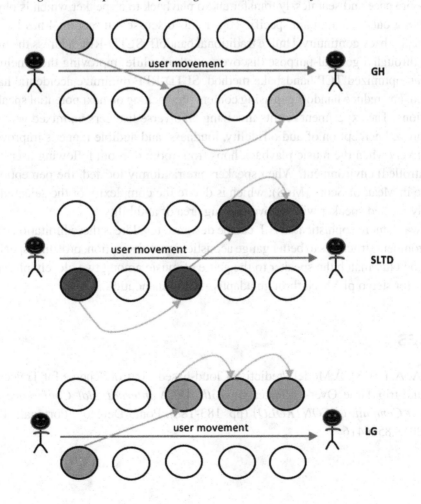

from three acoustic benchmarking metrics. Fidelity is a measure of the precision and clarity of speech and voices. Loudness is a measure on the effect on listening experience due to changes in amplitude. Audibility is a measure on whether audio is perceptible across obstacles or when user moves towards certain distance away from the speakers. Table 3 shows the average perception score, ranging from 1-5 (higher is better).

Table 3. The average of MoS from 50 listeners on the playback experience using speaker continuity

Metrics	Fidelity	Loudness (changes in)	Audibility	MoS
Score	4.5	4.3	4.8	4.53

CONCLUSION

This chapter discussed a use case on IoT devices continuity of smart speakers using a novel device discovery and rapid handoff techniques. Leveraging on IoT connectivity, Smart speakers can now accurately track users in an indoor space and seamlessly transfer audio playback to a speaker which is physically closer to the user. Ironing out some domain specific constraints discussed in section 4 has led to perceptible improvement in playback continuity. Unlike traditional handoff, SLTD-RPF address the interoperability of IoT devices through a general-purpose discovery method while improving the timeliness of device handoff using an optimized TCP handshake method. SLTD-RPF minimize accidental handoff using a hold-out method, and reduce handoff gap using content pre-caching on next potential speaker leveraging on A.I. predictions. The experiment results involving 50 diverse listeners on mixed genres collectively showed an improved perception of audio fidelity, loudness, and audible range is improved to 4.5, 4.3. and 4.8 respectively when the music playback hops from room to room following user movement in a simulated (controlled) environment. When speakers are randomly located, the perception test showed a minor decline in Mean of Score (MoS); which is due to the complexity of the selection algorithm in deciding closely located speaker with an overlapping area of audibility.

Moving forward, more sophisticated A.I. can be designed to address these limitations; like modeling the actual environment structures to better gauge acoustic signal absorption, profiling speakers' technical specifications to better match the speaker to the genre of music among two closely placed speakers, or to pair speakers for stereo playback through adaptive recommendation.

REFERENCES

Alessandretti, A. A. (2018). A Model Predictive Cloud-based Control Scheme for Trajectory-Tracking: Effects of Round-trip Time Over-estimates. In *13th APCA International Conference on Automatic Control and Soft Computing (CONTROLO)* (pp. 183-188). Ponta Delgada, Portugal: IEEE. 10.1109/CONTROLO.2018.8516416

Barnaghi, P. S., & Sheth, A. (2016). On Searching the Internet of Things: Requirements and Challenges. *IEEE Intelligent Systems, 31*(6), 71–75. doi:10.1109/MIS.2016.102

Bashah, N. S. (2011). A Mobile Service Architecture for improving Availability and Continuity. In *IEEE Symposium on Computers & Informatics* (pp. 380-384). Kuala Lumpur, Malaysia: IEEE. 10.1109/ISCI.2011.5958945

Chu, T. S. (2012). Acoustic Sensor Array for Determination of Undersea Acoustic Signatures. In *IEEE International Conference on Electro/Information Technology*. Indianapolis, IN: IEEE. 10.1109/EIT.2012.6220770

Datta, L. (2016). A new Task Scheduling method for 2 Level Load Balancing in homogeneous distributed system. In *International Conference on Electrical, Electronics, and Optimization Techniques (ICEEOT)* (pp. 4320-4325). Chennai, India: IEEE. 10.1109/ICEEOT.2016.7755534

Dawod, A., Georgakopoulos, D., Jayaraman, P. P., & Nirmalathas, A. (2019). Advancements Towards Global IoT Device Discovery and Integration. In *IEEE International Congress on Internet of Things (ICIOT)* (pp. 147-155). IEEE. 10.1109/ICIOT.2019.00034

Dong, Y. L. (2016). *Depth Map Up-sampling with Texture Edge Feature via Sparse Representation. In Visual Communications and Image Processing (VCIP)*. Chengdu, China: IEEE.

Dutta, A. M. (2006). GPS Assisted Fast-Handoff Mechanism for Real-Time Communication. In *IEEE Sarnoff Symposium*. Princeton, NJ: IEEE. 10.1109/SARNOF.2006.4534769

Evers, C. M. (2016). Acoustic simultaneous localization and mapping (A-SLAM) of a moving microphone array and its surrounding speakers. In *IEEE International Conference on Acoustics, Speech and Signal Processing (ICASSP)* (pp. 6-10). Shanghai, China: IEEE. 10.1109/ICASSP.2016.7471626

Fathima, N., A. A. (2017). Optimized Neighbor Discovery in Internet of Things (IoT). In *International Conference on Electrical, Electronics, Communication, Computer and Optimization Techniques (ICEEC-COT)* (pp. 594-598). IEEE. 10.1109/ICEECCOT.2017.8284573

Fortunato, M. C.-M. (2019). Enabling High Accuracy Dynamic Applications in Urban Environments Using PPP and RTK on Android Multi-Frequency and Multi-GNSS Smartphones. In *European Navigation Conference (ENC)*. Warsaw, Poland: IEEE. 10.1109/EURONAV.2019.8714140

Gu, C. S. (2009). GPS information assisted handoff mechanism in heterogeneous wireless networks. In *IEEE International Conference on Communications Technology and Applications*. Beijing, China: IEEE.

Hashem, B. K. (2000). A new algorithm to reduce the deviation in the base stations transmitted powers during soft handoff in CDMA cellular systems. In *IEEE Wireless Communications and Networking Conference. Conference Record (Cat. No.00TH8540)*. Chicago, IL: IEEE. 10.1109/WCNC.2000.904620

Hong, H. (2017). From Cloud Computing to Fog Computing: Unleash the Power of Edge and End Devices. In *IEEE 9th International Conference on Cloud Computing Technology and Science* (pp. 331-334). IEEE.

Huang, C. M. (1997). Handoff Architectures Ahkd Protocols For Transmitting Compressed Multimedia Information In Mobile PCSs. In *International Conference on Consumer Electronics* (pp. 784-794). Rosemont, IL: IEEE.

Joshi, N. K. (2018). Implementation of Novel Load Balancing Technique in Cloud Computing Environmen. In *International Conference on Computer Communication and Informatics (ICCCI)*. Coimbatore, India: IEEE. 10.1109/ICCCI.2018.8441212

Kang, J. S. (2013). Universal UPnP Bridge for Embedded Non-IP Device with Heterogeneous Network Interfaces. In *13th International Conference on Control, Automation and Systems (lCCAS 2013)* (pp. 561-563). Gwangju, Korea: IEEE. 10.1109/ICCAS.2013.6704002

Karakuşak, M. Z. (2016). The use of RSS and NI Filtering for the Wireless Indoor Localization and Tracking of Mobile Robots with Different Motion Models. In *24th Signal Processing and Communication Application Conference (SIU)*. Zonguldak, Turkey: IEEE. 10.1109/SIU.2016.7496088

Kaur, S. S. (2018). Efficient Load Balancing using Improved Central Load Balancing Technique. In *Proceedings of the Second International Conference on Inventive Systems and Control (ICISC 2018)* (pp. 1-5). Coimbatore, India: IEEE. 10.1109/ICISC.2018.8398857

Këpuska, V. (2018). Next-Generation of Virtual Personal Assistants (Microsoft Cortana, Apple Siri, Amazon Alexa and Google Home). In *IEEE 8th Annual Computing and Communication Workshop and Conference (CCWC)* (pp. 99-103). Las Vegas, NV: IEEE.

Kho, Y. H. (2015). Exploiting RF Signal Attenuation for Passive Indoor Location Tracking of an Object. In *IEEE 2015 International Conference on Computer, Communication, and Control Technology (I4CT 2015)* (pp. 152-156). Kuching, Malaysia: IEEE.

Klems, M. T. (2010). Automating the Delivery of IT Service Continuity Management through Cloud Service Orchestration. In *IEEE Network Operations and Management Symposium - NOMS 2010*. Osaka, Japan: IEEE. 10.1109/NOMS.2010.5488437

Lee, W. C. (2016). RSS-based Localization Algorithm for Indoor Patient Tracking. In *IEEE 14th International Conference on Industrial Informatics (INDIN)* (pp. 1060-1064). Poitiers, France: IEEE.

Lu, Y. F. (2009). Home Networking and Control based on UPnP: An Implementation. In *Second International Workshop on Computer Science and Engineering* (pp. 385-389). Qingdao, China: IEEE.

Luzuriaga, J. E. (2015). *Handling Mobility in IoT applications using the MQTT protocol*. Internet Technol. Appl.

Marbukh, V. (2019). Towards Fog Network Utility Maximization (FoNUM) for Managing Fog Computing Resources. In *IEEE International Conference on Fog Computing (ICFC)* (pp. 195-200). Prague, Czech Republic: IEEE. 10.1109/ICFC.2019.00032

Martin, E. Z. (2015). Rapid spatial mapping of the acoustic pressure in high intensity focused ultrasound fields at clinical intensities using a novel planar Fabry-Pérot interferometer. In *IEEE International Ultrasonics Symposium (IUS)*. Taipei, Taiwan: IEEE. 10.1109/ULTSYM.2015.0229

Moon, Y. H. (2018). *A Methodology of NB-IoT Mobility Optimization. In Global Internet of Things Summit (GIoTS)*. Bilbao, Spain: IEEE.

Morhart, C. B. (2009). Cooperative Multi-User Detection and Localization for Pedestrian Protection. In *German Microwave Conference*. Munich, Germany: IEEE. 10.1109/GEMIC.2009.4815863

Nishad, L. S., Kumar, S., & Bola, S. K. (2016). Round Robin Selection of Datacenter Simulation Technique Cloudsim and Cloud Analsyt Architecture and Making it Efficient by Using Load Balancing Technique. In *3rd International Conference on Computing for Sustainable Global Development (INDIACom)*. New Delhi, India: IEEE.

Pham, C. L. (2018). A Platform for Integrating Alexa Voice Service Into ECHONET-based Smart Homes. In *IEEE International Conference on Consumer Electronics-Taiwan (ICCE-TW)*. Taichung, Taiwan: IEEE. 10.1109/ICCE-China.2018.8448893

Sharma, P. K. (2018). Secure and Soft Handoff Techniques of IoT: A Review. In *Proceedings of the 2nd International Conference on Trends in Electronics and Informatics (ICOEI 2018)* (pp. 271-276). Tirunelveli, India: IEEE. 10.1109/ICOEI.2018.8553740

Tianfield, H. (2018). Towards Edge-Cloud Computing. In *IEEE International Conference on Big Data (Big Data)* (pp. 4883-4885). IEEE. 10.1109/BigData.2018.8622052

Valarmathi, M. L. (2016). A Survey on Node Discovery in Mobile Internet of Things(IoT) Scenarios. In *International Conference on Advanced Computing and Communication Systems (lCACCS -2016), Jan. 22 & 23, 2016, Coimbatore*. Coimbatore, India: IEEE. 10.1109/ICACCS.2016.7586400

Venkataram, P. L. (2000). A Method of Data Transfer Control during Handoffs in Mobile Multimedia Networks. In *IEEE International Conference on Personal Wireless Communications. Conference Proceedings (Cat. No.00TH8488)*. Hyderabad, India: IEEE. 10.1109/ICPWC.2000.905774

Vishwakarma, S. K. (2019). Smart Energy Efficient Home Automation System Using IoT. In *4th International Conference on Internet of Things: Smart Innovation and Usages (IoT-SIU)*. Ghaziabad, India: IEEE. 10.1109/IoT-SIU.2019.8777607

Vongchumyen, C. T. (2019). Home Appliances-Controlled Platform with HomeKit Application. In *5th International Conference on Engineering, Applied Sciences and Technology (ICEAST)*. Luang Prabang, Laos: IEEE.

Weirathmueller, M. W. (2007). *Acoustic Positioning and Tracking in Portsmouth Harbor, New Hampshire. In OCEANS*. Vancouver, Canada: IEEE.

Wong, S. P. (2008). Service Continuity for Audio Visual Service. In *IEEE International Symposium on Consumer Electronics*. Vilamoura, Portugal: IEEE.

Wright, O. (1995). Local acoustic probing using mechanical and ultrafast optical techniques. In *IEEE Ultrasonics Symposium. Proceedings. An International Symposium* (pp. 567-575). Seattle, WA: IEEE.

Xu, W. W. (2017). *Depth Map Super-resolution via Multiclass Dictionary Learning with Geometrical Directions. In IEEE Visual Communications and Image Processing (VCIP)*. St. Petersburg, FL: IEEE.

Yin, J. B. (2012). SNMP-based network topology discovery algorithm and implementation. In *9th International Conference on Fuzzy Systems and Knowledge Discovery (FSKD 2012)* (pp. 2241-2244). IEEE. 10.1109/FSKD.2012.6233879

Chapter 6
IoT Security:
To Secure IoT Devices With Two-Factor Authentication by Using a Secure Protocol

Khuda Bux Jalbani

Riphah Institute of Systems Engineering, Riphah International University, Islamabad, Pakistan

Akhtar Hussain Jalbani

Department of Information Technology, Quaid-e-Awam University of Engineering, Science, and Technology, Pakistan

Saima Siraj Soomro

Department of Information Technology, Quaid-e-Awam University of Engineering, Science, and Technology, Pakistan

ABSTRACT

The usage of the internet of things (IoT) devices is growing for the ease of life. From smart homes to smart cars, from smart transportation to smart cities, from smart hospitals to smart highways, these IoT devices send and receive highly sensitive data regarding the privacy of users or other information regarding the movement of users from one location to another location. The timing traces users when present at home and out of the home. But how does one secure this information from the attacker? There is a need for IoT devices security. As there are three layers of IoT devices—the application layer, network layer, and perception layer—three layers to be secure. IoT devices are heterogeneous and constrain energy consumption. The proposed solution in this chapter is three-way authentication of IoT devices by generating tokens from the device serial number and from the few configuration devices at the network layer. For high availability of IoT device services, the protection against distributed denial of service attack is implemented at the network layer.

DOI: 10.4018/978-1-7998-2803-7.ch006

INTRODUCTION

The Internet of Things (IoT) usage is growing rapidly to get more benefits from this technology with less interaction by any human. These IoT devices are used for smart homes, smart home appliances, smart cars, safe cities, sensors for medical, smart agriculture devices, and smart highways/motorways for safe roads. The IoT networks can be categorized as distributed, hybrid, universal, and vehicular sensor networks, etc. Sensors are used everywhere, from home security to water level observation of agriculture, from containers tracking to patient's health condition monitoring, from driverless cars to vehicle speed checking on motorways. In the early design of the Internet, security was not considered a major part. Today the same security threats and vulnerabilities are faced with IoT on each layer. Distributed data collection, processing, aggregation and analysis performed on that particular data is mainly performed from cloud services. This data is gathered from the sensors which are deployed as a service. A security breach threat exists, as these IoT devices are deployed at the customer's premises. These devices are not updated timely for the bug fixes in firmware and other required settings for the latest vulnerabilities fixes from vendors.

The business community wants to market these devices as early as possible. They only consider related laws and rules regarding stimulated manufacturing, but hardly pay any attention to security considerations. This leads to vulnerable IoT devices designing which opens doors for attackers. The IoT device apps gathering data or processing any function for the user or environment may put them at risk. Like, with the taxi service app, user location can be traced. House doors locking/unlocking, heaters on/off, car doors locking/unlocking without user permission are potential threats for IoT devices. For IoT devices security different tools and techniques have been used at every layer. For data transmission security between IoT devices, the asymmetric cryptographic algorithm is used. The asymmetric algorithm uses public-key algorithms because it will provide the key management, node authentication, third party key management, and security. For secure communication, a lightweight secure key distribution is needed. The key distribution technique is utilized for Wireless Sensor Networks (WSN) as communicating, gathering, master and shared key appropriation (Jing et al., 2014). A major constraint of IoT devices is low power computation and storage. From bigger to wearable devices, power storage is embedded inside. Due to this low power storage, these heavy security algorithms cannot be implemented. The solid cryptographic technique or digital signatures are proposed for information confirmation, gathering, and distribution, which needs trust management (Jing et al., 2014). The IoT is a reconciliation of different heterogeneous systems and from now on has its own one of a kind closeness and security issues. It is hard to perceive trusted in hubs in a heterogeneous domain. Heterogeneity, nature of IoT devices is the major hurdle in security standards adoption (Roman et al., 2013). The secured access control is an essential test in an IoT. For the most part, the information in the cloud is collected by various components and procedures. In like manner, the granularity level for getting comparable data differs for different retrievers. It is basic to offer security to the billions of customers in IoT frameworks. The anonymity of the customer must be kept up. The Access control once-over must be kept up by an expert. Security must be given its due centrality in the entire IoT life cycle. A centralized or associated IoT system has isolated information obtaining aloof substances, which give the gathered information to a brought together cloud computing that carries out the responsibility of gathering, preparing, investigating and circulating. In addition, the data ñow to the focal expert pursues a various leveled design. This has better-united security control anyway once presented to feebleness, the entire structure is undermined. As the developing number of IoT gadgets arrangement step by step, it is at high danger of information ruptures, Distributed Daniel of

Service DDoS assault, data fraud, security and protection of these gadgets. There is a need for security of IoT at its every layer. These layers are known as the application layer, network slayer and perception layer. The secure apps should be developed for the IoT devices to keep in view the privacy (Almusaylim, & Jhanjhi, 2019) of users. The main part of the IoT device is a network layer, where all configuration regarding IoT devices or sensors is performed. So this layer should be secured from attackers with the usage of two or three-factor authentication. This authentication should be implemented for adding new devices or sensors in the IoT network and apps used for gathering the information. As all existing security threats for cloud computing, internet and Wireless Sensor Networks WSN same are applicable for the IoT networks, because IoT is a combination of devices, sensor networks and cloud computing where the data is stored, processed, and analyzed (Jeyanthi et al., 2019). And detection of unauthorized use, and inspecting user actions with Intrusion Detection Systems in IoT devices (Anthony et al., 2018).

The idea of IoT was proposed by the Auto-ID Laboratory of Massachusetts Institute of Technology MIT in 1999 (Jeyanthi, 2016). As the nature of IoT devices is heterogeneous and constrains energy consumption, due to this the security methods designed for servers or computer systems cannot be applied to them. For secure communication between machines 2 machines, devices to the network and devices to apps the Quick UDP Internet Connection (QUIC) protocol (Hamilton et al., 2016) with public key authentication is recommended. Secondly, for fake devices protection, the two-factor authentication is recommended in this chapter. The two-factor authentication will be used with the username and pin code. The pin code will be generated from the physical address of devices and from gateway media access control (MAC) address. For the high availability of services, the protection against DDoS implemented with the assistance of a firewall knock operator (fwknop) open-source framework (Rash, 2007). In this chapter, the security-related threats, availability of IoT services and to secure them will be discussed.

RELATED WORK

What are the current devices and systems for the security, protection, as well as accessibility of IoT gadgets that will be talked about in this section? The analysts have recommended various apparatuses and strategies for the security, protection of IoT gadgets and for the high accessibility of IoT services. The safety of IoT devices and the environment cannot be determined by any software and framework that its implementation is safe and secure. The researcher proposed SOTERIA (Celik et al., 2018), a framework intended to check the models of IoT applications. The SOTERIA subsequently removes a state model from a SmartThings IoT application and applies model checking to find property infringement. The author proposed the solution Tyche (Rahmati et al., 2018), a protected improved approach that uses this instinctive hazard asymmetry, and gathering physical devices activities into likeness classes of risk. The Blockchain (BC) is proposed by the scholars without the concept of Proof of Work (POW) besides the need for currencies (Dorri et al., 2017). Authors have used the security and protection of Blockchain to the particular need for IoT. The researcher has proposed a novel structure IotSan (for IoT Sanitizer) (Nguyen et al., 2018). The IotSan uses model checking as an essential structure block. Towards easing the state space blast issue related with model checking (Clarke et al., 2011), the authors planed two improvements inside IotSan to (I) just consider applications that cooperate with one another, and (II) take out superfluous interleaving that is probably not going to yield valuable appraisal of dangerous practices. As the heterogeneity of the information produced by IoT devices another front for the current information preparing instruments. Hence, to tackle the estimation of the IoT-created information, new systems are required. In this unique circumstance, Machine Learning (ML) is viewed as one of the most appropriate computational ideal models to give implanted insight into the IoT gadgets (Mahdavinejad et al., 2018). ML strategies have been utilized in tasks, for example, characterization and relapse thickness estimation. An assortment of utilizations, for example; computer vision, extortion location, bio-informatics, malware discovery, validation, and discourse acknowledgment use ML calculations and strategies. Along these lines, ML can be utilized in IoT for giving smart administrations. The researchers have proposed the usage of ML (Hussain et al., 2019) in giving security and privacy of services to the IoT systems. The IoTMon (Ding, & Hu, 2018) has been proposed by analysts that can get all potential physical correspondences transversely over applications and enable safe coordinated effort controls on IoT stages. To report the issues achieved by unexpected physical affiliations. The IoTMon primary plays out a within application collaboration investigation utilizing static program examination to separate essential application data, including triggers, gadgets, and activities, for structure intra-application associates. Notwithstanding the static investigation of utilizations, IoTMon likewise utilizes Natural Language Processing (NLP) frameworks toward separate application delineations to perceive physical channels on the IoT organize, then at that point associate intra-application communications through physical and framework channels to produce between application communication chains. The confined gadget assets of IoT hubs instigated the improvement of physical unclonable function (PUF) (Suh, & Devadas, 2007). The PUF be able to extricate remarkable incentives as of integrated circuits (ICs) commencing procedure varieties that happen through assembling procedure and measure inward bungles utilizing binary successions. The online key generation or validation is used by the PUF. The analysts have proposed, two XOR-based reconfigurable PUF circuits (explicitly, an XOR-based reconfigurable bistable ring PUF (XRBR PUF) and an XOR-based reconfigurable ring oscillator PUF (XRRO PUF)) (Liu et al., 2019) are proposed as savvy justification reconfigurable PUF (RPUF) plans. The two plans are executed off Field-Programmable Gate clusters (FPGAs) and contrasted and past RPUF structures. The research commitments are triple: to start with, this assessment applies the operationally fundamental danger, resource and weakness assessment (OCTAVE) (Ali, & Awad, 2018) a technique is known as the OCTAVE Allegro hazard evaluation framework to perceive security dangers beginning from inside and outside brilliant homes. Second, it considers a widely inclusive point of view on both computerized and physical security hazards inside the IoT-based smart home territory. Third, the examination proposes a couple of countermeasures for easing the perceived security threats. The authors (Ammar et al., 2018) chose a set of IoT platforms: AWS IoT from Amazon, ARM Bed from ARM and various associates, Azure IoT Suite from Microsoft, Brillo/Weave from Google, Calvin from Ericsson, HomeKit from Apple, Kura from Eclipse, and SmartThings from Samsung. These platforms are a selection of due to mentioned measures: (1) notoriety with the seller's product plus hardware businesses, (2) the help of quick application advancement and the number of utilizations on the store, (3) the incorporation and utilization of the structure, and its distinction in the IoT advertise. As the author (Bhattacharjya et al., 2019) selected Datagram Transport Layer Security (DTLS) for the security protocol which relies upon standard protocol stack. The same security needs in traditional frameworks, for example, the Internet, based on three security objectives for IoT (Authentication, Integrity, and Confidentiality). DTLS accomplishes those objectives. The validation is developed during a totally affirmed DTLS handshake and depends upon an exchange of X.509 certiðcates containing Rivest–Shamir–Adleman (RSA) keys. As an unimpeded system (UCN) is traditionally signiðed by the Internet, while the IoT including a low-control a remote individual area mastermind (LoWPAN) signiðes the constrained territory. An IoT section put on the edge among the obliged framework (CN) and the UCN changes the correspondence among these two regions. Its activity regularly encompasses the change between various convention layer executions. The scientist's (Mukherjee et al., 2018) addresses the wide-running IoT-based application security needs and grouped framework edge resource objectives by proposing a novel structure of an adaptable IoT security middleware for from beginning to end cloud–fog correspondence. This will probably, basically secure the framework arranged at the customer fogs i.e., where the IoT gadgets are found. In any case, it will include security closeness with a present center cloud framework using System Level or Application-Level game plan thoughts of middleware. The middleware uses a novel Optimal Scheme Decider calculation that empowers customers to structure the best start to finish security contrive decision that matches with a given game plan of contraption resource necessities. The researcher proposed a security framework SIOTOME (Haddadi et al., 2018) this will learn and adjusts to the evolving condition, and responds to startling occasions in a brisk and self-sufficient way, by methods for gathering information, performing an investigation, making system access rules, furthermore controlling traffic in like manner for a guard. As unique IoT danger discovery requires a nearby view on traffic from the clients' gadgets, this should utilize security examination techniques that assurance protection of crude clients' information. Besides, we need to create instruments that ensure against a wide scope of system based assaults, for example; helplessness checking, interruption assaults, arrange listening in, information modification, just as Denial-of-Service (DoS) assaults. The SIOTOME will helpful to design between the edges organize and the ISP for early identification and alleviation of security vulnerabilities and dangers due to IoT gadget misconðgurations and malignant assaults. The FACT (Lee et al., 2017) is proposed by creators, usefulness is driven access control system to administer IoT contraptions securely. In FACT, the basic unit of control and use isn't the contraption, yet the convenience. This convenience-driven technique settles the security issues of the current IoT frameworks. To begin with, FACT analyzes whether an application has the benefit to get to the functionalities it solicitations to forestall unapproved get to. The Clients never again need to stress about security issues got from unprivileged applications. Second, FACT separates every usefulness of IoT gadgets to augment the general accessibility of the functionalities. Notwithstanding the attack of a vindictive or bartered application to handiness (e.g., DoS assault), the separation checks the attack from affecting the remainder of the functionalities with the ultimate objective that the functionalities can be given to various applications. As the development of Machine Learning ML (Xiao et al., 2018) and savvy attacks, IoT devices need to pick a watched approach and choose the key parameters in the security shows for the tradeoff in the heterogeneous and dynamic systems. ML procedures including oversaw learning, independent learning and support learning RL have been comprehensively associated with improve sort out security. To fill the hole, the specialist (Zhou et al., 2018) discusses and researches the IoT security issues from another perspective - IoT features. "IoT features" suggests the uncommon features of IoT contraptions, sort out, besides, applications, which are special with phones moreover, personal computers. For example, IoT contraptions have considerably less figuring limits, amassing resources, and power supply, in this manner "Constrained" is an IoT feature.

PROPOSED METHODOLOGIES AND SOLUTIONS FOR IOT SECURITY

In this chapter different types of frameworks, tools and methods are defined for the security of IoT devices. These tools or frameworks will provide a solution for security issues at different layers of IoT. To protect IoT users from personal identity information (PII), user locations, health information, and another financial information breach etc. The security issues, threats, and attacks exist on each layer of IoT networks. These attacks can carry out as active or passive attacks. The active attacks are easy to handle because these are the open enemy and by these attacks, the IoT network services will be unavailable. On the other hand, passive attacks are too hard to detect because they are the hidden enemy. These types of attacks are more dangerous for IoT networks or on other Internet services. The main feature of user privacy will be compromised due to these passive attacks.

Basic IoT Architecture Overview

Before describing the IoT security issues, challenges and threats there is a need to understand the basic IoT architecture as depicted in Figure 1. There are various perspectives on the structure of the Internet of things, explicitly on the layers of IoT (Madakam et al., 2015). Various analysts, in any case, have considered three-layer designing of IoT. These three layers are insinuated as the Perception, System, and Application layers. Each layer has its own usefulness in IoT structure.

Figure 1. Basic Design of IoT

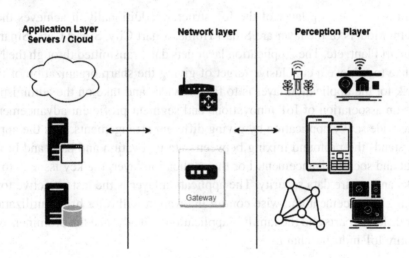

Perception Layer

The Perception layer generally expects the activity of social occasion besides, transmitting data to the Network layer. Various sorts of sensors joined to IoT gadgets can measure significant physical amounts, for instance, temperature, wetness, light power, furthermore, strong. The assembled data may be preprocessed in the Observation layer before they are transmitted The Perception layer may similarly engage contraptions to collaborate with various gadgets related to a short-extend arrange. Barely any gadgets are referenced here remote sensor organize (WSN), radio recurrence distinguishing proof (RFID), and last controlling segment. The application layer fuses two shadowiness scanner label marks see the device, RFID name, camera openings' sensor, and machine 2 machines (M2M) terminal, handheld terminal, sensor mastermind and sensor door. What the recognition layer should break anyway is to get the touchier and reasonable wisdom aptitude and deal with the issue as to low-control, downsizing and low-esteem point of view.

Network Layer

The Network Layer expects the activity of directing and transmitting the data assembled by the Perception layer by methods for arranging headways. The data is transmitted to various gadgets or IoT focuses on the Internet. A couple of cases of the system advances that are commonly used are WiFi, Bluetooth, 3G/LTE, Zigbee, Lora, etc. As described earlier IOTs network layer is built up based on the current mobile media transmission and Internet. Its principle highlight is to pass on the data between a long distance. The network layer involves different correspondence arrange and incorporated system dependent on the Internet, which is by and large viewed as the most developed part. Moreover, it incorporates the part that cleverly forms gigantic data. The administration focus of IoT data focus fog-cloud computing, stage, master framework and so forth that is to state network layer not just has the capability of system activity, yet additionally improves the capability of data activity.

Application Layer

The Application Layer is the top layer of the IoT structure additionally, it achieves the last target of serving the system. Models of the layer are Smart Home, Smart City, Smart Cars, Smart Grids, Smart Hospitals, and Smart Plant, etc. The Application layer gets data transmitted through the Network Layer, and it uses the data to achieve a conclusive target of giving the sharp organization of the IoT system. The principal task for the application layer is to find services and take on the administration. The application layer is an association of IoT innovations and segment proficient advancements and a layer to understand the wide savvy application by giving different arrangements. It is the application layers that at last understands the profound mixing between data innovation and part, and broadly affect the national financial and social advancement. For the application layer, the key issue is to share the data with the networks and secure data security. The application layer is the last objective for IoT advancement, programming advancement and wise control innovation will offer bright utilization of IoT. The advancement for different parts and the family's application will advance the prominence of the IoT and will profit the entire IoT industry chain.

IoT Security Problems

The IoT security-related problems remain not only for the security of wireless, WSN and the Internet. Yet in addition to IoT gadgets get to control, approval, the respectability of data, accessibility and security issues for their clients.

- **Power constraint in embedded devices:** The main concern of IoT users or researchers the computational power and storage size of these devices. To run security cryptographic algorithms requires high computation power and storage size which are heavy and expensive. Due to this, these cryptographic algorithms cannot be executed on resource-constrained devices such as embedded devices, wearables, sensors and on other wireless devices.

- **Heterogeneous devices or protocols:** As the heterogeneous idea of IoT gadgets, it is hard to oversee them from the focal framework in light of the fact that each seller is fabricating them according to their need with no widespread standard for these gadgets. With this constraint of IoT devices and protocols are managed on distributed systems.

- **The integrity of data:** For the integrity of data required which is collected and shared with other applications or devices. To ensure the authenticity of received data the cryptographic algorithms and digital signatures are recommended (Jing et al., 2014). To handle this computation power and storage size is big constrained for IoT devices.

- **Access control security:** The protected access control of the IoT network is a major undertaking. By and large, the information in the cloud is gotten to by various components and techniques. Moreover, the granularity level for getting comparable data appears differently in relation to different retrievers. Consequently, deðning the entrance control approach and checking the passage is one of the genuine difficulties (Roman et al., 2013).

- **Authentication controlling:** It is required to curiously recognize an IoT contraption and give both verification and endorsement for all of the devices. Confirmation ensures the authenticity of the data that ñows through the device and endorsement ensures checked access control. The components in an IoT framework may be incorporated logically and therefore, character the board with approval ends up being impressively progressively troublesome.

- **Circulated IoT networks:** A brought together or related IoT organize has separate data acquirement latent components, which give the accumulated data to a concentrated cloud administration that does the obligation of gathering, getting ready, dismembering and appropriating. Also, the information ñow to the central master seeks after a different leveled plan. This has better-bound together security control anyway once presented to vulnerabilities, the entire structure is undermined. In a passed on IoT organize every component is able to complete the obligation of data gathering, taking care of, looking at and scattering information and consequently is an attack vector.

- **Physical environment:** IoT systems are sent in a physical domain which is unusual. Along these lines, physical assaults have joined the rundown of conventional security dangers. Such as the insertion of fake devices on the network or theft of devices.

- **Trust management:** Trust the board accepts a basic activity in correspondence over substances and between an element and customer. Reputation calculation is required to choose a trusted in the substance. The total point of view on a central component helps in making sense of the reputation of the remainder of the substances. The irregularities in the notoriety worth might be settled by sharing the trust data from different focal substances. Mostly trust management between entity and client is provided by the third party, for example, public-key cryptography authentication for secure communication.

- **Privacy Issues:** The big threat to users of IoT their privacy, the user location, in/out time at household, and other personal information can be leaked. It is fundamental to offer insurance to the billions of customers in IoT frameworks. The anonymity of the customer must be kept up. Access control once-over must be kept up by any expert community. The Protection must be given its due importance in the entire IoT life cycle.

IoT Security Challenges

The large difficulties of IoT security rely upon the imprisonments of gadgets, programming, arrange, and physical area. The gadget hindrances are, computational and vitality prerequisite, memory basic and change safe packaging. Obstructions on writing computer programs are embedded programming constraints and a unique security fix. The Confinements on network connections are versatility, adaptability, an assortment of gadgets and correspondence medium, multi-network protocols and system topology.

IoT Devices

IoT devices incorporate sensors, wearable gadgets, advanced devices; microcontrollers similar to Arduino, Raspberry pi with inserted equipment. IoT gadgets are there available with the clients, embedded in some other gadget and may be used as a wearable device or may be accessible related with the web fantastic. In this manner, these gadgets are progressively defenseless against security assaults and can be effectively messed with. Equipment gadget producers are increasingly worried about the planning part of IoT gadgets instead of the security perspective. Thus the clients are presented to more hazards (Veracode, 2019). The decreased size and handling ability restrain the security highlights of an IoT gadget (Hajdarbegovic, 2019). Because of the basic proximity of IoT gadgets, it is hard to give an item fix to security revives. Because of the absence of institutionalization before assembling, in addition to uncovering the IoT equipment to security dangers. IoT equipment is presented to assaults to which all web associated gadgets are presented to, for example, DOS, and DDoS.

So as to secure the equipment, issues, for example, equipment lifecycle, programming refreshes, get to control and gadget validation ought to be managed. The Ventures should step up and validate all IoT devices configurations, perform defenselessness clear and check to sort out affiliations (Lewis, 2015). The big worry about the development of IoT is related to implanted framework security. Diverse IoT consortiums are managing deðning a structure to realize a character, contraption exposure, confirmation and security controls in a consistent way. Care should be taken to verify the private data present in hardware before they are discarded. When picking a gear to organize, the security worries, for instance, its intriguing character and confirmed amassing for encryption keys are to be veriðed. Evaluation to be done to check that it is so hard to change the confirmation set away in the gear.

Man-in-Middle Attack

The IoT network layer is a main threat for the man-in-middle assault. Because of the low computational intensity of IoT gadgets, this is done due to feeble encryption or no utilization of that vehicle encryption is executed. With this assault, the security of clients will be undermined and the uprightness of data on IoT systems. The listening stealthily will be trailed by this assault. This assault in nature is latent with the goal that the aggressor can investigate the traffic, and observing it additionally passively.

Eavesdropping

Due to insecure communication between source and destination, the information can be compromised and that is known as eavesdropping. The attacker will mask the identity of the user on the network by using eavesdropping.

Availability of Services

Accessibility implies that sensors keep on gather information whenever without any interruption. Cloud user is completely reliant upon the cloud service providers for their information and data as they store their data at remote area claimed by the service providers. Once in a while, the framework disappointment on the supplier's end can make it hard for the information proprietor to get to the information at the required time. Any sort of flooding assaults (e.g., Denial of Service) can bring about the interference of the services for a specific timeframe (Bhandari, & Zheng, 2018).

IoT Firmware and Applications

IoT applications segment incorporates the implanted programming, working frameworks utilized in IoT, for example, Android, Tiny OS, fog computing, Nimbis, and Hadoop. The vast majority of IoT programming manages information gathering, incorporating gadgets, applications, what's more, process interface, and continuous examination. IoT gadgets associated with the Internet have a working framework inserted in ðrmware. These working systems are not organized with security concerns and subsequently are feeble against malware ambushes. The implanted data in machines, PDAs and wearable contraptions with systems administration limits are dynamically feeble against outside assaults. This is in light of the fact that they share the data with other related devices and the introduced data lives for a greater number of periods than the hardware themselves. The security perspective is rejected by the undertaking as the cost of gear is significantly not as much as programming and security refreshes. Improperly conðgured limits devices related to the framework and are used from home are a similarly critical wellspring of hazard. There is a huge volume of data made from these devices. It is hard to pick if the data must be verified or not. Trojan steed or worms may be used to mix threatening code into programming.

The most monetarily wise response for verifying the embedded writing computer programs is to screen, in addition, secure the traffic at the entrance. The insurances threat for the wearable devices used in human administrations and amassing parts can be restricted by disabling Bluetooth of correspondence, geo-fencing, as far as possible correspondence, additionally, get the chance to control with external applications. Old working structure and programming without a fix must be kept up a vital good way to ensure security.

Plan-text Communication

Inferable from the immense number of IoT devices related to the framework, custom framework security, character, and key organization parts are hard to execute. Any device or method added to an IP address or URL has a related danger with it. It is hard to bring the entire IoT contraption related under the point of confinement of a controlled ðrewall, considering the way that an attacker may use a singular dealt center point to ambush the entire association in a flat manner. The observing and seclusion of IoT gadgets required to the private virtual local area network VLAN or system fragment may lessen security danger. Work organize is proposed as an answer for associating IoT gadgets since it is Self-sorting out, self-healing what's more, versatile. Unexpected increment in transfer speed necessity because of the enormous volume of information created from person to person communication destinations and IoT will imitate the assault, for example, DoS. Remote correspondence among IoT hubs subjects them to both dynamic and uninvolved assaults. A work system is framed by interfacing remote gadgets without any foundation. The cross-section in IoT empowers the IoT components to convey among themselves without ðxed foundation for correspondence. This is exceptionally useful if there ought to be an event of low power and uninformed rate applications in social protection, mechanical additionally, home motorization applications. IoT masterminds in an undertaking are mistreated to defenselessness if suitable Enterprise Mobility Management (EMM) course of action isn't deðned to alleviate the risk of essential corporate data spilled to the outside world.

Interoperability of Devices

The significantly focused nature of the IoT makes interoperability between things even a progressively irksome task to achieve. Moreover, remote correspondence advancements are progressing and developing rapidly. This adds to the flightiness of making interoperable interchanges in the IoT moreover (Elkhodr et al., 2016). The certainty brings about diverse gadgets that can't speak with each other which raises numerous mix issues in the IoT. Service depictions, regular practices, benchmarks and revelation components are among the numerous different difficulties that additionally should be considered before empowering interoperable associations between things. The IoT is tested by a divided, regularly erratic, arrangement of a blend of gadgets (for example low-control gadgets with low capacities versus increasingly proficient gadgets). This is, believe it or not, sets up a potential limit to achieving interoperability in the IoT. Likewise, the present-centered market in the low-control remote zone, where each affiliation is endeavoring to drive their standard forward is growing the peril of non-interoperability between IoT contraptions making compromise issues. While it is essential to outfit the end-customer with more determinations of headways, irritation should be kept up. This infers the IoT anticipates that the measure should engage even stages that are transmittable, operable and programmable transversely over contraptions, offering little appreciation to their make, model, maker, or mechanical applications.

Data Loss in Fog Computing

Data is put away in a cloud with a fundamental point of view of sharing. Decidedly affirmed sources in the Access Control List are required to get to the data. A specialist organization is accountable for any data spillage from the cloud. A misconfigured cloud will provoke data misfortune. External access to fragile data and logs must be restricted. An undermining specialist may get to any internal server and adventures, re-proper certain organizations with the potential danger of data misfortune. Cloud condition demands endless watching and interference distinguishing proof. It requires watching and logging virtual machine logs and shared organizations. Interference disclosure and balancing activity systems are recommended for the cloud to keep up a vital good way from data spill.

SOLUTIONS AND RECOMMENDATIONS

To secure the IoT devices is a big challenge for the research community and manufacturers of these devices. It is because of the heterogeneous nature of devices, low computational power, the small size of storage and battery backup constrains. As the usage of IoT devices, sensors, and RFIDs is growing day by day, so that they need security. These devices are generating a high volume of data on less secure networks. To protect that communication is necessary between machines 2 machines, devices to the network, or network to applications for the user's privacy, other secret information regarding the user's location and in/out timing from home. For this QUIC protocol along with public key authentication is recommended for the secure communication and integrity of information. Another challenge is fake device or gateway on the IoT network because of physical location is open to attackers. For this less computational power and with low overheard authentication is needed. Two-factor authentication will be used in this chapter. To protect the IoT network from DDoS attack the Fwknop an open-source tool has been used.

Secure Communication

The high volume of information is generated by IoT devices on the network. To secure this information of devices during communication a lightweight protocol is used. And for the low computational power of devices, the public key encryption authentication is used along with QUIC (Hamilton et al., 2016) protocol at the place traditional Hyper Test Transfer Protocol (HTTP) or DTLS (Ammar et al., 2018). QUIC is another multiplexed and secure transport protocol on UDP, planned to start from the earliest stage and advanced for HTTP/2 or HTTP/3 semantics. QUIC gives multiplexing and stream control proportionate to HTTP/2, sanctuary identical to TLS, also association semantics, unwavering quality, and congestion control equal to TCP. QUIC handshakes every now and again require zero roundtrips before sending payload, when contrasted with 1-3 roundtrips for TCP+TLS as presented in Figure 2. As QUIC client wants to connect with the server, then the client needs to perform a 1-roundtrip to initiate the connection in order to gather the required information to finish the handshake.

Figure 2. QUIC Handshake

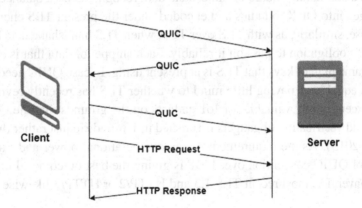

The client will send a request with an empty client hello (CHLO) message to the server. After that server will send a rejection (REJ) message in response to the *required* information to the client for the connect establishment. That information contains the server's certificates, a source address token for the verification of the client's Internet Protocol (IP) on a succeeding CHLO. If a client sends a CHLO message the second time, the cached messages will be used from the early connection to quickly send secure requests to the server. QUIC has pluggable blockage control, and more unrestrained motioning than TCP infers that it can give progressively luxurious information to the clog control calculation than TCP. The QUIC convention is constantly validated with scrambled headers and payloads. While a couple of bits of the QUIC parcel header are not scrambled, they are up 'til now affirmed by the recipient so as to thwart any bundle mixture or control by untouchables. QUIC shields relationship from witting or incidental middlebox control of through and through correspondence. Then again Transmission Control Protocol (TCP) headers appear in plaintext on the wire and not approved, causing a lot of implantation and header control issues for TCP, for instance, get window control and arrangement number overwriting. While a part of these is dynamic attacks, others are frameworks used by middleboxes in the framework from time to time attempting to clearly improve TCP execution.

Secure QUIC for Information Security

To verify the data of IoT gadgets for start to finish correspondence secure QUIC is utilized with Transport Layer Security TLS 1.3. TLS (Thomson, & Turner, 2019) gives two endpoints with a way to deal with setting up a strategy for correspondence over an untrusted medium (that is, the Internet) that ensures that messages they exchange can't be examined, changed, or manufactured. Records are solely crypto-graphically verified and a short time later transmitted over a strong vehicle (ordinarily TCP) which gives sequencing and guaranteed conveyance. The privacy and honesty security of bundles will be overseen by the QUIC. The TLS records, for example, TLS Handshake and Alert messages are yielded legitimately on the QUIC transport. The obligation of all TLS record layer will be taken by QUI, as the basic piece of the security and execution of QUIC relies upon the TLS validation and exchange of parameters. As opposed to TLS over TCP, QUIC applications that need to send data don't send it through TLS "application information" records. Or on the other hand, possibly, they send it as QUIC STREAM diagrams which are then passed on in QUIC bundles. QUIC passes on TLS handshake data in CRYPTO outlines, all of which include a contacting square of handshake data recognized by a balance and length. Those housings are packaged into QUIC bundles and encoded under the present TLS encryption level (Jager et al., 2015). Likewise, similarly, as with TLS over TCP, when TLS handshake data has been passed on to QUIC, it is QUIC's obligation to pass on it reliably. Each snippet of data that is conveyed by TLS is identified with the game plan of keys that TLS is at present using. In case QUIC needs to retransmit that data, it must use the equal keys paying little mind to whether TLS has recently revived to increasingly current keys. It is exceptionally valuable for IoT gadgets on the grounds that the QUIC convention is taking fewer assets and verification of gadgets is finished in 1-roundtrip just rather than 3-roundtrip (for TCP) (Lopez et al., 2015). As the requirement is low computational power and little stockpiling size with the utilization of QUIC convention over UDP is giving the best outcomes. Furthermore, with the utilization of this convention most recent TLS 1.3 and HTTP/2 or HTTP/3 likewise executed.

Two Factor Authentication

To protect from forging or fake devices there is a need for strong authentication of IoT devices on the network. As current two-factor authentication is using physical unclonable function PUF (Suh, & Devadas, 2007) only, but we have recommended register devices along with its user/administrator email address and serial number or other physical address of devices. In this chapter, the personal home page PHP and MySQL databases have been used for the two-factor authentication of devices. And here just core three functions written in PHP are discussed. With these recommended functions for two-factor authentication, the issue of low storage size in IoT devices will not be faced.

Device Registration

First of all, the registration of devices is necessary which will be used in the IoT network. The program used here is developed in PHP and MySQL database has been used for storing the records. For the registration of devices, the email and serial number or physical address of devices required in this function given bellow. This serial number or physical address will be saved into the database against the email address of already registered users or administrators of that IoT network. If any field of the required information is empty for device registration, then that device will not be registered at the network. These all programs are stored at the gateway which is Debian 9 based along with firewall and fwknop of single packet authorization.

```php
//The function to Register Devices for IoT network
function registerDevice()
 {
$request=$_POST;
$email = isset($request['email'])? $request['email']: '';
$serial_number = isset($request['serial_number'])? $request['serial_number']:
'';
if(! empty($email) ||! empty($serial_number)) {
registerDevice($email, $serial_number);
response("Success", 1);
} else {
response("Failure", 0);
}
 }
```

PIN Generation, Storage, and Administrator Login

The core function of this recommend solution is the Personal Identification Number (PIN) code generation of the IoT devices. In previous PHP functions the devices are registered which will be used on the network. As the network administrator or user of IoT network login for the installation and configuration of these devices. They will receive a PIN code via email for those registered devices on the network. The PHP rand function will generate a unique PIN code for these devices against the email address and serial number or physical address of devices. This PIN code will be stored in databases for verification of devices as two-factor authentication. The free application program interface API has been used for sending PIN code via email, for the SMS there are paid API available. The PIN code will be expired within a half hour to ensure the security of devices from forging or fake devices.

```php
//The function for storing PIN Code against User email address and serial number
function adminLogin()
 {
 $request=$_POST;
```

```
$email = isset($request['email']) ? $request['email']: '';
if (!empty($email)) {
$code = rand(200000, 999900);
updateDevicePINCode($email,$code);
////// SEND EMAIL TO Admin or User of IoT devices //////
$message="Use ".$code." to verif Admin login";
$subject = "PIN Code ";
send_email($subject, $message, $email]);
response("Approved", 1);
} else {
response("Fail", 0);
}
}
```

Device Verification

As the login of a network administrator or user of a device is approved. After that, the verification of devices is validated by the function given below. For the verification process, both the email address and PIN code are necessary if any field is missing then the verification of devices will be failed. The PIN code is generated against email address and serial number or physical is 5 characters for strong security. Then after three wrong attempts for device PIN code then that device will be blocked for 48 hours on the network. Due to these functions, the fake or forged devices have been blocked on the network.

```
function device Verified()
 {
 $request=$_POST;
 $email = isset($request['email']) ? $request['email']: '';
 $pin_code = isset($decoded['pin_code']) ? $request['pin_code']: '';
 if (!empty($email) && !empty($pin_code)) {
//The PIN code will be generated and stored into databases of admin login
 $cust=getCustomerDetail($email, 'pin_code');
//The verification of PIN code which is already generated for registered de-
vices
 if (empty($cust) || $cust['pin_code'] != $pin_code) {
response("Invalid Pin code",0);
 return ;
 }
response("PIN Verified", 1);
} else {
response("Invalid Pin",0);
}
}
```

DDoS Attack Protection

For the protection from DDoS attack on IoT network, the Single Packet Authorization (SPA) along with fwknop has been used at the gateway. In this implementation, the Debian 9 is used as a firewall and gateway. Due to low computational power and less storage size IoT devices and generating a high volume of information because of this, a big threat of DDoS attack exists. Already the Debian 9 base firewall has been implemented to secure the IoT network. But this firewall only is a defense for the blocking of malicious source addresses or filters in/out packets on the network. So to add an extra security layer for the protection of DDoS attack fwknop with SPA is recommended as it is shown in Figure 3. The fwknop already implemented by Michael Rash (Rash, 2004, Rash, 2006) . Fwknop (developed in Perl) at the time of start port knocking was used, as a new concept of the single packet authorization invented now, it is a default mode of operation on UDP (but it supports TCP and ICMP also).

Figure 3. Fwknop with SPA implementation on IoT network

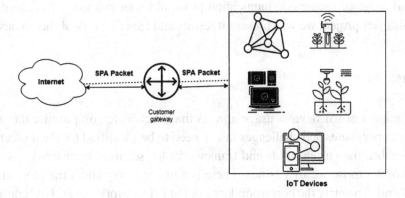

This gives effective confirmation of the client referencing endorsement to the server, and verifies against replay, disregarding the way that the timestamp used in fwknop isn't generally checked with time as the clock on the server. Both the timestamp and the discretionary data ðelds are used as fresh characteristics or 'randomizers' which help ensure that each endorsement parcel will yield an uncommon MD5 whole which can be logged to check for replays. These issues of 'DDoS and replay' assaults can be decreased by speaking to a 'window of acknowledgment' against which the timestamp is checked before any action is performed. The window of affirmation can be set to compensate for standard clock glide, yet a client with an inappropriate time may experience refusal of an organization as the client's timestamp won't arrange the authentic-time on the server when the timestamp is checked. By checking the timestamp and ensuring that it's inside the window of affirmation, the server can expel any potential replays that are outside the recognized time parcel, and the SPA is less asset eager when contrasted with port thumping. Single Packet Authorization, or SPA, has unclear destinations from port thumping, simultaneously, as opposed to encoding affirmation information in a movement of port numbers, it encodes it in the pay-load of a lone UDP datagram. Since UDP administrations are not required to respond to messages that they get, and the show doesn't thusly make any response, a non-responding UDP administration on an open port on a structure that discreetly drops unexpected parcels is dubious from a nearby port to a port range. A SPA server can thusly be made as a common framework organization, without hoping to go to package sniffers or any stage express parts. Since only a solitary parcel must be sent before opening an association, an SPA approval exchange takes significantly less time. It is less frail against group setback than port pounding, other than being invulnerable to bundle reordering.

FUTURE RESEARCH DIRECTIONS

There is still a ton of work that should be accomplished for the security of the physical layer of the IoT arrange in light of the fact that the gadgets are introduced in an open territory for the keen house, brilliant vehicles, savvy interstates, and shrewd urban areas. There ought to be a standard body that proposes the special standard conventions for these gadgets for correspondence and data sharing. As at present each producer of these gadgets is planning conventions or methods of correspondence according to their needs. Because of the idea of heterogeneous gadgets, it is very hard to completely execute the security on IoT arrange. The implementation of our recommended two-factor authentication, protection against DDoS attack, and usage of secure communication protocol under process. After the deployment it in SmartHomes industries project we will present it results and functionality of this in next version.

CONCLUSION

As the growing number of IoT devices usage attracts the attackers to compromise the security of these devices. So the security issues and challenges of IoT need to be identified for the protection of its users. This chapter described the current tools and frameworks for security, security issues of IoT, its challenges and solution for those security issues. There is a major worry about the protection and security of IoT gadgets clients. To verify the correspondence of the IoT networks, the QUIC convention has been prescribed, in light of the fact that QUIC works over UDP for HTTP/2 or HTTP/3 alongside TLS 1.3 to encode all traffic including handshake bundles. The QUIC is lightweight establishes the connection from a client to the server with 1-roundtrip which best for the low computational power and less size storage in IoT devices, due to this authentication and integrity of information ensured on the IoT network. For the protection from fake devices, the two-factor authentication has been recommended. The registration of IoT devices is done with the information of email address and physical address or serial number. The PHP program and MySQL is used for the PIN code generation against the registered devices at the gateway system. For the high availability of the IoT network, the fwknop with single packet authorization has been used for the DDoS attack protection.

ACKNOWLEDGMENT

Thankful to Dr. Muhammad Abid Saleem, visiting faculty member, Riphah Institute of System Engineering Islamabad, Pakistan for empowering us in such manner and offer valuable comments for this book chapter.

REFERENCES

Ali, B., & Awad, A. (2018). Cyber and physical security vulnerability assessment for IoT-based smart homes. *Sensors (Basel), 18*(3), 817. doi:10.339018030817 PMID:29518023

Almusaylim, Z. A., & Jhanjhi, N. Z. (2019). Comprehensive Review: Privacy Protection of User in Location-Aware Services of Mobile Cloud Computing. *Wireless Personal Communications, §§§*, 1–24.

Ammar, M., Russello, G., & Crispo, B. (2018). Internet of Things: A survey on the security of IoT frameworks. *Journal of Information Security and Applications, 38*, 8–27. doi:10.1016/j.jisa.2017.11.002

Anthony, O., Odeyabinya, J., & Emmanuel, S. (2018). Intrusion detection in internet of things (IoT). *International Journal of Advanced Research in Computer Science, 9*(1).

Bhandari, B., & Zheng, J. (2018). *A Preliminary Study On Emerging Cloud Computing Security Challenges.* arXiv preprint arXiv:1808.04143

Bhattacharjya, A., Zhong, X., Wang, J., & Li, X. (2019). Security challenges and concerns of Internet of Things (IoT). In *Cyber-Physical Systems: Architecture, Security and Application* (pp. 153–185). Cham: Springer. doi:10.1007/978-3-319-92564-6_7

Celik, Z. B., McDaniel, P., & Tan, G. (2018). Soteria: Automated IoT Safety and security analysis. In *2018 {USENIX} Annual Technical Conference ({USENIX}{ATC} 18)* (pp. 147-158). USENIX.

Clarke, E. M., Klieber, W., Nováček, M., & Zuliani, P. (2011, September). Model checking and the state explosion problem. In *LASER Summer School on Software Engineering* (pp. 1–30). Berlin: Springer.

Ding, W., & Hu, H. (2018, October). On the safety of IoT device physical interaction control. In *Proceedings of the 2018 ACM SIGSAC Conference on Computer and Communications Security* (pp. 832-846). ACM. 10.1145/3243734.3243865

Dorri, A., Kanhere, S. S., Jurdak, R., & Gauravaram, P. (2017, March). Blockchain for IoT security and privacy: The case study of a smart home. In *2017 IEEE international conference on pervasive computing and communications workshops (PerCom Workshops)* (pp. 618-623). IEEE.

Elkhodr, M., Shahrestani, S., & Cheung, H. (2016). *The internet of things: new interoperability, management, and security challenges.* arXiv preprint arXiv:1604.04824

Haddadi, H., Christophides, V., Teixeira, R., Cho, K., Suzuki, S., & Perrig, A. (2018, April). SIOTOME: An edge-ISP collaborative architecture for IoT security. Proc. IoTSec.

Hajdarbegovic, N. (2019). *Are we creating an insecure IoT? Secure challenges and concerns.* Retrieved from https://www.toptal.com/it/are-we-creating-an-insecure-internet-of-things

Hamilton, R., Iyengar, J., Swett, I., & Wilk, A. (2016). Quic: A udp-based secure and reliable transport for http/2. *IETF, draft-tsvwg-quic-protocol-02.*

Hussain, F., Hussain, R., Hassan, S. A., & Hossain, E. (2019). *Machine Learning in IoT Security: Current Solutions and Future Challenges.* arXiv preprint arXiv:1904.05735

Jager, T., Schwenk, J., & Somorovsky, J. (2015, October). On the security of TLS 1.3 and QUIC against weaknesses in PKCS# 1 v1. 5 encryption. In *Proceedings of the 22nd ACM SIGSAC Conference on Computer and Communications Security* (pp. 1185-1196). ACM.

Jeyanthi, N. (2016). Internet of things (IoT) as interconnection of threats (IoT). In *Security and Privacy in the Internet of Things (IoT)* (pp. 21–39). CRC Press. doi:10.1201/b19516-3

Jeyanthi, N., Abraham, A., & Mcheick, H. (2019). *Studies in Big Data 47 Ubiquitous Computing and Computing Security of IoT*. Springer. doi:10.1007/978-3-030-01566-4

Jing, Q., Vasilakos, A. V., Wan, J., Lu, J., & Qiu, D. (2014). Security of the Internet of Things: Perspectives and challenges. *Wireless Networks*, 20(8), 2481–2501. doi:10.100711276-014-0761-7

Lee, S., Choi, J., Kim, J., Cho, B., Lee, S., Kim, H., & Kim, J. (2017, June). FACT: Functionality-centric access control system for IoT programming frameworks. In *Proceedings of the 22nd ACM on Symposium on Access Control Models and Technologies* (pp. 43-54). ACM. 10.1145/3078861.3078864

Lewis, N. (2015). *Prevent IoT security threats and attacks before its too late*. Retrieved from https://internetofthingsagenda.techtarget.com/tip/Prevent-IoT-security-threats-and-attacks-before-its-too-late

Liu, W., Zhang, L., Zhang, Z., Gu, C., Wang, C., O'Neill, M., & Lombardi, F. (2019). XOR-based low-cost Reconfigurable PUFs for IoT Security. *ACM Transactions on Embedded Computing Systems*, 18(3), 25. doi:10.1145/3274666

Lopez, J. A., Sun, Y., Blair, P. B., & Mukhtar, M. S. (2015). TCP three-way handshake: Linking developmental processes with plant immunity. *Trends in Plant Science*, 20(4), 238–245. doi:10.1016/j.tplants.2015.01.005 PMID:25655280

Madakam, S., Ramaswamy, R., & Tripathi, S. (2015). Internet of Things (IoT): A literature review. *Journal of Computer and Communications*, 3(05), 164–173. doi:10.4236/jcc.2015.35021

Mahdavinejad, M. S., Rezvan, M., Barekatain, M., Adibi, P., Barnaghi, P., & Sheth, A. P. (2018). Machine learning for Internet of Things data analysis: A survey. *Digital Communications and Networks*, 4(3), 161–175. doi:10.1016/j.dcan.2017.10.002

Mukherjee, B., Wang, S., Lu, W., Neupane, R. L., Dunn, D., Ren, Y., & Calyam, P. (2018). Flexible IoT security middleware for end-to-end cloud–fog communication. *Future Generation Computer Systems*, 87, 688–703. doi:10.1016/j.future.2017.12.031

Nguyen, D. T., Song, C., Qian, Z., Krishnamurthy, S. V., Colbert, E. J., & McDaniel, P. (2018, December). IotSan: fortifying the safety of IoT systems. In *Proceedings of the 14th International Conference on emerging Networking EXperiments and Technologies* (pp. 191-203). ACM. 10.1145/3281411.3281440

Rahmati, A., Fernandes, E., Eykholt, K., & Prakash, A. (2018, September). Tyche: A risk-based permission model for smart homes. In 2018 IEEE Cybersecurity Development (SecDev) (pp. 29-36). IEEE. doi:10.1109/SecDev.2018.00012

Rash, M. (2004). Combining port knocking and passive OS fingerprinting with fwknop. *USENIX; login. Magazine*, 29(6), 19–25.

Rash, M. (2006). Single packet authorization with fwknop. Login. *The USENIX Magazine, 31*(1), 63–69.

Rash, M. (2007). Single packet authorization. *Linux Journal, 156*, 1.

Roman, R., Zhou, J., & Lopez, J. (2013). On the features and challenges of security and privacy in distributed internet of things. *Computer Networks, 57*(10), 2266–2279. doi:10.1016/j.comnet.2012.12.018

Suh, G. E., & Devadas, S. (2007, June). Physical unclonable functions for device authentication and secret key generation. In *2007 44th ACM/IEEE Design Automation Conference* (pp. 9-14). IEEE.

Thomson, M., & Turner, S. (2019). Using TLS to Secure QUIC. *Internet Engineering Task Force, Internet-Draft draft-ietf-quic-tls-22.*

Veracode white paper. (2019). *The internet of things: a security research study.* Retrieved from https://www.veracode.com/sites/default/files/Resources/Whitepapers/internet-of-things-whitepaper.pdf/

Xiao, L., Wan, X., Lu, X., Zhang, Y., & Wu, D. (2018). *IoT security techniques based on machine learning.* arXiv preprint arXiv:1801.06275

Zhou, W., Jia, Y., Peng, A., Zhang, Y., & Liu, P. (2018). The effect of IoT new features on security and privacy: New threats, existing solutions, and challenges yet to be solved. *IEEE Internet of Things Journal, 6*(2), 1606–1616. doi:10.1109/JIOT.2018.2847733

ADDITIONAL READING

Celik, Z. B., Babun, L., Sikder, A. K., Aksu, H., Tan, G., McDaniel, P., & Uluagac, A. S. (2018). Sensitive information tracking in commodity IoT. In *27th {USENIX} Security Symposium ({USENIX} Security 18)* (pp. 1687-1704).

Dehghantanha, A., & Choo, K. K. R. (Eds.). (2019). *Handbook of Big Data and IoT Security.* Springer. doi:10.1007/978-3-030-10543-3

Fernandes, E., Jung, J., & Prakash, A. (2016, May). Security analysis of emerging smart home applications. In *2016 IEEE Symposium on Security and Privacy (SP)* (pp. 636-654). IEEE. 10.1109/SP.2016.44

He, W., Golla, M., Padhi, R., Ofek, J., Dürmuth, M., Fernandes, E., & Ur, B. (2018). Rethinking access control and authentication for the home internet of things (IoT). In *27th {USENIX} Security Symposium ({USENIX} Security 18)* (pp. 255-272).

Hu, F. (2016). *Security and privacy in the Internet of things (IoTs): Models, Algorithms, and Implementations.* CRC Press. doi:10.1201/b19516

Jain, A., & Singh, T. (2020). Security Challenges and Solutions of IoT Ecosystem. In *Information and Communication Technology for Sustainable Development* (pp. 259–270). Singapore: Springer. doi:10.1007/978-981-13-7166-0_25

Khan, M. A., & Salah, K. (2018). IoT security: Review, blockchain solutions, and open challenges. *Future Generation Computer Systems, 82*, 395–411. doi:10.1016/j.future.2017.11.022

Khanna, A., Arora, S., Chhabra, A., Bhardwaj, K. K., & Sharma, D. K. (2019). IoT Architecture for Preventive Energy Conservation of Smart Buildings. In *Energy Conservation for IoT Devices* (pp. 179–208). Singapore: Springer. doi:10.1007/978-981-13-7399-2_8

KEY TERMS AND DEFINITIONS

Authentication: In computing the procedure or activity of confirming the identity of a client or process.

Availability: Ensures that systems, applications, and information are accessible to clients when they need them.

Cryptography: The change of information into a secret code for transmission over public systems.

Fog Computing: Is a term for a choice to cloud computing that puts a few sorts of exchanges and assets at the edge of a network, as opposed to setting up channels for cloud storage and use.

Integrity: It includes keeping up the consistency, precision, and dependability of information over its whole life cycle.

Security: Is the protection of data systems from burglary or harm to the equipment, the product, and to the data on them, just as from interruption or redirection of the services they give.

Sensors: A device that reacts to a physical boost, (for example, heat, light, stable, weight, attraction, or a specific movement) and transmits a subsequent impulse (with respect to estimation or working a control).

Chapter 7
A Survey on Intrusion Detection in Wired and Wireless Network for Future IoT Deployment

Vasaki Ponnusamy
Universiti Tunku Abdul Rahman, Malaysia

Said Bakhshad
Universiti Tunku Abdul Rahman, Malaysia

Bobby Sharma
Don Bosco University, Assam, Malaysia

Robithoh Annur
Universiti Tunku Abdul Rahman, Malaysia

Teh Boon Seong
Universiti Tunku Abdul Rahman, Malaysia

ABSTRACT

An intrusion detection system (IDS) works as an alarm mechanism for computer systems. It detects any malicious activity that happened to the computer system and it alerts an alarm message to notify the user there is malicious activity. There are IDS that are able to take action when malicious or anomalous networks are detected, which include suspending the traffic sent from suspicious IP addresses. The problem statement for this project is to find out the most accurate machine learning algorithm and the types of IDS with different placement strategies. When it comes to the deployment of a wireless network, IDS is not as easy a task as deploying a traditional network IDS. There are many unexpected complexities of the problem of reliable intrusion detection in a wireless network. The motivation of this research is to find the most suitable classification techniques that are able to increase the accuracy of an IDS. Machine learning is useful for the upcoming trend; it provides better accuracy in the detection of malicious traffic.

DOI: 10.4018/978-1-7998-2803-7.ch007

INTRODUCTION

An IDS is a monitoring system which observes the network and pushes a notification to the administrator in case of suspicious or malicious activity. Additional to an Intrusion Detection System, another system which will have a role similar to intrusion detection system with the additional feature to reject or drop the malicious network traffic packet, however, the focus of this project is limited to Intrusion Detection. The accuracy of an intrusion detection system is determined by the 4 states of Intrusion Detection, which are listed as True Positive, True Negative, False Positive and False Negative. The scenario where the detection refers to an attack vector in the form of a malicious packet coming into network and is detected by the intrusion detection system, followed by a notification to the administrator, is known as True Positive. The True Negative state describes the absence of attack vectors within the network traffic. The False Positive state refers to the IDS responding with actions normally prescribed to the event of an Intrusion Detection, while in reality, the network traffic is normal. The most concerning of these states is the False Negative, whereby a negative result is posted by the IDS during its network monitoring, unable to raise any notification to the administrator regarding the potentially network damaging malicious traffic.

In order to allay the risks posed by the states of detection, this paper creates a survey on Intrusion Detection System as shown in Figure 1 using insights from the results of the Machine Learning process, the goal of which is to establish a model able to predict malice or normalcy of the incoming network traffic. Classifiers such as decision Tree Classifier, Random Forest and Naïve Bayes, consisting of different kinds of network-traffic predicting algorithms, are used within this project to develop the Machine Learning environment. The focus will be on wired, wireless and ad hoc networks as shown in Figure 2 and based on the types on intrusion detection systems as shown in Figure 3 with different deployment methods as shown in Figure 8.

Figure 1. Focus of Intrusion Detection System

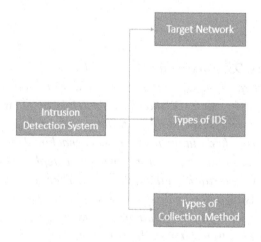

Figure 2. Target Network

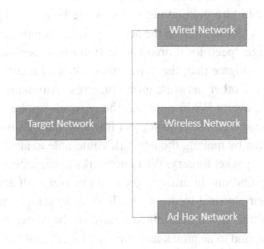

SURVEY ON INTRUSION DETECTION

Wired Network

A wired network consists of a group of computers or devices connected via physical network links, with the objective of data transmission between computers or devices using optical cables or transmission medium or to share resources. Wired network are less exposed to attack as compared to wireless network due to physical access to network via the required hardware being needed to access the data transmitted, which makes wired network comparatively more secure to wireless network. However, it cannot be claimed impervious to attacks absolutely, as malevolent users with legitimate access to the network and data may pose a risk from within. Being advantageous in speed, the cost is primarily ascertained by the network element features, such as number of computers and cable requirements, making wired networks cheaper and more affordable rather than using wireless network. Additionally, interference to the wireless network may cause signal loss or fading (Radja, 2015). That being said, wired networks are vulnerable to causing system-wide collapse in event of partial network immobility, as witnessed in the coal production safety being affected due to wired network failure. (Zhang & Mao 2015).

Wireless Network

The modern era has seen smartphone connectivity operation use a variety of wireless networks, such as wireless Local Area Network(Wi-Fi), cellular and Bluetooth, extensively. The said technology is employed by Social media, chat and video streaming applications to transmit data. Being universally accessible, easily available and budget-friendly has enabled Wi-Fi and cellular networks to be used predominantly among the wireless networks. (Rattagan, 2016) While bringing a market edge to an application by virtue of Wireless Local Area Network by virtue of the smartphone user connecting to public Wi-Fi wireless internet connection, it does expose the user to Wi-Fi to attacks and/or intrusion vulnerability. A hacker may be able to to harm a user by stealing personal information, further culminating into identity theft as well as the potential to commit fraud. An attacker can establish a rogue access point as a genuine internet access point in order to lure unknowing users, while being used to monitor the communications by the Access point users, going through the access point. (Vanjale & Mane & V.Patil, 2015). The extensive use of Wi-Fi for high-speed local area connectivity has seen an exponential increase in the attacks being carried out. To mitigate that, the Wi-Fi uses IDS as a security implement, which is used widely to provide security over other network infrastructures (Aminanto et al. 2017) . With enough traffic observed and collected over a Wi-Fi network, the network can be cracked with minimal effort, owing to its cryptography weakness. The requirement for non-encryption of the protocol design at the data link layer manifests further by making the network vulnerable to attacks such as Denial of Service (DOS), which are achieved via packet forgery. Wi-Fi networks using access point pre-authentication are implemented by corporate institutions in order to provide the user with access point connectivity over a large area, regardless of their physical location. While the said setup continues to remain vulnerable to DOS attacks and packet forgery, the distributed nature of the network implementation allows the administrator to be able to respond to an attack ascertain the location of the attacker within the network, restricting the damage to the network(Satam, 2017).

Existing Researches Regarding The Intrusion Detection In Wireless Network

The usage of Internet in everyone's daily life has significantly increases throughout the years. Companies such as Google, Facebook and Twitch had used the Internet to provide various services to their customers ranging from emails, online payments, social media, etc. However, wireless network comes with all sorts of security vulnerabilities. For instance, DoS attack can be carrried out by the hacker to overload the network with floods of traffics, consuming the resources of the network which ultimately results in the crippling of the entire network. Therefore, Intrusion Detection System and Intrusion Prevention System has been developed to detect and prevent malicious traffic packets from accessing the network. (Bradley, CISSP-ISSAP, 2018), (Pirc, 2017). There are many researches in IDS has been carried out such as Humayun et al 2020, SH Kok et al 2019 and Adeyemo et al 2019.

Ad Hoc Network

A network consisting of mobile nodes which can communicate amongst each other without the presence of specified infrastructure is known as an ad-hoc network. Self-sufficient mobile nodes communicating among themselves via a wireless link is called a Mobile Ad-Hoc Network. As such, ad-hoc networks have limited physical range within which they communicate, owing to the data packets being forwarded from its source to the nearby hosts, ultimately delivering to its destination. However, Mobile Ad-Hoc Network(MANET) holds the edge in security attack detection sensitivity due to limited constrictions for physical protection, making reputation management a more suitable security implementation rather than traditional intrusion detection, as per the claim of some researchers. The short-lived nature of the connections within an Ad hoc network shift the focus of the IDS on distributed design. Intrusion detection based on signatures is a suitable method for Ad hoc network IDS deployment, whereby the intrusion detection system is on a constant lookout for traffic patterns that are specific to misbehavior, resulting in the advantage of a low rate of false positive detection results, due to the system only responding to malicious behavior known beforehand (within the signature archives), while a normal node displaying no signatures similar to an attack. Alternately, the fact that this technique has a pre-requisite set of details within a pattern it has to match against its own data-store proves to be its drawback, where it has to detail all attack vectors within its dictionary and keep it updated with present threats, which in itself is challenging. The efficiency of the signature based intrusion detection depends on the length of the signature, with longer signatures requiring greater resources such as memory and processor, for detection. Accurate and through information of an outside attacker's signature during the course of network penetration makes this an effective approach(Mitchell & Ing-ray 2014). Ad-hoc networks are found to have 2 kinds of architectures; isolated and integrated. Nodes communicate among themselves within the same physical network is called an isolated ad-hoc network, which is further bifurcated into 2 types, namely large and small scale isolated ad-hoc network. A large scale isolated adhoc network may consist of nodes numbering in thousands, with high architecture costs and low performing traffic, making it unsuitable for volumetric data transmission because of security concerns, which is amongst the weaknesses of this type of network. Small scale isolated ad hoc network able to raise the uses in commercial such as smart home, business meeting place, hotspots and some private area. Internet Hotspots on digital devices and GPRS are a practical example of Integrated Adhoc networks, both of which can be used to provide connectivity to the internet to computers, phones and other devices. Although GPRS has a comparatively lower data-transfer rate than Hotspot, it does provide connectivity to users in unconventional places such as public transport hubs (Airports, Railway stations) (Sharmilla & Shanthi, 2016).

TYPES OF INTRUSION DETECTION SYSTEM

Signature-Based Intrusion Detection System

Signature based IDS (Figure 4) detects intrusion by matching the currently observed network traffic patterns to the attacks signature within its IDS database. In case the traffic has a signature pattern that matches the attack signatures of its database, the IDS flags it as malicious traffic and detects an attack. Comparison tools authenticate the data by matching it against the IDS database, allowing the data packet through to its network destination if it does not display a malicious pattern. The signature matching mechanism of the similarly named IDS results in a lower probability of generating a false positive alert, as well as making it a more suitable detection methodology against patterns previously known about, due to a non-compromised node lacking the attack signature pattern (B.I. Santoso et. al. 2016). Additionally, a signature based IDS provides better security against external threats due to the specific pattern of an attacker when making attempts at compromising the network. The improved performance of a signature based IDS does however establish the need to keep the database and/or dictionary of attack patterns currently updated with the latest malicious patterns. A failure to do so may witness a new malicious traffic signature being used by a potential attacker, which may be overlooked by the IDS, due to it having no query to match against (Mitchell & Ing-Ray 2014) .

Anomaly-Based Intrusion Detection System

Anomaly based IDS (Figure 5) performs the task of detecting intrusion by identifying any discrepancies within the network traffic, having established the features of normal traffic via observing the traffic accumulated over a period of time. Any activity within the traffic that is not in congruence with the

Figure 3. Types of Intrusion Detection System

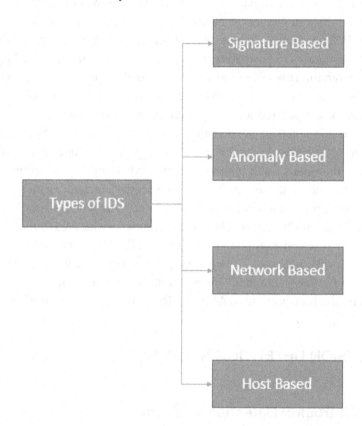

previously observed normal interaction of the network will be indicative of an intrusion, with the data being routed back to the attacker as a response (N.T Van & T.N Thinh & L.T. Sach 2017). Data mining methodologies, namely, association rule learning, clustering, classification and regression are used by a variety of anomaly detection environments. Anomaly detection techniques built on clustering methods works by grouping together data points which have a similar characteristic from a dataset, which enables algorithms based on clustering to be able to detect intrusions without any prior information about it.

Figure 4. Aumreesh et al. (2017) describe Misuse/ Signature Based IDS

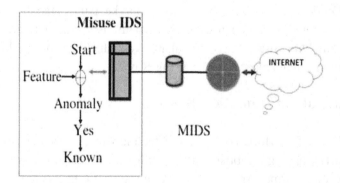

Figure 5. Aumreesh et al. (2017) describe Anomaly Based IDS

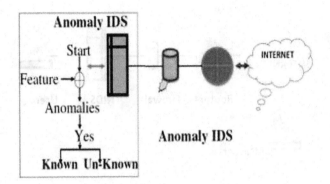

Classification based anomaly detection work by identifying the class of data being monitored on the basis of a dataset with known category members, it has been trained against. A classification implementing algorithm is known as a classifier, considered to be an illustration of supervised learning. In the event of a single algorithm being unable to deliver suitable results, different algorithms maybe joined in a hybrid approach. Supervised anomaly detection is a supervised training method in which the prediction of a training dataset labelled with classes such as normal or anomaly is assessed, so that a predictive model for further comparison between normal and anomaly classes can be created (Amanpreet & Mishra & Kumar 2012). Supervised anomaly detection gives way to two problems, which are the number of normal instances in the training dataset being higher than the number of anomaly instances, and the second being the difficulty in setting accurate and representative labels for anomaly classes. The first problem arises due to an imbalanced class distribution within the data mining. Using only normal class for training, Semi-Supervised anomaly detection doesn't require a level for anomaly classes and is a more suitable machine learning method compared to supervised learning. Conventionally, the class associated to normal behavior is modelled under this approach, in order to determine any anomaly within the test data. Unsupervised anomaly detection functions without any guidance, without requiring training data, making it applicable to most scenarios. The implied assumption of test data normal instances being higher than anomaly occurrences poses the risk of a high rate of false positives in case of an incorrect assumption (Mitchell & Ing-Ray 2014).

Network-based Intrusion Detection System

Methods implemented network-wide in order to detect an intrusion is known as a Network-based IDS (Figure 6) which monitors the entirety of traffic being routed through the network. The ability to provide real-time network attack detection and the subsequent reduced network damage due to the attack make it a cost-efficient solution (Muhammad K. Asif et. al.2013). Additionally, a network-based IDS is also able to provide security to other computers (which may be using their own IDS) within the network, while an external machine maybe monitored with its routing information provided to the IDS. However, a data-packet is rendered illegible to the network based IDS if it is encrypted via an encryption algorithm, which is a major handicap (A.T Taha et. al. 2015). With that said, having a vantage point for observing attacks while monitoring the entire network traffic, a network based IDS has an advantage of providing enhanced intrusion detection due to its constant vigilance (Aumreesh el al. 2017).

Figure 6. Aumreesh el al. (2017) describe Network IDS

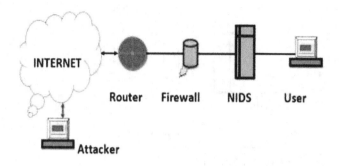

Host-based Intrusion Detection System

Deployed on a particular host within a network, Host based IDS (Figure 7) approaches intrusion detection by providing protection to a single computer, preventing malicious code from being executed on the said system. The host-based IDS selects the metric which is then supplied as an input to the decision engine. Data collected from various log files of activities that take place on the system provide a justification for the metric being used. (Sandeep & Thaksen 2016) The IDS generates an intrusion notification in case of any attribute value of a new record is above the system-measured threshold. Multivariate statiscal analysis on audit records is used to To identify anomalies. Besides, frequency distribution based anomaly detection can be used in shell commands logs. Additionally, there exists another kind of host-based IDS which trains a separate algorithm on the behaviour of normal software called by the system, raising a notification of detected anomaly upon observing unknown software behaviour. (Murtaza et al. 2013) A prime advantage of Host-based IDS is its ability to analyse attacks which have successfully intruded into the network. The system-subordinate framework can create a precautionary area about any activity that is closely related to the attack. Upon jumbling up of any arranged activity, the entrance of movement in a decoded shape that are done by the host-based observing framework. (Aumreesh el al. 2017) The usage of log files however does expose a few weaknesses, such as interpreted data represented by log files produced by system activity monitoring daemon programs delivering a skimmed data source. Additionally, the efficacy of disk zones in regards to the creation and management of log files which

Figure 7. Aumreesh el al. (2017) describe Host Based IDS

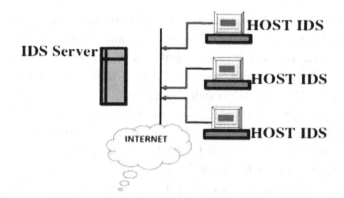

Figure 8. Deployment of IDS

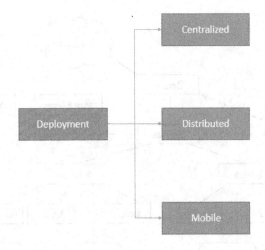

contain a large volume of equally prioritised to critical data, yet potentially irrelevant data also adds to the inconveniences faced by host-based IDS. (Creech & Hu 2014)

DEPLOYMENT OF INTRUSION DETECTION SYSTEM

Centralized Intrusion Detection System

In a Centralized IDS (Figure 9), the packet analysis is conducted on one or a small number of nodes, with the audit component distributed, however, the accumulated audits will be forwarded to a specified location for analysis to happen. (Toulouse & Minh & Curtis 2015) With Centralized IDS, various kinds of alerts are generated with the network node or host analysed by agents, followed by the alert being transferred to a central C&C handler responsible for analysing and arriving at the correct conclusive decision. (L.N. Tidjon & M. Frappier & A. Mammar 2019).

Distributed Intrusion Detection System

Distributed IDS (Figure 10) can be established by bundling a bunch of intrusion detection systems over a large network, with communications established between a singular server and multiple clients via the centralization communication method. (J. Amudhavel et al. 2016) this centralized architecture of the distributed IDS enables the detection of a coordinated attack on an organization as well as any related distributed resources. (Vandana P et. al. 2014) A distributed IDS is the amalgamated manifestation of a network-based IDS and host-based IDS. Detection mechanism and correlation manager are the primary components of an IDS, where the entire network traffic being checked and/or monitored by the detection mechanism, with the information collected being transfer to the correlation manager, which performs a global correlation against information collected from different IDS and issue an alert notification in case of an intrusion and/or attack. The global correlation for distributed intrusion detection, coupled with

Figure 9. Ghorbani et al. (2009) describes Centralized IDS

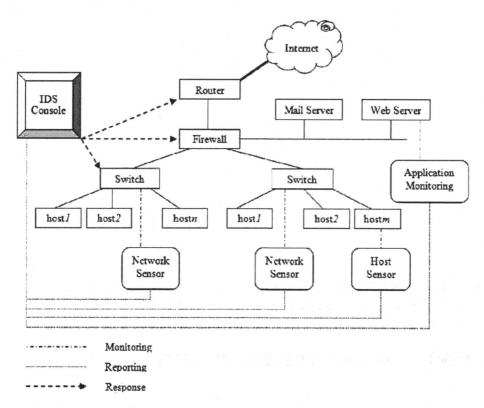

detection mechanisms for individual intrusion detection make distributed IDS useful to cloud computing environments. (Y. Mehmood et. al. 2015)

Figure 10. Huang et al. (2010) describes Distributed IDS

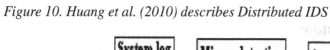
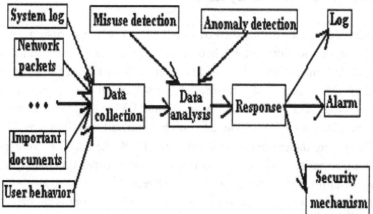

Mobile Agent Intrusion Detection System

A mobile agent (Figure 11) is an automated entity that is able to do different tasks in order to achieve some target. Able to operate despite the user not being connected to the network, the mobile agent is a piece of software that is able to traverse the network and achieve the goals defined by the user (Figure 12). The capability of a mobile agent to control itself by executing its decision structure regarding direction of movement enables it to carry out the tasks identified by the user, which differentiates an agent from an application. (Y. EL. Mourabit et. al. 2014) Mobile agent present some distinct advantages, of which, a reduced network load by virtue of the processing algorithm being executed by the agent itself instead of routing the entire data to the data pre-processing unit, is the most obvious one. Furthermore, the issue of network latency can be subdued due to quicker response times in case of direct host operations by the agent in comparison to information being routed to a central controller which is not on the same network, through a tree branch architecture. Additionally, the agent is dynamically adaptive, with reconfigurable mobility permissions which enable it to get in different environment, independent of operating system, for layer insertion. Data is collected from the attack location by deploying special agent. Scalability, by virtue of network load reduction due to the mobile agent replacing the central processing unit and load division to different machines is the final advantage observed by utilising a mobile agent. (Yousef EL Mourabit et. al. 2014)

Figure 11. Gao & Jin (2010) describes Mobile Agent

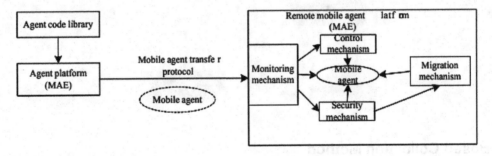

Figure 12. Gao & Jin (2010) describes Lifecycle of Mobile Agent

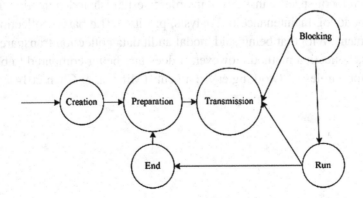

DATA COLLECTION METHODS

Behavior Based Collection Method

Amongst data collection methods (Figure 13), behaviour based collection analyses the node maintained logs and/or other audit data, in order to ascertain any compromise to the network security. A big benefit of the said data collection approach is its ability to scale up in order to handle the loads of large scale networks such as wireless sensor networks and mobile telephony. Moreover, the decentralized, infrastructure non-reliant state of operations in behavior based collection approach makes it more suitable for adhoc networks. The .collection method, with all its noted advantages, however, is susceptible to an increased workload for the intrusion system, owing to the additional effort involving in collecting the data. Furthermore, the behavior based data collection method is observed to be comparatively lesser effective than traffic based collection method (Mitchell & Chen 2014).

Figure 13. Data Collection Method

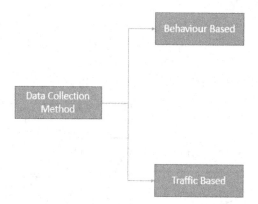

Traffic Based Collection Method

Traffic based data collection is another form of data collection, whereby the network activity is studied in an either general or protocol-specific inspection in order to establish node infection. Free of the requirement of individual node log maintenance or analysis, profits traffic based collection method in terms of resource management. With that being said, nodal audit data collection transparency is restricted in the traffic based data collection method, however, it does fare better compared to behavior based data collection methods for wireless networking environments (Mitchell & Chen 2014).

INTERNET OF THINGS (IOT)

Stemming from two words "Internet" and "Things", the term "Internet of Things" is immediately recognizable as IoT, where the primary word "Internet" refers to system interfaces that capitalize standard internet protocols like IP and TCP for connectivity, while the second term "Things" refers to any real world object. There is no singular user community adequate definition accessible for internet of things .(Madakam and Ramaswamy 2015), (Elrawy et al., 2018) "An open and far reaching system of wise items that have the ability to auto-sort out, exchange data, information and assets, responding and acting in face of circumstance and change in nature"

The Internet of Things (IoT) functions by providing global networking connectivity to uniquely identified entities. Iinterfacing with real world objects and implanting the knowledge into the framework, IoT intelligently processes the item-explicit data in order to make related decisions in a self-contained manner. IoT enables coordination between the internet and physical items over a particular physical area, which can be seen in applied examples such as home computerization, mechanical procedures, human well-being and ecological observation. Developing a proximity to Internet-associated gadgets in daily human interactions, providing a variety of advantages, it does provoke identified security issues. Intrusion Detection Systems (IDS) have been a significant device for system and data framework assurance for over two decades. That being said, conventional IDS methods applied to IoT is problematic due to features specific to IoT, such as the principles, compelled asset gadgets, and explicit convention stacks. Conventional security countermeasures don't perform as well as expected in IoT frameworks due to the various benchmarks and correspondence stacks included, the restricted figuring power and the high number of interconnected gadgets. This makes the provision of an explicit safety solution for IoT imperative in order to allow clients (individual and associations) to embrace it in its full potential (Sicari et al., 2015).

Intrusion Detection in IoT (IDS)

Intrusion detection within an IoT environment is a systematic procedural exercise that stays on the lookout for vindictive acts or maltreatment of administrative arrangements and information development in an organised manner, upon identification of which, it gives feedback to the administrative end for important activity. It monitors the development of all the information that possibly travels to and from the system in order to identify any malevolently designed data which may cause a disruption. The degree to which the Internet of Things is debilitated against assaults is exposed by IDS, which also outlines assault recognition for safety from extraordinary harm. It identifies attackers by highlighting risk, powerlessness, assaults and potential strategies in order to protect the framework against ongoing damage.

Intrusion & Intruder

A Masquerader, a user disallowed to use the system yet entering the security framework pretending to be a genuine user, is the primary form of an Intruder. It is seconded by Misfeasor, which is further classified in two types; an application-specific permission restrained legitimate user and a privilege-abusive authentic client. The third type of intruder is Clandestine which may either be inner or outer, but this kind of intruder attempts to utilize the administrator credentials in order to access the system. The open access and information sharing nature of the IoT environment makes the creation of a secured system with data movement a pivotal task for IDS (Gandhi et.al. 2018), which is a cumbersome task faced by

Table 1. Attacks Associated to IoT

Name of Attack's	Description	Technique	Purposes Intrusion in IoT
Botnets	systems Network of a group to distribute malware to be controlled remotely	Controlled by botnet operation and command and control server(C&C Server)	Criminals uses it for stealing private data, Misuse of online banking data, DDos attacks, spam and phishing email
Man-In-The Middle of IoT attack	Separate network device Interaction and interruption breach via a fake message in order to achieve Intrusion.	Interrupts network device and grasp original message to send his own fake message	Hacked vehicles, smart refrigerators, smart TVs and machinery, automatic door ect.
Data and Identity Theft IoT network attack	unauthorized source data collection. Most often the people safekeep their internet connected devices such as smart phone, laptop, and smart watch etc. the hacker easily stolen data to lunch an identity theft.	Identity theft (from internet connected devices of users)	Steal personal user data to uses it for their own purposes
Denial of service (DoS) attacks	Shorten a service that is viable from target	Distributer Denial of Service (DDoS). normally achieved using botnet.	Causes a widespread disruption of legitimate internet activity.
Social Engineering	To get confidential information such as bank information password.	Act of manipulating users or by secretly installing malicious software	Phishing emails, disclose relevant information. or redirect user to some important sites and websites by cleverly to get their detail information

current researchers. Despite various attempts at securing IoT environments, further work is still required in order to furnish an effective and secured IoT network.

Some types of attacks associated to IoT environments are tabulated as:

Vulnerabilities in Internet of Things Network

The vulnerabilities of an IoT network which are benefited by intruders enabling intruder to be effective in IoT network. These security concerns within the IoT network the increase the ratio of IoT network intrusion proportionately against the number of devices on the IoT network. There is a multitude of Internet of Things security vulnerabilities (Okpe et. al. 2018), however, some of the basic vulnerabilities are described below.

1. Vulnerable Internet of Things Network Interface: Most Internet of Things (IoT) organize client over-depends on default secret key, frail secret phrase or utilizing remiss secret word recuperation usefulness. Different highlights prompting unreliable web interface incorporates cross-website scripting, cross-webpage demand fabrication just as SQL injection.
2. **Inadequate Authentication or Authorization**: The verification process to confirm the user. Conventionally, the user is asked by the system for ID and password in order to perform authentication, whereas, authorization is the process of user approval in order to perform a particular action. The user access to an IoT interface represents some hazard. The authorization method of a user is very important for the security of an IoT network. Unapproved clients getting access to the

system interface is a security risk and may prove harmful to the network. This makes the presence of suitably enhanced authentication and authorization procedures imperative for the secure usage of the IoT network, with all other entities such as server, user and gadget having their own unique identity to use the network safely.

3. **Insecure assistance of IoT**: The open ports of all connected gadgets need examination and verification to ensure that the devices are not vulnerable to intrusion, thus improving the protection of the IoT network against cyber-attack.

4. **Poor Transport Encryption/Integrity Verification:** Strategies such as managing network and portable application data movement, and disallowing any data to move into the transport layer via encryption protocols such as secure sockets layer (SSL) and updated Transport layer security (TLS) can be utilised in order to subdue such a vulnerability.

5. **Vulnerable Cloud Interface:** Primarily, a check against rudimentary vulnerabilities needs to be conducted on all cloud interfaces. The default username and password is preferred by most unskilled users, which is an instance that needs to be avoided in order to make the security of a cloud interface more robust.

6. **Vulnerable Mobile Interface:** The ease of wireless network connectivity for IoT devices via a mobile interface requires a validation security guideline in order to check information presentation associated to remote systems.

7. **Scarcity of appropriate Security Configuration:** Multiple strategies such as provision of a diverse degree of access to network clients, encryption and usage of a robust secret key can be availed in order to forty the security design of the IoT network, enabling it to perform rudimentary interruption identification to the network.

8. **Insecure Software/Firmware:** Constantly updating with time and circumstances, as well as the dynamic nature of needs in an IoT environment, IoT devices need to ensure that the update documents of IoT devices are encoded and transmitted via encrypted interface. Further, updates as well as the update server from which they originate should be signed and confirmed in order to reduce the chances of IoT networked device intrusion.

9. **Low Physical Security:** The probability of an intrusion into the IoT network is inversely proportional to the physical security of the IoT network. The physical mediums being utilized within the network need to secure against rudimentary replacement, data encryption and its subsequent storage, and abstaining port access from malevolent users. Strong gadget assembly to protect against device dismantling also needs to be ensured.

Suggested Intrusion Detection Techniques for IOT

*   **SVELTE intrusion detection system in IoT:** Designed for IOT network, this type of IDS utilises the network mapping information for analysis in order to identify any intrusion to the IoT network. Consisting of an incorporated firewall and 6LoWPAN Mapper to collect information regarding IoT network and build it by using RPL (IPv6 routing Protocol for Low-Power), it is a resource friendly and successful IDS.
    SVELTE (Figure 14) is a real-time IDS which is specifically geared to meet the requirement for IPv6-connected IoT devices (Shahid Raza, Linus Wallgren and Thiemo Voigt, 2013). SVELTE collects information regarding to its connected nodes to create a network graph (Figure 15). Once it detects

Figure 14. STELTE's components
(Shahid Raza, Linus Wallgren and Thiemo Voigt, 2013)

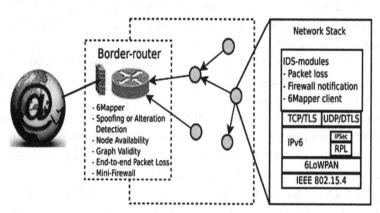

Figure 15. The concept of Three layer Artificial Neural Network
(Elike Hodo, Xavier Bellekens, Andrew Hamilton, Pierre-Louis Dubouih, Ephraim Iorkyase, Chistos Tachtazis and Robert Atkinson, 2016)

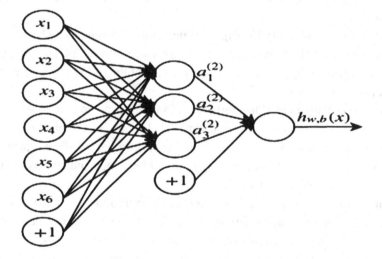

inconsistent pattern in the network, it will block the traffic from entering the network and flag the attacks. SVELTE is capable to detect attack such as spoofing, sinkhole and selective-forwarding.

- **Automata Based Intrusion Detection Method:** Using the automata model (Figure 16) for intrusion detection in extensive heterogeneous IoT network, the IDS uses this technique for the detection of a variety of attacks, notably, false attacks, reply attacks and jam attacks, with automatic attack reporting concerning the attacks identified.

Automata based IDS uses automata transitions to monitor and map the traffic flows of the different cases of IoT to an algebra space (Yulong Fu, Zheng Yan, Jin Cao, Ousmane Kone and Xuefei Cao, 2017). This concept of IDS applies to all sorts of network such as Wireless Sensor Network, MANET and etc due to the generalization of algorithms used in the IDS.

Figure 16. The architecture of Automata based IDS
(Yulong Fu, Zheng Yan, Jin Cao, Ousmane Kone and Xuefei Cao, 2017).

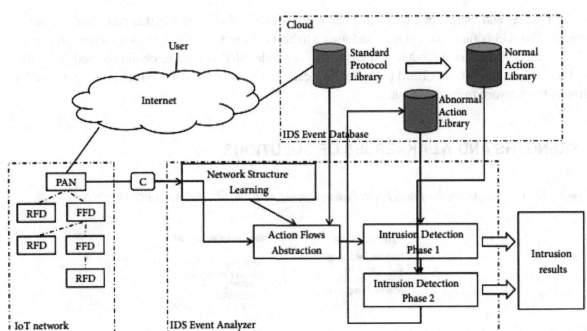

- **Hybrid Intrusion Detection strategy:** Using the Game model, which consists of intruder and normal user, for IDS in IoT, this strategy detects both signature and anomaly intrusion in IoT network.
- **Complex Event-Processing IDS:** Proposed by J. Chen and C. Chen for Real-time IoT networked devices, the matching pattern system, unlike convention IDS techniques, capitalises the Complex Event Processing (CEP) that focuses on the utilization features of the event stream and minimises the number of false positives in order to inspect the IoT network intrusions .
- **Artificial Neural Network (ANN) Intrusion Detection System**: This is a supervised type of ANN and multilevel perception that prepared to utilizing packet tracer of internet and was surveyed on its capability to stop Distributed Denial of Service (DDoS/DoS) attacks in interconnected devices network that is known as IoT devices [20].The processes of intrusion detection actually based on the pattern of attach and classification of normal pattern. It had the option to distinguish effectively various sorts of assaults and indicated great exhibitions as far as obvious and false positive rates.

Artificial Neural Network (ANN) is to create an IDS that can function offline to detect DDoS attacks. It manages this by gathering information from the IoT network and analyzed them for intrusion pattern/ signatures. The IDS consists of a Three layer ANN as shown in figure 2.14. ANN can learn about the attacks using 2 algorithms which is Feed forwarding Learning Algorithm and The Backward Learning Algorithm. Elike Hodo, Xavier Bellekens, Andrew Hamilton, Pierre-Louis Dubouih, Ephraim Iorkyase, Chistos Tachtazis and Robert Atkinson had conducted test toward their design and came out with a 99% detection rate for the attacks.

Novel IDS for IoT

Pavan Pongles and Gurunath Chavan had came out with a IDS (Figure 17) that can detect wormhole attacks. The IDS is functional in ipv6 and uses a hybrid approach for the detection method. It consists of 2 modules: Centralized module and Distributed module. 6BR is used to obtain the node's location and ID information and uses RSSI to locate the location of attack once detected. This allows the IDS to protect the network from inside out.

STRENGTHS AND WEAKNESSES OF SOLUTIONS

Figure 17. The architecture of novel IDS Pavan Pongle and Gurunath Chavan (2015).

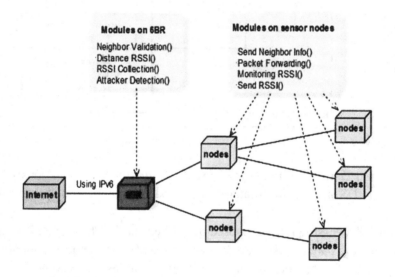

IoT DEEP LEARNING

Known as Deep Learning, advance machine learning is a cutting edge section within AI with a high investigative capability, capitulated by IoT applications such as PC vision, bioinformatics, and natural language processing (Otoum et.al.2019). It exhibits critical execution enhancement over some ML calculations and has recently been used by IoT applications in edge computing and fog computing. The significant volume of data to requiring transferral the IoT network by the aforementioned applications with DL preferring broad information execution over ML. Further, human interaction is not necessary in order for DL to work with new insights and take care of issue.

Recently, a number of IoT applications have risen in regards to varying aspects of smart life, i.e. smart home, city education, health, auto. Transportation, smart farming, and so forth. AI learning techniques for forecast (i.e., relapse, arrangement, and bunching), record mining, information investigation, and model acknowledgement are a primary component of a large portion of these applications. Among numerous machine learning approaches, Deep Learning (DL) has been effectively used in numerous IoT applications as of late (Diro & Chilamkurti, 2018). The technology advancements have made DL and

Table 2.

Type of IDS	Strengths
Anomaly-based Detection IDS	
Statistical based	Capable to prevent unknown attack from attacker
Knowledge based	Very low false alarm rate.
Machine Learning based	IDS is capable to learn about new attacks
Signature-based Detection IDS	
	Capable of recognizing known attacks in quick succession
	Less resources consumption because it only responsible to detect intrusive event
Specification-based Detection IDS	
	Able to detect known attack with signature detection system
	Able to detect unknown attack with anomaly detection system
Host-based IDS	
	Provide system logs and audit traits of operating system
Network-based IDS	
	Easy to implement into the network..
	Real-time detection in the network
VMM/Hypervisor-based IDS	
	Can function in virtual network.
	Act as a platform for communication at various level (VM to hypervisor, VM to VM)
Distributed IDS	
	Flexibility
	Can handle both known and unknown attacks due to the present of multiple IDS.
Automata based IDS for IoT	
	Able to detect wide ranges of attacks
	Can be used in different network (WSN, Manet) due to the generalization of algorithms
SVELTE in IoT	
	Low power, can be deployed in WSN
	Low memory and processor consumption
Artificial Neural Network IDS for IoT	
	High detection rate
	Can function offline
	Self learning capability
Novel IDS for IoT	
	Low power
	High detection rate
	Detection for internal or external attack

Table 3.

Type of IDS	Weaknesses
Anomaly-based Detection IDS	
Statistical based	High bandwidth consumption
Knowledge based	Cannot work without data sets Data sets takes a lot of time to make
Machine Learning based	High computational complexity High computational power to maintain.
Signature-based Detection IDS	
	Requires constant updates of the signature database in order to detect new attacks
	IDS is rendered useless if attacker attacks the signature database first.
Specification-based defense IDS	
	It takes time to calibrate the system to become optimal. (less false alarm, more detection)
	Requires specialized knowledge in IT to maintain the IDS
Host-based IDS	
	Consume a lot of resources on the host
	The agent is useless if the host is infected.
	High cost to deploy (every devices in the network has to install the software)
Network-base IDS	
	NIDS is not capable to process encrypted packets Will not function in Virtual network
VMM/Hypervisor-based IDS	
	Requires specialized knowledge regarding the technology.
	High network load
Distributed IDS	
	Takes a lot of time to calibrate the system to become viable for normal usage.
	Still vulnerable to attacks that target the IDS used, signature server attack that render that part of DIDS not able to function.
Automata based IDS for IoT	
	Complex algorithms
	High power, memory and processor consumption
SVELTE in IoT	
	Limited type of attack can be detected by the system
Artificial Neural Network IDS for IoT	
	Long teaching time
	Need a lot of reference data for attack patterns
Novel IDS for IoT	
	Can only detect Wormholes attack

IoT to be listed among the three main key innovation patterns reported for 2017, as declared at Gartner Symposium/ITxpo2016

The inability for conventional ML mechanisms to tackle the increasing investigative requirements of IoT frameworks has been an indirect cause for the concentrated attention for DL. The hierarchy of IoT information generation and executives have resulted in diversified, modern information systematic schematics and intelligently computerized reasoning methods being required by IoT frameworks. Normally, DL models are bifurcated into three classes; generative, discriminative, and hybrid models (Figure 18). Not a hard and fast rule, discriminative models primarily produce administered learning, while generative models are utilized for unaided learning. The Hybrid model cumulates the advantages of both the discriminative and generative models (Mohammadi et al, 2018). The semi supervised model of DL are the techniques that uses partial supervised and partial unsupervised data and get benefits of utilizing both. It enhances the ability to be more accurate this is the reason it is known as a hybrid model. The explanation of all these models is illustrated in Figure 18. In the given diagram the discriminative models are fully supervised technique and hybrid models are semi supervised, while the generative model can be supervised, unsupervised or semi supervised such as RBM, DBN and VEN respectively.

Figure 18. Mostly used types of Deep Learning Models in IoT

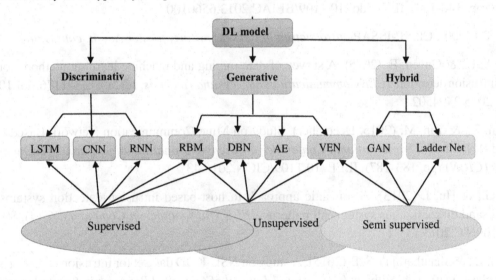

CONCLUSION

Recently, deep learning has become well known and grab the attention of many. Deep learning can be considered as the subset of machine learning as it functions in quite similar ways compare to machine learning but there is a distinction between them. Both the ML models and deel learning model will become better after training no matter what their function is. But in ML, when prediction return is inaccurate, it requires human to help to fine-tune. On the other hands, deep learning model could justify the outcome is precise or not by itself. Deep model is designed to frequently analyse the data in a logic way like how a person conclude on something. For this to be possible, deep learning uses layered structure of algorithm which is known as the artificial neural network (ANN). The survey work presented in this paper can be a good guideline for designing a deep learning intrusion detection in IoT networks. This survey work is an extension to the previous published works (Ponnusamy. V et al. 2020) on cybersecurity governance and secured systems needing a good intrusion detection systems.

REFERENCES

Agrawal, S., & Agrawal, J. (2015). Survey on anomaly detection using data mining techniques. *Procedia Computer Science*, *60*, 708–713. doi:10.1016/j.procs.2015.08.220

Amudhavel, J., Brindha, V., Anantharaj, B., Karthikeyan, P., Bhuvaneswari, B., & Vasanthi, M. (2016). A survey on intrusion detection system: State of the art review. *Indian Journal of Science and Technology*, *9*(11), 1-9.

Anthony, O., Odeyabinya, J., & Emmanuel, S. (2018). Intrusion detection in internet of things (IoT). *International Journal of Advanced Research in Computer Science*, *9*(1).

Asif, M. K., Khan, T. A., Taj, T. A., Naeem, U., & Yakoob, S. (2013, April). Network intrusion detection and its strategic importance. In 2013 IEEE Business Engineering and Industrial Applications Colloquium (BEIAC) (pp. 140-144). IEEE. doi:10.1109/BEIAC.2013.6560100

Bradley, T. (2000). CISSP-ISSAP. *Introduction to Packet Sniffing, former About. com Guide.*

Buczak, A. L., & Guven, E. (2015). A survey of data mining and machine learning methods for cyber security intrusion detection. *IEEE Communications Surveys and Tutorials*, *18*(2), 1153–1176. doi:10.1109/COMST.2015.2494502

Changsen, Z., & Yan, M. (2015, December). Study on Mine Communication Network Based on Ethernet and WSN. In *2015 International Conference on Computational Intelligence and Communication Networks (CICN)* (pp. 183-187). IEEE. 10.1109/CICN.2015.43

Creech, G., & Hu, J. (2013). A semantic approach to host-based intrusion detection systems using contiguousand discontiguous system call patterns. *IEEE Transactions on Computers*, *63*(4), 807–819. doi:10.1109/TC.2013.13

Dhanabal, L., & Shantharajah, S. P. (2015). A study on NSL-KDD dataset for intrusion detection system based on classification algorithms. *International Journal of Advanced Research in Computer and Communication Engineering*, *4*(6), 446–452.

Diro, A. A., & Chilamkurti, N. (2018). Distributed attack detection scheme using deep learning approach for Internet of Things. *Future Generation Computer Systems*, *82*, 761–768. doi:10.1016/j.future.2017.08.043

El Mourabit, Y., Toumanari, A., & Zougagh, H. (2014). A Mobile Agent Approach for IDS in Mobile Ad Hoc Network. *International Journal of Computer Science Issues*, *11*(1), 148.

Elijah, Abdullah, Jhanjhi, Supramaniam, & Abdullateef. (2019). Ensemble and Deep-Learning Methods for Two-Class and Multi-Attack Anomaly Intrusion Detection: An Empirical Study. *International Journal of Advanced Computer Science and Applications, 10*(9), 520-528.

Elrawy, M. F., Awad, A. I., & Hamed, H. F. A. (2018). Intrusion detection systems for IoT-based smart environments: A survey. *Journal of Cloud Computing, 7*(1), 1–20. doi:10.118613677-018-0123-6

Freeman, I., Haigler, A., Schmeelk, S., Ellrodt, L., & Fields, T. (2018). What are they Researching? Examining Industry-Based Doctoral Dissertation Research through the Lens of Machine Learning. In *2018 17th IEEE International Conference on Machine Learning and Applications (ICMLA)* (pp. 1338-1340). IEEE.

Fu, Y., Yan, Z., Cao, J., Koné, O., & Cao, X. (2017). An automata based intrusion detection method for internet of things. *Mobile Information Systems, 2017.*

Gandhi, U. D., Kumar, P. M., Varatharajan, R., Manogaran, G., Sundarasekar, R., & Kadu, S. (2018). HIoTPOT: Surveillance on IoT devices against recent threats. *Wireless Personal Communications, 103*(2), 1179–1194. doi:10.100711277-018-5307-3

Garg, A., & Maheshwari, P. (2016, January). A hybrid intrusion detection system: A review. In *2016 10th International Conference on Intelligent Systems and Control (ISCO)* (pp. 1-5). IEEE. 10.1109/ISCO.2016.7726909

Geetha, V., Aithal, S., & ChandraSekaran, K. (2006). Effect of Mobility over Performance of the Ad hoc Networks. In *2006 International Symposium on Ad Hoc and Ubiquitous Computing* (pp. 138-141). IEEE. 10.1109/ISAHUC.2006.4290661

Gupta, G. (2014). A self explanatory review of decision tree classifiers. In *International conference on recent advances and innovations in engineering (ICRAIE-2014)* (pp. 1-7). IEEE.

Hodo, E., Bellekens, X., Hamilton, A., Dubouilh, P. L., Iorkyase, E., Tachtatzis, C., & Atkinson, R. (2016). Threat analysis of IoT networks using artificial neural network intrusion detection system. In *2016 International Symposium on Networks, Computers and Communications (ISNCC)* (pp. 1-6). IEEE. 10.1109/ISNCC.2016.7746067

Humayun, M., Niazi, M., Jhanjhi, N. Z., Alshayeb, M., & Mahmood, S. (2020). Cyber Security Threats and Vulnerabilities: A Systematic Mapping Study. *Arabian Journal for Science and Engineering*, 1–19. doi:10.100713369-019-04319-2

Janeja, V. P., Azari, A., Namayanja, J. M., & Heilig, B. (2014). B-dids: Mining anomalies in a Big-distributed Intrusion Detection System. In *2014 IEEE International Conference on Big Data (Big Data)* (pp. 32-34). IEEE. 10.1109/BigData.2014.7004484

Jing, X., Yan, Z., & Pedrycz, W. (2018). Security data collection and data analytics in the Internet: A survey. *IEEE Communications Surveys and Tutorials, 21*(1), 586–618. doi:10.1109/COMST.2018.2863942

Kok, Abdullah, Jhanjhi, & Supramaniam. (2019). A Review of Intrusion detection System Using Machine Learning Approach. *International Journal of Engineering and Research, 12*(1), 8-15.

Kurundkar, G. D., Naik, N. A., & Khamitkar, S. D. (2012). Network intrusion detection using Snort. *International Journal of Engineering Research and Applications, 2*(2), 1288–1296.

Madakam, S., Ramaswamy, R., & Tripathi, S. (2015). Internet of Things (IoT): A literature review. *Journal of Computer and Communications, 3*(05), 164–173. doi:10.4236/jcc.2015.35021

Mehmood, Y., Shibli, M. A., Kanwal, A., & Masood, R. (2015). Distributed intrusion detection system using mobile agents in cloud computing environment. In *2015 Conference on Information Assurance and Cyber Security (CIACS)* (pp. 1-8). IEEE. 10.1109/CIACS.2015.7395559

Mitchell, R., & Chen, R. (2014). A survey of intrusion detection in wireless network applications. *Computer Communications*, *42*, 1–23. doi:10.1016/j.comcom.2014.01.012

Mohammadi, M., Al-Fuqaha, A., Sorour, S., & Guizani, M. (2018). Deep learning for IoT big data and streaming analytics: A survey. *IEEE Communications Surveys and Tutorials*, *20*(4), 2923–2960. doi:10.1109/COMST.2018.2844341

Mourabit, Y. E., Toumanari, A., Bouirden, A., Zougagh, H., & Latif, R. (2014). Intrusion detection system in Wireless Sensor Network based on mobile agent. In *2014 Second World Conference on Complex Systems (WCCS)* (pp. 248-251). IEEE. 10.1109/ICoCS.2014.7060910

Murtaza, S. S., Khreich, W., Hamou-Lhadj, A., & Couture, M. (2013). A host-based anomaly detection approach by representing system calls as states of kernel modules. In *2013 IEEE 24th International Symposium on Software Reliability Engineering (ISSRE)* (pp. 431-440). IEEE. 10.1109/ISSRE.2013.6698896

Otoum, S., Kantarci, B., & Mouftah, H. T. (2019). *On the feasibility of deep learning in sensor network*. Academic Press.

Parveen Sadotra & Sharma. (2016). A Review on Integrated Intrusion Detection System in Cyber Security. Academic Press.

Pongle, P., & Chavan, G. (2015). Real time intrusion and wormhole attack detection in internet of things. *International Journal of Computers and Applications*, *121*(9).

Ponnusamy, V., Jhanjhi, N. Z., & Humayun, M. (2020). Fostering Public-Private Partnership: Between Governments and Technologists in Developing National Cybersecurity Framework. In Employing Recent Technologies for Improved Digital Governance (pp. 237-255). IGI Global.

Ponnusamy, V., Selvam, L. M. P., & Rafique, K. (2020). Cybersecurity Governance on Social Engineering Awareness. In *Employing Recent Technologies for Improved Digital Governance* (pp. 210–236). IGI Global. doi:10.4018/978-1-7998-1851-9.ch011

Prasad. (2015). Intrusion Detection Systems. *Tools and Techniques-An Overview*, *8*(35), 1–2.

Radja. (2015). *The overview of wired and wireless networks and the need for the transition from wired to wireless networks*. Academic Press.

Rattagan, E. (2016). Wi-Fi usage monitoring and power management policy for smartphone background applications. In *2016 Management and Innovation Technology International Conference (MITicon)*. IEEE. 10.1109/MITICON.2016.8025223

Raza, S., Wallgren, L., & Voigt, T. (2013). SVELTE: Real-time intrusion detection in the Internet of Things. *Ad Hoc Networks*, *11*(8), 2661–2674. doi:10.1016/j.adhoc.2013.04.014

Santoso, B. I., Idrus, M. R. S., & Gunawan, I. P. (2016. Designing Network Intrusion and Detection System using signature-based method for protecting OpenStack private cloud. In *2016 6th International Annual Engineering Seminar (InAES)* (pp. 61-66). IEEE. 10.1109/INAES.2016.7821908

Satam, P. (2017). Anomaly Based Wi-Fi Intrusion Detection System. In 2017 IEEE 2nd International Workshops on Foundations and Applications of Self* Systems (FAS*W) (pp. 377-378). IEEE. doi:10.1109/FAS-W.2017.180

Saxena, A. K., Sinha, S., & Shukla, P. (2017). General study of intrusion detection system and survey of agent based intrusion detection system. In *2017 International Conference on Computing, Communication and Automation (ICCCA)* (pp. 471-421). IEEE. 10.1109/CCAA.2017.8229866

Selvam, L. M. P., Ponnusamy, V., & Rafique, K. (2020). Democratic Governance: A Review of Secured Digital Electoral Service Infrastructure. In Employing Recent Technologies for Improved Digital Governance (pp. 256-272). IGI Global. doi:10.4018/978-1-7998-1851-9.ch013

Shalev-Shwartz, S., & Ben-David, S. (2014). *Understanding machine learning: From theory to algorithms*. Cambridge university press. intrusion detection. *IEEE Networking Letters*, *1*(2), 68–71.

Sharmila, S., & Shanthi, T. (2016). A survey on wireless ad hoc network: Issues and implementation. In *2016 International Conference on Emerging Trends in Engineering, Technology and Science (ICETETS)* (pp. 1-6). IEEE. 10.1109/ICETETS.2016.7603071

Sicari, S., Rizzardi, A., Grieco, L. A., & Coen-Porisini, A. (2015). Security, privacy and trust in Internet of Things: The road ahead. *Computer Networks*, *76*, 146–164. doi:10.1016/j.comnet.2014.11.008

Tchakoucht, T. A., Ezziyyani, M., Jbilou, M., & Salaun, M. (2015). Behavioral appraoch for intrusion detection. In *2015 IEEE/ACS 12th International Conference of Computer Systems and Applications (AICCSA)* (pp. 1-5). IEEE. 10.1109/AICCSA.2015.7507118

Van, N. T., Thinh, T. N., & Sach, L. T. (2017). An anomaly-based network intrusion detection system using deep learning. In *2017 International Conference on System Science and Engineering (ICSSE)* (pp. 210-214). IEEE.

Vanjale, S. B., Mane, P. B., & Patil, S. V. (2015). Wireless LAN Intrusion Detection and Prevention system for Malicious Access Point. In *2015 2nd International Conference on Computing for Sustainable Global Development (INDIACom)* (pp. 487-490). IEEE.

Wang, Y., Xia, S. T., Tang, Q., Wu, J., & Zhu, X. (2017). A novel consistent random forest framework: Bernoulli random forests. *IEEE Transactions on Neural Networks and Learning Systems*, *29*(8), 3510–3523. PMID:28816676

Wang, Z.-Q. (2016). Research on Distributed Intrusion Detection System. Academic Press.

Yang, H., Xu, A., Chen, H., & Yuan, C. (2014). A Review: The Effects of Imperfect Data on Incremental Decision Tree. In *2014 Ninth International Conference on P2P, Parallel, Grid, Cloud and Internet Computing* (pp. 34-41). IEEE.

Yeo, L. H., Che, X., & Lakkaraju, S. (2017). *Understanding Modern Intrusion Detection Systems: A Survey*. arXiv preprint arXiv:1708.07174

Zhao, S., Li, W., Zia, T., & Zomaya, A. Y. (2018). A dimension reduction model and classifier for anomaly-based intrusion detection in internet of things. *Proceedings - 2017 IEEE 15th International Conference on Dependable, Autonomic and Secure Computing, 2017 IEEE 15th International Conference on Pervasive Intelligence and Computing, 2017 IEEE 3rd International Conference on Big Data Intelligence and Computing and 2017 IEEE Cyber Science and Technology Congress, DASC-PICom-DataCom-CyberSciTec 2017, 2018-January,* 836–843. 10.1109/DASC-PICom-DataCom-CyberSciTec.2017.141

Zulfikar, W. B., Gerhana, Y. A., & Rahmania, A. F. (2018, August). An Approach to Classify Eligibility Blood Donors Using Decision Tree and Naive Bayes Classifier. In *2018 6th International Conference on Cyber and IT Service Management (CITSM)* (pp. 1-5). IEEE. 10.1109/CITSM.2018.8674353

Chapter 8
Comprehensive Survey of Routing Protocols for Wireless Body Area Networks (WBANs)

Ali Raza

Quaid-e-Awam University of Engineering, Science, and Technology, Pakistan

Pardeep Kumar

Quaid-e-Awam University of Engineering, Science, and Technology, Pakistan

Adnan Ahmed

Quaid-e-Awam University of Engineering, Science, and Technology, Pakistan

Umair Ali Khan

Quaid-e-Awam University of Engineering, Science, and Technology, Pakistan

ABSTRACT

Wireless body area networks (WBANs) are one of the applications of IoT that deal with the remote transmission of patient data. The health-related data is of highly sensitive nature. The loss of critical data packets might lead a patient to an embarrassing position. Therefore, WBANs require a secure and efficient data transmission mechanism. However, wireless transmission traditionally remains vulnerable to many security attacks such as node misbehavior attack. Routing protocols play a key role in the extended network lifetime. However, efficient data routing in WBAN is a challenging task. In addition, sensor nodes due to wireless communication produce electromagnetic radiation that is absorbed by the human body and results in temperature rise. Therefore, routing protocols along with security issues must consider temperature rise to ensure safe wireless transmission. In this chapter, the authors present a comprehensive review of most relevant security and privacy concerns and relevant routing protocols addressing the aforementioned routing issues.

DOI: 10.4018/978-1-7998-2803-7.ch008

INTRODUCTION

The wireless technology has evolved over the years, today most of the electronic appliances and gadgets at home and offices are wirelessly operated. The group of devices that record data subjected to the application and transmit the recorded data wirelessly to the base station is called wireless sensor networks (WSNs). Initially, the scope of WSNs was limited to military, science and engineering experiments. However, today WSNs are applicable to various other fields such as water monitoring systems for managing river water level, fire monitoring system for protecting the forest from disasters, earthquake monitoring, habitat monitoring, military, etc. Although the sensor nodes are not rich in resource possession such as memory and processing capabilities, the large-scale deployment of these sensor nodes over an unattended area helps to monitor a larger geographical area. Similarly, Healthcare applications of WSNs have witnessed revolutionary changes and have got a significant acceptance in the recent past. The low cost, hazardless and extremely small size invasive and non-invasive sensor nodes are capable to indicate any abnormal health condition instantly to the patient himself, hospital management system or in some cases directly to the physician.

The network of these tiny biosensor sensor nodes placed on, around and inside the human body is called wireless body area networks (WBANs). The prime objective of WBANs is to provide health management facilitations to the patients/elderly peoples at low cost and ease. However, sensor nodes in WBANs have limited resources in terms of memory, processing power, battery storage, communication range, etc. Therefore, WBANs are considered quite different from traditional resource-efficient WSNs in terms of scalability, reliability, deployment, etc. The WSN is typically a standalone network in which sensor nodes are capable to adjust themselves to the condition. The homogeneous sensor nodes are deployed at a large scale to cover a significant geographical area and data rate is mostly application dependent, whereas nodes in a WBAN are of heterogeneous nature, the deployment of nodes is limited to the size of the human body and most of the time high data rate is required to monitor physiological characteristics like ECG and Blood pressure (Kumar & Lee, 2012). To better understand the difference between the two technologies, a brief comparison is presented in the following sub-section that highlights the key features of WBANs and their associated constraints before formally adopting WBANs for the betterment of human life. As nodes in a WBAN, are required to transmit the patient's data to the destination node in a cooperative manner using a multi-hop environment. Therefore, routing protocols play a key role in the extended network lifetime. Various routing protocols can be found in WSNs that routes data efficiently. However, these routing protocols in their original form cannot be applied in WBANs for patients' data transmission. The comparison between WSN and WBAN will unfold various characteristics of WBAN that demands to develop entirely new efficient routing protocols for WBANs.

Comparison of WSN and WBAN

Although WBAN is considered to be the subfield of WSN, they are not the same. Both of these technologies exhibit some unique constraints and challenges. The distinguishing features of both WSN and WBAN are described in detail in Table 1 (Khan & Pathan, 2018; Latré, Braem, Moerman, Blondia, & Demeester, 2011; Movassaghi, Abolhasan, Lipman, Smith, & Jamalipour, 2014). However, some of the unique challenges that differentiate WSNs from WBANs are briefly described below.

- **Network Size:** The network size of WSNs can vary from a few meters to kilometers where thousands of redundant sensor nodes can be deployed depending on monitored area and application. However, the network size of body area network is limited to the size of the human body. A typical BAN may contain few heterogeneous invasives or non-invasive biomedical sensor nodes to record physiological characteristics of the human body.

- **Resource limitations:** Sensor nodes in WSN possess rich resources in terms of power supply, processing and computational power and memory storage when compared to WBANs. However, resources in WBANs are limited due to the size of the nodes. The implantable nodes with limited resources are almost impossible to be replaced even for a device that requires a long lifetime.

- **Data Requirements:** The redundant nodes in WSN are required to gather data based on event detection. However, sensor nodes in WBANs are required to transmit data to the base station on a periodic base or when base station inquires for the data.

- **Signal Propagation:** In WSN, wave propagation is application dependent; their signal can travel up to kilometers. On the other hand, signals around the human body are attenuated before reaching their receiver node due to the lossy nature of the human body. Therefore, signals can travel up to a few meters.

- **Security:** The security is a prime concern in WBANs, as patient data is life-critical and requires reliable transmission to the base station. Whereas, security in WSN is required at a low level and is application dependant.

Table 1. Comparative Analysis of WSN and WBAN

Criteria	WSN	WBAN
Network Size	Hundreds to thousand nodes in an area of kilometers	Few nodes limited to the size of the human body
Topology Design	Random some time fixed and static	One or multi-hop star topology
Node Size	Small size preferred	Miniaturization is required
Accuracy	Achieved using redundant node	Each node is independent of other nodes and requires high accuracy and robustness
Node Replacement	Very easy	Invasive nodes very difficult, Non Invasive nodes very Easy
Bio-Compatibility	Not a concern in most applications	Essential for implanted nodes
Power source & Battery	Replaceable and can be charged via solar power	Difficult to replace in case of implanted nodes, a battery can be charged via body temperature
Node Lifetime	Years/Months/weeks	Years/Months
Wireless Technology	WLAN, Zig-bee, Bluetooth, GPRS and RF	IEEE 802.15.6, Zig-bee, Bluetooth
Date Rate	Homogenous	Heterogeneous
Security	Application dependent low-level security in most cases	Highly sensitive data requires reliable data transmission

Applications of WBANs

WBAN aims to enhance the quality of life; therefore, it supports various healthcare and consumer electronic applications. However, IEEE 802.15.6 [13] broadly categorizes WBAN into medical and non-medical applications. Patient health monitoring, assessing soldier fatigue, athlete fitness monitoring, etc. are some common medical applications of WBAN. On the other hand, gesture detection, driving assistance, entertainment are some common non-medical applications of WBANs.

Medical Applications

WBANs have a tremendous potential of transforming current healthcare systems into a real-time proactive healthcare management system, as it provides an easy-to-use healthcare system that is capable of diagnosing diseases at their preliminary stage. For example, chronic diseases like cardiovascular, cancer, asthma and so on are required to be monitored in real-time for providing assistance to the patient at any stage. The medical application of WBANs could be categorized into wearable, implantable and remotely controlled WBANs.

- **Wearable WBANs:** The sensor nodes which can be placed on the body to record physiological attributes like assessing soldier fatigue in the battlefield, observing athlete fitness level during training, sleep disorder, asthma monitoring, etc.
- **Implantable WBANs:** The sensor nodes which can be implanted inside the body beneath the skin to record physiological attributes. The devices like pacemakers, drug pumps, implanted cardiac defibrillators are some common devices that have been extensively used in the human body.
- **Remotely control WBANs:** Remote health monitoring is considered one of the most appealing applications of WBAN. The prime and core objective of such applications is to provide support for elderly peoples so that these peoples might be able to live independently. Telemedicine, smart homes, smart apartments are some common example of ambient assisted living (AAL).

Non-Medical Applications

This category of applications includes real-time streaming (video and audio capturing), entertainment, gaming applications on social networking sites, emotion detection, secure authentication (fingerprints, iris detection, facial recognition), emergency systems installed in homes (fire and smoke detection systems) and many more. Table 2 (Ullah et al., 2012) describes the attributes and characteristics of medical and non-medical applications of WBAN.

Therefore, by looking at the vast scope of WBAN and its applications several groups have developed various health monitoring projects such as CodeBlue (Welsh, Matt; Moulton, Steve; Fulford-Jones, Thaddeus; Malan, 2004), MobiHealth (Wac et al., 2009), Alarm-Net (Wood et al., 2008), UbiMob (Jwp, Lo, & Wells, 2004), ReMoteCare (Fischer, Lim, Lawrence, & Ganguli, 2008), Lifeguard (Montgomery et al., 2005), AID-N (T. Gao et al., 2007), CareNet (Jiang et al., 2009). These projects suggest that the healthcare systems are the most attracted applications of WBANs that could benefit human beings at any place i.e., home, hospitals, office, disasters sites, etc.

Table 2. Medical and Non-medical Applications and their Characteristics

Application Area	Biomedical Sensor Nodes	Data Rate	Power Utilization	QoS Support	Privacy
Implanted Medical Application	Glucose Sensor	Few Kbps	Extremely Low	Yes	High
	Pacemaker	Few Kbps	Low	Yes	High
	Endoscope Capsule	> 2 Mbps	Low	Yes	Medium
On Body Medical Application	ECG	3 Kbps	Low	Yes	High
	SpO2	32 Kbps	Low	Yes	High
	Blood Pressure	< 10 bps	High	Yes	Medium
Wearable Non-Medical Application	Music for Headsets	1.4 Mbps	Relatively High	Yes	Low
	Forgotten Things Monitor	256 Kbps	Low	No	Low
	Social Networking	< 200 bps	Low	No	High

CHALLENGES AND REQUIREMENTS OF WBANs

Even though wireless technology evolved a lot, the technological and social requirements of WBANs are quite challenging and different from other wireless technologies. The unique challenges and constraints must be addressed before formally adopting these networks. Table 3 enlists a few of the fundamental requirements of a typical WBAN.

Security and Privacy Requirements of WBANs

The first communication standard developed for WBANs is IEEE 802.15.6 and its first draft was presented in April 2010 by keeping in view the requirements of medical and consumer electronics within the close proximity of a human body (Latré et al., 2011). The draft was officially approved in 2012 with the aim to formulate a communication standard for the wireless devices that could operate within the vicinity of the human body. However, there are some unique challenges that need to be addressed before fully adopting WBANs such as secure and reliable data transmission, node mobility, real-time data delivery, tissue heating in case of implanted nodes and power management (He, Chen, Chan, Bu, & Vasilakos, 2012; Jamil, Iqbal, Amin, & Kim, 2019; Karthik & Ananthanarayana, 2018; Kim et al., 2018). Moreover, the sensitive nature of medical data demands the safety and privacy of patient data all the way from source to the destination node. For example, if a patient is suffering from chronic diseases, his/her data leakage might bring him/her in an uncomfortable situation. Moreover, sometime a patient may lose his/her job if sensitive information regarding chronic diseases is leaked. Thus it can be concluded that the misuse of patient data by an adversary for malafide intentions could lead to life-threatening risks for the patient. In some situation, an adversary may public the patient's medical data on social networking sites as shown in figure 1.

Certainly adopting WBANs in future healthcare systems remarkably reduce healthcare cost and benefits patient without cussing any discomfort. However, managing the security and privacy of patients' record is a big challenge for future healthcare systems (Al-Janabi, Al-Shourbaji, Shojafar, & Shamshirband, 2017; Kang & Adibi, 2015; Saleem, 2009). Moreover, traditional security mechanisms developed for WSNs cannot be adopted in WBANs because of limited resources (He et al., 2012). The authors in

Table 3. Technical Requirements of WBANs

WBAN Characteristics	Requirements
Data Rate	The scalable data rate is required for different WBAN applications, its expected range lies between Kbps to Mbps.
Effective Area	Sensors may be placed on, around and inside the human body, however, the max network size is limited to human body size.
Network Lifetime	Network lifetime is application dependent; The typical lifetime for implanted nodes should be around multiple years. However, for wearable nodes around a few weeks.
Security	Highly sensitive and confidential patients' data require strong but lightweight security solutions due to limited resource.
Setup Time	Extremely fast setup time probably less than a few seconds is required.
Biocompatibility	The sensor node must be approved by the regulatory bodies and should be compatible with the human body.
Fault Management	The network should be capable of recovering from any fault. The nodes must have self-healing capability.
Customization	The sensor nodes should be reconfigurable with the capability of remotely accessible.
Topology design	Typically star, mesh or hybrid topology with Multi-Hop abilities.
QoS	Reliable communication, higher throughput and delay control mechanism
Energy & Power	The node should consume the least energy while communication; The power consumption should be under 0.1mW at standby mode and 30mW in active mode.
Compatibility	Communication capabilities with other electronic devices

Figure 1. Patient privacy breach

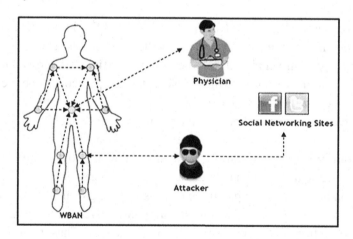

(Movassaghi et al., 2014) discussed the comprehensive security requirements of WBANs that must be addressed before adopting WBANs for patients' welfare systems.

Secure Management

In WBANs the operations related to the encryption and decryption require some secure management at the coordinator node for safe key distribution. Furthermore, the coordinator node adds and remove sensor nodes while association and disassociation process, therefore, it requires secure management.

Data Availability

Patient data is highly sensitive that must be available all the time to the caregiver. However, any attack against data availability could be dangerous for a patient's life. Therefore, healthcare systems should confirm data availability all the time by switching to other WBANs in case of any mishaps to data availability.

Data Authentication

Data authentication is one of the key requirements for WBANs. Therefore, both the coordinator and the sensor nodes before participating in packet forwarding should confirm that the received data comes from a trusted node.

Data Integrity

An adversary may participate in packet forwarding between the source and the coordinator node in order to send modified data to the central location/ or directly to a physician that could lead to the wrong diagnosis of a patient's health. Therefore, data integrity must be assured by all the means.

Data Confidentiality

The medical applications of WBAN transmit sensitive patient's data via a vulnerable and insecure wireless medium. Therefore, eavesdropping and disclosure of a patient's data is quite possible that might results in an embarrassing situation for the patient. For example, an eavesdropper may disclose a patient's data on a social network site that may cause him/her in losing his job. Data confidentiality can be achieved via data encryption using the shared key between the sensor and the coordinator node participating in packet forwarding.

Data Freshness

Data freshness ensures that the recorded physiological attributes of the patient are fresh and resent. An adversary by some means has not replayed the old messages. The data freshness requirement can be achieved by *strong-freshness* and *weak-freshness*. Strong-freshness confirms delay-free and correct ordering of data frames, while, weak freshness only conforms correct ordering of data frames.

Security Attacks on WBANs

Sensitive nature of patient data demands secure and reliable communication. However, due to wireless communication WBANs are vulnerable to many security attacks such as node misbehavior attack. A misbehaving node behaves abnormally by dropping packets prior to the destination node. Partially modified data reaching the central station for analysis by the physician could result in the wrong diagnosis and may endanger a patient's life. Therefore, a WBAN must guarantee the security and privacy of patient data. In the following subsection, some of the most common security attacks that could be harmful to the wireless healthcare systems are briefly discussed. The detail description of these attack models can be found in (Khan & Pathan, 2018; Kumar & Lee, 2012).

Monitoring and Eavesdropping Attack

This is the most common type of attack on patient privacy where an attacker by snooping patient's vital signs could be able to discover patient information. Furthermore, in some situation, an eavesdropper might be able to track the physical location of the patient and might result in severe consequences for the patient. Therefore, monitoring and eavesdropping is considered as the most serious concern to patient privacy (Dimitriou & Ioannis, 2008; P. Zhang & Ma, 2018).

Message Corruption Attack

This attack may be called as an advanced version of the eavesdropping attack. In this attack, an attacker might be able to partially modify or delete some data. Therefore, it results in the message corruption that could be useless for further processing [8].

Impersonate Attack

Attacker by some means represents the identity of a legitimate node in the network. After a successful impersonation attack, an attacker gets access to patient data that might be used for illegal means [8].

Message Replay Attack

The attacker node depletes the network precious resources by sending received signals for a repeated number of times [8].

Node Misbehavior Attack

The node misbehavior attack is one of the most divesting attacks in WBANs in which, an attacker node represents itself as a most suitable node for the communication having enough resource to meet all the requirements. However, after receiving data packets it behaves abnormally by dropping some or all of the received packets prior to the destination node [15].

Secure Routing Mechanisms in WBANs

The process of detecting, preventing and recovering from a security attack is called a security mechanism. Several security mechanisms developed for WSNs, however, these security mechanisms in their original form could not be applied in WBANs, as they are mostly developed for resource-efficient sensor networks and most of them are based on conventional cryptographic and authentication based mechanisms. The short summary of existing security mechanisms developed for WBANs is described in the bellowing subsection.

Cryptography

The transmission of highly personal and sensitive patients' data over a wireless medium is vulnerable to many security threats discussed in the previous section. Therefore, robust cryptographic functions are the absolute requirement of secure applications for wireless sensor networks. Cryptographic functions provide strong security mechanisms to protect against various security threats. However, these functions require extensive computational resources, therefore, these mechanisms in their original form are not suitable for WBANs (Le, Khalid, Sankar, & Lee, 2011). Thus, developing strong cryptographic functions for resource constraint networks such as WBANs is quite a challenging task. The availability of resources must be considered while designing and developing secure cryptographic functions for WBANs.

Key Management

Key management is another fundamental requirement for the development of secure routing schemes for WBANs. In the key management scheme, several cryptographic keys are distributed amongst sensor nodes across the network. The key management protocols can be categorized into three key management schemes (i.e., trusted server, key pre-distribution and self-enforcing) (Ng, Sim, & Tan, 2006; Shaikh, Lee, Khan, & Song, 2006). The trusted server routing protocol exclusively depends on the trusted base station for maintaining the trust key agreement in the entire network. However, these types of protocols are vulnerable to a single point of failure. Therefore, these routing protocols are inappropriate for WBANs (Ng et al., 2006).

Secure Routing

Secure data transmission is one of the fundamental issues in the wireless network. Data transmission by means of the wireless medium is vulnerable to many security attacks, such as DoS attack and malicious routing attack. Various secure routing protocols have been developed for WSNs but none of them fulfill the stringent requirements of WBANs (Nasser & Chen, 2007). Moreover, most of these routing protocols have been designed for static WSNs, thus mobility issue remains unsolved which is an ultimate requirement for WBANs.

Resilience to Node Capture

The network in a WBAN is comprised of small sensor nodes which are placed on the human body and some of which are installed in the hospital premises to collect environmental data. Due to wireless communication among nodes, the network nodes are exposed to many security threats. For example, an attacker by some means captures a sensor node and accesses its embedded data and reprograms it to behave maliciously. The abnormal behavior of a compromised node could results in the wrong diagnosis thereby endangering patient life (Ekong & Ekong, 2016). The cryptographic algorithm performs very well in protecting against outsider attack. However, these schemes cannot detect the compromised node instantly, therefore, the percentage of data loss until the detection of a compromised node is very high. Furthermore, these algorithms are unable to counter node misbehavior attacks where a legitimate node could behave abnormally.

Secure Localization

The biomedical sensor nodes are required to monitor the patient's physiological attributes and transmit these attributes to the central location. The continuous recording of patient's physiological attributes while moving requires determining the patient's exact location and is called localization. The author in (Boukerche, Oliveira, Nakamura, & Loureiro, 2008), discussed various localization issues and possible attacks on localization systems in WBANs. Therefore, while developing a secure mechanism that supports mobility in WBANs, one must understand localization issues and their countermeasures.

Trust Management

The reliable and secure transmission of patient record always remains a challenging task in wireless body area networks. To address the reliable data delivery researchers explore new mechanisms to transmit data reliably to the central location. Thus the term trust has been coined for providing reliable data delivery for resource constraint wireless sensor networks. The authors in (Boukerche & Ren, 2009), defined trust as "the degree to which a node should be trustworthy, secure or reliable during any interaction with the other node". However, trust mechanisms have not been extensively exploited in healthcare systems; therefore issues regarding trust evaluation must be resolved before implementing such mechanisms in WBANs.

Robustness to Denial of Service Attack

In Dos attack, the network communication is disrupted by an attacker by broadcasting an infinite number of high energy signals to overload the communication channel, which might have been available for other nodes in the network. The researchers have discussed various mechanisms to overcome the DoS attack. However, most of the solutions have been developed for resource efficient WSN. Therefore these proposed solutions in its original form are not suitable for WBANs. Furthermore, WBANs applications are mobile in nature thus requires further explorations to deal with DOS attacks in WBANs.

From the above discussion, it observed that numerous robust and efficient security mechanisms have been designed to deal with security issues in WSNs. However, these solutions in their original form are not suitable for resource constraint WBANs. Therefore, countermeasures for security issues in WBANs require further explorations to fulfill the security gaps. The following section further elaborates the challenges specifically related to secure routing in WBANs.

ROUTING CHALLENGES OF WBANs

The past decades have witnessed various routing protocols for WSNs and MANET. WBANs exhibit similar characteristics as of MANETs in terms of topology change. However, WBAN supports group-based movement in contrast to WSN that supports node-based movement due to the fact that nodes in a WBAN are installed on the human body. However, WBANs are resource-limited networks, therefore, have more strict energy constraint than WSNs and MANETs in terms of transmit power. In some situations, nodes are implanted inside the body tissues; the quick energy depletion of such implanted nodes would certainly require surgery that is quite a complex task. Therefore, it is necessary for WBANs to remain operational for a longer duration of time to avoid frequent node replacement. Thus, it can be concluded that due to unique characteristics and challenges the routing protocols developed for WSN and adhoc networks in their original form cannot be applied to WBANs (Ullah et al., 2012). Following are the most common routing challenges need to be addressed while developing routing protocols for WBANs, as discussed in (Movassaghi et al., 2014).

Postural Body Movements

Although the position of nodes is fixed on the human body, the nature of the network is mobile due to various body movements. Due to frequent topology changes the link quality between node varies with respect to time, therefore, intensifies the complexity of Quality of service (QoS) (Maskooki, Soh, Gunawan, & Low, 2011). Moreover, the signal attenuation is very high due to the nature of the human body and clothing which results in a signal blockage. Therefore, routing protocols to be developed for WBANs should be adaptive to frequent topology changes.

Temperature Rise and Interference

The electromagnetic radiation absorbed by the human body results in temperature rise around sensitive body tissues. The high temperature for a prolonged period of time could result in sensitive tissues damage (Tang, Tummala, Gupta, & Schwiebert, 2005a). Therefore, to protect sensitive tissues the routing protocols should be designed with extremely low transmit power (Ullah et al., 2012).

Local Energy Awareness

The tiny size of sensor nodes in WBANs have a very limited amount of energy, therefore, it requires the efficient design of routing algorithm that should uniformly distribute data packets across the network to protect quick energy depletion of certain nodes.

Global Network Lifetime

In some situation sensor nodes are installed inside the human body through a surgical operation, hence, node replacement due to quick energy depletion is not feasible at all. Therefore, node energy in a WBAN is of more importance than other sensor networks and require extended network lifetime probably for years.

Efficient Transmission Range

It is a known fact that higher transmission range of the sensor node requires more power for packet transmission and lower transmission range consume less energy. However, lower transmission range could result in frequent network partitioning and disconnections. This certainly requires a higher number of retransmissions. Therefore, a careful and efficient transmission range according to application requirement should be considered.

Packet Hop-Count Limitation

IEEE 802.15.6 draft suggests that the topology design for WBANs should follow one or two hop star topology and up to 256 nodes could be installed on the human body (Kwak, Ullah, & Ullah, 2010). However, from a realistic point of view, the deployment of sensor nodes in a WBAN is limited to the size of the human body. The fact is single-hop communication requires larger transmit power for transmitting packets. Whereas, multi-hop communication certainly increases the system complexity and results in higher energy consumption (Braem, B., Latre, B., Moerman, I., Blondia, C., & Demeester, 2006). Therefore, careful selection of topology with added relay nodes might be a preferable choice to save energy precious resource (Liang, Ge, Feng, Ni, & Phyo Wai, 2012).

Heterogeneous Environment

In a WBAN, sensor nodes are installed to record various attributes of the human body. However, these sensor nodes are of heterogeneous nature and are designed to perform a dedicated task only. Therefore, to meet the QoS requirements in WBAN is more difficult than WSNs.

TRUST OVERVIEW

The WBANs have received remarkable acceptance in our life due to the cost-effective and proactive health monitoring system. The sensor nodes are installed on the human body to record various body attributes which are wirelessly transmitted to the hospital management systems or directly to the caregiver who is available at the remote location for both diagnosis and future use. The patient's recorded data is highly personal and of sensitive nature, therefore, it must be protected adequately. However, meeting strict security and performance requirements in WBANs is a challenging task. Since the security and reliability of patient data must be ensured all the way, therefore, WBANs require secure mechanisms to protect against malicious intervention in the healthcare systems. For example, attacks by which an eavesdropper intercepts the wireless communication and by some means modify the patients' sensitive data, which results in patient privacy breach and dis-trust in such systems. Moreover, in some circumstances, modified data could lead to serious threats to the patient's life. To protect patients' sensitive data various secure routing protocols have been introduced by the researchers (Agha, Khan, Shams, Rizvi, & Qazi, 2018; Raja & Kiruthika, 2015; Ramli, Ahmad, & Abdollah, 2013; H. Wang, Fang, Xing, & Chen, 2011; Xuemin Shen, Rongxing Lu, Kato, Xiaodong Lin, & Nemoto, 2009). However, most of these routing protocols exploit conventional authentication and cryptographic based routing mechanisms and originally were developed for the resource-rich sensor networks. Therefore, these routing protocols, in their original form cannot be used for resource constraint WBANs. In addition, the cryptographic and authentication schemes are incapable to handle node misbehavior attacks (Boukerche & Ren, 2009; Y. Gao & Liu, 2014a; Karthik & Ananthanarayana, 2018; Kumar, Lee, & Lee, 2012).

In the recent past, the concept of trust-based routing schemes has been introduced in WBANs for addressing the misconduct of nodes, specifically, node misbehavior attacks (Y. Gao & Liu, 2014a; He et al., 2012). Trust-based routing provides secure and reliable data transmission without using traditional cryptographic and authentication based routing approach (Bhangwar, Kumar, Ahmed, & Channa, 2017; Devisri & Balasubramaniam, 2013). Trust in a wireless system is maintained by recording transactions of nodes in a network. The value of trust helps in determining the future action of the node and is calculated from the record that is maintained for each node in the network. The trust-based routing approach for countering misconducts of the node has proved to be a lightweight and effective as compared to traditional cryptographic approaches (Karthik & Ananthanarayana, 2018). The nodes in a trust-based routing scheme can be classified as trustworthy or untrustworthy nodes based on their past behavior. A node is considered as a trustworthy node if it behaves positively by forwarding all of the received packets. On the contrary, if a certain node behaves abnormally by dropping most of the received packets then that node will be considered as an untrustworthy node. The concept of trust has been extensively applied in many popular wireless networks such as WSN (Liu, Dong, Ota, & Liu, 2016; Yang, Xiangyang, Peng, Tonghui, & Leina, 2018), MANET (Devi & Hegde, 2018; Merlin & Ravi, 2019), VANET (S. Ahmed et al., 2018; Xia, Zhang, Li, Li, & Cheng, 2018), DTN (Singh, Juyal, & Saggar, 2017) and WMSN (Aswale & Ghorpade, 2015). However, research on trust-based routing in WBANs is still in an infancy stage. Prior to discussing the various factors involved in trust estimation and dissemination, it is necessary to discuss how it affects wireless networking systems.

Taxonomy of Node Misbehavior Attacks

The development of wireless medical sensor networks (WMSNs) is imperative for e-healthcare systems, but security in terms of reliability and privacy is a formidable challenge yet to be resolved. The fact that the wireless nature of communication amongst sensor nodes exposes WMSNs to the verity of node misbehavior attacks, an adversary may overtake some critical nodes and reprogram it to behave abnormally. Consequently, the compromised node might result in the revelation of patient critical information and may disrupt the overall communication in the network. The misbehaving nodes are mainly classified into selfish nodes and malicious nodes. The selfish node behaves abnormally by not participating in packet forwarding due to varied reasons such as insufficient resources. Whereas, the malicious node intents to destroy the network resources. An extensive review of node misbehavior attack is presented in (Sun & Li, 2017). However, node misbehavior attacks are mainly classified in the following perspectives.

Capabilities and Resources in Possession

In this type of classification, the attacks are classified as outsider and insider attacks. In outsider attacks, an adversary doesn't belong to the network systems and requires authentication and key information to access the network resources. Therefore, such attacks can easily be countered by using traditional authentication and cryptographic approaches. However, in insider attacks, an adversary is part of the network and possesses all network related information such as authentication keys and cryptographic information; therefore, it can't be addressed with the conventional approaches.

Trust Management and Network-Related Attacks

In the trust management related attacks, adversary intents to destruct the trust management system so that the trust management system couldn't make a correct decision regarding nodes behavior; whereas in network-related attacks, an adversary intents to completely disrupt the performance of the network. For example, adversary captures and reprograms a node that drops all packets. Trust management systems have the capability to counter such types of attacks.

The Efficiency of Countermeasure

Node misbehavior attacks can also be classified on the basis of security solutions to counter such attacks, such as traditional authentication and cryptographic approach and trust-based approach. A comparative analysis of traditional and trust-based security approach to counter node misbehavior attacks is presented in Table 4 (Adnan Ahmed, Abu Bakar, Channa, Haseeb, & Khan, 2015).

Table 4. Efficacy of Traditional vs Trust-based approach against Node Misbehavior Attacks

Attack Types	Insider Attacks	Outsider Attacks	TM-Related Attacks	Network Related Attacks	Traditional Solutions	Trust Based Solutions
Selective Forwarding	Yes	No	Yes	No	No	Yes
Hello Flood	No	Yes	No	Yes	Yes	No
Wormhole	Yes	No	No	Yes	No	Yes
Sybil	Yes	No	Yes	No	No	Yes
Grayhole	Yes	No	No	Yes	No	Yes
Blackhole	Yes	No	No	Yes	No	Yes
Routing Loop	No	Yes	No	Yes	Yes	No
Packet Injection	No	Yes	No	Yes	Yes	No
Conflicting behavior	Yes	No	Yes	No	No	Yes
Packet delay	Yes	Yes	Yes	No	Yes	Yes
Bad Mouth	Yes	No	Yes	No	No	Yes
Selfishness	Yes	No	Yes	No	No	Yes
On-Off attack	Yes	No	Yes	No	No	Yes
DoS	Yes	Yes	No	Yes	Yes	Yes

Trust Estimation Factors

There are various factors which can be used in estimating the trust of a node such as bootstrapping, trust evidence, trust evaluation and decision making. A detailed discussion of such factors is presented in (Gonzalez, Anwar, & Joshi, 2011). Amongst them bootstrapping is the first step in any Trust and Reputation Manager (TRM) system. There are three possible ways to initialize TRM system such as (i) considering each network node as trustworthy nodes by assigning high trust values initially (ii) considering each node as untrustworthy node by assigning low trust values initially and (iii) considering each node as neutral node, neither trustworthy nor untrustworthy by assigning neutral trust values initially. Each method of assigning trust values have their own advantages and disadvantages for instance, assigning high trust values initially results in taking some considerable amount of time in decreasing trust degree of misbehaving nodes. Whereas, assigning low trust value results in taking some amount of time in increasing trust degree of good behaving nodes. On the other hand, assigning neutral trust values initially, have the advantage of identifying and isolating misbehaving nodes in considerably less amount of time as compared to other both approaches. The trust evaluation in TRM may be based on *direct-trust* only, which is evaluated by nodes themselves by their own personal experience with their neighboring nodes or it may be based on an *indirect-trust* only, which is obtained from neighboring nodes having their own observations for their direct neighbors or it may be a combined approach of having both direct and indirect trust. For example, the authors in (Channa & Ahmed, 2011; Gidijala, Datla, & Joshi, 2010; Reddy & Selmic, 2011) have exclusively considered using only the direct-trust, whereas, in (Buchegger, n.d.) authors have only considered using the indirect-trust. However, most of the researcher's emphasis on using a combined approach of direct and indirect trust due to the added advantage of getting trust convergence at a rapid pace (Adnan Ahmed, Ashraf, Tunio, Abu Bakar, & Al-Zahrani, 2018; Airehrour, Gutierrez, & Ray, 2019; Yang et al., 2018).

There are many trust evaluation approaches proposed by researchers such as probability-based, game theory-based, weighting-based, neural network-based, Bayesian-based and entropy-based, etc. amongst them, probability-based trust evaluation approaches have been widely used in WSNs. However, in probabilistic based approaches, the Beta distribution amongst others (Gaussian, Poison and Binomial distribution) has a significant acceptance to researchers because of its simple and easy trust estimation mechanism. The decision-making component in TRM is used for excluding untrustworthy nodes from the network. There are mainly three widely used methods for decision making in TRM, i.e., Ranking-based, Weight-based and Threshold-based (Gonzalez et al., 2011). In the ranking-based methods, the nodes are assigned some ranks on the basis of their behavior, the value of the assigned ranks help in determining trustworthy and untrustworthy nodes (Manikandan & Manimegalai, 2013). In weight-based methods, the decision regarding nodes is based on the aggregated value of their reputations (Zahariadis, Trakadas, Leligou, Maniatis, & Karkazis, 2013). Whereas, the threshold-based methods filter out information collected from other nodes in the network (Sun & Li, 2017). For example, in a threshold-based method, each node in the network is associated with a trust value which determines the extent of trustworthiness of that node. The value of trust in a trust-based system depends upon the packet-forwarding behavior of a node and its value is increased on successful forwarding of each packet. Therefore, in order to determine the node's trustworthiness its trust value is compared with the predefined trust threshold value. If evaluated trust value is found to be greater than the trust threshold then that node will be considered as a trusted node. Otherwise, it is considered as a distrusted node which might behave abnormally during packet transmission. The next section presents the state-of-the-art secure routing protocols for WBANs exploiting the aforementioned trust estimation factors while evaluating the trustworthiness of nodes.

SECURE ROUTING PROTOCOLS FOR WBANs

This section presents a critical review of the most relevant literature in pursuit of reliable communication in WBANs based on both traditional security approaches and trust-aware routing schemes.

Secure Routing Schemes Based on Traditional Security Primitives

Secure data routing is one of the prime concerns for WBANs, as patient privacy must be guaranteed all the way. One of the key practices for secure data transmission in WBNAs is known to be via biometric. Biometrics is the process of examining and analyzing the humans' physiological characteristics to uniquely identify the person such as DNA, iris recognition, fingerprint, retina, etc. For example, the electrical activity of the heart can be recorded by using electrodes strategically placed on the body for diagnosing the heart-related diseases. The activity of the heart is basically a signal, by using these signals cryptographic keys can be generated that can uniquely identify the person (Ramli et al., 2013; Z. Zhang, Wang, Vasilakos, & Fang, 2012). Several routing schemes based on human biometrics have been developed for secure data transmission in WBANs. A brief summary of such schemes is given as follows.

A distributed key management scheme for secure routing in WBANs based on human biometrics, commonly known as BARI+ (Muhammad, Lee, Lee, & Lee, 2010). BARI+ introduced key refreshment schedules for managing the key amongst entire nodes in the network. The system model of the BARI+ comprised of sensor nodes (SNs) strategically placed on the body for collecting physiological attributes, a personal server (PS) that might be any handheld device or laptop to collecting data from SNs and relays collected information to the medical server (MS). PS is responsible for periodically issuing key refreshment schedules and have the authority of exempting any node from key management responsibilities due to low energy resource. For managing the WBAN, this scheme makes use of four different keys shared amongst SNs and MNs such as the communication key, the administrative key, the basic key and the secret key. This scheme works around three different phases such as initial deployment phase, re-keying phase and node addition phase. In the initial deployment phase, all initial keys are deployed in PS, MS and WBAN. In the re-keying phase, PS broadcast an encrypted value in the entire network that is obtained from patient biometric for refreshing the communication key. In the node addition phase, The MS is responsible to inform PS if a new node is added in the network by sending its identity, basic key and other related information to the PS. Moreover, for maintaining confidentiality, this scheme incorporate RC5 block cipher and SHA-1 for hashing.

A lightweight middleware scheme based on highly reusable codes is proposed in (Waluyo, Pek, Chen, & Yeoh, 2009). The common features of this middleware scheme are data acquisition, sensor reconfiguration on the fly, plug and play capabilities and resource management. Furthermore, this scheme ensures the security of the patient's critical data against unauthorized users. Moreover, for ensuring the confidentiality, a 64-bit SkipJack light-weight block cipher cryptosystem has been used.

Authors in (Huang, Hsieh, Chao, Hung, & Park, 2009), proposed a secure access mechanism architecture for WBSN. The proposed architecture is comprised of a sensor tier, a mobile tire and a backend network. The author claims that the proposed architecture is suitable for in-home applications, hospital-based networks and nursing home. The physiological attributes and environmental characteristics are collected by using biosensor nodes and wireless motes respectively. However, the collected information is broadcasted to the upper layers securely by sensor nodes and motes. The sensor nodes broadcast the collected information by using an advanced encryption standard (AES) and polynomial-based encryption is used for point-to-point communication between WSMs. The data packets are routed in a multi-hop fashion to the local station at mobile tier by mobile computing devices (MCD) such as PDA. Whereas, the backend tier is coupled with a fixed station and servers is responsible for providing application-level services for lower tiers.

An Elliptic Curve Cryptography (ECC) based mutual authentication scheme for WBANs is proposed in (Le et al., 2011). The network in this scheme is comprised of a *sensor layer* to collect physiological attributes using biomedical sensor nodes installed on the body and then transmits the recorded information to the *coordinator layer*. The coordinator layer forwards the received data to the *data access layer* for future record. The data access layer manages all data in a database server and makes sure that data is accessible to the authorized physician whenever it is required. The scheme is capable of handling attacks such as DoS attack, however, the patient privacy issues have not been addressed in this scheme.

A secure scheme for WMSNs is proposed in (Malasri & Wang, 2009). This scheme proposed a two-tier authentication scheme to protect against spoofing and physical compromise of mote that is based on the patient biometric and physiological data. The symmetric key sharing between biosensor nodes and the base stations is carried out using elliptic curve cryptography (ECC). Data confidentiality and integrity is ensured by using symmetric encryption and decryption based algorithms. Each mote is connected with a fingerprint scanner device to record patient biometrics for recognizing its identity at the base station. The proposed scheme is robust enough to handle spoofing attacks and against physical capture. However, there is significant computational overhead is involved when it comes to real implementation.

A cluster-based routing protocol for cardiac healthcare patient monitoring systems referred to as telecardiology sensor network (TSN) proposed in (Hu, Jiang, Wagner, & Dong, 2007). The scheme was originally designed for the U.S. healthcare community for the purpose of collecting health-related data of elderly peoples. The network is formed by installing nodes on the human body to record patient's physiological attributes such as ECG data and then the recorded information is wirelessly transmitted to the ECG server. The scheme divides the network into clusters to save energy resources. TSN maintain patient privacy by facilitating confidentiality and integrity and protect patient's physiological data by using the SkipJack block cipher cryptography algorithm. A ZigBee based secure architecture for healthcare systems in smart homes is proposed in (Dağtaş, Pekhteryev, Şahinoğlu, Çam, & Challa, 2008). The main features of the proposed scheme are: (i) the proposed scheme dynamically detects the signals within the area of body sensor network (BSN), (ii) reliable communication is ensured by using ZigBee which requires low transmit power, (iii) patient data is securely transmitted over the body sensor network (BSN); (iv) an efficient allocation of medium over wireless network and (v) an optimized data analysis by using an adaptive framework that enhances both computational and processing capabilities. The secure sessions are ensured by using secure key management protocol and patient's mobility is supported by using some authentication algorithm between the handheld device and sensor nodes installed on the body and ensure the security of patient's physiological data. However, the author has not mentioned the cryptographic algorithm which has been used in this scheme. However, energy efficiency is not investigated in this scheme while considering security services.

A secure scheme to ensure the content and contextual privacy in e-healthcare systems referred to as SAGE is proposed in (Xuemin Shen et al., 2009). In this system, the patient's health-related information is recorded by the sensor nodes are transmitted to the central database. The recorded data is then broadcasted to the entire physicians registered in the system. However, information is only accessible to a legitimate physician. In order to achieve access control, only legitimate patients and physician are allowed to store and retrieve information from the database. Furthermore, the elliptic curve cryptography is used to provide privacy solutions.

In (Cherukuri, Venkatasubramanian, & Gupta, 2003), authors have proposed a key distribution scheme based on the human biometrics for securing the communication. The pseudo-random number generated is based on human biometrics for encryption and decryption purpose. The author claims that the prosed scheme is suitable for WBANs as compared to the conventional cryptographic approaches due to the limited available resources. A lightweight security framework for WBANs based on human biometric to ensures secure communication is proposed in (H. Wang et al., 2011). The data is authenticated by using the time-efficient classification model. The biometric key is selected from the senders ECG signals and biometric features are differentiated by using Wavelet Domain Hidden Markov Model (HMM). Moreover, a light-weight encryption method is incorporated for achieving communication confidentiality in wireless body area networks.

It has been observed from the literature that the biometric-based secure routing schemes are lightweight in terms of resource consumption, however, these schemes are less accurate as the percentage of key recoverability is always less than the 100% (Mana, Feham, & Bensaber, 2011). Furthermore, these cryptographic-based secure routing protocols are unable to handle misbehaving nature of the node and might result in exposing/losing critical health-related data. Using biometric-based cryptographic approaches could be helpful in securing data from external attack. However, the network might remain vulnerable to an insider attack. On the other hand, Trust-based routing schemes are capable to counter insider attack and ensure that only trustworthy nodes could participate in packet forwarding. Moreover, trust-based routing schemes require too few resources in terms of computational and processing power, memory and energy resources in comparison to cryptographic base secure routing schemes (Adnan Ahmed, Bakar, Channa, Haseeb, & Khan, 2015).

Trust-Based Secure Routing Schemes for Reliable Communication in WBANs

Trust-based routing schemes unlike traditional security primitives are lightweight and provides security without using complex and resource inefficient cryptographic and authentication based algorithms, where trustworthiness of node is evaluated from its past behavior. A novel multicast trust-based routing protocol referred to as TrE for the healthcare system is proposed in (Boukerche & Ren, 2009). The TrE incorporated a distributed trust model to evaluate trust in a decentralized manner. Furthermore, a secure multicast mechanism based on trust evaluation (TrE) model is proposed for communication amongst sensor nodes in the network. TrE incorporates symmetric cryptographic algorithms for confidentiality protection and asymmetric algorithms for authentication. The trust evaluation of each node is based on historical records. The combined approach of secure multicast mechanism and trust evaluation process makes sure that only trustworthy nodes participate in the packet forwarding. However, this scheme only considers using the direct trust for evaluating nodes behavior, which not only makes it vulnerable to node collaboration attacks but the process of trust convergence is very slow. Therefore, misbehaving nodes might remain in the system for an extended duration, which undermines the feasibility of using such protocols in resource constraints body sensor networks.

A lightweight secure routing scheme based on trust commonly known as ReTrust for medical sensor network is proposed in (He et al., 2012). In this scheme, a two-tier architecture is proposed to reduce to various complexities involved in the architecture of WBAN for secure routing. The author claims that ReTrust is a lightweight routing scheme as it doesn't consider any calculation overhead over resource-limited sensor nodes (SNs), all the calculations regarding trust evaluation is carried out by master nodes (MNs) in the network. The scheme works around two topologies i.e., intracell and intercell. In Intracell the MN is responsible for managing the trust record of all SNs whereas, in Intercell the MN is responsible for managing the trust record of its neighboring MNs. The trust calculation in this scheme is based on direct trust, recommendations and an indirect trust. A sliding time window mechanism has been considered for calculating updated trust values. Although ReTrust is claimed to be a lightweight secure routing scheme, managing master nodes is bit complex, furthermore, failure of a master node in any cell might result in loss of patients' critical data.

A Tsallis entropy-based trust evaluation model for evaluating the trustworthiness of paths for medical sensor networks is proposed in (Y. Gao & Liu, 2014b). A two-layer architecture is considered for dividing the network into different clusters where a master node in each cluster is responsible for trust evaluation and forwarding packet to master nodes of neighboring clusters. Simulation results confirm that the proposed scheme successfully evaluates most trusted paths and avoid low trust master nodes. However, managing clusters and master nodes in each cluster requires extra resources; therefore, adaptability of such a scheme for resource constraints sensor networks is questionable.

In (Tajeddine, Kayssi, Chehab, Elhajj, & Itani, 2015), an efficient trust-based routing scheme for WSN commonly known as CENTERA is proposed. The CENTERA evaluates the trustworthiness of nodes in the network based on the packet forwarding behavior. CENTERA incorporate MAC for ensuring the validity of nodes and sensed data packets. The nodes in the network is required to periodically broadcast its neighborhood information along with their packet forwarding behavior to the base station. Moreover, the sensor nodes are further required to sign the generated packets before forwarding them to the destination node. However, a verification process is carried out by every intermediate node to verify the received packet with its own key, before the packet reaches the base station. This scheme has the capability to defend against replay, modification and impersonating attack. However, this scheme is unable to defend against internal attacks. CENTRA scheme is based on a centralized trust concept where the base station is required to filter out the malicious nodes from the system. Hence, trust convergence is a bit slow. Also, it does not provide any mechanism for preventing a legitimate but compromised node from exchanging wrong information about trusted nodes, thus affecting the degree of the trustworthiness. Moreover, encryption is carried out by each intermediate node while discovering routes, which results in, increased computational cost, overhead and energy consumption. Furthermore, CENTRA due to centralized nature is vulnerable to a single point of failure.

In (B. Wang, Chen, & Chang, 2014), a novel trust-based quality of service (QoS) aware routing algorithm (TQR) is proposed for ad hoc on-demand wireless network. The trustworthiness of nodes in the network is evaluated using direct trust and indirect trust. In addition, to meet the QoS requirements the link quality is estimated by using expected transmission count (ETX). Each node in this scheme is required to broadcast a probe packet after a fixed time interval for calculating ETX metric along with a packet containing the information regarding the count of the total number of probe packets which have been received from each of their neighboring nodes in the last time interval. However, frequent exchange of probe and hello packets results in high overhead. Moreover, link quality is a dynamic entity its incorporation in trust estimation process could result in taking an inappropriate decision, due to the varying nature of wireless links. A trust-aware routing framework commonly known as TSRF to address the node misbehavior attacks is proposed in (Duan, Yang, Zhu, Zhang, & Zhao, 2014). A watchdog mechanism is incorporated to evaluate the trustiness of the neighboring. TSRF implies an inconsistency check mechanism to circumvent false recommendations. Initially, a neutral trust value is assigned to each node in the network which increases with each successful packet forwarding and decreases otherwise. TSRF successfully identifies and excludes misbehaving nodes from the network. However, energy consideration and other related factors are ignored in this scheme, due to which it exhibits low network lifetime. Moreover, un-optimized route results in the selection of longer paths, which incurs high probability of route instability and delays.

A Reputation-Aware AODV routing protocol referred to as (RAAODV) to address selfish behavior of nodes is proposed in (Al-hamadani & Allen, 2014). A selfish node doesn't cooperate in the packet forwarding due to various reasons such as low energy. This scheme is comprised of three main components. (i) a monitoring component to perceive nodes behavior based on packet forwarding via watchdog mechanism (ii) a reputation manager to assess the trustiness of nodes (iii) a path manager for establishing trusted routes and initiating route maintenance if a node behaves abnormally in an active route or link breakage due to congestion or network fault. To safeguard against false reporting attack, RAAOD only employs direct trust mechanism. However, RAAODV sets a redemption interval time to allow misbehaving nodes to be part of the network after re-assigning neutral reputation values. The RAAODV only addresses the selfish behavior of nodes. However, no significance is given to scare energy resource and path length, thus results in low network lifetime and longer end-to-end route selection. Furthermore, incorporating only direct trust mechanism results in slow trust convergence as nodes are only capable of observing the behavior of its 1-hop neighbor, thus selfish nodes detection and isolation from the network is a bit slow. Moreover, the redemption mechanism enables misbehaving nodes to participate in packet forwarding; therefore, packets are lost at frequent pace until the misbehaving node is again isolated from the network.

A trust-aware secure routing scheme for WSN to protect from the malicious node is proposed in (Eissa, Abdul Razak, Khokhar, & Samian, 2013), commonly known as Fr-AODV. The trustworthiness of nodes is evaluated on the basis certain features containing certain attribute number which is exchanged with each forwarded packet. The scheme verifies the authenticity of nodes by exchanging Hello messages. The trust model in this scheme may result in tacking incorrect decision if an authenticated compromised node deceives in exchanging false information regarding features' attributes number. Furthermore, Fr-AODV only considers using the direct trust model which results in slow trust convergence. Therefore, incurs high communication overhead due to frequent route maintenance calls and exchange of hello packets. In (Marchang & Datta, 2012), a secure routing protocol based on trust referred to as LTB-AODV is proposed to counter blackhole and grayhole attacks. An intrusion detection system (IDS) is used to estimate the trustworthiness of node. Each node in the network is required to observe the activities of each of its direct neighboring nodes for evaluating the trust. Moreover, besides direct trust, the LTB-AODV makes use of indirect trust which is gained through interaction from other neighboring nodes. The use of IDS for trust estimation is the main drawback of the scheme; as IDS is vulnerable to node misbehavior attack in which a legitimate compromised node may drop a random number of packets or may send false route request; thus, showing inconsistent traffic pattern. Whereas IDS works on the assumption, that the traffic pattern remains consistent all the time. Furthermore, this scheme doesn't provide any mechanism to counter *false reporting attack* where a compromised sensor node might exchange wrong information in the network regarding the trusted node. Incorporating IDS for evaluating the trust might result in a storm of false alarms which may results in quick energy depletion thus, affecting the network lifetime.

Another trust-based routing protocol to defend against malicious and faulty nodes is proposed in (Channa & Ahmed, 2011) named as R-AODV. The nodes exchange packet forwarding statistics for their neighboring nodes in promiscuous mode and evaluate the trustworthiness of node based on aggregated packet forwarding ratio. However, trust computation is only based on the direct trust. R-AODV works fine in terms of malicious node detection. However, too many route maintenance call results in increased communication overhead. Furthermore, incorporating only direct trust results in slow trust convergence. Moreover, R-AODV does not share traffic load amongst the entire trusted node in the network; thus results in quick energy depletion of the trusted node on an active route thereby compromise network lifetime.

Table 5. Assessment of Secure Routing Schemes based on Trust

Scheme	Model	Trust Convergence	False Reporting Mechanism	Energy Aware	Network Overhead	Fault Detection
TrE (Boukerche & Ren, 2009)	Aggregated sum of packet forwarding ratio	No	No	No	High	No
Re-Trust (He et al., 2012)	Aggregated sum of packet forwarding ratio	No	No	No	High	No
BeTrust (Y. Gao & Liu, 2014a)	Weight-based Aggregated sum of packet forwarding ratio	No	No	No	High	No
CATMS (Karthik & Ananthanarayana, 2018)	Weight-based Aggregated sum of packet forwarding ratio	No	No	No	High	Yes
CENTRA (Tajeddine et al., 2015)	Aggregated sum of packet forwarding ratio	Slow	No	No	High	No
TQR (B. Wang et al., 2014)	Weight-based aggregated sum of direct and indirect trust	Moderate	No	No	High	No
TSRF (Duan et al., 2014)	Weight-based aggregated sum of direct and indirect trust	Moderate	Yes	No	Low	No
RAAODV (Al-hamadani & Allen, 2014)	Aggregated sum of packet forwarding ratio	Slow	No	No	Moderate	No
FR-AODV (Eissa et al., 2013)	Feature Attributes (Repute and identity)	Slow	No	No	Moderate	No
LTB-AODV (Marchang & Datta, 2012)	Intrusion Detection System	Moderate	Yes	No	High	No
R-AODV (Channa & Ahmed, 2011)	Aggregated sum of packet forwarding ratio	Slow	No	No	High	Yes
SORI (Qi He et al., 2008)	Aggregated sum of packet forwarding ratio	Slow	No	No	High	No

To protect against selfish behavior of nodes a secure routing scheme referred to as SORI is proposed in (Qi He, Dapeng Wu, & Khosla, 2008). SORI introduced punishment and reward-based system to encourage nodes for participating in packet forwarding. The scheme is comprised of three main components (i) the monitoring component to observe the behavior of neighboring nodes (ii) the reputation propagation component is responsible for evaluating the trustworthiness of nodes (iii) the punishment component that penalizes the selfish node for their misconduct. A node drops the received packet from a node whose reputation value is below the threshold value and decreases its reputation value. Furthermore, it is responsible for informing the selfish behavior of nodes to other nodes in the network, so that it should be punished by other nodes as well. SORI authenticate each node and packet by incorporating one hash function and Message Authentication Code (MAC). However, incorporating these complex methods in resource constraint wireless sensor network is not feasible.

The summary and comparison of the above trust-aware routing schemes in tabular form in terms of most common parameters related to trust is shown in Table 5 re-drawn from (Adnan Ahmed, Abu Bakar, et al., 2015)

THERMAL AND ENERGY-AWARE ROUTING PROTOCOLS FOR WBANs

Thermal-aware routing protocols are developed with the aim to minimize the temperature rise of sensor nodes across the network by routing packets from different routes. Thus, the temperature of nodes in the network remains under a predefined threshold value that avoids sensitive tissue damage due to overheating. However, dispersing packets on various routes increase complexity and overhead. The main reason behind the temperature rise is the absorption of electromagnetic radiation by the human tissue due to wireless communication consequently results in sensitive tissue damage (Tang et al., 2005a). In recent past, several thermal-aware schemes have been suggested for WBSNs with the aim to reduce temperature rise and refrain frequent hotspots nodes (i.e., a node whose temperature reaches above a specified temperature threshold). To the best of our knowledge, the first temperature-aware scheme to deal with temperature issue in WBANs is referred to as TARA proposed in (Tang, Tummala, Gupta, & Schwiebert, 2005b). TARA maintains the leadership history of cluster nodes and the location of the sensor nodes to reduce the temperature rise around sensitive tissues inside the human body. In TARA, node estimates the temperature change of their nearby nodes by overhearing the total number of forwarded packets, the estimation of radiation energy absorbed by the human body and the consumption of the power. TARA detour the packets to alternate paths to avoid hotspots (the area whose temperature is above a certain threshold value). TARA defines a packet withdrawn policy to return earlier received packets if next hop towards the destination is discovered as hotspot node. However, the temperature of the hotspot node goes down after remaining silent for a short while and that node will be considered for future routing. TARA incorporated Finite-Difference Time-Domain (FDTD) (Tang et al., 2005a) method and Penne's bioheat Equation (Hirata, Matsuyama, & Shiozawa, 2000) to estimate the temperature rise and specific absorption rate. The simulation results reveal that maximum temperature-rise is low. However, packet retransmission is very high due to packet withdrawn policy from the hotspot region. Thus, results in high packet loss ratio, low network lifetime, high delay and low reliability.

In (A. Bag & Bassiouni, 2006), a least temperature route (LTR) routing algorithm for body sensor networks to deal with temperature rise issue and packet delivery delay is proposed. Similar to TARA, LTR also defines hotspot as an area having a high temperature at that moment. In this scheme, each node maintains the temperature record for each of its neighboring node and forward packets to the coolest neighbor towards the sink. Moreover, each packet has an associated hop-count filed that increments by one when the packet is forwarded by any node. However, a max-hop count field is also defined for each packet. The packet is dropped in a case if its hop-count exceeds packets max-hop field. As packets are forwarded via least temperature nodes there is a significant chance that most of the nodes in the network remain involved in packet forwarding, consequently, leading to temperature rise in the network. Moreover, there is no guaranty that the packets will always be forwarded to the intended destination node while following the policy of least temperature routes in the network. Therefore, routes towards the destination node may not be optimal. Thus this scheme experience high network delay. An upgraded version of LTR is Adoptive LTR in which a max-hop adaptive field is introduced for each packet. Unlike LTR in which packets are dropped if exceeding its max-hops count filed. In ALTR, if packet exceeds its max hop adaptive than the packet is forwarded using shortest hop routing. Moreover, nodes in ALTR use delaying strategy to cool down the temperature. The packet is delayed for one unit of time if the temperature of its neighboring node is high which contributes to high end-to-end delay. Furthermore, it is also possible that the shortest hop routing strategy may result in selecting the route containing the hotspot node, thus results in wasting precious resources.

In (Takahashi, Xiao, & Hu, 2007), a hybrid scheme for WBANs is proposed that aims to optimize routes based on total route temperature rise and redundant hops in the network. In this scheme, the temperature of each node is assigned as a weighted-graph and later on, these weights are transferred to the outgoing edges of connected nodes. The least temperature routes are selected using Dijkstra's algorithm based on the minimum temperature of nodes in the network. Finally, routes are updated on a periodic basis in order to avoid an excessive temperature rise of sensor nodes. Authors in (A. Bag & Bassiouni, 2006), have compared simulation results of LTRT with LRT and ALTR and draw a conclusion that LTRT performs better than both LTR and ALTR. In (A. Bag & Bassiouni, 2007), a Hotspot Preventing Routing Algorithm referred to as HPR has been proposed for WBANs with the aim to deliver packets to the destination node with least packet delivery delay. In HPR, the temperature change of the neighboring node is estimated by counting the total number of packets forwarded by a certain node in a specific session. The packets forwarding in HPR is based on shortest hop routing algorithm unless the existence of the hotspot node on the active route. However, a packet can be forwarded up to packet's max-hop count and will be dropped in the case it exceeds its max-hop field. In addition, for avoiding routing loops, a list of most recently traversed nodes is maintained by each packet. The route selection process is comprised of two phases. In the first phase, the network nodes are required to exchange their initial temperature by using the shortest hop routing towards the destination node. In the second phase, each node is allowed to forward packets. However, if next-hop is the destination node then packets are forwarded immediately. Otherwise, packets are forwarded by following shortest hop routing to the next-hop node whose temperature is comparatively less as of the current node and value of the temperature threshold. Else the current node realizes that the next-hop temperature is somehow above the temperature threshold value. Thus, this route goes through hotspot node, therefore, it forward packets to the second coolest and unvisited node. The simulation results reveal that HPR experiences very low-temperature rise, low packet delivery delay and almost zero packet loss ratio as compared to TARA.

In (a. Bag & Bassiouni, 2008), a fault-tolerant and efficient routing algorithm referred to as RAIN is proposed. The scheme is designed in such a way that it functions effectively and independently regardless of some node's energy depletion. The RAIN operates in three different phases. The first phase is the network initialization phase, where each node is required to generate some random number that will serve as node-id and will be shared amongst all the nodes via hello message. However, "0" node-id is reserved for the sink node and cannot be assigned to any other node in the network. In the second phase, the packets are routed from source node to the sink node where a hop-count is associated with each packet that increments by "1" at each node to avoid routing to an infinite loop. Moreover, each node is required to maintain a queue to record packet-ids of the packets which have been received in the last time interval. In addition, the temperature of each node is estimated by counting the total number of packets transmitted by a neighboring node by overhearing its packet transmission. A node upon receiving packets performs following actions stepwise:

- Drop the packet if hop-count > TTL
- Drop the packet if its id is already available in the queue.
- Record the packet-id for the received packet in the queue if (*hop-count > hop_threshold* && *packet-id* is not available in the id-queue).
- Deliver the packet to the destination node, if it is available in the neighbor's list. Otherwise, packets are forwarded to the nth neighboring node with the probability of *Pn* that is inversely proportional to the estimated temperature of neighboring nodes.
- Finally, forward the packet to the coolest neighboring node or the node having the least temperature.

In the third phase, the sink node upon receiving a packet broadcasts an update message containing the packet-id of its neighboring nodes. Any node upon receiving an update message is bound to add the *packet-id* in the *id-queue*.

The authors claim that the energy consumption of RAIN is very low due to the least probability of duplicate packets and packet forwarding towards the hotspot node. This positively effects on minimizing end-to-end delay and high throughput.

Authors in (Tabandeh, Jahed, Ahourai, & Moradi, 2009), proposed a temperature aware routing protocol for body sensor networks referred to as TSHR, with the aim to reduce temperature-rise while forwarding packets with least packet delivery delay and least power consumption. The TSHR has been exclusively designed for WBANs application which requires high priority of packet delivery. Furthermore, TSHR supports packet retransmission if some packets are dropped during communication. The scheme works around two different phases, *a route setup phase* to initialize network nodes and building routing table and a *routing phase* where each node in the network transmit packets to the destination node using shortest hop routing. TSHR floats the idea of defining two threshold values for controlling the temperature of nodes in the network such as (i) T_s and (ii) T_{Dn}. T_s is fixed for all the nodes and each node is bound to restrict their temperature under this threshold, whereas, T_{Dn} is dynamic temperature threshold which is based on nodes own temperature and the average temperature of neighboring nodes. If the temperature of a certain node i.e., T_s is found to be greater than the T_{Dn} then that node is considered as a hotspot node. Simulation results reveal that network life time of TSHR is high and its packet loss ratio is almost zero. However, HPR performs better in terms of packet delivery delay than TSHR.

In (A. Ahmed et al., 2014), authors have proposed a temperature-aware and energy-efficient routing scheme referred to as M-ATTEMPT for WBANs with the aim to reduce nodes' temperature rise and packet delivery delay of critical data packets. In this scheme, the network topology is designed carefully in such a way that the sink node is reachable to every node at1-hop. However, sensor nodes placement at the body is according to their data rate such that the nodes with critical data packets can send data packets directly to the sink node with least possible delay; while ordinary data packets are routed in multi-hop fashion using shortest hop routing with high energy nodes. Moreover, a temperature threshold is also defined for controlling the temperature rise. A node has to break all the routes with their neighboring nodes if it finds that its temperature exceeds the threshold value. However, it is bound to resend the received packet to its previous node. Furthermore, at any stage during packet transmission, it is revealed that the temperature of a certain node has reached the threshold value then it will be the responsibility of the previous node to mark high-temperature node as a hotspot node.

The tiny size of sensor node with a limited amount of energy demands careful utilization of available energy resource, as in some situation, biomedical sensor nodes are implanted inside the human body that requires surgery, which is quite a complex task. Therefore, routing protocols to be designed for WBANs must be energy efficient and remain strict with energy conservation goals. To address the limited energy issues in WBANs, several energy-efficient schemes have been developed some of them are discussed as follows.

In (Movassaghi, Abolhasan, & Lipman, 2012), a routing scheme referred to as ETPA for WBANs has been proposed to deal with quick energy depletion and sensitive tissues damage due to temperature rise. In this scheme, a cost function is introduced based on node energy, temperature and received signal strength for the selection of efficient routes. The network nodes are required to broadcast a hello message containing their temperature and energy level for the network initialization. However, each node is only permitted to transmit packets in their allocated time slot. After the network initialization, each node computes the signal strength of the hello packet that is received from their nodes and then calculates the value of the cost function. Finally, in the next frame, a node forwards packets to the neighboring node with the least value of the cost function. Moreover, a packet could be forwarded to the next hop until it reaches its max-hop-count. The simulation results show better performance than the compared schemes, however, no justification has been given for the equal distribution of network load

In (Ha, 2016), an efficient routing scheme for WBANs is proposed to improve network lifetime and address path loss issue at the backside of the body, due to postural body movements. This scheme achieves even energy consumption goal by considering the standard deviation of residual energy of the forwarder node. A forwarder node is elected on the basis of least value of the standard deviation. The scheme is comprised of the four main phases.

- **Initialization phase:** In this phase, each node is required to broadcast a hello packet containing hop-count to the sink node.
- **Routing phase:** In this phase, each node is required to establish a route to the sink node.
- **Scheduling phase:** in this phase, each node is assigned a time slot using a TDMA scheme for data transfer.
- **Data transmission phase:** In this phase, an on-demand period is assigned for data transmission based on allocated time-slots. In addition, frequent route disconnection due to postural body movements is addressed by using multi-hop routing strategy by using the "selection_optimal_route" procedure.

In (Khanna, Chaudhary, & Gupta, 2018), a cluster-based routing scheme for WBANs is proposed by introducing a combined approach of using single and multi-hop based routing for packet transmission to achieve energy conservation goals. This scheme works around two phases, a setup phase to initialize network nodes and an operational phase in which a node having data packet selects a forwarder node based on two available choices (i) if the distance of next-hop node towards the destination node is less than the distance of node itself and the sink node and energy level above the threshold value. (ii) If the destination is in direct range of the source node itself the packets should be forwarded directly using single-hop communication. In (Mohammadani et al., 2018), an energy-efficient routing protocol is proposed for WBANs. The architecture of the scheme is comprised of eight sensor nodes amongst them two sensor nodes are dedicated for recording only critical data packets while other six nodes perform the dual task of sensing event and forwarding data packets. The critical data packets are forwarded by using the single-hop routing scheme, whereas, normal data packets are transmitted via a multi-hop routing scheme. However, in multi-hop, the next-hop is elected having the least distance to the sink node with maximum available energy resource. Nevertheless, nodes are only allowed to send packets in their assigned time slot i.e., TDMA.

The summary of temperature and energy-aware routing schemes is presented in Table 6 (Bangash, Abdullah, Anisi, & Khan, 2014; Movassaghi et al., 2014) Highlighting the overall goal, the extent of temperature-rise, end-to-end delay, packet delivery ratio and energy consumption of each routing scheme.

Table 6. Comparison of temperature-aware routing protocols

Protocol	Goal	Temperature Rise	Delay	PDR	Energy Consumption
TARA (Tang et al., 2005b)	To reduce the possibility of overheating	V. High	V. High	V. Low	V. High
LTR (A. Bag & Bassiouni, 2006)	Temperature minimization and energy conservation	High	High	Low	High
ALTR (A. Bag & Bassiouni, 2006)	Temperature rise issue, energy consumption & delay	High	Intermediate	High	High
LTRT (Takahashi et al., 2007)	To find the route with the minimum temperature	Low	Low	V. High	Low
HPR (A. Bag & Bassiouni, 2007)	To avoid hotspot formation & and minimize packet delivery delay	V. Low	Low	High	High
RAIN (a. Bag & Bassiouni, 2008)	To reduce avg. temp. rise & Avg. Delay	V. Low	Low	High	Low
TSHR (Tabandeh et al., 2009)	To reduce temp. rise, energy depletion & delay	V. Low	Intermediate	V. High	Low
M-ATTEMPT (A. Ahmed et al., 2014)	To reduce temp. rise, Energy depletion, & delay	Low	Low	High	Low
ETPA (Movassaghi et al., 2012)	Energy Efficiency and Temperature minimization	Low	Low	High	Low
EECBR (Ha, 2016)	To reduce packet loss ratio, & energy depletion.	Not addressed	Low	Low	low
M-SIMPLE (Khanna et al., 2018)	Energy Efficiency	Not. addressed	High	Low	high
EER (Mohammadani et al., 2018)	Energy efficiency	Not addressed	High	Low	low

SUMMARY

The literature review highlights the importance of health-related data, its security requirements and vulnerabilities and categorizes routing attacks into two broad categories i.e., insider and outsider attacks. A comprehensive review of secure routing protocols that deal with the security issues in WBANs is presented in detail and it has been observed that these routing schemes mainly rely on conventional security approaches where authentication and cryptographic keys are derived from human biometrics. Although these routing schemes have been considered as lightweight routing schemes; these are only capable of countering against external attacks. On the other hand, a legitimate node inside the network with all network-related privileges and possession of authentication and cryptographic keys might behave abnormally and could result in loss of critical data packets. This negatively affects and could lead to wrong diagnosis or privacy breach. Therefore, to address internal attacks, the concept of trust-aware routing schemes have been widely used in recent past and have proved to be a promising approach for providing security without using complex cryptographic approaches.

Moreover, it has been observed the sensor nodes due to wireless communication produce electromagnetic radiation which is absorbed by the human body, consequently, the temperature inside the human body is raised, which is harmful specifically for sensitive tissues. Therefore, secure and temperature aware routing protocols are of prime importance for WBANs. However, temperature-aware routing schemes mainly emphasis on reducing temperature-rise, while overlooking other critical factors such as energy, security, reliability and QoS. Therefore, it results in reduced network lifetime, higher transmission delays, frequent formation of hotspot nodes, low network throughput. The literature review highlights that dealing with security, temperature and energy issues individually is not an appropriate choice for WBANs, hence, it requires a novel routing approach to deals with diverse issues in WBANs.

REFERENCES

Agha, D. S., Khan, F. H., Shams, R., Rizvi, H. H., & Qazi, F. (2018). A Secure Crypto Base Authentication and Communication Suite in Wireless Body Area Network (WBAN) for IoT Applications. *Wireless Personal Communications*, *103*(4), 2877–2890. doi:10.100711277-018-5968-y

Ahmed, A., Abu Bakar, K., Channa, M. I., Haseeb, K., & Khan, A. W. (2015). A survey on trust based detection and isolation of malicious nodes in ad-hoc and sensor networks. *Frontiers of Computer Science*, *9*(2), 280–296. doi:10.100711704-014-4212-5

Ahmed, A., Ashraf, U., Tunio, F., Abu Bakar, K., & AL-Zahrani, M. S. (2018). Stealth Jamming Attack in WSNs: Effects and Countermeasure. *IEEE Sensors Journal*, *18*(17), 7106–7113. doi:10.1109/JSEN.2018.2852358

Ahmed, A., Bakar, K. A., Channa, M. I., Haseeb, K., & Khan, A. W. (2015). TERP: A Trust and Energy Aware Routing Protocol for Wireless Sensor Network. *IEEE Sensors Journal*, *15*(12), 6962–6972. doi:10.1109/JSEN.2015.2468576

Ahmed, A., Javed, N., Qasim, U., Ishfaq, M., Khan, Z. A., & Alhamdi, T. (2014). RE-ATTEMPT: A New Energy-Efficient Routing Protocol for Wireless Body Area Sensor Networks. *International Journal of Distributed Sensor Networks*, *464010*(4), 464010. doi:10.1155/2014/464010

Ahmed, S., Rehman, M. U., Ishtiaq, A., Khan, S., Ali, A., & Begum, S. (2018). VANSec: Attack-Resistant VANET Security Algorithm in Terms of Trust Computation Error and Normalized Routing Overhead. *Journal of Sensors*, *2018*, 1–17. doi:10.1155/2018/6576841

Airehrour, D., Gutierrez, J. A., & Ray, S. K. (2019, April). SecTrust-RPL: A secure trust-aware RPL routing protocol for Internet of Things. *Future Generation Computer Systems*, *93*, 860–876. doi:10.1016/j.future.2018.03.021

Al-hamadani, A., & Allen, W. H. (2014). RAAODV: a reputation-aware AODV for mobile ad hoc networks. In *Proceedings of the 2014 ACM Southeast Regional Conference on - ACM SE '14* (pp. 1–6). New York: ACM Press. 10.1145/2638404.2638462

Al-Janabi, S., Al-Shourbaji, I., Shojafar, M., & Shamshirband, S. (2017). Survey of main challenges (security and privacy) in wireless body area networks for healthcare applications. *Egyptian Informatics Journal*, *18*(2), 113–122. doi:10.1016/j.eij.2016.11.001

Aswale, S., & Ghorpade, V. R. (2015). Survey of QoS Routing Protocols in Wireless Multimedia Sensor Networks. *Journal of Computer Networks and Communications*, *2015*, 1–29. doi:10.1155/2015/824619

Bag, A., & Bassiouni, M. A. (2006). Energy efficient thermal aware routing algorithms for embedded biomedical sensor networks. In *2006 IEEE International Conference on Mobile Ad Hoc and Sensor Systems, MASS* (Vol. 1, pp. 604–609). 10.1109/MOBHOC.2006.278619

Bag, A., & Bassiouni, M. A. (2007). Hotspot Preventing Routing Algorithm for Delay-Sensitive Biomedical Sensor Networks. In *2007 IEEE International Conference on Portable Information Devices, PIDs 2007* (pp. 1–5). 10.1109/PORTABLE.2007.30

Bag, A., & Bassiouni, M. A. (2008). Routing algorithm for network of homogeneous and id-less biomedical sensor nodes (RAIN). In *2008 IEEE Sensors Applications Symposium* (pp. 68–73). IEEE.

Bangash, J. I., Abdullah, A. H., Anisi, M. H., & Khan, A. W. (2014). A survey of routing protocols in wireless body sensor networks. *Sensors (Switzerland)*, *14*(1), 1322–1357. doi:10.3390140101322 PMID:24419163

Bhangwar, A. R., Kumar, P., Ahmed, A., & Channa, M. I. (2017). Trust and Thermal Aware Routing Protocol (TTRP) for Wireless Body Area Networks. *Wireless Personal Communications*, *97*(1), 349–364. doi:10.100711277-017-4508-5

Boukerche, A., Oliveira, H. H. A. B. F., Nakamura, E. F., & Loureiro, A. A. F. (2008). Secure localization algorithms for wireless sensor networks. *IEEE Communications Magazine*, *46*(4), 96–101. doi:10.1109/MCOM.2008.4481347

Boukerche, A., & Ren, Y. (2009). A secure mobile healthcare system using trust-based multicast scheme. *IEEE Journal on Selected Areas in Communications*, *27*(4), 387–399. doi:10.1109/JSAC.2009.090504

Braem, B., Latre, B., Moerman, I., Blondia, C., & Demeester, P. (2006). The wireless autonomous spanning tree protocol for multihop wireless body area networks. In *Networking & Services, 2006 Third Annual International Conference* (pp. 1–8). Academic Press.

Buchegger, S. (n.d.). Performance Analysis of the CONFIDANT Protocol (Cooperation Of Nodes : Fairness In Dynamic Ad-hoc NeTworks) Background : the DSR Protocol. In Components (pp. 226–236). Academic Press.

Channa, M. I., & Ahmed, K. M. (2011). A reliable routing scheme for post-disaster ad hoc communication networks. *Journal of Communication*, *6*(7), 549–557. doi:10.4304/jcm.6.7.549-557

Cherukuri, S., Venkatasubramanian, K. K., & Gupta, S. K. S. (2003). Biosec: A biometric based approach for securing communication in wireless networks of biosensors implanted in the human body. In *Proceedings of the International Conference on Parallel Processing Workshops* (pp. 432–439). 10.1109/ICPPW.2003.1240399

Dağtaş, S., Pekhteryev, G., Şahinoğlu, Z., Çam, H., & Challa, N. (2008). Real-time and secure wireless health monitoring. *International Journal of Telemedicine and Applications*, *2008*, 1–10. doi:10.1155/2008/135808 PMID:18497866

Devi, V. S., & Hegde, N. P. (2018). Multipath Security Aware Routing Protocol for MANET Based on Trust Enhanced Cluster Mechanism for Lossless Multimedia Data Transfer. *Wireless Personal Communications*, *100*(3), 923–940. doi:10.100711277-018-5358-5

Devisri, S., & Balasubramaniam, C. (2013). Secure Routing Using Trust Based Mechaniam in Wireless Sensor Networks (WSNs). *International Journal of Scientific and Engineering Research*, *4*(2), 1–7.

Dimitriou, T., & Ioannis, K. (2008). Security issues in biomedical wireless sensor networks. In *2008 1st International Symposium on Applied Sciences in Biomedical and Communication Technologies, ISABEL 2008* (pp. 1–5). 10.1109/ISABEL.2008.4712577

Duan, J., Yang, D., Zhu, H., Zhang, S., & Zhao, J. (2014). TSRF: A trust-aware secure routing framework in wireless sensor networks. *International Journal of Distributed Sensor Networks*, *2014*(1), 209436. doi:10.1155/2014/209436

Eissa, T., Abdul Razak, S., Khokhar, R. H., & Samian, N. (2013). Trust-based routing mechanism in MANET: Design and implementation. *Mobile Networks and Applications*, *18*(5), 666–677. doi:10.100711036-011-0328-0

Ekong, V., & Ekong, U. (2016). A Survey of Security Vulnerabilities in Wireless Sensor Networks. *Nigerian Journal of Technology*, *35*(2), 392. doi:10.4314/njt.v35i2.21

Fischer, M., Lim, Y. Y., Lawrence, E., & Ganguli, L. K. (2008). ReMoteCare: health monitoring with streaming video. In *Proceedings - 7th International Conference on Mobile Business, ICMB 2008, Creativity and Convergence* (pp. 280–286). 10.1109/ICMB.2008.16

Gao, T., Massey, T., Selavo, L., Crawford, D., Chen, B. R., Lorincz, K., ... Welsh, M. (2007). The advanced health and disaster aid network: A light-weight wireless medical system for tiage. *IEEE Transactions on Biomedical Circuits and Systems*, *1*(3), 203–216. doi:10.1109/TBCAS.2007.910901 PMID:23852414

Gao, Y., & Liu, W. (2014a). *BeTrust : A Dynamic Trust Model Based on Bayesian Inference and Tsallis Entropy for Medical Sensor Networks*. Academic Press.

Gao, Y., & Liu, W. (2014b). BeTrust: A dynamic trust model based on Bayesian inference and Tsallis entropy for medical sensor networks. *Journal of Sensors*, *2014*, 1–10. doi:10.1155/2014/649392

Gidijala, N. S., Datla, S., & Joshi, R. C. (2010). *A Robust Trust Mechanism Algorithm for Secure Power Aware AODV Routing in Mobile Ad Hoc Networks*. doi:10.1007/978-3-642-14834-7_4

Gonzalez, J. M., Anwar, M., & Joshi, J. B. D. (2011). Trust-based approaches to solve routing issues in ad-hoc wireless networks: A survey. In *Proc. 10th IEEE Int. Conf. on Trust, Security and Privacy in Computing and Communications, TrustCom 2011, 8th IEEE Int. Conf. on Embedded Software and Systems, ICESS 2011, 6th Int. Conf. on FCST 2011* (pp. 556–563). 10.1109/TrustCom.2011.72

Ha, I. (2016). Even energy consumption and backside routing: An improved routing protocol for effective data transmission in wireless body area networks. *International Journal of Distributed Sensor Networks*, *12*(7), 1–11. doi:10.1177/1550147716657932

He, D., Chen, C., Chan, S., Bu, J., & Vasilakos, A. V. (2012). ReTrust: Attack-resistant and lightweight trust management for medical sensor networks. *IEEE Transactions on Information Technology in Biomedicine*, *16*(4), 623–632. doi:10.1109/TITB.2012.2194788 PMID:22531816

He, Q., Wu, D., & Khosla, P. (2008). SORI: a secure and objective reputation-based incentive scheme for ad-hoc networks. In 2004 IEEE Wireless Communications and Networking Conference (IEEE Cat. No.04TH8733) (vol. 2, pp. 825-830). doi:10.1109/wcnc.2004.1311293

Hirata, A., Matsuyama, S. I., & Shiozawa, T. (2000). Temperature rises in the human eye exposed to EM waves in the frequency range 0.6-6 GHz. *IEEE Transactions on Electromagnetic Compatibility*, 42(4), 386–393. doi:10.1109/15.902308

Hu, F., Jiang, M., Wagner, M., & Dong, D. C. (2007). Privacy-preserving telecardiology sensor networks: Toward a low-cost portable wireless hardware/software codesign. *IEEE Transactions on Information Technology in Biomedicine*, 11(6), 619–627. doi:10.1109/TITB.2007.894818 PMID:18046937

Huang, Y. M., Hsieh, M. Y., Chao, H. C., Hung, S. H., & Park, J. H. (2009). Pervasive, secure access to a hierarchical sensor-based healthcare monitoring architecture in wireless heterogeneous networks. *IEEE Journal on Selected Areas in Communications*, 27(4), 400–411. doi:10.1109/JSAC.2009.090505

Jamil, F., Iqbal, M., Amin, R., & Kim, D. (2019). Adaptive Thermal-Aware Routing Protocol for Wireless Body Area Network. *Electronics (Basel)*, 8(1), 47. doi:10.3390/electronics8010047

Jiang, S., Cao, Y., Iyengar, S., Kuryloski, P., Jafari, R., Xue, Y., … Wicker, S. (2009). *CareNet: An Integrated Wireless Sensor Networking Environment for Remote Healthcare*. doi:10.4108/icst.bodynets2008.2965

Jwp, Lo, B., & Wells, O. (2004). Ubiquitous monitoring environment for wearable and implantable sensors (UbiMon). In *Imperial College London* (pp. 3–4). Retrieved from http://ubicomp.org/ubicomp2004/adjunct/posters/ng.pdf

Kang, J., & Adibi, S. (2015). *A Review of Security Protocols in mHealth Wireless Body Area Networks*. WBAN. doi:10.1007/978-3-319-19210-9_5

Karthik, N., & Ananthanarayana, V. S. (2018). Context Aware Trust Management Scheme for Pervasive Healthcare. *Wireless Personal Communications*, 105(3), 725–736. doi:10.100711277-018-6091-9

Khan, R. A., & Pathan, A. S. K. (2018). The state-of-the-art wireless body area sensor networks: A survey. *International Journal of Distributed Sensor Networks*, 14(4). doi:10.1177/1550147718768994

Khanna, A., Chaudhary, V., & Gupta, S. H. (2018). Design and Analysis of Energy Efficient Wireless Body Area Network (WBAN) for Health Monitoring. Lecture Notes in Computer Science, 10990, 25–39. doi:10.1007/978-3-662-58039-4_2

Kim, B.-S., Shah, B., Al-Obediat, F., Ullah, S., Kim, K., & Kim, K.-I. (2018). An Enhanced Mobility and Temperature Aware Routing Protocol through Multi-Criteria Decision Making Method in Wireless Body Area Networks. *Applied Sciences (Basel, Switzerland)*, 8(11), 2245. doi:10.3390/app8112245

Kumar, P., & Lee, H. J. (2012). Security issues in healthcare applications using wireless medical sensor networks: A survey. *Sensors (Basel)*, 12(1), 55–91. doi:10.3390120100055 PMID:22368458

Kumar, P., Lee, S. G., & Lee, H. J. (2012). E-SAP: Efficient-strong authentication protocol for healthcare applications using wireless medical sensor networks. *Sensors (Basel)*, 12(2), 1625–1647. doi:10.3390120201625 PMID:22438729

Kwak, K. S., Ullah, S., & Ullah, N. (2010). An overview of IEEE 802.15.6 standard. In *2010 3rd International Symposium on Applied Sciences in Biomedical and Communication Technologies, ISABEL 2010* (pp. 2–7). 10.1109/ISABEL.2010.5702867

Latré, B., Braem, B., Moerman, I., Blondia, C., & Demeester, P. (2011). A survey on wireless body area networks. *Wireless Networks, 17*(1), 1–18. doi:10.100711276-010-0252-4

Le, X. H., Khalid, M., Sankar, R., & Lee, S. (2011). An Efficient Mutual Authentication and Access Control Scheme for Wireless Sensor Networks in Healthcare. *Journal of Networks, 6*(3), 355–364. doi:10.4304/jnw.6.3.355-364

Liang, L., Ge, Y., Feng, G., Ni, W., & Phyo Wai, A. A. (2012). Experimental study on adaptive power control based routing in multi-hop Wireless Body Area Networks. In *GLOBECOM - IEEE Global Telecommunications Conference* (pp. 572–577). 10.1109/GLOCOM.2012.6503174

Liu, Y., Dong, M., Ota, K., & Liu, A. (2016). ActiveTrust: Secure and Trustable Routing in Wireless Sensor Networks. *IEEE Transactions on Information Forensics and Security, 11*(9), 2013–2027. doi:10.1109/TIFS.2016.2570740

Malasri, K., & Wang, L. (2009). Design and implementation of a secure wireless mote-based medical sensor network. *Sensors (Basel), 9*(8), 6273–6297. doi:10.339090806273 PMID:22454585

Mana, M., Feham, M., & Bensaber, B. A. (2011). Trust key management scheme for wireless body area networks. *International Journal of Network Security, 12*(2), 75–83.

Manikandan, S. P., & Manimegalai, R. (2013). Trust based routing to mitigate black hole attack in MANET. *Life Science Journal, 10*(SUPPL.4), 490–498.

Marchang, N., & Datta, R. (2012). Light-weight trust-based routing protocol for mobile ad hoc networks. *IET Information Security, 6*(2), 77. doi:10.1049/iet-ifs.2010.0160

Maskooki, A., Soh, C. B., Gunawan, E., & Low, K. S. (2011). Opportunistic routing for body area network. *2011 IEEE Consumer Communications and Networking Conference. CCNC, 237*–241. doi:10.1109/CCNC.2011.5766463

Merlin, R. T., & Ravi, R. (2019). Novel Trust Based Energy Aware Routing Mechanism for Mitigation of Black Hole Attacks in MANET. *Wireless Personal Communications, 104*(4), 1599–1636. doi:10.100711277-019-06120-8

Mohammadani, K. H., Hussain, J., Khan, R. A., Arain, T. H., Soomro, A. A., Khan, S., & Zafar, H. (2018). An Energy Efficient Routing Protocol for Wireless Body Area Sensor Networks. *Wireless Personal Communications, 99*(4), 1443–1454. doi:10.100711277-018-5285-5

Montgomery, K., Mundt, C., Thonier, G., Tellier, A., Udoh, U., Barker, V., … Kovacs, G. (2005). *Lifeguard - a personal physiological monitor for extreme environments.* doi:10.1109/iembs.2004.1403640

Movassaghi, S., Abolhasan, M., & Lipman, J. (2012). Energy efficient thermal and power aware (ETPA) routing in Body Area Networks. *IEEE International Symposium on Personal, Indoor and Mobile Radio Communications, PIMRC, 13*(3), 1108–1113. 10.1109/PIMRC.2012.6362511

Movassaghi, S., Abolhasan, M., Lipman, J., Smith, D., & Jamalipour, A. (2014). Wireless body area networks: A survey. *IEEE Communications Surveys and Tutorials, 16*(3), 1658–1686. doi:10.1109/SURV.2013.121313.00064

Muhammad, K. (2010). BARI+: A biometric based distributed key management approach for wireless body area networks. *Sensors (Basel), 10*(4), 3911–3933. doi:10.3390100403911 PMID:22319333

Nasser, N., & Chen, Y. (2007). Secure multipath routing protocol for wireless sensor networks. *Proceedings - International Conference on Distributed Computing Systems.* 10.1109/ICDCSW.2007.72

Ng, H. S., Sim, M. L., & Tan, C. M. (2006). Security issues of wireless sensor networks in healthcare applications. *BT Technology Journal, 24*(2), 138–144. doi:10.100710550-006-0051-8

Raja, K. S., & Kiruthika, U. (2015). An Energy Efficient Method for Secure and Reliable Data Transmission in Wireless Body Area Networks Using RelAODV. *Wireless Personal Communications, 83*(4), 2975–2997. doi:10.100711277-015-2577-x

Ramli, S. N., Ahmad, R., & Abdollah, M. F. (2013). Electrocardiogram (ECG) signals as biometrics in securing wireless body area network. In *2013 8th International Conference for Internet Technology and Secured Transactions, ICITST 2013* (pp. 536–541). 10.1109/ICITST.2013.6750259

Reddy, Y. B., & Selmic, R. (2011). Trust-based Packet Transfer in Wireless Sensor Networks. *International Journal on Advances in Network Security, 4*(3), 198–207. doi:10.2316/p.2010.726-009

Saleem. (2009). On the Security Issues in Wireless Body Area Networks. *International Journal of Digital Content Technology and Its Applications, 3*(3), 1–4. doi:10.4156/jdcta.vol3.issue3.22

Shaikh, R. A., Lee, S., Khan, M. A. U., & Song, Y. J. (2006). LSec: Lightweight Security Protocol for Distributed Wireless Sensor Network. In *IFIP International Conference on Personal Wireless Communications* (pp. 367–377). 10.1007/11872153_32

Shen, X., Lu, R., Kato, N., Lin, X., & Nemoto, Y. (2009). Sage: A strong privacy-preserving scheme against global eavesdropping for ehealth systems. *IEEE Journal on Selected Areas in Communications, 27*(4), 365–378. doi:10.1109/JSAC.2009.090502

Singh, A. V., Juyal, V., & Saggar, R. (2017). Trust based Intelligent Routing Algorithm for Delay Tolerant Network using Artificial Neural Network. *Wireless Networks, 23*(3), 693–702. doi:10.100711276-015-1166-y

Sun, B., & Li, D. (2017). A Comprehensive Trust-Aware Routing Protocol with Multi-Attributes for WSNs. *IEEE Access: Practical Innovations, Open Solutions, 6*, 4725–4741. doi:10.1109/ACCESS.2017.2786944

Tabandeh, M., Jahed, M., Ahourai, F., & Moradi, S. (2009). A thermal-aware shortest hop routing algorithm for in vivo biomedical sensor networks. In *ITNG 2009 - 6th International Conference on Information Technology: New Generations* (pp. 1612–1613). 10.1109/ITNG.2009.274

Tajeddine, A., Kayssi, A., Chehab, A., Elhajj, I., & Itani, W. (2015). CENTERA: A centralized trust-based efficient routing protocol with authentication for wireless sensor networks. *Sensors (Switzerland), 15*(2), 3299–3333. doi:10.3390150203299 PMID:25648712

Takahashi, D., Xiao, Y., & Hu, F. (2007). LTRT: Least total-route temperature routing for embedded biomedical sensor networks. In *GLOBECOM - IEEE Global Telecommunications Conference* (pp. 641–645). IEEE. 10.1109/GLOCOM.2007.125

Tang, Q., Tummala, N., Gupta, S. K. S., & Schwiebert, L. (2005a). Communication scheduling to minimize thermal effects of implanted biosensor networks in homogeneous tissue. *IEEE Transactions on Biomedical Engineering*, *52*(7), 1285–1294. doi:10.1109/TBME.2005.847527 PMID:16041992

Tang, Q., Tummala, N., Gupta, S. K. S., & Schwiebert, L. (2005b). TARA: Thermal-Aware Routing Algorithm for Implanted Sensor Networks. In *Proceedings of 1st IEEE International Conference Distributed Computing in Sensor Systems* (pp. 206–217). 10.1007/11502593_17

Ullah, S., Higgins, H., Braem, B., Latre, B., Blondia, C., Moerman, I., ... Kwak, K. S. (2012). A comprehensive survey of wireless body area networks on PHY, MAC, and network layers solutions. *Journal of Medical Systems*, *36*(3), 1065–1094. doi:10.100710916-010-9571-3 PMID:20721685

Wac, K., Bults, R., Van Beijnum, B., Widya, I., Jones, V. M., & Konstantas, D., ... Hermens, H. (2009). Mobile patient monitoring: The MobiHealth system. In *Proceedings of the 31st Annual International Conference of the IEEE Engineering in Medicine and Biology Society: Engineering the Future of Biomedicine, EMBC 2009* (pp. 1238–1241). 10.1109/IEMBS.2009.5333477

Waluyo, A. B., Pek, I., Chen, X., & Yeoh, W. S. (2009). Design and evaluation of lightweight middleware for personal wireless body area network. In Personal and Ubiquitous Computing (Vol. 13, pp. 509–525). doi:10.100700779-009-0222-y

Wang, B., Chen, X., & Chang, W. (2014). A light-weight trust-based QoS routing algorithm for ad hoc networks. *Pervasive and Mobile Computing*, *13*, 164–180. doi:10.1016/j.pmcj.2013.06.004

Wang, H., Fang, H., Xing, L., & Chen, M. (2011). An integrated biometric-based security framework using wavelet-domain HMM in wireless body area networks (WBAN). In *IEEE International Conference on Communications*. 10.1109/icc.2011.5962757

Welsh, M., Moulton, S., Fulford-Jones, T., & Malan, D. J. (2004). CodeBlue : An Ad Hoc Sensor Network Infrastructure for Emergency Medical Care. In *International Workshop on Wearable and Implantable Body Sensor Networks* (p. 5). Retrieved from http://nrs.harvard.edu/urn-3:HUL.InstRepos:3191012

Wood, A. D., Stankovic, J. A., Virone, G., Selavo, L., He, Z., Cao, Q., ... Stoleru, R. (2008). Context-aware wireless sensor networks for assisted living and residential monitoring. *IEEE Network* (Vol. 22). doi:10.1109/MNET.2008.4579768

Xia, H., Zhang, S., Li, B., Li, L., & Cheng, X. (2018). Towards a Novel Trust-Based Multicast Routing for VANETs. *Security and Communication Networks*, *2018*, 1–12. doi:10.1155/2018/7608198

Yang, T., Xiangyang, X., Peng, L., Tonghui, L., & Leina, P. (2018). A secure routing of wireless sensor networks based on trust evaluation model. *Procedia Computer Science*, *131*, 1156–1163. doi:10.1016/j.procs.2018.04.289

Zahariadis, T., Trakadas, P., Leligou, H. C., Maniatis, S., & Karkazis, P. (2013). A novel trust-aware geographical routing scheme for wireless sensor networks. *Wireless Personal Communications*, *69*(2), 805–826. doi:10.100711277-012-0613-7

Zhang, P., & Ma, J. (2018). Channel characteristic aware privacy protection mechanism in WBAN. *Sensors (Switzerland)*, *18*(8), 2403. doi:10.339018082403 PMID:30042302

Zhang, Z., Wang, H., Vasilakos, A. V., & Fang, H. (2012). ECG-cryptography and authentication in body area networks. *IEEE Transactions on Information Technology in Biomedicine*, *16*(6), 1070–1078. doi:10.1109/TITB.2012.2206115 PMID:22752143

Chapter 9
A Critical Study on Internet of Medical Things for Secure WBAN

Saima Sultana
Hamdard University, Pakistan

Shamim Akhtar
Majmaah University, Saudi Arabia

Sadia Nazim
Hamdard University, Pakistan

Pardeep Kumar
https://orcid.org/0000-0002-8624-9020
Quaid-e-Awam University of Engineering, Science, and Technology, Pakistan

Manzoor Ahmed Hashmani
University Technology PETRONAS, Malaysia

Syed Sajjad Hussain Rizvi
Hamdard University, Pakistan

ABSTRACT

During the recent decade, wireless body area network (WBAN) was developed and prioritized. This gives reliability, energy efficiency, and guaranteed results. Moreover, internet of medical things (IoMT) also enhances the significance of WBAN networks. To achieve high throughput, performance, and efficiency, WBAN deserves a new protocol definition as compared to general wireless sensor network along with a more enhanced framework. The standard 802.15.6 with PHY and MAC layers follow the standardization of WBAN. The wireless nature of the network and various varieties of sensors in the presence of IoMT made it possible to develop new, effective, innovative, and demand-driven solutions for health improvement and quality of service. In the recent literature, the researchers have proposed an IoMT-based secure framework for WBAN. In this chapter, an in-depth and comprehensive depiction of the security issues of IoMT-based framework of the wireless network is highlighted that incorporates security measures in different levels of the WBAN network.

DOI: 10.4018/978-1-7998-2803-7.ch009

INTRODUCTION

he rising population in the world hits the paradigm of discovered technology to drive solutions to the problematic era. At the edge of decay, various automated phases of human life interact concisely with technological enhancements to seek worth, pleasure, and comfortability in an effective manner. According to a survey total population in Pakistan is about 207,774,000, as of July 2019, based on the latest United Nations estimation. Pakistan's population equals to 2.65% of the total world population. It declares a noticeable and markable figure for elderly people included. Figure 1 shows the graphical comparison between ages and available population in percentage while Table 1 shows further specification. To survive a healthy life, elderly persons endure one of the major issues as high healthcare costs. This is very crucial to take care of either an elderly person or a patient who is not fit physically may have some healthcare issues(Singh & Singh, 2016). With some dominant aspects, his caregiving lies in cost, security, comfort and reliability issues. In many cases like an injury or after a severe accident, it is mandatory for the patient to care deeply and sensitively. To stay at the hospital sometime gives anxiety and frustration. Cost, privacy and limitation on patients are other major concerns (Hayajneh, Almashaqbeh, Ullah, & Vasilakos, 2014) (Van Daele, Moerman, & Demeester, 2014).

The available proposed solution could be the use of technology as some tiny, cheap and less weight intelligent sensors are invented. Those sensors could be worn up or embedded in the side or around the body (Cavallari, Martelli, Rosini, Buratti, & Verdone, 2014). These sensors send their data that is a vital sign to an attached server, either wired or wireless. The wired one is much complex and costly for deployment and maintenance too. The wireless system is much cost-effective and easy to use. In lieu to achieve wireless system through sensors on or inside the body wireless sensor network works. Specifically to get entire achievements a new network comes into being, named Wireless Body Area Network (WBAN) (Van Daele et al., 2014). For transmission of vitals bring together from the patient to the medical expert, present in a remote location. An efficient, secure, reliable, up to date framework is required. So in this research paper, an IoMT based secure framework for WBAN is proposed.

Figure 1. Age paradigm

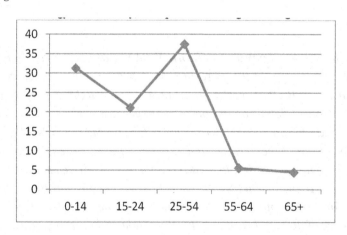

Table 1. Population Criteria

Age	% Age	Male	Female
0-14 years	31.36%	33,005,623	31,265,463
15-24 years	21.14%	22,337,897	20,980,455
25-54 years	37.45%	39,864,417	36,907,683
55-64 years	5.57%	5,739,817	5,669,495
65+	4.48%	4,261,917	4,910,0945

The proposed framework is consisting of three layers; Tier 1, Tier 2 and Tier 3. All three hierarchal tiers work together to form a secure framework.

This term WBAN was first coined by Van Dam et al. WBAN comprises some small intelligent nodes, called sensing nodes. These nodes are attached to a GUI device may be a tab or smart cellular phone. This device is sometimes called a gateway, which provides a connection between WBAN sensors and the internet (Van Daele et al., 2014).

Now a day, WBAN is most attractive for the researchers as WBAN, the noninvasive nature of the network makes it easy to get the status of patient health automatically without interrupting the personal life and then report it to any nearby coordinator node.

This node is basically responsible to forward vitals of a patient to the hospital or medical professionals. Such monitoring mechanism saves time, saves cost, trigger alerts on time can save one's life to get enter in a crucial stage without interrupting (Hayajneh et al., 2014).

WBAN is a convenient, reliable, non-invasive and accurate network that provides a good solution for e-health issues. WBAN is used to diagnose different life-threatening diseases. Work in close vicinity, on and inside the human body as well. WBAN protects a patient from previous and upcoming dangers of illness as well as a precast alert through its intelligent behavior.

Patients experience more mobility and are not advised to stay at the hospital for a longer time. As far as the technological era is spreading, the world moves aggressively and speedily toward easiness and comfort. So tracking patients is being more and easier. WBAN is a network consists of nodes, which gather and process as required information from the patient and deliver it to a centralized smart device, they consume energy. This smart device could be a chip, smartphone or computer, tasked to communicate the vitals properly in a timed manner. Now the issue is to save/consume less energy. For that purpose, different techniques are used. IETF (Internet Engineering Task Force) defined WBAN standard that is 802.15.6. This new and attractive standard was proposed to define the first physical (PHY) and second medium access control (MAC) layer for WBAN (Kwak, Ullah, & Ullah, 2010).

Research Motivation

The basic research motivation is to study an IoMT based security framework of WBAN by discussing its application areas and identifies common issues and highlights security concerns of IoMT based framework of WBAN. Rest of the paper is organized as follows, WBAN is covered in the first section, Second section focuses on secure framework or architecture, the Third section finalizes taxonomy and security concerns of WBAN, the Fourth section covers open issues and challenges of the IoMT based framework for WBAN and the fifth section concludes the research along with future direction.

INTERNET OF MEDICAL THINGS

Internet of Medical Things (IoMT) is a scheme of interconnected physical devices, whose availability occurs through the internet (Senthilkumar, Manikandan, Devi, & Lokesh, 2018).

Subsidy of IoMT

- Continuous monitoring regardless of time and location.
- Proves efficiency in an emergency situation when immediate steps of health care needed
- Works efficiently and perfectly when a medical expert is at a remote location.
- Manages the system's diversity and interoperability (Senthilkumar et al., 2018).

WIRELESS BODY AREA NETWORK

WBAN is a new charming technology to the world so a consequence domain of WBAN is in its research and development phase and not very clear (Latré, Braem, Moerman, Blondia, & Demeester, 2011). WBAN is basically an extended and specialized form of Wireless Sensor Network WSN. WBAN enhances the market of WSN besides its design is affected by new paradigms and protocols (Cavallari et al., 2014). Wireless body area network WBAN is also called wireless sensor network WSN or BSN body sensor network, consisting of sensors computing devices attached through a LAN or ad hoc network is either embedded inside or attached outside of the body. These sensor devices can either be saved in hand or in the pocket is connected to a tab or pad which provides GUI and data hub devices (Hayajneh et al., 2014).

In order to gather vitals and send them to the concerned one involves the interaction of the human body and computer devices. For the communication of data, the requirement of a network arises. Different techniques from Wireless Sensor Network WSN and ad hoc networks are used that make communication possible through sensor devices. These sensors could be an implant or deployed on the human body and attached to a network that the network uses the techniques of WSN and called Wireless Body Area Network WBAN. But many commonalities and some differences as well, to highlight basic elements Table 1 is used with some basic parameters. Although WBAN is derived from WSN so a comparison table clarifies it in detail with parameters affecting both (Arya & Bilandi, 2007) (Fernández-Caramés & Fraga-Lamas, 2018). IoMT works somewhere above the framework of WBAN. Continuous monitoring in emergency situations is only possible through it.

A Comparison of WBAN and WSN

See Table 2.

Table 2. A Comparison between WBAN & WSN

Parameters	WBAN	WSN
Deployment	Many devices, more added when needed	Many more devices to compensate for node failure
Mobility	Easy, share the same pattern	Static, stationary
Data Rate	Periodic, stable data rates, heterogeneous	Event based monitor, irregular, homogenous
Scale	Cm/m	m/km
Number of Nodes	Few, limited	Redundant
Accuracy of Result	By node accuracy	By node redundancy
Life of Node	Several Years	Several Years
Node Task	Multiple Task	Dedicated Task
Node Size	Small is essential	Small is preferable
Network Topology	Movable	Fixed, stationary
Node Placement	Difficult	Easy
Power Supply	Inaccessible, difficult to manage	Accessible, easy to maintain
Power Demand	Low, difficult	Large, energy supply easy
Bio-Compatibility	Must	Not considered
Security Level	High, for patients data	Low
Technology	Low power technology required	Bluetooth, Zigbee, WLAN, GPRS

LITERATURE REVIEW

(Singh & Singh, 2016) Provides a review of existing work in the field of Wireless Body Area Network (WBAN). The efficient, reliable and secure network communication between sensor nodes consumes energy. To cope up with energy related issues many ways explored and very few were found effective. Cluster head selection becomes a major issue for some energy efficient protocols. After wards data loss is a big issue, which causes latency. Some of major components along with various devices is discussed.

(Hayajneh et al., 2014) Provides an extensive study about E-health monitoring, which becomes very popular during previous some decays. For probabilistic channel access, various mathematical analysis of WBAN related formulae derived. WBAN architecture with coexistence is elaborated for some real life consequences.

(Van Daele et al., 2014) According to study the fame captured by Internet of things is due to cumulative size of wireless networks dwindling of electrical devices. Both sanction simultaneous maturity of WBAN. This paper is provided for an extensive study of status and opportunities of WBAN. It equates two examples of progression towards internet of things. The study elaborates challenges of WBAN and WBAN beautifully, along with available testbeds.

(Cavallari et al., 2014) In the research WBAN's main applicability technologies, various standards, highlighted design issues and evolutionary updates are provoked effectively. Case studies for investigation and testimony articles have been elaborated.

(Kwak et al., 2010) For the calibration of WBAN IEEE 802.15.6 is developed as communication standard augmented for tiny squat powered sensors. The communication standard takes place its core values at Medium Access Layer(MAC) along with physical (PHY) layer. Some of security concerns elaborated for communication at distinct frequency bands to make the communication safe.

(Senthilkumar et al., 2018) This study proves a good comparison of advantage and disadvantage of IoMT along with their impacts. The study reveals many technological aspects of wireless communication laterally highlight many customized application areas of WBAN.

(Latré et al., 2011) The research paper compels the agility comforts of patients with advent of WBAN. Also depicts minute variances of WBAN with WSN along with WBAN architectural advents. Propose innovative ubiquitous notion impression with a number of protocols. Requirement with latest trends are underlined by being encircled of WBAN turf.

(Arya & Bilandi, 2007) The focused study depicts a brief intro with multiple angle of applicability, limitations and challenges of WBAN. Patient care and nursing for elderly persons with many add on facilities is worded with existing MAC and network protocols. It also covers cryptographically considerable issues for making the WBAN safe and secure.

The article of (Fernández-Caramés & Fraga-Lamas, 2018) analyze the importance of smart clothing as an advent of WBAN. From smart to IoT empowered clothing, various aspects of life are prompted towards automation. This study demonstrates various past and future aspects of smart clothing.

(Yaseen et al., 2018) Emphasises on work flow of sensor nodes amongst various versions of communication age. These sensors are vision with an angle of e-health care system. The survey motivates some of security concerns for accurate communication over networks. A taxonomy of open issues and future challenges is also debated with respect to precise security metrics.

(Salayma, Al-Dubai, Romdhani, & Nasser, 2017) Represents 2 foremost concerns of WBAN. Initially it depicts the essentiality of reliability for WBAN, afterwards it delivers key encounters of current sate of art.

(Qureshi & Krishnan, 2018) Expresses the reasons behind the popularity of IoMT as sufficient use of technology, posh digits of medical health care expenses, stretched pausing delay time, less grasp of perception about cultivating quality of life. This study endeavors the hardware machineries of IoMT devices, required in fusion of WBAN and IoMT.

A Taxonomy is draft through different gathered collection of WSN, depicts various services offered according to its angle of usability. Various WSN applications along with its characterization features are discussed in Taxonomical order.

(N. & H., 2016) Discovers various applications of Body Area Network, provides an exhaustive survey of state of the art research work. The current covered aspects of security is underscored in eesence of making the WBAN strongly secure.

(Movassaghi, Abolhasan, Lipman, Smith, & Jamalipour, 2014) Led to multiple sectors of WBAN. It classifies numerous applications in other than medical arena side by side detailed specification of protocols for communication channels with respect to energy harvesting and secure transmission. Current state of the art is included.

(Khan & Pathan, 2018) Discusses the evolvement of WBAN after mature existence of WSN. This convent possiblity took place only with due reason of adherence to tremendous technological achievements. Tiny electronic components works magically, so gained significant courtesy in topical, mostly are towards human health paradigm.

(Al-Janabi, Al-Shourbaji, Shojafar, & Shamshirband, 2017) This study is a virtuous addition in WBAN to complement with various types of sensor nodes along with their uses and a multi domain architectural view of WBAN in terms of data transmission flow is discussed. The multilevel accessing hierarchy addicts worthy information to WBAN. The research decently deploys security concerns from multiple angles for effective communication among sensor nodes. Also discusses some security threats and their possible solutions. This study clarifies important security measures and their updated solutions in the lightening of contemporary necessities.

(Anwar, Bakhtiari, Zainal, Hanan Abdullah, & Qureshi, 2014) Provides a concurrent study concerns about wireless sensor network, its considerable security issues and threats bouts. The study depicts that numerous vital threats and attacks raids the security violence in slighter time domain. Initially it discovers chief design encounters for wireless sensor networks, afterwards it displays integral classification of security attacks. Some of main and mark able threats and attacks are deliberated deeply with end to end their technical clarifications.

(Abdullah, Butt, Ashraf, Qureshi, & Ullah, 2018) Covers the viable issues, reasonable concerns and challenging data privacy in WBANs. A digital signature cryptographic technique based hybrid security solution is proposed for secure communication. State of the art security and privacy mechanisms are evaluated and analyzed in terms of acting functionality. On the basis of digital signature mechanism an integrated Biometric security system is anticipated. An in depth judgement of secure surviving protocols of WBAN are gauged for performance criticality.

(Al Ameen, Liu, & Kwak, 2012) Depletion of a network associated with healthcare grasp typical attention. Various viable aspects of measuring health condition play a critical role in futuristic condition. This study's main focus is at emerging technology and reliable secure communication of WBAN. The foremost attention of the research is data security alarming triggers and their measures in consideration with architectural interpretation. An in depth study reveals the facts and figures of WSN chipset market sale to impose the rate of growth and revenue generation in millions.

(Seliem & Elgazzar, 2019) Comes with a reliable framework IoTeWay for IoT based IPv6 Low Power networks, experimenting smart home applications while theory probe security resiliency. This application is trisected into smart devices tier, platform and infrastructure tier, and the application tier. To mitigate huge data cloud supporting tier is able to serve.

(Hudson & Clark, 2019) Focuses the essential part of medical devices of WBAN and provides an enhanced study of implantable and wearable standards.

(Uluagac, Lee, Beyah, & Copeland, 2008) This research reveals the fact that among numerous network routing protocols only some are developed in deliberation of security. Less power and storage are considerable issues for WBAN devices hence asymmetric cryptographic algorithms are inappropriate. Obstacle security threats are intensively discussed with their common cons and pro according to WSN.

(Kang & Adibi, 2015) It is a WBAN survey review study which unveil the knots of security and confidentiality for mHealth. Also postulates observations and comparisons for human health as WBAN, WSN, CT and MC. The research continues to make aware about individual and cumulative attacks on WBAN or WSN which results unrepairable damage to patient health or leads to life threats. Also points some of security threat target area and divides the knowledge in OSI layers with applicability of WBAN, WSN, MC and CT.

(Mary & Kannammal, 2017) Here it is a comparative study among multiple WSN security protocols, taking an essence of architecture and security disputes follows common OSI architecture. In contrast to corresponds between application and security requirements of WSN more or less all related security protocols are compared on the basis of their distinct features.

(Mainanwal, Gupta, & Upadhayay, 2015) Compares a number of diversified security threatening issues.

ELEMENTAL VIEW OF WBAN

Although the wireless body area network is a complete system, assigned for specific tasks, functionality and performance depend upon the basic elements the whole system is comprised of.

Sensing Node

The main purpose of the sensing node is to sense, observe, and take samples from the human body or its surroundings. This attribute could be physical, chemical, biological or psychological. They are supervised and controlled by a coordinator node (Hayajneh et al., 2014). Then after sensing this input signal/signals is processed and stored temporarily. Afterward, it is passed over to gateways using the wireless network. This data is then transmitted over WLAN, GPRS, and Radio network for processes in real-time for analysis or maybe diverted back (Singh & Singh, 2016). The goal is to provide the health aware and risk-free survival to the patients without interrupting their routines (Hayajneh et al., 2014). These sensing nodes are placed on or inside the body with an ability of mobility (Yaseen et al., 2018). Sensors and their taxonomy are as below.

Figure 2. WBAN elemental Description

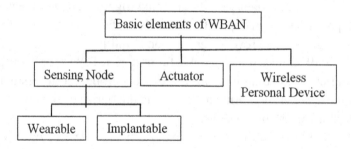

Sensing nodes consist of four components, transceiver, battery, microprocessor, and a sensing component (Salayma et al., 2017). Sensing device which senses the signal, equipped by sensing hardware, power device, and a transceiver. The second part is an actuator which is categorically hardware, responsible for taking a single or set of actions on the response of the sensing node, according to its function description. May consists of a

Medication supplier, an inventory holder, and a memory card accordingly. The third device is a Personal Device; this could be a computer, a tab or a cellular phone. The main purpose of this device is to save and process information of the sensing node and actuator (Singh & Singh, 2016). WBAN comprises of few or much low range (in body 3 m & 3 on the body to body) very tiny sensors, which falls basically in 2 types. (Cavallari et al., 2014) (Qureshi & Krishnan, 2018)

Wearable Sensor: As the word describes wearable so these are the electromagnetic sensors that are deployed on the body or sewed within the clothes that even could be worn for gathering vital signs (Arya & Bilandi, 2007). Like body temperature, blood pressure and SpO2 which checks oxygen saturation level and relates to the cardiac cycle. Both protect a person from an expected heart attack. ECG sensor also takes vitals of heartbeat according to time. EEG sensor senses the activity of the brain and alerts for the upcoming situation (Fernández-Caramés & Fraga-Lamas, 2018) (Salayma et al., 2017).

Implementable Sensor: These devices could be injected as prescribed by a physician, under the skin or implanted inside the body with transplanted or affected organ to monitor the functionality and observe the impurities (Arya & Bilandi, 2007). Implantable devices could be an insulin pump, Cardiac Defibrillators /pacemakers, deep brain neuron stimulators, cancer detection, Gastric Simulators, Foot Drop implants (Salayma et al., 2017).

Actuators

Actuators are the movable part of WSN activated upon receiving data from the sensor. Their structure is similar to sensors consists of a transceiver, battery, memory, and an actuator unit. Actuators are used to provide the drug to a patient periodically prescribed by a physician in a predefined order or upon a sensor detection of an abnormality. That drug could help to maintain or control sugar level in blood, body temperature level or could be used for a stretch in jaws and left the upper side of the body as an indication of a possible upcoming heart attack (Qureshi & Krishnan, 2018) (Salayma et al., 2017).

Wireless Personal Device (PD)

PD behaved like a bridge between sensors, actuators and a processing device (a laptop, a computer or a smartphone) (Yaseen et al., 2018). It consists of a transceiver, rich power source, a processor and large memory (Salayma et al., 2017). This sophisticated unit is named as Body Controller Unit (BCU), a sink, a body gateway (Arya & Bilandi, 2007).

COMMUNICATION ARCHITECTURE

The 802.15.6 Standard

For transmitting and reception of signaling data in WBAN latest available standard specified by Task Group TG6 (November 2007) is IEEE 802.15.6 standard (Cavallari et al., 2014). An updated version later released in February 2012. It ranges between 400 MHz to 11.2 GHz. It provides communication among low power, low cost with minimum data rate devices to work with, on, and inside the human body. It comprises 2 layers of PHY and MAC (Kwak et al., 2010).

Table 3. IEEE 802.15.6

Technology	IEEE 802.15.6
Standard	Body Area Network
Frequency Band	402 – 50MHz
Data rate	0.9714Mbps
Coverage Range	2 to 5 m
Modulation Scheme	DPSK
Network Topology	Star or 2 hoptree

PHY Layer

3 bands in the physical layer available due to a vast range of applications, the Narrow Band (NB), the Ultra-Wide Band (UWB) and Human Body Communication (HBC) (Kwak et al., 2010) (Cavallari et al., 2014) (Hayajneh et al., 2014). The PHY frame header contains a synchronization header with a preamble (SFD), (PHR) with a fixed payload size of 127 bytes. The total frame size should be less than 127 bytes (Perillo & Heinzelman, 2005).

Table 4. Physical Layer Bands

Band	Frequency	Application
NB	400,800,900 MHz 2.3,2,4GHz	Protects adjacent channel interference
UWB	3.1-11.2 GHz	For authorized users
HBC	10-50 GHz	Video, voice stream not support

MAC Layer

The IETF has defined only a single MAC layer to get channel access for all three flavors of physical layers. The Medium Access Control (MAC) layer defines how to access the medium in an efficient, reliable and fruitful fashion. The MAC layer should provide flexibility, less power consumption, and less latency as much as possible (Arya & Bilandi, 2007). MAC layer is all about to access the channel which is consisting of superframes. The basic channel accessing mechanism is occupied through a superframe. A superframe structure covers the whole channel and consists of a beacon period. A Beacon period provides a boundary to the entire superframe. To support possible data flow in WBAN combines both Contention Access and Contention Free techniques. WBAN 802.15.6 works in Active and Inactive modes. The inactive mode is for no communication. In the case of active mode Wireless, Personal Device chose one of 3 modes to operate. Beacon Mode with Beacon Period (Superframe), Non-Beacon mode with Superframe and Non-Beacon Mode without Superframe. A body area coordinator or Wireless personal device depicts to operate in one of three modes (Yaseen et al., 2018) (Qureshi & Krishnan, 2018) (Salayma et al., 2017) (Cavallari et al., 2014).

Figure 3. A Superframe structure

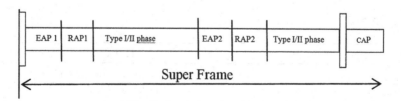

Beacon Mode with Beacon Period (Superframe)

Figure 3 shows a superframe structure which is divided into different phases that is Exclusive Access Period(EAP1), Random Access Period(RAP1), Type I/II phase, Exclusive Access Period(EAP2), Random Access Period(RAP2) and Contention Access Period(CAP). During the periods EAP, RAP and CAP transmission is occurred by contention for allocation of resources using the CSMA/CA mechanism. This CSMA/CA mechanism is basic for wireless transmission. In wireless transmission, data traffic could be of 2 types Normal/regular or emergency data. RAP1, RAP2, and CAP all play with normal regular traffic only. While EAP1, EAP2 are used during an emergency. In WBAN nodes sensor gather the vitals in a regular manner. But in case of any abnormality found in taken vitals so to get samples of vitals repeats periodically in a rapid manner and resultantly data traffic becomes high or dense during an emergency. Type I/II phase both dedicated to interval allocation for uplink, downlink, bi-link and delay bi-link. It uses polling for resource allocation. Wireless Personal Device keeps control of all allocation of intervals and can disable by setting 0 to any interval (Qureshi & Krishnan, 2018) (N. & H., 2016)

Non Beacon Mode With Superframe

This access mode enables WBAN nodes to communicate in either phase. i.e I or II.

Non Beacon Mode Without Superframe

During this mode Wireless, Personal Device is allowed to communicate only in type II unscheduled (Kwak et al., 2010) (Cavallari et al., 2014) (Qureshi & Krishnan, 2018).

THE PROPOSED COMMUNICATION ARCHITECTURE OF WBAN

The architecture of WBAN depends concisely on the deployment of the node, and the IoMT device is application-specific and demand-driven. The basic framework of IoMT nodes is distributed in, on or around the body. Node placement specifically not static as the body moves run so the architecture of the WBAN framework dynamically changes in a topological manner. Mostly WBAN follows a star or multi-hop routing schemes. But IoMT based framework remains unchanged. According to the research protocol definition of WBAN spans communication from the IoMT node attached with the body (elderly person) to the concerned body (hospital, physician, emergency) through the IoMT devices. Because of the traveling of data, IoMT framework architecture can be divided into 3 tiers as defined in (Latré et al., 2011) (N. & H., 2016) (Hayajneh et al., 2014) (Movassaghi et al., 2014) (Khan & Pathan, 2018). The design goal of the framework is based on security, availability. Figure 4 also shows a clear concept.

Tier 1: WBAN Intra structure: Encompasses intra body communication between nodes and their gateway as a wireless personal device, connected with IoMT and nodes to nodes themselves. It consists of many tiny sensor devices, actuators, and wireless personal device. The criticality factor is high as very near to the human body, which ranges about 3m. Tier 1 target is the transformation of data securely to the access point present in the next tier called IoMT (Fernández-Caramés & Fraga-Lamas, 2018) (Movassaghi et al., 2014).

Figure 4. Multitier WBAN in IoMT Environment

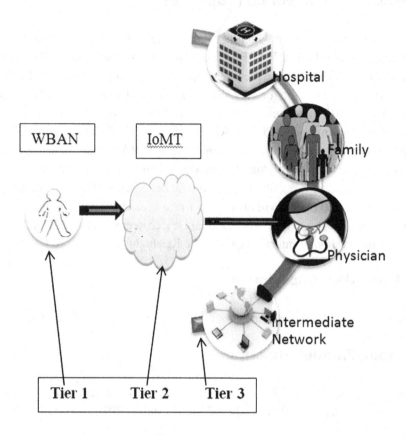

Tier 2: WBAN Inter structure: Tier 2 bridges the gap between tier 1 and tier 3. It is IoMT. It connects WBAN intra structure with beyond the structure through IoMT devices for communication. Tier 2 acts as a bridge for secure transmission between the wireless personal device and an external network.

Tier 3: WBAN Beyond structure: Connect WBAN to the concern staff/ caretaker/ medical persons through IoMT devices and transfer information. Stores received data on the medical server in the database so that on the basis of entities containing values appropriate decisions could be trigged in a timely manner.

TAXONOMY

See Figure 5.

Figure 5. Taxonomy of WBAN

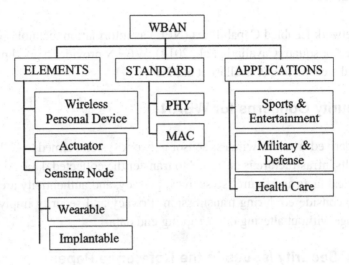

APPLICATIONS OF WBAN

Although there are so many aspects of deployment of WBAN on or around the body area, the main areas are as follows (N. & H., 2016) (Khan & Pathan, 2018).

Health Care

At first glance, it is enough attractive fields for WBAN deployment, through which an elderly person or a patient is acknowledged to the concerns. Treated and get sufficient and required attention as early in a continuous and regular fashion. WBAN is deployed through sensor nodes inside or around the body infinite number that helps to collect the data in the form of vital signs from a patient such as continuous monitoring of heart and brain, keep an eye on the sugar level, etc. By deploying WBAN neither an irregularity can be missed nor can any unusual foreseen be happened. WBAN also works for electrocardiogram (ECG), electroencephalogram (EEG), electro mammogram (EMG), pulse oximetry, drug delivery, postoperative and temperature monitoring, glucose level, toxin, blood level, etc (Cavallari et al., 2014)

Sports & Entertainment

WBAN could also be deployed in the sports and entertainment field. WBAN takes data like vital signs for assessment of blood pressure, heartbeat rate, friction in the movement of major joints, attack of viruses, etc. WBAN could also trigger an alarm for any unforeseen changes in spinal and brain activities. So that could help in maintaining a truly healthy lifestyle and prevent injuries in essence with freedom. WBAN help to make the entertainment industry much more sparkling. Movement of body parts is controlled by the motion capturing technique by means of gyroscopes and accelerators connected to a central node and worn by the actor and relevant team. In the gaming zone, WBAN controls the movement of a body not only geographically but specifically also with aspects of creativity. (Cavallari et al., 2014)

Military and Defense

The military uses Network Enabled Capabilities (NEC) as information technology to enhance the performance of individual or squad (Cavallari et al., 2014). WBAN provides a good presumption of movements, whether friendly or hostile. (Cavallari et al., 2014)

IoMT Based Security Concerns for WBAN

A WBAN system is derived from the wireless sensor network system, aimed to collect life-sensitive and critical patient data. Its infrastructure is designed to transfer the collected data. As patients data consist of important and critical facts and figures so secrecy, privacy, and authenticity are key majors and significant factors to be considered during transmission. Privacy and security imply the data collection, processing, and storage without altering or corrupting end data.

A Comparison of Security Issues in the Reference Paper

Table 5. A Comparison of Security issues in various referencs

Security Issue/Reference	11	12	13	14	15	16	17	18	19	20	21	22	23	24
Data Confidentiality	√		√	√	√			√						
Data Integrity	√	√	√		√	√	√		√	√		√	√	√
Data Freshness	√		√		√	√	√	√		√	√	√	√	
Data Authentication	√						√	√	√	√	√	√	√	√
Availability	√	√	√					√		√		√	√	
Data Encryption							√	√	√	√		√		√
Secure Management	√			√				√		√		√		
Dependability	√									√				
Secure Localization	√		√				√	√		√		√	√	
Accountability	√													
Flexibility	√							√	√	√				

- **Data Confidentiality:** Data confidentiality refers to the protection of a patient's data from altering and must be protected against unauthorized access and alteration; otherwise it may cause hazards (Al-Janabi et al., 2017). Sometimes wireless sensor network contains sensitive and crucial data so higher grades of confidentiality is needed (Anwar et al., 2014) (Abdullah et al., 2018) and could be achieved through data encryption techniques (Moshaddique Al Ameen, Jingwei Liu, 2015) which includes digital signatures and certificates, along with passcodes. The system is accessible only through authentication (Seliem & Elgazzar, 2019).
- **Data Integrity:** Data integrity consists of the factors considered for data protection. Unlike data confidentiality, it protects the unauthorized modification of data (Khan & Pathan, 2018) (Hudson & Clark, 2019). Data modification is simply manipulation, integration or hiding facts. These

modifications could be a consequent of any type of attack (Al-Janabi et al., 2017) (Uluagac et al., 2008). Data integrity uses multiple techniques of authentication to allow a receiver in a wireless environment(Anwar et al., 2014) . The data originating point of access authentication rejects fakeness (Moshaddique Al Ameen, Jingwei Liu, 2015). The data storage database tables have to be equipped with confidential keys (Kang & Adibi, 2015). The data transmitted should be received without modification. To ensure it a message authentication code (MAC) is generated (Mary & Kannammal, 2017). However, prevention from data modification is not an easy task, so error control mechanisms are used (Yaseen et al., 2018) (Mainanwal et al., 2015). The system works only with secure data transmission, can be accessed only through authentication (Seliem & Elgazzar, 2019).

- **Availability:** All WBAN data is sphered with crucial, important and significant vitals, which need to be transmitted accurately in a timely manner to the practitioner with the user network checks whether the targeted nodes are in active mode or not (Anwar et al., 2014). All services facilitated in a wireless network are presumed to be executed (Yaseen et al., 2018) (Mainanwal et al., 2015). IoMT provides a basic feature of availability that benefits in the form of successful execution of the system (Seliem & Elgazzar, 2019).

- **Data Encryption:** The vital issue of the WBAN system is to secure medical information of the patient. To maintain data confidentiality, data is transmitted by applying encryption algorithms to various channels (Mary & Kannammal, 2017). A patient's vital data has to be secure not only from disclosure to the nonentity but protected by external and neighboring networks (Khan & Pathan, 2018) (Mary & Kannammal, 2017) (Mainanwal et al., 2015) (Hudson & Clark, 2019).

- **Secure Management:** WBAN is consists of nodes managed by the coordinator node. The coordinator node is responsible for the secure association of corresponding new nodes and disassociation of old unusable nodes (Al-Janabi et al., 2017). To manage the whole network securely many cryptographic techniques are smeared. Work with many types of cryptographic keys(Abdullah et al., 2018) (Mainanwal et al., 2015).

- **Protection against unauthorized access:** For the sake of privacy, a patient's information is not shared with insurance companies as this step leads towards the restraining of policy coverage. WBAN sensors generate more critical and sensitive data, in case of data incorrect, corrupted, altered by any means or any flaw found then tempering causes mistreatment by the practitioner to the patient could face unpredictable circumstances or even death. Leakage of data leads to mental distortion, social humiliation, and job loss (Al-Janabi et al., 2017) (Abdullah et al., 2018).

- **Data Freshness:** Is a technique that ensures data confidentiality and integrity are safely played. This technique protects stale information to transmit over WBAN. As stale information leads to unwanted or omitted data (Al-Janabi et al., 2017). To ensure freshness a time stamp ensures validity (Anwar et al., 2014). For freshness assurance, a status code is validated for an interval (Moshaddique Al Ameen, Jingwei Liu, 2015) .Age of the data should be defined for denial of duplication(Yaseen et al., 2018) (Khan & Pathan, 2018) (Perillo & Heinzelman, 2005) (Mainanwal et al., 2015) (Kang & Adibi, 2015).

- **Data Authentication:** In a WBAN system data authentication is ought to perform at each node, coordinator node on data reception. This could be done through the matching of a secret code (Khan & Pathan, 2018) (Al-Janabi et al., 2017). It is highly recommended in a wireless sensor network environment that data required and provided to the real or original sources, to which communication is desired (Mary & Kannammal, 2017). In absence of authenticity wireless networks could be directed to fake actions (Yaseen et al., 2018) (Perillo & Heinzelman, 2005) (Mainanwal et al., 2015) .

- **Dependability:** Reliability and assurance are the key features of the WBAN system, where ever reliability loses during data transmission a life-threatening scenario could be seen (Al-Janabi et al., 2017).
- **Secure Localization:** In an emergency, WBAN location accuracy is a prerequisite. Taking advantage of leakage in current location information anyone could transmit altered or fake signals (Khan & Pathan, 2018) (Al-Janabi et al., 2017). To ensure all systems operational in any geographical region wireless sensor network uses its unique feature of localization (Anwar et al., 2014). Localization is the strategic technology for wireless networks (Yaseen et al., 2018) (Mainanwal et al., 2015)
- **Accountability:** All medical records are personal, needs to be hidden possibly from superfluous uses and discourage further abuses (Al-Janabi et al., 2017).
- **Flexibility:** The access control of the WBAN system should be flexible. In any uncertain circumstances, the data could be transferred to a physician for a second opinion, not authorized probably (Al-Janabi et al., 2017) (Mary & Kannammal, 2017) .

Open Issues and Challenges

WSN converts to a special type of network is WBAN, although there are a number of issues that require an adequate solution. The basic and main objective of WBAN is to minimize delay and maximize throughput in order to achieve a network that has the capability of reliability and is a fault-tolerant network (Salayma et al., 2017). Concerns with WBAN are the correct deployment of sensors, gathering real and authentic resultant data and saving the battery power when not needed or adopting less communication policy. Entire research only highlights concerns about power saving which is a major issue (Mary & Kannammal, 2017).

Power Optimization

WBAN is used in many different fields but deployment in the medical field is most promising. A patient is monitored because of some health issues, the monitoring devices need energy supply and it is one of the most important issues, to reduce stress caused by the energy supply/battery replace which needs surgery in some cases (Cavallari et al., 2014).

With the increase of WBAN in a new era, energy conservation is a challenge. Once a node is installed it should be alive up to several years or even decades for implanted devices (Van Daele et al., 2014), in case of energy deficiency of a single node affects the whole network so each node should be transmitting, receiving, idle or sleep. Furthermore, it is impossible for many devices (especially for embedded sensors) to recharge or change the batteries throughout life. Some algorithm and routing schedules handle these as if any node is transmitting, receiving or idle it consumes energy. If any node is sleeping it saves energy (Singh & Singh, 2016) (Van Daele et al., 2014). The problem of reducing energy consumption could be solved by using an energy-efficient MAC and PHY layer.

Devices in WBAN are usually battery-powered, consumes an amount of energy in performing a task. Sensing, communication, and data processing are the main tasks. Among all communication consumes the major amount of energy (Latré et al., 2011) (Arya & Bilandi, 2007). Once WBAN is deployed energy supply is a critical issue. When choosing the wireless technology power constraints must be considered. Wireless technologies focus on minimizing current drawn by various reliable techniques. Requirement and consumption of power vary from application to application. In fact, some of the WBAN sensors are implanted inside the body so energy supply touches the critical bottom. Nodes to be implanted are assigned for multiple years. So either it is mandatory to design ultra-low power transceivers or a new protocol definition for WBAN is mandatory, which consumes an adequate amount of energy. Another possible solution is to send the node in the sleeping mode when not in use. That lowers the duty cycle (Salayma et al., 2017).

In order to save energy low power microsensors are invented, they are cost-effective, but reliability is not assured. But still, their size and cost attract many applications to embed hundreds and thousands of systems for fault tolerance and quality. Costly macro sensors guarantee assurance (Singh & Singh, 2016) (Khan & Pathan, 2018).

Performance Dependency

WBAN is basically invented for functional enhancement and ease of use in telemedicine. It is either embedded or mounted fixed using wearable technology. WBAN works for wearable technology, so in the case of movement, WBAN should be robust against the topological change(Van Daele et al., 2014). Performance dependency of WBAN is not only relying on the cluster head, but it also includes different parameters such as the distance between nodes, power consumption during data transfer (Singh & Singh, 2016). During data transfer, high reliability and lowest delay are required to get high performance (Fernández-Caramés & Fraga-Lamas, 2018) (Van Daele et al., 2014).

CONCLUSION

The entire research depicts WBAN smartly from multiple angles. Discussed many application areas and highlights multiple security issues. An IoT based framework for WBAN along with major security concerns described in detail. The taxonomy of WBAN is described in the hierarchical format. Multitier division of IoMT framework architecture clarifies the data flow from the sensor node to the physician, caregiver, through the IoMT network. The research also defined layers of communication of WBAN.

REFERENCES

Abdullah, A. H., Butt, R. A., Ashraf, M. W., Qureshi, K. N., & Ullah, F. (2018). Securing Data Communication in Wireless Body Area Networks Using Digital Signatures. *Technical Journal, 23*(2), 50–55. Retrieved from https://tj.uettaxila.edu.pk/index.php/technical-journal/article/view/757

Al Ameen & Liu. (2015). Security and privacy issues in wireless sensor networks for healthcare. *Lecture Notes of the Institute for Computer Sciences, Social-Informatics and Telecommunications Engineering, 150*, 223–228. doi:10.1007/978-3-319-19656-5_32

Al Ameen, M., Liu, J., & Kwak, K. (2012). Security and privacy issues in wireless sensor networks for healthcare applications. *Journal of Medical Systems*, *36*(1), 93–101. doi:10.100710916-010-9449-4 PMID:20703745

Al-Janabi, S., Al-Shourbaji, I., Shojafar, M., & Shamshirband, S. (2017). Survey of main challenges (security and privacy) in wireless body area networks for healthcare applications. *Egyptian Informatics Journal*, *18*(2), 113–122. doi:10.1016/j.eij.2016.11.001

Anwar, R. W., Bakhtiari, M., Zainal, A., Hanan Abdullah, A., & Qureshi, K. N. (2014). Security issues and attacks in wireless sensor network. *World Applied Sciences Journal*, *30*(10), 1224–1227. doi:10.5829/idosi.wasj.2014.30.10.334

Arya, A., & Bilandi, N. (2007). A Review: Wireless Body Area Networks for Health Care. *International Journal of Innovative Research in Computer and Communication Engineering*, *3297*(4), 3800–3806. Retrieved from www.ijircce.com

Cavallari, R., Martelli, F., Rosini, R., Buratti, C., & Verdone, R. (2014). A survey on wireless body area networks: Technologies and design challenges. *IEEE Communications Surveys and Tutorials*, *16*(3), 1635–1657. doi:10.1109/SURV.2014.012214.00007

Fernández-Caramés, T. M., & Fraga-Lamas, P. (2018). Towards the internet-of-smart-clothing: A review on IoT wearables and garments for creating intelligent connected E-textiles. *Electronics (Switzerland)*, *7*(12), 405. doi:10.3390/electronics7120405

Hayajneh, T., Almashaqbeh, G., Ullah, S., & Vasilakos, A. V. (2014). A survey of wireless technologies coexistence in WBAN: analysis and open research issues. In Wireless Networks (Vol. 20). doi:10.100711276-014-0736-8

Hudson, F., & Clark, C. (2019). Wearables and Medical Interoperability: The Evolving Frontier. *Computer*, *51*(9), 86–90. doi:10.1109/MC.2018.3620987

N., S., & H., R. (2016). Recent Research on Wireless Body Area Networks: A survey. *International Journal of Computers and Applications*, *142*(11), 42–48. doi:10.5120/ijca2016909893

Kang, J., & Adibi, S. (2015). A review of security protocols in mhealth wireless body area networks (WBAN). *Communications in Computer and Information Science*, *523*, 61–83. doi:10.1007/978-3-319-19210-9_5

Khan, R. A., & Pathan, A. S. K. (2018). The state-of-the-art wireless body area sensor networks: A survey. *International Journal of Distributed Sensor Networks*, *14*(4). doi:10.1177/1550147718768994

Kwak, K. S., Ullah, S., & Ullah, N. (2010). An overview of IEEE 802.15.6 standard. *2010 3rd International Symposium on Applied Sciences in Biomedical and Communication Technologies, ISABEL 2010*, 2–7. 10.1109/ISABEL.2010.5702867

Latré, B., Braem, B., Moerman, I., Blondia, C., & Demeester, P. (2011). A survey on wireless body area networks. *Wireless Networks*, *17*(1), 1–18. doi:10.100711276-010-0252-4

Mainanwal, V., Gupta, M., & Upadhayay, S. K. (2015). A survey on wireless body area network: Security technology and its design methodology issue. *ICIIECS 2015 - 2015 IEEE International Conference on Innovations in Information, Embedded and Communication Systems*, (1), 1–5. 10.1109/ICIIECS.2015.7193088

Mary, J. R., & Kannammal, N. (2017). *A Comparative Study of Security protocols in Wireless Sensor Networks, 2*(5), 573–578.

Movassaghi, S., Abolhasan, M., Lipman, J., Smith, D., & Jamalipour, A. (2014). Wireless body area networks: A survey. *IEEE Communications Surveys and Tutorials, 16*(3), 1658–1686. doi:10.1109/SURV.2013.121313.00064

Perillo, M., & Heinzelman, W. (2005). *Wireless Sensor Network Protocols*. 36-813-36–842. doi:10.1201/9781420035094.sec8

Qureshi, F., & Krishnan, S. (2018). Wearable hardware design for the internet of medical things (IoMT). *Sensors (Switzerland), 18*(11), 3812. doi:10.339018113812 PMID:30405026

Salayma, M., Al-Dubai, A., Romdhani, I., & Nasser, Y. (2017). Wireless Body Area Network (WBAN): A survey on reliability, fault tolerance, and technologies coexistence. *ACM Computing Surveys, 50*(1), 1–35. doi:10.1145/3041956

Seliem, M., & Elgazzar, K. (2019). IoTeWay: A Secure Framework Architecture for 6LoWPAN Based IoT Applications. *2018 IEEE Global Conference on Internet of Things, GCIoT 2018*, 1–5. 10.1109/GCIoT.2018.8620137

Senthilkumar, T., Manikandan, B., Devi, M. R., & Lokesh, S. (2018). CSEIT1835133 | Technologies Enduring in Internet of Medical Things (IoMT) for Smart Healthcare System. *International Journal of Scientific Research in Computer Science, Engineering and Information Technology, 5*(3), 2456–3307.

Singh, R., & Singh, A. (2016). *A Review : Wireless Body Area Network Performance Dependency*. Academic Press.

Uluagac, A. S., Lee, C. P., Beyah, R. A., & Copeland, J. A. (2008). Article. *Designing Secure Protocols for Wireless Sensor Networks, 6*(5), 503–514. doi:10.1007/978-3-540-88582-5_47

Van Daele, P., Moerman, I., & Demeester, P. (2014). Wireless body area networks: Status and opportunities. *2014 31th URSI General Assembly and Scientific Symposium, URSI GASS 2014*, 2–5. 10.1109/URSIGASS.2014.6929369

Yaseen, M., Saleem, K., Orgun, M. A., Derhab, A., Abbas, H., Al-Muhtadi, J., ... Rashid, I. (2018). Secure sensors data acquisition and communication protection in eHealthcare: Review on the state of the art. *Telematics and Informatics, 35*(4), 702–726. doi:10.1016/j.tele.2017.08.005

Chapter 10
Network Security and Internet of Things

Shahzadi Tayyaba
Department of Computer Engineering, University of Lahore, Pakistan

Salman Ayub Khan
Department of Computer Engineering, University of Lahore, Pakistan

Muhammad Tariq
iD https://orcid.org/0000-0003-2787-8334
Superior University, Lahore, Pakistan

Muhammad Waseem Ashraf
iD https://orcid.org/0000-0002-7776-2746
Department of Physics (Electronics), GC University, Lahore, Pakistan

ABSTRACT

Information security is the most critical component of the information system. It is also a challenge of the organizations to build a secure network. Every organization that developed its organizational network has faced security attacks, security risks, and vulnerabilities. Internet of things (IoT) is based on smart devices that connect with each other to formulate a complex network. Therefore, in order to build a secure traditional network and IoT network, understanding the basics of the network layers, network security, and different types of network attacks is essential for network security beginners who are interested in working in the field of information security. In this chapter, the authors reviewed the essential and most important concepts of information security, IoT, and explained these topics in an easy-to-understand way. Furthermore, the chapter discussed the basic level of information security challenges to familiarize the undergraduates and postgraduate students and IoT information security practitioners about it.

DOI: 10.4018/978-1-7998-2803-7.ch010

INTRODUCTION

Meaningful data is called information. The Internet is a source to share and distribute information worldwide. The Internet is called internetworking. The Internet connects people with each other and provides help to find useful information. Network to network communication is also called internetworking. The network consists of host and end systems. The host and end system can be a computer, laptop, mobile phone, tablet, and all other devices that have the capability to connect on the internet. Routers and switches are used to connect the host and end systems. Information can be transmitted through wired or wireless media. The network can be classified into two common types such that Local Area Network (LAN) and Wide Area Network (WAN).

Connection of devices with each other in the same network of the same building, company, and organization is called a LAN. Each host has a unique address or identifier in a LAN. The spanning of LAN into small areas is shown in figure 1. The figure depicts the simple architecture of the LAN. Hosts are connected with the switch in the same network and can communicate with each other. A switch is used in the same building and supports the hosts to communicate with each other in terms of secure transmission. The switch is a layer two device that linked the hosts. It can take a decision for the route of information. There is no need for a router to transmit the information between the hosts in the same network.

Figure 1. Block Diagram of LAN

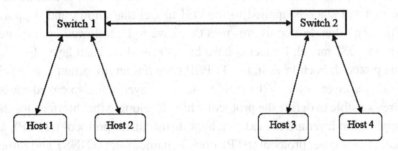

WAN is also used to link the devices. WAN connects routers and switches with each other. WAN connects organizations, cities and worldwide. Routers are used to link the LAN to the WAN. Switches are used to connect hosts with each other to share the information. Switches are used in the local area network. Figure 2 shows the architecture of internetworking. A WAN is used to communicate outside the organization, city, and country. A router is an intelligent device that is used to transmit information far away and can decide the shortest path to go to the destination. A router is a layer three device. The network is identified by the router. Router A at the left-hand side is connected to Router B. Hosts are connected in the local area network with switch and switch is connected with the router. The User 1 as host desires to connect with User 4 as host. User 1 and User 4 have different networks that can be the same class or different classes. Router A will route the information to Router B. Router B will send this information to the host 4. This is secure communication.

Medium is a significant part of the network. Transmission media can be guided and unguided. Guided media can be categorized into three types that Unshielded twisted pair (UTP), Shielded twisted

Figure 2. Architecture of Internetwork

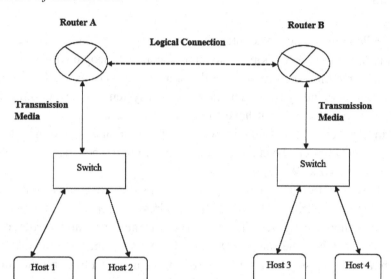

pair (STP), coaxial cable and fiber optics. Unguided media is free space or air. The antenna is required to transmit the information. The electromagnetic wave is used to carry information. The data transmission rate of guided media is larger than unguided media. TCP/IP protocol suite is used to communicate the devices and host with each other. Open system interconnection (OSI) is used to design the network architecture. The protocol stack is applied to the OSI model that allows and supports the devices to communicate with each other. Protocols are rules that have to be followed by the internet user. There are seven layers in the OSI model. Protocols have been defined for each layer. Five layers are used to have a stack of the protocol. Each layer in the TCP/IP suite has an important role. Each layer can work independently. The user layer in the OSI model is the first layer and also called the application layer. The developer is responsible to define the protocol while developing the interface for the user. Protocols defined for the application layer are named as a hypertext transfer protocol (HTTP), a worldwide web (www), secure shell, file transfer protocol (FTP), domain name system (DNS), and Simple Mail Transfer Protocol (SMTP). The transport layer is used to give transportation of data from source to destination. The transport layer is the second layer in which port numbers are used on both sides. The port number defines the destination address. Protocols used to connect the source and destination can be classified into two types that are Transmission Control Protocol (TCP) and User Datagram Protocol (UDP). TCP/IP suite has a network layer also called the internet layer. A router is a device that is used to route the information from one host to another host. A router is used to find the shortest path in the network to save time and distance. The protocol that has been defined for the network layer is an internet protocol (IP). IP is a unique identifier. It contains information, source, and destination address. The IP addresses can be classified into five classes. Each class has an important role. Each class defines the number of users in the organization. The TCP/IP suite has a linked layer and is also called the data link layer. The data link layer has no specific protocol. Switches are used as a link in the data link layer. Switches link the devices with each other. The data link layer uses the ethernet protocol. The physical layer is the last layer in the TCP/IP suite. The physical layer has not any protocol (Behrouz, Network Model, 2013).

Figure 3. Working of Layers in TC/IP suite

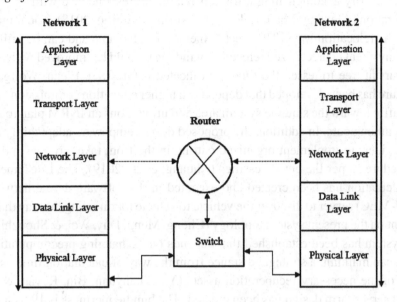

Figure 3 depicts the simple architecture of the two networks. Network 1 and Network 2 can communicate with each other. There is two-way communication between networks. The user at network 1 sends the message by using an application layer that is the user layer. The communication is moved to the transport layer. The information is used to break into small parts called segments. The port number and header are attached to segments. Segments are changed into an IP address at the network layer that is also called a packet. Packets are changed to frame at the data link layer. Error detection and flow control are the responsibilities of the data link layer. The frame is an envelope that has to be transmitted. The frame at the physical layer is converted into bits. Bits can not be transmitted to the receiver. Transmission media is the lowest layer in the architecture. It is used to transmit signals. Bits are converted into signals and then transmitted to the receiver. The receiver repeats the same process in down to up approach. The message is seen by the user on the device. The process of converting messages to signals and signals to message is done at the back end. Users can only see their messages on the front end or user interface. Virtual-ARP (VARP) system presents noteworthy focal points like better security, lower steering overheads, and higher adaptability when contrasted with traditional impromptu directing conventions (Mehran, Mahrokh, Wei, Abbas, & Negin, 2018). It is reported that the procedure of participation encompasses two phases, the determination of connectors and the production of interconnections. These two are led by requests. Furthermore, a joint foundation of the organized frame has been developed by four regular complex system models utilizing the designed methodology. The procedure performs better for fulfilling the requests and the technique can be applied to some other requests by changing the estimations of factors (WANQING, XIANGMING, LUHAN, & ZHAOMING, 2018). Fog radio area network (F-RAN) is developed that can accomplish the most noteworthy throughput for cell-edge UEs and furthermore keep up the best execution in the greater part of the rest of the zone. This prompts the most powerful procedure for distributing the radio assets in thick little cells coordinate with poor backhaul channel while moving the weight from sign handling servers to the edges of the system (ZIFAN, MIHAIL, & XUESONG, 2018). The residue defined network architecture has been developed that is ready to offer transporter grade security accomplishing ultra-dependable correspondence with sub-milliseconds for discontent recuperation (Alextian, Magnos, Roberta, Arash, & Emilio, 2018). The migration method is used to discover the relocation ways. The created method is adaptable and can be utilized for a movement study with any client characterized relocation window. It could be improved with a heuristic-based pruning of the pursuit tree to lessen the time multifaceted nature (Sai, Elena, Wolfgang, & Carmen, 2019). The structure has been developed that depends on higher education commission and useful split to coordinate the traffic toward the suitable system area and utilizations an INRM plan to assign and share the system assets among cuts. In addition, the proposed design empowers adaptability and dynamicity, utilizing the HEC idea, to implement organized cutting in the front take, arrange and adjust the asset designation procedure as per the cut necessities (Chuang, et al., 2019). The LifeTime-based Network State Routing calculation has been created and executed in the software define network-mobile edge computing (SDN-MEC) server to discover the vehicle to vehicle for directing the way that has the longest lifetime dependent on the present system topology (Chung, Meng, Duy, Wei, & Shouzhi, 2018). The fast transformation system has been established that depends on exchanging precomputation in the server farm organize. It can maintain a strategic distance from the way of calculation time as well as ensures the accessibility of the necessary recuperation assets (Yu, Yuanyuan, Bin, Ruyan, & George, 2018). The latent optical server farm design has been created. The bundle inertness is 19 µs and accomplishes 100% throughput. It shows lower inactivity and higher throughput even at high info loads contrasted and electrical data center network (Maotong, Chong, & Suresh, 2018). Hypercube based server has been created. It is used to find some kind of harmony among distance across, division width, steady versatility, cost and vitality utilization rather than the best in class server farm arrange structures (Zhen, et al., 2019). The applications of traditional machine learning calculations in software define network-based systems and the current system applications dependent on software define network design. The related ML algorithm has been discussed (Yanling, et al., 2019).

Information Security

Every person and organizations want to secure information. The information must be confidential and secure from unauthorized access. Nowadays data can be shared and also spread worldwide. A few years ago, data is collected by the organization and save in a file that was confidential and authorized persons are allowed to access, can change this data. The invention of the computer from the last decade. Information is used to keep in the hard drive of the computer (Behrouz & Debdeep, Introduction, 2015).

Computer networks are the 5th generation technology that is used to share the information from far away. The distributed information must be secure. Network and database administrator is responsible to change, retrieve, and delete the information for every organization.

Public and private organizations have information to be secured from theft. The purpose of secure information is to make it confidential mean to say that hide the information from an unknown person. Organizations want their data to encapsulate from unauthorized persons. Banks hide the customer accounts related information and did not give to any unknown person. Military data is also secret and does not want to share with malicious persons. Data hiding is not only for information stored in the computer, but it also applies when data to be transmitted over the network.

Another objective of information security is honesty. The information can be changed by everyone. But the only authorized person has the right to change the data that is confidential. The last goal is the obtainability of information for the authorized person. The information that is not available to the authorized person such that if a person has an account in a bank and he is not able to access it then it could be destructive for the organization. In this case, the organization has the lake of encapsulation of information as shown in Figure 4.

Figure 4. Role of Organization

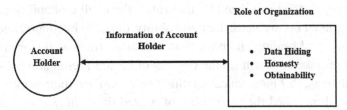

The international organization of telecommunication has designed the standards that provide the services and their solution to keep the information secure from unauthorized persons. There are five services provided by ITU and the standard is X.800. The defined services are used to cover the objective of information security.

Services can be used for one or more objectives to protect the information of the organization. Services can be categorized as data encapsulation, prevention of any change, authorization, retention, and password-based authentication. Retention service provides protection of sender and receiver information. The sender or receiver provides the proof of creation and identification of each other. Password-based authentication means to protect the data and is also called access control. The organization also provides data way to protect the information and support the services that cover the objective of information security. They need to secure the data. For this purpose, cryptography is used to encapsulate the data from an unauthorized person and is also called encipherment. A three-way handshaking mechanism is used to protect any change in the information. It generates some random values and compares these values at both ends. Another way to protect the data is to sign electronically and it is called a digital signature. The sender sends the signature and the receiver has to verify the signature. Public and private keys are used for certification. Insertions of raw data are done during transmission to make fool with the attacker. The modification of the path of data involves the honest person during transmission between two organizations so that both organizations can not be denied later. The grid-based unordered total mark plot has been reported. The created plan utilizes the crossing point technique and tackles the unordered total issue of grid marks with various open keys. It is utilized to maintain a strategic distance from both the marking request restriction and the danger of single mark phony. The plan has pursued the improved security model (Xiuhua, Wei, Qiaoyan, Zhengping, & Wenmin, 2018). The encipherment system named as Copker has been structured that is utilized to actualize open key encipherment altogether inside the focal handling unit without putting away any plain-content delicate information in the volatile memory. It is utilized to give encipherment administrations that can be verified against cold-boot assaults and presented sensible overhead (Le, et al., 2018). The SensorAuth based client validation framework has been created, for constant confirmation of clients dependent on their personal conduct standards, by utilizing the accelerometer and gyrator universally incorporated with cell phones. The SensorAuth can be played out the profoundly precise and time-proficient persistent confirmation, by arriving at the most reduced middle equivalent blunder pace of 4.66% and devouring a short validation time of around 5 sec (Yantao, Hailong, & Gang, 2018). The arrangement of the security dangers has been talked about that are explored from physical layer points of view since physical layer security advances have the upsides of accomplishing immaculate mystery, low computational intricacy, and asset utilization, and great adjustment for channel changes. In particular, the safe wiretap coding, asset assignment, signal preparation, and multi-hub collaboration, alongside physical layer key age and verification, to adapt to the rising security challenges has been broke down (Dong, et al., 2019). The youngsters wellbeing condition alliance survey method is utilized to distinguish the in all probability center human blunder causes that could bring about occurrences, their probability, the in all likelihood undertakings that could be influenced, recommended healing and protection measures, frameworks or procedures that can be influenced by human mistake and built up the degrees of hazard presentation. The reactions are provided by the representatives, that hierarchical spotlight on its kin and their workplace can be improved the data safety act and diminished the probability of related data safety episodes through a decrease in human mistake (Mark, et al., 2019). The insurance of authoritative data resources has required the cooperation of all worker's data safety synchronized struggle the endeavors of representatives so as to alleviate the impact of data safety ruptures and occurrences. The information examination is uncovered that individual standards, association, and promise to their association essentially impact the workers' disposition towards data security cooperation expectation (Nader, Carsten, Tim, & Steve, 2018). The validations of data hypothetical safety for the key natives in encipherment: private key encipherment and key understanding have been broke down (Mitsugu, Kazuo, & Junji, 2018). The data safety coincidental evaluations in the PC review are performed to PC frameworks, inside it to the database frameworks, regularly utilizing subjective strategies. The model has been created by utilizing the fuzzy logic for the calculation of the data safety threat in the database framework and the created model is valuable and expands the outcomes in the assessment of the data security chance (Yasser, Vivian, & Natalia, 2018).

Network Security

Two or more network devices connected with each other is called a network. Organizations can have wired or wireless networks to store and share information. Each employee of the organization has a dedicated computer in-network and all work stations can be controlled by the server. Hardware and software are installed in computer networks to protect the information. If workstations are connected with the internet that is not secure then the attacker can easily steal the information. The AID rearranging instrument dependent on Group-purchasing Auction for Identifier Network has been built up that is utilized for mapping servers, getting to exchanging switches and terminals. The designed module can get the upgraded arrangement with the most reduced calculation multifaceted nature and accomplished the biggest number of effective exchanges while ensuring the properties, for example, singular objectivity, spending equalization and honesty (Jianfeng, Ying, Su, & Lili, 2019).

The regular weakness that exists in both wired and remote systems is "unknown access" to a system. An aggressor can associate his gadget to a system however unbound center/switch port. In such a manner, a remote system is viewed as less secure than a wired system, since the remote system can be effectively gotten to with no physical association. There are five layers in the TCP/IP suite. Unexpectedly, in TCP/IP based system correspondence, in the event that one layer is hacked, different layers don't get mindful of the hack and the whole correspondence gets traded off. Thus, there is have to utilize security controls at each layer to guarantee complete security. Minimal worry for the security perspective during the structure and execution of conventions has transformed into a fundamental driver of dangers to system security. There exists an enormous number of vulnerabilities in the system. Along these lines, during transmission, information is profoundly helpless against assaults. The security threats and protection of IoT systems have been discussed in detail also described and analyzed the security measurements in the software-defined network and network function virtualization for IoT systems (Ivan, Tarik, Yacine, & Jaeseung, 2018).

An aggressor can emphasize the transmission over the network, obtain the material, and read the equivalent or re-embed a bogus message to accomplish his loathsome points. The security is not only used to secure the information; nonetheless, it plans to pledge that the entire system is safe. The security of the network is involved to confirm the comfort of routine, firm excellence, uprightness, and security of structure and material. To implement the security successfully that is used to overcome a range of risks from incoming or outgoing on a network. The security component intended to work at an upper layer can't give a guarantee to information at the lowest layers. Consequently, it might be important to convey different security systems for improving system security. A methodology has been defined toward the planned implementation of safety methods in organize capacities virtualization systems and dynamic adjustment to arrange changes. The methodology is based on a refinement model that is used to permit the dynamic change of elevated level security necessities into setup settings for system security capacities, and enhancement models that are used to permit the ideal determination of the system security capacity (Cataldo, Fulvio, Antonio, Diego, & Antonio, 2019). The staggered disseminated checking and remediation structure for software define networks has been developed. With a special security pipeline, It offers lightweight permeability over countless streams. The low dormancy recognition and assurance capacity and the potential for versatile observing in huge systems have been evaluated (Lyndon, Sandra, Matthew, & Andrew, 2018). The security methodologies for vehicle systems have been made. The pecking orders of the system are established by the product characterized thought to disentangle organize the executives and decay the control and information planes. The security plans can be utilized to accomplish better system execution as far as system throughput and control overhead contrasted and the typical system without security the system load limit fluctuates (Rong, Xiaojie, & Jun, 2018). The long term evolution network architecture, the attacks on the network, and security methods have been discussed in detail. The secure data center and its security measurements have been introduced for secure data transmission (Limei, Zheng, & Mohammed, 2018). The network security coding system has been designed with key generation methods and the adaptive quantitative algorithm is applied for the key generation process in NSCS (Yuanyuan, Bin, Feng, & Zhen, 2018). The system security-related information assortment is basic for the recognition of system assaults and interruptions, in this way adding to guarantee the security of an entire system framework.the scientific categorization and grouping of information assortment innovations. With respect to information assortment advancements, for the most part, assessed information assortment hubs, information assortment apparatuses, and explicit information assortment instruments. The current information assortment advances have examined with respect to the developed practical and security destinations so as to investigate their benefits and negative marks (Huaqing, Zheng, Yu, & Lifang, 2018). The Node Security Quantification model has talked about. The hub security capability comprises a security metric model that joins gatecrasher cautions with the system correspondence example to assess the security level of compelled hubs and the sensor information devoured by clients. The security mindfulness gave by the hub security capability measurements bolsters clients' and system directors' basic leadership. The experimental result has illustrated that the hub security capability is precisely evaluated security level with extremely low vitality and execution overhead (Alex, Ronaldo, Raimir, & Joel, 2019). The conveyed security approach system, in view of the ideal situation of security usefulness caught through network distributed security policy and security organization limitations, have created. The created structure that is increasingly proficient regarding system and figuring assets and versatility for all the secured situations have been demonstrated by the test result (Alireza, Yosr, Makan, & Mohamed, 2016). The protected path perfection rule in brilliant home systems dependent on distributed motion administration is profoundly expected to be significant portability of the board arrangement in the 5G and security mechanism with Burrows–Abadi–Needham rationale and Automatic security examination device have been analyzed (Daemin, et al., 2019). The strategy based security mechanism for disseminated software define network has been built up that is utilized to empower the safe interchanges and streams between various end has over different areas (Vijay, Kallol, Uday, & Michael, 2018). The appropriation framework security locale is applied to security mindfulness and the security separation strategy has created. The upsides of the area technique are to keep away from complex iterative tasks and decrease the calculation conveyed organize all the while (Jun, Baoqiang, & Fengzhang, 2019). The security assaults in remote sensor systems and grouped them into various kinds dependent on network layers. The arrangement of assessment criteria as far as both security information assortment and assault recognition have been organized (Haomeng, Zheng, Zhen, & Mohammed, 2018).

Figure 5 depicts the simple architecture of the protected network. The organization server is connected with LAN and WAN. Internet service providers give the internet facility to small or large organizations as per the requirement of the organization. The organization server is used to control the whole network

Figure 5. Simple Diagram of Secure Network Architecture

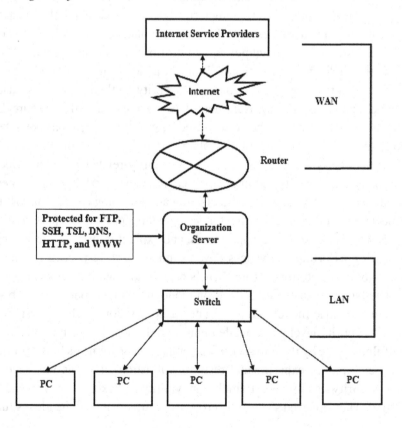

for secure transmission. All rules and rights apply to the server for the user. The router that is connected to the router of ISP must be secured by installed firmware software or hardware.

NETWORK SECURITY ATTACK

System security assaults are unknown events against isolated, company or legislative information technology assets in order to smash them, alter them or take sensitive data. As more adventures invite delegates to get to data from phones, frameworks become defenseless against data theft or complete destruction of the data or framework (William, 2017). The security problems recognized with the undercover network applied to mechanical structures have been discussed, and distinguishing the new powerlessness focuses when data innovation merge with operational advances (Cristina, Giuseppe, Federica, Javier, & Roberto, 2019). The significant properties of the capacity function of the arbitrarily varying wiretap channel have been investigated, such that, coherence and super-additivity. These properties are significant for the plan of hearty secure correspondence structure and for the streamlining of the Medium Access Control (Holger & Christian, 2018). The digital-physical design custom-made for direct current microgrids and abusing the correspondence potential dwelling in the microgrid electrical gear. The developed structure can be used to improve the security (vigor against disavowal of administration assaults) and control quality (determination of a VSCs set that advances a pre-characterized metric) (Pietro, Marko, Čedomir, & Tomislav, 2018). The negative effect of the remote channel blackouts on the demand side management unwavering quality is evaluated by the AN-aided scheme and the vitality request estimation mistake money related misfortune estimated in dollars. It is used to increase the encoding plan as far as improving the demand side management's security and decreasing the financial misfortune to the utility (Ahmed, Dusit, Ridha, & Naofal, 2017). The innovative remote interruption identification framework has developed, by consolidating portion thickness estimation and shrouded Markov model through a couple of line with feedback. The exhibition of the developed strategy has been tentatively approved and it is discovered that the projected technique can identify the previously mentioned assaults with 98% precision (Sibi, Sangeetha, & Vaidehi, 2019). The three types of calculations with the end goal that system schedulers, irregular early recognition, and arbitrary exponential checking has been examined. The dynamic line calculations have been demonstrated, for example, arbitrary early discovery, and irregular exponential denoting that can show more grounded safeguard capacities than the uninvolved line calculation under the medium-and little scale denial of service assaults (Wei, Houbing, Huihui, & Xiumei, 2017). There two types of network security attacks as given.

- Vigorous Attacks
- Submissive Attacks

Vigorous Attacks

Vigorous assault endeavors to adjust framework assets or impact their tasks. Dynamic assault includes some modification of the material flow or the making of bogus proclamation. Active attacks can be sensed easily. Actives assault is used to destruct the information system in a network. The security objectives are threatened by active attacks. Active attacks can be categorized into two groups that perform to change the information. A three-organize Stackelberg game methodology has been intended to display the practices of the aggressor, and the rivalries among the transmitter, transfers, and assailant. Through finding the Stackelberg balance of the created methodology, real clients can accomplish helpful correspondence to improve the mystery limit and to guard against full-duplex dynamic listening in assaults (He, Li, Yulong, Xianbin, & Kim, 2018). The exhibition of secure physical-layer communication methodologies has been researched for preparing based transfer helped enormous multiple inputs and multiple outputs downlink with the incompletely evaluated confidential signal with channel estimation mistakes, dynamic pilot tainting and spatially-connected blurring at the various receiving wire clusters. The effect of dynamic pilot defilement assaults has been evaluated by inferring the attainable mystery rates. the anonymous rate hole between detached listening stealthily and dynamic assaults have been explored. The investigation uncovers that the dynamic pilot sullying assaults can harshly security (Dhanushka, Santosh, & Gayan, 2019). The tale dynamic site fingerprinting assault has been performed at a controlled section hub. By effectively deferring hypertext move convention demands, and improve the exactness. Two calculations are utilized to explore the usefulness and contrasted by using the kNN classifier with acquiring the most extreme exactness that is 0.9864 (Ming, Xiaodan, Zhen, Changxin, & Junzhou, 2017).

Integrity Threating

Various types of attacks are used to destruct the information.

- It suggests that some part of a data is altered or that message is delayed or reordered to deliver an unknown impact. The account holder of the bank is required an online money transfer to his employee but the information by the attacker and bank transfer money to the attacker account. This is called the modification of data at the receiver end as shown in figure 6.

Figure 6. Data Modification

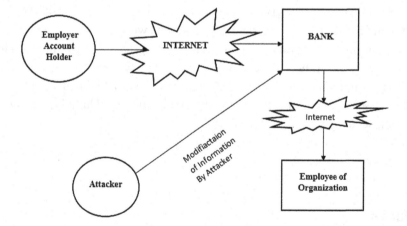

- Parodying happens when the aggressor imitates another person. If the attacker achieved the password of the bank customer and tell the bank that he/she is a customer of this bank. Attackers show their identity because of the password and online transfer the money. This type of attack is called spoofing as shown in figure 7.

Figure 7. Attacker Hack the Password

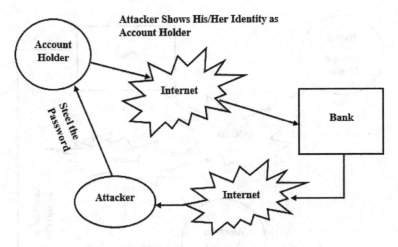

- The assailant acquires a duplicate of a message sent by a client and later attempts to replay it. Suppose Mr. Hallen sends a message to the back that to transfer money to the Aleeza. Aleeza behaves like an attacker and uses the same message for another transaction. This type of attack is called replaying as shown in figure 8.
- This stabbing is ended by correspondent or collector. The correspondent or recipient can reject later that he/she has sent or obtain information. The consumer asks his Bank "To move an add up to the individual" and far along on the correspondent reject that he had made such a solicitation. Figure 9 depicts the process of disclaimer. Collin has bought a product and paid the money to the seller whose name is Donald by the bank. After some time, Donald denied receiving payment and claim to the buyer through the bank to give him money for the product. This type of attack is called refutation.

These types of attacks are used for modification and destruct the integrity of data.

- It envisions the conventional use of correspondence workplaces. This attack may have a specific target. For example, a component may cover all messages composed to a particular objective. Another kind of organization refusal is the unsettling influence of an entire framework recoil by debilitating the framework or by over-troubling it by messages to degenerate execution as shown in figure 10.

Submissive Attacks

Submissive assault activities are used to acquire or exploit information as of the system yet don't affect system resources. Aloof Bouts are in the clue of snooping stealthily on or glance of transmission. The goal of the contending is to acquire a message that is used to transmit over the network. The powerlessness of searchable encryption plans has been explored that is in view of the suppositions on how much earlier information an aggressor is permitted to accomplish. A few uninvolved assaults, which just utiliz-

Figure 8. Receiver act as an attacker

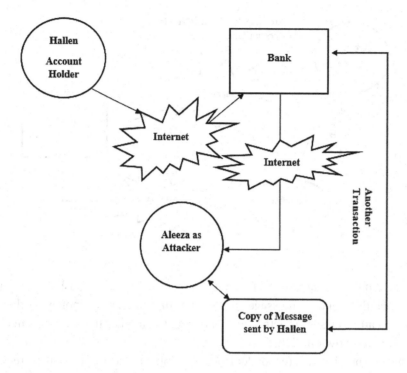

Figure 9. Simple Architecture of Repudiation by Donald

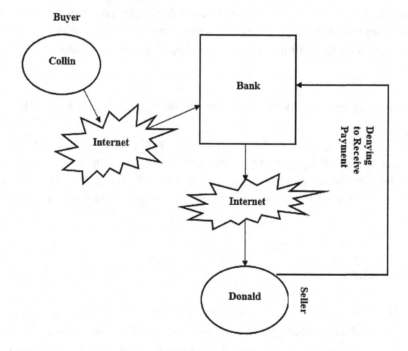

Figure 10. Structure of Danial of Service

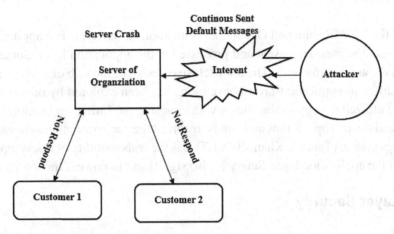

ing inactive information to uncover the relationship between watchword and search token. The detached assaults can be propelled to a unique kind of searchable encryption plan, which fizzles to "cover-up" the record get to design and to adequately break question (Jianting, Jia, Kaitai, Fan, & Ee, 2018).

- Telephonic discussion, an electronic mail communication or a moved file can have delicate or classified information. We should prevent a foe from learning the substance of these transmissions.
- Suppose that we had a technique for covering information, with the objective that the aggressor paying little respect to whether got the message couldn't expel any information from the message. The adversary could choose the region and character of the granting host and could watch the repeat and length of messages being exchanged. This information might be important in estimating the possibility of the correspondence that was happening. Information is sent by the Laxman to David that information can be confidential. The attacker continuously monitors the information sent by Laxman over the network. This type of attack destruct data confidentiality as shown in figure 11. Submassive attacks do not disturb the network transmission. These are used to monitor and acquire the data. Passive attacks are not easy to detect. Passive attacks are prevented by the encapsulation of data.

Figure 11. Simple Diagram of Traffic Monitoring

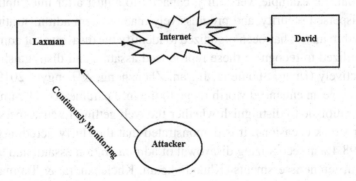

APPLICATION LAYER

The first layer of the TCP/IP suite and OSI model is an application layer. The application layer is also called the user layer. The message is sent and processed at the application layer. Some predefined protocols are used in the application layer. The nonexclusive design of the web of video things-based video observation and different application-layer conventions has been explored by ongoing testing. The investigation can be utilized to support the clients with choosing the fitting application layer conventions in different reconnaissance applications and can be resolved their appropriateness at various hubs of the web of video things system (Tanin & Khan, 2019). This is the responsibility of a developer to define rules and regulations at the application layer. Safety is also significant to process the information of the user.

Application Layer Security

The server is used to provide the service to each computer that is connected with a server in a network. The server provides the security of information during transmission. Organizations have a client-server architecture. The client has to follow the rules and regulations that are applied by the server in a network. There are a lot of services provided by a server such that email service, web service, DNS service, and DHCP. The server keeps a record of the web, email, and data. The thorough plan has been built up that permits the unification of various security instruments, in this manner expelling the weight of verification, common confirmation, persistent validation, and session the executives from the application advancement life-cycle. It is utilized to kill the requirement for session treats, session tokens and any comparative system presently being used (Zahoor, Hasan, Malik, Shahzaib, & Klaus, 2019). The complete band of application-layer denial of service occurrences using perilous structures has been inspected that how these occurrences can be implemented. The protection policies have also deliberated with distinct importance on the structures that are used to provide support in the uncovering of diverse attacks (Amit & P., 2018). The compelling resistance framework has been created, which is used the sketch material edifice to rapidly identify and moderate application-layer forswearing of administration assaults. The created model of the defense system that is painstakingly assessed its adequacy utilizing genuine assault information gathered from an enormous scale web bunch. The defense system can be utilized to diminish noxious solicitations while representing a constrained effect on ordinary clients (Chenxu, Tony, Xiapu, & Jinhe, 2017). The presentation model has been produced for a business gadget that can ready to perform propelled application-layer sifting, specifically of transmission control protocol traffic. The great communication of the evaluated exhibition with the gadget real conduct is demonstrated by various experiments (Manuel, Luca, Lucia, & Adriano, 2018). Different perspectives have been talked about, for example, versatility, capacity to adjust after interruptions, heterogeneous substrate systems, dispersed security, and progressively made system administrations (Jörg, Majid, & Tony, 2019). The rhythm matrix has been organized to identify the disavowal of administration assaults. The model can be utilized to recognize these reproduced assaults and distinguish the malevolent has precisely and productively (Huan, Shoufeng, Jiayan, Zhenzhong, & Fengyu, 2019). The Genetic Algorithm is utilized to give an enhanced worth range to the info parameters. The improved qualities are applied to the fuzzy rationale to distinguish whether the web getting to customers shows the conduct of assault, typical or streak occasions. It is demonstrated that the fluffy hereditary calculation model gives a precision of 98.4% in recognizing disavowal of administration assault and 97.3% in identifying streak occasions by different assessments (Khundrakpam, Khelchandra, & Tanmay, 2018). The great spam model utilizing the original Senshi network data has been made that can reap a 7.62% active visitor clicking percentage. gather email addresses from the Internet, complete email proprietor data utilizing their open interpersonal organization profile information, and break down the reaction of customized spam sent to clients as indicated by their profile utilizing a phony site (Enaitz, Urko, & José, 2017). The purpose of section client gadget confirmation systems that utilize characteristic client association has been discussed. The server provides email security (Napa, Jonathan, Nasir, Janusz, & Prakash, 2019). To secure the email at the application layer, there are two protocols name as PGP and SMIME that is used to secure the email system

Email Exchange Structure

Electronic mail is one-way communication. The sender sends the message and the receiver responds to this message of the sender. Organizations have an email server to perform communication between two users and keep records of email. Suppose Mr. Halen is working as a duty manager recruitment in an educational institute. He sends an email to Mr. Laxman for the vacancy announcement. The server is used to provide the path of communication between two persons. There are three agents are required to transmit the email. One is the user agent that is used to send and receive the email to the server. The mail transfer agent is used to transfer the message to the receiver mailbox. The agent is known as MTA is the part of the delivery server and it acts at both the sender and receiver side. Communication obtain agent is known as MAA is used to receive the email in the mailbox and show it to the user agent at the receiver side as shown in figure 12.

Email System Security

Creating usage of email correspondence for huge and pressing trades demands the game plan of certain essential security benefits as the going with. The electronic mail should not be scrutinized by anyone

Figure 12. Simple Block Diagram of Email System

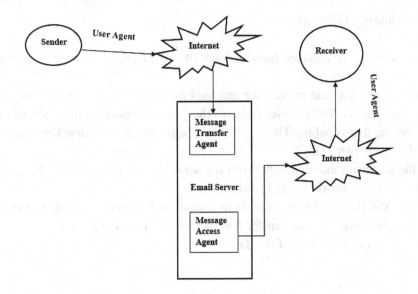

anyway the normal. The recipient electronic mail must check the confirmation of the sender. Attestation to the recipient that the message has not been adjusted since it was imparted by the transmitter. An email beneficiary can demonstrate to an organization who is responsible for an email system that the sender truly sent the message. The correspondent gets the affirmation that the message is given to the mail conveyance framework. Correspondent gets an affirmation that the beneficiary got the electronic mail. The new phishing electronic mail discovery model has been developed named THEMIS, which is utilized to display messages at the header, body, character level, and the word level all the while dependent on improved repetitive convolutional neural systems model with staggered vectors and consideration component. The general precision of THEMIS arrives at 99.848% is evaluated by experiments (Yong, Cheng, Cheng, Liang, & Yue, 2019). The disadvantage of the manual strategy to accomplish user confirmation can be utilized to defeat by a computerized procedure. The certifications are to approve the user has a programmed system foundation and it is acquired from the unique resilient power (Krishna, Balachandra, & Vasundhara, 2019). The methodology has been talked about to identify sidelong lance phishing assaults in associations progressively. The methodology is utilized to separate the highlights from area information and examine the attributes that are relating to such assaults, joined with their scoring strategy which takes a shot at the non-named group of data (Aniket & Sunil, 2019). Public key encipherment is used to provide a secure facility. There are two protocols used for safety services.

- PGP
- MIME

Pretty Good Privacy

It provides the security service to the email during communication. PGP is used to provide confidentiality, correspondent verification, message honesty, and proof of message. Alongside these security managements, it likewise gives information and key administration support. PGP utilizes existing encipherment calculations.

Pretty Good Privacy Algorithm

The working principle of PGP is given as:

- Information sends to the receiver. Information will in the form of plain text. The receiver receives the information in the mailbox.
- The sender generates a random number and uses its private key to send the data with a random number to the receiver. The receiver receives the data and validates the material using the secret key of the sender that is public. There is the symmetric and asymmetric key of the correspondent used to validate the material.
- Transmit the data and random number over the network after compressing them. This doest creat overwhelms on the network during transmission.
- There can be ASCII codes in an email. PGP is also sued to convert the ASCII characters. ASCII characters can be hidden before transfer it to the receiver over the system.
- PGP is used to uniform the size of the data.

Pretty Good Privacy protocol uses the RSA public key algorithms. RSA algorithm is used for encryption of data. IDEA is symmetric key algorithms are used for cryptography. MD5 is a hash algorithm used for authentication of message called a message digest. The information compress using the ZIP algorithm. Compression does not provide security of data. It just improves the flow of information, which becomes fast due to the small size of data.

The key authentication is regularly settled through a chain of beliefs. Any client can go about as a guaranteeing authority. Any pretty good privacy client can affirm another pretty good privacy client's open key. In any case, such authentication is just legitimate to another client if the client perceives the certifier as a reliable introducer. A few issues exist with such an accreditation strategy. It might be hard to discover a chain driving from a known and confided in broad daylight key to wanted key. Likewise, there may be various chains that can prompt various keys for the wanted client. X.509 is a certificate used for a reliable consultant to any credential. The sender sends data in the form of plain text to receive. Encryption performs at the plain text to secure the data and send encrypted data to the receiver. Hashing algorithm and a public key of the sender used for decrypt the data into plain text. The receiver receives the information as shown in figure 13.

Figure 13. Architecture of Pretty Good Privacy Protocol

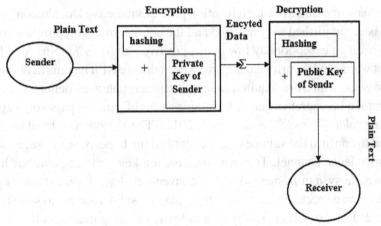

Multipurpose Internet Mail Extension

The simple rules that enhance the procedure of information of electronic mail in characters set, also sounds, videos, and pictures. The information contains various part and the address can be resolute into ASCII characters. Multipurpose internet mail extension along with data of electronic mail is usually sent with protocols such that SMTP, POP (password-based authentication protocol), and IMAP (three-way handshaking protocol in the client-server paradigm).

In spite of the fact that the multipurpose internet mail extension content was structured for the most part for simple mail transfer protocol, its substance types are likewise significant in other correspondence conventions. In the HyperText Transfer Protocol for the World Wide Web, servers embed a MIME header field toward the start of any Web transmission. Customers utilize the substance type or media type header to choose a proper watcher application for the kind of information showed. Multipurpose internet mail extension header consists of four-part. The header field is combined with a message and transmit to the receiver. The header field defines the format of the message.

The multipurpose internet mail extension version is defined as "1.1". Content-type defines the media format. Using the multipart type, multipurpose internet mail extension permits the information to have parts orchestrated in a tree structure where the leaf hubs are any non-multipart content sort and the non-leaf hubs are any of an assortment of multipart types. The first multipurpose internet mail extension details just portrayed the assembly of information. They didn't report the subject of presentation styles. The inline content-mien, which implies that it ought to be consequently shown when the message is shown, or an attached content-mien, in which case it isn't shown naturally and requires some type of activity from the client to open it. Characterized a lot of techniques for binary information other than ASCII content arrangement. Transfer encodings characterize the qualities demonstrated as follows, which are not case delicate. Note that '7bit', '8bit', and '0&1' imply that no parallel to-content encoding over the first encoding was utilized. In these cases, the header field is really repetitive for the email customer to unravel the message body, however, it might, in any case, be helpful as a marker of what kind of article is being sent. Qualities 'cited printable' and 'base64' tell the email customer that a paired to-content encoding plan was utilized and that suitable beginning interpreting is important before the message can be perused with its unique encoding. The AL-DOCX, a structure is built up that is utilized for precise identification of new obscure malignant Docx documents that can proficiently upgrade the system's discovery capacities after some time. The high location pace of vindictive Docx records (94.44% complete physical reaction) is accomplished as contrasted and the counter infection programming (85.9% all-out physical reaction)- with an exceptionally low bogus positive rate (0.19%) (Nir, Aviad, & Yuval, 2016). The different secret words and security dangers have been discussed. The ramifications of results, investigation, and discoveries, which are required to help both secret phrase clients and framework heads to increase a more profound comprehension of the helplessness of genuine passwords against best in class secret word breaking calculations (Shouling, et al., 2017). The Various validated key trade conventions have been proposed to confirm the validness of a client and the honesty of messages sent over an uncertain remote correspondence channel. The two confirmation key trade conventions have been planned by Tsai et al. for remote system frameworks. The conventions have been examined powerless against disconnected secret phrase speculating assaults by displaying solid assaults, in spite of their cases (Min, Xiaotong, Li, Kim, & Debiao, 2017). The system to battle phishing messages has been made. Safe PC has been intended for identifying new phishing efforts, which are developed from earlier ones (Christopher, Taegyu, Raffaele, Jeffrey, & Dan, 2018). The arrangement has been created to distinguish and report possible risky situations identified with cell phones dependent on Android, and it has built up an application that checks the cell phone scanning for hazardous client setups dependent on a predefined list (Klever, Edejair, & Fernando, 2017). The transparent policies are utilized to give another way to deal with creating conventions without a technique. Another convention has been created for a guaranteed electronic-mail dependent on a blockchain without a regular methodology that is incorporated with the ordinary email foundation. The convention is secure, effective, and reasonable from a pragmatic point of view (M, Josep, & Llorenç, 2019).

Secure Multipurpose Internet Mail Extension

SMIME is used to provide a security service than simple MIME. The content type is added to provide security service to MIME. This type of content includes public key encipherment. The Security services are provided by SMIME such that validation, information honesty, verification of sender using the electronic signature, confidentiality, and encapsulation of message. SMIME has a content type that is used to wrap the data in a single entity.

The honesty of data is provided by signed-data content means digital signature. The digital signature can be the various type of binary numbers. The secrecy of data can be provided by wrapping the data into a single object. The digest is generated by the content. Data contents are used to encapsulate by using any key. The information can be verified by using the Message Authentication Code key. The encipherment algorithms are required to give the security of the email system using S/MIME.

- Sender support triple data encryption standard or public-key encryption and receiver also use the same encryption standard.
- RSA public-key encryption algorithm is used for session encryption.
- The SHA-1 is used for information authentication.
- DSS scheme is used to produce for the random number is called a digest.
- Message Authentication Code and secure hash algorithm-1 are used for message authentication at both sides.

TRANSPORT LAYER

The transport layer is the 2nd layer in the TCP/IP suite and 4th layer in the open system interconnection model. The transport layer is used to establish a connection between network devices. A port number is used to define the address of the source and destination. Port number is combined with IP address and send to the destination is called a socket. Source port number can be dynamic because the operating system generates it in every time interval. The destination port number does not change, for example, the port number of HTTP is 80 and HTTPS is 443. The range of port numbers is 2^16 (65535). Security is provided to the socket for secure data transmission over the network. The conventional behavior of the multi-figure set and in reverse similarity security of transport layer security 1.3 has been examined. The cross-figure suite assault with respect to transport layer security in the model, and proved that the transport layer security 1.3 handshake convention has fulfilled the multi-figure set security, featuring the exacting need of remembering more data for the mark (Xiao, Jing, Zhen, & Wen, 2017). The equipment has been structured and actualized for the datagram TLS convention to permit start to finish safety for IoT. A significant part of this plan that can be used to configure the prime field elliptic encipherment quickening agent that is more vitality proficient contrasted with programming and cutting edge equipment (Utsav, et al., 2019). The gathering focused start to finish security has been grown, together with the presentation of another security mode. To be specific, a security affiliation is built up between an obliged application convention customer and a gathering of compelled application convention servers, in any case, fine-grained get to control can be authorized so each obliged application convention customer can get to a predetermined number of compelled application convention servers in the gathering. An open key activity, be that as it may, isn't required for the consequent datagram TLS handshakes, so the general computational weight can be decreased (Chang & Wang, 2018).

Transport Layer Security

TLS is used to apply above to the transport layer is called socket layer security as shown in figure 14. It is used for web security to provide security of data between the web browser of client and server. The server is used to provide services and the webserver is used to keep a record of web sites.

Figure 14. Block diagram of TSL in TCP/IP suite

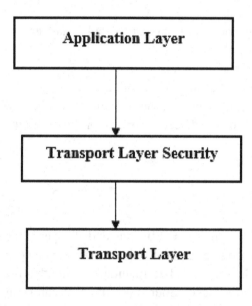

There are four types of the protocol used by a secure socket layer such that SSL record protocol, connection-oriented protocol, state transition protocol, and alert. The secure socket protocol stack belongs to the TCP/IP suite. It provides service to create a link among users to users and users to the mainframe for data transmission. The session is also created between the client and the server. The temporary time period is a lot to the session. The session created and finished using the handshake protocol. The session can consist of multiple connections.

The parameter of the session is given as:

- Session identifier
- Client certificate (X.509 public key or signature parameters)
- The compression method to decrease the size of data it does not provide security but reduces the destructive transmission.
- The cipher space where the encryption algorithm is used for data encapsulation and Message Authentication Code is used for confidentially of data.
- The master secret key is used to share between client and server.

- 1s Resemble Flage is used to indicate the status of the connection.

These parameters are used to share each link among users and servers. The connection state parameters are given as:

- The random byte sequent is done between the server and the client.
- The MAC secret is generated at the sender server for authentication.
- The MAC secret is generated at the sender client for authentication.
- The sender is used to generate the secret key by using conventional encryption methods.
- The client writes the key that is a shared key.
- The initialization vector is used to create a connection.
- Sequence Number

Secure Socket layer is implemented using the group of protocols. SSL record protocol is implemented above the transmission control protocol because of connection-oriented. SSL record protocol is used for data safety.

Working Principle of Secure Socket Layer Record Protocol

The implementation of the SSL record protocol is given as:

- The message at the application layer is being processed to the transport layer.
- Data is broken down into segments
- Apply the compression function at fragmented data. The compression function can ZIP code.
- Add the Message Authentication Code with compressed data. MAC can be generated using the hash function (MD5 or Secure hash algorithm-1).
- Apply conventional encryption methods to encapsulate the MAC and compressed data.
- Append SSL header with encrypted data and send it to the receiver.

Figure 15 depicts the process of SSL record protocol.

SSL Record Header

SSL record header is consists of four fields that is formate of data, maximum type: 3, minimum type: 0, and trampled length.

- The format of data is used to define the fragmentation process.
- The version of the SSL record header is 3:0.
- The maximum compressed length is 4 byte

How to calculate the Message Authentication Code by using MD-5 or SHA-1 Hash(message authentication-key// appending-2// hash (message authentication-key key//appending -1// sequence-number//SSL compressed length//SSL compressed type//SSL compressed fragmentation)) message authentication-key = Collective key Appending bits-2: 0101 0110 (48 times for MD-5) repeated & (40 times for secure

Figure 15. Simple Flow Diagram of SSL Record Protocol

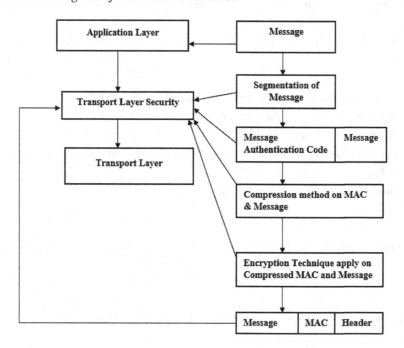

hash algorithm-1) repeated Appending bits-1: 0111 0110 ((48 times for MD-5) repeated & (40 times for secure hash algorithm-1) repeated.

Handshake Protocol

There are three fields involve in handshake protocol that is named as content type, length of data, and contents.

- The size of the content type is 1 byte. It is used to apply at higher layers for the fragmentation process.
- The length of the message is a maximum of 3 bytes.
- The length of the parameter associated with a message can be greater than 0 bytes.

The communication is done in four phases between client and server. Phases are used to establish the link among users and servers.

Phase-One

The purpose of phase one is to initialize the cipher suite, compression method, and protocols.

- The client sent a message to the server for establishing the connection. This message is called a hello message.
- The server responds to the client in terms of hello message.

Phase-Two

Server and Client exchange the certificate in phase two.

- Credential of mainframe computer directed to the client.
- Server exchange the key with the client.
- The server sent a request to the client for the certificate.
- The alive message is done by the server

Phase-Three

- Client exchange the certificate to the server.
- Client exchange the key.
- The certificate is verified by the server.

Phase-Four

- Change-cipher specifications have been finished by the client and server.

At the end of phase-4, the connection has been established between client and server. The information is being transmitted over the network.

The improved elliptic curve Diffie hellman-based handshake convention has been intended for the product characterizes system remote refreshing plan, specifically, the lopsided Open function handshake convention. The convention moves noteworthy calculation undertakings from the restricted IoT gadget to the power focus. The security of the convention is dissected. It can be demonstrated by the test that the elliptic curve Diffie hellman is a lot of lightweight than the transport layer security handshake convention and secure socket layer handshake convention (Jiaren, et al., 2018). The green supportive cloud correspondence worldview has been created holding fast to the idea of cloud interchanges profits by consolidating the created calculations and virtualization schematics by increasing a straight option in the quantity for the client with insignificantly expanded power utilization and included security. it has seen a general increment in control utilization during the correspondence time frame in the created convention (H, S, U, & B, 2017). The long spread postponement is utilized in the submerged acoustic channel and the sparsity of the system topology and formalized the conditions for which a hub can transmit in any event, when it is situated inside the correspondence scope of a hub taking part in a correspondence session. limitations have been planned dependent on conditions and present a conveyed impact evasion handshake-based convention, which, by together applying spatial and time reuse procedures, enormously improves channel use (Roee, Wenbo, Wee, & Lutz, 2013). The safe wrist-worn shrewd gadget blending plan has been structured by mistreating the movement sign of the gadgets that are produced by the handshake to arrange a dependable key between clients. a novel fluffy cryptography calculation has been made to guarantee the security of key arrangements. The created handshake speeding up based matching plan is vigorous, secure, and proficient that can be demonstrated by broad trials (Qi, et al., 2019). The structure has been built up that is utilized to advance transporter logic numerous entrance remote systems by designing distinctive handset parameters to give more prominent spatial reuse while wiping out concealed terminals. The ideal model for two-interface topologies and an inexact calculation for general topologies have been organized. The convention has the ability to totally dispense with ruinous cooperations bringing about enormous upgrades in throughput and postponement (Vinay, Saquib, & Nael, 2014).

Change Cipher Protocol

It defines the state of the cipher. Value is 1 byte for change cipher statement. It transforms the pending state to the current state.

Alerts

There are two fields are used such that level and alert field. The length of the level is 1 byte. The level can be classified into two types such that warning and fatal error.

The server generates an error in the form of the following messages:

- Unpredicted data
- Useless record-Message Authentication Code
- Unsuccessful data compression
- Unsuccessful linking
- Illegitimate Constraints

The server sends to the client in the form of the warning message that can be:

- Notification to close the credential
- Unverified Documentation
- Retract
- Unlicensed
- Unidentified

NETWORK LAYER

This is the 3rd layer in the TCP/IP suite and 5th layer in the OSI model. The responsibility of the network layer is to route the packet. The router is used at the network layer. The protocol has been defined network is called internet protocol. The router is an intelligent device that finds the shortest path for IP. IP is consists of the source address, destination address, and data that has to be transmitted. The network layer does not provide error control and flow control of IP.

Network Layer Security

The router is used to route the packet. The packet must be secured while the transmission over the network. The protocol has been defined for packet security that is called IP security. The network layer is secured by IPsec. IPsec is used to implement the above network layer and below the transport layer. IPsec can be implemented in various parts. It can be used to provide security to the application programs. Security service is provided to the transport layer by the IPsec. It provides security to each node in a network such as intradomain or inter-domain protocols. It used to encapsulate the information. It stopes the interference of any other communication channel. It provides data authentication from the origin and verifies that the data has been transmitted to the receiver. It permits to exchange the secret key and manage it. In a perfect world, any establishment would need its very own private system for correspondence to guarantee security. Be that as it may, it might be expensive to set up and keep up such a private system over the topographically scattered zone. It would require to oversee a composite foundation of correspondence links, switches. IPsec gives a simple component to executing the Virtual Private Network for such organizations. VPN innovation permits the establishment's official traffic to be sent over the open Internet by scrambling traffic before entering the open Internet and coherently isolating it from other network transmissions.

Mode of IPsec

The IPsec can be worked in two ways such that transport or tunnel mode. Transport mode is used to secure the packet that is coming from the transport layer. It provides security to the information at the network layer that is coming from the transport layer. The header is not protected by IPsec in transport mode as well as a complete packet. It provides protection to the information in the entire packet. IPsec is used to protect the peer to peer transmission.

The information has been encrypted at the upper layer and comes to the network layer. A new header is used to add with encrypted data in tunnel mode. IPsec is applied to a complete packet including the IP header. The original header is different from the newly added header. Tunnel mode is used for a wide area network, which means that the routers can be communicated with other routers or hosts with a different network. The tunnel is created between the sender and receiver for secure data transmission. This is the imaginary path to protect the initial IP header.

Protocol of IPsec

IPsec has two protocols that are used to provide the security to the header and information in entire packets. The protocols are AH and ESP. AH, the protocol does not provide secrecy of information. It is used to provide the source verification and also give the validation of information in the packet. The hash function (MD5) is used for authentication and conventional private key. AH, is added by the message digest. The mode of operation is used to define the location of AH for transmission. The length of AH is 32 bits. The real limit of the internet protocol header is 51. The AH is comprised of six fields such as the next header, information span, set aside, safety constraints, categorization quantity, and hashing for authentication.

Each field has its own responsibility. The next header is used to define the formate of information that is carrying in the IP packet. The size of the next header is eight-bit. The value of the header is 51 before the encryption of data. The length of data in AH can be multiple of four-bytes but it does not contain the first eight bits. From security associations, when it is distinguished that the security convention is AH, the parameters of the AH header are determined. The process is associated with the security parameter index. And the maximum length has been defined for SPI is 32 bits. The sequence number can be 32 bit long and defines the flow of information. When IP transmit again so sequence number does not change, it does not repeat its sequence. The hash function is used for authentication of data and it has a variable length.

The AH, protocol does not care about the secrecy of data. In this case, IPsec has introduced another protocol named as encapsulation security information protocol. It is used to provide the source verification, the validity of data and secrecy of data. To make the determination easier, the data of verification is used to add at the last position of the IP packet. The value of the protocol in the header is 50. Encapsulation header and trailer are added in the IP packet. The header in encapsulation security information has two fields that are SPI and sequence number. 32 bits long is the size of the header. The characteristics of the header are similar to the authentication header. 32 bits long is the trailer of encapsulation. The field has been defined for the trailer is padding and length. The working principle of encapsulation security information is given as:

- The Information is added by the trailer.
- The Information and trailer are used to encapsulate by using conventional symmetric key algorithms.
- Haeder is being added before transmission.
- The verification of data is generated by the header, information, and trailer of encapsulation security information.
- The MD5 algorithm is used to create the authentication data.
- The generated digest is used to add at the last place of the trailer.
- Finally, the header of IP is appended after the modification of the protocol and the value is 50 that is assigned to the header.

The origination of IPsec transmission is based on security associations. The connection is generated by the sender and the receiver is the functionality of the security association. When connection successfully linked then data is being transferred. The encapsulation of data and verification of data is done in various ways. IPsec is used to provide options for data hiding and confirmation. Security association helps to determine the algorithm of encapsulation as well as the hash algorithm for both users. Security association gives the parameter that defines the relationship between systems. The two-way communication between the systems can be done with the help of security associations. SPI is used to determine the security association at the system. IPsec is used to transmit data fastly.

The maximum size of the SPI is 32 bit long. It set the value of the security association that can be a maximum 32 bit long. It is used to give a difference between two security associations with similar IPsec. IPsec has two types of database named as safety association record and safety strategy record. The safety association record saves the condition of the security association of endpoints. There are nine conditions that have been defined in SAD.

The sequence number for outbound transmission as well as overflow flag is used for authentication header and encapsulation security information. The maximum length can be 32 bit long. The prevention of reply is determined by a separate window. The time to live for security association is defined in the database. The header algorithm of authentication and encapsulation security information is used to define the database. The working of IPsec also defines in the database. The prevention of fragmentation is also done in the database.

The security association database has three parts that are SPI, parameter, and destination IP address. The purpose of the security policy database is to route the packet. It indicates the security association in the database. It also indicates the traffic that is used to bypass the IPsec protocol. The security policy database is used to filter the packet where the schedules absolute upon are the stimulation of security association procedures.

IPsec also provides security services to information at the network layer to satisfy the objective of information security. The security association database is used for access control. The IP is discarded if there is no security association at the destination. The accuracy of information is conserved by two protocols of IPsec. The receiver is checked the authentication code sent by the sender that is created by the hash algorithm. The origin of the information is authenticated by both protocols in IPsec. The confidential information is provided by encapsulation security information. The attack that is used to repeat the information can be prevented by the authentication header and encapsulation security information protocol.

SECURITY SYSTEM

This is fundamental for all connotations to secure their structures on the off chance that they target transmission the managements demanded by representatives and customers. This, over the long haul, confirms the unsavory reputation of your company. With the help of software and turning out to be a more brilliant phase by phase, the requirement to use organize safety apparatus turns out to be more and more feeble. There are various ways to protect the network of an organization. The following systems are required to secure the information over the network in an organization.

- The software is required to protect the system is called antivirus and antimalware. The antivirus is used to scan the system for any threat, worms, and viruses. It is used to fix the worms and viruses and give complete protection to the files in the system.
- The security of the application is essential to take request safety meanwhile no request is completed splendidly. This effective for any request to comprise susceptibilities that are utilized by aggressors to go in your structure. The Request safety along these lines includes the merchandise, apparatus, and measures your choice to finish those programs that have been started.
- So as to recognize an unusual structure manner, you must realize the resembles of behavior. Conduct examination instruments are able to do obviously perceiving workouts that deviate from the rules. Your safety people will hence have the option to prolifically distinguish pointers of the conciliation that represent a possible problem and rapidly solve the dangers.
- Associations should confirm that their employee doesn't show delicate data to an unauthorized network. Employees must hence utilize data loss protection in advance, organize protection exertions, that have individuals as of shifting, distribution, or in any event, letterpress indispensable data in a hazardous technique.
- Electronic mail entryways are observed as the core risk for a safety rupture. Assailants use public deceitful tactics and separate statistics so as to paradigm sophisticated efforts to deceive receivers and later direct them to locales helping up the virus. The electronic mail safety measure is suitable for obstructive stabbings and monitoring the mails so as to avert the forfeiture of sensitive material.
- Firewalls have placed an obstruction between you're confined in the inner structure and unworthy from external structures, like an internetworking. Various guidelines are used to allow transmis-

sion. There are two types of firewall used in a network to protect the information such that software and hardware firewall. The free firewall productively supervises the transmission on your personal computer, laptop, and verifies all links when are browsing the information.

- The intrusion protection system is a protection system that is used for inspection of transmission so as to efficiently detect stabbings. The intrusion protection system is used to design the ruleset refreshes for splutter. It can possible to design the ruleset refreshes that allow them to subsequently run at precise interludes and these keep informed.

- Cell phones and software are increasingly actuality absorbed by the attackers. The information technology links could very in a little while helping the company program on close to home gadgets. There is, in reality, the requirement for you is to switch the gadgets that can get to your system. It is also imperative to structure their affiliations to keep compose the private transmission.

- Programming categorized partition is used to organize traffic into shifted commands and makes it simpler for the detection of unapproved transmission. The polices can be contracted that are reliant on the zone, trade, and with the goal that the right individuals get the accessibility and distrustful devices are in the controllable behavior.

- The Safety of data and occasion organization software are used to bond all the required data by your safety crew so as to recognize and respond to threats. This type of software is local in a different scheme, including computer-generated and corporeal gadgets and network programs.

- A VPN is a type of safety structure equipped for encoding the company to protect the complete system, or for the most part over the network. A faraway system to a virtual private network is commonly utilized internet protocol security so as to verify the correspondence among systems and gadgets.

- An ideal network safety procedure will help in supervisory your team's network use, repudiating reachability to the malevolent web, and delaying.

- The arrange safety process encourages to switch who can access the network. It is essential to notice each device and consumer so as to keep out possible aggressors. This will assist you in implementing your security policies. The rebellious device can be simply jammed.

- Specialized Grid Shield is utilized to secure information inside the system. Specialized structure insurance monitors both put away and in-travel information from malignant programming and from unapproved people.

- Physical Network Security is a system security measure intended to keep unapproved individuals from physically meddling with arranging parts. Entryway locks and ID passes are basic parts of physical system security.

- Authoritative System Safety is a security technique that switches a client's system conduct and access. It additionally gives a standard working methodology to IT officials when executing changes in the IT framework. Organizational approaches and systems are types of organizational system insurance.

The physical layer safety can be accomplished by multi-jump helpful for the remote communication whose identical channel lattice can be utilized as the safe estimation grid. Expanding the number of bounces will build the mystery rate (Lyu, Han, & Fu, 2018). The physical layer safety in ultra-thick structures as the closeness of the clients to the phones has been researched. The random spatial pattern is utilized so as to give tractable articulations to the normal mystery rate where Rician blurring diverts are considered in the principle and the spillage joins (Mahmoud & Walaa, 2017). The physical layer safety model has been intended to keep different transmitted messages secure. The assisted ideal beamforming plan is created to ensure layered data security. The arrangement raised estimate based calculation is utilized to handle the nonconvexity of the issue and afterward, a low-unpredictability zero-driving beamforming plan is examined. The mystery execution advancement in Layered physical security can be demonstrated by scientific displaying (Wei, Jian, Yonghong, & Yuchen, Artificial-Noise-Aided Optimal Beamforming in Layered Physical Layer Security, 2018). An epic plan for instigating counterfeit intersymbol interference at a foe with constrained assets at real gadgets has been created and explored (Sasi & Ranjan, 2019). The physical layer safety investigates different capable fifth-generation advances that have been examined, including physical layer safety programming, gigantic MIMO, millimeter-wave exchanges, mixed structures, unbalanced numerous entrance, two-way communication (Yongpeng, et al., 2018). The encrusted physical layer safety model has been created, which is the expansion of the customary physical layer safety to the area of different layer data security. The data security structure that can be utilized to transmit the message that has a security level, while each client has a trusted status. The messages must be decoded by the client with security levels lower than or equivalent to their freedom, else, they will be esteemed as meddlers (Wei, Jian, Yonghong, & Yuchen, Transmit Beamforming for Layered Physical Layer Security, 2019). The structure articulation for the mystery blackout likelihood has been talked about, which can be considered the blurring attributes of the remote condition, the area and the number of interferers, just as the transmission intensity of the base station and the obstruction (Dimitrios, Alexandros, George, & Arumugam, 2017). The mystery execution of the remote portable sensor correspondence arranges that is dependent on a source, reliable beneficiary, and a nuisance model over the two-weakening of remote sign crossing various ways has been explored. the accurate secure blackout likelihood and the likelihood of carefully positive mystery limit articulations for two transmit receiving wire choice plans have been driven and Cumulative the quantity of transmitting reception apparatuses can be investigated and improved the mystery execution by reenactments (Han, Lingwei, Wenzhong, Pingping, & Ruhong, 2019). The digital protection structure has been talked about for remote clients in cell systems, where every client paid a premium to a backup plan for future money related remuneration if a blackout jumps out at a person. The remnant's likelihood of the safety net provider can be adequately diminished by preparing a bigger number of reception apparatuses at the base stations or expanding system recurrence salvage (Xiao, Dusit, Nicolas, Hai, & Ping, 2018). The physical layer safety plot for portable registering level in versatile wellbeing digital-physical framework has been created utilizing instruments from stochastic geometry. The articulations for the transmission area around a commonplace portable client have been inferred that fulfill a mystery likelihood, an objective blackout likelihood, and postpone edge limitations (Rachad, et al., 2017).

FUNDAMENTAL OF IOT AND ARCHITECTURE OF IOT

The network of the network called the internet is used to connect the objects and devices. Sensors or radio connected devices are used to transmit data over the network. The sensory system can be automatic wireless reconfigurable to sense the data and send it to the user application. By the invention of IPv6, the things are addressable. Every object has an IP address to browse it any time. Internet of things use three types of protocol for communication purpose that can be classified as human to human, things to human and things to things. Things can be machines, tools or devices as well. Ubiquitous computing is required for processing and control through the feedback system. The user interface is required to process and display the results. The user interface can be a graphical user interface or menu-driven architecture.

The internet of things is nothing but menu driver architecture that can compose of three main components list as an embedded system, cloud based system, and user end. These three components can be further divided into three layers. Each layer has a specific role in complete architecture. The first layer is the application layer that can be the user layer to see the parameters that have to be measured. The parameters in smart earth that have to be controlled and measured at any time and place can be temperature, humidity, the flow of water, retaining and logistics, smart homes, and cities. The application is developed to support the user to monitor and control every device that is connected on the internet.

The last layer is the embedded system layer. This layer is composed of sensors, devices to locate the position, and radio frequency tags. Sensors are used to sense the physical parameter and transmit to the second layer. Sensors are wirelessly connected to monitor and control the parameters such that air pressure, fire, and smoke detection. The Wireless sensors network also called nodes that are distributed at a different place and collects the sensed information to send it through the internet. Wireless technologies are used to monitor and control named as Zigbee, Bluetooth, GSM/GPRS, and Wifi with different data rates and frequency. Radiofrequency identification is a foundation of the internet of things. RFID tags are used to locate and track objects. IP is used to track and browse the information of objects automatically all over the world. Courier service is an example of IoT to provide complete information of objects that have been tagged. Computers can automatically detect the tagged objects. GPS is used to provide location-based services to users. GPS is known as a global positioning system that is used by the real-time tracking. Radars are used to locate using electromagnetic waves. Lidar is used to locate using optical signals. Sonar is used to detect the object based on acoustic signals. A system strength mindful grouping convention for intellectual radio systems has been developed. Range elements and vitality utilization are just because all the while incorporated into the convention plan of system security mindful bunching (Meng, Si, Wei, & Min, 2019) (Almusaylim & Zaman, 2019) (Hussain & Hussain, 2019) (Humayun, Niazi, Jhanjhi, Alshayeb, & Mahmood, 2020).

One of the major concerns with the IoT is to make sure the security of the IoT related devices connected with the network. IoT has several advantages like stay connected, efficient usage of electricity, row safety, healthcare, cost efficiency, security, privacy, consistent, quick response, interoperability, Resiliency, consistent, reduce complexity, and more convenience. The IoT has also disadvantages like Data Massively, environment issues, data security, personal privacy, lesser jobs, losing control over life, yields environment, high risk of leakage of data, complex, human labor reduces, lifestyle is going to technology-driven, and one extra point of failure. In the recent past, various IoT security incidents already happened and IoT users are still worried about their data. To enhance the security, IT administrators should run IoT security tests regularly, deploy access controls, implement IoT security standards in the organization, deploy risk management specifically for IoT networks, IoT identify spoofing attack measures, secure network connections, avoid initiation of network connection first by the IoT devices, build own IoT network, implement strong encryption method on Wi-Fi, give router a specific and unique name, set up a separate guest IoT network, change factory default user names and passwords, keep setting safe, update all software of IoT, conduct regular audit of the IoT network, implement two-factor authentication, implement network monitoring tools, keep track network bandwidth usage, and also implement security measures into supply chain regarding IoT. The IoT devices also face challenges, like security, connectivity, standards, intelligent analysis & actions, authentication, access control, policy enforcement, trust, mobile security, secure middleware, confidentiality, confidentiality, law and regulations, business policies, IoT vendors, network connectivity, expert team, infrastructure, implementation issues, technological enhancement, High fees of implementation, protection worries, uncertainty, dataflow, loss of business, ethical issues, unique addressing, standardization, lack of skills, storage, processing power and time, scalability, local and compliance, organization size, awareness and adoption, latency and complexity, device authentication, secure communication, policy enforcement, lack of budget, cybersecurity, cybercrime, intellectual property laws, communication laws, attack detection and real-time protection.

The devices that are connected over the network through mobile, and information network. Cloud Computing is playing a crucial rule in IoT. Cloud computing is the middle layer of a complete model. Cloud computing is used to store the information sent by devices that are connected over the network. This information is available to the user at any time and any place of the entire world. Clouds can be a web or grid system that provides service-oriented architecture. The forward a multi-layered answer for safely setting up start to finish TCP/IP based Internet of Things interchanges over long term evaluation cell-based systems. This system comprises guidelines based interlocking useful components sent in a safely architected transporter organize giving a protected end to the end correspondences channel for the Internet of Things gadgets and applications (Craig & Andrea, 2019). The author has discussed the advance engineering design, architecture, and internet of things also cyber-physical systems (Kai, Geoffrey, & Jack, 2012). Figure 16 demonstrates the architecture of IoT.

Verifying the IoT is a multi-faceted exertion that requires enormous moves just as little changes in accordance with guarantee systems, frameworks, information, and gadgets are secured. The purpose of IoT is to provide support to the human being. To secure the devices and transmission over the network is

Figure 16. Architecture of the Internet of Things

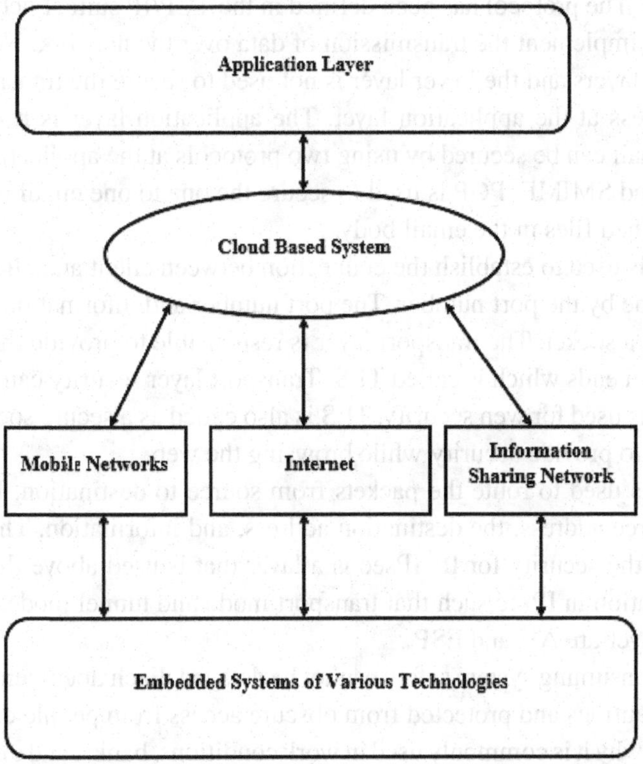

more important. There is a kind of way to protect the devices and information over the network such that don't connect to the network if you don't need to send or review the information because the information is an asset. To secure the information of the device it is necessary to keep a strong password. When browsing or sharing the information no need to turn on the plug and play button. It is recommended to install the latest firmware and used secure cloud services to store the information over the network.

DISCUSSION AND RECOMMENDATION

The devices are connected with each other to perform some tasks and it is called a network. The network can be wired or wireless. The network is used to share or distribute the information and people can take advantage of meaningful information. The use of the network is important for faster transmission of data. Organizations want to secure the information while transmitting over the network that is called information security. There are three objectives of information security that are the secrecy of data, truthfully of data and accessibility of data to the authorized person.

The network is designed by the OSI model and protocols are applied to the OSI model for the implementation of the network. OSI model is robust and easy to implement in designing the network. The user writes a message on the application layer. The message processes to the transport layer and is divided into small parts over there. The network layer is used to deal with IP. The IP is also called as a packet that has a source and destination addresses along with information to be transmitted. The data link layer is used to create a frame to encapsulate the packets. The physical layer is used to transform the frame into bits, furthermore, bits change into a single form for transmission.

The network is to be secured for the achievement of the objective of information security that is called network security. The protocol has been defined in the TCP/IP suite. Each layer has a predefined protocol that is used to implement the transmission of data over the network. Network security is used to implement at higher layers and the lower layer is not used to secure the transmission. The electronic mails are used to process at the application layer. The application layer is responsible to secure the email contents. The email can be secured by using two protocols at the application layer and the names of protocols are PGP and SMIME. PGP is used to secure the one to one email message and SMIME is used to secure the attached files in the email body.

The transport layer is used to establish the connection between client and client or client and server. The transmission is done by the port number. The port number and information are combined together in a single entity called a socket. The transport layer is responsible to provide the security to the socket at source and destination ends which is called TLS. Transport layer security can be implemented above the transport layer and is used for wen security. TLS is also called as a secure socket layer. TSL has four protocols that are used to provide security while browsing the web.

The network layer is used to route the packets from source to destination. IP is called an internet protocol that has a source address, the destination address, and information. The network layer is also responsible to provide the security for IP. IPsec is a layer that is used above the network layer. There are two modes of operation in IPsec such that transport mode and tunnel mode. The protocols that are defined for the IPsec layer are AH and ESP .

The obligation for consuming system safety cannot be delayed. Each document, material and separate statistics are endured cautious and protected from obscure access from people existing on the structure and outside of it. That's why it is commonly used in work conditions, banks, and different affiliations. The blueprints and other approaches of system safety help the system authority to screen any sort of abuse, change or unapproved access of a PC make. Private frameworks can be given protection from outside attacks by stopping them from the web. Framework Safety makes them safe from dangerous attacks.

The Internet of things provides support to monitor and control the smart earth. The Internet of things is the latest technology used to track the required information. IoT is the solution to reduce complexity, enhance the performance of the system in the logistics, health care, and cyber systems. The Internet of things is supported by pervasive computing to process the information and display the required result graphical user interface. Cloud computing is a database system that can be used to access information at any time and place of the world. To provide security it is essential to protect the device using firewall, password and VPN as well.

CONCLUSION

The Internet is a source to share important information worldwide. To secure the information over the internet is called network security. Rules and regulations are used to stop the access of unauthorized individuals. There are some goals such that availability, confidentially and integrity to secure data from the attacker during the network transmission. Network security is adopted by organizations that can be used to secure private data or open access for the public. Various types of network security are used to protect the whole information over the network from an intruder like web security, email security, and wireless security. Keys or passwords are used for authentication. The advantage of network security is to save the information and can be useful at any instance of time.

Objects, and devices that are connected through a network to communicate with each other known as the internet of things. The invention of IPv6 makes it addressable to control, monitor and recognize the objects using wireless technologies. IoT security is to protect the data that is transmitted over the channel. The IoT provides quality of life, reduces complexity and enhances the efficiency of the system.

In this book chapter, the author will emphasize the fundamental concept of network, information security, and network security, introduce the possible network security attacks, discuss the application layer security in detail, the transport layer and its security protocol briefly discuss, IP security above the network layer describes, security system, fundamentals of IoT and architecture of IoT and final discussion, and recommendations.

REFERENCES

Ahmed, E. S., Dusit, N., Ridha, H., & Naofal, A. (2017). Impact of the Wireless Network's PHY Security and Reliability on Demand-Side Management Cost in the Smart Grid. *IEEE Access: Practical Innovations, Open Solutions*, 5, 5678–5689. doi:10.1109/ACCESS.2017.2695520

Alex, R., Ronaldo, T. P., Raimir, H. F., & Joel, J. P. (2019). Enabling Online Quantitative Security Analysis in 6LoWPAN Networks. *IEEE Internet of Things Journal*, 6(3), 5631–5638. doi:10.1109/JIOT.2019.2904302

Alextian, L., Magnos, M., Roberta, L. G., Arash, F. B., & Emilio, S. (2018). RDNA: Residue-Defined Networking Architecture Enabling Ultra-Reliable Low-Latency Datacenters. *IEEE eTransactions on Network and Service Management, 15*(4), 1473–1487. doi:10.1109/TNSM.2018.2876845

Alireza, S., Yosr, J., Makan, P., & Mohamed, C. (2016). Efficient Provisioning of Security Service Function Chaining Using Network Security Defense Patterns. *IEEE Transactions on Services Computing, 12*(4), 534–549.

Almusaylim, Z. A., & Zaman, N. (2019). A review on smart home present state and challenges: Linked to context-awareness internet of things (IoT). *Wireless Networks, 25*(6), 3193–3204. doi:10.100711276-018-1712-5

Amit, P., & P., S. (2018). DDoS Attacks at the Application Layer: Challenges and Research Perspectives for Safeguarding Web Applications. *IEEE Communications Surveys and Tutorials, 21*(1), 661–685.

Aniket, B., & Sunil, B. (2019). Detecting lateral spear phishing attacks in organisations. *IET Information Security, 13*(2), 133–140. doi:10.1049/iet-ifs.2018.5090

Behrouz, A. F. (2013). Network Model. In *Data Communication and Networking* (pp. 74–80). New York: Mc Graw Hill.

Behrouz, A. F., & Debdeep, M. (2015). Introduction. In *Cryptogarphy and Network Security* (pp. 1–2). New York: Mc Graw Hill.

Cataldo, B., Fulvio, V., Antonio, L., Diego, R. L., & Antonio, P. P. (2019). Adding Support for Automatic Enforcement of Security Policies in NFV Networks. *IEEE/ACM Transactions on Networking, 27*(2), 707–720. doi:10.1109/TNET.2019.2895278

Chang, S. P., & Wang, S. P. (2018). A Group-Oriented DTLS Handshake for Secure IoT Applications. *IEEE Transactions on Automation Science and Engineering, 15*(4), 1920–1929. doi:10.1109/TASE.2018.2855640

Chenxu, W., Tony, T. N., Xiapu, L., & Jinhe, W. (2017). SkyShield: A Sketch-Based Defense System Against Application Layer DDoS Attacks. *IEEE Transactions on Information Forensics and Security, 13*(3), 559–573.

Christopher, N. G., Taegyu, K., Raffaele, D. C., Jeffrey, A., & Dan, G. (2018). Learning from the Ones that Got Away: Detecting New Forms of Phishing Attacks. *IEEE Transactions on Dependable and Secure Computing, 15*(6), 988–1001. doi:10.1109/TDSC.2018.2864993

Chuang, S., Min, Z., Yueying, Z., Danshi, W., Luyao, G., Wei, L., ... Siya, X. (2019). Hierarchical Edge Cloud Enabling Network Slicing For 5G Optional Fronthaul. *Journal of Optical Communications and Networking, 11*(4), B60–B70. doi:10.1364/JOCN.11.000B60

Chung, M. H., Meng, S. C., Duy, T. D., Wei, L. S., & Shouzhi, X. (2018). V2V Data Offloading for Cellular Network Based on the Software Defined Network (SDN) Inside Mobile Edge Computing (MEC) Architecture. *IEEE Access: Practical Innovations, Open Solutions, 6*, 17741–17755. doi:10.1109/ACCESS.2018.2820679

Cristina, A., Giuseppe, B., Federica, P., Javier, L., & Roberto, S. (2019). Covert Channels-Based Stealth Attacks in Industry 4.0. *IEEE Systems Journal, 13*(4), 3980–3988. doi:10.1109/JSYST.2019.2912308

Daemin, S., Keon, Y., Jiyoon, K., Philip, V. A., Jeong, N. K., & Ilsun, Y. (2019). A Security Protocol for Route Optimization in DMM-Based Smart Home IoT Networks. *IEEE Access: Practical Innovations, Open Solutions, 7*, 142531–142550. doi:10.1109/ACCESS.2019.2943929

Dhanushka, K., Santosh, T., & Gayan, A. A. (2019). Secure Communication in Relay-Assisted Massive MIMO Downlink With Active Pilot Attacks. *IEEE Transactions on Information Forensics and Security, 14*(11), 2819–2833. doi:10.1109/TIFS.2019.2901825

Dimitrios, S. K., Alexandros, A. A., George, K. K., & Arumugam, N. (2017). Physical Layer Security in the Presence of Interference. *IEEE Wireless Communications Letters, 6*(6), 802–805. doi:10.1109/LWC.2017.2743716

Dong, W., Bo, B., Kai, L., Wenbo, Z., Yanping, Y., & Zhu, H. (2019). Enhancing Information Security via Physical Layer Approaches in Heterogeneous IoT With Multiple Access Mobile Edge Computing in Smart City. *IEEE Access: Practical Innovations, Open Solutions, 7*, 54508–54521. doi:10.1109/AC-CESS.2019.2913438

Enaitz, E., Urko, Z., & José, M. G. (2017). A study of the personalization of spam content using Facebook public information. *Logic Journal of the IGPL, 25*(1), 30–41. doi:10.1093/jigpal/jzw040

Guan, W., Wen, X., Wang, L., & Lu, Z. (2018). On-Demand Cooperation Among Multiple Infrastructure Networks For Multi-Tenant Slicing: A Complex Network Perspective. *IEEE Access: Practical Innovations, Open Solutions, 6*, 78689–78699. doi:10.1109/ACCESS.2018.2885143

H, D. M., S, N. M., U, B. D., & B, M. B. (2017). Green Symbiotic Cloud Communications: Virtualized Transport Layer and Cognitive Decision Function. *IEEE Access, 5*, 13409 - 13421.

Han, W., Lingwei, X., Wenzhong, L., Pingping, X., & Ruhong, W. (2019). Physical Layer Security Performance of Wireless Mobile Sensor Networks in Smart City. *IEEE Access: Practical Innovations, Open Solutions, 7*, 15436–15443. doi:10.1109/ACCESS.2019.2895338

Haomeng, X., Zheng, Y., Zhen, Y., & Mohammed, A. (2018). Data Collection for Security Measurement in Wireless Sensor Networks: A Survey. *IEEE Internet of Things Journal, 6*(2), 2205–2224.

He, F., Li, X., Yulong, Z., Xianbin, W., & Kim, K. R. (2018). Three-Stage Stackelberg Game for Defending Against Full-Duplex Active Eavesdropping Attacks in Cooperative Communication. *IEEE Transactions on Vehicular Technology, 67*(11), 10788–10799. doi:10.1109/TVT.2018.2868900

Holger, B., & Christian, D. (2018). Secure Identification Under Passive Eavesdroppers and Active Jamming Attacks. *IEEE Transactions on Information Forensics and Security, 14*(2), 472–485.

Huan, L., Shoufeng, C., Jiayan, W., Zhenzhong, C., & Fengyu, W. (2019). Identifying Application-Layer DDoS Attacks Based on Request Rhythm Matrices. *IEEE Access: Practical Innovations, Open Solutions, 7*, 164480–164491. doi:10.1109/ACCESS.2019.2950820

Huaqing, L., Zheng, Y., Yu, C., & Lifang, Z. (2018). A Survey on Network Security-Related Data Collection Technologies. *IEEE Access: Practical Innovations, Open Solutions, 6*, 18345–18365. doi:10.1109/ACCESS.2018.2817921

Humayun, M., Niazi, M., Jhanjhi, N. Z., Alshayeb, M., & Mahmood, S. (2020). Cyber Security Threats and Vulnerabilities: A Systematic Mapping Study. *Arabian Journal for Science and Engineering, §§§,* 1–19. doi:10.100713369-019-04319-2

Hussain, K., Hussain, S. J., Jhanjhi, N. Z., & Humayun, M. (2019, April). SYN Flood Attack Detection based on Bayes Estimator (SFADBE) For MANET. In *2019 International Conference on Computer and Information Sciences (ICCIS)* (pp. 1-4). IEEE. 10.1109/ICCISci.2019.8716416

Ivan, F., Tarik, T., Yacine, K., & Jaeseung, S. (2018). A Survey on Emerging SDN and NFV Security Mechanisms for IoT Systems. *IEEE Communications Surveys and Tutorials, 21*(1), 812–837.

Jianfeng, G., Ying, Z., Su, Y., & Lili, W. (2019). AID Shuffling Mechanism Based on Group-Buying Auction for Identifier Network Security. *IEEE Access: Practical Innovations, Open Solutions, 7,* 123746–123756. doi:10.1109/ACCESS.2019.2936043

Jianting, N., Jia, X., Kaitai, L., Fan, Z., & Ee, C. C. (2018). Passive Attacks Against Searchable Encryption. *IEEE Transactions on Information Forensics and Security, 14*(3), 789–802.

Jiaren, C., Xin, H., Jie, Z., Jiawei, Z., Yaxi, L., Dawei, L., & Xiaofeng, M. (2018). A Handshake Protocol With Unbalanced Cost for Wireless Updating. *IEEE Access: Practical Innovations, Open Solutions, 6,* 18570–18581. doi:10.1109/ACCESS.2018.2820086

Jörg, L., Majid, V., & Tony, Y. Z. (2019). Elements of Application-Layer Internetworking for Adaptive Self-Organizing Networks. *Proceedings of the IEEE, 107*(4), 797–818. doi:10.1109/JPROC.2019.2894291

Jun, X., Baoqiang, Z., & Fengzhang, L. (2019). Distribution Network Security Situation Awareness Method Based on Security Distance. *IEEE Access: Practical Innovations, Open Solutions, 7,* 37855–37864. doi:10.1109/ACCESS.2019.2906779

Khundrakpam, J. S., Khelchandra, T., & Tanmay, D. (2018). Detection and differentiation of application layer DDoS attack from flash events using fuzzy-GA computation. *IET Information Security, 12*(6), 502–512. doi:10.1049/iet-ifs.2017.0500

Klever, R. P., Edejair, V., & Fernando, A. A. (2017). An Integrated Solution for the Improvement of the Mobile Devices Security based on the Android Platform. *IEEE Latin America Transactions, 15*(11), 2171–2176. doi:10.1109/TLA.2017.8070423

Krishna, P., Balachandra, M., & Vasundhara, A. (2019). Automated User Authentication in Wireless Public Key Infrastructure for Mobile Devices Using Aadhar Card. *IEEE Access: Practical Innovations, Open Solutions, 7,* 17981–18007. doi:10.1109/ACCESS.2019.2896324

Le, G., Jingqiang, L., Ziqiang, M., Bo, L., Luning, X., & Jiwu, J. (2018). Copker: A Cryptographic Engine Against Cold-Boot Attacks. *IEEE Transactions on Dependable and Secure Computing, 15*(5), 742–754. doi:10.1109/TDSC.2016.2631548

Limei, H., Zheng, Y., & Mohammed, A. (2018). LTE/LTE-A Network Security Data Collection and Analysis for Security Measurement: A Survey. *IEEE Access: Practical Innovations, Open Solutions, 6,* 4220–4242. doi:10.1109/ACCESS.2018.2792534

Lyndon, F., Sandra, S., Matthew, B., & Andrew, W. (2018). Tennison: A Distributed SDN Framework for Scalable Network Security. *IEEE Journal on Selected Areas in Communications, 36*(12), 2805–2818. doi:10.1109/JSAC.2018.2871313

Lyu, Q., Han, G., & Fu, X. (2018). Physical Layer Security in Multi-Hop AF Relay Network Based on Compressed Sensing. *IEEE Communications Letters, 22*(9), 1882–1885. doi:10.1109/LCOMM.2018.2853101

M, F. H., Josep, L. F., & Llorenç, H. (2019). A Solution for Secure Certified Electronic Mail Using Blockchain as a Secure Message Board. *IEEE Access, 7,* 31330 - 31341.

Mahmoud, K., & Walaa, H. (2017). Physical Layer Security in Ultra-Dense Networks. *IEEE Wireless Communications Letters, 6*(5), 690–693. doi:10.1109/LWC.2017.2731840

Manuel, C., Luca, D., Lucia, S., & Adriano, V. (2018). Performance Evaluation and Modeling of an Industrial Application-Layer Firewall. *IEEE Transactions on Industrial Informatics, 14*(5), 2159–2170. doi:10.1109/TII.2018.2802903

Maotong, X., Chong, L., & Suresh, S. (2018). PODCA: A passive optical data center network architecture. *Journal of Optical Communications and Networking, 10*(4), 409–420. doi:10.1364/JOCN.10.000409

Mark, E., Ying, H., Cunjin, L., Iryna, Y., Helge, J., & Leandros, A. M. (2019). Employee Perspective on Information Security Related Human Error in Healthcare: Proactive Use of IS-CHEC in Questionnaire Form. *IEEE Access: Practical Innovations, Open Solutions, 7,* 102087–102101. doi:10.1109/ACCESS.2019.2927195

Mehran, A., Mahrokh, A., Wei, N., Abbas, J., & Negin, S. (2018). A Routing Framework for Offloading Traffic From Cellular Networks to SDN-Based Multi-Hop Device-to-Device Networks. *IEEE eTransactions on Network and Service Management, 15*(4), 1516–1531. doi:10.1109/TNSM.2018.2875696

Min, L., Xiaotong, Z., Li, L., Kim, K. R., & Debiao, H. (2017). Security Analysis of Two Password-Authenticated Multi-Key Exchange Protocols. *IEEE Access: Practical Innovations, Open Solutions, 5,* 8017–8024. doi:10.1109/ACCESS.2017.2698390

Ming, Y., Xiaodan, G., Zhen, L., Changxin, Y., & Junzhou, L. (2017). An active de-anonymizing attack against tor web traffic. *Tsinghua Science and Technology, 22*(6), 702–713. doi:10.23919/TST.2017.8195352

Mitsugu, I., Kazuo, O., & Junji, S. (2018). Security Formalizations and Their Relationships for Encryption and Key Agreement in Information-Theoretic Cryptography. *IEEE Transactions on Information Theory, 64*(1), 654–685. doi:10.1109/TIT.2017.2744650

Nader, S. S., Carsten, M., Tim, W., & Steve, F. (2018). Information security collaboration formation in organisations. *IET Information Security, 12*(3), 238–245. doi:10.1049/iet-ifs.2017.0257

Napa, S., Jonathan, W., Nasir, M., Janusz, K., & Prakash, I. (2019). Emerging NUI-Based Methods for User Authentication: A New Taxonomy and Survey. *IEEE Transactions on Biometrics, Behavior, and Identity Science, 1*(1), 5–31. doi:10.1109/TBIOM.2019.2893297

Nir, N., Aviad, C., & Yuval, E. (2016). ALDOCX: Detection of Unknown Malicious Microsoft Office Documents Using Designated Active Learning Methods Based on New Structural Feature Extraction Methodology. *IEEE Transactions on Information Forensics and Security*, 12(3), 631–646.

Pietro, D., Marko, A., Čedomir, S., & Tomislav, D. (2018). Software-Defined Microgrid Control for Resilience Against Denial-of-Service Attacks. *IEEE Transactions on Smart Grid*, 10(5), 5258–5268.

Qi, J., Xiaohan, H., Ning, Z., Kuan, Z., Xindi, M., & Jianfeng, M. (2019). Shake to Communicate: Secure Handshake Acceleration-Based Pairing Mechanism for Wrist Worn Devices. *IEEE Internet of Things Journal*, 6(3), 5618–5630. doi:10.1109/JIOT.2019.2904177

Rachad, A., Lingjia, L., Jonathan, A., Michael, J. M., John, D. M., & Yang, Y. (2017). A Physical Layer Security Scheme for Mobile Health Cyber-Physical Systems. *IEEE Internet of Things Journal*, 5(1), 295–309.

Roee, D., Wenbo, S., Wee, S. S., & Lutz, L. (2013). Joint Time and Spatial Reuse Handshake Protocol for Underwater Acoustic Communication Networks. *IEEE Journal of Oceanic Engineering*, 38(3), 470–483. doi:10.1109/JOE.2012.2229065

Rong, G., Xiaojie, W., & Jun, L. (2018). A Software Defined Networking-Oriented Security Scheme for Vehicle Networks. *IEEE Access: Practical Innovations, Open Solutions*, 6, 58195–58203. doi:10.1109/ACCESS.2018.2875104

Sai, K. P., Elena, G., Wolfgang, K., & Carmen, M. M. (2019). Rational Agent-Based Decision Algorithm For Strategic Converged Network Migration Planning. *Journal of Optical Communications and Networking*, 11(7), 371–382. doi:10.1364/JOCN.11.000371

Sasi, V. P., & Ranjan, B. (2019). Channel-Aware Artificial Intersymbol Interference for Enhancing Physical Layer Security. *IEEE Communications Letters*, 23(7), 1182–1185. doi:10.1109/LCOMM.2019.2915076

Shouling, J., Shukun, Y., Xin, H., Weili, H., Zhigong, L., & Raheem, B. (2017). Zero-Sum Password Cracking Game: A Large-Scale Empirical Study on the Crackability, Correlation, and Security of Passwords. *IEEE Transactions on Dependable and Secure Computing*, 14(5), 550–564. doi:10.1109/TDSC.2015.2481884

Sibi, C. S., Sangeetha, D., & Vaidehi, V. (2019). Intrusion detection system for detecting wireless attacks in IEEE 802.11 networks. *IET Networks*, 8(4), 219–232. doi:10.1049/iet-net.2018.5050

Tanin, S., & Khan, A. W. (2019). Choice of Application Layer Protocols for Next Generation Video Surveillance Using Internet of Video Things. *IEEE Access: Practical Innovations, Open Solutions*, 7, 41607–41624. doi:10.1109/ACCESS.2019.2907525

Utsav, B., Andrew, W., Chiraag, J., & Madeleine, W. (2019). An Energy-Efficient Reconfigurable DTLS Cryptographic Engine for Securing Internet-of-Things Applications. *IEEE Journal of Solid-State Circuits*, 54(8), 2339–2352. doi:10.1109/JSSC.2019.2915203

Vijay, V., Kallol, K., Uday, T., & Michael, H. (2018). A Policy-Based Security Architecture for Software-Defined Networks. *IEEE Transactions on Information Forensics and Security*, 14(4), 897–912.

Vinay, K., Saquib, R., & Nael, B. A. (2014). Interaction Engineering: Achieving Perfect CSMA Handshakes in Wireless Networks. *IEEE Transactions on Mobile Computing, 13*(11), 2552–2565. doi:10.1109/TMC.2014.2314130

Wei, W., Houbing, S., Huihui, W., & Xiumei, F. (2017). Research and Simulation of Queue Management Algorithms in Ad Hoc Networks Under DDoS Attack. *IEEE Access: Practical Innovations, Open Solutions, 5*, 27810–27817. doi:10.1109/ACCESS.2017.2681684

Wei, Z., Jian, C., Yonghong, K., & Yuchen, Z. (2018). Artificial-Noise-Aided Optimal Beamforming in Layered Physical Layer Security. *IEEE Communications Letters, 23*(1), 72–75.

Wei, Z., Jian, C., Yonghong, K., & Yuchen, Z. (2019). Transmit Beamforming for Layered Physical Layer Security. *IEEE Transactions on Vehicular Technology, 68*(10), 9747–9760. doi:10.1109/TVT.2019.2932753

William, S. (2017). Computer and Network Security Concept. In *Cryptography and Network Security: Principle and Practice* (pp. 37–40). Uttar Pradesh, India: Pearson.

Xiao, L., Dusit, N., Nicolas, P., Hai, J., & Ping, W. (2018). Managing Physical Layer Security in Wireless Cellular Networks: A Cyber Insurance Approach. *IEEE Journal on Selected Areas in Communications, 36*(7), 1648–1661. doi:10.1109/JSAC.2018.2825518

Xiao, L., Jing, X., Zhen, F. Z., & Wen, T. Z. (2017). Investigating the Multi-Ciphersuite and Backwards-Compatibility Security of the Upcoming TLS 1.3. *IEEE Transactions on Dependable and Secure Computing, 16*(2), 272–286.

Xiuhua, L., Wei, Y., Qiaoyan, W., Zhengping, J., & Wenmin, L. (2018). A Lattice-Based Unordered Aggregate Signature Scheme Based on the Intersection Method. *IEEE Access: Practical Innovations, Open Solutions, 6*, 33986–33994. doi:10.1109/ACCESS.2018.2847411

Yanling, Z., Ye, L., Xinchang, Z., Guanggang, G., Wei, Z., & Yanjie, S. (2019). A Survey of Networking Applications Applying the Software Defined Networking Concept Based on Machine Learning. *IEEE Access: Practical Innovations, Open Solutions, 7*, 95397–95417. doi:10.1109/ACCESS.2019.2928564

Yantao, L., Hailong, H., & Gang, Z. (2018). Using Data Augmentation in Continuous Authentication on Smartphones. *IEEE Internet of Things Journal, 6*(1), 628–640.

Yasser, A. B., Vivian, E. S., & Natalia, M. S. (2018). Artificial intelligence techniques for information security risk assessment. *IEEE Latin America Transactions, 16*(3), 897–901. doi:10.1109/TLA.2018.8358671

Yong, F., Cheng, Z., Cheng, H., Liang, L., & Yue, Y. (2019). Phishing Email Detection Using Improved RCNN Model With Multilevel Vectors and Attention Mechanism. *IEEE Access: Practical Innovations, Open Solutions, 7*, 56329–56340. doi:10.1109/ACCESS.2019.2913705

Yongpeng, W., Ashish, K., Chengshan, X., Giuseppe, C., Kai, K. W., & Xiqi, G. (2018). A Survey of Physical Layer Security Techniques for 5G Wireless Networks and Challenges Ahead. *IEEE Journal on Selected Areas in Communications, 36*(4), 679–695. doi:10.1109/JSAC.2018.2825560

Network Security and Internet of Things

Yu, X., Yuanyuan, L., Bin, Z., Ruyan, W., & George, N. R. (2018). SDN enabled restoration with triggered precomputation in elastic optical inter-datacenter networks. *Journal of Optical Communications and Networking*, *11*(1), 24–34.

Yuanyuan, K., Bin, L., Feng, C., & Zhen, Y. (2018). The Security Network Coding System With Physical Layer Key Generation in Two-Way Relay Networks. *IEEE Access: Practical Innovations, Open Solutions*, *6*, 40673–40681. doi:10.1109/ACCESS.2018.2858282

Zahoor, A. A., Hasan, T., Malik, H. M., Shahzaib, T., & Klaus, M. (2019). Key-Based Cookie-Less Session Management Framework for Application Layer Security. *IEEE Access: Practical Innovations, Open Solutions*, *7*, 128544–128554. doi:10.1109/ACCESS.2019.2940331

Zhen, Z., Yuhui, D., Geyong, M., Junjie, X., Laurence, T. Y., & Yongtao, Z. (2019). HSDC: A Highly Scalable Data Center Network Architecture for Greater Incremental Scalability. *IEEE Transactions on Parallel and Distributed Systems*, *30*(5), 1105–1119. doi:10.1109/TPDS.2018.2874659

Zifan, L., Mihail, L. S., & Xuesong, Q. (2018). Fog Radio Access Network: A New Wireless backhaul Architectuer For Small Cell Networks. *IEEE Access: Practical Innovations, Open Solutions*, *7*, 14150–14161.

Chapter 11
Security of Wireless Sensor Networks:
The Current Trends and Issues

Mumtaz Qabulio

(iD) https://orcid.org/0000-0002-9294-2657

Institute of Information and Communication Technology, University of Sindh, Jamshoro, Pakistan

Yasir Arfat Malkani

Institute of Mathematics and Computer Science, University of Sindh, Jamshoro, Pakistan

Muhammad S. Memon

Department of Information Technology, University of Sindh, Dadu Campus, Pakistan

Ayaz Keerio

Institute of Mathematics and Computer Science, University of Sindh, Jamshoro, Pakistan

ABSTRACT

Wireless sensor networks (WSNs) are comprised of large collections of small devices having low operating power, low memory space, and limited processing capabilities referred to as sensor nodes. The nodes in WSNs are capable of sensing, recording, and monitoring environmental conditions. Nowadays, a variety of WSNs applications can be found in many areas such as in healthcare, agriculture, industries, military, homes, offices, hospitals, smart transportation, and smart buildings. Though WSNs offer many useful applications, they suffer from many deployment issues. The security issue is one of them. The security of WSNs is considerable because of the use of unguided medium and their deployment in harsh, physically unprotected, and unattended environments. This chapter aims to discuss various security objectives and security attacks on WSNs and summarizes the discussed attacks according to their categories. The chapter also discusses different security protocols presented to prevent, detect, and recover the WSNs from various security attacks.

DOI: 10.4018/978-1-7998-2803-7.ch011

INTRODUCTION

The WSNs are closely deployed self-organizing and self-healing networks. WSNs are composed of tiny devices called sensor nodes. Those nodes are equipped with limited power, memory and processing capabilities (Mumtaz Qabulio, 2015). The sensor nodes are designed to measure environmental conditions such as light, temperature, heat, pressure, smoke, fire, dust, humidity, soil, object motion and human activity recognition (Jordao, Torres, & Schwartz, 2018), etc. Nowadays, the WSNs are getting popular and are being deployed extensively due to the range of applications they support and due to the decline in their costs. Some of the attractive and emerging applications of WSNs are found in environment monitoring, in environmental control (e.g. fire detection, air pollution monitoring, flood, traffic control Systems) in military (e.g. monitoring of equipments), in wearable computing (e.g. wrist-worn integrated health monitoring device), in context-aware ubiquitous applications (e.g. Sentient Computing, Ambient Intelligence, Interactive Games and Toys, Augmented reality). The WSNs are also powerful technology in enabling Internet of Things (IoT) (Khalil, Abid, Benhaddou, & Gerndt, 2014; Patil & Chen, 2017). Figure 1 presents an abstract architecture of the WSNs which is comprised of three layers (e.g. sensor field layer, end-user layer and internet/satellite layer). The sensor field is composed of sensor nodes; sensor nodes are basic and essential part of the wireless sensor networks (Michal, 2013) because they are responsible to perform core tasks for the network (e.g. sensing, communication, processing).

Figure 1. High Level Architecture of WSNs

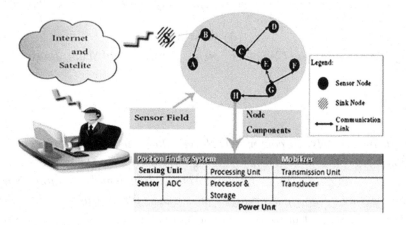

The sensor nodes are equipped with various units (e.g. sensing, processing, communication and power units). These nodes might have position finding and mobilizer modules too (Mishra & Thakkar, 2012). All sensor node units and modules are also presented in figure 1. Each of the unit and module is supposed to perform specific task such as the sensing unit accommodates sensors in order to measure environmental conditions and analogue-to-digital converter in order to convert received analogue signal in the digital form. The processing-unit is comprised of a processor and multiple memories such as RAM and ROM for storing the data and for performing data processing operations. The communication unit constitutes of a radio transceiver for sending and receiving data to and from other network nodes. The power-unit accommodates the energy-source and is ought to provide uninterrupted power supply to all sensor node units. The position finding system via GPS device is responsible detect location of the sensor node in the network (Malkani, Keerio, Mahar, Memon, & Keerio, 2015). Along with this, it is also responsible to discover neighboring nodes for a particular node of the network (Shikha, 2016). Furthermore, the node's location information is also used by various routing protocols in order to identify route information for the respective node. Various location based routing protocols are discussed in (Niculescu & Nath, 2003; Roychowdhury & Patra, 2010; Xing, Lu, Pless, & Huang, 2004; Yu, Govindan, & Estrin, 2001; Zorzi & Rao, 2003). However, there are location-free routing protocols as well. In the end, the sensor node may have a mobilizer or actuator; the mobilizer is used to provide locomotion ability to the sensor nodes.

Furthermore, functionality wise the WSNs nodes are classified as sink node or base station (BS) and ordinary nodes of the network. The ordinary nodes have limited processor, power and storage resources. These nodes are supposed to sense environmental conditions in analog form and transform them into digital form and relay the sensed data to the base station. Ordinary nodes may perform processing on data before transmitting the date towards the sink node. The BS in contrast, is powerful node and is equipped with better and higher processing, storage and power resources. The sink nodes have faster processors, high storage and are connected with better or constant power supplying source (e.g. grid station than batteries). Base station could be a personal computer or desktop computer, a laptop machine, a PDA device or any powerful sensor node equipped with better and reliable resources (Malkani, et al., 2015). The base station is like a conciliator between network nodes and the end-users .This not only is responsible to relay sensor data to the end user however it also ought to analyze the and present the received data in understandable form to the end user. The security of WSNs is a major concern due to the following mentioned issues (D. S. Dr. G. Padmavathi, 2009):

1. Unguided Medium: Unguided or wireless mediums are by default less secure as compared to wires ones, where intruders can easily drop packets, modify them or replace real packets with malicious ones. As being wireless in nature, the WSNs have adopted these challenges from existing Wireless Networks.

2. Ad-hoc Deployment: WSN has dynamic topology, which keeps changing as motes are failed, added or replaced. Nothing is known about topology before addition of node. Consequently, network itself must be self configuring and sustainable within such a highly dynamic environment.

3. Hostile Environment: WSNs are deployed in real time and open environment wherein their nodes can be accessed physically or can easily be damaged. Even rough weather can harm the sensor motes. Consequently, the sensor node needs to be self-healing and self organizing in the nature.

4. Resource Scarcity: As sensor nodes have limited resources, designing an effective security mechanism with constrained computation, power and memory resources is again a big challenge in wireless sensor networks.

5. Unattended Operation: It's again a challenge to make sure that all nodes are attended specially when nodes are managed remotely and there is no any central assistance for nodes. If a node remains unattended for longer time period then there are possibilities that a node has been attacked.

Due to the aforementioned challenges, WSNs are prone to numerous security attacks. Those security attacks are majorly classified as active-attacks and passive-attacks. Passive-attacks violate confidentiality of data; in passive attacks the adversary monitors and listens the communication during transmission, hence they are less harmful for the network. However, the data gathered through passive attacks is used launch active attacks in the network. Eavesdropping, traffic analysis, traffic monitoring, decryption of weakly encrypted traffic (Chelli, 2015) are examples of passive security attacks.

The active attacks on the other hand are supposed to alter the system's intended behavior. In these attacks the adversary tries to get complete control over the network hence they are more harmful for the network and target the integrity, data freshness, and availability objectives of the network security. Furthermore, the security attacks can also be categorizes as security attribute they target (attribute-oriented), the OSI layer they operate (layer-oriented) and as location of attacking device (location-oriented). However, before describing aforementioned type of attacks, there is need to explain the WSNs security attributes, the layered communication stack of the WSNs node and locations of the attacking devices. Consequently, section below defines all these concepts.

SECURITY OBJECTIVES OF THE WSNS

As being the network, the WSNs have similar security objectives (CIAA) as of traditional networks. The term CIAA stands for confidentiality, integrity, availability and authenticity. However capabilities and applications of WSNs are different from the traditional one. That is why, in addition to the primary security objectives there are defined secondary security objectives for WSNS as well. Section bellow discusses the primary and security objectives for WSNs found in literature (Chelli, 2015; D. S. Dr. G. Padmavathi, 2009; Kirar, 2014). Figure 2 presents list of primary and secondary security attributes for the WSNs.

Primary Security Objectives

Confidentiality

The confidentiality objective ensures secrecy and privacy of the data. It ensures that the data should not be revealed and accessed by the unauthorized users on the network. The confidentiality is the basic yet core objective of the network security.

Integrity

The aim of the integrity security objective is to safeguard data from being changed by the unauthorized users. The integrity objective also maintains intended behavior of the system and guarantees that the system must respond to the network the way it supposed to be.

Availability

The *availability* attribute ensures and maintains the uninterrupted, continuous and reliable provision of system services to requesting entity and it guarantees that the system should not deny the services if they are requested by legitimate and authorized entities of the network.

Authenticity

The aim of authenticity objective is to verify identity of each entity uniquely on a network. It makes certain that the entity is what it is claiming.

Secondary Security Objectives

Data Freshness

The aim of the data freshness objective is to ensure novelty of the messages; it guaranties that the message is not replayed or delayed. The adversary can violate this objective by capturing messages transmitted from legitimate nodes of the network, and then keep on resending captured messages back to the network nodes in order to launch flooding attacks.

Self-Organization

The WSNs are positioned at unprotected, harsh and unreachable environments. Wherein, no any physical assistance and maintenance is supplied to network nodes. Consequently, the sensor nodes themselves need to be robust for fixing the occurred problems and to recovering themselves from the state of the attack.

Time Synchronization

The WSNs are collection of heavily deployed sensor nodes, those nodes collectively work for a common cause. The sensor nodes either sends their data to the BS or to the cluster heads (CH) (powerful sensor node in terms of resilient power) then after CH aggregates and sends data towards base station (powerful sensor node, PDA, laptop or personal computer). The base station finally processes the data and produces the end results. Hence, all the sensor nodes needs to be time synchronized (M. D. S. Dr. G. Padmavathi, 2009).

Secure Localization

The WSNs are made up of enormous collection of nodes spread at wide region on various areas. Localization is the technique of recognizing the correct location of sensor node in the network. Secure localization is significant in wireless sensor networks because of their applications in routing, key distribution schemes, in data aggregation an in location-based authentication schemes. Not only this, but the localization plays important role in many WSNs applications such as object tracking, vehicle tracking, environment monitoring, health monitoring, disaster management etc. As a result, it is equally important for WSNs security to correctly and timely locate the location of the sensor node the network (Chelli, 2015).

Non-Repudiation

Non- repudiation makes certain that, any network entity shouldn't refuse to send data and messages which were previously generated and transmitted by it.

Figure 2. Primary and Secondary Security Objectives of the WSNS

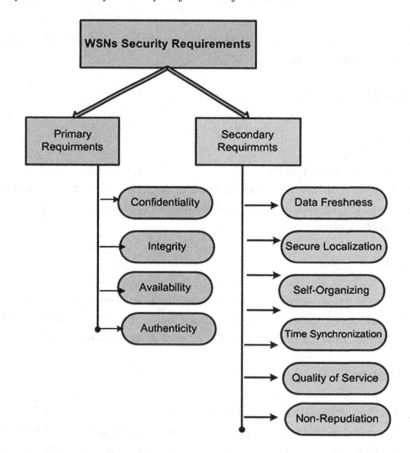

Quality of Services

This objective of network security guarantees the uninterrupted and trusted transmission as well as reception of data packets between network nodes. It focuses on optimizing the transmission speed and quality of data. This majorly focuses on latency, throughput and jitter attributes of the data transmission.

WSNs Node Communication Stack

The protocol stack for WSNs nodes is composed of different layers which include physical, data link, network, transport and application layers respectively. Wherein every layer of the communication stack has distinct responsibilities which are defined bellow. Figure 3 shows communication attack for WSNs.

Physical Layer

This layer in WSNs communication stack provides means to transmit bit-stream over a communication medium. The core responsibilities of physical layers include modulation, generation of carrier frequency, transmission and reception of bits, selection of frequency band, signal diversion of the data. The physical layer also provides mean of interaction with MAC layer(Yick, Mukherjee, & Ghosal, 2008).

Figure 3. WSNs Protocol Stack
(Kocakulak & Butun, 2017)

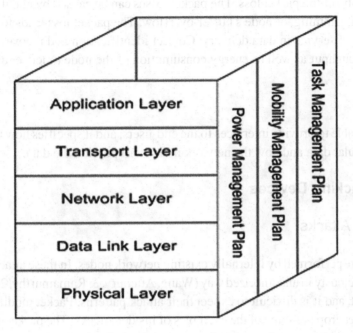

Data Link Layer

This layer of communication stack is accountable for data transferring between nodes sharing single communication channel/link. This layer furthermore provides services like multiplexing, frame-detection, medium access control, data-encryption, error-control and flow-control. Furthermore, data link layer is also responsible to ensure reliable connections of the point-to-point and point-to-multipoint communication. The MAC layer provides interaction with physical layer for detecting and correcting the frame errors(Yick, et al., 2008).

Network Layer

This layer assigns the addresses to the network nodes and is also accountable to route the network packets between source and destination. The routing protocols for WSNs needs to be different from routing protocols of the IP based networks because the nodes in sensor networks are not assigned IP addresses. Consequently, routing protocols for WSNs must meet the network's memory, power, bandwidth and processing constraints efficiently. Furthermore those protocols are supposed to be scalable and should be capable of managing the data transmission between various network nodes effectively (Yick, et al., 2008).

Transport Layer

This layer is accountable for secure packet transport and data encryption. The transport layer ensures that data at source and sink are reliable and of quality. Multiple implementations, variable-reliability, packet-loss recovery and congestion control mechanism should be supported by this layer in the network.

The transport layer protocols must be general and application independent. As each application of the WSNs has distinct ratio of the packet loss. The packet losses can be caused by nodal failure, link congestion, packet collision, jamming, or node's buffer-overflow. The packet loss leads to energy wastage and degrades the quality of service in data delivery. Correct identification and recovery of the lost packets will improve the throughput as well as energy consumption of the node (Yick, et al., 2008).

Application Layer

This layer is accountable to provide interfaces to the end-users, and it specifies how the users can request and query the particular data and how the network nodes will provide the data.

Location of Attacking Devices

Internal or Inside Attacks

The insider attacks are performed by internally existing network nodes. In these attacks a legitimate node of the WSNs act maliciously in unauthorized way (Wang, Attebury, & Ramamurthy, 2006). Insider attacks are difficult to detect, and it is difficult to expect their attack patterns. Packet modification, misrouting, eavesdropping /packet drop are some of the examples of insider attacks. The packet drop attacks can also be categorized as black-hole, gray-hole sink hole and worm-hole attacks. These attacks will be proved critical threat for safety critical applications (e.g. military surveillance, battle field management) which are responsible for monitoring the battlefields and other critical infrastructures (Chelli, 2015) .

External or Outside Attacks

External or outside attacks are launched by outside nodes of the WSNs. the attacker by utilizing these external nodes can launch eavesdropping, jamming and various flooding attacks to overwhelm the network resources, consequently, cause the denial of services attacks.

Security Attacks on WSNs   .

This section of the chapter comprehensively discusses various security attacks launched on the WSNs in order to compromise their security. The section first explains various attacks and, in the end it summarizes discussed attacks according to their category.

Eavesdropping

In eavesdropping attack the attacker secretly listens the communication through communication line by intercepting the packets during transmission. The attacker then reveals the contents of the dropped packet which can violet the confidentiality of the data. The revealed data can be used to launch various active attacks (e.g. replay and modification attacks) on a network. bellow figure 4 shows a scenario of eavesdropping attack.

Figure 4. Eavesdropping Attack

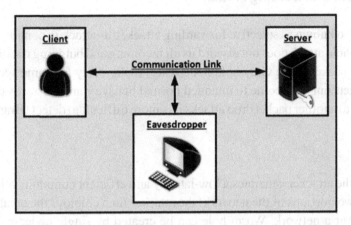

Black Hole Attack

The Black hole attack is one of the packets drop attacks in this attack the compromised node discards all its incoming packets. The black hole node also discards its outgoing packets rather than forwarding them to the intended receiver without acknowledging the sender node about this intentional dropping of packets. This underlying attack suppresses reaching of the important data to the BS, to the cluster head or to other legitimate nodes of the, hence significantly degrades the network performance (Brar & Angurala, 2016). Figure 5 depicts the idea of black hole attack.

Figure 5. Black-hole Attack

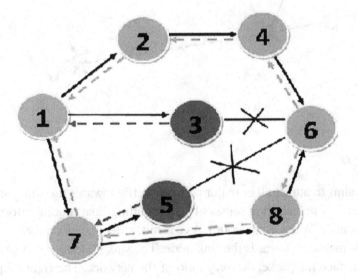

Grey-Hole/Selective Forwarding Attack

Grey-hole attack is also known as selective forwarding attack, this attack in contrast to the black hole attack the node in grey-hole attack does not discard its all incoming and outgoing traffic rather it selectively discards the network packets. The Grey-hole node reacts maliciously for some specific period of time by dropping the packets but may come to intended normal behavior and forwards the received packets. Therefore in contrast to another packet drop attacks it is more difficult to detect (Brar & Angurala, 2016).

Wormhole Attack

In wormhole attack, the attacker generates a low-latency and efficient communication link between two devices or between two portions of the network. the attacker than employs the created link to replay the received messages over a network. Worm hole can be created by single node, or by non-neighboring nodes of the network or by multiple nodes of the network residing at different locations of the network (Palacharla, Chandan, GnanaSuryaTeja, & Varshitha, 2018). The wormhole node replays the old messages at different parts of the network by means of tunnel. The figure 6 shows illustration of the wormhole attack

Figure 6. Wormhole attack
(Shaon, 2015)

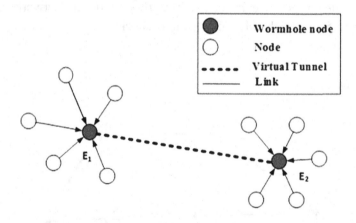

Sinkhole Attack

The sinkhole attack aims to attract all or major network traffic towards the single malicious node. That malicious node fascinates neighboring sensors by transmitting fake routing information to show best path towards the sink node(Wang, et al., 2006). As a result, other network nodes choose malicious node for transmitting their messages towards the sink node. The sink node then can easily drop the packets that can ultimately reduce the packet delivery ratio of the network. The figure 7 presents scenario of sinkhole attack.

Figure 7. Sinkhole Attack
(Choi, Cho, Kim, Hong, & Kim, 2009)

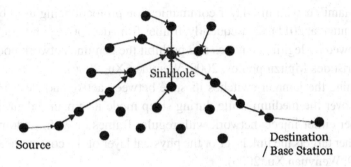

Node Malfunction

In this attack, a network node produces in consistent and inaccurate data hence exploits integrity of the sensor node. This attack can be proved quite harmful if data aggregating or cluster head node starts malfunctioning.

Node Outage Attack

In this type of the attack the sensor node denies from performing its assigned and intended functions. The discussed attack can be launched by two ways. First by physically destroying the node, secondly by using some techniques or other attacks (e.g. flooding attacks, black-hole or sinkhole attack) which leads towards un-functioning of the targeted node (Raja Waseem Anwar, 2014).

Jamming

Jamming is one of the common attacks on WSNs. The jamming is intentional interference that aims to jam either specific link or the complete network. Consequently it leads to the DoS attacks in the networks (G. Jayanthi Lakshmi, 2013). In jamming, the attacker jams the network links/channels through broadcasting random bit patterns or random signal over the medium or via redirecting the sent traffic back to the sending transmitter/node of the network (Messai, 2014). The Jamming attacks further leads to radio interference, resource exhaustion and denial-of-services attacks in the network. The jamming attacks can be launched on physical and data-link layers both (Law, et al., 2009). Jamming is common at physical layer, though jamming can affect data-link layer too. Link layer jamming damages MAC frames and utilizes smart jammers for launching energy efficient jamming. The jamming at link layer is critical to deal with as compared to physical layer jamming. The jamming attacks are further classified as constant, random, reactive and deceptive jamming.

The **constant** jamming targets physical layer, wherein the jamming device constantly transmits high power random bits on a medium. Those bits do not use any protocol format (e.g. MAC). These jammers try to keep channel busy and prohibit the legitimate network nodes to access the medium. As a result, this endless transmission ultimately brings the network in DoS situation (G. Jayanthi Lakshmi, 2013).

The **deceptive** jamming is link layer jamming wherein the deceptive jammer constantly injects the medium with regular though fake frames or replays the old frames on a network. these jammers are smart jammers as they are familiar with link-layer communication protocol being used by the nodes (Law, et al., 2009; S.M.K .Chaitanya, 2011). Consequently, frames from deceptive jammers follow same protocol format which is followed by legitimate nodes and prohibit the genuine network nodes to send their data over the medium (Aristides Mpitziopoulos, 2009; Wenyuan Xu, 2006).

In **random** jamming the jammer switches its state between active and sleep modes. During active mode its sends data over the medium while during sleep mode it remains silent. However, during active mode the jammer either injects network with regular frames or with random bits. Consequently, random jamming either targets the link layer or the physical layer of the communication stack (Aristides Mpitziopoulos, 2009; Wenyuan Xu, 2006).

Figure 8. Jamming Attacks [31]

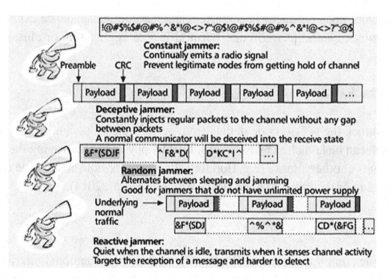

In **reactive** jamming the jammer remains silent until any activity is sensed over the medium, Here the jammers constantly keeps itself in the receiving mode and listens the network medium for activities, the jammer transmits the jamming signal as soon as it preamble bit patters are detected.m As reactive jammers are not energy efficient jammers as they always remain in active state (e.g. in receiving mode) (S.M.K .Chaitanya, 2011). Some form of the reactive jammers instead of being in receiving mode constantly, use channel sensing mechanisms. Wherein these jammers remain in sleep mode and whenever any activity is detected on the channel, they immediately start sending data for producing collision on the network (Aristides Mpitziopoulos, 2009; Wenyuan Xu, 2006).

Collision

The collision is one of the common attacks or condition in networked environments, collision is caused n network when two nodes simultaneously send their data over same medium. When collided packets are received at destination side, they have mismatched checksum value. Consequently, the destination discards the received collided packet.

Sybil Attack

In this attack the attacked node intentionally and illegally replicates its identity, with Sybil attack the compromised node adopts multiple ids and pretends itself as multiple different nodes of the network. A node can adopt multiple identities either by generating fake ids or by stealing ids from the legitimate network nodes. Bellow figure 9 depicts the Sybil attack.

Figure 9. Sybil Attack
(R. Singh, Singh, & Singh, 2016)

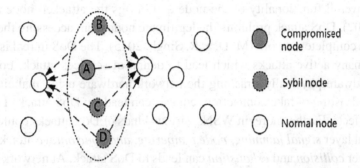

Node Tempering or Node Capture Attack

In this attack, the attacker physically acquires/captures the sensor node from the network and obtains complete control over compromised entity. By deploying this attack, the attacker can get unlimited access over the compromised and can easily get data and shared keys stored on nodes local memory. The attacker then by using captured shared keys can establish fake connections with rest of the legitimate nodes of the network.

Environment Tampering

Through this attack the attacker violets integrity of sensor data. the attacker here can tamper with network's deployment area by installing a magnet over the magnetometer, he/she can also tamper with proximity, temperature, pressure or soil sensors deployed in the network so that these sensors could produce inaccurate readings in the network (Roosta, 2008).

Node Replication or Clone Node Attack

This is an active and internal type of attack, wherein the adversary at first physically catches one or many network nodes, retrieves security related information (e.g. keys and ID) stored on node's memory, duplicated that information onto various nodes of the network and redeploys those clone nodes at strategic locations of network (Mumtaz Qabulio, 2015). The adversary furthermore can utilize those clones to launch other various attacks such as sinkhole attacks(Zhang, Liu, Bai, & Zheng, 2018), wormhole attacks(Giri, Borah, & Pradhan, 2018), grey-hole attack, black hole attacks (Kaur & Kumar, 2018), jamming attacks, replay attacks, selective forwarding attacks, modification attacks on a network etc.

Node Malfunctioning Attack

In node malfunctioning attack, the attacked node produces incorrect, bogus and inconsistent data. This attack violets *integrity* of the sensor node and can violet the *data freshness* of the sensor network.

Denial of Services (Dos) Attack

This is type of an active attacks, it can be launched internally or externally from the network. DoS attack compromises overall functionality of the node and brings the attacked node into non-functional state (Stankovic, 2002). DoS attack prohibits the legitimate node from accessing the network resources and may crashes the complete network (M. D. a. R. Singh, 2015). The DoS in real is not a single attack; however there are many active attacks which lead to denial of services attack. For example, damaging the network hardware physically, crashing the network hardware using malicious codes, resource exhaustion and broadcasting of fake connection requests can leads to DoS attack. The jamming attacks also produce DoS affects. Furthermore, in WSNs various kinds of DoS attacks could be performed. For example, on physical layer *signal jamming, node tampering, and node outage* attacks may leads to DoS situation, on link layer *collision* and *exhaustion* can leads to DoS attack. At network layer *black hole attacks, sinkhole, grey hole, wormhole* attacks will bring the network in DoS condition. Finally at transport layer *acknowledgment flooding, HELLO Flooding, SYN flooding* and *de-synchronization Attacks could produce DoS attack on the network (D. S. Dr. G. Padmavathi, 2009).*

Exhaustion of Resources Attack

Exhaustion attack aims to overwhelm the resources of victim node. This can be done by either engaging the victim node in excessive processing and calculations, or to transmit flood of unnecessary traffic to the victimized node (Messai, 2014).

Flooding Attacks

Flooding attacks are active and internal type of attacks, flooding attacks aims to flood the network with fake traffic for overwhelming the network that ultimately leads to DoS attacks. Flooding attacks include HELLO Flood Attack, acknowledgement flooding attacks. In these attacks the attacking node requests for the fake connection which are never completed (Chelli, 2015). Hello flood attack is depicted bellow in figure 10.

Figure 10. Hello Flooding Attack

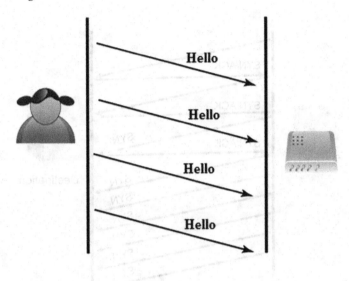

De-synchronization Attacks

In De-synchronization attack, the attacked node endlessly requests for re-transmission of the missed frames, consequently the sender node will re-transmit the packet. If attacker maintains correct timings it can prohibit the legitimate nodes to transmit their data (Chelli, 2015).

SYN Flooding Attack

As SYN flooding attack is one of the flooding attacks, here the attacker also constantly sends bogus SYN requests to the BS. This attack aims to overwhelm the BS resources in order to make it unresponsive for the requests from legitimate nodes of the network (Hussain, Hussain, Jhanjhi, & Humayun, 2019). Figure 11 presents graphical representation of the attack.

Altered, Replayed Packets Attack

Message reply and message alteration are collectively referred as message modification attack. In former attack, the adversary gathers messages sent from the legitimate nodes of the network by launching eavesdropping, wormhole or sinkhole attacks. The attacker than resends the captured messages to the networks nodes pretending itself as an authorized node. In latter attack, the attacker modifies the contents of the captured messages by either playing with the order of the messages or just holding the messages, and resending them after some delay in order to cause unwanted results (Almusaylim & Zaman, 2019).

The table 1 bellow summarizes discussed security attacks based on attack location, the security attribute they compromise and the layer they target.

Figure 11. SYN Flooding Attack

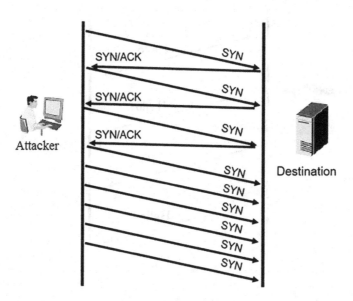

TRADITIONAL SECURITY MECHANISMS

Symmetric Cryptography

Symmetric cryptography employs secret information (e.g. key or information required to generate key) which is pre-loaded into local memory of the node before its deployment in the WSNs. The legitimate nodes then use that common key for secure communication. However with this scheme there is serious security threat that is if adversary successes to physically compromise any of the networks, then the attacker can get access over the pre-loaded key consequently can bypass the authentication check. As a reason various researchers have used and suggested usage of pair-wise keys instead of single global key for establishing secure communication in WSNs. following are some of the protocols based on pair-wise keys to govern secure communication in WSNs.

Pggerrig et al. in (Perrig, Szewczyk, Tygar, Wen, & Culler, 2002) have proposed the key management protocol called *SPINS* which employs a trusted sink node to distribute the pair-wise keys. The SPINS supports many security services including semantic security, authentication, replay protection, data freshness. The SPINS has minimal communication overheads and is suitable for networks with limited resources.

LEAP stands for Localized Encryption and Authentication Protocol (Alsoufi, Elleithy, Abuzaghleh, & Nassar, 2012) is one of the key management protocol. It uses four secret keys (e.g. individual, pair-wise, cluster, and group). All keys are shred with different network node, such as the respective node shares its individual key with base station; the node shares its pair-wise key with all of its neighbor nodes. Cluster key is shared among all nodes belongs to same cluster. The group key is a global key and is common between entire nodes of the network. Use of different keys enhances level of authenticity, and makes the network communication more secure. TinySec (Link Layer Security Architecture) (Karlof, Sastry, & Wagner, 2004) is a light weight security package and is proposed to ensure authentication in

Table 1. Summary of Security attacks

Attack	Attack Nature	Compromised Security Attribute	Targeted Network Layer	Attack Location
Signal/Radio Jamming	Active	Availability	Physical	External, internal
Eavesdropping	Passive	Confidentiality	Physical	External
Node Capture or Node Tempering Attack	Active	Availability, confidentiality, integrity authenticity,	Physical	External
Node Malfunctioning	Active	Integrity	Physical	Internal
Node Outage attack	Active	Availability	Physical	Internal
Clone Node Attack	Active	Confidentiality, Integrity, availability, data freshness	Physical	Internal
Collision	Active	Availability	Data link layer	Internal, external
Exhaustion of Resources Attack	Active	Availability	Data link layer	External
Black-hole Attack	Passive	Confidentiality, integrity, availability, non-repudiation	Network layer, routing attack	Internal
Worm hole attack	Passive	Confidentiality, Integrity, data freshness	Network layer, routing attack	Internal
Sink hole attack	Passive	Confidentiality, Integrity, Availability	Network layer	Internal
Grey-hole/Selective forwarding Attack	Active	Integrity, Non-repudiation	Network layer	Internal
Altered, replayed packets Attack	Active	Integrity, data freshness	Network layer	Internal
Flooding Attack	Active	Availability, Data freshness	Transport layer	Internal
De-synchronization Attack	Active	Availability	Transport layer	Internal
SYN Flooding Attack	Active	Availability	Transport layer	Internal attack
Sybil attack	Active	Authentication,	Network layer	Internal attack
Acknowledgement spoofing Attack	Active	Availability, data freshness	Transport layer	Internal
Denial of Services	Active	Availability, Non-repudiation	All layers	Internal, external

the networks. It comes with premium distributions of the TinyOS. BROSK (BROadcast Session Key negotiation protocol) (Lai, Kim, & Verbauwhede, 2002) is another pair-wise key management protocol wherein each network node is supposed to broadcast a message accommodating the nonce. Then after, the neighboring nodes in the network generate the common-key such that the key is a function of their nonces. The node uses pre-deployment key in order to authenticate each other, that key is supposed as secure key and is supposed to be unreachable to the captured nodes.

Eschenauer and Gligor in (Yagan, 2012) have proposed a random key pre-distribution based scheme. In their proposed solution, each node prior to its deployment picks set of key and id from given key pool. After that, for authenticating each other, whenever two neighboring nodes encounter each other in the network, they first exchange their ids with each other and then find out the of identities and keys from their stored key chains.

Asymmetric Cryptography

The existing symmetric cryptographic solutions relaying on efficient way of establishing keys between different network nodes, in these solutions keys once assigned are never refreshed, which is limitation of symmetric cryptographic solutions. In contrast to symmetric cryptographic solutions, the asymmetric cryptography focuses on refreshing the keys which makes key management dynamic and boosts the level of secure communication. in addition to this, the symmetric solutions are not scalable and does not consider cases of node capture attacks (Wang, et al., 2006). However, asymmetric cryptography involves heave mathematical operations, which might overwhelm the resources constrained sensor node. But recent studies have shown successful implementation of the asymmetric cryptography in those low power and processing sensing devices. Gura et al. According to Wandar in (Wander, Gura, Eberle, Gupta, & Shantz, 2005) both of the asymmetric cryptographic schemes (e.g. RSA and elliptic curve cryptography) can be implemented on limited resource devices without any hardware up-gradation. In CPUs with 8-bit processor the ECC shows better performance as compared to RSA. In addition to this, the ECC's supports 160-bit key size which results shorter messages during transmission than 1024-bit RSA keys. Watro et al. in [34] have discussed that limited version of the RSA can be successfully applied over the WSNs nodes.

Malan et al. in (Malan, Welsh, & Smith, 2004) have implemented the Diffie-Hellman employing Elliptic Curve Discrete Logarithm Problem. The authors also have shown that the public keys are possible to generate within period of 34 seconds, and the generated keys can easily be dispersed between network nodes with nodes having just over 1 KB of static-RAM and 34 kilobytes of the ROM. Joseph et al. in (Liu, Baek, Zhou, Yang, & Wong, 2010) have implemented Pairing-based Cryptography (PBC) primitives for an 8-bit processor in TinyPBC. They have shown that TinyPBC takes 5.45s only to compute pairings on ATmega128L processor bases mote (e.g.MicaZ).

LAYER WISE SECURITY MEASURES

Security Against Physical Layer Attacks

Jamming is one of the primary attacks on WSNs at physical layer, though WSNS are prone to environment tampering and node capturing attacks as well. The node capture attacks further leads to clone node attacks, node malfunctioning and node outage attacks. There are very few attacks which target the physical layer, though they are most difficult to prevent because wireless sensor networks are populated in open, harsh and physically unattended environments wherein they can easily to be captured and compromised by the attacker. Physical layer attacks compromise availability attribute of the security. That means any the physical layer security attacks ultimately leads to denial of services attack (Chelli, 2015). The table below present security mechanisms and protocols proposed to deal with physical layer attacks or physical attacks.

Spreading techniques (FHSS, CDMA) are traditional methods to deal with jamming in WSNs. In FHSS the data is transmitted employing multiple carrier frequencies rather than single frequency. The CDMA employs coding scheme, wherein each of the transmitter is allocated a code. Though, these solutions are computationally intensive and FHSS requires multiple frequencies, however sensor nodes are limited resource device and usually use single carrier frequency; that is why WSNs are highly prone to jamming attacks. As far as node capture and clone node attacks are considered, they are even trickier to deal with. The node capture attacks are basis clone node and other tampering attacks. In the literature (Bekara & Laurent, 2007; Bryan Parno; Chakib Bekara; Chia-Mu Yu, 2012; Glory Rashmi. A1; Mauro Conti; Ming Zhang, 2009; Wazir Zada Khan, 2013; Xiaoming Deng)some of the solutions are found to deal with clone node and node capture attacks which are presented in table below.

Table 2. Various Attacks on Physical Layer and Countermeasures

Attack	Countermeasure
Jamming Attack	Spreading Techniques (Frequency hopping, code spreading)
Eavesdropping Attack	Cryptography
Node Capture Attack and clone node attacks	Randomized multicast, Node2node broadcast, line selected multicast, Deterministic Multicast, Randomized Efficient Distributed, RAndom WaLk, Table-assisted RAndom WaLk, Randomly Directed Exploration, Compressed sensing-base clone node identification

Security Against Data Link Layer Attacks

Resource exhaustion and collision are two attacks which target the data link layer. One of the solutions for dealing with collision attacks is to use error-correcting codes, many of the error-correcting codes work best with collisions caused by environmental interferences or by probabilistic error. Furthermore, the error-codes are also able to detect malicious and intentional collisions. Though, no any separate sophisticated defenses against malicious collision are proposed yet (Wang, et al., 2006). In order to mitigate resource exhaustion attack, the limitations on no of request for MAC protocols needs to be applied by limiting the rate of the MAC can save power utilization of the node. Another solution of this attack is utilization of time division multiplexing which restricts the network nodes to access medium on their turn and for specified period of time (Wang, et al., 2006).

Security Against Network Layer Attacks

Two different types of attacks are possible to launch on network layer, the packet drop attacks (e.g. sink hole, black hole, worm hole, Grey-hole/selective-forwarding) and modification attacks (e.g. Spoofing, Alteration, or Replay attacks). An attacker can alter or spoof the messages or can replay the packets on a network. The attacker can also can spoof, alter, or replay the routing information (e.g. creating routing loops, extending and shortening the source routes) for disrupting the network traffic. The secure routing

Table 3. Summary of Various Attacks on Data-Link Layer and Their Countermeasures

Attack	Countermeasure
Collision	Error correcting-codes
Resource exhaustion	Time division multiplexing, Limiting MAC for dealing with excessive request

protocol is required to deal both type of attacks. There are various routing protocols proposed to deal with routing attacks in WSNs. However, cluster based hierarchical protocols are considered energy efficient protocols (Sharma & Jena, 2011). Following are presented various cluster based protocol proposed to mitigate various packet drop and reply attacks on WSNs. The table bellow summarizes proposed protocols along with the attack they mitigate and the security objective they meet.

Furthermore in order to mitigate WSNs from altering, spoofing of messages, traditional methods such as hash functions, digital signatures and MAC (message authentication code) are used. However in order to maintain freshness of data and defending against replay attacks timestamps are attached with messages (Wang, et al., 2006).

Table 4. Summary of Various Hierarchical Routing Protocols to Deal Packet Drop and Modification Attacks

Protocol	Security Attribute	Mitigated Attack
SLEACH (Islam, Islam, & Islam, 2007)	Integrity, Authenticity	Replay/Modification, selective forwarding, sink-hole
F-LEACH(Zheng & Hu, 2009)	Confidentiality, Integrity, data freshness, Authenticity	Replay/Modification, Sybil
R-LEACH(Sundararajan & Arumugam, 2015)	Confidentiality, Integrity, Authenticity	Replay/Modification, selective forwarding, sink-hole, Sybil, worm-hole
Sec-LEACH (Sharma & Jena, 2011)	Confidentiality, Integrity, data freshness, Authenticity	Replay/Modification, selective forwarding, Sybil
SS-LEACH (Sharma & Jena, 2011)	Confidentiality, Integrity, Authenticity	Replay/Modification, selective forwarding, Sybil
SRPSN (Ouafaa, Mustapha, Salah-ddine, & Jalal, 2016)	Confidentiality, Integrity, Authenticity	Replay/Modification, selective forwarding
LHA-SP (Oliveira, Wang, & Loureiro, 2005)	Confidentiality, Authenticity	..
ESMR (Vijendran & Gripsy, 2014)	Confidentiality	Replay/Modification
SRPBCG (Ouafaa, Mustapha, Salah-ddine, & Said, 2016)	Confidentiality, Authenticity	Replay/Modification
M. Bohang et al.	Integrity, Authenticity	Replay/Modification
SHEER (Ouafaa, Mustapha, Salah-ddine, & Jalal, 2016)	Confidentiality, Integrity, data freshness, Authenticity	Replay/Modification, selective forwarding, Sybil

Security Against Transport Layer Attacks

This layer is majorly prone to flooding attacks, acknowledgement spoofing and de-synchronization attacks. The flooding attacks can be prevented via connection authentication. For de-synchronization attacks, each type of network packet (e.g. control packet and data packet) needs to be authenticated. Header or full packet authentication can be useful for preventing de-synchronization attacks. Here firewalls can b useful to protect network from flooding and de-synchronization attacks. The firewalls aim to provide reliable, authenticated and secure connection between two data transmitting nodes. . AEGIS (Hossain & Raghunathan, 2010) and S_Firewall (Ma, Yi, Zhong, & Zhang, 2006) are two firewalls proposed in the literature to provide secure data transmission between nodes and to filter out fake incoming and outgoing traffic. Moreover to this, in (Hussain, et al., 2019) the authors have proposed an AI based approach called SFADBE to deal with SYN flooding attacks in wireless sensor networks as well. Here Puzzle algorithms are also used to limit creation of the fake connections. In puzzle algorithms if any user intended to establish the connection s ought to solve a puzzle before establishing the new connection. Solving a puzzle for each connection requires time; consequently, the it will not be possible for an adversary to open multiple connections fast enough to overwhelm the network nodes (Wang, et al., 2006). Finally in (Almulhim & Zaman, 2018) the authors have proposed light-weight authentication scheme. It is based on session key agreement between the network node and the BS. Their scheme is especially able to protect a network from man-in-the-middle and masquerade attacks.

CONCLUSION

This chapter delineates the wireless sensor networks along with their architecture and vital applications. The major objective of this chapter was to provide comprehensive details on security issues of WSNs. In compliance to that objective, the chapter first depicted primary and secondary objectives of the WSNs security and discussed most of the security attacks that compromises and violets the security of the WSNs. the chapter finally provides some of the countermeasures used to protect the WSNs from discussed attacks.

REFERENCES

Almulhim, M., & Zaman, N. (2018). *Proposing secure and lightweight authentication scheme for IoT based E-health applications*. Paper presented at the 2018 20th International Conference on Advanced Communication Technology (ICACT).

Almusaylim, Z. A., & Zaman, N. (2019). A review on smart home present state and challenges: Linked to context-awareness internet of things (IoT). *Wireless Networks*, 25(6), 3193–3204. doi:10.100711276-018-1712-5

Alsoufi, D., Elleithy, K. M., Abuzaghleh, T., & Nassar, A. (2012). *Security in wireless sensor networks-Improving the leap protocol*. Academic Press.

Anwar, Zainal, Abdullah, & Qureshi. (2014). Security Issues and Attacks in Wireless Sensor Network. *World Applied Sciences Journal*, 30(10).

Bekara, C., & Laurent, M. (2007). *Defending against nodes replication attacks on wireless sensor networks*. Paper presented at the SAR-SSI 2007: 2nd Conference on Security in Network Architectures and Information Systems.

Brar, S., & Angurala, M. (2016). Review on grey-hole attack detection and prevention. *International Journal of Advance research. Ideas and Innovations in Technology*, 2(5), 1–4.

Chaitanya, Ayyappa, & Ravindra. (2011). Analysis and Study of Denial of Service Attacks in Wireless Mobile Jammers. *International Journal of Computer Science and Telecommunications, 2*(5).

Chelli, K. (2015). Security issues in wireless sensor networks: Attacks and countermeasures. *Proceedings of the World Congress on Engineering.*

Choi, B. G., Cho, E. J., Kim, J. H., Hong, C. S., & Kim, J. H. (2009). *A sinkhole attack detection mechanism for LQI based mesh routing in WSN.* Paper presented at the 2009 International Conference on Information Networking.

Conti, Mancini, & Mei. (n.d.). Distributed Detection of Clone Attacks in Wireless Sensor Networks. *IEEE Transactions on Dependable and Secure Computing.*

Deng & Chen. (n.d.). *Mobility-assisted Detection of the Replication Attacks in Mobile Wireless Sensor Networks.* Academic Press.

Dr, G., & Padmavathi, D. S. (2009). A Survey of Attacks, Security Mechanisms and Challenges in Wireless Sensor Networks. *International Journal of Computer Science and Information Security, 4*(1).

Dr, G., & Padmavathi, M. D. S. (2009). A Survey of Attacks, Security Mechanisms and Challenges in Wireless Sensor Networks. *International Journal of Computer Science and Information Security, 4*(1).

Giri, D., Borah, S., & Pradhan, R. (2018). *Approaches and Measures to Detect Wormhole Attack in Wireless Sensor Networks: A Survey. In Advances in Communication, Devices and Networking* (pp. 855–864). Springer. doi:10.1007/978-981-10-7901-6_92

Hossain, M. S., & Raghunathan, V. (2010). *Aegis: A lightweight firewall for wireless sensor networks.* Paper presented at the International Conference on Distributed Computing in Sensor Systems. 10.1007/978-3-642-13651-1_19

Hussain, K., Hussain, S. J., Jhanjhi, N., & Humayun, M. (2019). *SYN Flood Attack Detection based on Bayes Estimator (SFADBE) For MANET.* Paper presented at the 2019 International Conference on Computer and Information Sciences (ICCIS). 10.1109/ICCISci.2019.8716416

Islam, J., Islam, M., & Islam, N. (2007). *A-sleach: An advanced solar aware leach protocol for energy efficient routing in wireless sensor networks.* Paper presented at the Sixth International Conference on Networking (ICN'07). 10.1109/ICN.2007.14

Jordao, A., Torres, L. A. B., & Schwartz, W. R. (2018). Novel approaches to human activity recognition based on accelerometer data. *Signal, Image and Video Processing, 12*(7), 1–8. doi:10.100711760-018-1293-x

Karlof, C., Sastry, N., & Wagner, D. (2004). TinySec: a link layer security architecture for wireless sensor networks. *Proceedings of the 2nd international conference on Embedded networked sensor systems.* 10.1145/1031495.1031515

Kaur, T., & Kumar, R. (2018). *Mitigation of Blackhole Attacks and Wormhole Attacks in Wireless Sensor Networks Using AODV Protocol.* Paper presented at the 2018 IEEE International Conference on Smart Energy Grid Engineering (SEGE). 10.1109/SEGE.2018.8499473

Khalil, N., Abid, M. R., Benhaddou, D., & Gerndt, M. (2014). *Wireless sensors networks for Internet of Things.* Paper presented at the Intelligent sensors, sensor networks and information processing (ISSNIP), 2014 IEEE ninth international conference on. 10.1109/ISSNIP.2014.6827681

Khan, Saad, & Xiang. (2013). Detection and Mitigation of Node Replication Attacks in Wireless Sensor Networks: A Survey. *International Journal of Distributed Sensor Networks.*

Kirar, V. P. S. (2014). A Survey of Attacks and Security Requirements in Wireless Sensor Networks. *International Journal of Computer, Electrical, Automation, Control and Information Engineering, 8*(12), 2198–2203.

Kocakulak, M., & Butun, I. (2017). *An overview of Wireless Sensor Networks towards internet of things.* Paper presented at the Computing and Communication Workshop and Conference (CCWC), 2017 IEEE 7th Annual. 10.1109/CCWC.2017.7868374

Lai, B., Kim, S., & Verbauwhede, I. (2002). *Scalable session key construction protocol for wireless sensor networks.* Paper presented at the IEEE Workshop on Large Scale RealTime and Embedded Systems (LARTES).

Lakshmi, Rao, Mohan, & Kumar. (2013). Jamming Attacks Prevention in Wireless Sensor Networks Using Secure Packet Hiding Method. *International Journal of Advanced Research in Computer and Communication Engineering, 2*(9).

Law, Y. W., Palaniswami, M., Hoesel, L. V., Doumen, J., Hartel, P., & Havinga, P. (2009). Energy-efficient link-layer jamming attacks against wireless sensor network MAC protocols. *ACM Transactions on Sensor Networks, 5*(1), 6. doi:10.1145/1464420.1464426

Liu, J. K., Baek, J., Zhou, J., Yang, Y., & Wong, J. W. (2010). Efficient online/offline identity-based signature for wireless sensor network. *International Journal of Information Security, 9*(4), 287–296. doi:10.100710207-010-0109-y

Ma, J., Yi, P., Zhong, Y., & Zhang, S. (2006). *S_Firewall: A firewall in wireless sensor networks.* Paper presented at the 2006 International Conference on Wireless Communications, Networking and Mobile Computing. 10.1109/WiCOM.2006.280

Malan, D. J., Welsh, M., & Smith, M. D. (2004). *A public-key infrastructure for key distribution in TinyOS based on elliptic curve cryptography.* Paper presented at the 2004 First Annual IEEE Communications Society Conference on Sensor and Ad Hoc Communications and Networks, 2004. IEEE SECON 2004. 10.1109/SAHCN.2004.1381904

Malkani, Y., Keerio, A., Mahar, J., Memon, G., & Keerio, H. (2015). Localization, Routing and Data Gathering in Wireless Sensor Networks (WSNs). *Sindh University Research Journal, 44*(1).

Messai, M.-L. (2014). *Classification of Attacks in Wireless Sensor Networks.* Paper presented at the International Congress on Telecommunication and Application.

Michal, M. (2013). *Base station for Wireless sensor network* (Unpublished Diploma Thesis). Masryk University.

Mishra, S., & Thakkar, H. (2012). Features of WSN and Data Aggregation techniques in WSN: A Survey. *Int. J. Eng. Innov. Technol., 1*(4), 264–273.

Mpitziopoulos, DKonstantopoulos, & Pantziou. (2009). *A Survey on Jamming Attacks and Countermeasures in WSNs.* Paper presented at the IEEE Communications Surveys & Tutorials.

Mumtaz Qabulio, Y. (2015). On Node Replication Attack in Wireless Sensor Networks. *Mehran University Research Journal of Engineering & Technology, 34*(4).

Niculescu, D., & Nath, B. (2003). Trajectory based forwarding and its applications. *Proceedings of the 9th annual international conference on Mobile computing and networking.*

Oliveira, L. B., Wang, H. C., & Loureiro, A. A. (2005). *LHA-SP: Secure protocols for hierarchical wireless sensor networks.* Paper presented at the 2005 9th IFIP/IEEE International Symposium on Integrated Network Management, 2005. 10.1109/INM.2005.1440767

Ouafaa, I., Mustapha, E., Salah-ddine, K., & Jalal, L. (2016). *An advanced analysis on secure hierarchical routing protocols in wireless sensor network.* Paper presented at the 2016 International Conference on Engineering & MIS (ICEMIS). 10.1109/ICEMIS.2016.7745375

Ouafaa, I., Mustapha, E., Salah-ddine, K., & Said, E. H. (2016). Secure Hierarchical Routing Protocols in Wireless Sensor Networks: A Comparative Analysis. *International Journal of Software Engineering and Its Applications, 10*(11), 95–108. doi:10.14257/ijseia.2016.10.11.08

Palacharla, S., Chandan, M., GnanaSuryaTeja, K., & Varshitha, G. (2018). Wormhole Attack: a Major Security Concern in Internet of Things (Iot). *International Journal of Engineering & Technology, 7*(3.27), 147-150.

Patil, H. K., & Chen, T. M. (2017). *Wireless Sensor Network Security: The Internet of Things. In Computer and Information Security Handbook* (3rd ed., pp. 317–337). Elsevier. doi:10.1016/B978-0-12-803843-7.00018-1

Perrig, A., Szewczyk, R., Tygar, J. D., Wen, V., & Culler, D. E. (2002). SPINS: Security protocols for sensor networks. *Wireless Networks, 8*(5), 521–534. doi:10.1023/A:1016598314198

Rashmi. (n.d.). A1, M. C. M. Detection of Node Replication Attacks in Mobile Sensor Networks Using Efficient Localized Detection Algorithm. *International Journal of Engineering Research and Applications.*

Roosta, T. G. (2008). *Attacks and defenses of ubiquitous sensor networks.* Academic Press.

Roychowdhury, S., & Patra, C. (2010). *Geographic adaptive fidelity and geographic energy aware routing in ad hoc routing.* Paper presented at the International Conference.

Shaon, M. (2015). *A computationally intelligent approach to the detection of wormhole attacks in wireless sensor networks.* Academic Press.

Sharma, S., & Jena, S. K. (2011). A survey on secure hierarchical routing protocols in wireless sensor networks. *Proceedings of the 2011 international conference on communication, computing & security.* 10.1145/1947940.1947972

Shikha. (2016). A Study for Finding Location of Nodes in Wireless Sensor Networks. *International Journal of Computer Science & Engineering Technology, 7*(3).

Singh, M. D. R. (2015). A Review of Security Issues and Denial of Service Attacks in Wireless Sensor Networks. *International Journal of Computer Science and Information Technology Research, 3*(1).

Singh, R., Singh, J., & Singh, R. (2016). TBSD: A defend against Sybil attack in wireless sensor networks. *International Journal of Computer Science and Network Security, 16*(11), 90–99.

Stankovic, D. W. a. J. A. (2002). Denial of Service in Sensor Networks. *IEEE Computer, 35*(10).

Sundararajan, R. K., & Arumugam, U. (2015). Intrusion detection algorithm for mitigating sinkhole attack on LEACH protocol in wireless sensor networks. *Journal of Sensors, 2015,* 2015. doi:10.1155/2015/203814

Vijendran, A. S., & Gripsy, J. V. (2014). *Enhanced secure multipath routing scheme in mobile adhoc and sensor networks.* Paper presented at the Second International Conference on Current Trends In Engineering and Technology-ICCTET 2014. 10.1109/ICCTET.2014.6966289

Wander, A. S., Gura, N., Eberle, H., Gupta, V., & Shantz, S. C. (2005). *Energy analysis of public-key cryptography for wireless sensor networks.* Paper presented at the Third IEEE international conference on pervasive computing and communications. 10.1109/PERCOM.2005.18

Wang, Y., Attebury, G., & Ramamurthy, B. (2006). *A survey of security issues in wireless sensor networks.* Academic Press.

Xing, G., Lu, C., Pless, R., & Huang, Q. (2004). On greedy geographic routing algorithms in sensing-covered networks. *Proceedings of the 5th ACM international symposium on Mobile ad hoc networking and computing.* 10.1145/989459.989465

Xu, Trappe, & Zhang. (2006). Jamming Sensor Networks: Attack and Defense Strategies. *IEEE Network.*

Yagan, O. (2012). Performance of the Eschenauer–Gligor key distribution scheme under an ON/OFF channel. *IEEE Transactions on Information Theory, 58*(6), 3821–3835. doi:10.1109/TIT.2012.2189353

Yick, J., Mukherjee, B., & Ghosal, D. (2008). Wireless sensor network survey. *Computer Networks, 52*(12), 2292–2330. doi:10.1016/j.comnet.2008.04.002

Yu, L., & Kuo. (2012). *CSI: Compressed Sensing-Based Clone Identification in Sensor Networks.* Paper presented at the 8th IEEE International Workshop on Sensor Networks and Systems for Pervasive Computing. 10.1109/PerComW.2012.6197497

Yu, Y., Govindan, R., & Estrin, D. (2001). *Geographical and energy aware routing: A recursive data dissemination protocol for wireless sensor networks.* Academic Press.

Zhang, M. (2009). Memory Efficient Protocols for Detecting Node Replication Attacks in Wireless Sensor Networks. Academic Press.

Zhang, Z., Liu, S., Bai, Y., & Zheng, Y. (2018). M optimal routes hops strategy: Detecting sinkhole attacks in wireless sensor networks. *Cluster Computing,* 1–9.

Zheng, G., & Hu, Z. (2009). *A Clustering Protocol Based on the Probability Fading Strategy in WSNs.* Paper presented at the 2009 International Conference on Information Engineering and Computer Science. 10.1109/ICIECS.2009.5366020

Zorzi, M., & Rao, R. R. (2003). Geographic random forwarding (GeRaF) for ad hoc and sensor networks: Energy and latency performance. *IEEE Transactions on Mobile Computing, 2*(4), 349–365. doi:10.1109/TMC.2003.1255650

ADDITIONAL READING

Al-Suhail, G. A., Mehdi, J., & Nikolakopoulos, G. (2017). A Practical Survey on Wireless Sensor Network Platforms. *Journal of Communications Technology. Electronics and Computer Science, 13,* 23–30.

Atwady, Y., & Hammoudeh, M. (2017). *A survey on authentication techniques for the internet of things.* Paper presented at the Proceedings of the International Conference on Future Networks and Distributed Systems. 10.1145/3102304.3102312

Dhand, G., & Tyagi, S. (2016). Data aggregation techniques in WSN: Survey. *Procedia Computer Science, 92,* 378–384. doi:10.1016/j.procs.2016.07.393

Han, G., Jiang, J., Zhang, C., Duong, T. Q., Guizani, M., & Karagiannidis, G. K. (2016). A survey on mobile anchor node assisted localization in wireless sensor networks. *IEEE Communications Surveys and Tutorials, 18*(3), 2220–2243. doi:10.1109/COMST.2016.2544751

Li, M., Li, Z., & Vasilakos, A. V. (2013). A survey on topology control in wireless sensor networks: Taxonomy, comparative study, and open issues. *Proceedings of the IEEE, 101*(12), 2538–2557. doi:10.1109/JPROC.2013.2257631

Mateen, A., Javaid, N., & Iqbal, S. (2019). *Towards energy efficient routing in blockchain based underwater WSNs via recovering the void holes.* MS thesis, COMSATS University Islamabad (CUI), Islamabad 44000, Pakistan.

Ndiaye, M., Hancke, G., & Abu-Mahfouz, A. (2017). Software defined networking for improved wireless sensor network management: A survey. *Sensors (Basel), 17*(5), 1031. doi:10.339017051031 PMID:28471390

Rashid, B., & Rehmani, M. H. (2016). Applications of wireless sensor networks for urban areas: A survey. *Journal of Network and Computer Applications, 60,* 192–219. doi:10.1016/j.jnca.2015.09.008

Chapter 12
A Process Framework to Migrate Legacy Application to Cloud:
LAMP2C

Sanjeev Kumar Yadav

Jyoti Vidyapeeth University, Jaipur, India

Akhil Khare

CSED MVSR Engineering College, Hyderabad, India

Kavita Choudhary

Jyoti Vidyapeeth University, Jaipur, India

ABSTRACT

An enterprise has a challenge in keeping pace with the quickly evolving technology. The biggest challenge comes in terms of legacy application migration to technologies like cloud. Legacy application migration should be well thought out at the very start (i.e., pre-migration and supported by migration framework). In this chapter, the author proposes a legacy application migration framework with a focus on pre-migration area. A robust technical and business analysis of existing/legacy applications, based on the enterprise's focus parameters, during pre-migration sets the migration path for subsequent area of framework. The proposed pre-migration mathematical assessment helps an enterprise to understand a legacy application's current state and also helps in unearthing the information with respect to candidate application and helps in taking well-informed decisions like GO or NO-GO w.r.t legacy application migration. Considering application migration a journey, it is important that it reaches its destination, so pre-migration is an important area of the migration journey.

DOI: 10.4018/978-1-7998-2803-7.ch012

INTRODUCTION

Technology landscape is evolving ever since it came into existence but since the arrival of internet technology landscape is changing at a faster pace than ever before. Keeping pace with changing technology has become a challenge in itself for an enterprise, however important is that enterprise can't ignore these technological enhancement i.e. it has to adopt these new technologies to keep themselves competitive and make most out of an existing application or portfolio of applications.

Legacy application were developed using hardware, software and coding platform that were relevant during that point of time. These application were enterprises backbone and same holds good today as well, however with the technology technological enhancement multiple other challenges are faced by enterprises in terms of shortage of skilled manpower availability, knowledge retention, cost increase with respect to maintenance of software and hardware, unable to scale the software, reduced efficiencies and effectiveness of operators, which will effect business progress, customers impression or understanding and company's image agility to serve customer (Ali Khajeh-Hosseini, *et al.*, 2010). Challenges highlighted are specific either to enterprise or legacy application however few challenges which remains common irrespective to the enterprise size, software, hardware, etc. Ref. Figure *1*

Figure 1. Legacy Application Maintains and Enhancement Challenge

1. Customer
   a. Application is an important factor in addressing the competition. Enterprise business interest may get influenced due to Application inefficiency.
   b. Application may not meet customer expectation in terms of
      i. Application efficiency, which may lead to dissatisfied customer and may effect on future business.
      ii. Functionality/feature, which will provide an edge to competition i.e. application is not able to keep up with business growth.
      iii. Inefficient application, will lead to dissatisfied customer.
2. Knowledge
   a. Lack of extensive legacy application knowledge may impact on:
      i. Adding additional functionality to application
      ii. Enhancements of the application and.
      iii. System maintenance
   b. Non-availability of many legacy application knowledgeable resources may face challenges in terms of sharing legacy application knowledge and its best practices.
   c. Knowledge concentration within set of people increases the dependency on fixed number of people.
3. Resources
   a. Reduction in resource's pool due to attrition or their desire to learn market-relevant technology (Rashmi Rai, *et al.,* 2013) or any other reason, will impact resource availability in market for legacy application maintenance, it includes enhancement.
   b. As application knowledge and understanding gets concentrated within limited number of resources; people retention cost will increase. Related aspect will be - getting resource with higher cost in required technology.
4. Technology
   a. Existing enterprise critical application may be using multiple technology, so application maintenance cost will be high in terms of skilled manpower, licenses, etc. (Rashmi Rai, *et al.,* 2013)
   b. Non-existence of product support from product vendor, may impact to support activities of legacy application. It will also have direct impact on the availability of skilled man power.
   c. Applications are device dependent i.e. these applications are not accessible on any other machine/device than office computers.
5. Compliance
   a. If no enhancement is made to legacy applications; it may lead it to become regulatory non-compliance (Rashmi Rai, *et al.,* 2013).
   b. Regulatory non-compliance is bigger risk to an enterprise than adopting relevant technology by migrating legacy application to.
6. High Operating Cost (Support and maintenance)
   a. Legacy system operating cost increases due to hardware, staff's training, inefficiency, outages, etc. some of the costs which are generally not stated in budget are customer's loyalty, employee's satisfaction and brand image.

b. Revenue earned using better tools and technology, by competitor, should be considered as lost revenue due to inability of using relevant technology. However, it may not be possible to arrive at the loss of revenue an enterprise is making due to non-investment in latest technology.

With all these challenges big question, which arises with respect to legacy software or hardware is; what should an enterprise do with legacy applications/software or hardware? In other words, how enterprise can avoid legacy pitfalls as they may not be in a situation to discard legacy applications due to various reason such as these applications has become core to business over a period of time, large enough to be understood by an individual, etc. so What are the options available with an enterprise in this situation to deal with legacy application.

As regard to enterprise long-term goal for legacy application; an enterprise has below mentioned three prominent options, post initial development phase and maintenance phase, with respect to their legacy applications:

1. Migrate - Migrate existing application to new platform.
2. Replace - Replace existing application, which are referred as legacy application, with any suitable off-the-shelf application i.e. standard commercial application available in market.
3. Re-develop - Re-develop the existing application all over again, in any of the market-relevant technology.

replace or *re-develop* may not be the viable option as companies are unlikely to develop an application from scratch, which has become kind of organization's heart line, so viable option for a company is to *migrate* present software to new technology and/or new platform. Enterprises are aware of the fact that migration of their current application is in there interest and way to go however biggest challenge with legacy application migration is to retain the current investments made on the application i.e. reusing existing capabilities in a renewed environment.

Cloud computing is among the most sought after platforms of all the latest emerging technologies due to various advantages it provides to an enterprise. Enterprise planning for migration to cloud may have unique and different migration's reason from other enterprise, however there are two challenge;

1. One is without throwing away their current investments i.e. reusing most of the existing capabilities in a renewed or more stable environment. And
2. Two, cloud computing concepts and approach differs from that of traditional approach.

Application migration is not so straight forward as it seems to be (Rashmi, *et al.,* 2012; Stavros, *et al.,* 2013), because all cloud layers are covered unlike legacy application particularly when legacy application is tightly coupled (Muhammad Aufeef, *et al.,* 2012; Jesus Bisbal, *et al.,* 1997) as compare to cloud application. Hence migration requires structured approach to assure consistent value realization. Proposed migration framework **LAMP2C**, expanded form is "Legacy Application **M**igration **P**rocess **F**ramework to **C**loud". One of the focus area of LAMP2C is Pre-Migration area whereas LAMP2C as a whole acts as one stop shop for the migration process that address the migration related activities.

BACKGROUND

Undertook the study of related research papers freely available over internet to understand research taken place till now in legacy application migration to cloud.

1. Arooj Hussain, *et al.*, 2017; author is of view that companies are migrating their data and resources to the cloud because of multiple benefits cloud computing offers. Author highlights that company may encounter challenges, while switching from a traditional system to a cloud-based system along with various issues and incompetence that cloud computing brings with itself, which can give nightmares to the company's team opting for migrating legacy application to cloud. At the same time author, highlight that all these issues and challenges can be taken care, if proper care is taken during the migration and maintenance phase.

2. Muhammad Shoaib, *et al.*, 2017; author examined and reviewed the current migration framework, keeping in view process, activities, challenges and their solutions, which provides guidelines to enhance migration process. Author is of view that due to fast technological enhancement organizations need to migrate from a platform to another such as cloud-based migration however due to unavailability of resources, migration may not be performed optimality. Risks are also involved while migration activity is performed but these risks can be reduced, if migration is done appropriately. Comparison of multiple selected studies was carried out to point out the existing gap and explore future directions of work. It was concluded that a common framework need to be proposed with respect to software migration and software engineering.

3. Khadija SABIRI and Faouzia BENABBOU, 2015; author highlights the benefit cloud computing provides due to which many companies look forward to migrate their application to cloud however small and medium size company gets discouraged to migrate to cloud due to challenges, which are expected to come and due to the migration project's potential size and complexity. At the same time author commented that barely any directions are existing for legacy application migration to cloud, so it will be in the interest of organization to plan for challenges which are expected while moving legacy application to cloud.

4. Flavio Corradini, *et al.*, 2015; Author highlight the fact that the new paradigm (Cloud technology and application/service hosting in Cloud) has led to re-engineering phase of migrating existing software to cloud environment. According to author, it is important to analyse application's cloud compliance and post migration expectation along with effort required for moving software to cloud, before migration procedure gets initiated. At present author decided to consider only the technological part of the migration while ignoring business aspects.

5. K C Gouda, *et al.*, 2014; as per author cloud migration can be categorized as Big Bang Migration and Trickle Migration. Author also suggests twelve migration patterns classified. Users can chose any suggested migration pattern as per requirement best suited for migration requirement, to cloud. Migration patterns can be best chosen by individuals' interest. Author is of view that, if migration is not carried out in proper way than it can damage the secured data and applications along with other inconveniences are unavoidable else it bring wonders.

6. Pooyan Jamshidi, *et al.*, 2013; author selected 23 studies published from 2010 to 2013 for systematic literature review. Framework characterization is taken as a base for these selected studies for their classification and comparison with a Focus on effort required for migration of on-premise legacy application to cloud. Requirement of migration framework is apparent in this paper; it exposes the

fact that people do not trust cloud migration because of non-existence of frameworks however its existence can help in restoring the trust in cloud migration. Author's review also shows the absence of tools to support automated migration and its tasks.

7. Muhammad Aufeef Chauhan and Muhammad Ali Babarhas, 2012; Author highlights that successful migration happens only if supported by defined processes. It helps a) identify migration challenges, if any and address the same b) platform evaluation strategy and any domain specific requirements. A framework is shared in this paper based on migrating experience that supports migration of an Open Source System (OSS). Author explains the process with the help of relative analysis of efforts required for migration, reports the possible challenges, suitable solutions and lesson learned. Author expect these experiences to serves as guiding principle for individuals devising to migrate legacy application.

8. Juncal Alonso, *et al.*, 2013; Author is of view that a) many companies are putting plans to migrate in-house hosted application to cloud and b) migrating to cloud is a risky proposition due to uncertainty, especially when companies are unaware of whether investment will be recovered or not. Paper presents a modernization assessment framework to assess companies which are planning to migrate there products to Cloud on factors like cost estimations, ROI, effort and migration. In addition proposed assessment framework provides insight to companies about the required effort and cost for migration to cloud, it also provides information about organizational processes change because of migration. It will help companies to decide, whether they need to migrate or need to start from scratch.

FRAMEWORK OVERVIEW

Migration requires structured approach to assure consistent value realization; LAMP2C acts as a guiding principle and provides process guidelines that needs to go along while legacy application is getting migrated. Framework support migration in efficient way, which increases the likelihood of a successful cloud migration by having elaborate upfront comprehensive migration plan, along with continuous and pertinent communications among stakeholders and their involvement in entire migration journey. LAMP2C suggest to follow phased manner approach and never compels to follow activities cover-to-cover. LAMP2C support all migration related activities and helps in speeding up migration effective and efficient manner. It can be used to evaluate and enhance enterprise existing migration processes.

Proposed LAMP2C framework is divided into three parts. At highest level is **Area**. Area is sub-divided into **Phases**. Phases are further sub-divided in **Activities.** Ref. Figure 2.

1. **Area** – Area is the highest unit in the proposed framework. LAMP2C follow four area approach, which cut across three cloud layers:

    a. Pre-migration Area - Activities required to be completed, before real migration are bundled in this area of LAMP2C.

It helps stakeholders to analyze the enterprise's current IT landscape identified for migration in detail. It helps to take well informed decisions based on various parameters, which matters to enterprise. Outcome of pre-migration area will be the ultimate answer of GO or NO-GO w.r.t application migration.

Figure 2. LAMP2C - Components

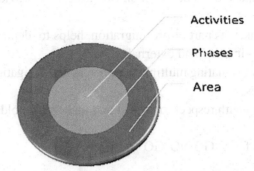

b.   Migration Area -. Migration area is the second and most happening area of the LAMP2C framework. It can be called the heart of LAMP2C framework as actual migration takes place in this area of framework.

c.   Post Migration Area – Activities required to be completed, after real migration stays bundled in this area of LAMP2C. Actions in post-migration area are based previous areas of framework i.e. Pre-migration and Migration.

d.   Governance Area. - Governance area, one of the important area of LAMP2C, which cut across all three area of framework. Governance is generally the system of rules, practice and process by which enterprise gets directed and controlled so governance area helps to keep a check on the progress with respect to migration across layers.

Area is the collection of one or more than one Phases.

2.   **Phase** – Area is divided into Phases with falls within the given Area. Phase is the collection of activities.

3.   **Activities** – Activities is the smallest unit of the framework and is an actionable item under Phase. Activities can't be further sub-divided.

PRE-MIGRATION

Pre-Migration area is starting point of the migration project and most crucial area of LAMP2C framework; starting point for the migration journey (Juncal Alonso, *et al.,* 2013). Migration project success is highly depends upon the initial assessment made before embarking on the journey of actual legacy application migration. Assessment, during pre-migration area must be performed thoroughly, it helps stakeholders to understand whether legacy application migration to cloud is economically feasible and beneficial or there is a need to choose/identify alternate methods (Juncal Alonso, *et al.,* 2013). Assessment should uncover dependencies or gap at high-level; failing to uncover dependencies or gaps can jeopardize the project's viability.

Let us understand some of the benefits of Pre-migration, before discussing the pre-migration in details:

1. Validate and support stakeholder's decision on the project by providing quality information and facts.
2. Feasibility study undertaken as part of pre-migration, helps to identify constraints, if any, project may face, which includes internal and external.
3. Success rate improves by evaluating multiple parameters and mitigating factors early on that could affect the project's success.
4. Helps in decision-making with respect to project and make stakeholder better prepared to embark on migration journey.
5. Provides important facts for a "GO/NO-GO" decision

In pre-migration area, enterprise is required to look at the application or application portfolio keeping in view enterprise's strategic business objective (Juncal Alonso, *et al.,* 2013). At high-level pre-migration assessments is carried out, depending on enterprise requirement and focus, under categories a) Technical assessment, b) Business assessment or c) Both. Process flow is detailed out in Figure 3.

Figure 3.

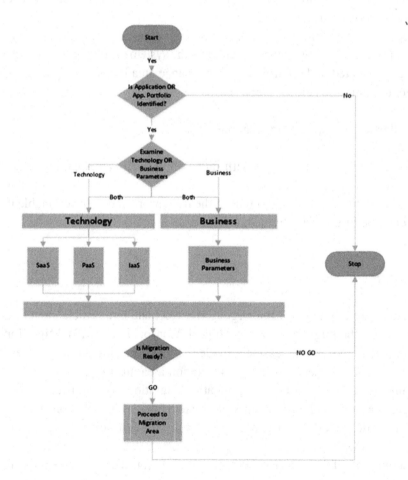

Before embarking on migration journey via pre-migration; as part of pre-migration enterprise need to decide on what kind of assessment needs to be undertaken; Technical Assessment or Business Assessment or perform both the assessment. Assessment decision is organization specific however for discussion purpose both will be considered.

Parameters which are important or are considered to be important for the portfolio or application are clubbed into assessment categories because:

1. Technical Assessment provides an early insight to application migration requirements and dependencies, which needs to be taken care during migration journey, with respect to technical attribute of legacy application or portfolio.

2. Business assessment provides an early insight to application migration potential cost organization may incur to carry out the migration to the cloud, with respect to business attribute of legacy system or portfolio.

Underline target of pre-migration area is to identify business and technical benefits with respect to migration cost (Leire Orue-Echevarria, *et al.,* 2012). And helps stakeholders to take, ultimate, well informed decision with respect to application migration i.e. application migration is a GO or NO-GO.

Pre-Migration assessment provides:

1. Inputs for creating a legacy application migration strategy, if ultimate assessment answer is GO for migration.
2. Inputs detailing out the risk and issues involved in the application or portfolio migration so that appropriate mitigation plan or strategies can considered for minimizing potential extra costs.
3. Inputs to create migration road-map and execution plan.
4. Inputs to create a RACI matrix for the entire duration of migration project.

Technical Feasibility Assessment

Technical feasibility assessment of the proposed legacy application or portfolio is very critical which helps to determine if migration is "technically" viable or not. It in turn provides the application snapshot in term of its architecture, dependencies, risk factors, list application integrated, etc. (Juncal Alonso, *et al.,* 2013). Its focus is to understand, 'can it be done' or "will it work?" and at the same time it will also help to identify gap, if any.

Technical Feasibility helps in identify areas of strengths and weakness along with assessment of the software, hardware, and other requirements of proposed system. It aids to know where to direct further planning and resources.

Apart from list of benefits any assessment feasibility brings; Technical Feasibility Assessment benefits are as follows:

1. Increases the success rate by multiple parameters evaluation.
2. Feasibility study helps to un-earth constraints, if any, migration project may face. Constrains includes both, internal and external constrains.
3. Unearth the area which will need special attention.

4. Identifies legacy application modules that are affected by migration and efforts required for migrating these modules.
5. Helps in decision-making keeping in view the constrains, if any

Cloud cover three service model so important is that technical feasibility should cover all the required parameters linked to three service model and its related aspects to un-cover the gaps, if any. Stakeholders are free to choose or add any additional parameter based on the service model considered as within migration project scope and/or chosen assessment area.

Parameters considered for assessment will be based on enterprise environment, project requirement, etc. while identifying parameter, it will be a good practice to categories parameter it service model so that mapping will be easy in next area of LAMP2C framework i.e. Migration Area.

Common Parameters

Common parameters are those parameters which cut across more than one service models and considered for assessment. All these parameters are clubbed into one as "Common Parameters", if required. It helps to avoid consideration of similar parameter(s) across service model and save the assessment effort. However, it depends upon individual as to how they would like consider these common parameters for pre-migration analysis.

Mathematical Assessment Methodology

Technical feasibility assessment of LAMP2C's pre-migration area is a parameter-based mathematical assessment methodology; parameters which are important or considered to be relevant for enterprise and application. It is referred as LAMP2C-ASK, a vital component, if to be called so, of LAMP2C. LAMP2C-ASK helps company to examine there IT landscape holistically and analyse its application portfolio in detail.

LAMP2C-ASK, it is divided into five phases, which needs to be performed in a sequential order as each phase output acts an input for the next phase except the 1st phase where parameters are getting identified:

1. Identify Parameter
2. ASK Point
3. ASK Confidence Level
4. ASK Belt and
5. Plot Chart

All the above phases gets executed sequentially as shown in Figure 4.

Identify Parameters

LAMP2C-ASK has parameter-based approach; required and relevant parameters and sub-parameters, needs to be isolated and listed, to start with. Identifying parameters and preparing a comprehensive list of parameters will be one of the most tedious tasks as being a legacy application, many of the informa-

Figure 4. LAMP2C-ASK Pre-migration Flow

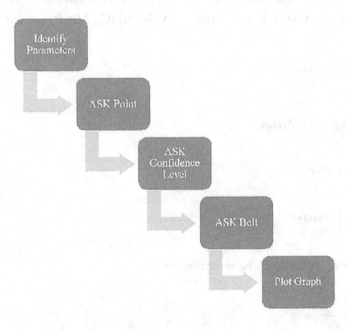

tion required may not be easily available, if available, then it may not be complete due to various reasons such as documentation is missing, resources (man-power) are not available, etc.

ASK Points

Once parameters are identified than parameter are assigned "Impact Rating" that is parameter's importance based on the parameter's impact for the specific application, as in Table 1. Importance ranges between "Very Low" to "Very High" and its impact rating ranges from 0.1 and 5.0. 0.1 is the lowest and 5.0 is the highest "Impact Rating".

Table 1. Impact Rating Range

Importance	Impact Rating Range
Very high	4.1 to 5.0
High	3.1 to 4.0
Neutral	2.1 to 3.0
Low	1.1 to 2.0
Very Low	0.1 to 1.0

Assume parameters namely C1, C2, C3, and so on till Cn. "n" is maximum number of parameter. Impact Rating is assigned based on the important of each parameter, which ranges from 0.1 to 5.0. Adding all and dividing them by the total parameters count (in this example is "n") will yield the mean value of the considered parameter. It is referred as "**ASK Point**" (ASKP) i.e. μ_c.

$$ASKP = \mu_c = \frac{\int C_{1+\int C_2 + \int C_3 + \int C_4 ... + \int C_n}}{n}$$

$$ASKP = \mu_c = Parameters' \, Mean$$

$$n = number \, of \, parameters$$

$$i = importance \, of \, parameter$$

In summarized form; formula can be re-written as:

$$ASKP = \mu_c = \sum_1^n \frac{\int C_n}{n}$$

ASK Confidence Level

Calculate the standard deviation using the same data. Standard deviation is referred as **ASK Confidence Level (ACL)**. ACL is calculated by adding the square of the value after subtracting ASKP for each parameter value, summed value when divided by the total number of parameters gives standard deviation σ_c i.e. ACL.

$$ACL = \sigma_c = \frac{\left(\int C_1 - \mu_c\right)^2 + \left(\int C_2 - \mu_c\right)^2 + \left(\int C_3 - \mu_c\right)^2 + ... \left(\int C_n - \mu_c\right)^2}{n}$$

$$ACL = \sigma_c = Parameters' \, Standard \, Deviation$$

$$ASKP = \mu_c = Parameters' \, Mean$$

$$n = number \, of \, parameters$$

In summarized form formula can be re-written as:

$$ACL = \sigma_c = \sum_1^n \frac{\left(\int C_n - \mu_c\right)^2}{n}$$

ASK Belt

ASKB has two part; one ASKB Right i.e. $ASKB_R$ and second is ASKB Left i.e. $ASKB_L$. $ASKB_R$ and $ASKB_L$ can be calculated as shown below:

$ASKB_R =$ ASKP + ACL

$ASKB_L =$ ASKP - ACL

ASK Belt (ASKB) helps to create boundary for identified parameter with the help of ASKP and ACL. ASKP, ASKB ($ASKB_R$ and $ASKB_L$) and ACL helps to calculate $f(x)$ using the below formula:

$$f(x) = \frac{1}{\sqrt{2\pi\sigma_c^2}} e^{\frac{-(x-\mu_c)^2}{2\sigma_c}}$$

Constant values and other values for the above given formula are as below:

$\pi = 3.14$

$e = 2.71$ and

$x =$ Parameter Impact

$\mu_c =$ ASKP

$\sigma_c =$ ACL

Plot Graph

Arranged parameters' $f(x)$ value in ascending order of impact rating for graph plotting. Plotting $f(x)$ values vs x values, gives the bell curve as below:

List of parameters which falls within $ASKB_R$ and $ASKB_L$ range can be considered safely as migration scope, where are outside will be considered as out-side migration scope. However list of parameters which falls outside the limit needs to be re-looked at or special attention need to be given to these parameters or

Figure 5. Bell Curve (In-Scope / Out-Scope parameters)

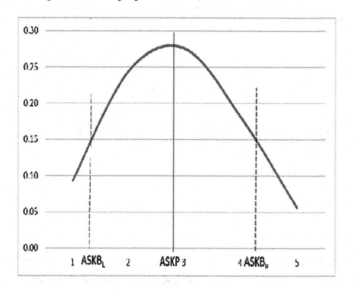

appropriate decision need to be taken by enterprise to move them within the migration scope, if required as they have better understanding of ground realities.

Business Feasibility Assessment

Real concern for many stakeholders in an enterprise is about the actual cost of moving legacy application to cloud with respect to investment made on on-premise infrastructure and software. It is generally believed and discussed widely that existing systems i.e. legacy system migration to cloud can or will reduce the capital expenses which are related to costs of hardware (servers and other), operating system environment, operating system and database products license costs, database products deployment and hiring staff for maintaining the system and its operational expense. Nevertheless challenge is that an enterprise, who want to commence migration journey needs to measure return-on-investment (ROI) before start of migration journey but issue is that there is no right and easy way to calculate ROI because migration to cloud impacts cost and people heavily along with speed which makes it tougher to evidently recognize value of cloud.

Business Feasibility Assessment reveal and evaluate to answer "should it be done" from business perspective. Keeping this in view, it is critical for an enterprises to understand the economics (potential cost and the efforts required of the organization to carry out the migration to the cloud) behind the belief that will help them to make the right decisions before embarking on migration journey. In order to understand the economics, it requires an elaborate analysis of cost and its benefit that involves infrastructure, infrastructure support, legal requirements, operation staff, and security. In addition, it is important to understand on-premises infrastructure a) current state of utilization, b) why enterprise is having extra capacity and c) whether these are getting utilized at optimum level.

Business Feasibility Assessment will support enterprise's decision makers in terms of estimated costs, migration's operational risk, benefits, etc. in other words it will help understand whether financial benefits will clearly exceed the migration costs or not. At this point, would like to highlight that:

1. Investments required for migration can be of diverse kind such as revenue increasing, cost-reduction or mandatory investments w.r.t compliance. Cloud investments generally falls into categories of revenue increasing and cost-reduction.
2. Organizations need to make change in their processes and policies for changes to be effective as Cloud required is less asset investment as compare to on premise.
3. As no high capital investments is required, so it will change the method of budgets spending or allocation or its management, which means that a transition from CapEx to OpEx.

In KPMG article "Journey to the cloud" in 2017 lists series of reasons for enterprises to adopt cloud computing however costs saving is at third position only. It shows that companies are taking strategic longer term perspective instead of instant cost savings. (David Conroy, *et. al*, 2017). Key question for any enterprise on journey of migrating legacy application to cloud is its measurement of return-on-investment". Challenge is that there is no easy or right way to calculate the return-on-investment.

Multiple number of metrics are available and are used by enterprises for financial evaluation. These metrics can be divided into two; a) one which are static and does not takes risk and time into consideration for example Payback Period or Average Annual Rate and b) additionally which are dynamic and takes risk and time into consideration for example Net Present Value (NPV) or Internal Rate of Return (IRR). Each financial assessment is a measurement method for capital's productivity that relates profit to capital investment or cash-flow to expenditure. Higher the return, more value is being created with the capital. Ultimate goal for any enterprise is earning a return against cost of capital.

Technical and Business Feasibility Assessments should help/assist:

1. Stakeholder to have clear understanding of each of the parameter identified or considered to conduct the migration feasibility
2. Stakeholder to obtain answer for one important question "Whether to migrate application to cloud or not?" i.e. whether to GO or NO-GO with the cloud migration.
3. Stakeholder to understand, if legacy application in full is not ready to move to cloud than which parts of the application can be moved to Cloud in the current paradigm.
4. In providing inputs to develop migration strategy and high-level migration road map, which can act as a bible for the migration journey along with documented known challenges (risk and issues) that are taken into consideration.

FUTURE RESEARCH DIRECTIONS

LAMP2C framework intended to help organization to adopt cloud technology, which is a long term process, so proposed framework can be further enhanced by putting a robust Gating criteria at every stage of framework. It can also be enhanced to cater the requirement of migrating application from one cloud provider to another provider.

CONCLUSION

Keeping pace with fast changing technology landscape is a challenge for an enterprise, which brings in multiple other challenges such as skilled manpower availability i.e. shortage, knowledge retention, increase in cost of software and hardware maintenance, etc. Keeping in view challenges arises due to changing technology landscape, investment made in legacy application over a time period; best available option is, migrate the legacy application to new technology or platform.

LAMP2C framework's Pre-migration area provides systematic mathematical formula based approach for Technical and Business Feasibility. Mathematical approach helps in identifying the critical parameters which are key for migration success. Approach suggested as part of LAMP2C framework is easy to implement, independent of parameter number and is flexible due to which all or anyone of three cloud service model can be considered. It has the flexibility either to consider all the model at one go or cloud service model individually as appropriate for legacy application migration. LAMP2C framework's Pre-migration area, while help and guide to embarking on a migration journey and provides required information to stakeholders, so that stakeholder can take informed decision with respect to proceed for migration or not i.e. GO or NO-GO decision. In addition, proposed migration framework LAMP2C a) will act as one stop solution for the migration process b) will help significantly in decision making c) will address the migration related activities and d) will help in enhancing the migration execution.

REFERENCES

Alonso, J., Arrieta, L. O.-E., Escalante, M., Gorroñogoitia, J., & Presenza, D. (2013). Cloud modernization assessment framework: Analyzing the impact of a potential migration to Cloud. *2013 IEEE 7th International Symposium on the Maintenance and Evolution of Service-Oriented and Cloud-Based Systems.* 10.1109/MESOCA.2013.6632736

Bisbal, J., Lawless, D., Wu, B., Grimson, J., Wade, V., & Richardson, R. (1997). An Overview of Legacy Information System Migration. *Asia-Pacific Software Engineering Conference.*

Chauhan & Babar. (2012). Towards Process Support for Migrating Applications to Cloud Computing. *International Conference on Cloud Computing and Service Computing.*

Conroy, D., Williams, J., Chauhan, S., Harmson, G., Snyder, M., & Symons, C. (2017). *Journey to the cloud - The creative CIO Agenda.* Retrieved from KPMG: https://assets.kpmg.com/content/dam/kpmg/xx/pdf/2017/02/the-creative-ciosagenda-journey-to-cloud.PDF

Corradini, F., De Angelis, F., Polini, A., & Sabbatini, S. (2015). Cloud Readiness Assessment of Legacy Application. *5th International Conference on Cloud Computing and Services Science (CLOSER2015).* 10.5220/0005443301190126

Gouda, Dwivedi, Patro, & Bhat. (2014). Migration Management in Cloud Computing. *International Journal of Engineering Trends and Technology, 12*(9).

Hussain, A., Bashir, S., Akhter, K., & Rashid, I. (2017). Issues Encountered During Migration from Existing Systems to Cloud Based Systems. *IJCSMC, 6*(6).

Jamshidi, Ahmad, & Pahl. (2013). Cloud Migration Research: A systematic Review. *Cloud Computing, IEEE Transaction on.*

Khajeh-Hosseini, Sommerville, & Sriram. (2010). *Research Challenges for Enterprise Cloud Computing.* Academic Press.

Orue-Echevarria. Alonso, Escalante, & Schuster. (2012). Assessing the Readiness to Move into the Cloud. Academic Press.

Rai, Mehfuz, & Sahoo. (2013). Efficient Migration of Application to Clouds: Analysis and Comparison. *GSTF Journal on Computing, 3*(3).

Rashmi, Mehfuz, & Sahoo. (2012, April). A five-phased approach for cloud migration. *International Journal of Emerging Technology and Advanced Engineering, 2*(4).

Sabiri & Benabbou. (2015). Methods Migration from On-premise to Cloud. *IOSR Journal of Computer Engineering, 17*(2), 58-65.

Shoaib, M., Ishaq, A., Ahmad, M. A., Talib, S., Mustafa, G., & Ahmed, A. (2017). Software Migration Frameworks for Software System Solutions: A Systematic Literature Review. *International Journal of Advanced Computer Science and Applications, 8*(11), 2017. doi:10.14569/IJACSA.2017.081126

Stavru, S., Krasteva, I., & Ilieva, S. (2012). *Challenges for Migrating to the Service Cloud Paradigm: An Agile Perspective.* Academic Press.

Chapter 13
Light Fidelity:
Data Through Illumination

Neha
Jamia Hamdard, India

Pooja Gupta
ⓘ https://orcid.org/0000-0003-4594-0840
Jamia Hamdard, India

ABSTRACT

This chapter discusses the relevant effects of li-fi technology in data transfer. The chapter should enable the reader to identify and relate to evolving data transmission technology. The chapter gives details of the basic components of li-fi. This chapter also discusses data transmission through light. The chapter should enable the reader to identify the difference between VLC and li-fi communication. The chapter also discusses the important properties, misconceptions, and limitations of this emerging technique. Furthermore, how various modulation techniques used in li-fi and its advantages over wi-fi technology has been mentioned in this chapter. The authors elucidate the major challenges and application areas of li-fi.

INTRODUCTION

Wireless technology has developed strikingly which make progressing communication. Today, encouraged by Radio Frequency circuit fabrication and numerous switching techniques, moderate rapid media transmission has been to a great extent conveyed over the world. Wireless communication faces speed problem when associated with various devices. Fixed transmission capacity limits high data transfer rates and interfaces with a secured system. Presently, the increasing enthusiasm for Wireless communication, the existing radio range beneath 10 GHz has turned out to be insufficient. Expected to relentlessly growing stipulation for wireless communication, Wi-Fi is going up against numerous troubles clog, density, safety, cost sufficiency, accessibility, effectiveness, and security.

Li-Fi is developed to transmit information at high rate up to 14 Gbps. To overcome the looming spectrum crunch frequency reuse concept may be adopted. This methodology has been utilized effec-

DOI: 10.4018/978-1-7998-2803-7.ch013

tively and introduces the concept of small cell. Be that as it may, decreases in cell sizes are progressively hard to accomplish because of the high infrastructure cost for data link. For these reasons, the optical resources are copious as appeared in Figure.1. Also, it is license-free. As of now, no regulation exists for the spectrum of infrared as well as visible light. It can offer bandwidth up to 780THz (Kuppusamy, P., Muthuraj, S., & Gopinath, S. 2016; Ramadhani, E., & Mahardika, G. P. 2018). The advancement of Li-Fi is to overcome the lack of existing technology.

Li-Fi is the condensing of light fidelity and was communicated by Harald Hass, a German physicist in his concept of "wireless data from every light". In Li-Fi, data is transferred using light signals instead of radio waves. It outfits well data transmission. In the coming age, this innovation will be utilized for transmitting information through the light in a closed territory. It is an innovation that uses a light emitting diode (LEDs) to transmit information remotely.

It uses a bidirectional light and wireless method of communication. The transceiver will play an important role to establish a proper communication link between points/nodes. The function of Transceiver is to relay and receive data in the Li-Fi system. The modulation technique used in transceiver allows the LED used in the system to know how to use the light. This technology is appropriate for highly dense information area. It is also suitable for minimizing radio interference problem in a constrained region.

Figure 1. The Electromagnetic spectrum

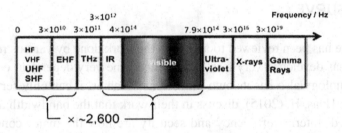

The electromagnetic spectrum can be classified from radio waves to gamma rays shown in Figure 1. The authors of Sharma, R. R., & Sanganal, A. (2014) and Kavehrad, M. (2010). have discussed in their research some spectrums which are mentioned below:

1. Radio waves (30 Hz-300GHz): This becomes insufficient for increasing data. Also, due to spectrum cost Radio waves are expensive. It is less safe due to interference.
2. Infra-red (300GHz-400THz): Generally, it is useful for Low power application and analysis of organic compounds. Safety is the major concern while using Infrared at high power. So it is advised to use Infrared with less power.
3. Visible light (400THz–790THz): This spectrum range is detected by the human eye. It is that part of the electromagnetic spectrum that has not been used until now.
4. Ultra Violet (800THz-30PHz): It causes chemical reaction and also adversely affects the human body. It has a tendency to penetrate the skin. However, this may be considered for the purposes of on-the-spot communication without individuals.
5. X-rays (30PHz-30EHz): Generally, used in medical and security purpose.

6. Gamma Rays (greater than 10EHz): Typically, used for clinical imaging in nuclear medicine. Gamma rays are unsafe and risky because of their adverse impacts on human

Kuppusamy et al. (2016) has seen that the range from 300 GHz to 790 THZ i.e. IR to Visible is much higher than the radio range.

Using visible light for communication has the potential to transform this technology into how we access the Internet. There will be no unfavorable impact on security as data cannot be retrieved in the absence of light. Since Radio Frequency communication is prone to eavesdropping whereas this technology can be excellently used in high-security zones.

The frequency extends that is open to us, including numerous waves, for example, X-beams, gamma beams, UV, infrared, visible light beams, radio waves, etc. Any wave could be selected for communication, but why the only the visible range is chosen? The clarification for this is the easier reach and less destructive impacts that these wave causes. VLC utilizes light between 400 THz (780 nm) and 800 THz (375 nm) as a medium that is less unsafe to high-power applications. Subsequently, the visible light (from red to blue) of the electromagnetic range does no solicitation to the individuals as the rays are sheltered to utilize, vast data transfer capacity and moreover ensuing period in the communication area (Sarkar, A., Agarwal, S., & Nath, A., 2015).

LITERARTURE SURVEY

Li-Fi related literature has been reviewed to ascertain the work done by various researchers. In the last few decades, Wi-Fi has developed very fast. We have become very dependent on this technology day by day. But this technology also has its own limitations. Such as, it can only serve a certain distance. Also, Dimitrov, S., & Haas, H. (2015). discuss in their work that the bandwidth and speed used in this technology are limited. Internet efficiency and security are now the major concern. Thus RF-based Wi-Fi technology isn't the ideal route to achieve the latest capabilities. Harald Hass introduced a new methodology known as Light Fidelity (Li-Fi). The design flexibility of Li-Fi aids to overcome the disadvantages of WiFi in the context of adaptability, speed, and ease of use. Ramadhani, E., & Mahardika, G. P. (2018) has mentioned in their paper that LiFi technology has been implemented in Paris. Sarkar et.al (2015) and Neha, Gupta, P. (2017). discuss in their work that this methodology has used VLC and LEDs as media for fast information transfer. LED lights utilized in Li-Fi are pocket-friendly, safe, and durable. Also, it has good performance and better lifetime. Paul, S., & Sharma, S. (2014) has mentioned in their research that VLC is liberated from any health concerns, as it is environment friendly, green technology instead of the microwave, which has an adverse effect on human bodies.

Haas, H.(2018) in "LiFi is a paradigm-shifting 5G technology." has explained various misconceptions and represent the possible effects of this technique. This research article additionally predicts a shift in the existing wireless communication while moving from millimeter wave to Nanometer wave range.

He has also compared VLC and Li-Fi.

Khanda, D., & Jain, S. (2014) presented a research article "Li-fi (light fidelity): The future technology in wireless communication." in which they have explained that every bulb can be performed as a receptor in the Li-Fi technique. This paper also mentions that the exchange of data and signals can be accomplished using light and radio waves simultaneously.

Kavehrad, M. (2010) in "Sustainable energy-efficient wireless applications using light." gives an outline of sustainable wireless applications Since replacing traditional bulbs with LEDs reduces CO_2 emissions.

Li-Fi technique makes use of LED. Therefore, this communication technology also reduces global warming. This article provides a brief description of optical wireless communications by using UV, IR and light spectrum. His paper also supports that this emerging technology includes fewer hardware and configurations that make it economical and adaptable.

Dimitrov, S., & Haas, H. (2015) in "Principles of LED light communications: towards networked Li-Fi.",provides a balanced theoretical and practical approaches required to develop highly efficient light communication. Additionally, it also has extensive analysis of spectral and power efficiencies and data rate as well.

Karthika, R., & Balakrishnan, S. (2015) in "Wireless communication using Li-Fi technology", gives an idea to transmit data using VLC as serial data using UART. Karthika et.al (2015) employed a microcontroller that toggles LED at the transmitter side. The appropriate file to be recognized by PC software for binary conversion at the receiver side.

IEEE Standards Association maintains service quality. It also follows existing frequency bands that are recognized by national medical regulatory authorities and utilizes their standard. It provides an international standard for reliable wireless communications used for close proximity.

According to the study paper published by FN Division, TEC (n.d.) has discussed the various applications of this sustainable technology. It also specifies the VLC (IEEE 802.15.7) standard.

THE COMPONENT OF THE SYSTEM

The mode of information media is the same for Li-Fi as well as VLC i.e. light. However, they differ in the range of operating spectrum which is visible range only for VLC and Visible, UV and IR for Li-Fi. They also differ in mode of data flow which is unidirectional and point-to-point in case of VLC and bidirectional in case of Li-Fi. VLC is best suited for low data rate while Li-Fi is for swift wireless communication.

According to Sharma, R. R., & Sanganal, A. (2014), Khan, L. U. (2017) and FN Division, TEC (n.d) the fundamental components of Li-Fi are:

1. LEDs: A light emitting diode (LED) that have semiconductor property can transmits light when an electric current is passed through it. The basic LED family is used to power information transfer in Li-Fi technology. Light is given when particles that collect electric current (known as electrons and holes) together inside a semiconductor material. White LED light bulbs are commonly used in the execution of Li-Fi. By applying steady current to such devices through the LED it can be used for illumination.

Fast and simple current shifts can be made to isolate optical outputs at very high speeds. The LED can be turned ON/OFF through which various combinations of digital 0s and 1s can be made easily. Thus, it can be used as a source. To the human eye its response appears consistent due to the fast flickering of LED.

2.   Photodiode: A photodiode also has semiconductor property and it converts light into an electric current when photons are absorbed in it. It operates in the reverse bias state. When photons are consumed, the current is spread over the photodiode and less current measurement is done when current is not lit. A silicon photodiode acts as a receiver with a good response to visible light.

3.   Image Sensor: It consists an enormous number of photodiodes. It is a photosensitive electronic device that converts an optical image into an electronic signal. . It can be used as a picture receiver in digital imaging devices. CMOS sensors are the most popular image sensors used in Li-Fi. It is usually embedded in camera modules and imaging devices.

WORKING PRINCIPLE

The working of light fidelity technology is much unmingled. The principle of Li-Fi is discussed by Saini, H. (2016) in their research work as Li-Fi depends on sending modulating signal in an organized manner. Due to the working speed of LED being less than 1 microsecond, human eyes cannot identify the LED on and off. When LED is ON state digital and 1 'is being transmitted and when it is in OFF state digital is 0' is being transmitted. Moreover, these LEDs can be turned on and off swiftly. This closure action empowers information transmission using binary code. Li-Fi is suitable and well efficiently operated to achieve speed up to 1Gbps or more. Additionally, Li-Fi varies from fiber-optic since Li-Fi protocol layers are apt for short distance (up to 10 meters) at high speed. Ramadhani, E et.al (2018) discuss that at high speeds, the protocol layers in Li-FI are suitable for short distances .

Figure 2. Block Diagram of Li-Fi Information Transmission

Figure 2 indicates information transmission using Li-Fi. First, information from the source is initiated for transmission on the system. In this system, transmitter (LED) and internet are connected .The data is then adjusted and afterward coordinated to the LED light. The LED light illuminates the light for additional information. The photodetector captures the light and receives the signal from the transmitter.

The data is in the form of light that is received at the end of the collector (photodetector / light sensor).

The received data is decrypted at the collector end. The decrypted information then appeared on the device connected to the receiver. Receivers such as cell phone cameras and digital cameras that contain photodetector receive signals from light sources. The received data stream is fed into the demodulator. At long last, information is received at the end is in the format the same as transmitted.

Properties of Li-Fi

1. The Unused electromagnetic range is used: This system uses a portion of the electromagnetic range that has not yet been used extensively. i.e. Visible spectrum.
2. Light-based Wi-Fi: According to Sarkar et.al (2015) Light is used in the transmission in Li-Fi instead of radio waves. The LEDs used in transceiver can only transmit and receive data within a room. Since basic lights are used there can be N-numbers of access points.
3. No significant mal impact: Light does not have any real ill impact.

MODULATION SCHEME

The use of Li-Fi depends on light communication as well as optical wireless communication (OWC) systems. The modulated signal that contains the data is used to switch the LED at the ideal frequencies. Various modulation schemes are available for Li-Fi which can communicate in an orderly manner even in the absence of light. It also helps to communicate in low-intensity area. Variation in light intensity as reported in the information signal.

1. Single Carrier Modulation (SCM): In this modulation scheme, microwave and optical wave is used as subcarrier and carrier respectively. It is worthy of a low and medium data rate. On-off keying (OOK), pulse-position modulation (PPM), and pulse-amplitude modulation (PAM) are the notable modulation technique used in SCM.
2. Multiple Carrier Modulation (MCM): The achievement of SCMs increases its spectral potential. This requires a complex process when SCM is brought into action at high data rates. The development of MCMs overcomes the loss of SCMs. OFDM is a popular variant of MCM. The Optical orthogonal frequency division multiplexing (O-OFDM) is the carrier use as a part in optical wireless communication (OWC).

The authors of Haas, H (2015), Dimitrov et.al (2015) and Khanda(2014) Major characteristics of SCM and MCM is discussed. Some important characteristics are mentioned in table 1.

CHALLENGES

Li-Fi is experiencing some issues, shown in Figure 3, for example, modulation, availability, capacity, efficiency, coverage, interruption and security, etc. In addition to the many points of interest in Wi-Fi technology, Ayyash, M., Elgala, H., Khreishah, A., Jungnickel, V., Little, T., Shao, S. & Freund, R. (2016) and Kuppusamy et al. (2016) has discussed some difficulties. Some are enlisted below:

1. Li-Fi must require line of sight for successful information transmission. A slight difference indicates an interference in transmission.
2. The receiver is unaware to send the information back to the transmitter.
3. External light sources for example bulbs, daylight may cause interference during information transmission. This indicates a decrease in quality.

Table 1. The different characteristics of SCM and MCM

Modulation Scheme	Modulation	Characteristics
Single Carrier Modulation (SCM)	Pulse Amplitude Modulation (PAM)	Prone to signal distortion, it is combined with other modulation for better result.
	Pulse Position Modulation (PPM)	Provide efficient and support at low illumination level.
	On-Off Keying (OOK)	At low intensity, continuous ON/OFF of the light-emitting diode will reduce reliability of the transmitted information. Also increase and decrease of the brightness of the light-emitting diode will reduce the data rate.
Multiple Carrier Modulation (MCM)	Orthogonal Frequency Division Multiplexing (OFDM)	Best suited when multiple transmitters are used at the same time. Interference could be reduced by shifting bandwidth to higher frequency.

4. There is a need to figure out how to manage surroundings changes if the mechanical assembly is set up outside.
5. As visible light can't infiltrate through walls it can be effortlessly hindered by someone essentially strolling before LED source.

Interference

In optical lighting dependent on data communication, the most difficult part is to provide optical uplink service. According to Sharma, R. R., & Sanganal, A. (2014) This is on the basis that the uplink can

Figure 3. Challenges in Li-Fi

intrude on the downlink signal. This is a matter of concern on the issue of interference. This problem can be avoided if directional transfer of data can be achieved by the transmitter.

Security

Li-Fi may suffer from eavesdropping. This can happen if the light gets diffused from any spacing e.g. spacing between the door and the floor. Cracks and shielded windows can also cause a leak.

Infrastructure

The indoor and open space is the infrastructure in Li-Fi. Similar to optical characteristics, Li-Fi additionally exerts shading effects during transmission. This shading effect will affect sending and receiving information.

Modulation

The primary concerns in Li-Fi are modulation and light intensity i.e. illumination/dimming. There are several approaches for modulation, illumination, and dimming. In Li-Fi, modulation is attained by switching on / off of the LED. One difficulty is the means by which modulation is empowering the illumination of LEDs with the goal that data can be sent when the light power is excessively low. While the darkening procedure is proportional to the brightness of the LEDs.

Coverage

Li-Fi is an innovation that performs well in closed infrastructure. Coverage in the outer territory can be enhanced by associating it with some other communication system supporting outdoor network access. Li-Fi, if integrated with Wi-Fi, may well deliver better performance everywhere.

COMPARISON OF LI-FI WITH WIFI

The authors of Elbasher, W. S., Mustafa, A. B., & Osman, A. A. (2015), Neha, Gupta, P. (2017) and Paul, S., & Sharma, S. (2014) has discussed comparison of Li-Fi and Wi-Fi based on various parameters. Table 2 shows the comparison of Li-Fi with Wi-Fi system.

SHORT COMINGS OF RADIO WAVE TRANSMISSION, MISCONCEPTION, ADVANTAGES OF LI-FI & LIMITATIONS

Short Comings of Radio Wave Transmission

The authors Ayyash et.al (2016) and Kuppusamy et.al (2016) has mentioned several constraints of radio waves in their research work. The basic issues of transmission of radio waves are as:

Table 2. Li-Fi vs Wi-Fi

Features	Li-Fi	Wi-Fi
Acronyms	Light Fidelity	Wireless Fidelity
Transmitter	LED	Antenna
Receiver	LED	Antenna
Frequency band	1000 times frequency spectrum of the radio waves(in the range of THz)	2.4GHz,4.9GHz and 5GHz
Working Principle	Direct Binary Data serving	Various Technologies
System components	LED bulb (lamp) and photo detector	Need to install router, subscriber devices (laptops, PDAs, desktops)
Signal-to-Noise Ratio	Very High	May be more
No of users	Area under the Light source	Rely upon access point
Data Transfer speed	1Gbps	Offers 150Mbps(WLAN)
Coverage Area	10 meters	20 - 100 meters vary depending on transmission power and antenna type
Interference	No/less interference	Interference with nearby routers/devices
Topology	Point to point	Point to multipoint
Communication	Based on Visible Light Communication	Based on Radio Frequency Communication.
Availability	Anywhere	Confined
Secure(Privacy)	Data transfer is secured because Light is interrupted by walls.	Privacy is required as walls cannot hinder RF signals
Power consumption	Low	High
Efficiency	Since the energy consumption of LED is very less. This makes Li-Fi more efficient	As such radio base stations consume higher energy making the system less efficient.
Environment Impact	Low	Medium
Data Density	Interference is low and can go through in dense region	Interference is more and it can pass through in Less dense region

1. Energy Efficiency: In Li-Fi at base station a great deal of energy is required for cooling purposes. This makes the base stations less efficient.
2. Capacity: The radio wave is used for data transmission in wireless communication that is limited as well as expensive. It also has an obliged transmission limit. With rapidly growing technologies and improvement in generations like 3G, 4G, 5G and so on we are also facing a shortage of radio spectrum.
3. Availability: The penetration of radio waves is a key concern. Also, it is not suitable for using radio waves in aerospace and high altitude. It can produce severe / catastrophic results where radio interference is high.
4. Security: Since radio waves can easily penetrate the opaque structures, it is vulnerable and can be misused by cyber criminals. RF communication is susceptible to cyber-attacks. This causes notable security concerns for Wi-Fi.

Advantages of Li-Fi

The Li-Fi is a new technology that showed up in 2011 and depends on light transmission as a mode of communication. It is described by minimal cost and suitable for a point-to-point operation (Ayyash et.al, 2016). The potential advantage of such technology is that it uses light sources which are connected in many areas.

The Li-Fi technology has the following advantages:

1. Prevents piggybacking.
2. Scalable network
3. Eliminates neighbouring system interference.
4. VLC can be utilized viably without influencing the carrier signals during the movement.
5. Other electronics devices do not interfere with Li-Fi that make it better for use in situations such as emergency clinics and aircraft. Security is increased because light cannot penetrate opaque structures. Li-Fi Internet access provides protection from information misuse. It is restricted beyond the operating area. This allows greater security and protection to the transmitted data as it travels shorter distances and cannot penetrate walls.
6. Li-Fi requires few components for its operation. Additionally, it uses almost negligible power for the information transmission.
7. LED can operate on small amounts of electricity and is easily available and accessible everywhere. The use of LED light can restrict the use of energy. Consequently, the conveyance of information requires very less power. This makes it more productive from cost and energy point of view.
8. Because of low interference, high transmission bandwidth and high output, this technique is equipped for conveying high information rates. Li-Fi can effectively accomplish information transmission rate up to 10 Gbps.
9. The light source is available in abundance due to which accessibility is not a problem. Internet connectivity will always be available if there is presence of light source. Lights are easily accessible that can be used as media for data transmission. It is used in all areas, for example, infrared, Bluetooth, Wi-Fi and Internet providers.

Li-Fi Misconceptions

Li-Fi technology has numerous misconceptions associated with it some of which are mentioned below:

1. Illumination Flicker: The minimal frequency at which the illumination is rectified is in the range of 1MHz. Refresh rate is about 100Hz. This implies that Li-Fi light has higher (by 10000) flicker rate as compared to a screen. Hence, there is no apparent flicker.
2. Illumination cannot be reduced: Advanced modulation technologies can empower the function of Li-Fi near the turn-on voltage of the LED. This implies Li-Fi can also function at output levels generating low light and can still maintain considerably high data rates.
3. This is only for downlink: One important plus point is that Li-Fi can be conjoined with LED lights. However, this does not imply that the two tasks of lighting and internet connectivity should be used simultaneously. These two can be easily alienated. Thus, uplink communication, where there is no requirement of light, can also be performed using Li-Fi.

4. Li-Fi does not operate in daylight conditions since daylight establishes a stable interference signal outside the transmission bandwidth being used for modulation. The operating frequency of Li-Fi is over 1MHz. In this way, continuous daylight can be expelled with the help of electrical filters. In fact, daylight is largely helpful because it can empower Li-Fi receivers based on solar cell and this solar cell will be used for receiving the information as well for collecting energy from sunlight.

5. Li-Fi is disruptive in nature: Any technique that puts an already established technology out of place and originates a completely new business is considered to be disruptive. For example, social networking has disrupted telephone. Li-Fi is not disruptive. Instead it is complementary to Wi-Fi in the sense that prevailing Wi-Fi networks can be utilized to achieve web connectivity with enhanced speed and security (Ayyash et.al, 2016).

Limitations of Li-Fi

Li-Fi technique has a few limitations as well some of which are mentioned below:

1. In Li-Fi technology, availability of a light source is must to operate internet. This can curb areas and situations where Li-Fi can be utilized.
2. A close or immaculate line-of-sight is required for information transmission.
3. Opaque interface blocks communication hence opaque barriers en route can affect information transmission. Hence, the range of signals is restrained.
4. Speed of information transmission may well get affected by sunlight, Natural light.
5. Interference with different source of light may be possible. One of the possible drawbacks is the blocking of signal from outside. Interference of sunlight can cause an intrusive internet. Natural light, sunlight and general electric lighting can also influence speed of transmission.
6. Reliability of operation because of interference from other light sources, for example, daylight, electrical bulbs etc.
7. Acquiring the inability of devices to react back through light transmission technology.
8. Wi-Fi offers more range of operation since in Li-Fi, light waves cannot propagate through walls.
9. Set-up establishment cost is high.
10. Development of an entirely different framework would be required for Li-Fi.
11. Large-scale implementation is still in pipeline.

VARIOUS APPLICATIONS OF LI-FI

Li-Fi technology has wide ranging applications some of which are mentioned below:

1. Academia: Li-Fi is the recent development that has enhanced internet access speed with its fast transmission capacity. Hence, academic institutions can employ it in smart classrooms, for video conferencing and for digital tutorial downloads etc. (Ramadhani et. al, 2018)
2. Catastrophe Management: Li-Fi can be introduced in catastrophic situations such as earth quack, tidal wave, wave or tropical storms, tsunami. Li-Fi bulbs can be mounted on the road to provide web connectivity as well as lighting on both sides of the street.

3. Smart Cities: Li-Fi has multiple applications in smart cities ranging from fast, reliable web connectivity to waste management, smart agriculture, smart traffic management etc. It can be appended to street lights which can then function as Li-Fi hotspots and sensor structures can be utilized to control light and data.

4. Hazardous Environments: Communication based on Radio Frequency can prove to be dangerous in places like mines. For such situations, Li-Fi gives a shielded substitute to electromagnetic impedance. (Gupta, N. P. 2017).

5. Mobile Connectivity/ Super-fast wireless internet: Electronics devices like mobile laptops etc. can connect explicitly using Li-Fi. In addition, Li-Fi provides better security in short-range with high transmission rate. The light coming from various sources can be utilized for accessing the web. Li-Fi also provides quick access to internet than Wi-Fi. This is particularly helpful in applications like uploading and downloading audio/video, conferencing, etc.

6. Underwater communication: Acoustic signals also affect marine life. Although its transmission rate is low, it has adverse effects on marine life. The use of RF in water is inappropriate due to strong signal ingestion. In such environments Li-Fi is best suited for information exchange

7. Traffic Management: LED is used in headlights and backlight indicators of the vehicles. Nearby vehicles can then communicate using these LED lights. It shows the possibility of accident by exchange of data. So, Li-Fi is also helpful in reducing the accidents.

8. Defence: In RF technology, signals can be ceased and trapped. Development of authentic communication network is not possible without appropriate RF devices. Li-Fi communication supports such situations because light is accessible everywhere. However, Li-Fi communication does not have such limitations.

9. Applications in Sensitive Areas: Some areas such as petrochemical industry become severe when exposed to RF wave. Wi-Fi is exceptionally dangerous for fragile locations. Li-Fi creates better security wireless networks in such plants where other transmission media are risky.

10. Aviation: Since Li-Fi does not cause interference with the radio signals being used in aircraft, quick transmission of information can be achieved that to at low cost. The cable system can be minimized and hence the weight thus allowing more space and flexibility for the seating. It supports the functioning of In-Flight entertainment (IFE) structures and integration with passengers' phones.

11. Hospital and Healthcare: Wi-Fi emits exceptionally high-risk radio waves. Since Wi-fi is used in operation theatres and radio waves are used in many medical devices, it can cause health issues to patients. For such scenario, Li-Fi can be deployed instead of Wi-Fi to achieve network connectivity. The electromagnetic interference is negligible in Li-Fi hence, no interference with assistive devices or with the MRI scanner.

CONCLUSION

Numerous wireless technologies are developing and emerging due to increased interest towards quick information transmission. Li-Fi can prove to be a suitable answer for this scenario for light is its fundamental structure. Limitless, precise, quick, safe and cost efficient, Li-Fi might be the successor of Wi-Fi upon further improvement. This technology has immense potential because of its proficient and economical nature and ability to solve existing challenges such as deficiency of radio frequency for data transmission. Its applications go broadly from toys to communication and can discover uses in fields like military and medication due to its capability of providing communication authenticity. Future application of Li-Fi include Smart home automation, Smart Cities, Smart transportation system, Security application, Data communication for IoT network and many more.

REFERENCES

Ayyash, M., Elgala, H., Khreishah, A., Jungnickel, V., Little, T., Shao, S., ... Freund, R. (2016). Coexistence of WiFi and LiFi toward 5G: Concepts, opportunities, and challenges. *IEEE Communications Magazine, 54*(2), 64–71. doi:10.1109/MCOM.2016.7402263

Dimitrov, S., & Haas, H. (2015). *Principles of LED light communications: towards networked Li-Fi.* Cambridge University Press. doi:10.1017/CBO9781107278929

Division, F. N. TEC. (n.d.). *Study Paper on LiFi (Light Fidelity) & its Applications*. Retrieved from http://tec.gov.in/pdf/Studypaper/lifi%20study%20paper%20-%20approved.pdf

Elbasher, W. S., Mustafa, A. B., & Osman, A. A. (2015). A Comparison between Li-Fi, Wi-Fi, and Ethernet Standards. *International Journal of Scientific Research (Ahmedabad, India), 4*(12), 1–4.

Gupta, N. P. (2017). Electromagnetic pollution its impact and control. *International Journal of Engineering Applied Sciences and Technology, 2*(7), 61–65.

Haas, H. (2018). LiFi is a paradigm-shifting 5G technology. *Reviews in Physics, 3,* 26–31. doi:10.1016/j.revip.2017.10.001

IEEE Standards Association. (2012). IEEE standard for local and metropolitan area networks-part 15.6: wireless body area networks. *IEEE std, 802*(6), 2012.

Karthika, R., & Balakrishnan, S. (2015). Wireless communication using Li-Fi technology. *SSRG International Journal of Electronics and Communication Engineering, 2*(3), 32-40.

Kavehrad, M. (2010). Sustainable energy-efficient wireless applications using light. *IEEE Communications Magazine, 48*(12), 66–73. doi:10.1109/MCOM.2010.5673074

Khan, L. U. (2017). Visible light communication: Applications, architecture, standardization and research challenges. *Digital Communications and Networks, 3*(2), 78–88. doi:10.1016/j.dcan.2016.07.004

Khanda, D., & Jain, S. (2014). Li-fi (light fidelity): The future technology in wireless communication. *International Journal of Information & Computation Technology, 4*(16), 1686–1694.

Kuppusamy, P., Muthuraj, S., & Gopinath, S. (2016, March). Survey and challenges of Li-Fi with comparison of Wi-Fi. In *2016 International Conference on Wireless Communications, Signal Processing and Networking (WiSPNET)* (pp. 896-899). IEEE. 10.1109/WiSPNET.2016.7566262

Neha, Gupta, P. (2017). A Study on Future of Communication: Li-Fi. *International Journal of Innovative Research in Science. Engineering and Technology, 6*(6), 12195–12202.

Paul, S., & Sharma, S. (2014). *Future of telecommunication technologies: WI-FI vs. WI-MAX vs. Li-Fi vs. GI-FI. ISTP Journal of Research in Electrical and Electronics Engineering.*

Ramadhani, E., & Mahardika, G. P. (2018, March). The Technology of LiFi: A Brief Introduction. *IOP Conference Series. Materials Science and Engineering*, 325(1), 012013. doi:10.1088/1757-899X/325/1/012013

Saini, H. (2016). Li-Fi (Light Fidelity)-The future technology In Wireless communication. *Jisuanji Yingyong*, 7(1), 13–15.

Sarkar, A., Agarwal, S., & Nath, A. (2015). Li-fi technology: Data transmission through visible light. *International Journal of Advance Research in Computer Science and Management Studies*, 3(6), 1–12.

Sharma, R. R., & Sanganal, A. (2014). Li-Fi Technology: Transmission of data through light. *International Journal of Computer Technology and Applications*, 5(1), 150.

Chapter 14
Semantic Analysis of Videos for Tags Prediction and Segmentation

Umair Ali Khan

Quaid-e-Awam University of Engineering, Science, and Technology, Pakistan

ABSTRACT

Due to the growing volume of multimedia data generated these days, it has become extremely difficult to manually analyze the data and extract useful information from it. Especially the analysis of videos pertaining to different fields such as surveillance, videos, social media, education, etc. cannot be done efficiently by manual methods. This requires automatic analysis algorithms that can intelligently analyze videos and derive salient information from them. This information can be useful in a number of tasks such as video segmentation, incident detection, anomaly detection, query-based video retrieval, and content censorship. This chapter provides a detailed review of the techniques proposed for video analysis to provide a compact set of video tags. This chapter considers it a joint tag-segmentation problem and critically analyzes the relevant literature to highlight their respective pros and cons. At the end, potential research areas in this domain and suggestions for improvement are discussed.

INTRODUCTION

The huge amount of multimedia data generated these days makes it an ordeal to envisage techniques which can automatically check the contents of multimedia data to ascertain their authenticity and classify them accordingly. Especially, retrieval of required information from multimedia data and assignment of appropriate tags largely depends on manual processing. Hence, the quality of the assigned tags follows a subjective criterion and varies from person to person. Our preliminary experiments (Khan, 2017) in this regard demonstrate that human-generated meta data can not suffice to give full insight into the main contents of a video and/or shows inconsistency due to the lack of precision in human's ability of information recall. In addition, manually-generated semantic tags are less accurate and present irregularities. Our preliminary experiments on this topic further reveal that this ostensibly trivial task entails an intelligent

DOI: 10.4018/978-1-7998-2803-7.ch014

analysis of a video to predict its representative tags without human intervention. This automatically extracted information has immense applications in optimizing video search, automatically retrieving scenes from videos based on user's query, object detection and localization, automatic text/subtitles generation for videos, detecting specific events in videos, action recognition, behavior recognition, recommendation systems, etc. Among these applications, scene-driven retrieval is particularly important in the sense that it not only helps in content-censorship (e.g., automatically censoring the scenes containing nudity, sex, violence, smoking, etc), but also in on-demand retrieval of desired scenes from a given video (e.g., making highlights of a soccer match which contain all the goal events). At the same time, scene-driven retrieval is equally important for video summarization, e.g., removing all boring or unwanted scenes.

Segmenting a video in the major constituent topics does require a precise identification of these topics in the first place. This information can then be used for on-demand scene selection, content-censorship and other tasks. In this chapter, the author specifically addresses the problem of predicting key information from a video in the form of small number of tags which describe the overall contents of the video. For this purpose, it is essential not only to understand the semantic meaning of individual video frames, but also to predict a compact set of the video's representative topics. The predicted information can be utilized in a number of ways such as videos categorization, context-based search, content-censorship (e.g., nudity, violence and sex in kid videos). Apart from this, the predicted tags for a video can be further utilized to segment the video according to the user's choice.

VIDEO TAGGING & SEGMENTATION

The problem of video tagging and segmentation has not been addressed in combination, though its applications are ostensible. The existing approaches of video segmentation operate on surficial level and/or are focused on specific videos. As the related work in this domain in the coming sections will show that the approaches dependent on the hand-crafted image features do not suffice to deliver an adequate level of accuracy in this problem, an intelligent algorithm for this semantic analysis is required. At the same time, the problem of video segmentation in the context of video tagging needs to be re-formulated.

Applying the traditional approaches of object detection on the individual video frames will be inefficient as we will end up with low-level information (e.g., the localization of objects in the individual frames instead of the contextual relationship among them). In addition, processing each video frame will also introduce computational inefficiency and result in redundant information. This problem can only be addressed by a machine learning algorithm which can be trained to predict the high-level, representative features of video scenes.

The tremendous advancements in the field of machine learning have paved the way for finding patterns in complex data with an accuracy which, in some cases, even surpasses human's pattern matching performance. The cheap and scalable parallel processing technique utilizing Graphical Processing Units (GPUs) have made possible to efficiently apply machine learning techniques for image/video analytics (Charniak, 2019). That said, applying machine learning to learn the traditional image features for our problem is not efficient due to the well-known issues related to these features such as requirement of mathematical modeling, limited generalization, scale- and rotation variance, inability to maintain performance under different conditions, etc.

Instead of learning the hand-crafted image features, it is more efficient to discover the underlying features in the individual video frames. Deep learning (Zhao, 2019) can serve this purpose, as it does not require a priori information of image features. Instead, it learns the underlying patterns in complex data during training. Apart from this, a deep learning model trained on a large dataset can be retrained using transfer learning (Yang, 2020) for a different classification task with a much smaller dataset and training time. Considering the promising features of deep learning, this chapter formulates the problem of video tags prediction as a deep learning based classification. The author investigates the applicability and potential of deep learning for predicting a set of key tags for a video and thereby segmenting the video with respect to the predicted tags.

The rest of the chapter first provides a critical survey of the existing techniques of video tagging and their respective merits and demerits. Subsequently, the techniques of video segmentation are reviewed and analyzed. This discussion is followed by the potential of machine learning, in particular deep learning, for video tagging and segmentation. At the end suggestion in this domain are proposed.

Existing Approaches of Video Tagging

We believe that video tags prediction and segmentation has not been well-studied in the literature. The related work in this domain is primarily targeted at video tagging on a limited scale. Qi et al. (2007) annotated certain concepts in a video using multi-label classification and the inter-class correlation. Another video labeling approach proposed by Siersdorfer et al. (2009) put to use the redundancy among YouTube videos for finding associations among videos and assigning tags to similar videos. The techniques proposed by Shen et al. (2011) and Liu et al. (2005) made use of the data captured by the smartphone sensors to generate video tags. Steiner et al. (2014) proposed technique identified basic objects in the images and videos of a digital camera and further exploited the geographical and date/time information to predict the relevant tags.

Ulges et al. (2008) first found the key frames from a video and then predicted several visual features for each key frame. The visual features were assigned scores which were later fused to generate a final probability for a certain tag in the video. The tagging performance in this approach largely depended on the feature modalities and thus had limited accuracy. Chen et al. (2010) proposed a video tagging technique which first found all the textual descriptions of a video from Internet sources and a graph model was applied on the descriptions to discover and score the key words serving as tags. This technique was dependent on the human-generated textual description. In a similar technique, Zhao et al. (2010) first found similar videos by local features. The tags from the similar videos were analyzed to pick the most relevant tags for the given video. It is palpable that this technique shared the same limitations as in (Chen, 2010).

Some techniques proposed by Aradhye et al. (2009), Toderici et al. (2010) and Yang et al. (2011) did not solely rely on the user-supplied tags, but also took into account the audiovisual features to train classifiers based on the correspondence between the contents and the user-annotated tags. Nevertheless, the incorporation of inconsistent user-supplied meta data introduced the aforementioned issues.

A large part of the relevant literature in this context relied on the user-annotated meta data. A similar technique pro- posed by Chu et al. (2011) first searched for the images on Flickr that has similar tags as those of the given video. A bipartite graph was used to describe the relationship between the key frames of the video and the tags associated with the images. The technique proposed by Acharya et al. (2012) selected one or more user-generated tags for a video which described its category. A transcript of plurality of words was generated along with their respective ranks. Based on the ranking of the plurality of words, one or more tags were generated. Chen et al. (2012) proposed a web video topic detection technique. This technique utilized the video related tag information to determine bursty tag groups based on their co-occurrence and temporal trajectories. The near-duplicate key frames predicted from the web videos were fused with these tag groups. Subsequently, the fused groups were further matched with the keywords obtained from the search engine to find the topics.

Some techniques (Kar, 2018) (Hoang, 2018) used the plot synopses and summaries of videos to predict a set of tags or video genres. These techniques required plot synopses of videos which are not always readily available with a video. In addition, the dataset was comprised of manually curated tags which share the same aforementioned limitations.

Due to the recent breakthroughs and advancements in deep learning, the research on semantic analysis of images and videos has been diverted to use complex neural architectures to learn hierarchical feature representations. The active research areas in this domain include converting visual data to textual representation (Donahue, 2015) (Venugopalan, 2014), (Venugopalan, 2015), (Pan, 2016), answering questions from videos (Antol, 2015), (Malinowski, 2015), and video classification (Karpathy, 2014), (Zha, 2015), (Yue, 2015), (Wu, 2015). The first two areas are different from tags prediction, as they entail more sophisticated architectures such as recurrent neural network (Donahue, 2015) in combination with Convolutional Neural Network (CNN) to discover the spatio-temporal connection between consecutive video frames. On the other hand, video classification does hold resemblance with video tagging, but it is mainly focused on predicting the major category a video falls in, rather than predicting an extended set of classes pertaining to a given video. Table 1 gives a summary of the existing approaches of video tagging.

Table 1. Summary of the existing approaches of video tagging

Technique	Description	Limitation
Concept annotation	Multi-label classification and inter-class correlation, finding association among videos.	Human-annotated meta data
Smartphone and digital camera sensors	Using the data of inertial measurment units to tag videos	Limited to the the sensor functions
Visual features	Detection of key frames and visual features	Dependent on feature modalities
Audio-visual features	Audio-visual features and the user-annotated tags to train classifiers	Human-annotated meta data. Feature modalities.
Correlation of meta data	Utilizing the annotated information to find appropriate tags	Human-annotated meta data

Existing Approaches of Video Segmentation

A number of video segmentation techniques have been studied in the relevant literature. Majority of these techniques use a common approach: finding the shot boundaries and merging the shots into uncategorized segments (scenes) based on their visual similarity. A shot is an elementary structural segment that is defined as a sequence of images taken without interruption by a single camera (Boccignone, 2005). Rasheed et al. (2003) clustered the shots based on their color similarity and found the segment boundaries based on the shot lengths and the motion contents. Some techniques (Rasheed, 2005), (Ngo,

2005), (Zhao, 2007) addressed the video segmentation by constructing a shot similarity graph using the color and motion information and subsequently segmenting the video by graph partitioning. Some shot clustering techniques (Zhai, 2005), (Zhai, 2006) also used Markov chain Monte Carlo technique for detecting segment boundaries, albeit the segments were uncategorized. In another shot clustering approach, Chasanis et al. (2009) applied a sequence alignment algorithm to detect the change in pattern of shot labels to determine segment boundaries. In another technique, Chasanis et al. (2009) first found the local in- variant descriptors of the key frames of all the shots and grouped them into clusters. Each cluster was treated as a visual word. The histograms of visual words were smoothed using Gaussian kernels whose local maxima represent the segment boundaries. In a different approach, Hoai et al. (2011) augmented video segmentation with action recognition. They first trained a recognition model using multi-class SVM on a labeled dataset. The segmentation and action recognition was done simultaneously using dynamic programming. This was the first approach of video segmentation with segment categorization, though in the form of limited number of action recognition. However, it did require the engineered image features for training the action recognition model.

Some approaches combined audiovisual features for scene segmentation. Sidiropoulos et al. (2011) addressed this issue with a semantic criterion by exploiting the audiovisual features of the key frames to construct multiple Scene Transition Graphs (STGs) (Yeung, 1998). A probabilistic merging process combined the results of the STGs to detect segment boundaries. In a similar approach, Bredin et al. (2012) extended this idea by combining speaker diarization and speech recognition with visual information. A drawback of these techniques is that the STGs exploit low-level visual features and provide no margin for augmenting heterogeneous feature sets. In addition, the heuristic settings of certain STG parameters are also required. In another technique, Baber et al. (2011) used frame entropy to find shot boundaries and determine the key frames of the shots. Afterwards, the SURF features of the neighboring key frames within a window were matched to determine the scene boundary. In a later approach Baber et al. (2013) the histogram of visual words for each shot were computed. The distance between the visual word histograms was calculated to merge the shots which are closer in space.

In a more recent approach, Yanai et al. (2014) found the relevant shots from web videos based on the given keywords. This technique first searched for the relevant web videos by matching their human-generated tags with the given key- words. It then segmented the selected videos into shots and ranked them according to the similarity of visual features. The top-ranked shots represented the shots of interest.

A detailed literature review in this domain reveals that video tagging and segmentation has not been studied in combination. Whereas the existing techniques of video tagging either depend on hand-crafted image features and user- annotated meta data or do not provide an extended set of the thematic points of a video, the semantic criteria in the video segmentation is largely ignored. The commonly used approach of matching the low-level visual and/or audio features of the successive shots (or their key frames) to determine the segment boundaries is too trivial to understand the semantic correlation among the shots. Additionally, segmenting and merging all the logical story units based on the semantic understanding of individual shots cannot be efficiently done by low-level, engineered audiovisual features. Hence, segmenting a video into constituent topics, which can be later retrieved by a query, requires an intelligent semantic analysis of each shot. This is only efficiently possible by a deep learning based algorithm which does not require a priori knowledge of the low-level features. Table 2 gives a summary of the existing appraoches of video segmentation.

VIDEO TAGGING & SEGMENTATION USING DEEP LEARNING

Due to the ability of deep learning to discover intricate pattern in complex data, it is most suitable to perform intelligent analytics on videos and derive salient information. However, a common challenge in training a deep learning model is the availability of training dataset which, in many cases, is difficult to obtain. Another challenge is the long training time required to train a deep learning model. These challenges can be addressed by utilizing transfer learning (Yosinski, 2014) which offers the possibility of retraining a pre-trained model with relatively much smaller amount of dataset and training time. The idea used in transfer learning is to utilize the knowledge acquired in one task of training to another task.

The technique proposed in (Xu, 2015) uses a combination of convolution neural network with recurrent neural networks for video captioning. The low-level output of the recurrent neural networks is enriched by tag embedding. The later step performs a scoring of the generated sentences with respect to their relevance. However, this task is tantamount to video translation and does not specifically perform tags prediction. Another video tagging technique (Xu, 2015) proposes an event ontology comprising of events and their concepts using deep learning. The proposed techniques enable ontology browsing, semantic event search, and video tagging via open web interfaces. Although this approach seems promising, the details of the deep learning model, training and tagging algorithm are largely missing.

Table 2. Summary of the existing approaches of video segmentation

Technique	Description	Limitation
Shot Clustering	Shot boundary detection and clustering based on the visual similarity of shots	Uncategorized shots. Hand-crafted features.
Action recognition	Trained recognition model using SVM	Engineered image features
Audio-visual features	Finding key frames and using their audio-visual features to construct multiple Scene Transition Graphs (STGs)	Exploitation of low-level visual features by STGs. Heuristic settings of certain STG parameters required.

Zhou et al. (2017) predict the video tags by first estimating the frame level tags using deep learning. The CNN outputs are fused through a learnable pooling function to predict tags at the video level. This is the first approach to use deep learning for video tagging which fuses the frame level predictions into a video level tags prediction. Although, the motion in formation in this process is ignored, yet the technique effectively tags videos. However, the algorithm still does not fulfill the problem addressed in this chapter in its entirety. Another technique proposed by Ilyas et al. (2019) first discovers the key frames in a video and uses these key frames to train a deep neural network to generate the most frequent tags.

A recent technique (Khan, 2020) proposed by the author of this chapter addresses the problem of video tagging and segmentation in combination. A technique is developed for frame level analytics and finally fusing and filtering the information to generate video level tags. Transfer learning is used to retraing a deep learning model on the static video frames representing a 50-tag vocabulary. Instead of running the inference on all the frames, only the representative frames are selected by a keyframe detection algorithm. A tag prediction algorithm reduces redundancy among the tags and assigns scores to all the tags. Finally, the tags having the highest scores are selected to be the representative tags of the video. The corpus generated by the tags prediction algorithm contains start and end of the video shots, individual tags for each shot, and the keyframes. This information is used to segment the videos with respect to the predict tags. Although this technique is basically proposed for video tags prediction and segmentation, it can be easily applied to other types of videos. The tag vocabulary is scalable and the deep learning model can be retrained with minimal effort to incorporate more tags.

LIMITATIONS AND CONSTRAINTS

The relevant literature does not address the problem discussed in this chapter in combination, except the technique proposed by Khan et al. (2020). However, this technique also does not incorporate motion information for tags prediction. For rapidly changing and highly dynamic scenes in the video, motion information plays a key role in accurate prediction of the scene.

Another limitation of the existing techniques for tags prediction using machine learning is their dependency on the human-annotated data. This data is not always the outcome of a rigorous, expert analysis. For instance, the meta data associate to the videos of popular video streaming services, such as Youtube, is recklessly assinged to videos. This limits the accuracy of the algorithm and results in inaccurate search results and video recommendations. Since a myriad of aforementioned tasks depend on the accurate tags, prediction of video tags needs a high level of accuracy.

The existing video segmentation techniques mainly segment videos by first finding the shot boundaries and subsequently clustering the shots into same cluster baed on the audio-visual similarity of their low-level, hand-crafter image features. Since engineered image features have known issue, these techniques do not efficiently segment videos.

POTENTIAL RESEARCH AREAS

The existing approaches of video tags prediction and segmentation using deep learning can be improved in the following aspects.

- The motion information can be incorporated to the feature learning by integrating a Long-Short Term Memory (LSTM) model with a convolutionl neural network. The LSTM models are useful to learn the spatio-temporal information and are expected to enhance prediction accuracy for highly dynamic scenes.
- The accurate prediction of some scenes also requires incorporating audio information. For example, comedy scenes in a video can only be accurately predicted by incorporating audio information. The LSTM models can be used to learn the audio features along with the visual features to predict the tags for such video segments.
- Video/video scripts, reviews or plots available on public database of videos can be used to further increase the tags prediction accuracy. This information is carefully written and usually reviewed by the database administrators. Hence, it can be useful to further increase the tags prediction accuracy.
- Youtube-8M dataset contains the visual features of 8 million videos. This dataset is freely available for training video classification algorithms. This dataset can be used to develop a much larger

and similar tag vocabulary as constructed Khan et al. (2020). Using a technique similar to the one developed by Khan et al. (2020), a video tagging and segmentation algorithm can be developed which can predict video tags with more accuracy and cover a wider range of video topics.

CONCLUSION

In this chapter, a review of the existing techniques of video tags prediction and segmentation was presented. The review showed that the existing video tagging techniques are largely dependent on the human-annotated data and/or do not address this problem in its entirety as formulated in this chapter. At the same time, video segmentation techniques largely depend on hand crafted image features which have known issues. It was concluded that this task can only be efficiently performed by a machine learning technique. More precisely, a deep learning based technique is most promising to achieve a higher efficacy in this context. In addition, the chapter also showed that combining video tags prediction with segmentation have a number of advantages and should be studied in combination. The issues pertaining to video tagging and segmentation were highlighted and the potential research areas for improvements were described.

REFERENCES

Acharya, S. (2012). *U.S. Patent No. 8,098,976*. Washington, DC: U.S. Patent and Trademark Office.

Antol, S., Agrawal, A., Lu, J., Mitchell, M., Batra, D., Lawrence Zitnick, C., & Parikh, D. (2015). Vqa: Visual question answering. In *Proceedings of the IEEE international conference on computer vision* (pp. 2425-2433). IEEE.

Aradhye, H., Toderici, G., & Yagnik, J. (2009, December). Video2text: Learning to annotate video content. In *IEEE International Conference on Data Mining Workshops* (pp. 144-151). IEEE.

Baber, J., Afzulpurkar, N., & Bakhtyar, M. (2011). Video segmentation into scenes using entropy and SURF. In *7th International Conference on Emerging Technologies* (pp. 1-6). 10.1109/ICET.2011.6048496

Baber, J., Satoh, S. I., Afzulpurkar, N., & Keatmanee, C. (2013, August). Bag of visual words model for videos segmentation into scenes. In *Proceedings of the Fifth International Conference on Internet Multimedia Computing and Service* (pp. 191-194). 10.1145/2499788.2499814

Boccignone, G., Chianese, A., Moscato, V., & Picariello, A. (2005). Foveated shot detection for video segmentation. *IEEE Transactions on Circuits and Systems for Video Technology, 15*(3), 365–377. doi:10.1109/TCSVT.2004.842603

Bredin, H. (2012, March). Segmentation of TV shows into scenes using speaker diarization and speech recognition. In *IEEE International Conference on Acoustics, Speech and Signal Processing (ICASSP)* (pp. 2377-2380). 10.1109/ICASSP.2012.6288393

Charniak, E. (2019). *Introduction to deep learning*. The MIT Press.

Chasanis, V., Kalogeratos, A., & Likas, A. (2009). Movie segmentation into scenes and chapters using locally weighted bag of visual words. In *Proceedings of the ACM International Conference on Image and Video Retrieval* (pp. 1-7). 10.1145/1646396.1646439

Chasanis, V. T., Likas, A. C., & Galatsanos, N. P. (2008). Scene detection in videos using shot clustering and sequence alignment. *IEEE Transactions on Multimedia, 11*(1), 89–100. doi:10.1109/TMM.2008.2008924

Chen, T., Liu, C., & Huang, Q. (2012). An effective multi-clue fusion approach for web video topic detection. In *Proceedings of the 20th ACM international conference on Multimedia* (pp. 781-784). 10.1145/2393347.2396311

Chen, Z., Cao, J., Song, Y., Guo, J., Zhang, Y., & Li, J. (2010). Context-oriented web video tag recommendation. In *Proceedings of the 19th international conference on World wide web* (pp. 1079-1080). 10.1145/1772690.1772813

Chu, W. T., Li, C. J., & Chou, Y. K. (2011). Tag suggestion and localization for web videos by bipartite graph matching. In *Proceedings of the 3rd ACM SIGMM international workshop on Social media* (pp. 35-40). 10.1145/2072609.2072621

Donahue, J., Anne Hendricks, L., Guadarrama, S., Rohrbach, M., Venugopalan, S., Saenko, K., & Darrell, T. (2015). Long-term recurrent convolutional networks for visual recognition and description. In *Proceedings of the IEEE conference on computer vision and pattern recognition* (pp. 2625-2634). 10.1109/CVPR.2015.7298878

Hoai, M., Lan, Z. Z., & De la Torre, F. (2011). Joint segmentation and classification of human actions in video. In CVPR 2011 (pp. 3265-3272). doi:10.1109/CVPR.2011.5995470

Hoang, Q. (2018). *Predicting movie genres based on plot summaries.* arXiv preprint arXiv:1801.04813

Ilyas, S., & Rehman, H. U. (2019). A Deep Learning based Approach for Precise Video Tagging. In *15th International Conference on Emerging Technologies (ICET)* (pp. 1-6). 10.1109/ICET48972.2019.8994567

Kar, S., Maharjan, S., & Solorio, T. (2018). Folksonomication: Predicting tags for movies from plot synopses using emotion flow encoded neural network. In *Proceedings of the 27th International Conference on Computational Linguistics* (pp. 2879-2891). Academic Press.

Karpathy, A., Toderici, G., Shetty, S., Leung, T., Sukthankar, R., & Fei-Fei, L. (2014). Large-scale video classification with convolutional neural networks. In *Proceedings of the IEEE conference on Computer Vision and Pattern Recognition* (pp. 1725-1732). 10.1109/CVPR.2014.223

Khan, U. A., Ejaz, N., Martínez-del-Amor, M. A., & Sparenberg, H. (2017, August). Movies tags extraction using deep learning. In *14th IEEE International Conference on Advanced Video and Signal Based Surveillance (AVSS)* (pp. 1-6). IEEE.

Khan, U. A., Martínez-Del-Amor, M. Á., Altowaijri, S. M., Ahmed, A., Rahman, A. U., Sama, N. U., ... Islam, N. (2020). Movie Tags Prediction and Segmentation Using Deep Learning. *IEEE Access: Practical Innovations, Open Solutions, 8*, 6071–6086. doi:10.1109/ACCESS.2019.2963535

Liu, X., Corner, M., & Shenoy, P. (2009). SEVA: Sensor-enhanced video annotation. *ACM Transactions on Multimedia Computing Communications and Applications, 5*(3), 1–26. doi:10.1145/1556134.1556141

Malinowski, M., Rohrbach, M., & Fritz, M. (2015). Ask your neurons: A neural-based approach to answering questions about images. In *Proceedings of the IEEE international conference on computer vision* (pp. 1-9). 10.1109/ICCV.2015.9

Miranda-Steiner, J. E. (2013). *U.S. Patent Application No. 13/298,310.* Washington, DC: US Patent Office.

Ngo, C. W., Ma, Y. F., & Zhang, H. J. (2005). Video summarization and scene detection by graph modeling. *IEEE Transactions on Circuits and Systems for Video Technology, 15*(2), 296–305. doi:10.1109/TCSVT.2004.841694

Pan, Y., Mei, T., Yao, T., Li, H., & Rui, Y. (2016). Jointly modeling embedding and translation to bridge video and language. In *Proceedings of the IEEE conference on computer vision and pattern recognition* (pp. 4594-4602). 10.1109/CVPR.2016.497

Qi, G. J., Hua, X. S., Rui, Y., Tang, J., Mei, T., & Zhang, H. J. (2007). Correlative multi-label video annotation. In *Proceedings of the 15th ACM international conference on Multimedia* (pp. 17-26). 10.1145/1291233.1291245

Rasheed, Z., & Shah, M. (2003). Scene detection in Hollywood movies and TV shows. In IEEE Computer Society Conference on Computer Vision and Pattern Recognition, 2003. *Proceedings., 2*, II-343.

Rasheed, Z., & Shah, M. (2005). Detection and representation of scenes in videos. *IEEE Transactions on Multimedia, 7*(6), 1097–1105. doi:10.1109/TMM.2005.858392

Shen, Z., Arslan Ay, S., Kim, S. H., & Zimmermann, R. (2011). Automatic tag generation and ranking for sensor-rich outdoor videos. In *Proceedings of the 19th ACM international conference on Multimedia* (pp. 93-102). 10.1145/2072298.2072312

Sidiropoulos, P., Mezaris, V., Kompatsiaris, I., Meinedo, H., Bugalho, M., & Trancoso, I. (2011). Temporal video segmentation to scenes using high-level audiovisual features. *IEEE Transactions on Circuits and Systems for Video Technology, 21*(8), 1163–1177. doi:10.1109/TCSVT.2011.2138830

Siersdorfer, S., San Pedro, J., & Sanderson, M. (2009). Automatic video tagging using content redundancy. In *Proceedings of the 32nd international ACM SIGIR conference on Research and development in information retrieval* (pp. 395-402). ACM.

Toderici, G., Aradhye, H., Pasca, M., Sbaiz, L., & Yagnik, J. (2010). Finding meaning on youtube: Tag recommendation and category discovery. In *IEEE Computer Society Conference on Computer Vision and Pattern Recognition* (pp. 3447-3454). 10.1109/CVPR.2010.5539985

Ulges, A., Schulze, C., Keysers, D., & Breuel, T. M. (2008). A system that learns to tag videos by watching youtube. In *International Conference on Computer Vision Systems* (pp. 415-424). Springer. 10.1007/978-3-540-79547-6_40

Venugopalan, S., Rohrbach, M., Donahue, J., Mooney, R., Darrell, T., & Saenko, K. (2015). Sequence to sequence-video to text. In *Proceedings of the IEEE international conference on computer vision* (pp. 4534-4542). IEEE.

Venugopalan, S., Xu, H., Donahue, J., Rohrbach, M., Mooney, R., & Saenko, K. (2014). *Translating videos to natural language using deep recurrent neural networks.* arXiv preprint arXiv:1412.4729

Wu, Z., Wang, X., Jiang, Y. G., Ye, H., & Xue, X. (2015). Modeling spatial-temporal clues in a hybrid deep learning framework for video classification. In *Proceedings of the 23rd ACM international conference on Multimedia* (pp. 461-470). 10.1145/2733373.2806222

Xu, H., Ye, G., Li, Y., Liu, D., & Chang, S. F. (2015). Large video event ontology browsing, search and tagging (eventnet demo). In *Proceedings of the 23rd ACM international conference on Multimedia* (pp. 803-804). 10.1145/2733373.2807973

Xu, R., Xiong, C., Chen, W., & Corso, J. J. (2015). Jointly modeling deep video and compositional text to bridge vision and language in a unified framework. *Twenty-Ninth AAAI Conference on Artificial Intelligence.*

Yanai, K. (2014). Automatic extraction of relevant video shots of specific actions exploiting Web data. *Computer Vision and Image Understanding, 118*, 2–15. doi:10.1016/j.cviu.2013.03.009

Yang, Q., Zhang, Y., Dai, W., & Pan, S. J. (2020). *Transfer learning.* Cambridge University Press. doi:10.1017/9781139061773

Yang, W., & Toderici, G. (2011). Discriminative tag learning on youtube videos with latent sub-tags. In CVPR 2011 (pp. 3217-3224). doi:10.1109/CVPR.2011.5995402

Yeung, M., Yeo, B. L., & Liu, B. (1998). Segmentation of video by clustering and graph analysis. *Computer Vision and Image Understanding, 71*(1), 94–109. doi:10.1006/cviu.1997.0628

Yosinski, J., Clune, J., Bengio, Y., & Lipson, H. (2014). How transferable are features in deep neural networks? In Advances in neural information processing systems (pp. 3320-3328). Academic Press.

Yue-Hei Ng, J., Hauaknecht, M., Vijayanarasimhan, S., Vinyals, O., Monga, R., & Toderici, G. (2015). Beyond short snippets: Deep networks for video classification. In *Proceedings of the IEEE conference on computer vision and pattern recognition* (pp. 4694-4702). 10.1109/CVPR.2015.7299101

Zha, S., Luisier, F., Andrews, W., Srivastava, N., & Salakhutdinov, R. (2015). *Exploiting image-trained CNN architectures for unconstrained video classification.* arXiv preprint arXiv:1503.04144

Zhai, Y., & Shah, M. (2005). A general framework for temporal video scene segmentation. In *Tenth IEEE International Conference on Computer Vision (ICCV'05)* (Vol. 2, pp. 1111-1116). 10.1109/ICCV.2005.6

Zhai, Y., & Shah, M. (2006). Video scene segmentation using Markov chain Monte Carlo. *IEEE Transactions on Multimedia, 8*(4), 686–697. doi:10.1109/TMM.2006.876299

Zhao, R., Yan, R., Chen, Z., Mao, K., Wang, P., & Gao, R. X. (2019). Deep learning and its applications to machine health monitoring. *Mechanical Systems and Signal Processing, 115*, 213–237. doi:10.1016/j.ymssp.2018.05.050

Zhao, W. L., Wu, X., & Ngo, C. W. (2010). On the annotation of web videos by efficient near-duplicate search. *IEEE Transactions on Multimedia*, *12*(5), 448–461. doi:10.1109/TMM.2010.2050651

Zhao, Y., Wang, T., Wang, P., Hu, W., Du, Y., Zhang, Y., & Xu, G. (2007). Scene segmentation and categorization using ncuts. In *IEEE Conference on Computer Vision and Pattern Recognition* (pp. 1-7). IEEE.

Zhou, Y., Sun, X., Liu, D., Zha, Z., & Zeng, W. (2017). Adaptive pooling in multi-instance learning for web video annotation. In *Proceedings of the IEEE International Conference on Computer Vision Workshops* (pp. 318-327). IEEE.

Chapter 15
ACO–Based Algorithms in Wireless Sensor Networks

Renu Jangra
Kurukshetra University, India

Ramesh Kait
Kurukshetra University, India

Sarvesh Kumar
ⓘ https://orcid.org/0000-0001-9459-1312
Poornima University, Jaipur, India

ABSTRACT

Wireless sensor networks (WSN) offer great expertise that club the sensing, execution, communication, and network technology along with microelectronics and micro-mechanical devices together to study the environment. It is a new concept and a consequence of few steps in the communication field. If the original prospect of this new network works according to the planned concept, it will recover the examining and control systems used these days in the environment for consumer, medical, industries, and military sectors. The wireless technology gives the advantage of decrease in cost that cabling operation has in recent systems and also makes it possible to perform measurements in unreachable places. Many applications can work on the concept of this technology.

INTRODUCTION

Batteries are used to generate current in the nodes. But, the batteries are discharge in fast manners which humiliate the network lifetime. Repeatedly usage of battery power corrupts the normal working of the whole network. The taxonomy of routing protocols in WSN is based on (a) style of functioning of nodes (b) the way of nodes participated in the network (c) the network structure. Therefore, the routing protocol is separated into hierarchical, data centric and location based on the foundation of the network structure. The energy efficient routing is based on the hierarchical structure. Many more algorithms also come

DOI: 10.4018/978-1-7998-2803-7.ch015

under this group. Till now, there are so many power efficient algorithms are executed by the researchers. These are LEACH, PEGASIS, TEEN, APTEEN, HPAR etc to get well from the energy issue. LEACH (Low Energy Adaptive

Clustering Hierarchy) is one of them. The base of routing protocols is different format such as clustering, chaining, cost based etc. The immense quantity of nodes present in wireless sensor network is sometimes tricky to handle. So, the best way is to combine some nodes and make a cluster. Making a cluster is a technique called clustering; which puts a limit on the energy usage by the sensor nodes. The communication and management of nodes in the cluster is handled with the aid of the cluster head. The choice of cluster head among cluster nodes is done by the probability rule which is based on ACO. The cluster nodes send data to the cluster head which further send related information to the base station. ACO-DEEC (Ant Colony Optimization based Distributed Energy Efficient Clustering protocol) calculates the probability rule to

select the cluster head that based on the parameters: distance and power of the nodes. This algorithm improves the energy usage, number of packets sent to the base station, dead nodes when evaluated with the existing protocol DEEC.

LEACH Protocol

LEACH protocol is based on the hierarchical topology that further belongs to the hierarchical network. The author (Heinzelman, 2002) has projected that a cluster always made up of more than two nodes and its size changes with the range of the network. For proper utilization of power in the network, among all the nodes present in the cluster, one is elected as cluster head based on round robin fashion. Every node catches the opportunity to become a cluster head. LEACH is a self-organizing network work as a protocol which uses the arbitrary allotment of energy between the nodes. The crowded network made up of thousands of nodes that have been separated into the cluster having the same size. The node considered as cluster head has been divided as coordinate nodes, cluster member, and normal nodes. LEACH uses TDMA schedule for assignment of energy to nodes. If one node becomes the cluster head (CH) constantly, its energy starts to drain. To overcome this state, other nodes also catch the possibility to become the cluster head after some round or after a particular time. All the nodes present in the cluster, forward their information to the cluster head and the CH collects all the data from its entire member nodes. At last, cluster head, gathers the data and pass this data to the base station for further process (Liao, 2013). The operation of LEACH is split into two phases: a) Setup Phase b) Steady State.

- **Setup phase**: In the setup phase, all the sensor nodes available in the network are scattered into different clusters and one cluster head is selected arbitrarily from each cluster. In a cluster, sensor nodes opt a random number between 0 and 1. The selected random number is then compared with the threshold value T (n), given in equation 1. If the opted value is less than the threshold (opted value < T (n)) value, then that node is considered as a cluster head or else that node remains as a cluster member. A message as knowledge is promoted by the cluster head once a node is selected as a cluster head.

$$T (n) = p/ 1- p * (r \bmod 1/p) \text{ if } n \in G \qquad (1)$$

0 otherwise

Where G is the grouping of that node which is not elected as CH in the last 1/p round; p is the probability for cluster head and n is the node and r is a current round of the process. LEACH protocol is related with rounds so after the execution of every cycle or after 1/p rounds, the nodes are qualified to participate in the selection process of the cluster head. As a result, each node gets the same opportunity to become a cluster head.

- **Steady State Phase**: Once the cluster is formed in the first setup phase, based on Time Division Multiple Access (TDMA) schedule, cluster head is allocated to all the member nodes of the cluster. On the basis of this schedule, the nodes send their related data to their particular CH. After receiving the data from nodes, CH calculates the sum of its own data and data received from other nodes. Then, it transmits this aggregated value to the base station (Khediri, 2014). The time taken by the steady state phase is higher than the setup phase. After every round, the new CHs are selected and the timeline operation composed of the steady-state phase and setup phase is applicable.

Energy Model

Primarily, the transmission model used to be a radio model that had been separated into two parts based on the transferring and receiving distance of the nodes that is a free space model and multipath fading model. There is an assumption in the free space propagation model that the transmitter and receiver antenna are positioned in an empty environment where absorbing obstacles and reflecting surfaces are not considered. But, in multipath the propagation model, obstacles and reflectors take into consideration. Therefore, the received signals have a set of reflections and/or direct wave each having its own degree of attenuation and delay. The formula for path loss is given by distance^n. The value of n ranges from about 2 (in corridors) to 6 (for cluttered and obstructed paths). The wireless communications mostly simulated through the use of the free space propagation model.

Figure 1. Energy Model

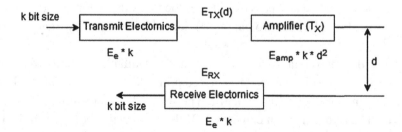

This model works on a straightforward hypothesis that the received signal power inversely proportional to the distance between the transmitter (TX) and the receiver (RX). The communication medium is supposed as symmetric by the protocol. The energy consumed in transferring `k' bits from one node to another at a distance d had been illustrated as

$$(k, d) = k * E_e + k * E_{fs} * d^2; d < d0$$

$$E_{TX}(k, d) = k * E_e + k * E_{amp} * d^4, d^3 d0$$

$$E_{RX}(k, d) = k * E_e$$

Where E_{TX} is the energy utilized by the transmitter to send the message of k bit in size, E is the energy utilized by the receiver to receive the message of k bit in size, E_e is the electronic energy utilized by the circuitry machine to send one bit of data during transmitting and receiving. The E depends on the features like filtering, modulation, digital coding, distance from the receiver and the bit rate (Correia, 2010). In energy model as given in Fig 1; the transmitter loses energy in power amplification and to run the radio electronics, and receiver loses energy in execution of radio electronics. Both space and multi-path model are used and both depend on the distance between the receiver and the transmitter. E_{fs} and E_{amp} are the parameters of amplification energy during transmission in free space model and multipath model, respectively. Threshold distance is represented by d_0.

$$d_0 = \ddot{O}Efs/Eamp$$

If $d \pounds d_0$ then the free space model is considered and energy consumption is multiple of d^2. If $d > d_0$ the multipath model is considered and energy consumption is multiple of d^4.

Modified ACO LEACH Protocol

Wireless Sensor network faces complex issues regarding the management of energy in sensor nodes. Many algorithms have been designed by researchers to resolve the related concern. LEACH protocol saves energy to a great extent because of the direct communication of nodes with the base station. It has improved the network lifetime around eight times than the direct transmission (Batra, 2014). Instead of this, the basic LEACH protocol suffers from the weakness of randomly selecting the cluster head and energy consumption. The cluster head is selected randomly after a few rounds in the LEACH. The residual energy of nodes varies; the nodes which are at the more distance from the base station consuming more energy compared to the other for the same length of data. When the same node is elected as cluster head, then it dies soon as of low energy, hence decreases the lifespan of the network. The proposed algorithm has been planned with the proper management the battery power of the sensor nodes and the selection of cluster head among the nodes is done by combining the existing LEACH with the ACO concept (Jangra, 2019)

In the proposed algorithm named as MALP (Modified Ant-based LEACH Protocol), ACO is applied to find the optimal path from the nodes to the base station for efficient transmission. While choosing the cluster head, the current energy and the residual energy of a node is multiplied by the number of nodes because the node that is selected as the cluster head has more battery power. ACO is used to discover the optimal path among the nodes and the BS. The optimal election probability formula for a node to select as a cluster head is as follows:

$$ENR = (E_0/E_{res} * NoOfNodes)^\rho;$$

Figure 2. Flowchart of LEACH

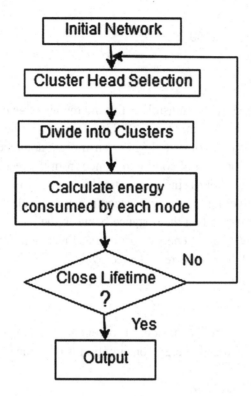

$$T(n) = p/ 1\text{-}p * (r \bmod 1/p) * ENR, \text{ if } n \in G \tag{2}$$

Zero otherwise

E_0 and E_{res} are the current energy and residual energy of the nodes, respectively. NoOfNodes is the number of nodes present in the network, rho is the initial pheromone value.

Proposed Algorithm

```
Begin
(Set Up Phase)
1. Create the network and initialize the initial probability (p), number of
nodes (n), initial energy E₀, ρ, E_fs, E_amp, E_TX, E_RX.
2. Calculate the energy consumption for cluster head and non cluster head by
equation (2).
3. The optimal distance between the nodes and base station is computed by ACO
algorithm.
4. If (E0 > 0) and r mod (1/p) ¹ 0 then that node is elected as the cluster
head for that round otherwise considered as a node itself and go to step 8.
```

5. Cluster head advertises the messages to nodes (Steady Phase).

6. If the node is cluster head, then it computes the received data from nodes aggregate it and send to the base station otherwise it is a node itself send data to the cluster head.

7. If (E_0 <0) then calculates dead nodes.

8. One round completed.

End

Table 1.

Parameter	Values
Protocol	LEACH and MALP
Area of the Network	100 m * 100 m
E_e	50 nJ/bit
E_{fs}	10pJ/bit/ m^4
E_{amp}	0.013pJ/bit/m^4
E_0	0.5 J/bit
Packet Size (CH to BS)	6400 bytes
Packet Size (node to CH)	200 bytes
p	0.1

In Table 2, the performance of different LEACH versions is discussed and shown in the table form. These LEACH versions are LEACH-C (C termed as Centralized), T-LEACH (T termed as Threshold), V-LEACH (V termed as Vice) and MALP (Modified Ant-based LEACH Protocol). The comparison is about the energy consumed by different protocols during their lifetime in the network, the number of nodes that are dying during the entire communication process, the time is taken by the algorithms to execute, the type of changes occur in existing LEACH to propose the new enhancements, cluster head selection criteria of the protocols, balanced clustering limit and self-organization capacity of the protocols (Jangra, 2019).

Table 2.

Scenerio	Existing LEACH	LEACH-C	T-LEACH	V-LEACH	MALP (Modified Ant based LEACH Protocol)
Energy Consumed	More	Lower	Lower	Lower	Least
Dead Nodes	More	Less than LEACH	Less than LEACH	Less than LEACH	Less
Execution Time	More	Lower	Lower	Lower	Least
Classification	Hierarchical	Hierarchical	Hierarchical	Chain	Hierarchical
Self-Organization	Yes	No	Yes	Yes	Yes
Enhancement w.r.t LEACH	NA	Consistent centralized clustering irrespective of the number of nodes in the cluster	Doing the cluster head selection by considering the remaining energy of the nodes.	The cluster formation stage is delayed and initiate when the server is dead and use a replaced node as cluster head.	It uses the term number of nodes, residual energy and pheromone value in cluster head selection probability formula.
Balanced Clustering	OK	Very Good	OK	OK	Very Good
Cluster Head Selection Criteria	Random	Pre-assigned	Remaining energy	Random/Pre-assigned	Residual energy and pheromone value

The protocols of routing available in wireless sensor networks have an immense part in maintaining the performance of the network as a good energy handling organization, boost the network's lifetime and so on. The base of routing protocols is different format such as clustering, chaining, etc. The immense quantity of nodes present in a wireless sensor network is sometimes tricky to handle. So, the best way is to combine some nodes and make a cluster. Making a cluster is a technique called clustering; which puts a limit on the energy used by the sensor nodes. The communication and management of nodes in the cluster are handled with the aid of the cluster head. The choice of cluster head among cluster nodes is done by the probability rule which is based on ACO. The cluster nodes send data to the cluster head, which further send related information to the base station. The proposed algorithm ACO-DEEC (Ant Colony Optimization based Distributed Energy-Efficient Clustering protocol) calculates the probability rule to select the cluster head that based on the parameters: distance and power of the nodes. This algorithm improves the energy usage, a number of packets received at the base station, dead nodes when evaluated with the existing protocol DEEC. The sensor nodes are considered at a highly valued component of the wireless sensor network (WSN). The energy of the sensor nodes is very limited that have an effect on the living period of the network. There is a base station (BS) inside or outside the field of nodes (Jangra, 2017). Many route finding protocols have been anticipated to enhance the existence of the network, the count of the packets/data transferred to the base station and to reduce the death of node too early and so on. The route finding protocols evaluated on clustering scheme has been used to get the required objective.

In clustering, combining of some nodes makes a cluster, among them one node is the cluster head (CH) and others are cluster node. The cluster head communicates with a cluster node in a direct way. The cluster head has the responsibility of filtering, aggregating and processing of the data sent by the cluster member nodes. The DEEC "Distributed energy efficient clustering" protocol is one among the clustering scheme based protocol. In DEEC, the cluster head has been selected as the prospect measure of the ratio of the residual energy and the average energy of the nodes (Elbhiri, 2010). The node with high residual and average energy has the most chance to be selected as a cluster head. The clustering based routing protocols identify the method of how to select the cluster head and how to minimize the communication path between CH and base station for energy efficient transmission of data. A bio-inspired clustering protocol has been proposed which estimates the suitable CHs. The wireless medium is considered less reliable in terms of reliability and robustness of the network compared to the wired medium. To improve this, the ideal model of the social insect swarm behavior for the blueprint of wireless networks takes into consideration (Jangra, 2017). In recent times, a trend has come to adopt bio-inspired criteria for WSN design (Jangra, 2017). Mainly the swarm-based routing algorithms are easy and vigorous to adapt the topological changes. The idea has been taken from foraging nature of the ant colony. In this, we have proposed the algorithm ACO-DEEC "Ant Colony Optimization based Distributed Energy-Efficient Clustering protocol" which calculates the probability law to select the cluster head depends on the parameters: distance and power of the nodes. The energy utilization, number of packets received at the base station and more dead nodes have been improved by this proposed algorithm as compared to the existing DEEC protocol.

- **ACO-DEEC**: In the proposed algorithm, we apply ant colony optimization on DEEC protocol and named as ACO-DEEC. In DEEC, the nodes are chosen as CH by applying the probability rule. They further based on the ratio of the remaining energy of the node to the average (standard) energy of the network. However, in the ACO-DEEC, the cluster head is selected by applying the probability function as well as the parameters that are the power of the node and the length between the node and a base station. It is considered that a large path between nodes will be having more energy and vice versa. The steps followed by the ants in the ACO-DEEC are: Ants selects the next cluster head using the start rule and select optimal one using revise rule.

- **Start Rule**: Let an ant is positioned on the cluster head node `i' and choose next cluster head node `j' using equations (1) and (2).

$$P = \frac{Distance_i * \alpha + Phero_i * \beta}{\sum_{i=0}^{N_i} \left(Distance_i * \alpha + Phero_i * \beta \right)} \tag{1}$$

where P = The probability function to select a cluster head among the nodes.
$Phero_i$ = Value of the pheromone.

$$Phero_i = \frac{\tau_{i,j}^{\alpha} * \eta_i^{\beta}}{\sum_{i=0}^{N_i} \tau_{i,j}^{\alpha} * \eta_i^{\beta}} \tag{2}$$

where, $\tau^{i,j}$ is the intensity of the pheromone, α and β are the controlling parameters, η_i is the heuristic information.

$$\eta_i = \frac{1}{I_e - e} \tag{3}$$

where, I - e = Original energy of the node.
e = Actual energy of the node.
If any node has less power, then it has less chance to select as a CH.

- **Revise Rule**: When an ant search the next CH then the value of pheromone on that node is updated according to equation (4).

$$\tau_{i,j}\left(t+1\right) = \left(1-\rho\right)\tau_{i,j}\left(t\right) + \rho\Delta\tau_{i,j}\left(t\right) \tag{4}$$

where $\Delta\tau_{i,j}\left(t\right)$ is the update in pheromone and ρ is used to stop the creation of extra pheromone.

Proposed Algorithm (ACO-DEEC)

```
Begin
1.      Create the network and initialize the initial probability (ρ), num-
```

ber of nodes (n), number of rounds r_{max}, Initial energy E_0, ρ, E_{fs}, E_{amp}, E_{TX} and E_{RX}.

2.   Compute the standard (average) energy of the network.

3.   Calculate the probability function of each node by taking into account the power of the node and the length of the node from the Base station.

4.   Probability function is calculated using formula.

$$P = \frac{Distance_i * \alpha + Phero_i * \beta}{\sum_{i=0}^{N_i} \left(Distance_i * \alpha + Phero_i * \beta \right)}$$

$$Phero_i = \frac{\tau_{i,j}^{\alpha} * \eta_i^{\beta}}{\sum_{i=0}^{N_i} \tau_{i,j}^{\alpha} * \eta_i^{\beta}}$$

$$\eta_i = \frac{1}{I_e - e}$$

5.   If a node is CH in the previous round, then the node is a part of group G wherever G is a set of those nodes which are qualified to turn into a CH and that node, choose an unsystematic number between zero and one else node become a cluster member node and transfer data to the relevant CH.

6.   If the chosen unsystematic number is less than the threshold function, then that node is a CH else node is a cluster member and sends data to the relevant CH.

7.   Calculate the energy left, dead nodes and packets received to the base station for the nodes.

SUMMARY

The Wireless Sensor Network is a network used to make an analysis of surroundings such as temperature, pressure, motion and so on by the help of its base station and thousands of sensor nodes that are deployed in the surrounding. The communication among sensor nodes taken place via a base station and wireless radios. The entity that does the job of sensing is named as a sensor. These sensors are competent in translating objects, things into signals that are effortlessly being analyzed and planned. The dimension, physical safety, power, memory storage, unpredictable communications, low expenses, energy efficient is the unique properties of a wireless sensor network. Beyond all these properties, there are numerous issues regarding the deployment of nodes, power consumption, heterogeneity, topology, reliability and scalability, a medium of transmission, etc. that have been faced by the wireless sensor network. Among the above challenges, the issue of management of power is the main concern. For the smooth working of the wireless sensor network, it is necessary that power should be stable throughout the network. Batteries are used to generate current in the nodes. But, the batteries are discharged in fast manners which humiliate the network lifetime. Repeated usage of battery power corrupts the normal working of the whole network. By enhancing the cluster head probability selection formula and using the ACO approach in the selection of the optimal path between the cluster head and the base station, MALP handles the proper energy utilization, better execution time and increment in the lifespan of the network.

The outline of diverse basic ant colony algorithms explained and it can also be used in getting the solution of upcoming investigating problems. ACO excellently works in the area of the metaheuristic optimization problem to provide better solutions. The main major concern in a wireless sensor network is better energy utilization in the sensor node by making it more efficient using the proposed algorithm MALP. By enhancing the cluster head probability selection formula and using the ACO approach in the selection of the optimal path between the

cluster head and the base station, MALP handles the proper energy utilization, better execution time and increment in the lifespan of the network. Hence, the overall performance of MALP is better than the existing LEACH. The main goal of LEACH is to improve the network lifetime and saves the energy consumption of nodes.

Clustering has been used in WSN routing protocol for saving the energy of the sensor nodes. The energy-based routing protocols DEEC and ACO-DEEC divide the large network into clusters. Wireless Sensor network is the fastest growing technology in the field of research. As with any other area, it also requires good security as its infrastructure is established in the inaccessible environment and it does the critical task of sensing, collecting, tracking, and processing of data. The research on WSN security is making progress at a remarkable speed. There is not any complete document that catalogs the security concern and the risk models which create exclusive threats to the wireless sensor networks. The establishment of the whole setup is only fruitful if there is a secure communication happened with it. So, the security of the network is required for the secure and correct delivery of data. Attackers are always ready either to steal the data or corrupt it for their own use. So, need security as these networks are constructed for isolated observation. An illegal change in the sensed data may lead to incorrect information to be reached at the judgment creator. It is a big deal to provide security to WSN as its infrastructure is set up in a remote place. As the literature studied, there are many security protocols designed to provide security in WSN. We also work on the same concern and designed a security protocol. We apply the cryptography algorithms AES and RSA as a security measure on our proposed algorithm ACO-DEEC and they named as AES ACO-DEEC and RSA ACO-DEEC. Also, compare both algorithms based on different parameters. The AES ACO-DEEC works better in most cases than RSA ACO-DEEC. In this thesis, the proposed algorithms provide energy-efficient, secure and good routing protocol.

Result Analysis

In our objective, we proposed the algorithm that wastes less energy, superior routing path and having good quality safety procedures with the aid of ACO algorithms and its variation, special tools, etc. that can facilitate the researchers to carry out their assignment or research. The analysis of basic ACO on TSP Problem shows that the best possible solution for the proposed algorithm results on the values provided in the parameters. The three alternatives of ACO is also discussed named as AS, ACS, and MMAS. We can explore and evaluate the variants of ACO on the basis of heterogeneous parameters setting. Analysis

Figure 3. Flowchart of Proposed Algorithm

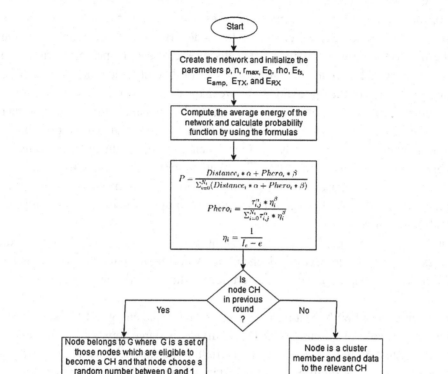

shows that the algorithm's behavior varied with the behavior of factors like a count of ants, a factor that makes a decision of controlling the concentration of pheromone on the path, pheromone controlling parameter (α), visibility deciding parameter (β), pheromone handling parameter (ρ) and iterations. In our experimental analysis, the conclusion is that the ant colony system performs superior among the three (AS, ACS, and MMAS) in comparison to other algorithms in the following manner. When there is an increase in the count of ants and iterations, then the expenditure of a path covered by ants and used time is less in case of ACS. The algorithm ACS is also working fine respective to the length of the path visited by the ants when manipulating besides a grouping of α and β parameters. When parameters values are initialized as α = 1; β = 1; ρ = 0.05; Q = 1; m (number of ants) = 40, then on increasing the number of iterations, at start of execution cost changes but after 100 iterations onward cost is unchanging and minimum. With increasing the number of ants, the cost goes down and after m=50 onward it remains constant. Our experimental analysis shows that at m=50, the best possible solution is generated in terms of cost and length of the tour. The selection of the values of α; β, m and ρ are opting on the basis of research and the literature study. The experimental results show the performance of ant colony algorithms when solving TSP problems. The assessment of the result of the algorithm is also evaluated on the basis of additional features like the iterations count, the time taken to execute the algorithm and so on. We also enlighten the fundamental theory of ant colony optimization that gets encouragement from the foraging conduct of ants. After evaluating the various algorithms of ACO, we terminate the discussion with the point that the variations of ACO algorithms are helpful in generating the solution for different combinatorial optimization problems nowadays; researchers generally apply ACO for standard NP-hard optimization problems, while some perform on related variations. The recent research is still going on and on simulation phase; the thorough arithmetical clarification and whole theoretical organization have not been officially formed so far about the algorithm. The ACO concepts are used to design these algorithms to get progress in removing the WSN disputes. The use of parameters varies according to the algorithms. The mainly used parameters are pheromone gathering, performance metric, and simulator and so on to acquire the optimal solution. The modified ACO representation compared with accessible conventional routing algorithms which are applicable in network routing problem. The proposed algorithm ACO-DEEC uses the ant colony optimization technique in the probability function to select the cluster head. ACO- DEEC works better than DEEC. The comparison is done between two using MATLAB simulation.

CONCLUSION

The main goal of Low Energy Adaptive Clustering Hierarchy (LEACH) is to improve the network lifetime and saves the energy consumption of nodes. But, apart from that, there are still some disadvantages with LEACH protocol. To remove or reduce these shortcomings, some new versions of LEACH are introduced which are LEACH-K, A-LEACH, O-LEACH, V-LEACH, EELBCRP, etc. The future researchers can also do reviews and research on these versions. The main major concern in a wireless sensor network is better energy utilization in the sensor node by making it more efficient using the proposed algorithm MALP. Hence, the overall performance of MALP is better than the existing LEACH. The proposed algorithm ACO-DEEC improves the energy usage, count of the packets received at the BS and reduce the dead nodes. Hence, it improves the energy and the working time of the network.

Future Work

ACO is one of the finest techniques for solving optimization difficulty. It has lots of advantages such as when there is a dynamic change in the graph, the ACO algorithms can be executed constantly and adjusts to transforming in the actual moment over simulated annealing and genetic algorithm, come near to related problems. The algorithms are good to provide solutions to small problems. The Ant Colony Optimization algorithm has appropriate for a broad collection of applications and resourceful for Traveling Salesman Problem and parallel problems. The constructive feedback explanation helps in quick detection of good solutions. Many algorithms are improved and projected to get a better solution. The previously done work needs better to perform in this area to generate a better solution to the problems. Nowadays, WSNs are a well-known study matter and gradually better practice. It monitors the industrialized event and biological over the previous two decades. Like this, ACO is also counting in modern researches. We elucidate the critical of the wireless sensor network, construction of sensor nodes, communication protocol, features, disputes, application, security concern, and attacks, direction-finding protocol, fundamental of ACO, and its algorithms. A combination of algorithms is anticipated to get the most favorable solution to the problem. In the upcoming time, researchers can also do the work on the ACO algorithm variations with another parameter domain that hopefully presents different performance and results.

REFERENCES

Batra, P. K., & Kant, K. (2014, October). Stable cluster head selection in leach protocol: a cross-layer approach. In *Proceedings of the 7th ACM India Computing Conference* (pp. 1-6). 10.1145/2675744.2675761

Correia, L. H., Heimfarth, T., Pereira, G. M., Silva, V. F., & de Santana, J. L. (2010). Radio channel model of wireless sensor networks operating in 2.4 GHz ISM band. *INFOCOMP*, *9*(1), 98–106.

Elbhiri, B., Saadane, R., & Aboutajdine, D. (2010, September). Developed Distributed Energy-Efficient Clustering (DDEEC) for heterogeneous wireless sensor networks. In *2010 5th International Symposium On I/V Communications and Mobile Network* (pp. 1-4). IEEE.

Heinzelman, W. B., Chandrakasan, A. P., & Balakrishnan, H. (2002). An application-specific protocol architecture for wireless microsensor networks. *IEEE Transactions on Wireless Communications*, *1*(4), 660–670. doi:10.1109/TWC.2002.804190

Jangra, R., & Kait, R. (2017). ACO Parameters Analysis of TSP Problem. *International Journal of Computer Science and Mobile Applications*, *8*(5).

Jangra, R., & Kait, R. (2017, February). Analysis and comparison among ant system; ant colony system and max-min ant system with different parameters setting. In *2017 3rd International Conference on Computational Intelligence & Communication Technology (CICT)* (pp. 1-4). IEEE.

Jangra, R., & Kait, R. (2017). Principles and Concepts of Wireless Sensor Network and Ant Colony Optimization: A Review. *International Journal of Advanced Research in Computer Science*, *8*(5).

Jangra, R., & Kait, R. (2019). Modified Ant System Solving TSP Problem. *International Journal of Innovative Technology and Exploring Engineering*, *8*, 328–331.

Jangra, R., & Kait, R. (2019). *Modified Energy Proficient ACO Based LEACH Protocol in Wireless Sensor Network*. Available at SSRN 3426948

Khediri, S. E., Nasri, N., Wei, A., & Kachouri, A. (2014). A new approach for clustering in wireless sensors networks based on LEACH. *Procedia Computer Science*, *32*, 1180–1185. doi:10.1016/j.procs.2014.05.551

Liao, Q., & Zhu, H. (2013). An energy balanced clustering algorithm based on LEACH protocol. *Applied Mechanics and Materials*, *341*, 1138–1143. doi:10.4028/www.scientific.net/AMM.341-342.1138

Chapter 16
Analysis of Climate Prediction and Climate Change in Pakistan Using Data Mining Techniques

Soobia Saeed

Department of Software Engineering, Universiti Teknologi Malaysia, Malaysia

N. Z. Jhanjhi

(iD) https://orcid.org/0000-0001-8116-4733

School of Computing and IT (SoCIT), Taylor's University, Malaysia

Mehmood Naqvi

Faculty of Electrical and Computer Engineering Technology, Mohawk College of Applied Arts and Technology, Canada

Vasaki Ponnusamy

Universiti Tunku Abdul Rahman, Malaysia

Mamoona Humayun

College of Computer and Information Sciences, Jouf University, Saudi Arabia

ABSTRACT

Weather forecasting is a significant meteorological task and has arisen in the last century from a rational and revolutionary point of view among the most difficult problems. The authors are researching the use of information mining techniques in this survey to measure maximum temperature, precipitation, dissipation, and wind speed. This was done using vector help profiles, decision tree, and weather data obtained in Pakistan in 2015 and 2019. For the planning of workbook accounts, an information system for meteorological information was used. The presentations of these calculations considered using standard implementing steps as well as the estimate that gave the best results for generating disposal rules for intermediate environment variables. Likewise, a prophetic network model for the climate outlook program, contradictory results, and true climate information for the projected periods have been created. The results show that with sufficient information on cases, data mining strategies can be used to estimate the climate and environmental change that it focuses on.

DOI: 10.4018/978-1-7998-2803-7.ch016

INTRODUCTION

The weather forecast has been among the most difficult logically and mechanically in the last century. This is the result of two elements: First, it is used in some human exercises, in addition to the feature provided by the various innovative developments that have been identified directly with this solid field of examination, similar to the evolution of calculation and change in estimation Frameworks. Accurate forecasting is one of the great difficulties facing the world of meteorology worldwide. Since ancient days and weather, expectations have been highlighted among the most interesting and wonderful space. Researchers have tried to estimate meteorological characteristics using different methods, and some of these strategies are more accurate than others.

The weather forecast involves predicting how the current environment will change. Use land visualizations, ship and aircraft visualizations, radio signals, Doppler radar and satellites, current weather conditions are collected. This data is sent to meteorological centers that gather, isolate and turn the information into a variety of tables, maps, and graphs. Quick and creative computers on surface and air maps share a large amount of visualization. With the aid of meteorologists reporting any mistakes, personal computers draw lines on charts. An analysis is called the final guide. Mapping computers and projecting what it eventually looks like. The climate calculation of a machine is regarded as a forecast of numerical weather.

Weather prediction has attracted much attention for its numerous exploration groups, as it helps defend human life and wealth. Estimating taking into account temperature and forecasts are crucial for agribusiness and therefore for traders within warehouse markets. Service organizations use temperature meters to evaluate demand in the coming days. External workouts are greatly reduced due to heavy rain, snow and thermal sensation, and guesses can be used to organize workouts on these occasions, organize them in advance and stay alive. Climate prediction has become a gradual necessity for researchers, farmers, livestock, global food, security and failures management and related societies to understand the natural wonders of organizing and organizing the future. Climate change is a significant and permanent change and the objective transition of climate examples over periods ranging from decades to a large number of years. Environmental change today is synonymous with human and abnormal climate change. However, in experimental journals, a change in global temperature indicates an increase in surface temperature, while environmental change involves serious atmospheric dedication and everything else that will affect the expansion of incubation gas amounts. Climate changes are obtained from changes in intermediaries, which are signs that reflect the atmosphere, for example, vegetation, ice centers, neuromorphology, ocean level change and icy geography. Part of this is useful for improving natural disasters, performing agricultural work, development, sea route, forest developments and protection purposes. Plane stations organize the primary airport organization in light of nearby weather conditions that have light parameters that can change in a short time. These parameters, for example, fog, precipitation level, etc. It can be very dangerous to flight safety and expense (S. Zainudin et.al, 2016).

To predict weather by numerical means, meteorologists have created inaccurate weather models using scientific and mathematical terms to describe how air temperature, weight, and humidity change after for a while. Mathematical data is modified on a computer and improved information on current barometric conditions on the computer. The computer analyzes mathematical data to decide how distinctive climate changes will change in the next few minutes. The computer re-applies this method over and over using one cycle performance as information for the next cycle. For some time to search later (12, 24, 36, 48, 72, or 120 hours), the computer prints its verified data. Then divide the information and draw the lines for the expected position of the different weight tires. The latest computer guesswork diagram is known as a graph or predictive program. The predictor uses the software as a weather forecast guide. There are many environmental models that talk to the atmosphere, and they all translate air in a slightly different way (A. M. Bagirov et.al, 2017).

To predict weather by numerical means, meteorologists have devised barometric models that change the environment using scientific comparisons to describe how air temperature, weight, and humidity change after a while. Sports data is modified on a computer and information about current weather conditions is fed from the computer. The computer detects comparisons to determine how distinct environmental variables change in the next few minutes. The computer application restores this system over and overusing one cycle performance as information for the next session. For some time required at a later time (12, 24, 36, 48, 72, or 120 hours), the computer prints its calculated data. Then search the information, and draw the lines for the expected position of the different weight tires. The most recent computerized guessing diagram is known as a prediction diagram. Weather prediction is used as a guide for weather prediction. There are many environmental models that talk to the air, and each decomposes the atmosphere in a marginally distinctive way (S. R. Kumar. (2017).

Data mining, also called a database discovery database (KDD), is an area to find new data and may be useful with lots of information. Unlike standard measurable strategies, information-seeking systems search for interesting information without asking prior theories, and the type of patterns that can be found depends on the information search assignments used. After all, there are two types of information exploration tasks: graphic data mining tasks that represent the general characteristics of current information and previous information mining tasks that strive to make forecasts in light of deriving accessible information. These strategies are regularly more adaptive and effective for exploratory research than measurement techniques. The procedures most used as part of information mining are artificial neural systems, genetic algorithms, induction of bases, closest neighborhood strategy, memory-based logical thinking, logistic regression, and discriminatory analysis and decision trees.

In this work, both the vector support device (SVM) and decision trees (DT) have been used to classify meteorological information accumulated in Pakistan over a 3-year period (January 2013 to December 2015), in order to create arrangement rules for applying data mining techniques in weather forecasting and parameters Climatic during the study period and to anticipate future weather conditions using recorded information that can be accessed. Prediction goals are those climate changes that affect us every day, such as minimum and most extreme changes in temperature, precipitation, disappearance, and wind speed (M. Ahmad et.al, 2018).

Decision Tree (DCT)

A decision tree is a flowchart like a tree structure. Each inner center means a test of a feature. Each branch talks about the test result. Paper cubes speak to the circulation. The choice tree structure provides an explicit text for "yes - then" criteria (as opposed to the numerical comparisons extracted), making the results easy to translate. In tree structures, leaves speak of groups and branches speak of the conjugation of the components that cause these commands. In an election test, the external election tree can be used explicitly to talk about elections and make decisions. The idea of adding data is used to choose an estimate of a portion of an internal position. The part that is estimated to give the largest increase in data is determined. Officially, the increase in data is entropy. In order to improve the accuracy and speculation of the assembly and relapse of trees, various strategies such as reinforcement and pruning were introduced. Boosting is a strategy to improve the accuracy of the prophetic capacity by applying the capacity over and over in agreement and boosting the performance of each power with a weighting to reduce the total predictive error or planting several independent trees in parallel and then adding together after creating each of the trees. Pruning on the tree to improve the span of the trees, in this way, the tolerances are reduced, a problem with comprehensive single tree models as the model begins to contain information. While this form is connected to information that has not been used to compile the form, the form will not be ready for a summary. There are several choice tree accounts and these include Alternative Decision Tree, Logitboost Alternative Decision Tree (LAD)(N. Mishra et.al, 2018).

Figure 1. Tree Diagram
(H. Vathsala et.al, 2017).

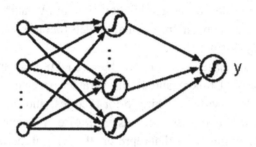

Support Vector Machines (SVM)

The calculation of the support vector machine is based on measurable learning assumptions. The Support Vector Machines standard is to define unique information X in an F component area with high dimensions through the ability to draw non-linear mapping and build the perfect hyperlink in a new space. SVM methods can be connected in order and relapse. In order, a perfect hyperlink was found to isolate information in two categories, while a hyperlink was created close to any number of foci reasonably predictable (H. Vathsala et.al, 2017).

$$G = \left\{ \left(xt, dt \right) \right\} Nt1 \tag{1}$$

The declining vector support (SVR) predicts the highest temperature in the region. Relapse is a matter of assessing capacitance in light of the specific set of information. Note that the information is where xi is the data vector, d is the desired result, and N is compared to the range of the information set. The general type of ability to evaluate the regression of the support vectors is (A. M. Bagirov et.al, 2017)

$$f = \left(\left(x \right) w \varnothing \left(x \right) \right) + b \tag{2}$$

Where w and b are the co-efficient that need to be estimated from information, where f(x) is the non-linear capacity in feature space.

METHOD OF DATA COLLECTION

The information used in this work was obtained from the Pakistan Meteorological Department, National Agricultural Center (NAMC). Status information was included within 8 months, i.e. from August 2015 to February 2016. The accompanying methods were adopted at this stage of the test: data cleaning, data selection, and data conversion as data and data extraction.

SAMPLING TECHNIQUE AND SAMPLE SIZE

Data Cleaning

At this stage, a future configuration was finally created; the customer information was converted into an appropriate institution (Pakistan Meteorological Department of the National Agromate Center (NAMC) to extract the information (M. Ahmad et.al, 2017).

Data Selection

At this point, the information that applies to the test has been resolved and retrieved from the data set. The meteorological data set contains 10 (10) characters, their classification and representation are given in Table 1, while an examination of the numerical traits appears in Table 2. Because of the shape of the cloud model information where both traits are identical and a high percentage of missing traits are not used in a booth Daylight information as part of the investigation (N. Mishra et.al, 2018).

Table 1. Attributes of Meteorological Dataset

Attribute	Type	Description
Year	Mathematical	Annual measured
Month	Mathematical	Month measured
Wind-speed	Mathematical	Airstream run in KM
Evaporation	Mathematical	Evaporation
Cloud Form	Mathematical	The mean cloud amount
Radioactivity	Mathematical	The quantity of radioactivity
Sunlight	Mathematical	The quantity of sunlight
Min-Temp	Mathematical	The monthly Smallest Temperature
Rainfall	Mathematical	Total monthly rainfall
Max-Temp	Mathematical	Extreme Temperature

Data Mining Stage

The data extraction stage was divided into three phases. Each account was used to classify meteorological data sets at each point. Information exploration focuses on exposing the dark properties of information. Characterization is a matter of determining which class behavior is in which another perception occurs, based on a set of knowledge that includes beliefs known to be involved in classification. In reducing quantifiable characteristics, known as various logical variables, highlights, etc., probability classifiers can be more effectively combined with large machine learning companies so that the propagation error problem is either reduced or avoided altogether (H. Vathsala and S. G. Koolagudi. (2017).

Statistical Technique and Evaluation Metrics

When selecting the control calculations and parameters that best shaped the climate, and defining the variable, the accompanying implementation measures were used for data mining and their calculation was used for the classification of meteorological data sets at each point. The shape of model information where both traits are identical calculations and also a high percentage of missing traits are not used in Daylight information as the control calculations and parameters give the best shape of climate through the usage of Statistical Technique and Evaluation Metrics.

Connection Coefficient

This measures the objective relationship between the expected values and real values. This technique is unique because it does not change with a scale of attributes for experiments. The higher number means a distinct model, meaning 1, an impeccable, measurable relationship and a significance of 0, there is no communication in any way for coefficient connection can be incorporated more effectively with larger machine learning companies so that the issue of propagation error is minimized or completely avoided (A. M. Bagirov et.al, 2017).

Mean Squared Error

The mean squared error appears among the most common achievement metrics for numerical prediction. This word is recorded by taking the normal state of the square discrepancies between each imaging quality and its correct estimate of comparison. Error%: The percentage of error with the following equation, the mean of the squared error is the square of the mean squared error. Half of the error square gives an estimate of the same dimensions as real and expected attributes (M. Ahmad, et.al, 2017).

% Error: The percent error characterized by the following equation

$$\%Error = 100 \; / \; NP \sum_{j-O}^{P} \sum_{i-o}^{n} \frac{dyij - ddij}{ddij}$$

Where

P = number of yield handling components
N = number of models in the data set
dyij = denormalized system yield for model i at handling component j
ddij = denormalized craved yield for the model I at preparing component

Experimental Design

The updated Weka Decision Tree workbook account was used on Weka to check meteorological information. The Weka algorithm was chosen to implement climate data extraction techniques after the results of the completed tests were correlated using CART and C4.5 calculations. SVM is used for those who are equipped to complete a time-saving examination specifically: SVM systems are used to predict future estimates of wind speed, evaporation, radiation, minimum temperature, maximum temperature, and rain given month and year (N. Mishra et.al, 2018).

MANAGEMENT ANALYSIS

The latest information management in the form of tables, general information and charts as after proposing the model, a study of weather forecasting and climate change was presented using a data mining strategy. Since the mid-fifties, it has been recognized that weather conditions affect the behavior of the driver and the way the transport tire must operate. By changing speeds, different types of progress and parameters, driver responses affect the overall tire implementation. This area offers a written review of a point about the characterization of severe weather conditions and their interpretation of objective quantifiable standards. Initially, the effect of such conditions on the current passage thickness is presented. This effect is related to a modification of the limit, delay, size and speed, and reflects the behavior of drivers in a particular street area. Once the amendment is understood in these criteria, the central part of the study is examined; the investigation considers the interaction of climate impacts with the time of the science, and the unmarked crossing points and variable message signs (VMS) are scanned. The researcher focused on weather data and was monitored and preserved. Recorded parameters are used to guess the weather. If there is a modification in any of the recorded parameters, such as wind path, wind speed, temperature, precipitation, adhesion, then the emerging climatic condition can be expected using faulty nervous systems, reverse diffusion methods. The expansion will also operate in vast areas (J. Wu, J et.al, 2015).

The effect of "weather conditions" on transport tires is a generic term that can represent some confusion. Specialists used distinct arrangement plans for climatic conditions, in light of the fact that these conditions contrast sharply with species and size. Some weather conditions are convincing in nature and, therefore, can lead to an alternative reaction of drivers. These excellent conditions are outside the fast center of the current study. Other unpleasant weather conditions (light, heavy rain, heavy and light snow, etc.) provide a less tight period of time for employers and allow drivers to maintain a satisfactory amount of control over their vehicles; this control may not be in completely "normal" conditions due to Physical elements, for example, perception, physical discomfort (hot or cold temperatures) and asphalt friction with tires when it rains or cold conditions. Most current studies do not show all "climate conditions" as objective quantifiable parameters, which makes it difficult to clarify or evaluate the impact of these conditions on transport tires and their clients. There are several studies that support the relevance of information search systems to climate forecasts (D. Gupta and U. Ghose. (2015).

The researcher investigated the data mining strategies and discovered that the criteria for assessing the climate, such as temperature, precipitation, disappearance and wind tempo, are the best. Performance can be improved with Neuro-Fuzzy models to provide climate change. Likewise, prior information, such as precipitation, wind speed, dew point, and temperature, is used to forecast the weather using the calculation of the nearest neighbor k. Create accurate results in advance in the weather forecast. Progress can be seen using examples. Learn about the design can be used. Additionally, using data mining systems, weather information was foreseen and a decision made. Time estimate parameter connections are discovered using information extraction procedures. Since meteorological information is massive and time-consuming, it is not only necessary to modify it by extracting the usual information, but it can also be changed using some different methods. As we mentioned, in a specific location, the best information is used to forecast the weather using learning dissemination. The history of the information must be preserved for the weather forecast. The framework should be versatile so that it can definitely be useful in the event of any sudden change of information. In this vital information exploration strategies are used. These techniques have to deal with a sudden weather change for recording information, radar, lid, and satellites are used. Some researchers have demonstrated a review of climate prediction using simulated neuron systems and consider the advantage of using it. It produces excellent results and can be considered a different choice for traditional meteorological methodology. The study reported the defective nervous system's ability to predict various climatic wonders, such as temperature, rainstorms, precipitation, and wind speed, and believed that real engineering such as BP, MLP, was adequate to foresee climate admiration. Nonetheless, the precision of the forecasts produced by these procedures is still below the level of good taste due to the non-linear form of the climate data set (D. Gupta and U. Ghose. (2015).

In addition, another scientist described a subtle strategic system that uses information mining to set temporary forecasts for precipitation in certain places. Three-month precipitation information is investigated in a particular area for a long time. Accurate and accurate climate prediction is a great test for a test group. The aggregation method is used to describe the purpose of precipitation at ground level. The aggregation strategy is used to aggregate the component that represents a specific region in which precipitation sites are involved and precipitation is expected in a particular region. Various models of direct relapse were received with an expectation; however, the results give precipitation information that has some estimated estimates, not estimated estimates. Gaurav suggested, however. Saul and Sunil R. Gupta simulate a nervous system to predict future weather in a given region. The post-proliferation neural network is used for the introductory presentation. At the time, Hopfield networks are encouraged by the result produced by the BPN model. Features include temperature, humidity and wind speed. Climate information is collected over a three-year period, including 15,000 cases and smaller prediction errors and fast learning procedure. This can be considered a different option for the usual meteorological methodologies. Both accounts are combined in a viable way. You can determine an indirect relationship that exists between the features of the recorded information and forecast the weather in the future.

Another world used a little computing in the CART weather forecast. The information collected is in Hong Kong. The information is recorded somewhere around 2002 and 2005. The information used in preparing the dataset includes parameters for the year, month, and normal weight, and relative humidity, amount of fog, precipitation, and normal temperature. WEKA, open-source data mining software, is used to implement the CART validation tree account. The check tree, results, and actual data are used to produce the weather forecast model. The way in which information about previous events is preserved is marked. A change of information is required by calculating the choice tree taking into account the ultimate goal that WEKA will use productively for weather forecasting. A framework has been proposed that uses the recorded climate information and applies the "K-Neighbor Neighbor (KNN)" information extraction account to provide this chronic information within a specified time range(M. A. Nayak and S. Ghosh. (2013).

Then the nearest time intervals are taken to forecast the climate in Sri Lanka. Daily weather information is collected for a whole year. It produces accurate results within a reasonable period of time for a large period of time in advance. It is concluded that KNN is useful for element information and information that progresses or is revised quickly and provides better implementation compared to alternative methods. The combination of light fixing systems can give more accurate results. Also, climate tire agitation on a submatrix scale is discussed based on performance elements in the NWP model that uses unrealistic information extraction methods via a typical MOS system. The information mining system, aggregation, when connected to the uniqueness and relative confusion, can give an early indication of the development of a flood. The average K group is used to obtain two-day information on real rainfall. An effort is being made to provide auspicious and concrete data at these events, using information mining strategies as part of the appendix to the PNT Templates. A deficiency that could not be used for long-range forecasts was found (M. A. Nayak and S. Ghosh. (2013).

When using selection trees, the information stored in the past is used to forecast the most promising atmosphere. With all parameters, expectations can be improved and fulfilled. In addition, the starting point for forecasts will not be limited. Likewise, the self-categorization of the information-extraction procedure called the Enhanced Group Data Management Method (e-GMDH) was used to forecast and estimate the weather. E-GMDH works effectively when it contradicts and validates more established information-extraction procedures. The GUI that is not fully configured in the account must be updated to include the current functionality. He also used the aggregation strategy using K-Neighbor Neighbor technology to define the hidden example within the huge set of data specified with the weather to exchange recoverable data in usable learning to arrange and forecast the atmosphere. Temperature and roughness are obtained during a specific time period. High prediction accuracy for temperature and humidity is obtained. The product can be included with the Lumberjack information frame to search and forecast parameters in remote areas. The learning revolution, however, extracts information from a specific place. For this purpose, the frame should be versatile so that, if there is any weather modification, it can also be suitable. Adaptive information mining techniques are used, such as cleaning and information management. In addition, MLPN, ERNN, HFM, and RBFN accounts are examined by research to select valid mean, median, and standard deviation indicators. Application to improve the forecast of objective information, the weather can be successfully estimated. On the other hand, the relationship test was investigated, which was related to the expectation of seasons in a specific location. The relationship between precipitation in a specific location and elements that influence future precipitation. Wind Anxiety is the primary parameter used as part of this document. The connected system is accurate, but at the same time, it is still being tested upon contact for a more comprehensive regional composition (R. Venkata Ramana et.al, 2013).

Data extraction methods are used to obtain climatic information and to put hidden examples within the big data set in order to exchange recovered data in usable learning to rank and forecast the climate condition. The information extraction procedure is related to the focus of learning the climate data set for Gaza City. This learning can be used to gain helpful expectations and support the cheese-making process.

There is a need to manufacture dynamic information mining techniques, which could gradually learn to coordinate the path of rapidly changing climatic nature and surprising events. Meanwhile, information mining systems are being explored to anticipate extreme temperatures, rainfall, wind dissipation, and wind speed. Calculation C4.5 checks tree and neurotransmitter manufacturer systems are used for prediction. Weather information is collected somewhere around 2009 and 2018 from the city of Ibadan, Nigeria. A meteorological information form is produced and used for the preparation of workbook accounts. The execution of each calculation is inconsistent and standard and measurements of implementation are used with the best result for producing disposal rules for intermediate climate variables. Additionally, a model of the prophetic nervous system is produced to predict the weather and contradict the results and true climate information for the planned period. The results show that with sufficient information prepared, the information extraction procedure can be used effectively for weather forecasting and environmental change studies. Likewise, data mining techniques are implemented to control the way ships are in midway. GPS is used to identify the area as part of the vessel that it is currently exploring. Climate information characteristics include atmosphere, turbidity, temperature, and storm. Your sun's climate report and current database are contradictory. The dissection dataset is delivered to a check tree account, C4.5 and ID3. The choice obtained in relation to weather conditions is related to the ship and the route is chosen as necessary. Close cooperation between realistic groups and a Couple of constant credits should be modified as ID3 can't specifically manage the persistent reaches (D. Gupta and U. Ghose. (2015).

The use of information in prospecting strategies is examined to search for examples in specially assigned climatic conditions, for example, weather, the month of the year, wind path, speed, and seriousness using a single region information sheet. Chronic climate information is being used, somewhere around 2008 and 2012, from telemetry devices that were introduced as part of vineyards in northern New Zealand. It has been demonstrated that the use of methods to extract information and nearby climatic conditions recorded in intermittent intermediate situations can provide new education, in line with wind designs for decision-making for the management of vineyardsFrom the information store; specific events are eliminated with the Kumeu River Vineyard for a period of four years (2008-2012). The collected information is cleaned to erase all readings outside Kumeu's record readings. The most recent events 86,418 are displayed and move within 12 months. The choice tree accounts used are C5, Quest, CRT, and CHAID. SOM is used for the reason of aggregation. Multilayer ANN is used for wind storm forecasting. Systems for extracting information and measurable strategies are implemented using SPSS. It gives a decent device to analyze an ethos dataset. ARCWMC later, use the aggregation system with the K-Nearest Neighbor strategy to define the hidden example within the massive set of data specified with the weather in order to exchange the recovered data in usable information to provide and predict the atmospheric state. Temperature and humidity are obtained during a specific time period. High-precision forecasts of temperature and humidity are obtained. The product can be installed with the Lumberjack information frame to search and forecast parameters in remote areas. In addition, the investigator expected the Assam rain month by one month using the information extraction system. Conventional quantifiable method: uses multiple linear regressions. The information includes a six-year period somewhere in 2007 and 2012 that is collected locally from the Regional Meteorological Center, Guwahati, Assam, and India. The information is divided into four months for each season. The parameters chosen for the model are the lowest temperature, maximum temperature, average ocean level, weight, wind speed, and precipitation. The implementation of this model is measured in a balanced R square updated in C #. Some parameters such as wind resistance are excluded due to the necessity of collecting information that can give a more accurate result. The prediction model provides sufficient accuracy in light of the various direct setbacks (D. Gupta and U. Ghose. (2015).

When using the data extraction method, the researcher expected year-end precipitation using the characteristic temperature of the four climatic elements, turbidity, weight and ocean level, and along these lines, the group used data to calculate possible drought results in Rajasthan. Some variables are eliminated using information mining systems. At this point, the relationship test is bound to the data set and the connection is in the variables. Elements with positive relationships are selected and used in re-lapse research. MLR is used for a relapse test to forecast precipitation. At this point, measurable research links with that information to discover the extent of drought potential. For the standard deviation of the probability of droughts, parameter fluctuations, and dry station listings are used, and the dry stations are recognized. The occurrence of prominent parameters is taken into account when studying the dry season case, while other weather components can influence the situation in a wide range. Later it is not very accurate. In this expansion, Z. Jean et al. New, accurate and up-to-date new seasonal frameworks have grown to bury annual atmospheric projections using the information exploration strategy, K-Neighbor Neighbor (KNN). Use chronic numerical information to anticipate the atmosphere of a particular region, city or nation in advance. The data set consists of 10 years of unforgettable information with 17 types, i.e. average temperature, maximum temperature, minimum temperature, wind speed, maximum wind speed, minimum wind speed, dew point, sea level, depth Snowfall, Fog, Explosion, SST, SLP, etc., with 40,000 records for 10 urban communities use the dataset cleansing information to manage loud and lost traits. It is saved in MS-ACCESS design. At the same time, you can expect an enormous array of properties with an unnatural state of accuracy. The expected posterior effect of KNN is less demanding to achieve this. It cannot be combined to reflect global changes (ENSO occasions), but it can work effectively with regions that do not tend to have these global impacts but at the same time. Likewise, precipitation is expected in the hour in a timely manner from anywhere on the earth efficiently. Rain injection is determined initially. At this point, only if there is some kind of precipitation, then the precipitation is expected per hour. Although he has become familiar with a large number of planned methodologies for hourly forecasts, most of them have limitations on implementation due to the existence of a wide range of information and restrictive information procedures. Truck and C4.5 are used to produce results, which can give secret and vital examples with direct reasons. About 18 variants of the climate season were used. For approval reasons, the 10-fold double acceptance strategy is implemented. The truck offers marginally better implementation on C4.5. Given the possibilities, there are only a few events to predict, which makes it difficult to predict (R. Venkata Ramana et.al, 2013).

In the same way, another scientist S has contributed to the creation of a technology to predict precipitation on a local or nearby scale for a river basin of extensive climate information. The CART model, which takes into account how the average K is combined with the choice tree calculation, is used to squeeze precipitation states based on environmental variables of large scale in a vessel of waterways. Daily rainfall situation is obtained from multi-site precipitation information recorded day after day using the K-mean system. The group's various legal metrics relate to monitoring precipitation information to obtain the ideal number of groups. The truck is used to prepare long-term rainfall situation information from day to day. This technique has been tested for the Indian River in India. The expected change in the pot of the current is due to the change in the global temperature by examining the number of days that fall under the various precipitation cases in the observed period and the expected future. The truck's calculation ended with the excellent expectation of daily rainfall in a vessel of watercourses using a measurable scale (SubanaShanmuganathan and Philip Sallis. (2014).

The Support Vector Machine (SVM) is set up and calculation for aggregating and relapsing databases, for example, SVM can be used to learn polynomial compilations, spiral hypothesis (RBF) and multi-layer visualization (MLP) 7. Vapnik initially recommended SVM in the 1960s from the last century of settlement, and more recently, it has become a dangerous set of exploration that can be inferred from improvements in procedures and assumptions associated with expansions of relapse and thickness estimate. SVM emerged from a realistic learning premise; the point is to deal only with the issue of enthusiasm without treating a more problematic issue as a transitional step. SVM relies on the additional risk reduction standard, which has been firmly identified with the regulation hypothesis. This standard fuse limits control of the anticipated temperature rise, and, accordingly, is a fractional response to changing the willingness to change the dilemma (V. B. Nikam and B. B. Meshram. (2013).

Two main components in using SVM are numerical programming techniques and cutting work. Parameters are found when explaining the problem of quadratic programming with direct restrictions on equality and inequality, rather than highlighting the problem of non-curved and unrestricted rationalization. The adaptability of the capabilities of the parts allows the SVM to search for a wide range of theoretical spaces. Here we focus on SVM to characterize two classes, with categories P, N for $= +1, - 1$ I and separately. This can be accomplished without many extensions to the separation arrangement k by developing k classifiers for the two classes 9. The engineering translation of the reinforcement vector arrangement (SVC) is that the calculation is looking for the ideal isolation surface, i.e. the super plane that can be said to be equal from the two classes 10. It is distinguished. This ideal ultra-insulating plane has many excellent realistic properties 9. SVC is offered first for the direct removable condition. The Portion capabilities are familiar with the development of uneven surfaces. Finally, to get noisy information, when the complete separation of the two categories is not attractive, stagnation variables are known taking into account the error setting (Pinky Saikia Dutta et.al, 2014).

COMPARISON OF DATA MINING TECHNIQUES

According to the best work done by scientists in the editorial survey, there should be a possible correlation. Various information mining systems are used to predict different weather parameters, such as humidity, temperature, and wind. The various credits used in the link are applications, creators, information extraction systems, accounts, properties, time period, dataset size, accuracy rate, points of interest and inconveniences. They produce diverse results with their downsides and teachers. The main result of this is planned by theory without "lunch", which states that there is no better calculation for extracting information. This leads to the need to choose the appropriate learning account for a specific problem. In terms of climate forecasts, the selection of trees selected and average k ends with a more accurate prediction of different methods of extracting information. The relapse strategy could not detect an accurate forecast estimate. If so, an inaccurate estimate can be recovered. He also notes that as the size of the data set expands, the accuracy first increases, but then decreases after a certain degree. It could be one of the reasons for overly tuning the set of data. The work is done by many scientists and examined by the doodle in table 2.

COMPARISON OF DATA MINING TECHNIQUES FOR WEATHER PREDICTION

See Table 2.

Table 2.

SNO.	Applications	Techniques	Algorithms	Attributes	Time Period	Dataset Size	Accuracy	Advantages	Disadvantages
1	Climate forecast for boat navigation.	Decision tree	C4.5, ID3	Climate, moisture, storm, temperature	4-5 location	20- 30 Instances	-	Checked results	Do not deal with a continuous range of data directly
2	Climate forecast	Decision tree	C_A_R_T	Pressure, the volume of clouds, rain, precipitation, temperature	4 years	48 Instances	83%	Great predictability	Data transfer is required. An additional account is required
3	Hourly rainfall forecast	Decision tree	C4.5, C_A_R_T	Temperature, the direction of wind, speed, rain, moisture, pressure	3 years	26280 Instances	99% and 93%	High precision forecast	Small data is left to predict
4	Daily rainfall forecast in the river basin	Decision tree, Clustering	CART, k-Mean clustering	Temperature, MSLP, heat, wind, precipitation	50 years	432000 Instances	-	Clustering of multi-site rainfall data	Small data is left to predict. Verification not implemented
5	Climate forecast and Climate Change Studies	Decision tree, ANN	C4.5, C_A_R_T, T_L_F_N	Temperature, rainfall, wind speed, evaporation	10 years	36000 Instances	82%	The best network for prediction is chosen	Accuracy varies greatly with the size of a training data set
6	Wind gust forecast	Decision tree, ANN	C5.0, CRT, Q_U_E_S_T, CHAID, S_O_M	Dew point, humidity, wind direction, temperature, wind speed	4 years	86418 Instances	99%and 85%	Perfect for ad hoc data set review	Data recorded at irregular intervals. Do not handle continuous data
7	Climate forecast general	ANN	B_P_N, Hopfield networks	Temperature, wind speed, humidity	3 years	15000 Instances	-	The combination of both provides better predictability	Attribute normalization is required
8	Climate prediction in Sri Lanka	ANN	K_N_N	Temperature, moisture, rainfall, wind speed	1 year	365 Instances	-	Advantageous for complex results.	You need to integrate feature selection techniques
9	humidity and temperature forecast	Lazy learning, clustering	K_N_N, K- mean clustering	Temperature, moisture	-	-	100% approx	Appropriate for multimodal groups	You cannot predict data in remote areas
10	Interannual climate forecast	Lazy learning	K_N_N	Wind speed, point of dew, seal, depth of snow, rain	10 years	40000 Instances	96%	Precise long-term performance with a wide range of attributes	It cannot be combined to reflect global changes
11	Meteorological data analysis	Clustering	K-mean clustering	Temperature, moisture, storm, wind speed	4years	8660 Instances	-	Good accuracy of prediction	Dynamic data mining methods are required
12	Cloud burst forecast	Clustering	K-mean clustering	Temperature, moisture	2 days	100% clustering	Supplement with NWP models.	Not good for long-term forecasts	K Pabreja [16]
13	Rainfall forecast	Regression	M_L_R	Min and maximum temperature, direction of wind, humidity, precipitation	6 years	72 Instances	63%	Satisfactory accuracy.	The removal of the attribute is required to improve accuracy
14	Short-term Rainfall forecast	Regression	M_L_R	Min and maximum temperature, direction of wind, humidity, precipitation	3 months for 5 years	450 Instances	52%	Can even work with a small set of data	Instead of exactly, an approximate value is recovered
15	Deficiency forecast	Regression	M_L_R	Regeneration, sea level, rain, temperature	1 year	365 Instances	-	There is also correlation and statistical analysis.	Verification is not done

RESULTS AND DISCUSSION

n this chapter, the researcher attempted that the C5 account (updated in weak programming) is the new change of ID3 and C4.5 account that Quinlan has made over the last two decades in the results of the weka decision tree detailed below:

Weka Decision Tree Results

The C5 account (updated in poor programming) is the new ID3 and C4.5 account change that Quinlan has made over the past two decades. The norm used for syllables in Weka's account is based on ideas about information theory and has been improved after a while. The basic idea is to pick a variable that offers more data in order to understand the appropriateness of grouping the setup category in each branch. One of the points of interest for decision tree classifiers is that it can be concluded that it is extremely beneficial to manage generated trees and lets customers understand their data. Weka will generate three trees of selection and rules of selection based on alternative choices. Trees and guidelines were generated using 10-fold acceptance and findings were collected in a collection of test information with minimal error. Table 3 provides a list of the executions and the tree of selection obtained from Execution No. 6, with the smallest error.

Table 3. Summary of choice tree results

Run No	No of Trees Generated	Error
1	20	57.2 percent
2	18	49.9 percent
3	20	40.6 percent
4	17	40.6 percent
5	15	743.0 percent
6	16	32.2 percent
7	14	57.2 percent
8	20	40.6 percent
9	17	57.2 percent
10	16	49.0 percent
Average	17.3	49.7 percent
Standard Deviation	0.6	3.7 percent

The results of the selected Weka tree can also be presented in the easiest to understand and use the type of guidelines (Weka rules), and each principle includes the following:

1. The principle number that only serves to distinguish the standard
2. Visions (n, lift x) or (n / m, lift x) presses the standard implementation

3. n is the number of preparedness cases guaranteed by the principle and indicates the number of cases that are not appropriate for the category provided by the standard. Principle accuracy is evaluated by the Laplace Ratio (n-m + 1) / (n + 2). Height x is the result of separating the estimated precision from the beginning by the relative frequency of the expected category in the setting group

4. One or more conditions that must be fulfilled to be a relevant principle

5. The expected layer in principle

6. A quality somewhere around 0 and 1 that establishes the certainty with which this prediction is made, and

7. The default layer is used when applying any of the principles.

The Weka guidelines for the Weka era are shown in the set of test information that uses cross-acceptance 10 times in Table 4 and shows twelve Operating Criteria 7 that contain minimal errors running the number of established rules

Table 4. Summary of aftereffects of Weka rules generation

Run No	No of Rules Generated	Error
1	13	58.3percent
2	16	50.0 percent
3	14	41.7 percent
4	16	50.0 percent
5	16	33.3 percent
6	13	58.3 percent
7	16	25.0 percent
8	17	33.3 percent
9	15	33.3 percent
10	20	41.7 percent
Average	15.6	42.5 percent
Standard Deviation	0.7	3.6 percent

Rule 1: indicates that the rotational speed during the 2015-2019 periods is more pronounced than 2.94 km / h, while the temperature ranges between 5.72 ° C and 19.36 ° C in February.

Rule 2: It proposes that the rotational speed during the 2015-2019 periods be between 3.28 km / h and 150.66 km / h, while the temperature ranges between 8.1 ° C and 19.1 ° C in March.

Rule 3: It is concluded that the rotational speed during the 2015-2019 period is more pronounced than 3.63 km/hour, the temperature ranges between 16.6 ° C and 27.22 ° C, and the precipitation is more pronounced from 33.1 mm in April.

Rule 4: It is concluded that the speed of rotation in the period 2015-2019 decreases between 37.98 km / h and 141.98 km / h, the temperature is clearer than 20.96 ° C and precipitation is clearer than 37.98 mm in May.

Rule 5: indicates that the rotational speed during the 2015-2019 periods is clearer than 37.22 km / h and the temperature ranges from 22.72 ° C to 37.22 ° C in June.

Rule 6: It is concluded that the rotational speed during the 2015-2019 period is more pronounced than 36.08 km / h, and solar radiation is more pronounced than 24.89 maximum temperatures at around 36.08 ° C in July.

Rule 7: indicates that the radiation during the 2015-2019 periods is around 19.87 and the maximum temperature is around 35.3 ° C in August.

Rule 8: indicates that the rotational speed during the 2015-2019 periods is more pronounced than 35.94 km / h and the temperature ranges from 27.89 ° C to 35.94 ° C in September.

Rule 9: The rotational speed during the period 2015-2019 is also conducting around 34.97 km / h, and the temperature ranges between 19.15 ° C and 34.97 ° C in October.

Rule 10: indicates that the rotational speed in the 2015-2019 periods is about 17.08 km / h and the temperature ranges between 10.1 ° C to 17.08 ° C in November.

Rule 11: indicates that the rotational speed during the 2015-2019 periods is about 12.16 km / h, the maximum temperature is more clear than 4.2 ° C and precipitation are about 12.16 mm in December.

It can be observed that the highest temperature during the study period between February and April is around 27 ° C and the lowest temperatures are 19.15 ° C in June and September. The wind speed is highest for more than 37.98 km / h in May. The minimum recorded precipitation is approximately 5.9 mm for September, and more pronounced than 34 mm in July.

For nervous system builders, different parameters were used to prepare the system, for example, the portions of the memory used, the number of processing components in the wrapped layer, etc., and the system that gave the best result was changed. These systems can show the problem, although the measurement of the information used has affected its accuracy.

CONCLUSION

In this work, a calculation of the arrangement of trees with a weak choice was used to produce selection trees and criteria for requesting climate parameters, for example, maximum temperature, lowest temperature, precipitation, dissipation and wind speed for month and year. The information used in Pakistan was obtained from the weather station somewhere around 2013 and 2015. The results indicate how these parameters affect the weather seen in these months during the study period. Looking at the information that followed the model over time, changes in climate examples were highlighted. SVM can identify connections between information variables and return generation in light of the observed designs inherent in the information without programming or creating complex comparisons to demonstrate these connections. Thus, adequately provided SVM information can identify the links between climatic parameters and use them to forecast future weather conditions. The results obtained were evaluated with a set of test information provided together with the preparation information and found to be sufficient given a small amount of information that can be accessed for preparation and testing. To obtain an excellent result, a wide range of information will be required that will include information gathered over many decades. In future explorations, thin nerve models will be used in the weather forecasting process. This work is necessary for climate change, taking into account the fact that a variety of weather conditions in terms of temperature, precipitation and wind rhythm can focus on using these information extraction strategies. This chapter presents a regression application for support vectors for predicting atmospheric temperature. SVM performance was compared to the DT decision tree for different orders. It was also noted that the choice of parameters in the case of SVM has a significant impact on model output Can be related by setting parameters correctly, Support Vector Machines can replace certain weather forecasting applications based on neural network models.

REFERENCES

Ahmad, M., Aftab, S., Ali, I., & Hameed, N. (2017). Hybrid Tools and Techniques for Sentiment Analysis. *RE:view*, *8*(3).

Ahmad, M., Aftab, S., Bashir, M. S., & Hameed, N. (2018). Sentiment Analysis using SVM : A Systematic Literature Review. IEEE.

Ahmad, Aftab, & Muhammad. (2017). Machine Learning Techniques for Sentiment Analysis: A Review. *Int. J. Multidiscip. Sci. Eng.*

Bagirov, A. M., Mahmood, A., & Barton, A. (2017).Prediction of monthly rainfall in Victoria, Australia: Clusterwise linear regression approach. Atmos. Res.

Chauhan, D., & Thakur, J. (2014). *Data Mining Techniques for Weather Prediction: A Review. International Journal on Recent and Innovation Trends in Computing and Communication.*

Dutta & Tahbilder. (2014). Prediction Of Rainfall Using Data mining Technique over Assam. *Indian Journal of Computer Science and Engineering (IJCSE).*

Gupta, D., & Ghose, U. (2015). A Comparative Study of Classification Algorithms for Risk Prediction in Pregnancy. Academic Press.

Kumar, S. R. (2017). Extensive evaluation of seven machine learning methods for rainfall prediction in weather derivatives. *Expert Systems with Applications.*

Mishra, Soni, Sharma, & Upadhyay. (2018). Development and Analysis of Artificial Neural Network Models for Rainfall Predictionby Using Time- Series Data. *Int. J. Intell. Syst. Applied.*

Mishra, N., Soni, H. K., Sharma, S., & Upadhyay, A. K. (2018). *Development and Analysis of Artificial Neural Network Models for Rainfall Prediction by Using Time-Series Data. Int. J. Intell. Syst. Appl.*, *10*(1), 16–23.

Nayak, M. A., & Ghosh, S. (2013).Prediction of extreme rainfall event using weather pattern recognition and support vector machine classifier. Theor. Appl. Climatol.

Nikam, V. B., & Meshram, B. B. (2013). Modeling Rainfall Prediction Using Data Mining Method: A Bayesian Approach. *2013 Fifth Int. Conf. Comput. Intell. Model. Simulation.* 10.1109/CIMSim.2013.29

Ramana, Krishna, Kumar, & Pandey. (2013). Monthly Rainfall Prediction Using Wavelet Neural Network Analysis. *Water Resources Management.*

Shanmuganathan & Sallis. (2014). *Data Mining Methods to Generate Severe Wind Gust Models*. Academic Press.

Vathsala, H., & Koolagudi, S. G. (2017). *Prediction model for peninsular Indian summer monsoon rainfall using data mining and statistical approaches. Comput. Geoscience.*

Wu, J., Long, J., & Liu, M. (2015). *Evolving RBF neural networks for rainfall prediction using hybrid particle swarm optimization and genetic algorithm. Neurocomputing.*

Zainudin, S., Jasim, D. S., & Baker, A. A. (2016). *Comparative Analysis of Data Mining Techniques for Malaysian Rainfall Prediction. Int. J. Adv. Sci. Eng. Inf. Technology, 6*(6), 1148–1153.

Chapter 17
A Survey on Algorithms in Deep Learning

Sindhu P. Menon

Jain College of Engineering and Technology, India

ABSTRACT

In the last couple of years, artificial neural networks have gained considerable momentum. Their results could be enhanced if the number of layers could be made deeper. Of late, a lot of data has been generated, which has led to big data. This comes along with many challenges like quality, which is one of the most important ones. Deep learning models can improve the quality of data. In this chapter, an attempt has been made to review deep supervised and deep unsupervised learning algorithms and the various activation functions used. Challenges in deep learning have also been discussed.

INTRODUCTION

A typical neural network will have a number of neurons interconnected in all possible ways just like how the neurons in our brain our connected. At any point of time, all neurons need not be active. The hidden layers which are present in-between the input and output layer play a very important role, as this number goes high, they are termed as Deep Neural Networks(DNN). The main advantage of DNN when compared with an artificial neural network is that in DNNs features are identified automatically. More the number of hidden layers, more number of features get identified. This results in better prediction accuracy. The number of neurons in the input layer depends on the number of features. For instance, Suppose we want to train the system to identify the image in Fig 1. This can be assumed to be a matrix of size 35*35 pixels. Hence the total number of pixels are 1225. The number of neurons, in the input layer will be 1225 as this is the number of features identified.

Algorithms for training such networks can be classified as Supervised and Unsupervised. In the next section an overview of these algorithms will be given.

The article contains the Introduction in Section 1, followed by Literature Survey in Section 2. A survey into deep learning models is discussed in Section 3 followed by the challenges in training them in Section 4. Finally, the article concludes in Section 5.

DOI: 10.4018/978-1-7998-2803-7.ch017

Figure 1. Image for Training
(Courtesy: Google)

LITERATURE SURVEY

A lot of surveys have been done on various areas like health, object detection, medical image analysis, cancer detection, agriculture, sentiment analysis and many more. Almost 300 papers were published only in medical imaging in 2016. The need for deep nets came from the fact that features had to be learnt efficiently. CNN was the first network introduced in this direction. Since early seventies, a lot of work on CNN has been done((Fukushima, 1980) and the same was developed on analysing medical image in 1995(Lo et al. (1995). Using this concept, they achieved success in LeNet, their first real world application to recognise hand written digits (LeCun et al., 1998). The number of layers in LeNet and AlexNet(t (Krizhevsky et al., 2012) hadtwo and five layers with a design such that larger layers were closer to input and smaller layers were closer to output. The activation function used in AlexNet was RLU. But it didn't gain enough momentum despite its success. The belief earlier was that it is very difficult to train deep nets. Momentum was gained in 2006 when it was shown by (Bengio et al., 2007; Hinton and Salakhutdinov, 2006; Hinton et al., 2006) that if it was trained layerwise, by stacking networks, the performance could be improved. More complex layers were stacked to improve the efficiency of these models. AN Inception model which has 22 layers (Szegedy et al. (2014) was introduced with varying size convolutions. This was also names as GoogLeNet.

A number of surveys exist in the field of agriculture (Deng & Yu, 2014), (Wan, et al., 2014), (Najafabadi, et al., 4 2015). To handle the issues related to agriculture, smart techniques for farming are needed(Tyagi, 2016). A survey on the agricultural practices and how to use them were discussed((Kamilaris, Gao, Prenafeta-Boldú, & Ali, 2016)

Similarly in the area of computer vision, we have object detection. Since many decades, a lot of research work is going on in this area(Fischler and Elschlager 1973). The basic idea in this is to identify and object and to return its position when encountered (Everingham et al. 2010; Russakovsky et al. 2015). In detecting objects, we have two types, the first is to detect instances and the other is to identify categories (Grauman and Leibe 2011; Zhang et al. 2013). A number of data sets exist for identifying objects. Few of them are MS COCO (Lin et al. 2014), ImageNet (Deng et al. 2009), PASCAL VOC (Everingham et al. 2010, 2015) and Open Images (Kuznetsova et al. 2018). In spite of such exhaustive work being done in the last couple of years, designing an efficient model is still an area which is unresolved.

DEEP LEARNING MODELS

Deep Networks can be classified as Supervised or Unsupervised. In Supervised Learning, we know well in advance the class to which each entity in the data set belongs to and on the basis of that we can classify them. In Unsupervised Learning, the output class is not known in advance. Only on the basis of certain features we classify them.

Auto Encoders

A basic type of Artificial Neural Network which belongs to the class of Unsupervised Learning algorithms is the Auto Encoder. This has two phases in it, the first being the encoding phase and the second being the decoding phase as shown in Fig 2.

Figure 2.

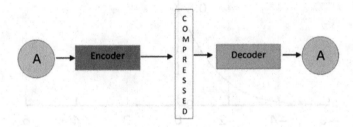

The encoder is a function which will take as input the set of features identified . For instance, if $a^1, a^2 \ldots \ldots a^n$ are the set of features identified wherein if we consider the example of Fig 1, 'n' is 1225. This can be written as

$$h^{(n)} = f \, \Theta(a^n) \tag{1}$$

where $h^{(n)}$ is the compressed representation of the feature vector. This is in turn fed to the decoder which will convert the features back to the corresponding input. The decoder is given by the function

$$x = g \, \Theta(h) \tag{2}$$

Once this output is obtained, the error is calculated using the Loss Function. The objective is to obtain the minimum reconstruction error. The parameters given as input to such a model are { W,E,W',D} where W and W' are the weight matrices and E and D are the encoder and decoder respectively.

A variation of this is the Stacked Auto Encoder wherein a number of autoencoders are Stacked on top of one another. Normally, the encoders and decoders produce output which is non-linear. To convert it to a linear format we use one of the activation functions. The various commonly used activation functions are Sigmoid Function, Tanh Function, Relu (Rectified Linear Unit) Function, Leaky Relu, Elu and Maxout. The most commonly used one at present is Leaky Relu. Sigmoid and tanh kills the gradient to zero. Hence Relu was introduced.

Sigmoid Function

Sigmoid Function is a squashing function which is used to squash the output between 0 and 1. When we have a data set which contains two classes, like 0 and 1, then we apply Sigmoid Function to predict the probability of the class. A typical Sigmoid Function appears as shown in Fig 3

Figure 3. Sigmoid Function

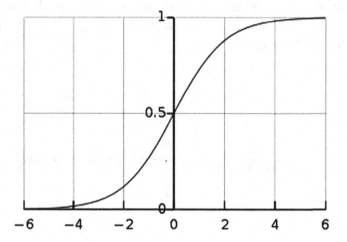

It is applied to every node in the neural network and computed using the equation

$$f(x) = \frac{1}{1 + e^{-x}}$$

(3)

where x is the output of the neuron.

Tanh Function

This is similar to the Sigmoid Function but the difference is the range of values is between -1 and 1. Fig 4 shows a tanh function

The function is given as

$$\tanh(x) = \frac{\sin(x)}{\cos(x)} = \frac{e^x - e^{-x}}{e^x + e^{-x}}$$

(4)

Figure 4. Tanh Activation Function
(Courtesy:Google)

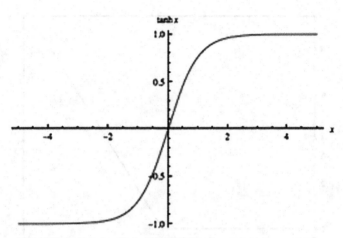

In Sigmoid and Tanh, when error is propagated back, it is done in drastic steps. At times, this results in losing the optimal error giving rise to the gradient descent problem

Rectified Linear Unit (ReLU)

This is the most widely used activation function since the former two namely sigmoid and tanh reduces the gradient to zero, i.e. the vanishing gradient problem. ReLU overcomes this problem. This function returns zero on inputting a negative value and the same value back if its positive as in Fig 5. It is represented as

$$a(i)= maximum(0,i) \tag{5}$$

This function allows complex relationships in data to be learnt. It can be represented using a simple if-else as

```
if(i>0):
        return i
else:
        return 0
```

Leaky ReLU

The difference between ReLU and Leaky ReLU is that in ReLU at times due to negative bias, the function becomes zero and once it falls, it can never recover from that whereas Leaky ReLU, always has some gradient left in it, hence it recovers from this problem. Hence training also becomes fast.

The function is given as

Figure 5. Rectilinear Activation Function
(Courtesy:Google)

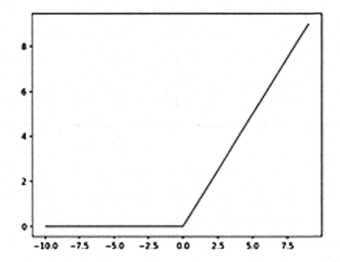

$$g(x) \begin{aligned} &= \alpha * j \quad if\ j < 0 \\ &= j \qquad if\ j >= 0 \end{aligned}$$

(6)

where α is a constant value.

Fig 6 shows the slope of Leaky ReLU.

Figure 6. Leaky ReLU
(Courtesy:Google)

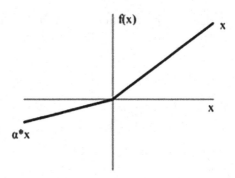

MaxOut: MaxOut is another activation function which is used to compute the maximum of the inputs. The output function for MaxOut neuron is the product of weights and inputs in matrix form. Fig 7 shows a MaxOut Activation function when n=2.

$$g(x) = max(w_1x_1, w_2x_2 \ldots \ldots w_nx_n)$$

(7)

Figure 7. MaxOut Activation Function
(Courtesy: Google)

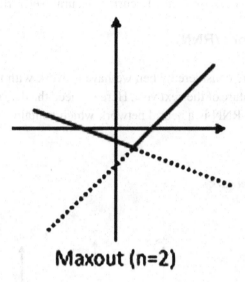

Maxout (n=2)

Convolution Neural Network[20]

Another widely used algorithm in deep learning is Convolution Neural Networks .It is basically used to work with large image set. LeNet style models were the basis for the origin of Convolution Neural Networks as discussed by LeCun Y et al.(1995).These models were layers of convolution networks. In pure mathematics, Convolution is when a new function transforms as the output of integration of two other functions where we can show how the shape of one function is altered by the other. There are three processes to be performed in any convolution operation (1) Read the input image (2) Obtain the feature detector (3) Input the feature map. The input image could a 3*3 matrix which contains of 1s and 0s. In order to learn features well, convolution operations were performed many times. Another architecture called Inception architecture also came into picture at the same time by Szegedy C et al.(2015) Several versions of Inception architecture came into existence. Initially it was Inception V1, later Inception V2 by C. Szegedy et al. (2016), Inception V3 by Szegedy C et al.(2016) and most recently Inception-ResNet by Szegedy C et al. (2017). These models were just like convolutions but they could learn quicker using lesser features.

The convolution layer takes the image as input, converts it into a sequential vector of the form $a= \{a1, a2.....aN\}$. The convolution layer is defined as

$$x_i = f(\mathring{a}_i \, K_{ij} \, \Theta \, a_i + b_j) \tag{3}$$

where x_i denoted the yth output of the layer, Θ represents the convolution operator and b_j denotes the bias. This network includes many convolution layers stacked upon one another and a sub sampling layer which will move the feature detector to the right one cell at a time. N. Kalchbrenner et al. (2014), H. Shi et al. (2016), O. Abdel-Hamid et al. (2012), Y. Qian et al. (2016), O. Abdel-Hamid et al. (2012) and P. Swietojanski et al. (2014) in their work have said that these networks are also highly used in Speech

Processing and Natural Language Processing. The disadvantage with these networks is that they do not consider time into account. To overcome this, Recurrent Neural Networks were introduced.

Recurrent Neural Network (RNN)

Recurrent Neural Networks are considered when we have to work with time series data. For instance, consider prediction of temperature of the next year. Here we need the data of previous years as illustrated by Menon SP et al. (2017). A RNN is a neural network which contains output, along with hidden and input layer.

Figure 8. Recurrent Neural Network

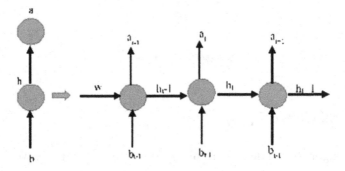

In Fig 8, $\{a_0, a_1 \ldots a_n\}$ indicates the output units, $\{h_1, h_2 \ldots h_n\}$ indicates the hidden layers and $\{b_0, b_1 \ldots b_n\}$ represents the input units. At time t, the network considers the current instance h_t and its previous h_{t-1} to predict the next value.

CHALLENGES IN TRAINING DEEP NETWORKS

We can witness more non linearity in the architectures when the abstraction increases. Some models which are actually very close to one another can be viewed differently because of the changes in their meaning. The features could appear complex because of the mapping from input to features. The relations between the mappings could be simple, linear or may be dependent on one another. Our belief would be to have a system which has easier concepts. This could be at the cost of a more complex training, which could involve the local minima too.

Initially, D. Erhan et al. (2010) had proposed that layer wise unsupervised training is better than supervised training . This was explained in the work of Bengio Y et al. (2009) wherein they have said that learning simpler concepts is much easier, then like a pyramid, where difficult concepts represent the base and the complex ones are built on top of it. But in some cases the top two layers of any neural network could over fit the training data. Then when the features are transferred from one level to the other level, the values could be very small. Bengio Y et al. (1994) said that this could result in gradients getting vanished which was the problem in Recurrent Neural Networks.

Lot of research by D.C. Ciresan et al. (2010), Glorot X et al. (2011), Krizhevsky A et al. (2012) and F. Seidearea et al. (2011) has led to the finding that lot of labelled data could be trained in a supervised manner effectively without any pretraining Related work has shown that in such cases supervised training excels over unsupervised training as the latter brought about no or little positive change.

CONCLUSION

The large volumes of data available today has led researchers to utilize them effectively which could result in results with greater accuracy. This has resulted in the birth of deep learning. Deep learning is used in many areas like Image Processing, Natural Language Processing and so on. In addition to this, due to the availability of high performing devices, training on such large data has becoming simple. Hence, many models are developed of late for deep learning. An insight into some of the models has been mentioned in this paper. Although data is available in abundance, its quality needs to be maintained. Hence the need of the hour is to explore more deep learning models.

REFERENCES

Abdel-Hamid, O., Mohamed, A. R., Jiang, H., Deng, L., Penn, G., & Yu, D. (2014). Convolutional neural networks for speech recognition. *IEEE/ACM Transactions on Audio, Speech, and Language Processing*, *22*(10), 1533–1545. doi:10.1109/TASLP.2014.2339736

Abdel-Hamid, O., Mohamed, A. R., Jiang, H., & Penn, G. (2012, March). Applying convolutional neural networks concepts to hybrid NN-HMM model for speech recognition. In *2012 IEEE international conference on Acoustics, speech and signal processing (ICASSP)* (pp. 4277-4280). IEEE.

Bengio, Y., Lamblin, P., Popovici, D., & Larochelle, H. (2007). Greedy layer-wise training of deep networks. Advances in Neural Information Processing Systems, 153–160.

Bengio, Y., Louradour, J., Collobert, R., & Weston, J. (2009, June). Curriculum learning. In *Proceedings of the 26th annual international conference on machine learning* (pp. 41-48). Academic Press.

Bengio, Y., Simard, P., & Frasconi, P. (1994). Learning long-term dependencies with gradient descent is difficult. *IEEE Transactions on Neural Networks*, *5*(2), 157–166. doi:10.1109/72.279181 PMID:18267787

Cireşan, D. C., Meier, U., Gambardella, L. M., & Schmidhuber, J. (2010). Deep, big, simple neural nets for handwritten digit recognition. *Neural Computation*, *22*(12), 3207–3220. doi:10.1162/NECO_a_00052 PMID:20858131

K. Deng, Z. Yu, S. Patnaik, & J. Wang (Eds.). (2018). Recent Developments in Mechatronics and Intelligent Robotics. In *Proceedings of International Conference on Mechatronics and Intelligent Robotics (ICMIR2018)* (Vol. 856). Springer.

Deng, L., & Yu, D. (2014). Deep learning: Methods and applications. *Foundations and Trends in Signal Processing*, *7*(3-4), 197–387. doi:10.1561/2000000039

Erhan, D., Bengio, Y., Courville, A., Manzagol, P. A., Vincent, P., & Bengio, S. (2010). Why does unsupervised pre-training help deep learning? *Journal of Machine Learning Research, 11*(Feb), 625–660.

Everingham, M., Eslami, S., Gool, L. V., Williams, C., Winn, J., & Zisserman, A. (2015). The pascal visual object classes challenge: A retrospective. *IJCV, 111*(1), 98–136. doi:10.100711263-014-0733-5

Everingham, M., Gool, L. V., Williams, C., Winn, J., & Zisserman, A. (2010). The pascal visual object classes (voc) challenge. *IJCV, 88*(2), 303–338. doi:10.100711263-009-0275-4

Fischler, M., & Elschlager, R. (1973). The representation and matching of pictorial structures. *IEEE Transactions on Computers, 100*(1), 67–92. doi:10.1109/T-C.1973.223602

Fukushima, K. (1980). Neocognitron: A self-organizing neural network model for a mechanism of pattern recognition unaffected by shift in position. *Biological Cybernetics, 36*(4), 193–202. doi:10.1007/BF00344251 PMID:7370364

Glorot, X., Bordes, A., & Bengio, Y. (2011, June). Deep sparse rectifier neural networks. In *Proceedings of the fourteenth international conference on artificial intelligence and statistics* (pp. 315-323). Academic Press.

Grauman, K., & Leibe, B. (2011). Visual object recognition. *Synthesis Lectures on Artificial Intelligence and Machine Learning, 5*(2), 1–181. doi:10.2200/S00332ED1V01Y201103AIM011

Hinton, G. E., Osindero, S., & Teh, Y.-W. (2006). A fast learning algorithm for deep belief nets. *Neural Computation, 18*(7), 1527–1554. doi:10.1162/neco.2006.18.7.1527 PMID:16764513

Hinton, G. E., & Salakhutdinov, R. R. (2006). Reducing the dimensionality of data with neural networks. *Science, 313*(5786), 504–507. doi:10.1126cience.1127647 PMID:16873662

Ioffe, S., & Szegedy, C. (2015). *Batch normalization: Accelerating deep network training by reducing internal covariate shift.* arXiv preprint arXiv:1502.03167

Kalchbrenner, N., Grefenstette, E., & Blunsom, P. (2014). *A convolutional neural network for modelling sentences.* arXiv preprint arXiv:1404.2188

Kamilaris, A., Gao, F., Prenafeta-Boldú, F. X., & Ali, M. I. (2016). Agri-IoT: A semantic framework for Internet of Things-enabled smart farming applications. In *3rd World Forum on Internet of Things (WF-IoT)* (pp. 442-447). Reston, VA: IEEE.

Krizhevsky, A., Sutskever, I., & Hinton, G. E. (2012). Imagenet classification with deep convolutional neural networks. In Advances in neural information processing systems (pp. 1097-1105). Academic Press.

Kuznetsova, A., Rom, H., Alldrin, N., Uijlings, J., Krasin, I., Pont-Tuset, J., . . . Ferrari, V. (2018). *The open images dataset v4: Unified image classification, object detection, and visual relationship detection at scale.* arXiv preprint arXiv:1811.00982

LeCun, Y., Bottou, L., Bengio, Y., & Haffner, P. (1998). Gradient-based learning applied to document recognition. *Proceedings of the IEEE, 86*(11), 2278–2324. doi:10.1109/5.726791

LeCun, Y., Jackel, L. D., Bottou, L., Cortes, C., Denker, J. S., Drucker, H., ... Vapnik, V. (1995). Learning algorithms for classification: A comparison on handwritten digit recognition. *Neural networks: the statistical mechanics perspective, 261,* 276.

Lin, T., Maire, M., Belongie, S., Hays, J., Perona, P., Ramanan, D., . . . Zitnick, L. (2014). Microsoft COCO: Common objects in context. In ECCV (pp. 740–755). Academic Press.

Lo, S.-C., Lou, S.-L., Lin, J.-S., Freedman, M. T., Chien, M. V., & Mun, S. K. (1995). Artificial convolution neural network techniques and applications for lung nodule detection. *IEEE Transactions on Medical Imaging, 14*(4), 711–718. doi:10.1109/42.476112 PMID:18215875

Menon, S. P., Bharadwaj, R., Shetty, P., Sanu, P., & Nagendra, S. (2017, December). Prediction of temperature using linear regression. In *2017 International Conference on Electrical, Electronics, Communication, Computer, and Optimization Techniques (ICEECCOT)* (pp. 1-6). IEEE.

Najafabadi, M. M., Villanustre, F., Khoshgoftaar, T. M., Seliya, N., Wald, R., & Muharemagic, E. (2015). Deep learning applications and challenges in big data analytics. *Journal of Big Data, 2*(1), 1. doi:10.118640537-014-0007-7

Qian, Y., Bi, M., Tan, T., & Yu, K. (2016). Very deep convolutional neural networks for noise robust speech recognition. *IEEE/ACM Transactions on Audio, Speech, and Language Processing, 24*(12), 2263–2276. doi:10.1109/TASLP.2016.2602884

Russakovsky, O., Deng, J., Su, H., Krause, J., Satheesh, S., Ma, S., ... Berg, A. C. (2015). Imagenet large scale visual recognition challenge. *International Journal of Computer Vision, 115*(3), 211–252. doi:10.100711263-015-0816-y

Seide, F., Li, G., & Yu, D. (2011). Conversational speech transcription using context-dependent deep neural networks. *Twelfth annual conference of the international speech communication association.*

Shi, H., Ushio, T., Endo, M., Yamagami, K., & Horii, N. (2016, December). A multichannel convolutional neural network for cross-language dialog state tracking. In *2016 IEEE Spoken Language Technology Workshop (SLT)* (pp. 559-564). IEEE. 10.1109/SLT.2016.7846318

Swietojanski, P., Ghoshal, A., & Renals, S. (2014). Convolutional neural networks for distant speech recognition. *IEEE Signal Processing Letters, 21*(9), 1120–1124. doi:10.1109/LSP.2014.2325781

Szegedy, C., Ioffe, S., Vanhoucke, V., & Alemi, A. A. (2017, February). Inception-v4, inception-resnet and the impact of residual connections on learning. *Thirty-first AAAI conference on artificial intelligence.*

Szegedy, C., Liu, W., Jia, Y., Sermanet, P., Reed, S., Anguelov, D., . . . Rabinovich, A. (2014). *Going deeper with convolutions.* arXiv:1409.4842

Szegedy, C., Vanhoucke, V., Ioffe, S., Shlens, J., & Wojna, Z. (2016). Rethinking the inception architecture for computer vision. In *Proceedings of the IEEE conference on computer vision and pattern recognition* (pp. 2818-2826). 10.1109/CVPR.2016.308

Tyagi, A. C. (2016). Towards a Second Green Revolution. *Irrigation and Drainage, 65*(4), 388–389. doi:10.1002/ird.2076

Wan, J., Wang, D., Hoi, S. C., Wu, P., Zhu, J., Zhang, Y., & Li, J. (2014). Deep learning for content-based image retrieval: A comprehensive study. In *Proceedings of the 22nd ACM international conference on Multimedia*. ACM.

Zhang, X., Yang, Y., Han, Z., Wang, H., & Gao, C. (2013). Object class detection: A survey. *ACM Computing Surveys, 46*(1), 10:1–10:53.

Chapter 18
Analyzing the Performance and Efficiency of IT-Compliant Audit Module Using Clustering Methods

Soobia Saeed

Department of Software Engineering, Universiti Teknologi Malaysia, Malaysia

N. Z. Jhanjhi

(iD) https://orcid.org/0000-0001-8116-4733

Taylor's University, Malaysia

Mehmood Naqvi

Faculty of Electrical and Computer Engineering Technology, Mohawk College of Applied Arts and Technology, Canada

Mamoona Humayun

College of Computer and Information Sciences, Jouf University, Saudi Arabia

Vasaki Ponnusamy

Universiti Tunku Abdul Rahman, Malaysia

ABSTRACT

Human beings have a knack for errors. Counter-effective actions rendered to specify and rectify such errors in a minimum period of time are required when effectiveness and swift advancement depends on the capability of acknowledging the faults and errors and repair quickly. The software as audit module application in IT complaint is in review in this commentary as is another significant instrument created in the field of data analysis that digs deep into quickly and successfully assessing the imprecisions or grievances identified by the users in a certain company. The target of this study is to evaluate the statistical significance in relationship between client reporting attitude and client reliability and to evaluate the impact of strong responsiveness on client reliability, to measure the statistically noteworthy effect of client grievance conduct on service quality, and to test the impact of service quality on client dedication.

DOI: 10.4018/978-1-7998-2803-7.ch018

INTRODUCTION

In a world where information technology is superseding all the other necessities of modern living by virtue of computers and other computing devices, personal information transferring tools like tablet PCs, mobile phones and others of the like, every diverse organization is inclined to acquiring the technological equipment that helps ease work in the most efficient way. Since the question of faults and errors remain unanswered due to human nature, unforeseen circumstances as well as natural occurrences, it is deemed most important to have a contingency plan to back up against such errors when reported and come up with a solution to the problems faced. Such complaint-handling programs are essentially required which could tackle such happenings against timely feedback. Such feedbacks and actions taken against them are the need of the managing body of any given organization from the private or public sector so as to review and assess important inputs given by the clients and take timely actions against any said error or unsatisfactory event. The prompt addressing of the issues and specific reporting of errors or malfunctioning aids workplaces accelerate their outcomes by reducing time consumption in error removing and efficiently assuaging mishaps and inadvertent failures and enhancing skills of personnel in their mundane activity. The difficulty is a sign of displeasure corresponded to an operational organization acknowledged with its substance, or the declarations handling of procedure in its own, where censure is promptly and thoroughly expected. A skillful complaint organizing structure has three major benefits for an office, it is helpful for an individual to report his concerns and get them resolved in an efficient and time-saving manner that his discontent is relieved to his utmost satisfaction and there is no commercial effect to the management. Valuable feedback and complaints are conveyed to the management for better developing their administrative short-comings. Where peevish matters looked after proficiently, an impressive structure can prosper the dishonor of an organization and amplify self-reliance and auto-reconciliation in the organization's managerial processes(K. Coussement and D. Van den Poel. (2015).

Statement of the Problem

The user wants a user-friendly complaint resolution process, Suitable consideration and appreciation, Due honoring and acknowledgment, An authentic analysis and conclusion, An apologetic confession, Prompt and efficient reply back in the least possible time. What a workplace demands necessarily, A convenient platform where complaints/comments could be received, Simplified solutions for the personnel to tackle any query raised, Platform's capacity to document each grievances for future references, To make the most of the complaints to avoid future occurrences and create smooth operations, To enhance administrative body's capability in addressing limitations/strengths of a certain department. This research in view is prepared with the idea of looking into the major areas of services against which a typical complaint is launched when the provision of services are not at par with the demands. Additionally, its objective is to investigate how effectively preventative measures could be taken to keep arousal of complaints from taking place, and if they occur, how positively to cope with those. We will do it by the Clustering Method, which is a type of grouping and data analysis. This will particularly be a study of assessments by customers and administrative reactions on the Complaint Audit Module. Through this, we can investigate both the review and its resolution. Hence, this refers to the major study target of these papers, which goes like: "What are the essential weaknesses that raise a client to get displeased and what is / should be the management's reaction to it?"(V. Bosch and F. Enriquez. (2015).

Background of the Research

The foundation of research relies on its governing principle i.e. tackling of grievances effectively and satisfying the consumer/complainer. In a workplace, it is beyond control to avoid inconvenient occurrences to take place. The job, and more importantly, the idea is to come up with a guideline which helps accommodate all concerned to get back from the setback faced due to conventional human error and remove those errors in such a way that any mishaps, after they are treated properly, cause no harm to the workplace's mundane activities. Problems/errors/complaints, are bound to happen; but learning from them and making all possible efforts in containing them is the key to a flouring work-environment. It is openly acknowledged that rigid bonds between consumer complaints and quick resolution to those problems create more satisfied users since it shows them they are given proper services by the organization they come into doing business with. It helps them make their mind about future interactions and continuing their business ventures time and again. And what does an organization look forward to? To gain customer's trust! That's their primary goal. Additionally, a satisfied user is a source of advertisement and can easily increase the clientele through his satisfied self. A happy customer gives good vibes to those who have not had a chance to doing business with the company in the review. Why would a satisfied customer want to try something new when all he can get, according to his requirements, from the same initial place he started doing business with. He knows that if for any reason he has some complaints, the company will resolve them in a jiffy as if those complaints never occurred in the first place. Hence, for any given business-place, work-place or organization, he is deemed essential to have a strong and responsive line-of-action prepared to give their consumers the help they need when they need it. The management of any organization must have this realized beforehand that clients who take the time to write a complaint to the organization are few out of millions of others who think it is their right to get reasonable anticipation from the company they are doing business with. A consumer can register their complaints via any method such as writing to the company through mail, giving a call on the complaint registration number via telephone or mobile phone or even sending an email. But out of all the above-stated methods, the one construed the most reliable for them will surely be an online complaint platform. This may sound a little over-exaggerated, but here is how we can testify(C. Chiao-Chen and C. Yang-Chieh. (2011):

A consumer/client is usually a layman who comes across a fault in the service or product provided by the company and he wants to complain about it. He does not know who to contact for this since he is only aware of what the problem is but he is certainly not aware which department/section of the company has caused the problem and which department is there to fix it. He may not know how to address his issue most simply and effectively so that he neither wastes his own time in writing about the complaint repeating him several times nor causes wastage of time to those who are going to read it. An advance complaint audit module can give the user the idea how to simply address his issue to the concerned department by going through an easy-to-use and comprehensible platform which allows user to precisely and distinctively notify the company about his concerns. A common user is not aware if his written complaint will be given the treatment it needs. He is unsure if it will be with the concerned department in time (if only the query the user has is time-bound). He is also not sure if he will give the reply back from the company and from whom? The user places a telephone call and anticipates his call is given a proper hearing and he is assured by the telephone operator/attendee about the resolution of his complaints in time. But as soon as the phone is hung up, he wonders if he could get back to the guy he talked before again and if he would actually remember him and his complaint since he did not have any certain time-frame for resolution of his grievance(s). Moreover, he is not going to tolerate it if he thinks he may have to repeat himself again before another person in the same fashion he did before in his earlier call, if only he is not replied to timely and had to call again(Abdelfattah and Samiha. (2008).

Research Objective

The objective of this research is to determine the analyses of performance and efficiency of client complaint actions, strong reactions and dealing quality on user's dependability from the audit module in information technology compliant. The specific objectives were to:

1. Determine the correlation among the client's complaint actions and solver tangibility from the audit module in information technology compliant.
2. Evaluate the affiliation concerning strong reactions and Client Faithfulness.
3. Observe the bond among client complaint performance and facility quality.
4. Determine the effect of stable replies on the affiliation among examination quality and client loyalty.

LITERATURE REVIEW

An Audit Module is essential for a workplace that is committed to professionalism by utilizing its resources in a minimum possible ways to compartmentalize tasks to the benefit of its employees for saving their time and efforts and also their clients for saving their time and trust in the company. Such a module can be devised in different efficient and effective manners according to the work-style and nature of the business of a certain organization. Unfortunately, lesser companies dig deep into coming up with an ideal complaint-resolving plan/procedure. Their realization and acknowledgment of the matter are so limited that they don't find it useful to have such a platform available with their work-place. Surprisingly, there is a very small amount of research available in this domain, which causes much loss of interest in the eyes of the management of a given company. Moreover, the platforms already in action are so stereotyped and monotonous that it is generally believed not working for any at all. Since the grounds are wide open in this particular area for ample research work and analysis to be carried out, it is commonly assumed there is not much to do in this regard. Linear works are available and thus are in vogue for others to follow. Such platforms are copied in a similar way and run by other users since the developers don't even bother applying their vast imaginations to bring the one-dimensional work to another level. We are well aware that any user expects more ease and less trouble in a program/software he is asked to run and use. User-friendliness has become an expression of idealism when it comes to doing something new, imaginative and unparalleled to the already developed platforms. After all that is said above, the most important question that arises is: What is an organization supposed to do and ask for from their developers to give them which could not only satisfy the needs of their internal working body – their employees – as well as the customer who is so courteous to bother and register a complaint online using the complaint module expecting to get a response back within his anticipated time-period? (De. Ruyter, and Wetzels. (2010).

Nowadays, organizations take a comparatively greater interest in knowing about the factors that motivate a customer to appraise his / her experience of doing business with that particular organization in terms of competitiveness and uniqueness of the service provided to them. Since the service division is responsible for meaningful participation in the development of the economy of recent days, it is the clients who enjoy the fruits of variety and effortless accessibility. It is obvious that the service division is prospering by virtue of competitiveness all for the moderation of commerce, and revolutionary developments in the advertising and marketing reforms within the division. Hence, it is inevitable for organizations to come up with a strategy to keep their customers trusting them and inflict them to induce trust for the company in the hearts of others. This is the most effective means of survival in the hands of the competition airing all around. Additionally, consumers are acknowledged and honored as the principal deciders for the service features to be acquired by organizations to match client demands. Still, service breakdown is unavoidable because of the type of services extended based on its volatility, uniformity, vulnerability and amalgamation (STAUSS, B., SCHOELER, (2004).

The two elements that lead a client to the decision of making a repurchase are the quality of services extended and how satisfied he/she is with those services. State that magnitude of the quality of services like understanding, receptiveness and trustworthiness considerably forecast on purchaser's faithfulness. Additionally, quality of service increases the effect of verbal advertisement conducted by the satisfied user and positive manners, more; the reimbursement of client devotion is broadly documented inside the trade. There is development in client preservation and boost in the bazaar divide; and in the reduction of the employ of capital, they state the product to their associates and would rather protest than a blemish. Extra remuneration of client allegiance comprises inferior expenses linked with containing obtainable clientele, rather than continually hiring fresh ones mainly inside older, spirited marketplaces, steadfast clients are further expected to increase their rapport in the product variety and so the booty from that assembly are extended tenure and increasing(Singh. J. January, (1988).

One other broadly apparent advantage of reliable consumers is a criticism that is considered to operate as data straits, casually connecting systems of associates, family and additional possible clients to the union. In calculation, devotion is a product of behavior in look for communication and clientele do again buy. Prospects of optimistic strengthening persuade relative behaviors.

Overhaul excellence has been established to effect together behavioral goals and conclusions. Purchasers buy several services from providers who have lofty excellence relations. Added, corporations employ faithfulness programs (like allowing free-of-cost airing, without charge SMS and complimentary internet service) that offer financial booty to improve client relations. Though, the dispute is that a disgruntled but satisfied or happy purchaser is miserable and may be unfaithful. "Clients are licentious when it is about dealings with organizations". They have established little customers are "faithful" (100 percent loyal) or "licentious" (no loyalty to any brand). Rather, most people are "multi-dimensional" (loyal to a collection of makes in a merchandise class). From this viewpoint, faithfulness is as distinct as "a continuing tendency to purchase the make, typically as one out of numerous"(Fornell, C. & Wernerfelt., 2013).

Client Grievance Conduct

Purchaser grievance presentation submits to the reactions activated by apparent displeasure which is neither sensitively conventional nor rapidly elapsed in the expenditure of merchandise or examination. The research proposes that client grievance conduct (CGC) is multifaceted occurrences that are mirrored in the amount of substitute meaning planned to clarify this sort of behavior. Conventionally, the ordinary determining of argumentative behavior was explained as displeasure because of insufficiencies of truthfulness, dependability, receptiveness, accessibility and more functionality. Therefore, customer discontent is an effect of the inconsistency between predictable and appreciated recital. Discontent is bottomed on disconfirmation of hope. It is a client practice which is lesser than the received anticipations (Aaker, D. A., Kumar, V. & Day. (2004).

Client grievance conduct is the use of displeasure. Research declares discontent is an important issue to donate to criticism. One research displeasure rooted by the unenthusiastic dissertation of buy outlook that guided to lawful grievance conduct. Numerous learning's relating to customer approval and unhappiness has engaged the discontent pattern. As per this pattern, customer pleasure or displeasure is the meaning of professed differences amid the previous prospect of the merchandise or tune-up and its authentic recital. Customer grievance conduct is connected to unconstructive discomfort – whereas the professed presentation sprays little anticipation, resulting in the buyer to happen to be disappointed (Adams. (2009).

Inspected the discomfort result on approval and its collision on revisit benefaction, and established those were connected to the after-sales manners like ill-talking or having no exploits. Additionally, an assessment of expenses and profits about a grievance is a further feature that twists displeasure to an achievement. If the expenditure and time used upon a grievance are alleged as beyond the reimbursements as an effect of grievances, clients will be inclined to remain hushed and do nothing. Non-grievers measured arguing was made by groups with nothing to act and understood it as ineffective (Ahluwalia. R. et.al, 2012).

Grieving is described as a proper term of disappointment with a lot of features of examining data. By grieving, clients can look for several likely results that could be brought together. A disgruntled consumer can influence a grievance, way out or stay dedicated to the corporation. Vocal reply basically pertains to grieving straight to the wrong service giver. A client who speaks to a service provider by himself, in black and white or by using the phone would like to have a vocal reply. On the contrary, exit gets placed whenever the buyer starts a self-reject against the service offered to keep from doing again the business which caused the discomfort. Inserts the "no complaint action" which is defined in this research as a pledge to the procurement of merchandise and services(Andreasen, 1998).

Compact Replies

It is declared that compact replies are corporation procedures completed in the sort of using major constructive attempts on grievance fulfillment and allegiance. Though, It is centered on six grievance treatment features which weight the alleged evenhandedness of the process. Those compact replies symbolize standards for clients like remedy, regret, special treatment, clarification, endeavor, facilitation and appropriateness and they influence after-sales client grievance conduct. The compact replies were abridged into 03 assemblies as worker performance, recompense and corporation dealings. There is nonetheless a question on the compact replies to grievance treatment which is nevertheless a road to probable input to compact replies journalism.

Worker attitude is defined as categorical, accountable and instructive conduct of the serving individual and wants for worker's capability and vigorous hearing abilities that appear to be more significant for grievers, worker conduct wraps up the communal feature of grievance treatment by accepting kindness and trustworthiness (such as the elucidation of the issue). Recompense engages repayments, substitutes, or a reply answer that the corporation extends to tackle a client grievance in shape of regret in terms of community loss to assist in reinstating societal evenhandedness. Explains recompense as an advantage or reply product that the corporations offer to deal with a client objection. It symbolizes a touchable advantage in the shape of financial and insubstantial reaction upshots which could be measured as emotional reparation like confession or regret. On a service malfunction, customers anticipate the service bringer to reimburse for any concrete failure endured as a reaction to that service collapse. Consumers look forward to several kinds of recompense related to how harshly the service collapse hurts. An upset client may anticipate a "reasonable compensation" for the crisis, while a customer feeling "maltreated" as a consequence of the service malfunction imagines a few special amends (Babakus et.al, 2003).

Corporate policies comprise of feasibility and appropriateness when grievance management procedures are handled in a competent and clear-cut mode. Swiftness relates to the instant and simple means of managing an objection. That account includes servicing and aptness that both submit to the skill of companies to manage grievance-treatment procedures in a proficient and uncomplicated style. This executive reply, though, is classified as "executive policies", which suitably serves the substance of mutual groupings, while the phrase "swiftness" is rather an alias of appropriateness. Additionally, capable attending workers ought to keep adequate service information and skill for superior communications; and to grow to be well-informed on organizing grievances parallel to resolving issues (Andreassen. (2001).

Provision Quality

Provision quality (PQ) as an observed judgment subsequent from an assessment procedure where clients match their prospects with the provision they observe to have conventional. PQ is a serious aspect of effectiveness. It is an idea that has created substantial attention and argument in the research collected works due to the trouble of individually describing and determining it, with no general agreement developing concerning either phase. The discussion on provision quality maybe because of its proportions of dependability, reassurance, reality, awareness, and understanding. The excellence of a specific provision is whatever the client perceives it to be(Karatepe,(2010).

Provision quality as apparent by the client may vary from the excellence of the provision actually carried. Provisions are individually knowledgeable procedures where construction and intake actions take place instantaneously. Relations, together with a sequence of instants of reality between the client and the facility provider arise. Such buyer-seller contacts or provision happenstances have a dangerous influence on the apparent package. Provision quality has been definite in a number of methods but one of the most general meanings is: "an assessment between the predictable facility and the supposed deal" (Bagire, V. A. (2012). This description is the user-based and great value of an examination is attained by reliable consultation or exceeding client's prospects. Now, the subject of the facility of assured provision in an appropriate, correct and reliable way needs maximum importance. Earlier researches designate that dependability absolutely and meaningfully affects clients' awareness of provision quality of mobile telephone handlers because the consistency of a provision has been recognized as the operator of mobile provision quality (Ballantyne, D., & Varey, R.J. (2006).

Client Faithfulness

It is described that client faithfulness as an intensely detained obligation to re-purchase or re-support a favorite invention/facility steadily in the upcoming, thereby producing repetitive same-product or same product-conventional acquiring although situational effects and presentation exertions having the probable to reason swapping behavior. Alternatively, devotion is described as the client's aim to remain to do occupational with an organization such as the re-procurement objective. Client faithfulness is a multidimensional impression that has grown over the years. Early research frequently highlighted the interactive dimension of faithfulness (such as recurrence acquisition of a given product), but also attitudinal and reasoning scopes have been documented. For example, it defines provision faithfulness as the mark to which a client displays recurrence acquiring behavior from a facility supplier, owns an optimistic attitudinal nature toward the supplier, and reflects using only this supplier when an essential for this provision exists. However, quality difficulties often principal to the oversight of real behavior in experimental research and emphasis is in supreme belongings on goals, supposing that objectives powerfully mark behavior(Baron, R.M. & Kenny, D. A. (1986).

A collective method in significant client faithfulness is to differentiate between a user's interactive faithfulness and attitudinal faithfulness. Interactive faithfulness is articulated as frequent dealings (or measurement of entire overheads in the class) and can occasionally be dignified quite basics with observational systems. Attitudinal faithfulness is often amorphous as an optimistic mark near both continuation of the association and the wish to continue in the connection and is occasionally distinct as corresponding to connection obligation. Communicative and attitudinal faithfulness are both extremely valued because they are extremely tangled: frequent acquisitions lead to optimistic marks, which clues to conative faithfulness. It is clarified that attitudinally faithful clients are plentiful less subject to damaging material about the product than non-loyal clients. When faithfulness to product growths, the returns torrent from faithful clients become more expectable and can develop substantially. Truthfully, organizations cannot finally remove the opportunity of provision failures. Notwithstanding the disappointments, clients may still endure faithfully to the acquisitions and practice of the corporate services. Devotion consequently mentions to the state in which the client chooses not to criticize, but stays loyal to a deal or to an invention compliant noiselessly and inertly its failure. It is significant to highlight that the term trustworthiness has, in this circumstance, no right or optimistic value. This resource that a client is faithful, notwithstanding the problems experienced and the subsequent disappointment, particularly when there is no accessible substitute. Faithfulness is one of those reasoning, non-behavioral answers which can mark users' observation of the problematic up to repudiating that displeasure exists. Dependability is consequently resolute by the strong point of the association between comparative assertiveness and replication support Festinger, L. (2015).

Clustering Methods

Data grouping by clustering method is a uniformed technique for learning how we can mine data in groups. If we have a large amount of distributed data by clustering algorithm we can convert this big number of information into the meaning full logical small amount of data in small time by making groups the same type of data has same properties which we can define globally .for grouping information this clustering algorithm is followed in many systems. It has fragment family construction for cluster skill, image division, statistics recovery, web contacts combination, market division, and technical and manufacturing examination. Many grouping techniques have been offered and they can be generally categorized into four classes: separating methods, classified methods, solidity-based approaches and grid built methods. Other grouping methods that do not fir in these groups have been established. They are fuzzy logics, simulated neural nets and basic algorithms (Fornell, C., & Wernerfelt, B. (2000).

Partitioned Algorithms

Algorithms of partition data is the first family member of grouping data by performing data mining in clustering method, K-means are usually used for group for the data mining of large application (CLARE) otherwise medias around data mining which we say PAM are used and CLARANS, application's data binding for large grouping technique are used. If we focused on k-means "k" is the group of infinite n objects from a set, so that the squared-error objective function is minimized. In this equation, Cluster is represented as Ci, cluster point is represented as p, and the above equation shows mi as the Ci group mean in the cluster. We can name vector to the mean of the Ci group. Which included, for every attribute, the vector value of k object data in this partition clustering group is the numeric value of parameter we inter in cluster, object of information is represented by k for this cluster and Response factor is the figure of bunches, k, and as a productivity the procedure proceeds the centers, or capitals, of all group Ci, maximum times not including the group characteristics of distinct points. The distance ratio generally active is the Euclidean distance. Individually for the enhancement standard and the contiguity index, there are no boundaries, and they can be definite according to the request or the operator's inclination(Orisingher,, 2010).

METHODOLOGY

For any organization, customer complaints clustering/segmentation is one of the most significant methods used in studies of data mining. Clustering is a technique in which data is gathered in the grouping. By using clustering algorithms we can get a definite meaning full smaller number of date groups from the big number of data information. The clustering method is classified into four classes: partitioning, density-based, grid base and hierarchical methods. In this research, we use the partitioning method and hierarchical method. The formulation criteria of both hierarchical method and partition method have been discussed in the literature review. The result of this research is based on both types of the clustering method. For gathering data from customers for this research are as under by using Audit module application data can be gathered in group step by step and can also do data simulation. Data simulation result are show in the result here we discuss how the Audit module application gathers data by clustering method (partitioning & hierarchical method). This study classifies existing customer complaints cluster/segmentation methods into methodology-oriented and application-oriented approaches. Most methodology driven studies used mathematical methodologies; e.g. statistics, neural net, generic algorithm (GA) and Fuzzy set to identify the optimized segmented group.

In recent years, it has been recognized that the partitioned clustering technique is well suited for clustering a large dataset due to their relatively low computational requirements. Behavioral clustering and segmentation help derive strategic marketing initiatives by using the variables that determine customer shareholder value. By conducting demographic clustering and segmentation within the behavioral segments, we can define a tactical way to organize customer complaint data. It is then possible to target those customers most likely to exhibit the desired behavior by creating predictive models.

In this work demographic clustering algorithm is used to identify the performance and efficiency of audit module in IT complaints, the user complaint data is cleansed and developed patterns using various parameters and subsequently profiled the data, developed the clusters and identified the performance and efficiency of audit module in IT complaints. The experimental results, it showed that the proposed approach would generate more useful patterns from large data.

Collection of Data

The raising organization of Pakistan Young's Private limited ranked highest in Karachi has been selected for the implementation of the Audit module in IT complaint to test efficiency and performance. After the implementation of application one-year data of end-user complaints has been gathered to test results according to our objective, Data contain shows the response from the corresponding administrator in the environment, were highlighted by audit module application in an organization. For data collection, we have given the access of the application to every single user to the response. In a graphical chart by using the clustering method we have simulated the performance and efficiency of the Audit Module in IT complaints.

Primary Data

The primary data of complaint has been gathered by the implementation Audit module application in organization Young's private limited by giving access to each end-user to fill main form "Complaint Form" on computer data has been stored in database result has been concluded by quarrying the data according to partitioning and hierarchical technique after the detail comparison of these two types clustering method with other different type like k-means, PAM (Partitioning Around Medias), CLARA (Clustering Large Applications), and CLARANS (Clustering Larger Application's) as discussed in literature review in Comparison and Summary.

Sample Technique

The sampling technique is applying the clustering method in the audit module application to get data from the end-user and manipulate it to known efficiency and performance.

Sample Size

For sample size, only one raising organization of Karachi has been focused in this research live data entry in the application is the way to collect data. The sample size of this research we have simulated one-year data of user complaints.

Instrument of Data Collection

The chain of command of the performance of the Audit Module is if an employer makes a blunder, he will take off a complaint that will range for his department head. The problem will be accepted and denoted to the Information Technology department's head, and then he will subject a time-frame for determination of the assumed complaint. This problem will additionally be focused on the applicable section where the problem will be controlled by the authorities for appropriate determining of the problem. Subsequently, the problem position will be displayed as 'done'. At that time, according to the order, the client who had raised complaints will be addressed he will then authenticate or recognize if the interrogation has been committed or remain need support from the significant department for more enhancement or supplementary feedback. If the problem is originated to have been magnificently determined, then the client who raised the problem will do sign off on this complaint specific code generated by the system accordingly as 'done' on his portion to concentrate to substance totally committed. If not, he will construct his comments on the original badly-behaved if demand unmoving remains unexplained as per the need of individual client throwing the objection. In this process, the significance and rank will be assumed to the complainer. On the other hand, on the methodical side, the consequence shall be known to the estimation of the company's software developer relatively than the singular initiation grievance.

Figure 1. Movements of Audit Module

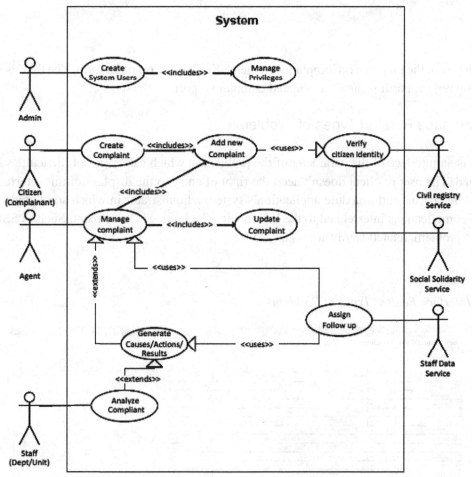

Part 1: Forms of Main Menu Items

The directly above figure 2 demonstrations of the elementary interface of the Audit System, there are two distinctive strip menus. The leading strip menu is named 'Complain', which involves four fundamental

Figure 2. Forms of Main Menu Items

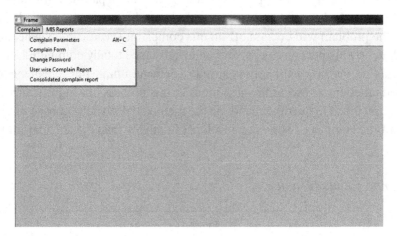

objects. These are the First one is Complain parameter. Second is Complain form. The third is User-wise complaining report. Forth is the Consolidated complain report.

Part 2: Interface Related Types of Problems

This form is an interface of the parameter of the problem in which categories of difficulties have been well-defined. The user or client doesn't need the right of entry to the displays of this interface. This is only controlled by the audit module application's system administrator in which sorts grade of all categories of complications interrelated to the Information Technology department. Such as SSS System, BI Reports problem, related Hardware issues etc.

Figure 3. Interface Related Types of Problems

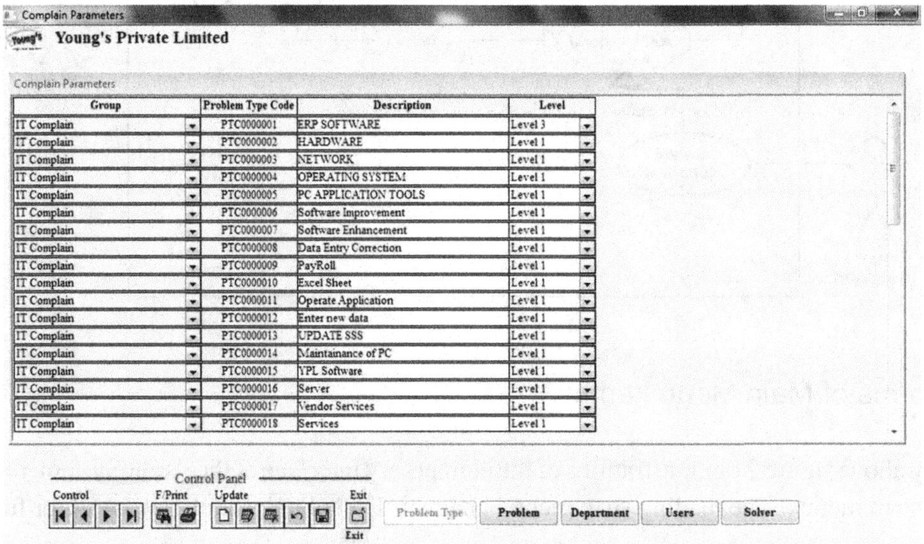

Part 3: Organization Department Related Interface

Figure 4 as above appearances the form or interface for the whole departments in an association. This form is only easily reached to the audit module application's system administrator without consuming any confession to the users. This interface is connected to the main form of user interface end-user con not directly access this form when users login to the application, the application will sense the department of the user through the database. In the database, there are two tables related to user personal information and department. The primary key of the department table which is department code is placed in the personal information table as subkey or foreign key.

Figure 4. Organization Department Related Interface

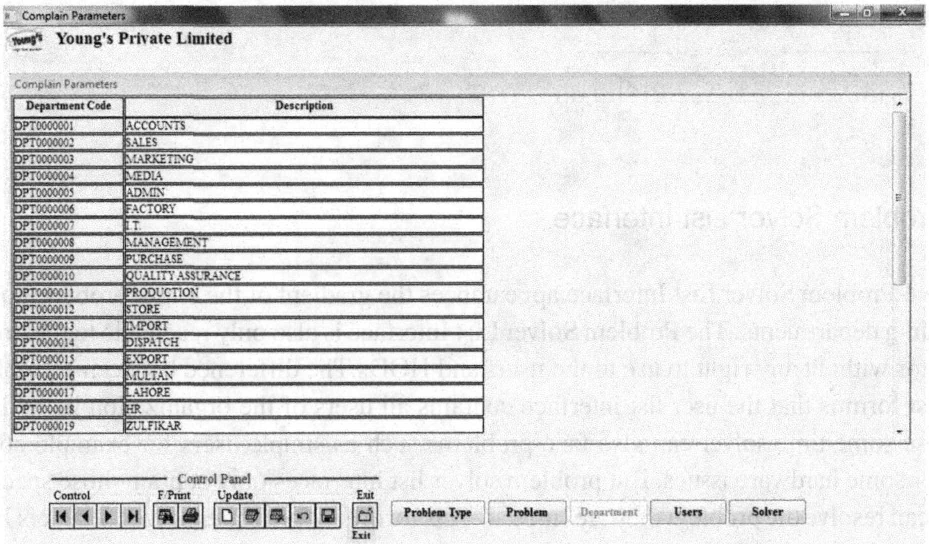

Part 4: Users List Form

The Figure 5 user list interface is definitely associated with the end-users of every single section of an organization; on the other hand, it only appearances the schedules/entrance of all potential users within the association. The right of entry of directly above form is also an organizational right of a structure superintendent; therefore, it is also not available to the users. This user list interface is compulsory to enhance the coordinator administrator with the indispensable data on the probable handlers/appellants. System administrator input data in this form and make login IDs and set passwords in the database. The database contains a table of passwords in which the user code and password field are mentions. User code is a foreign key from the user's personal information table. This is the beginning of the cycle of the Login Form hierarchy.

Figure 5. Users List Form

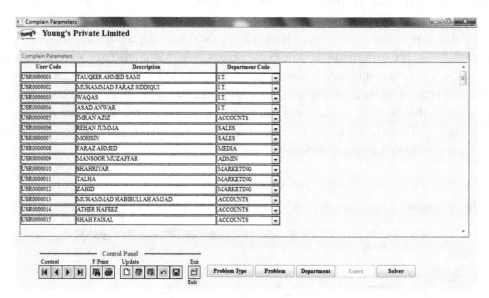

Part 5: Problem Solver List Interface

The Figure 6 Problem Solver List Interface appearances the gradient of the entire problem solvers from corresponding departments. The Problem Solver List Interface is also only reachable to the organization administrator without any right to use to the users and HODs.The difference between a problem solver and user list form is that the user list interface contains all users of the organization including solvers also because some time solver can also face problems such as simple users for example connectivity problems or some hardware issues. But problem solver list interfaces only contain those specific expert users who can resolve the problem they are limited. This form auto generates solver code it is linked with the main complaint form. Solver always log in with his user id and password but there is a drop-down

Figure 6. Problem Solver List Interface

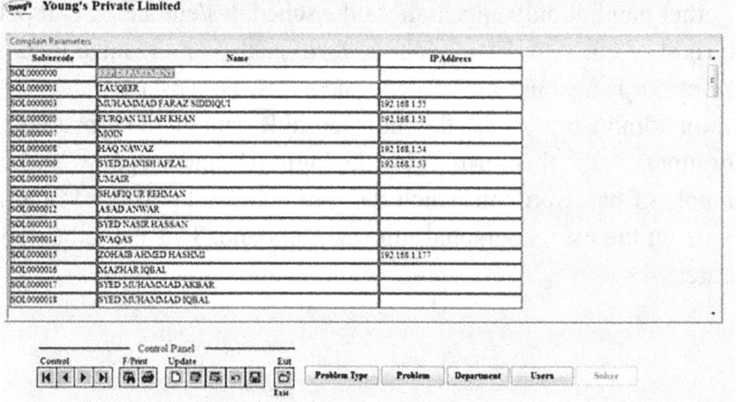

where solver selects his name to mention that this complaint is resolved by him. This solver code will also use H.O.Ds in main complaint form when they do the process of complaint delegation. When they refer the complaint to the specific expert user they will select solver code. On behave of this user code, we can measure the performance of the specific solver.

Part 6: Main Complaint Interface

Figure 7. Main Complaint Interface

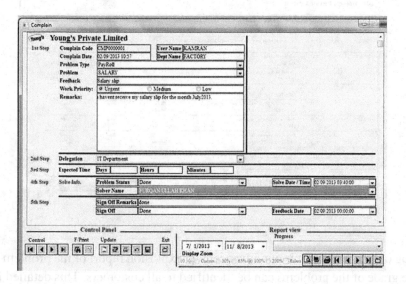

This is the key interface or objection form where an employer presents his / her objection. The leading mechanism an employer is obligatory to ensure here is to select the territory of the difficult type. Upon choosing, he shall be focused on a subordinate strip where the sub-classes or grouping or diversity of problematic categories associated with the category or province of the complaint, which is defined, as shown. The third strip cries for the suggestion of the substance problem or the detailed environment of the problematic. This problem will be focused on the department's Bosses of the operator or the appellant, which will additionally be promoted to the head of the Information Technology Department or the structure administrator, He will subject a time-frame for resolving of the assumed objection. This problem will additionally be absorbed near the significant subdivision where the objection will be controlled by the specialists for appropriate determining of the problem. After that, the problem position will be exposed as 'done'. At that time, according to the order, the appellant will be given a talk he will then validate or recognize if the interrogation has been committed or static must assist from the significant department for more enhancement or extra opinion. If the problem is initiate to have been magnificently determined, then the appellant will do sign off on raised complaint as 'done' on his portion to concentrate to substance completely committed. Or else, he will generate his comments on the opening problem if only the request still residues unexplained as per the need of the user initiation the problem. In this complete procedure, the urgency and significance will be specified to the appellant.

Then, in a procedural way, the significance shall be assumed to the estimation of the software developer reasonably the user launching problem.

Part 7: Log of All Complaint

Figure 8. Log of All Complaint

The Figure 8 Log of All Complaint is our advancement explosion report or the problem resolving status sheet, where the grade of the problems can be identified to all customers. This detailed log supports the appellant and other employers to know where a specific inquiry positions after its initiation.

Methodological Frameworks

See Figure 9.

Figure 9. Log of All Complaint

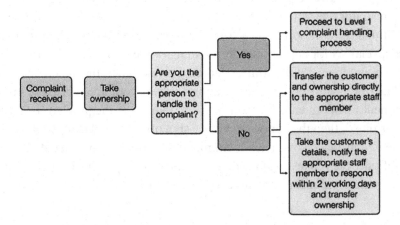

Requirements and Specification

- **Principles for firm structures -**There is an abnormal state of understanding fundamental rules that must form the establishments of an association. Objection and Efficiency Audit Module Application, tense from national published principles and from the practical and further effort:
- **Profoundly unmistakable processes** – containing clear information about step by step instructions to create furthermore, seek after dissension with a solitary purpose of association; clear and perfect response on how the grumbling is dealt with and uplifted.
- **Simple and unrestricted right to use** – an abstraction of all excessive right of entry barriers and facilitate the user.
- **Powerful business conventions**– succeed abnormal states of excellence declaration and execution. These must incorporate a part wide, surely knew and acknowledged meaning of what organizes an objection; flawless soundtrack techniques containing foundation of client reference numbers at the beginning; protected and effectual information management; monitor processes to check customer fulfillment with the way that protestations are controlled.
- **Reasonableness and stability** – treating all clients decently and with deference; taking dependable techniques for deciding grumblings and deciding results.
- **Reaction** – strong as well as suitable time bounds for deciding majority user protests and, essentially, elasticity managing troublesome dissensions together with keeping the complainant educated.
- **Organizational proprietorship and duty** – In a company, it is essentially required that the process of grumbling taking care of and general examination of grievances information is comprehended and bolstered at all stages and points. Drastic and effective endeavors should be rendered to make sure that the most effective organizational configurations and processes are intact, including vigorous workplace training and monitoring.

ISO Codes for Complaint Handling

1. **Visibility:** It should be publicly made known about how and where to make a complaint so that the common people find it easy to register their grievance, problems or obstacles.
2. **Accessibility:** A complaints-processing system must be easy to access to all appellants. All information should be made accessible in details to make and resolve grievances. The dissensions taking care of the procedure and backup details must comprehensible also useable. Info should simple dialect.
3. **Responsiveness:** acknowledgment of every single objection made known to pursuer right away. Objections ought to be cared for immediately as for now is the ideal time limitations. The plaintiff should be processed gallantly what's more, be kept educated of the advancement of their protestation through the dissensions taking care of framework.
4. **Independence:** Each grumbling ought to be tended to in a fair, objective and unprejudiced way through the dissensions taking care of the procedure.
5. **Custodies:** Access to the grievances taking care of procedure ought to be sans charge to the pursuer.
6. **Secrecy:** Secretive information ought not to be made accessible, yet just for the reasons of resolving the grievance inside of the association and ought to be extensively shielded from exposure, unless the complainant expressly concurs with its divulgence.

7. **Client-centered methodology:** the association ought to receive a client-centered methodology, ought to be interested in input including dissensions and ought to show responsibility for determining objections by its activities.
8. **Liability:** the association ought to ensure that registration equalization for and highlighting on the demonstrations and finishes of the association as for grievances treatment is obviously perceived
9. **Frequent enhancement:** repeated enhancement of grievances taking care of system and value of goods must perpetual goal of the association.

Issues of Mishandling Complaints

1. **Competence/impartiality consequence:** together problem resolution with equality of recompense.
2. **Entrance:** easiness of reaching for a proficient contact individual.
3. **Approachability:** civility, courteousness, correspondence style.
4. **Empathy:** preparation to take the customer's perspective, including understanding the client's disturbance.
5. **Individualized:** way to deal with grumbling taking care of.
6. Noticeable exertion: **determine the issue.**
7. **Dynamic criticism:** counting notifying about processes, postponements, results, etc.
8. **Dependability:** keeping assurances.
9. **Rate of reaction:** response to grievance and determination.

Figure 10. Total Usage Reliability Graph

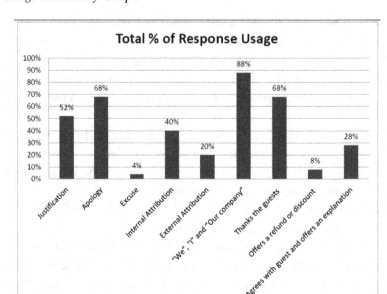

Reliability Test Analysis

Reliability test analysis of Audit module performance and efficiency is depend on justification 52%, Apology 68%, excuse 4%, internal & external attribution 40% to 20%,on organization 88%,clients 68%, refund and discount complaints 8%, client's problem explanation 28%.

RESULTS, FINDINGS, AND INTERPRETATION OF THE RESULTS

As in the literature review in comparison& summary, it is proved that an isolated system or any other data simulating technique will not give the best result without using the clustering method. By using clustering method in audit module application data has been gather as discussed in research methodology, after that grouped data has been stored in database of audit module in IT complaint management system simulation process has been done step by step by using quarries in database according to the clustering formulas we get our objective as discussed in chapter 1.

Figure 11. Summary of Complaint by Solver

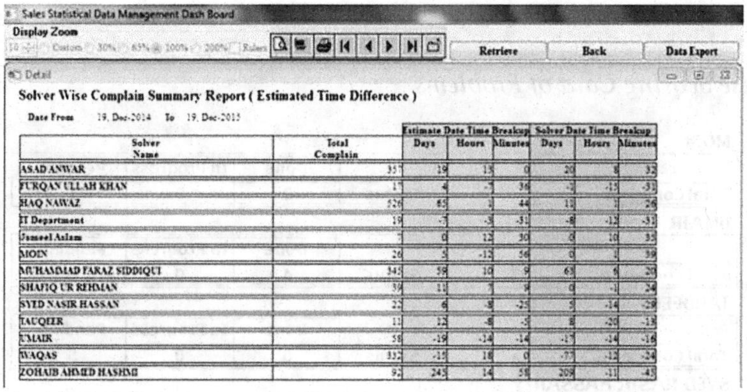

Sales Statistical Data Management Dash Board

Display Zoom

Retrieve | Back | Data Export

Detail

Solver Wise Complain Summary Report (Estimated Time Difference)

Date From 19, Dec-2014 To 19, Dec-2015

Solver Name	Total Complain	Estimate Date Time Breakup			Solver Date Time Breakup		
		Days	Hours	Minutes	Days	Hours	Minutes
ASAD ANWAR	357	19	13	0	20	8	32
FURQAN ULLAH KHAN	17	4	-7	36	-2	-15	-31
HAQ NAWAZ	526	65	1	44	12	1	26
IT Department	19	-7	-3	-31	-8	-12	-31
Jameel Aslam	7	0	12	30	0	10	35
MOIN	26	5	-12	56	0	1	39
MUHAMMAD FARAZ SIDDIQUI	345	59	10	9	63	6	20
SHAFIQ UR REHMAN	39	11	7	9	0	-1	24
SYED NASIR HASSAN	22	6	-8	-25	5	-14	-29
TAUQEER	11	12	-8	-5	8	-20	-13
UMAIR	58	-19	-14	-14	-17	-14	-16
WAQAS	332	-15	18	0	-77	-12	-24
ZOHAIB AHMED HASHMI	92	245	14	58	209	-11	-45

Figure 11 Summary of Complaint by Solver provides the complete measurements of whole problematic solvers' improvements or effectiveness status. It particularizes in what way and how much time Complaint solvers were assumed in entire to resolve an interrogation and how momentarily they completed their whole granted works. It also provides information on the number of problems determined by a person, solver. This is the result of solvers efficiency chart figure graphical representation of performance efficiency percentage are shown in figure 15 which is 92% out of 100% complaint.

Tangibility components were the main 1 trait, which was whined about with a percentage of 68%. The objections were primarily about the support of the organization inside, departments, Software and Hardware. The vast majority of the client protestations appeared to be supported anyway, a portion of the dissensions happened, on the grounds that the client misconstrued the organization's idea and in this manner had too exclusive standards to the administration conveyance. By the implementation of this application tangibility factor increases.

Figure 12 User-wise Scoring Card of Problems is the user-wise problem resolving status Table. This

Figure 12. Summary of Complaint Type

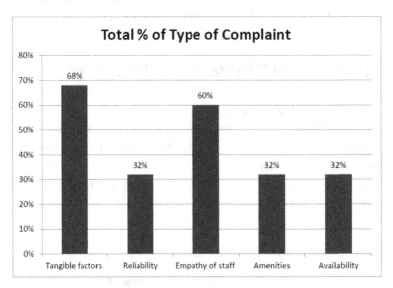

Figure 13. User-wise Scoring Card of Problems

MOIN

			Done	In Progress	Pending
Total Complains	3	Status	2	0	1

UMAIR

			Done	In Progress	Pending
Total Complains	4	Status	4	0	0

TAUQEER

			Done	In Progress	Pending
Total Complains	5	Status	0	0	5

SYED NASIR HASSAN

			Done	In Progress	Pending
Total Complains	10	Status	10	0	0

ASAD ANWAR

			Done	In Progress	Pending
Total Complains	19	Status	18	1	0

SHAFIQ UR REHMAN

			Done	In Progress	Pending
Total Complains	26	Status	26	0	0

ZOHAIB AHMED HASHMI

			Done	In Progress	Pending
Total Complains	29	Status	25	4	0

HAQ NAWAZ

			Done	In Progress	Pending
Total Complains	47	Status	44	2	1

MUHAMMAD FARAZ SIDDIQUI

			Done	In Progress	Pending
Total Complains	64	Status	63	0	1

WAQAS

			Done	In Progress	Pending
Total Complains	81	Status	81	0	0

clarifies how many problems solvers resolved overall; how many complaints are in progress or how many are pending.it can perform an audit of individual users that is known as a tracking system. This chart calculates the date of complaint status wise graphically representation of the percentage of efficiency of user complaint and solver cooperation is in figure 15 which is 98% out of 100% as shown below.

This data are cluster on solvers we can calculate the faith fullness of every solver there are 288 problems has been raised by users 276 problems have been resolved by a solver that's mean faithfulness of solver are 95% by using this application faithfulness of solver increases. These data are gathering by the manipulation of the hierarchical method as shown in this diagram.

The figure 13 summary of the progress of combine complaint designates synopses on the complications controlled Department-wise 92%, Solver-wise 98% and Problem-type-wise 91%. The department-wise instantaneous report stretches the measurements on the number of problems created in contradiction of a specific department, which shelters bright on the improvement of the specific department also. The Solver-wise instantaneous report provides the statistics on which problem solver grows more objections and how respectable he is intelligent to grip his amount of work. Problem-type-wise instantaneous particularizes the category of complications/errors which reasons more suffering than others and reduces trouble in efficiently implementing effort. This The difficulty is very critical checking which assistance cans growth the development of a specific department in direction to manage the complications regularly rising.

The Figure 14 Graphical Representation of Problems Status displays Complaint Detail Report Status Wise, which is a graphical demonstration of the problematic position. It sorts the number of grievances in classifications like done 98%, Pending 2%, Cancel 0%, In-progress 0%, Rejected 0%.

By using this application the crystal view of organization efficiency can b see accurately in the graphical representation of problem status is.

Figure 14. Summary of Progress of Combine Complaint

Department Wise

Department Name	Department Total
ACCOUNTS	4
SALES	7
MARKETING	4
I.T.	187
PURCHASE	1
PRODUCTION	3
HR	3
FINISH GOODS	3
MAINTANANCE DEPT	1
M.I.S	7
Total Complain	**220**

Solver Wise

Solver Name	Solver Total
MUHAMMAD FARAZ SIDDIQUI	17
MOIN	48
HAQ NAWAZ	29
UMAIR	13
SHAFIQ UR REHMAN	29
ASAD ANWAR	29
SYED NASIR HASSAN	2
WAQAS	38
ZOHAIB AHMED HASHMI	8
MAZHAR IQBAL	1
SYED MUHAMMAD AKBAR	3
Burhan	2
Total Solve Complain	**159**

Problem Type Wise

Problem Type Description	Problem Types Total
ERP SOFTWARE	4
HARDWARE	25
NETWORK	36
OPERATING SYSTEM	1
PC APPLICATION TOOLS	1
Software Improvement	1
PayRoll	1
Maintainance of PC	2
Server	19
Services	2
SSS Software	31
HRMS Software	4
ITC SOFTWARE	2
DYNAMICS SOFTWARE	28
MP SOFTWARE	1
Tertiary	2
DYNAMICS AX 2012 R3	23
DAILY TASKS	36
PURCHASING	1
Total Complain	**220**

Status Wise

Problem Status	Problem Status Total
Done	220
Total Complain	**220**

Figure 15. Graphical Representation of Problems Status

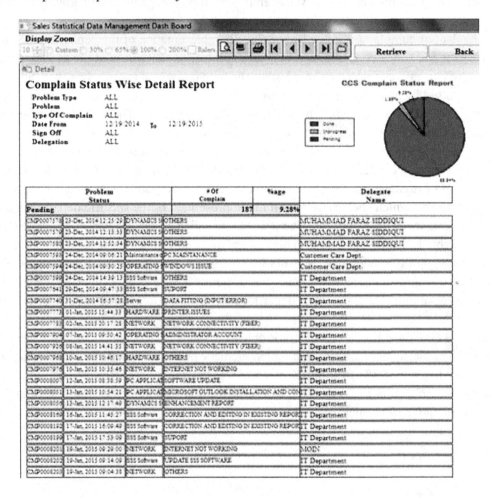

The diagram showed directly above is the three-monthly report on soft wares that are being practiced in a specified organization. This chart actually displays a whole audit report on the complete running software/applications in the association.

These are the topographies that the Analyzing Performance and Efficiency of Audit Module in IT Complaint Application include off, which can assist in supporting, decreasing and incapacitating the errors, mistakes and objections of employers in a forceful and progress-oriented association. It also supports document the complete information of each main and minor difficulties encountered by a particular department, customer and presentations. By simulate above result solver efficiency 98%, problem status "done" 98%, software streamline mean user's comfortability with their work on different application is increasing to 98% we can say this Audit Module is time-saving, time-effective, dependable, more approachable and target-oriented, which only reduces enhancement and productivity in a professional work environment for the comfort and peace-of-mind of its persons on grass-root levels to higher management level.

Figure 16. Summary of Application Performance

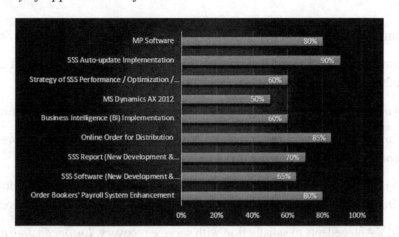

Experimental Assessment Summary

Experimental assessment summary of this research is that by using this tool in any organization work efficiency of employees can be increased as we see in above result in (figure 15) user satisfaction and organization graph reach to 88%, also note the problem solver tangibility as we show in result in (figure 15) tangibility factor increases to 68% by using this tool performance of other application in any organization can b track as track in (figure 21) Mp software 80%, Ms. Dynamics Ax 2012 50% etc. This is our objective 4 to the examination of quality also track the teamwork relationship between the user and problem solver as in objective 3 it is proved that complaint resolving progress is 98%.

CONCLUSION

Complain efficiency and audit module application provides important management information as in (4.2 Experimental Assessment Summary). By analyzing complaints and their root causes any organization users can learn from it, and then make improvements in performance and services as in (Figure 21). Complaint efficiency and audit module application will help to handle increasing complaint volumes as discussed in results see(a graphical representation of problem status figure 20). Although confirming compliance with the regulation . Improving worker productivity, It decreases time and cost in solving complaints see (figure19 Summary of Progress of Combine Complaint). Complaint efficiency audit application guides users through a best practice complaint follow up process so all users are handled in a consistent, fair manner see in (figure 5 Infrastructure of Audit Module). It confirms the process is properly followed and schedules met. Amount of work and performance controlling tool keep cases on track and confirm everyone knows accurately what required to be done, when and whom. The whole thing is kept in one place-all put in storage, protected and searchable.

REFERENCES

Aaker, D. A., Kumar, V. & Day. (2004). *Marketing Research* (7th ed.). John Willy & Sons.

Abdelfattah & Samiha. (2008). Toward E-Knowledge Based Complaint Management Tunis. *University of Tunis M., 273*, 293–295.

Adams. (2009). *Inequity in social exchange: Advances in social psychology*. Academic Press.

Ahluwalia, R., Unnava, H.R., & Brunkrant. (2012). *Towards Understanding the Value of a Loyal Customer: An Information-Processing Perspective*. Marketing Science Institute.

Andreasen. (1988). Consumer complaints and redress: what we know and what we don't know. In *The Frontier of Research in the Consumer Interest*. American Council on Consumer Interests.

Andreassen. (2001). Antecedents to satisfaction with service recovery. *European Journal of Marketing*.

Assael. (1992). *Consumer Behavior & Marketing Action* (4th ed.). PWS-Kent Publishing Company.

Atalik, O. (2007). Customer complaints about airline service: A preliminary study of Turkish frequent flyers. *Management Research News*.

Aydin, S. A., & Ozer, O. (2005). The analysis of antecedents of customer loyalty in the Turkish Mobile Telecom market. European Journal of Marketing.

Babakus, E., Yavas, U., Karatepe, O.M., & Avci, T. (2003). The effect of management commitment to service quality on employees' affective and performance outcomes. *Journal of the Academy of Marketing Science*.

Bagire, V. A. (2012). *Strategic configurations and performance of large non-Governmental organizations in Uganda* (PhD Thesis). University of Nairobi.

Ballantyne, D., & Varey, R.J. (2006). Creating value-in-use through marketing interaction: the exchange logic of relating, communicating and knowing. *Marketing Theory*.

Baron, R.M. & Kenny, D. A. (1986). The moderator Mediator Variable distinction in Social Psychological Research: Conceptual Strategic and statistical consideration. *Journal of Personality and Social Psychology*.

Bell, S.J., & Luddington, J.A. (2006). Coping with customer complaints. *Journal of Service Research*.

Bies R. J., Shapiro D. L., & Bernard, H. R. (2000). *Interactional fairness judgments: the influence of causal accounts*. Academic Press.

Bloemer, J., de Ruyter, K. M., & Wetzels, M. (2015). Linking perceived service quality and service loyalty: a multi-dimensional perspective. *European Journal of Marketing*.

Bosch, V., & Enriquez, F. (2015). TQM and QFD: Exploiting a customer complaint management system. *International Journal of Quality & Reliability Management, 22*(1), 30–37. doi:10.1108/02656710510572977

Chiao-Chen, C., & Yang-Chieh, C. (2011). *Comparing consumer complaint responses to online and offline environment*. Internet Research.

Coussement, K., & Van den Poel, D. (2015). *Improving customer complaint management by automatic email classification using linguistic style features as predictors*. Decision Support Systems.

De Matos, C.A. & Rossi, C.A.V. (2008). Word-of-mouth communications in marketing: a meta-analytic review of the antecedents and moderators. *Journal of Academy of Marketing Science*.

DeCarlo, T.E., Laczniak, R.N., Motley, C.M., & Ramaswami, S. (2007). Influence of image and familiarity on consumer response to negative word-of-mouth communication about retail entities. *Journal of Marketing Theory and Practice*.

Duffy, D. L. (2013). Internal and external factors which affect customer loyalty. Journal of Consumer Marketing.

Ehigie, B. (2016). Correlates of Consumer Loyalty to their bank: A case of Nigeria. *International Journal of Bank Marketing*.

Ehrenberg, A. S. C., & Scriven, J. A. (1999). Brand loyalty. In The Elgar Companion to Consumer Research and Economic Psychology. Edward Elgar.

Estelami, H. (2000). Competitive and procedural determinants of delight and disappointment on consumer complaint outcomes. *Journal of Service Research*.

Fairchild, A. J. & MacKinnon, D.P. (2009). *A General Model for Testing Mediation and Moderation Effects*. Academic Press.

Festinger, L. (2015). A theory of cognitive dissonance. Stanford, CA: Stanford University Press.

Fornell, C., & Wernerfelt, B. (1987). Defensive Marketing Strategy by Consumer Complaint Management: A Theorical Analysis. *JMR, Journal of Marketing Research*.

Fornell, C., & Wernerfelt, B. (2000). Defensive marketing strategy by customer complaint management: A theoretical analysis. *JMR, Journal of Marketing Research*.

Fornell, C., & Westbrook, R. A. (2010). *An exploratory study of assertiveness, aggressiveness, and consumer complaining behavior*. Ann Arbor, MI: Association for Consumer Research.

Karatepe. (2010). *The Practice of Social Research*. Wadsworth Publishers.

O'Neill, W., & Palmer, A. (2004). Cognitive dissonance and the stability of service quality perceptions. *Journal of Services Marketing*, *18*(6), 433–449. doi:10.1108/08876040410557221

Orisingher, C. Valentini, S. & Angelis, M. D. (2010). A meta-analysis of satisfaction and complaint handling services. *Journal of the Academy of Marketing Science*.

De Ruyter & Wetzels. (2010). Customer equity considerations in service recovery: A crossindustry perspective. *International Journal of Service Industry Management*.

Saeed & Jaffri. (2015). Information security in the modern education system in Pakistan. *IJTNR*, 1-7.

Sheth, & Bennett. (Eds.). (2010). Toward a theory of consumer complaining behavior. In Consumer and Industrial Buying Behavior. North-Holland Publishing.

Singh, J. (1988). Consumer Complaint Intentions and Behavior: A Review and Prospect. *Journal of Marketing. Social Research Methods: Qualitative and Quantitative Approaches.*

Stauss & Schoeler. (2004). Complaint management profitability: what do complaint managers know? Managing Service Quality.

Vazquez-Casielles, R. & Diaz-Martin, A.M. (2009). Satisfaction with service recovery: Perceived justice and emotional responses. *Journal of Business Research.*

Compilation of References

Aaker, D. A., Kumar, V. & Day. (2004). *Marketing Research* (7th ed.). John Willy & Sons.

Abdelfattah & Samiha. (2008). Toward E-Knowledge Based Complaint Management Tunis. *University of Tunis M.*, *273*, 293–295.

Abdel-Hamid, O., Mohamed, A. R., Jiang, H., & Penn, G. (2012, March). Applying convolutional neural networks concepts to hybrid NN-HMM model for speech recognition. In *2012 IEEE international conference on Acoustics, speech and signal processing (ICASSP)* (pp. 4277-4280). IEEE.

Abdel-Hamid, O., Mohamed, A. R., Jiang, H., Deng, L., Penn, G., & Yu, D. (2014). Convolutional neural networks for speech recognition. *IEEE/ACM Transactions on Audio, Speech, and Language Processing*, *22*(10), 1533–1545. doi:10.1109/TASLP.2014.2339736

Abdullah, A. H., Butt, R. A., Ashraf, M. W., Qureshi, K. N., & Ullah, F. (2018). Securing Data Communication in Wireless Body Area Networks Using Digital Signatures. *Technical Journal*, *23*(2), 50–55. Retrieved from https://tj.uettaxila.edu.pk/index.php/technical-journal/article/view/757

Abomhara, M., & Køien, G. M. (2014, May). Security and privacy in the Internet of Things: Current status and open issues. In *2014 international conference on privacy and security in mobile systems (PRISMS)* (pp. 1-8). IEEE.

Abomhara, M. (2015). Cyber security and the internet of things: Vulnerabilities, threats, intruders and attacks. *Journal of Cyber Security and Mobility*, *4*(1), 65–88. doi:10.13052/jcsm2245-1439.414

Abouzahir, S., Sadik, M., & Sabir, E. (2017). IoT-Empowered Smart Agriculture: A Real-Time Light-Weight Embedded Segmentation System. In Ubiquitous Networking. Cham: Springer International Publishing. doi:10.1007/978-3-319-68179-5_28

Acharya, S. (2012). *U.S. Patent No. 8,098,976*. Washington, DC: U.S. Patent and Trademark Office.

Adams. (2009). *Inequity in social exchange: Advances in social psychology*. Academic Press.

Advanced Control Corp. (n.d.). Retrieved from https://advancedcontrolcorp.com

Aftab, M., Chen, C., Chau, C.-K., & Rahwan, T. (2017). Automatic HVAC control with real-time occupancy recognition and simulation-guided model predictive control in low-cost embedded system. *Energy and Building*, *154*, 141–156. doi:10.1016/j.enbuild.2017.07.077

Agha, D. S., Khan, F. H., Shams, R., Rizvi, H. H., & Qazi, F. (2018). A Secure Crypto Base Authentication and Communication Suite in Wireless Body Area Network (WBAN) for IoT Applications. *Wireless Personal Communications*, *103*(4), 2877–2890. doi:10.100711277-018-5968-y

Agrawal, S., & Agrawal, J. (2015). Survey on anomaly detection using data mining techniques. *Procedia Computer Science*, *60*, 708–713. doi:10.1016/j.procs.2015.08.220

Ahluwalia, R., Unnava, H.R., & Brunkrant. (2012). *Towards Understanding the Value of a Loyal Customer: An Information-Processing Perspective*. Marketing Science Institute.

Ahmad, Aftab, & Muhammad. (2017). Machine Learning Techniques for Sentiment Analysis: A Review. *Int. J. Multidiscip. Sci. Eng.*

Ahmad, M., Aftab, S., Bashir, M. S., & Hameed, N. (2018). Sentiment Analysis using SVM : A Systematic Literature Review. IEEE.

Ahmad, M., Aftab, S., Ali, I., & Hameed, N. (2017). Hybrid Tools and Techniques for Sentiment Analysis. *RE:view*, *8*(3).

Ahmed, A., Abu Bakar, K., Channa, M. I., Haseeb, K., & Khan, A. W. (2015). A survey on trust based detection and isolation of malicious nodes in ad-hoc and sensor networks. *Frontiers of Computer Science*, *9*(2), 280–296. doi:10.100711704-014-4212-5

Ahmed, A., Ashraf, U., Tunio, F., Abu Bakar, K., & AL-Zahrani, M. S. (2018). Stealth Jamming Attack in WSNs: Effects and Countermeasure. *IEEE Sensors Journal*, *18*(17), 7106–7113. doi:10.1109/JSEN.2018.2852358

Ahmed, A., Bakar, K. A., Channa, M. I., Haseeb, K., & Khan, A. W. (2015). TERP: A Trust and Energy Aware Routing Protocol for Wireless Sensor Network. *IEEE Sensors Journal*, *15*(12), 6962–6972. doi:10.1109/JSEN.2015.2468576

Ahmed, A., Javed, N., Qasim, U., Ishfaq, M., Khan, Z. A., & Alhamdi, T. (2014). RE-ATTEMPT: A New Energy-Efficient Routing Protocol for Wireless Body Area Sensor Networks. *International Journal of Distributed Sensor Networks*, *464010*(4), 464010. doi:10.1155/2014/464010

Ahmed, E. S., Dusit, N., Ridha, H., & Naofal, A. (2017). Impact of the Wireless Network's PHY Security and Reliability on Demand-Side Management Cost in the Smart Grid. *IEEE Access: Practical Innovations, Open Solutions*, *5*, 5678–5689. doi:10.1109/ACCESS.2017.2695520

Ahmed, S., Rehman, M. U., Ishtiaq, A., Khan, S., Ali, A., & Begum, S. (2018). VANSec: Attack-Resistant VANET Security Algorithm in Terms of Trust Computation Error and Normalized Routing Overhead. *Journal of Sensors*, *2018*, 1–17. doi:10.1155/2018/6576841

Airehrour, D., Gutierrez, J. A., & Ray, S. K. (2019, April). SecTrust-RPL: A secure trust-aware RPL routing protocol for Internet of Things. *Future Generation Computer Systems*, *93*, 860–876. doi:10.1016/j.future.2018.03.021

Al Ameen & Liu. (2015). Security and privacy issues in wireless sensor networks for healthcare. *Lecture Notes of the Institute for Computer Sciences, Social-Informatics and Telecommunications Engineering*, *150*, 223–228. doi:10.1007/978-3-319-19656-5_32

Al Ameen, M., Liu, J., & Kwak, K. (2012). Security and privacy issues in wireless sensor networks for healthcare applications. *Journal of Medical Systems*, *36*(1), 93–101. doi:10.100710916-010-9449-4 PMID:20703745

Al-Ali, A., Zualkernan, I. A., Rashid, M., Gupta, R., & Alikarar, M. (2017). A smart home energy management system using Internet of Things and big data analytics approach. *IEEE Transactions on Consumer Electronics*, *63*(4), 426–434. doi:10.1109/TCE.2017.015014

Alattas, R. (2016). Detecting black-hole attacks in WSNs using multiple base stations and check agents. In 2016 Future Technologies Conference (FTC) (pp. 1020-1024). IEEE. doi:10.1109/FTC.2016.7821728

Alavi, A. H., Jiao, P., Buttlar, W. G., & Lajnef, N. (2018). Internet of Things-enabled smart cities: State-of-the-art and future trends. *Measurement*, *129*, 589–606. doi:10.1016/j.measurement.2018.07.067

Albright, D., Brannan, P., & Walrond, C. (2010). *Did Stuxnet take out 1,000 centrifuges at the Natanz enrichment plant?* Institute for Science and International Security.

Alessandretti, A. A. (2018). A Model Predictive Cloud-based Control Scheme for Trajectory-Tracking: Effects of Round-trip Time Over-estimates. In *13th APCA International Conference on Automatic Control and Soft Computing (CONTROLO)* (pp. 183-188). Ponta Delgada, Portugal: IEEE. 10.1109/CONTROLO.2018.8516416

Alex, R., Ronaldo, T. P., Raimir, H. F., & Joel, J. P. (2019). Enabling Online Quantitative Security Analysis in 6LoWPAN Networks. *IEEE Internet of Things Journal*, *6*(3), 5631–5638. doi:10.1109/JIOT.2019.2904302

Alextian, L., Magnos, M., Roberta, L. G., Arash, F. B., & Emilio, S. (2018). RDNA: Residue-Defined Networking Architecture Enabling Ultra-Reliable Low-Latency Datacenters. *IEEE eTransactions on Network and Service Management*, *15*(4), 1473–1487. doi:10.1109/TNSM.2018.2876845

Al-hamadani, A., & Allen, W. H. (2014). RAAODV: a reputation-aware AODV for mobile ad hoc networks. In *Proceedings of the 2014 ACM Southeast Regional Conference on - ACM SE '14* (pp. 1–6). New York: ACM Press. 10.1145/2638404.2638462

Ali, S., Khan, M. A., Ahmad, J., & Malik, A. W., & ur Rehman, A. (2018). Detection and prevention of Black Hole Attacks in IOT & WSN. In *2018 Third International Conference on Fog and Mobile Edge Computing (FMEC)* (pp. 217-226). IEEE. 10.1109/FMEC.2018.8364068

Ali, B., & Awad, A. (2018). Cyber and physical security vulnerability assessment for IoT-based smart homes. *Sensors (Basel)*, *18*(3), 817. doi:10.339018030817 PMID:29518023

Alireza, S., Yosr, J., Makan, P., & Mohamed, C. (2016). Efficient Provisioning of Security Service Function Chaining Using Network Security Defense Patterns. *IEEE Transactions on Services Computing*, *12*(4), 534–549.

Ali, S., & Kim, D.-H. (2013). Effective and comfortable power control model using Kalman filter for building energy management. *Wireless Personal Communications*, *73*(4), 1439–1453. doi:10.100711277-013-1259-9

Al-Janabi, S., Al-Shourbaji, I., Shojafar, M., & Shamshirband, S. (2017). Survey of main challenges (security and privacy) in wireless body area networks for healthcare applications. *Egyptian Informatics Journal*, *18*(2), 113–122. doi:10.1016/j.eij.2016.11.001

Almulhim, M., & Zaman, N. (2018). *Proposing secure and lightweight authentication scheme for IoT based E-health applications.* Paper presented at the 2018 20th International Conference on Advanced Communication Technology (ICACT).

Almusaylim, Z. A., & Jhanjhi, N. Z. (2019). Comprehensive Review: Privacy Protection of User in Location-Aware Services of Mobile Cloud Computing. *Wireless Personal Communications*, *§§§*, 1–24.

Almusaylim, Z. A., & Zaman, N. (2019). A review on smart home present state and challenges: Linked to context-awareness internet of things (IoT). *Wireless Networks*, *25*(6), 3193–3204. doi:10.100711276-018-1712-5

Alonso, J., Arrieta, L. O.-E., Escalante, M., Gorroñogoitia, J., & Presenza, D. (2013). Cloud modernization assessment framework: Analyzing the impact of a potential migration to Cloud. *2013 IEEE 7th International Symposium on the Maintenance and Evolution of Service-Oriented and Cloud-Based Systems.* 10.1109/MESOCA.2013.6632736

Alsoufi, D., Elleithy, K. M., Abuzaghleh, T., & Nassar, A. (2012). *Security in wireless sensor networks-Improving the leap protocol.* Academic Press.

Amasyali & El-Gohary. (2016). Building Lighting energy consumption prediction for supporting energy data analytics. *Procedia Engineering, 145,* 511-517.

Amit, P., & P., S. (2018). DDoS Attacks at the Application Layer: Challenges and Research Perspectives for Safeguarding Web Applications. *IEEE Communications Surveys and Tutorials, 21*(1), 661–685.

Ammar, M., Russello, G., & Crispo, B. (2018). Internet of Things: A survey on the security of IoT frameworks. *Journal of Information Security and Applications, 38,* 8–27. doi:10.1016/j.jisa.2017.11.002

Amudhavel, J., Brindha, V., Anantharaj, B., Karthikeyan, P., Bhuvaneswari, B., & Vasanthi, M. (2016). A survey on intrusion detection system: State of the art review. *Indian Journal of Science and Technology, 9*(11), 1-9.

Ananthi, N., Divya, J., Divya, M., & Janani, V. (2017). IoT Based Smart Soil Monitoring System for Agricultural Production. In 2017 IEEE Technological Innovations in ICT for Agriculture and Rural Development (TIAR). Chennai: IEEE. doi:10.1109/TIAR.2017.8273717

Andreasen. (1988). Consumer complaints and redress: what we know and what we don't know. In *The Frontier of Research in the Consumer Interest.* American Council on Consumer Interests.

Andreas, P. (2018). Efficient IoT-based sensor BIG Data collection–processing and analysis in smart buildings. *Future Generation Computer Systems, 82,* 349–357. doi:10.1016/j.future.2017.09.082

Andreassen. (2001). Antecedents to satisfaction with service recovery. *European Journal of Marketing.*

Aniket, B., & Sunil, B. (2019). Detecting lateral spear phishing attacks in organisations. *IET Information Security, 13*(2), 133–140. doi:10.1049/iet-ifs.2018.5090

Anthony, O., Odeyabinya, J., & Emmanuel, S. (2018). Intrusion detection in internet of things (IoT). *International Journal of Advanced Research in Computer Science, 9*(1).

Antol, S., Agrawal, A., Lu, J., Mitchell, M., Batra, D., Lawrence Zitnick, C., & Parikh, D. (2015). Vqa: Visual question answering. In *Proceedings of the IEEE international conference on computer vision* (pp. 2425-2433). IEEE.

Anwar, Zainal, Abdullah, & Qureshi. (2014). Security Issues and Attacks in Wireless Sensor Network. *World Applied Sciences Journal, 30*(10).

Anwar, R. W., Bakhtiari, M., Zainal, A., Hanan Abdullah, A., & Qureshi, K. N. (2014). Security issues and attacks in wireless sensor network. *World Applied Sciences Journal, 30*(10), 1224–1227. doi:10.5829/idosi.wasj.2014.30.10.334

Aradhye, H., Toderici, G., & Yagnik, J. (2009, December). Video2text: Learning to annotate video content. In *IEEE International Conference on Data Mining Workshops* (pp. 144-151). IEEE.

Aruul Mozhi Varman, S., & Arvind Ram Baskaran, S. (2017). Deep Learning and IoT for Smart Agriculture Using WSN. In *2017 IEEE International Conference on Computational Intelligence and Computing Research (ICCIC).* Coimbatore: IEEE. 10.1109/ICCIC.2017.8524140

Arya, A., & Bilandi, N. (2007). A Review: Wireless Body Area Networks for Health Care. *International Journal of Innovative Research in Computer and Communication Engineering, 3297*(4), 3800–3806. Retrieved from www.ijircce.com

Asif, M. K., Khan, T. A., Taj, T. A., Naeem, U., & Yakoob, S. (2013, April). Network intrusion detection and its strategic importance. In 2013 IEEE Business Engineering and Industrial Applications Colloquium (BEIAC) (pp. 140-144). IEEE. doi:10.1109/BEIAC.2013.6560100

Assael. (1992). *Consumer Behavior & Marketing Action* (4th ed.). PWS-Kent Publishing Company.

Aswale, S., & Ghorpade, V. R. (2015). Survey of QoS Routing Protocols in Wireless Multimedia Sensor Networks. *Journal of Computer Networks and Communications, 2015*, 1–29. doi:10.1155/2015/824619

Atalik, O. (2007). Customer complaints about airline service: A preliminary study of Turkish frequent flyers. *Management Research News*.

Atzori, L., Iera, A., Morabito, G., & Nitti, M. (2012). The social internet of things (siot)–when social networks meet the internet of things: Concept, architecture and network characterization. *Computer Networks, 56*(16), 3594–3608. doi:10.1016/j.comnet.2012.07.010

Avast smart home security report. (2019). Avast.

Aydin, S. A., & Ozer, O. (2005). The analysis of antecedents of customer loyalty in the Turkish Mobile Telecom market. European Journal of Marketing.

Ayyash, M., Elgala, H., Khreishah, A., Jungnickel, V., Little, T., Shao, S., ... Freund, R. (2016). Coexistence of WiFi and LiFi toward 5G: Concepts, opportunities, and challenges. *IEEE Communications Magazine, 54*(2), 64–71. doi:10.1109/MCOM.2016.7402263

Babakus, E., Yavas, U., Karatepe, O.M., & Avci, T. (2003). The effect of management commitment to service quality on employees' affective and performance outcomes. *Journal of the Academy of Marketing Science*.

Baber, J., Afzulpurkar, N., & Bakhtyar, M. (2011). Video segmentation into scenes using entropy and SURF. In *7th International Conference on Emerging Technologies* (pp. 1-6). 10.1109/ICET.2011.6048496

Baber, J., Satoh, S. I., Afzulpurkar, N., & Keatmanee, C. (2013, August). Bag of visual words model for videos segmentation into scenes. In *Proceedings of the Fifth International Conference on Internet Multimedia Computing and Service* (pp. 191-194). 10.1145/2499788.2499814

Bacco, M., Berton, A., Ferro, E., Gennaro, C., Gotta, A., Matteoli, S., . . . Zanella, A. (2018). Smart Farming: Opportunities, Challenges and Technology Enablers. In 2018 IoT Vertical and Topical Summit on Agriculture - Tuscany (IOT Tuscany). Tuscany: IEEE.

Bag, A., & Bassiouni, M. A. (2008). Routing algorithm for network of homogeneous and id-less biomedical sensor nodes (RAIN). In *2008 IEEE Sensors Applications Symposium* (pp. 68–73). IEEE.

Bag, A., & Bassiouni, M. A. (2006). Energy efficient thermal aware routing algorithms for embedded biomedical sensor networks. In *2006 IEEE International Conference on Mobile Ad Hoc and Sensor Systems, MASS* (Vol. 1, pp. 604–609). 10.1109/MOBHOC.2006.278619

Bag, A., & Bassiouni, M. A. (2007). Hotspot Preventing Routing Algorithm for Delay-Sensitive Biomedical Sensor Networks. In *2007 IEEE International Conference on Portable Information Devices, PIDs 2007* (pp. 1–5). 10.1109/PORTABLE.2007.30

Bagire, V. A. (2012). *Strategic configurations and performance of large non-Governmental organizations in Uganda* (PhD Thesis). University of Nairobi.

Bagirov, A. M., Mahmood, A., & Barton, A. (2017).Prediction of monthly rainfall in Victoria, Australia: Clusterwise linear regression approach. Atmos. Res.

Ballantyne, D., & Varey, R.J. (2006). Creating value-in-use through marketing interaction: the exchange logic of relating, communicating and knowing. *Marketing Theory*.

Bangash, J. I., Abdullah, A. H., Anisi, M. H., & Khan, A. W. (2014). A survey of routing protocols in wireless body sensor networks. *Sensors (Switzerland), 14*(1), 1322–1357. doi:10.3390140101322 PMID:24419163

Barnaghi, P. S., & Sheth, A. (2016). On Searching the Internet of Things: Requirements and Challenges. *IEEE Intelligent Systems, 31*(6), 71–75. doi:10.1109/MIS.2016.102

Baron, R.M. & Kenny, D. A. (1986). The moderator Mediator Variable distinction in Social Psychological Research: Conceptual Strategic and statistical consideration. *Journal of Personality and Social Psychology.*

Bashah, N. S. (2011). A Mobile Service Architecture for improving Availability and Continuity. In *IEEE Symposium on Computers & Informatics* (pp. 380-384). Kuala Lumpur, Malaysia: IEEE. 10.1109/ISCI.2011.5958945

Batra, P. K., & Kant, K. (2014, October). Stable cluster head selection in leach protocol: a cross-layer approach. In *Proceedings of the 7th ACM India Computing Conference* (pp. 1-6). 10.1145/2675744.2675761

Beek, C., Frosst, D., Greve, P., Gund, Y., Moreno, F., Peterson, E., & Tiwari, R. (2017). *Mcafee labs threats report. McAfee.* Santa Clara, CA: Tech. Rep.

Behrouz, A. F. (2013). Network Model. In *Data Communication and Networking* (pp. 74–80). New York: Mc Graw Hill.

Behrouz, A. F., & Debdeep, M. (2015). Introduction. In *Cryptogarphy and Network Security* (pp. 1–2). New York: Mc Graw Hill.

Bekara, C., & Laurent, M. (2007). *Defending against nodes replication attacks on wireless sensor networks.* Paper presented at the SAR-SSI 2007: 2nd Conference on Security in Network Architectures and Information Systems.

Bell, S.J., & Luddington, J.A. (2006). Coping with customer complaints. *Journal of Service Research.*

Belmonte-Hernandez, A., Hernandez-Penaloza, G., Alvarez, F., & Conti, G. (2017). Adaptive fingerprinting in multi-sensor fusion for accurate indoor tracking. *IEEE Sensors Journal, 17*(15), 4983–4998. doi:10.1109/JSEN.2017.2715978

Bengio, Y., Lamblin, P., Popovici, D., & Larochelle, H. (2007). Greedy layer-wise training of deep networks. Advances in Neural Information Processing Systems, 153–160.

Bengio, Y., Louradour, J., Collobert, R., & Weston, J. (2009, June). Curriculum learning. In *Proceedings of the 26th annual international conference on machine learning* (pp. 41-48). Academic Press.

Bengio, Y., Simard, P., & Frasconi, P. (1994). Learning long-term dependencies with gradient descent is difficult. *IEEE Transactions on Neural Networks, 5*(2), 157–166. doi:10.1109/72.279181 PMID:18267787

Bhandari, B., & Zheng, J. (2018). *A Preliminary Study On Emerging Cloud Computing Security Challenges.* arXiv preprint arXiv:1808.04143

Bhangwar, A. R., Kumar, P., Ahmed, A., & Channa, M. I. (2017). Trust and Thermal Aware Routing Protocol (TTRP) for Wireless Body Area Networks. *Wireless Personal Communications, 97*(1), 349–364. doi:10.100711277-017-4508-5

Bhattacharjya, A., Zhong, X., Wang, J., & Li, X. (2019). Security challenges and concerns of Internet of Things (IoT). In *Cyber-Physical Systems: Architecture, Security and Application* (pp. 153–185). Cham: Springer. doi:10.1007/978-3-319-92564-6_7

Bies R. J., Shapiro D. L., & Bernard, H. R. (2000). *Interactional fairness judgments: the influence of causal accounts.* Academic Press.

Billy, Wijerathne, Ng, & Yuen. (2017). Sensor fusion for public space utilization monitoring in a smart city. *IEEE Internet of Things Journal.*

Bisbal, J., Lawless, D., Wu, B., Grimson, J., Wade, V., & Richardson, R. (1997). An Overview of Legacy Information System Migration. *Asia-Pacific Software Engineering Conference.*

Bloemer, J., de Ruyter, K. M., & Wetzels, M. (2015). Linking perceived service quality and service loyalty: a multidimensional perspective. *European Journal of Marketing.*

Boccignone, G., Chianese, A., Moscato, V., & Picariello, A. (2005). Foveated shot detection for video segmentation. *IEEE Transactions on Circuits and Systems for Video Technology, 15*(3), 365–377. doi:10.1109/TCSVT.2004.842603

Bosch, V., & Enriquez, F. (2015). TQM and QFD: Exploiting a customer complaint management system. *International Journal of Quality & Reliability Management, 22*(1), 30–37. doi:10.1108/02656710510572977

Bosilj, Aptoula, Duckett, & Cielniak. (2019). Transfer Learning between Crop Types for Semantic Segmentation of Crops versus Weeds in Precision Agriculture. *Journal of Field Robotics.*

Boubiche, D. E., Pathan, A.-S. K., Lloret, J., Zhou, H., Hong, S., Amin, S. O., & Feki, M. A. (2018). Advanced Industrial Wireless Sensor Networks and Intelligent IoT. *IEEE Communications Magazine, 56*(2), 14–15. doi:10.1109/MCOM.2018.8291108

Boukerche, A., Oliveira, H. H. A. B. F., Nakamura, E. F., & Loureiro, A. A. F. (2008). Secure localization algorithms for wireless sensor networks. *IEEE Communications Magazine, 46*(4), 96–101. doi:10.1109/MCOM.2008.4481347

Boukerche, A., & Ren, Y. (2009). A secure mobile healthcare system using trust-based multicast scheme. *IEEE Journal on Selected Areas in Communications, 27*(4), 387–399. doi:10.1109/JSAC.2009.090504

Bradley, T. (2000). CISSP-ISSAP. *Introduction to Packet Sniffing, former About. com Guide.*

Braem, B., Latre, B., Moerman, I., Blondia, C., & Demeester, P. (2006). The wireless autonomous spanning tree protocol for multihop wireless body area networks. In *Networking & Services, 2006 Third Annual International Conference* (pp. 1–8). Academic Press.

Brar, S., & Angurala, M. (2016). Review on grey-hole attack detection and prevention. *International Journal of Advance research. Ideas and Innovations in Technology, 2*(5), 1–4.

Bredin, H. (2012, March). Segmentation of TV shows into scenes using speaker diarization and speech recognition. In *IEEE International Conference on Acoustics, Speech and Signal Processing (ICASSP)* (pp. 2377-2380). 10.1109/ICASSP.2012.6288393

BrickerBot Malware Emerges. (n.d.). *Permanently Bricks IoT Devices.* Retrieved from https://www.trendmicro.com/vinfo/us/security/news/internet-of-things/brickerbot-malware-permanently-bricks-iot-devices

Buchegger, S. (n.d.). Performance Analysis of the CONFIDANT Protocol (Cooperation Of Nodes : Fairness In Dynamic Ad-hoc NeTworks) Background : the DSR Protocol. In Components (pp. 226–236). Academic Press.

Buczak, A. L., & Guven, E. (2015). A survey of data mining and machine learning methods for cyber security intrusion detection. *IEEE Communications Surveys and Tutorials, 18*(2), 1153–1176. doi:10.1109/COMST.2015.2494502

Burg, A., Chattopadhyay, A., & Lam, K. Y. (2017). Wireless communication and security issues for cyber–physical systems and the Internet-of-Things. *Proceedings of the IEEE, 106*(1), 38–60. doi:10.1109/JPROC.2017.2780172

Campbell, B., Clark, M., DeBruin, S., Ghena, B., Jackson, N., Kuo, Y.-S., & Dutta, P. (2016). Perpetual Sensing for the Built Environment. *IEEE Pervasive Computing*, *15*(4), 45–55. doi:10.1109/MPRV.2016.66

Canales-Ide, F., Zubelzu, S., & Rodríguez-Sinobas, L. (2019). Irrigation Systems in Smart Cities Coping with Water Scarcity: The Case of Valdebebas, Madrid (Spain). *Journal of Environmental Management*, *247*, 187–195. doi:10.1016/j.jenvman.2019.06.062 PMID:31252223

Cataldo, B., Fulvio, V., Antonio, L., Diego, R. L., & Antonio, P. P. (2019). Adding Support for Automatic Enforcement of Security Policies in NFV Networks. *IEEE/ACM Transactions on Networking*, *27*(2), 707–720. doi:10.1109/TNET.2019.2895278

Cavallari, R., Martelli, F., Rosini, R., Buratti, C., & Verdone, R. (2014). A survey on wireless body area networks: Technologies and design challenges. *IEEE Communications Surveys and Tutorials*, *16*(3), 1635–1657. doi:10.1109/SURV.2014.012214.00007

Cekerevac, Z., Dvorak, Z., Prigoda, L., & Cekerevac, P. (2017). *Internet of Things and The Man-In the-Middle Attacks – Security and Economic Risks*. MEST Journal. doi:10.12709/mest.05.05.02.03

Celik, Z. B., McDaniel, P., & Tan, G. (2018). Soteria: Automated IoT Safety and security analysis. In *2018 {USENIX} Annual Technical Conference ({USENIX}{ATC} 18)* (pp. 147-158). USENIX.

Chaitanya, Ayyappa, & Ravindra. (2011). Analysis and Study of Denial of Service Attacks in Wireless Mobile Jammers. *International Journal of Computer Science and Telecommunications, 2*(5).

Chang, S. P., & Wang, S. P. (2018). A Group-Oriented DTLS Handshake for Secure IoT Applications. *IEEE Transactions on Automation Science and Engineering*, *15*(4), 1920–1929. doi:10.1109/TASE.2018.2855640

Changsen, Z., & Yan, M. (2015, December). Study on Mine Communication Network Based on Ethernet and WSN. In *2015 International Conference on Computational Intelligence and Communication Networks (CICN)* (pp. 183-187). IEEE. 10.1109/CICN.2015.43

Channa, M. I., & Ahmed, K. M. (2011). A reliable routing scheme for post-disaster ad hoc communication networks. *Journal of Communication*, *6*(7), 549–557. doi:10.4304/jcm.6.7.549-557

Charniak, E. (2019). *Introduction to deep learning*. The MIT Press.

Chasanis, V. T., Likas, A. C., & Galatsanos, N. P. (2008). Scene detection in videos using shot clustering and sequence alignment. *IEEE Transactions on Multimedia*, *11*(1), 89–100. doi:10.1109/TMM.2008.2008924

Chasanis, V., Kalogeratos, A., & Likas, A. (2009). Movie segmentation into scenes and chapters using locally weighted bag of visual words. In *Proceedings of the ACM International Conference on Image and Video Retrieval* (pp. 1-7). 10.1145/1646396.1646439

Chauhan & Babar. (2012). Towards Process Support for Migrating Applications to Cloud Computing. *International Conference on Cloud Computing and Service Computing*.

Chauhan, D., & Thakur, J. (2014). *Data Mining Techniques for Weather Prediction: A Review. International Journal on Recent and Innovation Trends in Computing and Communication*.

Chelli, K. (2015). Security issues in wireless sensor networks: Attacks and countermeasures. *Proceedings of the World Congress on Engineering*.

Chen, S., Xu, H., Liu, D., Hu, B., & Wang, H. (2014). A vision of IoT: Applications, challenges, and opportunities with china perspective. *IEEE Internet of Things Journal, 1*(4), 349-359.

Cheng, Z., Zhao, Q., Wang, F., Jiang, Y., Xia, L., & Ding, J. (2016). Satisfaction based Q-learning for integrated lighting and blind control. *Energy and Building, 127*, 43–55. doi:10.1016/j.enbuild.2016.05.067

Chen, T., Liu, C., & Huang, Q. (2012). An effective multi-clue fusion approach for web video topic detection. In *Proceedings of the 20th ACM international conference on Multimedia* (pp. 781-784). 10.1145/2393347.2396311

Chenxu, W., Tony, T. N., Xiapu, L., & Jinhe, W. (2017). SkyShield: A Sketch-Based Defense System Against Application Layer DDoS Attacks. *IEEE Transactions on Information Forensics and Security, 13*(3), 559–573.

Chen, Z., Cao, J., Song, Y., Guo, J., Zhang, Y., & Li, J. (2010). Context-oriented web video tag recommendation. In *Proceedings of the 19th international conference on World wide web* (pp. 1079-1080). 10.1145/1772690.1772813

Cherukuri, S., Venkatasubramanian, K. K., & Gupta, S. K. S. (2003). Biosec: A biometric based approach for securing communication in wireless networks of biosensors implanted in the human body. In *Proceedings of the International Conference on Parallel Processing Workshops* (pp. 432–439). 10.1109/ICPPW.2003.1240399

Chiao-Chen, C., & Yang-Chieh, C. (2011). *Comparing consumer complaint responses to online and offline environment.* Internet Research.

Choi, B. G., Cho, E. J., Kim, J. H., Hong, C. S., & Kim, J. H. (2009). *A sinkhole attack detection mechanism for LQI based mesh routing in WSN.* Paper presented at the 2009 International Conference on Information Networking.

Christopher, N. G., Taegyu, K., Raffaele, D. C., Jeffrey, A., & Dan, G. (2018). Learning from the Ones that Got Away: Detecting New Forms of Phishing Attacks. *IEEE Transactions on Dependable and Secure Computing, 15*(6), 988–1001. doi:10.1109/TDSC.2018.2864993

Chuang, S., Min, Z., Yueying, Z., Danshi, W., Luyao, G., Wei, L., ... Siya, X. (2019). Hierarchical Edge Cloud Enabling Network Slicing For 5G Optional Fronthaul. *Journal of Optical Communications and Networking, 11*(4), B60–B70. doi:10.1364/JOCN.11.000B60

Chung, M. H., Meng, S. C., Duy, T. D., Wei, L. S., & Shouzhi, X. (2018). V2V Data Offloading for Cellular Network Based on the Software Defined Network (SDN) Inside Mobile Edge Computing (MEC) Architecture. *IEEE Access: Practical Innovations, Open Solutions, 6*, 17741–17755. doi:10.1109/ACCESS.2018.2820679

Chu, T. S. (2012). Acoustic Sensor Array for Determination of Undersea Acoustic Signatures. In *IEEE International Conference on Electro/Information Technology*. Indianapolis, IN: IEEE. 10.1109/EIT.2012.6220770

Chu, W. T., Li, C. J., & Chou, Y. K. (2011). Tag suggestion and localization for web videos by bipartite graph matching. In *Proceedings of the 3rd ACM SIGMM international workshop on Social media* (pp. 35-40). 10.1145/2072609.2072621

Cireşan, D. C., Meier, U., Gambardella, L. M., & Schmidhuber, J. (2010). Deep, big, simple neural nets for handwritten digit recognition. *Neural Computation, 22*(12), 3207–3220. doi:10.1162/NECO_a_00052 PMID:20858131

Citing Images and Tables Found Online I UNSW Current Students. (2019). https://student.unsw.edu.au/citing-images-and-tables-found-online https://dzone.com/articles/the-internet-of-thingsgateways-and-next-generation

Clarke, E. M., Klieber, W., Nováček, M., & Zuliani, P. (2011, September). Model checking and the state explosion problem. In *LASER Summer School on Software Engineering* (pp. 1–30). Berlin: Springer.

Condry, M. W., & Nelson, C. B. (2016). Using Smart Edge IoT Devices for Safer. Rapid Response With Industry IoT Control Operations. *Proceedings of the IEEE*, 104(5), 938-946. 10.1109/JPROC.2015.2513672

Conoscenti, M., Vetro, A., & De Martin, J. C. (2016, November). Blockchain for the Internet of Things: A systematic literature review. In *2016 IEEE/ACS 13th International Conference of Computer Systems and Applications (AICCSA)* (pp. 1-6). IEEE. 10.1109/AICCSA.2016.7945805

Conroy, D., Williams, J., Chauhan, S., Harmson, G., Snyder, M., & Symons, C. (2017). *Journey to the cloud - The creative CIO Agenda*. Retrieved from KPMG: https://assets.kpmg.com/content/dam/kpmg/xx/pdf/2017/02/the-creative-ciosagenda-journey-to-cloud.PDF

Conti, Mancini, & Mei. (n.d.). Distributed Detection of Clone Attacks in Wireless Sensor Networks. *IEEE Transactions on Dependable and Secure Computing*.

Corradini, F., De Angelis, F., Polini, A., & Sabbatini, S. (2015). Cloud Readiness Assessment of Legacy Application. *5th International Conference on Cloud Computing and Services Science (CLOSER2015)*. 10.5220/0005443301190126

Correia, L. H., Heimfarth, T., Pereira, G. M., Silva, V. F., & de Santana, J. L. (2010). Radio channel model of wireless sensor networks operating in 2.4 GHz ISM band. *INFOCOMP*, 9(1), 98–106.

Coulibaly, S., Kamsu-Foguem, B., Kamissoko, D., & Traore, D. (2019). Deep Neural Networks with Transfer Learning in Millet Crop Images. *Computers in Industry*, 108, 115–120. doi:10.1016/j.compind.2019.02.003

Coussement, K., & Van den Poel, D. (2015). *Improving customer complaint management by automatic email classification using linguistic style features as predictors*. Decision Support Systems.

Creech, G., & Hu, J. (2013). A semantic approach to host-based intrusion detection systems using contiguousand discontiguous system call patterns. *IEEE Transactions on Computers*, 63(4), 807–819. doi:10.1109/TC.2013.13

Cristina, A., Giuseppe, B., Federica, P., Javier, L., & Roberto, S. (2019). Covert Channels-Based Stealth Attacks in Industry 4.0. *IEEE Systems Journal*, 13(4), 3980–3988. doi:10.1109/JSYST.2019.2912308

Daemin, S., Keon, Y., Jiyoon, K., Philip, V. A., Jeong, N. K., & Ilsun, Y. (2019). A Security Protocol for Route Optimization in DMM-Based Smart Home IoT Networks. *IEEE Access: Practical Innovations, Open Solutions*, 7, 142531–142550. doi:10.1109/ACCESS.2019.2943929

Dağtaş, S., Pekhteryev, G., Şahinoğlu, Z., Çam, H., & Challa, N. (2008). Real-time and secure wireless health monitoring. *International Journal of Telemedicine and Applications*, 2008, 1–10. doi:10.1155/2008/135808 PMID:18497866

Dale, B., & Dale, B. (2018, January 22). *Three Whitehat Countermeasures to the Botnet Threat*. Retrieved from https://observer.com/2016/11/mirai-bestbuy-popopret-imperva-cymmetria-virgil-security-spiffy/

Datta, L. (2016). A new Task Scheduling method for 2 Level Load Balancing in homogeneous distributed system. In *International Conference on Electrical, Electronics, and Optimization Techniques (ICEEOT)* (pp. 4320-4325). Chennai, India: IEEE. 10.1109/ICEEOT.2016.7755534

Dawod, A., Georgakopoulos, D., Jayaraman, P. P., & Nirmalathas, A. (2019). Advancements Towards Global IoT Device Discovery and Integration. In *IEEE International Congress on Internet of Things (ICIOT)* (pp. 147-155). IEEE. 10.1109/ICIOT.2019.00034

Daylighting: Whole Building Design Guide. (n.d.). Retrieved from https://www.wbdg.org/resources/daylighting

De Matos, C.A. & Rossi, C.A.V. (2008). Word-of-mouth communications in marketing: a meta-analytic review of the antecedents and moderators. *Journal of Academy of Marketing Science.*

De Ruyter & Wetzels. (2010). Customer equity considerations in service recovery: A crossindustry perspective. *International Journal of Service Industry Management.*

DeCarlo, T.E., Laczniak, R.N., Motley, C.M., & Ramaswami, S. (2007). Influence of image and familiarity on consumer response to negative word-of-mouth communication about retail entities. *Journal of Marketing Theory and Practice.*

Deng & Chen. (n.d.). *Mobility-assisted Detection of the Replication Attacks in Mobile Wireless Sensor Networks.* Academic Press.

K. Deng, Z. Yu, S. Patnaik, & J. Wang (Eds.). (2018). Recent Developments in Mechatronics and Intelligent Robotics. In *Proceedings of International Conference on Mechatronics and Intelligent Robotics (ICMIR2018)* (Vol. 856). Springer.

Deng, L., & Yu, D. (2014). Deep learning: Methods and applications. *Foundations and Trends in Signal Processing, 7*(3-4), 197–387. doi:10.1561/2000000039

Deogirikar, J., & Vidhate, A. (2017, February). Security attacks in IoT: A survey. In *2017 International Conference on I-SMAC (IoT in Social, Mobile, Analytics and Cloud)(I-SMAC)* (pp. 32-37). IEEE. 10.1109/I-SMAC.2017.8058363

Devisri, S., & Balasubramaniam, C. (2013). Secure Routing Using Trust Based Mechaniam in Wireless Sensor Networks (WSNs). *International Journal of Scientific and Engineering Research, 4*(2), 1–7.

Devi, V. S., & Hegde, N. P. (2018). Multipath Security Aware Routing Protocol for MANET Based on Trust Enhanced Cluster Mechanism for Lossless Multimedia Data Transfer. *Wireless Personal Communications, 100*(3), 923–940. doi:10.100711277-018-5358-5

Dhanabal, L., & Shantharajah, S. P. (2015). A study on NSL-KDD dataset for intrusion detection system based on classification algorithms. *International Journal of Advanced Research in Computer and Communication Engineering, 4*(6), 446–452.

Dhanushka, K., Santosh, T., & Gayan, A. A. (2019). Secure Communication in Relay-Assisted Massive MIMO Downlink With Active Pilot Attacks. *IEEE Transactions on Information Forensics and Security, 14*(11), 2819–2833. doi:10.1109/TIFS.2019.2901825

Dimitrios, S. K., Alexandros, A. A., George, K. K., & Arumugam, N. (2017). Physical Layer Security in the Presence of Interference. *IEEE Wireless Communications Letters, 6*(6), 802–805. doi:10.1109/LWC.2017.2743716

Dimitriou, T., & Ioannis, K. (2008). Security issues in biomedical wireless sensor networks. In *2008 1st International Symposium on Applied Sciences in Biomedical and Communication Technologies, ISABEL 2008* (pp. 1–5). 10.1109/ISABEL.2008.4712577

Dimitrov, S., & Haas, H. (2015). *Principles of LED light communications: towards networked Li-Fi.* Cambridge University Press. doi:10.1017/CBO9781107278929

Ding, W., & Hu, H. (2018, October). On the safety of IoT device physical interaction control. In *Proceedings of the 2018 ACM SIGSAC Conference on Computer and Communications Security* (pp. 832-846). ACM. 10.1145/3243734.3243865

Diro, A. A., & Chilamkurti, N. (2018). Distributed attack detection scheme using deep learning approach for Internet of Things. *Future Generation Computer Systems, 82*, 761–768. doi:10.1016/j.future.2017.08.043

Division, F. N. TEC. (n.d.). *Study Paper on LiFi (Light Fidelity) & its Applications*. Retrieved from http://tec.gov.in/pdf/Studypaper/lifi%20study%20paper%20-%20approved.pdf

Dlodlo, N., & Kalezhi, J. (2015). The Internet of Things in Agriculture for Sustainable Rural Development. In *2015 International Conference on Emerging Trends in Networks and Computer Communications (ETNCC)*. Windhoek, Namibia: IEEE. 10.1109/ETNCC.2015.7184801

Dobran, B. (2019). *The Ultimate Guide to Man in the Middle Attacks: Prevention is Key*. Retrieved from https://phenixnap.com/man-in-the-middle-attacks-prevention

Donahue, J., Anne Hendricks, L., Guadarrama, S., Rohrbach, M., Venugopalan, S., Saenko, K., & Darrell, T. (2015). Long-term recurrent convolutional networks for visual recognition and description. In *Proceedings of the IEEE conference on computer vision and pattern recognition* (pp. 2625-2634). 10.1109/CVPR.2015.7298878

Dong, W., Bo, B., Kai, L., Wenbo, Z., Yanping, Y., & Zhu, H. (2019). Enhancing Information Security via Physical Layer Approaches in Heterogeneous IoT With Multiple Access Mobile Edge Computing in Smart City. *IEEE Access: Practical Innovations, Open Solutions, 7*, 54508–54521. doi:10.1109/ACCESS.2019.2913438

Dong, Y. L. (2016). *Depth Map Up-sampling with Texture Edge Feature via Sparse Representation. In Visual Communications and Image Processing (VCIP)*. Chengdu, China: IEEE.

Dorri, A., Kanhere, S. S., Jurdak, R., & Gauravaram, P. (2017, March). Blockchain for IoT security and privacy: The case study of a smart home. In 2017 IEEE international conference on pervasive computing and communications workshops (PerCom Workshops) (pp. 618-623). IEEE.

Dr, G., & Padmavathi, D. S. (2009). A Survey of Attacks, Security Mechanisms and Challenges in Wireless Sensor Networks. *International Journal of Computer Science and Information Security, 4*(1).

Duan, J., Yang, D., Zhu, H., Zhang, S., & Zhao, J. (2014). TSRF: A trust-aware secure routing framework in wireless sensor networks. *International Journal of Distributed Sensor Networks, 2014*(1), 209436. doi:10.1155/2014/209436

Duffy, D. L. (2013). Internal and external factors which affect customer loyalty. Journal of Consumer Marketing.

Dutta & Tahbilder. (2014). Prediction Of Rainfall Using Data mining Technique over Assam. *Indian Journal of Computer Science and Engineering (IJCSE)*.

Dutta, A. M. (2006). GPS Assisted Fast-Handoff Mechanism for Real-Time Communication. In *IEEE Sarnoff Symposium*. Princeton, NJ: IEEE. 10.1109/SARNOF.2006.4534769

Edwards, S., & Profetis, I. (2016). Hajime: Analysis of a decentralized internet worm for IoT devices. *Rapidity Networks, 16*.

Ehigie, B. (2016). Correlates of Consumer Loyalty to their bank: A case of Nigeria. *International Journal of Bank Marketing*.

Ehrenberg, A. S. C., & Scriven, J. A. (1999). Brand loyalty. In The Elgar Companion to Consumer Research and Economic Psychology. Edward Elgar.

Eissa, T., Abdul Razak, S., Khokhar, R. H., & Samian, N. (2013). Trust-based routing mechanism in MANET: Design and implementation. *Mobile Networks and Applications, 18*(5), 666–677. doi:10.100711036-011-0328-0

Ekong, V., & Ekong, U. (2016). A Survey of Security Vulnerabilities in Wireless Sensor Networks. *Nigerian Journal of Technology, 35*(2), 392. doi:10.4314/njt.v35i2.21

El Mourabit, Y., Toumanari, A., & Zougagh, H. (2014). A Mobile Agent Approach for IDS in Mobile Ad Hoc Network. *International Journal of Computer Science Issues, 11*(1), 148.

Elbasher, W. S., Mustafa, A. B., & Osman, A. A. (2015). A Comparison between Li-Fi, Wi-Fi, and Ethernet Standards. *International Journal of Scientific Research (Ahmedabad, India), 4*(12), 1–4.

Elbhiri, B., Saadane, R., & Aboutajdine, D. (2010, September). Developed Distributed Energy-Efficient Clustering (DDEEC) for heterogeneous wireless sensor networks. In *2010 5th International Symposium On I/V Communications and Mobile Network* (pp. 1-4). IEEE.

Elijah, Abdullah, Jhanjhi, Supramaniam, & Abdullateef. (2019). Ensemble and Deep-Learning Methods for Two-Class and Multi-Attack Anomaly Intrusion Detection: An Empirical Study. *International Journal of Advanced Computer Science and Applications, 10*(9), 520-528.

Elkhodr, M., Shahrestani, S., & Cheung, H. (2016). *The internet of things: new interoperability, management, and security challenges.* arXiv preprint arXiv:1604.04824

Elrawy, M. F., Awad, A. I., & Hamed, H. F. A. (2018). Intrusion detection systems for IoT-based smart environments: A survey. *Journal of Cloud Computing, 7*(1), 1–20. doi:10.118613677-018-0123-6

Enaitz, E., Urko, Z., & José, M. G. (2017). A study of the personalization of spam content using Facebook public information. *Logic Journal of the IGPL, 25*(1), 30–41. doi:10.1093/jigpal/jzw040

Enertiv – Smart Building Soultions. (n.d.). Retrieved from https://www.enertiv.com

Erhan, D., Bengio, Y., Courville, A., Manzagol, P. A., Vincent, P., & Bengio, S. (2010). Why does unsupervised pre-training help deep learning? *Journal of Machine Learning Research, 11*(Feb), 625–660.

Estelami, H. (2000). Competitive and procedural determinants of delight and disappointment on consumer complaint outcomes. *Journal of Service Research.*

Everingham, M., Eslami, S., Gool, L. V., Williams, C., Winn, J., & Zisserman, A. (2015). The pascal visual object classes challenge: A retrospective. *IJCV, 111*(1), 98–136. doi:10.100711263-014-0733-5

Everingham, M., Gool, L. V., Williams, C., Winn, J., & Zisserman, A. (2010). The pascal visual object classes (voc) challenge. *IJCV, 88*(2), 303–338. doi:10.100711263-009-0275-4

Evers, C. M. (2016). Acoustic simultaneous localization and mapping (A-SLAM) of a moving microphone array and its surrounding speakers. In *IEEE International Conference on Acoustics, Speech and Signal Processing (ICASSP)* (pp. 6-10). Shanghai, China: IEEE. 10.1109/ICASSP.2016.7471626

Fairchild, A. J. & MacKinnon, D.P. (2009). *A General Model for Testing Mediation and Moderation Effects.* Academic Press.

Fathima, N., A. A. (2017). Optimized Neighbor Discovery in Internet of Things (IoT). In *International Conference on Electrical, Electronics, Communication, Computer and Optimization Techniques (ICEECCOT)* (pp. 594-598). IEEE. 10.1109/ICEECCOT.2017.8284573

Fayaz & Kim. (2018). *A Prediction Methodology of Energy Consumption Based on Deep Extreme Learning Machine and Comparative Analysis in Residential Buildings.* Academic Press.

Ferentinos, K. P. (2018). Deep Learning Models for Plant Disease Detection and Diagnosis. *Computers and Electronics in Agriculture, 145*, 311–318. doi:10.1016/j.compag.2018.01.009

Fernández-Caramés, T. M., & Fraga-Lamas, P. (2018). Towards the internet-of-smart-clothing: A review on IoT wearables and garments for creating intelligent connected E-textiles. *Electronics (Switzerland)*, *7*(12), 405. doi:10.3390/electronics7120405

Festinger, L. (2015). A theory of cognitive dissonance. Stanford, CA: Stanford University Press.

Fischer, M., Lim, Y. Y., Lawrence, E., & Ganguli, L. K. (2008). ReMoteCare: health monitoring with streaming video. In *Proceedings - 7th International Conference on Mobile Business, ICMB 2008, Creativity and Convergence* (pp. 280–286). 10.1109/ICMB.2008.16

Fischler, M., & Elschlager, R. (1973). The representation and matching of pictorial structures. *IEEE Transactions on Computers*, *100*(1), 67–92. doi:10.1109/T-C.1973.223602

Fornell, C., & Wernerfelt, B. (1987). Defensive Marketing Strategy by Consumer Complaint Management: A Theorical Analysis. *JMR, Journal of Marketing Research*.

Fornell, C., & Wernerfelt, B. (2000). Defensive marketing strategy by customer complaint management: A theoretical analysis. *JMR, Journal of Marketing Research*.

Fornell, C., & Westbrook, R. A. (2010). *An exploratory study of assertiveness, aggressiveness, and consumer complaining behavior*. Ann Arbor, MI: Association for Consumer Research.

Fortunato, M. C.-M. (2019). Enabling High Accuracy Dynamic Applications in Urban Environments Using PPP and RTK on Android Multi-Frequency and Multi-GNSS Smartphones. In *European Navigation Conference (ENC)*. Warsaw, Poland: IEEE. 10.1109/EURONAV.2019.8714140

Freeman, I., Haigler, A., Schmeelk, S., Ellrodt, L., & Fields, T. (2018). What are they Researching? Examining Industry-Based Doctoral Dissertation Research through the Lens of Machine Learning. In *2018 17th IEEE International Conference on Machine Learning and Applications (ICMLA)* (pp. 1338-1340). IEEE.

Fruhlinger, J. (2017). *What is Stuxnet, who created it and how does it work?* Retrieved from https://www.csoonline.com/article/3218104/what-is-stuxnet-who-created-it-and-how-does-it-work.html

Fu, Y., Yan, Z., Cao, J., Koné, O., & Cao, X. (2017). An automata based intrusion detection method for internet of things. *Mobile Information Systems, 2017*.

Fukushima, K. (1980). Neocognitron: A self-organizing neural network model for a mechanism of pattern recognition unaffected by shift in position. *Biological Cybernetics*, *36*(4), 193–202. doi:10.1007/BF00344251 PMID:7370364

Gandhi, N., Petkar, O., & Armstrong, L. J. (2016). Rice Crop Yield Prediction Using Artificial Neural Networks. In *2016 IEEE Technological Innovations in ICT for Agriculture and Rural Development (TIAR)*. Chennai, India: IEEE. doi:10.1109/TIAR.2016.7801222

Gandhi, U. D., Kumar, P. M., Varatharajan, R., Manogaran, G., Sundarasekar, R., & Kadu, S. (2018). HIoTPOT: Surveillance on IoT devices against recent threats. *Wireless Personal Communications*, *103*(2), 1179–1194. doi:10.100711277-018-5307-3

Gao, Y., & Liu, W. (2014a). *BeTrust : A Dynamic Trust Model Based on Bayesian Inference and Tsallis Entropy for Medical Sensor Networks*. Academic Press.

Gao, T., Massey, T., Selavo, L., Crawford, D., Chen, B. R., Lorincz, K., ... Welsh, M. (2007). The advanced health and disaster aid network: A light-weight wireless medical system for tiage. *IEEE Transactions on Biomedical Circuits and Systems*, *1*(3), 203–216. doi:10.1109/TBCAS.2007.910901 PMID:23852414

Gao, Y., & Liu, W. (2014b). BeTrust: A dynamic trust model based on Bayesian inference and Tsallis entropy for medical sensor networks. *Journal of Sensors*, *2014*, 1–10. doi:10.1155/2014/649392

Garg, A., & Maheshwari, P. (2016, January). A hybrid intrusion detection system: A review. In *2016 10th International Conference on Intelligent Systems and Control (ISCO)* (pp. 1-5). IEEE. 10.1109/ISCO.2016.7726909

Garlati, Z. (2016). *Owlet Baby Wi-Fi Monitor "Worst IoT Security of 2016"*. Retrieved from: https://www.information-securitybuzz.com/expert-comments/owlet-baby-wi-fi-monitor-worst-iot-security-2016/

Gebreslassie, B., Zayegh, A., & Kalam, A. (2017). Design, modeling of an intelligent green building using, actuator sensor interface network protocol. *Australasian Universities Power Engineering Conference (AUPEC)*, 1-6. 10.1109/AUPEC.2017.8282492

Geetha, V., Aithal, S., & ChandraSekaran, K. (2006). Effect of Mobility over Performance of the Ad hoc Networks. In *2006 International Symposium on Ad Hoc and Ubiquitous Computing* (pp. 138-141). IEEE. 10.1109/ISAHUC.2006.4290661

Ghazi, M., Mostafa, B. Y., & Aptoula, E. (2017). Plant Identification Using Deep Neural Networks via Optimization of Transfer Learning Parameters. *Neurocomputing*, *235*, 228–235. doi:10.1016/j.neucom.2017.01.018

Gidijala, N. S., Datla, S., & Joshi, R. C. (2010). *A Robust Trust Mechanism Algorithm for Secure Power Aware AODV Routing in Mobile Ad Hoc Networks*. doi:10.1007/978-3-642-14834-7_4

Giraldo, J., Urbina, D., Cardenas, A., Valente, J., Faisal, M., Ruths, J., ... Candell, R. (2018). A survey of physics-based attack detection in cyber-physical systems. *ACM Computing Surveys*, *51*(4), 76. doi:10.1145/3203245 PMID:31092968

Giri, D., Borah, S., & Pradhan, R. (2018). *Approaches and Measures to Detect Wormhole Attack in Wireless Sensor Networks: A Survey. In Advances in Communication, Devices and Networking* (pp. 855–864). Springer. doi:10.1007/978-981-10-7901-6_92

Glorot, X., Bordes, A., & Bengio, Y. (2011, June). Deep sparse rectifier neural networks. In *Proceedings of the fourteenth international conference on artificial intelligence and statistics* (pp. 315-323). Academic Press.

Goap, A., Sharma, D., Shukla, A. K., & Rama Krishna, C. (2018). An IoT Based Smart Irrigation Management System Using Machine Learning and Open Source Technologies. *Computers and Electronics in Agriculture*, *155*(September), 41–49. doi:10.1016/j.compag.2018.09.040

Gonzalez, J. M., Anwar, M., & Joshi, J. B. D. (2011). Trust-based approaches to solve routing issues in ad-hoc wireless networks: A survey. In *Proc. 10th IEEE Int. Conf. on Trust, Security and Privacy in Computing and Communications, TrustCom 2011, 8th IEEE Int. Conf. on Embedded Software and Systems, ICESS 2011, 6th Int. Conf. on FCST 2011* (pp. 556–563). 10.1109/TrustCom.2011.72

Gouda, Dwivedi, Patro, & Bhat. (2014). Migration Management in Cloud Computing. *International Journal of Engineering Trends and Technology, 12*(9).

Grauman, K., & Leibe, B. (2011). Visual object recognition. *Synthesis Lectures on Artificial Intelligence and Machine Learning*, *5*(2), 1–181. doi:10.2200/S00332ED1V01Y201103AIM011

Greer, C., Burns, M., Wollman, D., & Griffor, E. (1900). Cyber-Physical Systems & the Internet of Things. *NIST Special Publication*, *202*, 2019.

Guan, W., Wen, X., Wang, L., & Lu, Z. (2018). On-Demand Cooperation Among Multiple Infrastructure Networks For Multi-Tenant Slicing: A Complex Network Perspective. *IEEE Access: Practical Innovations, Open Solutions*, *6*, 78689–78699. doi:10.1109/ACCESS.2018.2885143

Gu, C. S. (2009). GPS information assisted handoff mechanism in heterogeneous wireless networks. In *IEEE International Conference on Communications Technology and Applications*. Beijing, China: IEEE.

Guo, X., Tiller, D., Henze, G., & Waters, C. (2010). The performance of occupancy-based lighting control systems: A review. *Lighting Research & Technology*, *42*(4), 415–431. doi:10.1177/1477153510376225

Gupta, D., & Ghose, U. (2015). A Comparative Study of Classification Algorithms for Risk Prediction in Pregnancy. Academic Press.

Gupta, G. (2014). A self explanatory review of decision tree classifiers. In *International conference on recent advances and innovations in engineering (ICRAIE-2014)* (pp. 1-7). IEEE.

Gupta, N. P. (2017). Electromagnetic pollution its impact and control. *International Journal of Engineering Applied Sciences and Technology*, *2*(7), 61–65.

H, D. M., S, N. M., U, B. D., & B, M. B. (2017). Green Symbiotic Cloud Communications: Virtualized Transport Layer and Cognitive Decision Function. *IEEE Access, 5*, 13409 - 13421.

Haas, H. (2018). LiFi is a paradigm-shifting 5G technology. *Reviews in Physics*, *3*, 26–31. doi:10.1016/j.revip.2017.10.001

Haddadi, H., Christophides, V., Teixeira, R., Cho, K., Suzuki, S., & Perrig, A. (2018, April). SIOTOME: An edge-ISP collaborative architecture for IoT security. Proc. IoTSec.

Ha, I. (2016). Even energy consumption and backside routing: An improved routing protocol for effective data transmission in wireless body area networks. *International Journal of Distributed Sensor Networks*, *12*(7), 1–11. doi:10.1177/1550147716657932

Hajdarbegovic, N. (2019). *Are we creating an insecure IoT? Secure challenges and concerns*. Retrieved from https://www.toptal.com/it/are-we-creating-an-insecure-internet-of-things

Hamilton, R., Iyengar, J., Swett, I., & Wilk, A. (2016). Quic: A udp-based secure and reliable transport for http/2. *IETF, draft-tsvwg-quic-protocol-02*.

Han, W., Lingwei, X., Wenzhong, L., Pingping, X., & Ruhong, W. (2019). Physical Layer Security Performance of Wireless Mobile Sensor Networks in Smart City. *IEEE Access: Practical Innovations, Open Solutions*, *7*, 15436–15443. doi:10.1109/ACCESS.2019.2895338

Haomeng, X., Zheng, Y., Zhen, Y., & Mohammed, A. (2018). Data Collection for Security Measurement in Wireless Sensor Networks: A Survey. *IEEE Internet of Things Journal*, *6*(2), 2205–2224.

Hashem, B. K. (2000). A new algorithm to reduce the deviation in the base stations transmitted powers during soft handoff in CDMA cellular systems. In *IEEE Wireless Communications and Networking Conference. Conference Record (Cat. No.00TH8540)*. Chicago, IL: IEEE. 10.1109/WCNC.2000.904620

Hayajneh, T., Almashaqbeh, G., Ullah, S., & Vasilakos, A. V. (2014). A survey of wireless technologies coexistence in WBAN: analysis and open research issues. In Wireless Networks (Vol. 20). doi:10.100711276-014-0736-8

He, Q., Wu, D., & Khosla, P. (2008). SORI: a secure and objective reputation-based incentive scheme for ad-hoc networks. In 2004 IEEE Wireless Communications and Networking Conference (IEEE Cat. No.04TH8733) (vol. 2, pp. 825-830). doi:10.1109/wcnc.2004.1311293

He, D., Chen, C., Chan, S., Bu, J., & Vasilakos, A. V. (2012). ReTrust: Attack-resistant and lightweight trust management for medical sensor networks. *IEEE Transactions on Information Technology in Biomedicine, 16*(4), 623–632. doi:10.1109/TITB.2012.2194788 PMID:22531816

He, F., Li, X., Yulong, Z., Xianbin, W., & Kim, K. R. (2018). Three-Stage Stackelberg Game for Defending Against Full-Duplex Active Eavesdropping Attacks in Cooperative Communication. *IEEE Transactions on Vehicular Technology, 67*(11), 10788–10799. doi:10.1109/TVT.2018.2868900

Heinzelman, W. B., Chandrakasan, A. P., & Balakrishnan, H. (2002). An application-specific protocol architecture for wireless microsensor networks. *IEEE Transactions on Wireless Communications, 1*(4), 660–670. doi:10.1109/TWC.2002.804190

Hern, C. (2016, October 23). *IoT Smart City – What is a Smart City?* http://www.infiniteinformationtechnology.com/IoT-smart-city-what-is-smart-home

Hierarchies, C. A. (Sun Directory Server Enterprise Edition 7.0 Reference). (n.d.). https://docs.oracle.com/cd/E19424-01/820-4811/gdzdp/index.html

Hinton, G. E., Osindero, S., & Teh, Y.-W. (2006). A fast learning algorithm for deep belief nets. *Neural Computation, 18*(7), 1527–1554. doi:10.1162/neco.2006.18.7.1527 PMID:16764513

Hinton, G. E., & Salakhutdinov, R. R. (2006). Reducing the dimensionality of data with neural networks. *Science, 2006*(313), 504–507. doi:10.1126cience.1127647 PMID:16873662

Hirata, A., Matsuyama, S. I., & Shiozawa, T. (2000). Temperature rises in the human eye exposed to EM waves in the frequency range 0.6-6 GHz. *IEEE Transactions on Electromagnetic Compatibility, 42*(4), 386–393. doi:10.1109/15.902308

Hoai, M., Lan, Z. Z., & De la Torre, F. (2011). Joint segmentation and classification of human actions in video. In CVPR 2011 (pp. 3265-3272). doi:10.1109/CVPR.2011.5995470

Hoang, Q. (2018). *Predicting movie genres based on plot summaries.* arXiv preprint arXiv:1801.04813

Hodo, E., Bellekens, X., Hamilton, A., Dubouilh, P. L., Iorkyase, E., Tachtatzis, C., & Atkinson, R. (2016). Threat analysis of IoT networks using artificial neural network intrusion detection system. In *2016 International Symposium on Networks, Computers and Communications (ISNCC)* (pp. 1-6). IEEE. 10.1109/ISNCC.2016.7746067

Holger, B., & Christian, D. (2018). Secure Identification Under Passive Eavesdroppers and Active Jamming Attacks. *IEEE Transactions on Information Forensics and Security, 14*(2), 472–485.

Hong, H. (2017). From Cloud Computing to Fog Computing: Unleash the Power of Edge and End Devices. In *IEEE 9th International Conference on Cloud Computing Technology and Science* (pp. 331-334). IEEE.

Hossain, M. S., & Raghunathan, V. (2010). *Aegis: A lightweight firewall for wireless sensor networks.* Paper presented at the International Conference on Distributed Computing in Sensor Systems. 10.1007/978-3-642-13651-1_19

Housley, R., & Polk, T. (2001). *Planning for PKI: best practices guide for deploying public key infrastructure.* John Wiley & Sons, Inc.

Huang, C. M. (1997). Handoff Architectures Ahkd Protocols For Transmitting Compressed Multimedia Information In Mobile PCSs. In *International Conference on Consumer Electronics* (pp. 784-794). Rosemont, IL: IEEE.

Huang, S., Zhou, C. J., Yang, S. H., & Qin, Y. Q. (2015). Cyber-physical system security for networked Industrial processes. *International Journal of Automation and Computing, 12*(6), 567–578. doi:10.100711633-015-0923-9

Huang, Y. M., Hsieh, M. Y., Chao, H. C., Hung, S. H., & Park, J. H. (2009). Pervasive, secure access to a hierarchical sensor-based healthcare monitoring architecture in wireless heterogeneous networks. *IEEE Journal on Selected Areas in Communications*, 27(4), 400–411. doi:10.1109/JSAC.2009.090505

Huan, L., Shoufeng, C., Jiayan, W., Zhenzhong, C., & Fengyu, W. (2019). Identifying Application-Layer DDoS Attacks Based on Request Rhythm Matrices. *IEEE Access: Practical Innovations, Open Solutions*, 7, 164480–164491. doi:10.1109/ACCESS.2019.2950820

Huaqing, L., Zheng, Y., Yu, C., & Lifang, Z. (2018). A Survey on Network Security-Related Data Collection Technologies. *IEEE Access: Practical Innovations, Open Solutions*, 6, 18345–18365. doi:10.1109/ACCESS.2018.2817921

Hudson, F., & Clark, C. (2019). Wearables and Medical Interoperability: The Evolving Frontier. *Computer*, 51(9), 86–90. doi:10.1109/MC.2018.3620987

Hu, F., Jiang, M., Wagner, M., & Dong, D. C. (2007). Privacy-preserving telecardiology sensor networks: Toward a low-cost portable wireless hardware/software codesign. *IEEE Transactions on Information Technology in Biomedicine*, 11(6), 619–627. doi:10.1109/TITB.2007.894818 PMID:18046937

Humayun, M., Niazi, M., Jhanjhi, N. Z., Alshayeb, M., & Mahmood, S. (2020). Cyber Security Threats and Vulnerabilities: A Systematic Mapping Study. *Arabian Journal for Science and Engineering*, 1–19. doi:10.100713369-019-04319-2

Hussain, A., Bashir, S., Akhter, K., & Rashid, I. (2017). Issues Encountered During Migration from Existing Systems to Cloud Based Systems. IJCSMC, 6(6).

Hussain, F., Hussain, R., Hassan, S. A., & Hossain, E. (2019). *Machine Learning in IoT Security: Current Solutions and Future Challenges*. arXiv preprint arXiv:1904.05735

Hussain, K., Hussain, S. J., Jhanjhi, N. Z., & Humayun, M. (2019, April). SYN Flood Attack Detection based on Bayes Estimator (SFADBE) For MANET. In *2019 International Conference on Computer and Information Sciences (ICCIS)* (pp. 1-4). IEEE. 10.1109/ICCISci.2019.8716416

IEEE Standards Association. (2012). IEEE standard for local and metropolitan area networks-part 15.6: wireless body area networks. *IEEE std, 802*(6), 2012.

IIOT. (2017). *An overview of the IoT Security Market Report 2017-2022*. Retrieved from: https://iiot-world.com/reports/an-overview-of-the-iot-security-market-report-2017-2022/

Ilyas, S., & Rehman, H. U. (2019). A Deep Learning based Approach for Precise Video Tagging. In *15th International Conference on Emerging Technologies (ICET)* (pp. 1-6). 10.1109/ICET48972.2019.8994567

Ioffe, S., & Szegedy, C. (2015). *Batch normalization: Accelerating deep network training by reducing internal covariate shift*. arXiv preprint arXiv:1502.03167

IoT explained: What is the internet of things? (n.d.). *IoT Agenda*. Retrieved February 23, 2020, from https://internetofthingsagenda.techtarget.com/feature/Explained-What-is-the-Internet-of-Things

Islam, J., Islam, M., & Islam, N. (2007). *A-sleach: An advanced solar aware leach protocol for energy efficient routing in wireless sensor networks*. Paper presented at the Sixth International Conference on Networking (ICN'07). 10.1109/ICN.2007.14

Ivan, F., Tarik, T., Yacine, K., & Jaeseung, S. (2018). A Survey on Emerging SDN and NFV Security Mechanisms for IoT Systems. *IEEE Communications Surveys and Tutorials*, 21(1), 812–837.

Jager, T., Schwenk, J., & Somorovsky, J. (2015, October). On the security of TLS 1.3 and QUIC against weaknesses in PKCS# 1 v1. 5 encryption. In *Proceedings of the 22nd ACM SIGSAC Conference on Computer and Communications Security* (pp. 1185-1196). ACM.

Jain, S., & Garg, V. (2018). A review of open loop control strategies for shades, blinds and integrated lighting by use of real-time daylight prediction methods. *Building and Environment, 135*, 352–364. doi:10.1016/j.buildenv.2018.03.018

Jamil, F., Iqbal, M., Amin, R., & Kim, D. (2019). Adaptive Thermal-Aware Routing Protocol for Wireless Body Area Network. *Electronics (Basel), 8*(1), 47. doi:10.3390/electronics8010047

Jamshidi, Ahmad, & Pahl. (2013). Cloud Migration Research: A systematic Review. *Cloud Computing, IEEE Transaction on.*

Janeja, V. P., Azari, A., Namayanja, J. M., & Heilig, B. (2014). B-dids: Mining anomalies in a Big-distributed Intrusion Detection System. In *2014 IEEE International Conference on Big Data (Big Data)* (pp. 32-34). IEEE. 10.1109/BigData.2014.7004484

Jangra, R., & Kait, R. (2017, February). Analysis and comparison among ant system; ant colony system and max-min ant system with different parameters setting. In *2017 3rd International Conference on Computational Intelligence & Communication Technology (CICT)* (pp. 1-4). IEEE.

Jangra, R., & Kait, R. (2019). *Modified Energy Proficient ACO Based LEACH Protocol in Wireless Sensor Network.* Available at SSRN 3426948

Jangra, R., & Kait, R. (2017). ACO Parameters Analysis of TSP Problem. *International Journal of Computer Science and Mobile Applications, 8*(5).

Jangra, R., & Kait, R. (2017). Principles and Concepts of Wireless Sensor Network and Ant Colony Optimization: A Review. *International Journal of Advanced Research in Computer Science, 8*(5).

Jangra, R., & Kait, R. (2019). Modified Ant System Solving TSP Problem. *International Journal of Innovative Technology and Exploring Engineering, 8*, 328–331.

Javed, A., Larijani, H., Ahmadinia, A., & Gibson, D. (2017). Smart Random Neural Network Controller for HVAC Using Cloud Computing Technology. *IEEE Transactions on Industrial Informatics, 13*(1), 351–360. doi:10.1109/TII.2016.2597746

Jeyanthi, N. (2016). Internet of things (IoT) as interconnection of threats (IoT). In *Security and Privacy in the Internet of Things (IoT)* (pp. 21–39). CRC Press. doi:10.1201/b19516-3

Jeyanthi, N., Abraham, A., & Mcheick, H. (2019). *Studies in Big Data 47 Ubiquitous Computing and Computing Security of IoT.* Springer. doi:10.1007/978-3-030-01566-4

Jianfeng, G., Ying, Z., Su, Y., & Lili, W. (2019). AID Shuffling Mechanism Based on Group-Buying Auction for Identifier Network Security. *IEEE Access: Practical Innovations, Open Solutions, 7*, 123746–123756. doi:10.1109/ACCESS.2019.2936043

Jiang, S., Cao, Y., Iyengar, S., Kuryloski, P., Jafari, R., Xue, Y., … Wicker, S. (2009). *CareNet: An Integrated Wireless Sensor Networking Environment for Remote Healthcare.* doi:10.4108/icst.bodynets2008.2965

Jianting, N., Jia, X., Kaitai, L., Fan, Z., & Ee, C. C. (2018). Passive Attacks Against Searchable Encryption. *IEEE Transactions on Information Forensics and Security, 14*(3), 789–802.

Jiaren, C., Xin, H., Jie, Z., Jiawei, Z., Yaxi, L., Dawei, L., & Xiaofeng, M. (2018). A Handshake Protocol With Unbalanced Cost for Wireless Updating. *IEEE Access: Practical Innovations, Open Solutions, 6*, 18570–18581. doi:10.1109/ACCESS.2018.2820086

Jing, Q., Vasilakos, A. V., Wan, J., Lu, J., & Qiu, D. (2014). Security of the Internet of Things: Perspectives and challenges. *Wireless Networks, 20*(8), 2481–2501. doi:10.100711276-014-0761-7

Jing, X., Yan, Z., & Pedrycz, W. (2018). Security data collection and data analytics in the Internet: A survey. *IEEE Communications Surveys and Tutorials, 21*(1), 586–618. doi:10.1109/COMST.2018.2863942

Jordao, A., Torres, L. A. B., & Schwartz, W. R. (2018). Novel approaches to human activity recognition based on accelerometer data. *Signal, Image and Video Processing, 12*(7), 1–8. doi:10.100711760-018-1293-x

Jörg, L., Majid, V., & Tony, Y. Z. (2019). Elements of Application-Layer Internetworking for Adaptive Self-Organizing Networks. *Proceedings of the IEEE, 107*(4), 797–818. doi:10.1109/JPROC.2019.2894291

Joshi, N. K. (2018). Implementation of Novel Load Balancing Technique in Cloud Computing Environmen. In *International Conference on Computer Communication and Informatics (ICCCI)*. Coimbatore, India: IEEE. 10.1109/ICCCI.2018.8441212

Jun, X., Baoqiang, Z., & Fengzhang, L. (2019). Distribution Network Security Situation Awareness Method Based on Security Distance. *IEEE Access: Practical Innovations, Open Solutions, 7*, 37855–37864. doi:10.1109/ACCESS.2019.2906779

Jwp, Lo, B., & Wells, O. (2004). Ubiquitous monitoring environment for wearable and implantable sensors (UbiMon). In *Imperial College London* (pp. 3–4). Retrieved from http://ubicomp.org/ubicomp2004/adjunct/posters/ng.pdf

Kalchbrenner, N., Grefenstette, E., & Blunsom, P. (2014). *A convolutional neural network for modelling sentences.* arXiv preprint arXiv:1404.2188

Kamilaris, A., Gao, F., Prenafeta-Boldú, F. X., & Ali, M. I. (2016). Agri-IoT: A semantic framework for Internet of Things-enabled smart farming applications. In *3rd World Forum on Internet of Things (WF-IoT)* (pp. 442-447). Reston, VA: IEEE.

Kamilaris, A., & Prenafeta-Boldú, F. X. (2018). Deep Learning in Agriculture: A Survey. *Computers and Electronics in Agriculture, 147*, 70–90. doi:10.1016/j.compag.2018.02.016

Kang, J. S. (2013). Universal UPnP Bridge for Embedded Non-IP Device with Heterogeneous Network Interfaces. In *13th International Conference on Control, Automation and Systems (ICCAS 2013)* (pp. 561-563). Gwangju, Korea: IEEE. 10.1109/ICCAS.2013.6704002

Kang, J., & Adibi, S. (2015). *A Review of Security Protocols in mHealth Wireless Body Area Networks.* WBAN. doi:10.1007/978-3-319-19210-9_5

Kar, S., Maharjan, S., & Solorio, T. (2018). Folksonomication: Predicting tags for movies from plot synopses using emotion flow encoded neural network. In *Proceedings of the 27th International Conference on Computational Linguistics* (pp. 2879-2891). Academic Press.

Karakuşak, M. Z. (2016). The use of RSS and NI Filtering for the Wireless Indoor Localization and Tracking of Mobile Robots with Different Motion Models. In *24th Signal Processing and Communication Application Conference (SIU)*. Zonguldak, Turkey: IEEE. 10.1109/SIU.2016.7496088

Karatepe. (2010). *The Practice of Social Research.* Wadsworth Publishers.

Karlof, C., Sastry, N., & Wagner, D. (2004). TinySec: a link layer security architecture for wireless sensor networks. *Proceedings of the 2nd international conference on Embedded networked sensor systems.* 10.1145/1031495.1031515

Karpathy, A., Toderici, G., Shetty, S., Leung, T., Sukthankar, R., & Fei-Fei, L. (2014). Large-scale video classification with convolutional neural networks. In *Proceedings of the IEEE conference on Computer Vision and Pattern Recognition* (pp. 1725-1732). 10.1109/CVPR.2014.223

Karthika, R., & Balakrishnan, S. (2015). Wireless communication using Li-Fi technology. *SSRG International Journal of Electronics and Communication Engineering, 2*(3), 32-40.

Karthik, N., & Ananthanarayana, V. S. (2018). Context Aware Trust Management Scheme for Pervasive Healthcare. *Wireless Personal Communications, 105*(3), 725–736. doi:10.100711277-018-6091-9

Kaur, T., & Kumar, R. (2018). *Mitigation of Blackhole Attacks and Wormhole Attacks in Wireless Sensor Networks Using AODV Protocol.* Paper presented at the 2018 IEEE International Conference on Smart Energy Grid Engineering (SEGE). 10.1109/SEGE.2018.8499473

Kaur, S. S. (2018). Efficient Load Balancing using Improved Central Load Balancing Technique. In *Proceedings of the Second International Conference on Inventive Systems and Control (ICISC 2018)* (pp. 1-5). Coimbatore, India: IEEE. 10.1109/ICISC.2018.8398857

Kavehrad, M. (2010). Sustainable energy-efficient wireless applications using light. *IEEE Communications Magazine, 48*(12), 66–73. doi:10.1109/MCOM.2010.5673074

Kaya, A., Keceli, A. S., Catal, C., Yalic, H. Y., Temucin, H., & Tekinerdogan, B. (2019). Analysis of Transfer Learning for Deep Neural Network Based Plant Classification Models. *Computers and Electronics in Agriculture, 158*, 20–29. doi:10.1016/j.compag.2019.01.041

Kelly, S. D. T., Suryadevara, N. K., & Mukhopadhyay, S. C. (2013). Towards the Implementation of IoT for Environmental Condition Monitoring in Homes. *IEEE Sensors Journal, 13*(10), 3846–3853. doi:10.1109/JSEN.2013.2263379

Këpuska, V. (2018). Next-Generation of Virtual Personal Assistants (Microsoft Cortana, Apple Siri, Amazon Alexa and Google Home). In *IEEE 8th Annual Computing and Communication Workshop and Conference (CCWC)* (pp. 99-103). Las Vegas, NV: IEEE.

Khajeh-Hosseini, Sommerville, & Sriram. (2010). *Research Challenges for Enterprise Cloud Computing.* Academic Press.

Khalil, N., Abid, M. R., Benhaddou, D., & Gerndt, M. (2014). *Wireless sensors networks for Internet of Things.* Paper presented at the Intelligent sensors, sensor networks and information processing (ISSNIP), 2014 IEEE ninth international conference on. 10.1109/ISSNIP.2014.6827681

Khan, R., Khan, S. U., Zaheer, R., & Khan, S. (2012). Future internet: the internet of things architecture, possible applications and key challenges. In *2012 10th international conference on frontiers of information technology*, (pp. 257-260). IEEE. 10.1109/FIT.2012.53

Khan, Saad, & Xiang. (2013). Detection and Mitigation of Node Replication Attacks in Wireless Sensor Networks: A Survey. *International Journal of Distributed Sensor Networks.*

Khanda, D., & Jain, S. (2014). Li-fi (light fidelity): The future technology in wireless communication. *International Journal of Information & Computation Technology, 4*(16), 1686–1694.

Khan, L. U. (2017). Visible light communication: Applications, architecture, standardization and research challenges. *Digital Communications and Networks, 3*(2), 78–88. doi:10.1016/j.dcan.2016.07.004

Khan, M. A., & Salah, K. (2018). IoT security: Review, blockchain solutions, and open challenges. *Future Generation Computer Systems, 82*, 395–411. doi:10.1016/j.future.2017.11.022

Khanna, A., Chaudhary, V., & Gupta, S. H. (2018). Design and Analysis of Energy Efficient Wireless Body Area Network (WBAN) for Health Monitoring. Lecture Notes in Computer Science, 10990, 25–39. doi:10.1007/978-3-662-58039-4_2

Khan, R. A., & Pathan, A. S. K. (2018). The state-of-the-art wireless body area sensor networks: A survey. *International Journal of Distributed Sensor Networks, 14*(4). doi:10.1177/1550147718768994

Khan, U. A., Ejaz, N., Martínez-del-Amor, M. A., & Sparenberg, H. (2017, August). Movies tags extraction using deep learning. In *14th IEEE International Conference on Advanced Video and Signal Based Surveillance (AVSS)* (pp. 1-6). IEEE.

Khan, U. A., Martínez-Del-Amor, M. Á., Altowaijri, S. M., Ahmed, A., Rahman, A. U., Sama, N. U., ... Islam, N. (2020). Movie Tags Prediction and Segmentation Using Deep Learning. *IEEE Access: Practical Innovations, Open Solutions, 8*, 6071–6086. doi:10.1109/ACCESS.2019.2963535

Khediri, S. E., Nasri, N., Wei, A., & Kachouri, A. (2014). A new approach for clustering in wireless sensors networks based on LEACH. *Procedia Computer Science, 32*, 1180–1185. doi:10.1016/j.procs.2014.05.551

Kho, Y. H. (2015). Exploiting RF Signal Attenuation for Passive Indoor Location Tracking of an Object. In *IEEE 2015 International Conference on Computer, Communication, and Control Technology (I4CT 2015)* (pp. 152-156). Kuching, Malaysia: IEEE.

Khundrakpam, J. S., Khelchandra, T., & Tanmay, D. (2018). Detection and differentiation of application layer DDoS attack from flash events using fuzzy-GA computation. *IET Information Security, 12*(6), 502–512. doi:10.1049/iet-ifs.2017.0500

Kim, B.-S., Shah, B., Al-Obediat, F., Ullah, S., Kim, K., & Kim, K.-I. (2018). An Enhanced Mobility and Temperature Aware Routing Protocol through Multi-Criteria Decision Making Method in Wireless Body Area Networks. *Applied Sciences (Basel, Switzerland), 8*(11), 2245. doi:10.3390/app8112245

Kirar, V. P. S. (2014). A Survey of Attacks and Security Requirements in Wireless Sensor Networks. *International Journal of Computer, Electrical, Automation, Control and Information Engineering, 8*(12), 2198–2203.

Kirby, Ahmad, Mainuddin, Khaliq, & Cheema. (2017). Agricultural Production, Water Use and Food Availability in Pakistan: Historical Trends, and Projections to 2050. *Agricultural Water Management, 179*, 34–46.

Klems, M. T. (2010). Automating the Delivery of IT Service Continuity Management through Cloud Service Orchestration. In *IEEE Network Operations and Management Symposium - NOMS 2010*. Osaka, Japan: IEEE. 10.1109/NOMS.2010.5488437

Klever, R. P., Edejair, V., & Fernando, A. A. (2017). An Integrated Solution for the Improvement of the Mobile Devices Security based on the Android Platform. *IEEE Latin America Transactions, 15*(11), 2171–2176. doi:10.1109/TLA.2017.8070423

Kocakulak, M., & Butun, I. (2017). *An overview of Wireless Sensor Networks towards internet of things.* Paper presented at the Computing and Communication Workshop and Conference (CCWC), 2017 IEEE 7th Annual. 10.1109/CCWC.2017.7868374

Kok, Abdullah, Jhanjhi, & Supramaniam. (2019). A Review of Intrusion detection System Using Machine Learning Approach. *International Journal of Engineering and Research, 12*(1), 8-15.

Kong, W., Dong, Z. Y., Hill, D. J., Luo, F., & Xu, Y. (2017). *Short-term residential load forecasting based on resident behavior learning, IEEE Transactions on Power Systems.* Pre-print. doi:10.1109/TPWRS.2017.2688178

Korolov, M. (2019). *What is a botnet? When armies of infected IoT devices attack.* Retrieved from https://www.csoonline. com/article/3240364/what-is-a-botnet.html

Krishna, P., Balachandra, M., & Vasundhara, A. (2019). Automated User Authentication in Wireless Public Key Infrastructure for Mobile Devices Using Aadhar Card. *IEEE Access: Practical Innovations, Open Solutions, 7,* 17981–18007. doi:10.1109/ACCESS.2019.2896324

Krizhevsky, A., Sutskever, I., & Hinton, G. E. (2012). Imagenet classification with deep convolutional neural networks. In Advances in neural information processing systems (pp. 1097-1105). Academic Press.

Kumar, A., & Hancke, G. P. (2014). An Energy-Efficient Smart Comfort Sensing System Based on the IEEE 1451 Standard for Green Buildings. *IEEE Sensors Journal, 14*(12), 4245–4252. doi:10.1109/JSEN.2014.2356651

Kumar, P., & Lee, H. J. (2012). Security issues in healthcare applications using wireless medical sensor networks: A survey. *Sensors (Basel), 12*(1), 55–91. doi:10.3390120100055 PMID:22368458

Kumar, P., Lee, S. G., & Lee, H. J. (2012). E-SAP: Efficient-strong authentication protocol for healthcare applications using wireless medical sensor networks. *Sensors (Basel), 12*(2), 1625–1647. doi:10.3390120201625 PMID:22438729

Kumar, S. R. (2017). Extensive evaluation of seven machine learning methods for rainfall prediction in weather derivatives. *Expert Systems with Applications.*

Kuppusamy, P., Muthuraj, S., & Gopinath, S. (2016, March). Survey and challenges of Li-Fi with comparison of Wi-Fi. In *2016 International Conference on Wireless Communications, Signal Processing and Networking (WiSPNET)* (pp. 896-899). IEEE. 10.1109/WiSPNET.2016.7566262

Kurundkar, G. D., Naik, N. A., & Khamitkar, S. D. (2012). Network intrusion detection using Snort. *International Journal of Engineering Research and Applications, 2*(2), 1288–1296.

Kuznetsova, A., Rom, H., Alldrin, N., Uijlings, J., Krasin, I., Pont-Tuset, J., . . . Ferrari, V. (2018). *The open images dataset v4: Unified image classification, object detection, and visual relationship detection at scale.* arXiv preprint arXiv:1811.00982

Kwak, K. S., Ullah, S., & Ullah, N. (2010). An overview of IEEE 802.15.6 standard. In *2010 3rd International Symposium on Applied Sciences in Biomedical and Communication Technologies, ISABEL 2010* (pp. 2–7). 10.1109/ISABEL.2010.5702867

Lai, B., Kim, S., & Verbauwhede, I. (2002). *Scalable session key construction protocol for wireless sensor networks.* Paper presented at the IEEE Workshop on Large Scale RealTime and Embedded Systems (LARTES).

Lakshmi, Rao, Mohan, & Kumar. (2013). Jamming Attacks Prevention in Wireless Sensor Networks Using Secure Packet Hiding Method. *International Journal of Advanced Research in Computer and Communication Engineering, 2*(9).

Langill, J., & Mitigation, S. (2010, November 17). *Defense in Depth Needed.* Retrieved from https://isssource.com/stuxnet-mitigation-defense-in-depth-needed/

Latré, B., Braem, B., Moerman, I., Blondia, C., & Demeester, P. (2011). A survey on wireless body area networks. *Wireless Networks, 17*(1), 1–18. doi:10.100711276-010-0252-4

Law, Y. W., Palaniswami, M., Hoesel, L. V., Doumen, J., Hartel, P., & Havinga, P. (2009). Energy-efficient link-layer jamming attacks against wireless sensor network MAC protocols. *ACM Transactions on Sensor Networks, 5*(1), 6. doi:10.1145/1464420.1464426

LeCun, Y., Jackel, L. D., Bottou, L., Cortes, C., Denker, J. S., Drucker, H., ... Vapnik, V. (1995). Learning algorithms for classification: A comparison on handwritten digit recognition. *Neural networks: the statistical mechanics perspective, 261*, 276.

LeCun, Y., Bengio, Y., & Hinton, G. (2015). Deep Learning. *Nature, 521*(7553), 436–444. doi:10.1038/nature14539 PMID:26017442

LeCun, Y., Bottou, L., Bengio, Y., & Haffner, P. (1998). Gradient-based learning applied to document recognition. *Proceedings of the IEEE, 86*(11), 2278–2324. doi:10.1109/5.726791

Lee, W. C. (2016). RSS-based Localization Algorithm for Indoor Patient Tracking. In *IEEE 14th International Conference on Industrial Informatics (INDIN)* (pp. 1060-1064). Poitiers, France: IEEE.

Lee, I., & Lee, K. (2015). The Internet of Things (IoT): Applications, investments, and challenges for enterprises. *Business Horizons, 58*(4), 431–440. doi:10.1016/j.bushor.2015.03.008

Lee, S., Choi, J., Kim, J., Cho, B., Lee, S., Kim, H., & Kim, J. (2017, June). FACT: Functionality-centric access control system for IoT programming frameworks. In *Proceedings of the 22nd ACM on Symposium on Access Control Models and Technologies* (pp. 43-54). ACM. 10.1145/3078861.3078864

Le, G., Jingqiang, L., Ziqiang, M., Bo, L., Luning, X., & Jiwu, J. (2018). Copker: A Cryptographic Engine Against Cold-Boot Attacks. *IEEE Transactions on Dependable and Secure Computing, 15*(5), 742–754. doi:10.1109/TDSC.2016.2631548

Leo, M., Battisti, F., Carli, M., & Neri, A. (2014, November). A federated architecture approach for Internet of Things security. In *2014 Euro Med Telco Conference (EMTC)* (pp. 1-5). IEEE. 10.1109/EMTC.2014.6996632

Letsoalo, E., & Ojo, S. (2017). Session hijacking attacks in wireless networks: A review of existing mitigation techniques. In 2017 IST-Africa Week Conference (IST-Africa) (pp. 1-9). IEEE. doi:10.23919/ISTAFRICA.2017.8102284

Lewis, N. (2015). *Prevent IoT security threats and attacks before its too late.* Retrieved from https://internetofthingsagenda.techtarget.com/tip/Prevent-IoT-security-threats-and-attacks-before-its-too-late

Le, X. H., Khalid, M., Sankar, R., & Lee, S. (2011). An Efficient Mutual Authentication and Access Control Scheme for Wireless Sensor Networks in Healthcare. *Journal of Networks, 6*(3), 355–364. doi:10.4304/jnw.6.3.355-364

Li, W., Lu, Y., Sun, J., Chen, Q., Dong, T., Zhou, L., . . . Wei, L. (2017). People counting based on improved gauss process regression. *Proc. of International Conference on Security, Pattern Analysis, and Cybernetics (SPAC)*, 603–608.

Liang, L., Ge, Y., Feng, G., Ni, W., & Phyo Wai, A. A. (2012). Experimental study on adaptive power control based routing in multi-hop Wireless Body Area Networks. In *GLOBECOM - IEEE Global Telecommunications Conference* (pp. 572–577). 10.1109/GLOCOM.2012.6503174

Liao, Q., & Zhu, H. (2013). An energy balanced clustering algorithm based on LEACH protocol. *Applied Mechanics and Materials, 341*, 1138–1143. doi:10.4028/www.scientific.net/AMM.341-342.1138

Lilis, G., Conus, G., Asadi, N., & Kayal, M. (2017). Towards the next generation of intelligent building: An assessment study of current automation and future IoT based systems with a proposal for transitional design. *Sustainable Cities and Society, 28*, 473–481. doi:10.1016/j.scs.2016.08.019

Limei, H., Zheng, Y., & Mohammed, A. (2018). LTE/LTE-A Network Security Data Collection and Analysis for Security Measurement: A Survey. *IEEE Access: Practical Innovations, Open Solutions, 6*, 4220–4242. doi:10.1109/ACCESS.2018.2792534

Lin, T., Maire, M., Belongie, S., Hays, J., Perona, P., Ramanan, D., . . . Zitnick, L. (2014). Microsoft COCO: Common objects in context. In ECCV (pp. 740–755). Academic Press.

Liu, J. K., Baek, J., Zhou, J., Yang, Y., & Wong, J. W. (2010). Efficient online/offline identity-based signature for wireless sensor network. *International Journal of Information Security*, *9*(4), 287–296. doi:10.100710207-010-0109-y

Liu, W., Zhang, L., Zhang, Z., Gu, C., Wang, C., O'Neill, M., & Lombardi, F. (2019). XOR-based low-cost Reconfigurable PUFs for IoT Security. *ACM Transactions on Embedded Computing Systems*, *18*(3), 25. doi:10.1145/3274666

Liu, X., Corner, M., & Shenoy, P. (2009). SEVA: Sensor-enhanced video annotation. *ACM Transactions on Multimedia Computing Communications and Applications*, *5*(3), 1–26. doi:10.1145/1556134.1556141

Liu, Y., Akram Hassan, K., Karlsson, M., Weister, O., & Gong, S. (2018). Active Plant Wall for Green Indoor Climate Based on Cloud and Internet of Things. *IEEE Access: Practical Innovations, Open Solutions*, *6*, 33631–33644. doi:10.1109/ACCESS.2018.2847440

Liu, Y., Dong, M., Ota, K., & Liu, A. (2016). ActiveTrust: Secure and Trustable Routing in Wireless Sensor Networks. *IEEE Transactions on Information Forensics and Security*, *11*(9), 2013–2027. doi:10.1109/TIFS.2016.2570740

Liu, Z., Chen, D. K., Peh, D. L., & Tan, D. K. W. (2017). A feasibility study of Building Information Modeling for Green Mark New Non-Residential Building (NRB): 2015 analysis. *Energy Procedia*, *143*, 80–87. doi:10.1016/j.egypro.2017.12.651

Lopez, J. A., Sun, Y., Blair, P. B., & Mukhtar, M. S. (2015). TCP three-way handshake: Linking developmental processes with plant immunity. *Trends in Plant Science*, *20*(4), 238–245. doi:10.1016/j.tplants.2015.01.005 PMID:25655280

Lo, S.-C., Lou, S.-L., Lin, J.-S., Freedman, M. T., Chien, M. V., & Mun, S. K. (1995). Artificial convolution neural network techniques and applications for lung nodule detection. *IEEE Transactions on Medical Imaging*, *14*(4), 711–718. doi:10.1109/42.476112 PMID:18215875

Lottes, P., Khanna, R., Pfeifer, J., Siegwart, R., & Stachniss, C. (2017). UAV-Based Crop and Weed Classification for Smart Farming. In *2017 IEEE International Conference on Robotics and Automation (ICRA)*. Singapore: IEEE. 10.1109/ICRA.2017.7989347

Lu, Y. F. (2009). Home Networking and Control based on UPnP: An Implementation. In *Second International Workshop on Computer Science and Engineering* (pp. 385-389). Qingdao, China: IEEE.

Lu, Y., Wu, Z., Chang, R., & Li, Y. (2017). Building Information Modeling (BIM) for green buildings: A critical review and future directions. *Automation in Construction*, *83*, 134–148. doi:10.1016/j.autcon.2017.08.024

Luzuriaga, J. E. (2015). *Handling Mobility in IoT applications using the MQTT protocol*. Internet Technol. Appl.

Lyndon, F., Sandra, S., Matthew, B., & Andrew, W. (2018). Tennison: A Distributed SDN Framework for Scalable Network Security. *IEEE Journal on Selected Areas in Communications*, *36*(12), 2805–2818. doi:10.1109/JSAC.2018.2871313

Lyu, Q., Han, G., & Fu, X. (2018). Physical Layer Security in Multi-Hop AF Relay Network Based on Compressed Sensing. *IEEE Communications Letters*, *22*(9), 1882–1885. doi:10.1109/LCOMM.2018.2853101

M, F. H., Josep, L. F., & Llorenç, H. (2019). A Solution for Secure Certified Electronic Mail Using Blockchain as a Secure Message Board. *IEEE Access, 7*, 31330 - 31341.

Ma, J., Yi, P., Zhong, Y., & Zhang, S. (2006). *S_Firewall: A firewall in wireless sensor networks*. Paper presented at the 2006 International Conference on Wireless Communications, Networking and Mobile Computing. 10.1109/WiCOM.2006.280

Madakam, S., Lake, V., Lake, V., & Lake, V. (2015). Internet of Things (IoT): A literature review. *Journal of Computer and Communications*, *3*(05), 164–173. doi:10.4236/jcc.2015.35021

Mahdavinejad, M. S., Rezvan, M., Barekatain, M., Adibi, P., Barnaghi, P., & Sheth, A. P. (2018). Machine learning for Internet of Things data analysis: A survey. *Digital Communications and Networks*, *4*(3), 161–175. doi:10.1016/j.dcan.2017.10.002

Mahmoud, R., Yousuf, T., Aloul, F., & Zualkernan, I. (2015, December). Internet of things (IoT) security: Current status, challenges and prospective measures. In *2015 10th International Conference for Internet Technology and Secured Transactions (ICITST)* (pp. 336-341). IEEE.

Mahmoud, K., & Walaa, H. (2017). Physical Layer Security in Ultra-Dense Networks. *IEEE Wireless Communications Letters*, *6*(5), 690–693. doi:10.1109/LWC.2017.2731840

Mainanwal, V., Gupta, M., & Upadhayay, S. K. (2015). A survey on wireless body area network: Security technology and its design methodology issue. *ICIIECS 2015 - 2015 IEEE International Conference on Innovations in Information, Embedded and Communication Systems*, (1), 1–5. 10.1109/ICIIECS.2015.7193088

Malan, D. J., Welsh, M., & Smith, M. D. (2004). *A public-key infrastructure for key distribution in TinyOS based on elliptic curve cryptography.* Paper presented at the 2004 First Annual IEEE Communications Society Conference on Sensor and Ad Hoc Communications and Networks, 2004. IEEE SECON 2004. 10.1109/SAHCN.2004.1381904

Malasri, K., & Wang, L. (2009). Design and implementation of a secure wireless mote-based medical sensor network. *Sensors (Basel)*, *9*(8), 6273–6297. doi:10.339090806273 PMID:22454585

Malinowski, M., Rohrbach, M., & Fritz, M. (2015). Ask your neurons: A neural-based approach to answering questions about images. In *Proceedings of the IEEE international conference on computer vision* (pp. 1-9). 10.1109/ICCV.2015.9

Malkani, Y., Keerio, A., Mahar, J., Memon, G., & Keerio, H. (2015). Localization, Routing and Data Gathering in Wireless Sensor Networks (WSNs). *Sindh University Research Journal, 44*(1).

Mana, M., Feham, M., & Bensaber, B. A. (2011). Trust key management scheme for wireless body area networks. *International Journal of Network Security*, *12*(2), 75–83.

Manic, M., Amarasinghe, K., Rodriguez-Andina, J. J., & Rieger, C. (2016). Intelligent Buildings of the Future: Cyberaware, Deep Learning Powered, and Human Interacting. *IEEE Industrial Electronics Magazine*, *10*(4), 32–49. doi:10.1109/MIE.2016.2615575

Manic, M., Wijayasekara, D., Amarasinghe, K., & Rodriguez-Andina, J. J. (2016). Building Energy Management Systems: The Age of Intelligent and Adaptive Buildings. *IEEE Industrial Electronics Magazine*, *10*(1), 25–39. doi:10.1109/MIE.2015.2513749

Manikandan, S. P., & Manimegalai, R. (2013). Trust based routing to mitigate black hole attack in MANET. *Life Science Journal*, *10*(SUPPL.4), 490–498.

Manuel, C., Luca, D., Lucia, S., & Adriano, V. (2018). Performance Evaluation and Modeling of an Industrial Application-Layer Firewall. *IEEE Transactions on Industrial Informatics*, *14*(5), 2159–2170. doi:10.1109/TII.2018.2802903

Maotong, X., Chong, L., & Suresh, S. (2018). PODCA: A passive optical data center network architecture. *Journal of Optical Communications and Networking*, *10*(4), 409–420. doi:10.1364/JOCN.10.000409

Marasco & Kontokosta. (2016). Applications of machine learning methods to identifying and predicting building retrofit opportunities. *Energy and Buildings,* 431-441.

Marbukh, V. (2019). Towards Fog Network Utility Maximization (FoNUM) for Managing Fog Computing Resources. In *IEEE International Conference on Fog Computing (ICFC)* (pp. 195-200). Prague, Czech Republic: IEEE. 10.1109/ICFC.2019.00032

Marchang, N., & Datta, R. (2012). Light-weight trust-based routing protocol for mobile ad hoc networks. *IET Information Security*, *6*(2), 77. doi:10.1049/iet-ifs.2010.0160

Mark, E., Ying, H., Cunjin, L., Iryna, Y., Helge, J., & Leandros, A. M. (2019). Employee Perspective on Information Security Related Human Error in Healthcare: Proactive Use of IS-CHEC in Questionnaire Form. *IEEE Access: Practical Innovations, Open Solutions*, *7*, 102087–102101. doi:10.1109/ACCESS.2019.2927195

Martin, E. Z. (2015). Rapid spatial mapping of the acoustic pressure in high intensity focused ultrasound fields at clinical intensities using a novel planar Fabry-Pérot interferometer. In *IEEE International Ultrasonics Symposium (IUS)*. Taipei, Taiwan: IEEE. 10.1109/ULTSYM.2015.0229

Mary, J. R., & Kannammal, N. (2017). *A Comparative Study of Security protocols in Wireless Sensor Networks, 2*(5), 573–578.

Maskooki, A., Soh, C. B., Gunawan, E., & Low, K. S. (2011). Opportunistic routing for body area network. *2011 IEEE Consumer Communications and Networking Conference. CCNC, 237–241.* doi:10.1109/CCNC.2011.5766463

Mehmood, Y., Shibli, M. A., Kanwal, A., & Masood, R. (2015). Distributed intrusion detection system using mobile agents in cloud computing environment. In *2015 Conference on Information Assurance and Cyber Security (CIACS)* (pp. 1-8). IEEE. 10.1109/CIACS.2015.7395559

Mehran, A., Mahrokh, A., Wei, N., Abbas, J., & Negin, S. (2018). A Routing Framework for Offloading Traffic From Cellular Networks to SDN-Based Multi-Hop Device-to-Device Networks. *IEEE eTransactions on Network and Service Management*, *15*(4), 1516–1531. doi:10.1109/TNSM.2018.2875696

Menon, S. P., Bharadwaj, R., Shetty, P., Sanu, P., & Nagendra, S. (2017, December). Prediction of temperature using linear regression. In *2017 International Conference on Electrical, Electronics, Communication, Computer, and Optimization Techniques (ICEECCOT)* (pp. 1-6). IEEE.

Merlin, R. T., & Ravi, R. (2019). Novel Trust Based Energy Aware Routing Mechanism for Mitigation of Black Hole Attacks in MANET. *Wireless Personal Communications*, *104*(4), 1599–1636. doi:10.100711277-019-06120-8

Messai, M.-L. (2014). *Classification of Attacks in Wireless Sensor Networks*. Paper presented at the International Congress on Telecommunication and Application.

Michal, M. (2013). *Base station for Wireless sensor network* (Unpublished Diploma Thesis). Masryk University.

Ming, Y., Xiaodan, G., Zhen, L., Changxin, Y., & Junzhou, L. (2017). An active de-anonymizing attack against tor web traffic. *Tsinghua Science and Technology*, *22*(6), 702–713. doi:10.23919/TST.2017.8195352

Min, L., Xiaotong, Z., Li, L., Kim, K. R., & Debiao, H. (2017). Security Analysis of Two Password-Authenticated Multi-Key Exchange Protocols. *IEEE Access: Practical Innovations, Open Solutions*, *5*, 8017–8024. doi:10.1109/ACCESS.2017.2698390

Mirakhorli, A., & Dong, B. (2016). Occupancy behavior based model predictive control for building indoor climate - A critical review. *Energy and Building*, *129*, 499–513. doi:10.1016/j.enbuild.2016.07.036

Miranda-Steiner, J. E. (2013). *U.S. Patent Application No. 13/298,310*. Washington, DC: US Patent Office.

Mishra, Soni, Sharma, & Upadhyay. (2018). Development and Analysis of Artificial Neural Network Models for Rainfall Predictionby Using Time- Series Data. *Int. J. Intell. Syst. Applied.*

Mishra, N., Soni, H. K., Sharma, S., & Upadhyay, A. K. (2018). *Development and Analysis of Artificial Neural Network Models for Rainfall Prediction by Using Time-Series Data. Int. J. Intell. Syst. Appl., 10*(1), 16–23.

Mishra, S., & Thakkar, H. (2012). Features of WSN and Data Aggregation techniques in WSN: A Survey. *Int. J. Eng. Innov. Technol., 1*(4), 264–273.

Mitchell, R., & Chen, I. R. (2014). A survey of intrusion detection techniques for cyber-physical systems. *ACM Computing Surveys, 46*(4), 55. doi:10.1145/2542049

Mitchell, R., & Chen, R. (2014). A survey of intrusion detection in wireless network applications. *Computer Communications, 42*, 1–23. doi:10.1016/j.comcom.2014.01.012

Mitsugu, I., Kazuo, O., & Junji, S. (2018). Security Formalizations and Their Relationships for Encryption and Key Agreement in Information-Theoretic Cryptography. *IEEE Transactions on Information Theory, 64*(1), 654–685. doi:10.1109/TIT.2017.2744650

Mocrii, D., Chen, Y., & Musilek, P. (2018). IoT-based smart homes: A review of system architecture, software, communications, privacy and security. *Internet of Things, 1–2*, 81–98. doi:10.1016/j.iot.2018.08.009

Mohammadani, K. H., Hussain, J., Khan, R. A., Arain, T. H., Soomro, A. A., Khan, S., & Zafar, H. (2018). An Energy Efficient Routing Protocol for Wireless Body Area Sensor Networks. *Wireless Personal Communications, 99*(4), 1443–1454. doi:10.100711277-018-5285-5

Mohammadi, M., Al-Fuqaha, A., Sorour, S., & Guizani, M. (2018). Deep learning for IoT big data and streaming analytics: A survey. *IEEE Communications Surveys and Tutorials, 20*(4), 2923–2960. doi:10.1109/COMST.2018.2844341

Mohapatra, A. G., & Lenka, S. K. (2016). Neural Network Pattern Classification and Weather Dependent Fuzzy Logic Model for Irrigation Control in WSN Based Precision Agriculture. *Procedia Computer Science, 78*, 499–506. doi:10.1016/j.procs.2016.02.094

Montgomery, K., Mundt, C., Thonier, G., Tellier, A., Udoh, U., Barker, V., ... Kovacs, G. (2005). *Lifeguard - a personal physiological monitor for extreme environments.* doi:10.1109/iembs.2004.1403640

Moon, Y. H. (2018). *A Methodology of NB-IoT Mobility Optimization. In Global Internet of Things Summit (GIoTS).* Bilbao, Spain: IEEE.

Morhart, C. B. (2009). Cooperative Multi-User Detection and Localization for Pedestrian Protection. In *German Microwave Conference.* Munich, Germany: IEEE. 10.1109/GEMIC.2009.4815863

Mosterman, P. J., & Zander, J. (2016). Industry 4.0 as a cyber-physical system study. *Software & Systems Modeling, 15*(1), 17–29. doi:10.100710270-015-0493-x

Mourabit, Y. E., Toumanari, A., Bouirden, A., Zougagh, H., & Latif, R. (2014). Intrusion detection system in Wireless Sensor Network based on mobile agent. In *2014 Second World Conference on Complex Systems (WCCS)* (pp. 248-251). IEEE. 10.1109/ICoCS.2014.7060910

Movassaghi, S., Abolhasan, M., & Lipman, J. (2012). Energy efficient thermal and power aware (ETPA) routing in Body Area Networks. *IEEE International Symposium on Personal, Indoor and Mobile Radio Communications, PIMRC, 13*(3), 1108–1113. 10.1109/PIMRC.2012.6362511

Movassaghi, S., Abolhasan, M., Lipman, J., Smith, D., & Jamalipour, A. (2014). Wireless body area networks: A survey. *IEEE Communications Surveys and Tutorials, 16*(3), 1658–1686. doi:10.1109/SURV.2013.121313.00064

Mpitziopoulos, DKonstantopoulos, & Pantziou. (2009). *A Survey on Jamming Attacks and Countermeasures in WSNs.* Paper presented at the IEEE Communications Surveys & Tutorials.

Muhammad, K. (2010). BARI+: A biometric based distributed key management approach for wireless body area networks. *Sensors (Basel), 10*(4), 3911–3933. doi:10.3390100403911 PMID:22319333

Mukherjee, B., Wang, S., Lu, W., Neupane, R. L., Dunn, D., Ren, Y., & Calyam, P. (2018). Flexible IoT security middleware for end-to-end cloud–fog communication. *Future Generation Computer Systems, 87*, 688–703. doi:10.1016/j.future.2017.12.031

Mumtaz Qabulio, Y. (2015). On Node Replication Attack in Wireless Sensor Networks. *Mehran University Research Journal of Engineering & Technology, 34*(4).

Murtaza, S. S., Khreich, W., Hamou-Lhadj, A., & Couture, M. (2013). A host-based anomaly detection approach by representing system calls as states of kernel modules. In *2013 IEEE 24th International Symposium on Software Reliability Engineering (ISSRE)* (pp. 431-440). IEEE. 10.1109/ISSRE.2013.6698896

Myers, T., Mohring, K., & Andersen, T. (2017). Semantic IoT: Intelligent Water Management for Efficient Urban Outdoor Water Conservation. Lecture Notes in Computer Science, 10675.

N., S., & H., R. (2016). Recent Research on Wireless Body Area Networks: A survey. *International Journal of Computers and Applications, 142*(11), 42–48. doi:10.5120/ijca2016909893

Nader, S. S., Carsten, M., Tim, W., & Steve, F. (2018). Information security collaboration formation in organisations. *IET Information Security, 12*(3), 238–245. doi:10.1049/iet-ifs.2017.0257

Najafabadi, M. M., Villanustre, F., Khoshgoftaar, T. M., Seliya, N., Wald, R., & Muharemagic, E. (2015). Deep learning applications and challenges in big data analytics. *Journal of Big Data, 2*(1), 1. doi:10.118640537-014-0007-7

Napa, S., Jonathan, W., Nasir, M., Janusz, K., & Prakash, I. (2019). Emerging NUI-Based Methods for User Authentication: A New Taxonomy and Survey. *IEEE Transactions on Biometrics, Behavior, and Identity Science, 1*(1), 5–31. doi:10.1109/TBIOM.2019.2893297

Nasser, N., & Chen, Y. (2007). Secure multipath routing protocol for wireless sensor networks. *Proceedings - International Conference on Distributed Computing Systems.* 10.1109/ICDCSW.2007.72

Navada, Adiga, & Kini. (2013). A Study on Daylight Integration with Thermal Comfort for Energy Conservation in a General Office. *IJOEE*, 18-22.

Nayak, M. A., & Ghosh, S. (2013).Prediction of extreme rainfall event using weather pattern recognition and support vector machine classifier. Theor. Appl. Climatol.

Neha, Gupta, P. (2017). A Study on Future of Communication: Li-Fi. *International Journal of Innovative Research in Science. Engineering and Technology, 6*(6), 12195–12202.

Ng, H. S., Sim, M. L., & Tan, C. M. (2006). Security issues of wireless sensor networks in healthcare applications. *BT Technology Journal, 24*(2), 138–144. doi:10.100710550-006-0051-8

Ngo, C. W., Ma, Y. F., & Zhang, H. J. (2005). Video summarization and scene detection by graph modeling. *IEEE Transactions on Circuits and Systems for Video Technology, 15*(2), 296–305. doi:10.1109/TCSVT.2004.841694

Nguyen, D. T., Song, C., Qian, Z., Krishnamurthy, S. V., Colbert, E. J., & McDaniel, P. (2018, December). IotSan: fortifying the safety of IoT systems. In *Proceedings of the 14th International Conference on emerging Networking EXperiments and Technologies* (pp. 191-203). ACM. 10.1145/3281411.3281440

Nguyen, V. L., Lin, P. C., & Hwang, R. H. (2019). Energy Depletion Attacks in Low Power Wireless Networks. *IEEE Access: Practical Innovations, Open Solutions, 7*, 51915–51932. doi:10.1109/ACCESS.2019.2911424

Niculescu, D., & Nath, B. (2003). Trajectory based forwarding and its applications. *Proceedings of the 9th annual international conference on Mobile computing and networking.*

Nikam, V. B., & Meshram, B. B. (2013). Modeling Rainfall Prediction Using Data Mining Method: A Bayesian Approach. *2013 Fifth Int. Conf. Comput. Intell. Model. Simulation.* 10.1109/CIMSim.2013.29

Nir, N., Aviad, C., & Yuval, E. (2016). ALDOCX: Detection of Unknown Malicious Microsoft Office Documents Using Designated Active Learning Methods Based on New Structural Feature Extraction Methodology. *IEEE Transactions on Information Forensics and Security, 12*(3), 631–646.

Nishad, L. S., Kumar, S., & Bola, S. K. (2016). Round Robin Selection of Datacenter Simulation Technique Cloudsim and Cloud Analsyt Architecture and Making it Efficient by Using Load Balancing Technique. In *3rd International Conference on Computing for Sustainable Global Development (INDIACom)*. New Delhi, India: IEEE.

Noman, H. A., Abdullah, S. M., & Mohammed, H. I. (2015). An Automated Approach to Detect Deauthentication and Disassociation Dos Attacks on Wireless 802.11 Networks. *International Journal of Computer Science Issues, 12*(4), 107.

O'Neill, W., & Palmer, A. (2004). Cognitive dissonance and the stability of service quality perceptions. *Journal of Services Marketing, 18*(6), 433–449. doi:10.1108/08876040410557221

Oliveira, L. B., Wang, H. C., & Loureiro, A. A. (2005). *LHA-SP: Secure protocols for hierarchical wireless sensor networks.* Paper presented at the 2005 9th IFIP/IEEE International Symposium on Integrated Network Management, 2005. 10.1109/INM.2005.1440767

Orisingher, C. Valentini, S. & Angelis, M. D. (2010). A meta-analysis of satisfaction and complaint handling services. *Journal of the Academy of Marketing Science.*

Orue-Echevarria. Alonso, Escalante, & Schuster. (2012). Assessing the Readiness to Move into the Cloud. Academic Press.

Otoum, S., Kantarci, B., & Mouftah, H. T. (2019). *On the feasibility of deep learning in sensor network.* Academic Press.

Ouafaa, I., Mustapha, E., Salah-ddine, K., & Jalal, L. (2016). *An advanced analysis on secure hierarchical routing protocols in wireless sensor network.* Paper presented at the 2016 International Conference on Engineering & MIS (ICEMIS). 10.1109/ICEMIS.2016.7745375

Ouafaa, I., Mustapha, E., Salah-ddine, K., & Said, E. H. (2016). Secure Hierarchical Routing Protocols in Wireless Sensor Networks: A Comparative Analysis. *International Journal of Software Engineering and Its Applications, 10*(11), 95–108. doi:10.14257/ijseia.2016.10.11.08

Palacharla, S., Chandan, M., GnanaSuryaTeja, K., & Varshitha, G. (2018). Wormhole Attack: a Major Security Concern in Internet of Things (Iot). *International Journal of Engineering & Technology, 7*(3.27), 147-150.

Pamina, J., & Beschi Raja, J. (2019). *Survey on deep learning algorithms.* Academic Press.

Pandharipande, A., & Caicedo, D. (2015). Smart indoor lighting systems with luminaire-based sensing: A review of lighting control approaches. *Energy and Building, 104*, 369–377. doi:10.1016/j.enbuild.2015.07.035

Pan, S. J., & Yang, Q. (2010). A Survey on Transfer Learning. *IEEE Transactions on Knowledge and Data Engineering*, *22*(10), 1345–1359. doi:10.1109/TKDE.2009.191

Pan, Y., Mei, T., Yao, T., Li, H., & Rui, Y. (2016). Jointly modeling embedding and translation to bridge video and language. In *Proceedings of the IEEE conference on computer vision and pattern recognition* (pp. 4594-4602). 10.1109/CVPR.2016.497

Parveen Sadotra & Sharma. (2016). A Review on Integrated Intrusion Detection System in Cyber Security. Academic Press.

Pasluosta, C. F., Gassner, H., Winkler, J., Klucken, J., & Eskofier, B. M. (2015). An emerging era in the management of Parkinson's disease: Wearable technologies and the internet of things. *IEEE Journal of Biomedical and Health Informatics*, *19*(6), 1873–1881. doi:10.1109/JBHI.2015.2461555 PMID:26241979

Pasqualetti, F., Dörfler, F., & Bullo, F. (2013). Attack detection and identification in cyber-physical systems. *IEEE Transactions on Automatic Control*, *58*(11), 2715–2729. doi:10.1109/TAC.2013.2266831

Patil, H. K., & Chen, T. M. (2017). *Wireless Sensor Network Security: The Internet of Things. In Computer and Information Security Handbook* (3rd ed., pp. 317–337). Elsevier. doi:10.1016/B978-0-12-803843-7.00018-1

Paul, S., & Sharma, S. (2014). *Future of telecommunication technologies: WI-FI vs. WI-MAX vs. Li-Fi vs. GI-FI. ISTP Journal of Research in Electrical and Electronics Engineering.*

Pérez, S., Hernandez-Ramos, J. L., Matheu-Garcia, S. N., Rotondi, D., Skarmeta, A. F., Straniero, L., & Pedone, D. (2018). A Lightweight and Flexible Encryption Scheme to Protect Sensitive Data in Smart Building Scenarios. *IEEE Access: Practical Innovations, Open Solutions*, *6*, 11738–11750. doi:10.1109/ACCESS.2018.2801383

Perillo, M., & Heinzelman, W. (2005). *Wireless Sensor Network Protocols*. 36-813-36–842. doi:10.1201/9781420035094.sec8

Perrig, A., Szewczyk, R., Tygar, J. D., Wen, V., & Culler, D. E. (2002). SPINS: Security protocols for sensor networks. *Wireless Networks*, *8*(5), 521–534. doi:10.1023/A:1016598314198

Pham, C. L. (2018). A Platform for Integrating Alexa Voice Service Into ECHONET-based Smart Homes. In *IEEE International Conference on Consumer Electronics-Taiwan (ICCE-TW)*. Taichung, Taiwan: IEEE. 10.1109/ICCE-China.2018.8448893

Pietro, D., Marko, A., Čedomir, S., & Tomislav, D. (2018). Software-Defined Microgrid Control for Resilience Against Denial-of-Service Attacks. *IEEE Transactions on Smart Grid*, *10*(5), 5258–5268.

Pongle, P., & Chavan, G. (2015). Real time intrusion and wormhole attack detection in internet of things. *International Journal of Computers and Applications*, *121*(9).

Ponnusamy, V., Jhanjhi, N. Z., & Humayun, M. (2020). Fostering Public-Private Partnership: Between Governments and Technologists in Developing National Cybersecurity Framework. In Employing Recent Technologies for Improved Digital Governance (pp. 237-255). IGI Global.

Ponnusamy, V., Jhanjhi, N. Z., & Humayun, M. (2020). Fostering Public-Private Partnership: Between Governments and Technologists in Developing National Cybersecurity Framework. In *Employing Recent Technologies for Improved Digital Governance* (pp. 237–255). IGI Global. doi:10.4018/978-1-7998-1851-9.ch012

Ponnusamy, V., Selvam, L. M. P., & Rafique, K. (2020). Cybersecurity Governance on Social Engineering Awareness. In *Employing Recent Technologies for Improved Digital Governance* (pp. 210–236). IGI Global. doi:10.4018/978-1-7998-1851-9.ch011

Prasad. (2015). Intrusion Detection Systems. *Tools and Techniques-An Overview, 8*(35), 1–2.

Public Key Infrastructure – Tutorials point. (n.d.). Www.Tutorialspoint.Com. https://www.tutorialspoint.com/cryptography/public_key_infrastructure.htm

Puranik, V., Sharmila, A. R., & Kumari, A. (2019). Automation in Agriculture and IoT. In *2019 4th International Conference on Internet of Things: Smart Innovation and Usages (IoT-SIU)*. Ghaziabad, India: IEEE. 10.1109/IoT-SIU.2019.8777619

Qian, Y., Bi, M., Tan, T., & Yu, K. (2016). Very deep convolutional neural networks for noise robust speech recognition. *IEEE/ACM Transactions on Audio, Speech, and Language Processing, 24*(12), 2263–2276. doi:10.1109/TASLP.2016.2602884

Qi, G. J., Hua, X. S., Rui, Y., Tang, J., Mei, T., & Zhang, H. J. (2007). Correlative multi-label video annotation. In *Proceedings of the 15th ACM international conference on Multimedia* (pp. 17-26). 10.1145/1291233.1291245

Qi, J., Xiaohan, H., Ning, Z., Kuan, Z., Xindi, M., & Jianfeng, M. (2019). Shake to Communicate: Secure Handshake Acceleration-Based Pairing Mechanism for Wrist Worn Devices. *IEEE Internet of Things Journal, 6*(3), 5618–5630. doi:10.1109/JIOT.2019.2904177

Qin, Z., Yu, F., Liu, C., & Chen, X. (2018). *How Convolutional Neural Network See the World - A Survey of Convolutional Neural Network Visualization Methods.* ArXiv:1804.11191 [Cs]

Qureshi, F., & Krishnan, S. (2018). Wearable hardware design for the internet of medical things (IoMT). *Sensors (Switzerland), 18*(11), 3812. doi:10.339018113812 PMID:30405026

Rachad, A., Lingjia, L., Jonathan, A., Michael, J. M., John, D. M., & Yang, Y. (2017). A Physical Layer Security Scheme for Mobile Health Cyber-Physical Systems. *IEEE Internet of Things Journal, 5*(1), 295–309.

Radja. (2015). *The overview of wired and wireless networks and the need for the transition from wired to wireless networks.* Academic Press.

Rahmati, A., Fernandes, E., Eykholt, K., & Prakash, A. (2018, September). Tyche: A risk-based permission model for smart homes. In 2018 IEEE Cybersecurity Development (SecDev) (pp. 29-36). IEEE. doi:10.1109/SecDev.2018.00012

Rai, Mehfuz, & Sahoo. (2013). Efficient Migration of Application to Clouds: Analysis and Comparison. *GSTF Journal on Computing, 3*(3).

Raja, K. S., & Kiruthika, U. (2015). An Energy Efficient Method for Secure and Reliable Data Transmission in Wireless Body Area Networks Using RelAODV. *Wireless Personal Communications, 83*(4), 2975–2997. doi:10.100711277-015-2577-x

Rajan, A., Jithish, J., & Sankaran, S. (2017). Sybil attack in IOT: Modelling and defenses. In *2017 International Conference on Advances in Computing, Communications and Informatics (ICACCI)* (pp. 2323-2327). IEEE. 10.1109/ICACCI.2017.8126193

Ramadhani, E., & Mahardika, G. P. (2018, March). The Technology of LiFi: A Brief Introduction. *IOP Conference Series. Materials Science and Engineering, 325*(1), 012013. doi:10.1088/1757-899X/325/1/012013

Ramana, Krishna, Kumar, & Pandey. (2013). Monthly Rainfall Prediction Using Wavelet Neural Network Analysis. *Water Resources Management.*

Ramli, S. N., Ahmad, R., & Abdollah, M. F. (2013). Electrocardiogram (ECG) signals as biometrics in securing wireless body area network. In *2013 8th International Conference for Internet Technology and Secured Transactions, ICITST 2013* (pp. 536–541). 10.1109/ICITST.2013.6750259

Rao, T. A. (2018). Security challenges facing IoT layers and its protective measures. *International Journal of Computers and Applications*, *975*, 8887.

Rasheed, Z., & Shah, M. (2003). Scene detection in Hollywood movies and TV shows. In IEEE Computer Society Conference on Computer Vision and Pattern Recognition, 2003. *Proceedings.*, *2*, II-343.

Rasheed, Z., & Shah, M. (2005). Detection and representation of scenes in videos. *IEEE Transactions on Multimedia*, *7*(6), 1097–1105. doi:10.1109/TMM.2005.858392

Rashid, F. Y. (2016). *NTP fixes denial-of-service flaws*. Retrieved from: https://www.infoworld.com/article/3144471/security/ntp-fixes-denial-of-service-flaws.html

Rash, M. (2004). Combining port knocking and passive OS fingerprinting with fwknop. *USENIX; login. Magazine*, *29*(6), 19–25.

Rash, M. (2006). Single packet authorization with fwknop. Login. *The USENIX Magazine*, *31*(1), 63–69.

Rash, M. (2007). Single packet authorization. *Linux Journal*, *156*, 1.

Rashmi, Mehfuz, & Sahoo. (2012, April). A five-phased approach for cloud migration. *International Journal of Emerging Technology and Advanced Engineering*, *2*(4).

Rashmi. (n.d.). A1, M. C. M. Detection of Node Replication Attacks in Mobile Sensor Networks Using Efficient Localized Detection Algorithm. *International Journal of Engineering Research and Applications*.

Rattagan, E. (2016). Wi-Fi usage monitoring and power management policy for smartphone background applications. In *2016 Management and Innovation Technology International Conference (MITicon)*. IEEE. 10.1109/MITICON.2016.8025223

Raykov, Y. P., Ozer, E., Dasika, G., Boukouvalas, A., & Little, M. A. (2016). Predicting room occupancy with a single passive infrared (PIR) sensor through behavior extraction. *Proceedings of ACM International Joint Conference on Pervasive and Ubiquitous Computing*, 1016–1027. 10.1145/2971648.2971746

Raza, S., Wallgren, L., & Voigt, T. (2013). SVELTE: Real-time intrusion detection in the Internet of Things. *Ad Hoc Networks*, *11*(8), 2661–2674. doi:10.1016/j.adhoc.2013.04.014

Reddy, Y. B., & Selmic, R. (2011). Trust-based Packet Transfer in Wireless Sensor Networks. *International Journal on Advances in Network Security*, *4*(3), 198–207. doi:10.2316/p.2010.726-009

Reka, S. S., & Dragicevic, T. (2018). Future effectual role of energy delivery: A comprehensive review of Internet of Things and smart grid. *Renewable & Sustainable Energy Reviews*, *91*, 90–108. doi:10.1016/j.rser.2018.03.089

Reshma, Juhi, & Pillai. (2016). Impact of Machine Learning and Internet of Things in Agriculture: State of the Art. In *International Conference on Soft Computing and Pattern Recognition*. Springer.

Reyna, A., Martín, C., Chen, J., Soler, E., & Díaz, M. (2018). On blockchain and its integration with IoT. Challenges and opportunities. *Future Generation Computer Systems*, *88*, 173–190. doi:10.1016/j.future.2018.05.046

Rios, F. C., Parrish, K., & Chong, W. K. (2016). Low-investment energy retrofit framework for small and medium office buildings. *Procedia Engineering*, *145*, 172–179. doi:10.1016/j.proeng.2016.04.057

Roee, D., Wenbo, S., Wee, S. S., & Lutz, L. (2013). Joint Time and Spatial Reuse Handshake Protocol for Underwater Acoustic Communication Networks. *IEEE Journal of Oceanic Engineering*, *38*(3), 470–483. doi:10.1109/JOE.2012.2229065

Roman, R., Zhou, J., & Lopez, J. (2013). On the features and challenges of security and privacy in distributed internet of things. *Computer Networks*, *57*(10), 2266–2279. doi:10.1016/j.comnet.2012.12.018

Rong, G., Xiaojie, W., & Jun, L. (2018). A Software Defined Networking-Oriented Security Scheme for Vehicle Networks. *IEEE Access: Practical Innovations, Open Solutions, 6*, 58195–58203. doi:10.1109/ACCESS.2018.2875104

Roosta, T. G. (2008). *Attacks and defenses of ubiquitous sensor networks.* Academic Press.

Roychowdhury, S., & Patra, C. (2010). *Geographic adaptive fidelity and geographic energy aware routing in ad hoc routing.* Paper presented at the International Conference.

Russakovsky, O., Deng, J., Su, H., Krause, J., Satheesh, S., Ma, S., ... Berg, A. C. (2015). Imagenet large scale visual recognition challenge. *International Journal of Computer Vision, 115*(3), 211–252. doi:10.100711263-015-0816-y

Sabaliauskaite, G., & Mathur, A. P. (2013). Intelligent checkers to improve attack detection in cyber physical systems. In *2013 International Conference on Cyber-Enabled Distributed Computing and Knowledge Discovery* (pp. 27-30). IEEE. 10.1109/CyberC.2013.14

Sabiri & Benabbou. (2015). Methods Migration from On-premise to Cloud. *IOSR Journal of Computer Engineering, 17*(2), 58-65.

Sadeghi, A. R., Wachsmann, C., & Waidner, M. (2015). Security and privacy challenges in industrial internet of things. In *2015 52nd ACM/EDAC/IEEE Design Automation Conference (DAC)* (pp. 1-6). IEEE. 10.1145/2744769.2747942

Saeed & Jaffri. (2015). Information security in the modern education system in Pakistan. *IJTNR*, 1-7.

Sai, K. P., Elena, G., Wolfgang, K., & Carmen, M. M. (2019). Rational Agent-Based Decision Algorithm For Strategic Converged Network Migration Planning. *Journal of Optical Communications and Networking, 11*(7), 371–382. doi:10.1364/JOCN.11.000371

Saini, H. (2016). Li-Fi (Light Fidelity)-The future technology In Wireless communication. *Jisuanji Yingyong, 7*(1), 13–15.

Salamon, J., & Bello, J. P. (2015). Unsupervised feature learning for urban sound classification. *Proceedings of IEEE International Conference on Acoustics, Speech and Signal Processing (ICASSP)*, 171–175. 10.1109/ICASSP.2015.7177954

Salayma, M., Al-Dubai, A., Romdhani, I., & Nasser, Y. (2017). Wireless Body Area Network (WBAN): A survey on reliability, fault tolerance, and technologies coexistence. *ACM Computing Surveys, 50*(1), 1–35. doi:10.1145/3041956

Saleem. (2009). On the Security Issues in Wireless Body Area Networks. *International Journal of Digital Content Technology and Its Applications, 3*(3), 1–4. doi:10.4156/jdcta.vol3.issue3.22

Sanislav, T., & Miclea, L. (2012). Cyber-physical systems-concept, challenges and research areas. *Journal of Control Engineering and Applied Informatics, 14*(2), 28–33.

Santoso, B. I., Idrus, M. R. S., & Gunawan, I. P. (2016. Designing Network Intrusion and Detection System using signature-based method for protecting OpenStack private cloud. In *2016 6th International Annual Engineering Seminar (InAES)* (pp. 61-66). IEEE. 10.1109/INAES.2016.7821908

Sarkar, A., Agarwal, S., & Nath, A. (2015). Li-fi technology: Data transmission through visible light. *International Journal of Advance Research in Computer Science and Management Studies, 3*(6), 1–12.

Sasi, V. P., & Ranjan, B. (2019). Channel-Aware Artificial Intersymbol Interference for Enhancing Physical Layer Security. *IEEE Communications Letters, 23*(7), 1182–1185. doi:10.1109/LCOMM.2019.2915076

Satam, P. (2017). Anomaly Based Wi-Fi Intrusion Detection System. In 2017 IEEE 2nd International Workshops on Foundations and Applications of Self* Systems (FAS* W) (pp. 377-378). IEEE. doi:10.1109/FAS-W.2017.180

Saxena, A. K., Sinha, S., & Shukla, P. (2017). General study of intrusion detection system and survey of agent based intrusion detection system. In *2017 International Conference on Computing, Communication and Automation (ICCCA)* (pp. 471-421). IEEE. 10.1109/CCAA.2017.8229866

Securityradware. (2017). *BrickerBot PDoS Attack: Back with A Vengeance.* Retrieved from: https://security.radware. com/ddos-threats-attacks/brickerbot-pdos-back-with-vengeance/

Seide, F., Li, G., & Yu, D. (2011). Conversational speech transcription using context-dependent deep neural networks. *Twelfth annual conference of the international speech communication association.*

Seliem, M., & Elgazzar, K. (2019). IoTeWay: A Secure Framework Architecture for 6LoWPAN Based IoT Applications. *2018 IEEE Global Conference on Internet of Things, GCIoT 2018*, 1–5. 10.1109/GCIoT.2018.8620137

Selvam, L. M. P., Ponnusamy, V., & Rafique, K. (2020). Democratic Governance: A Review of Secured Digital Electoral Service Infrastructure. In *Employing Recent Technologies for Improved Digital Governance* (pp. 256–272). IGI Global. doi:10.4018/978-1-7998-1851-9.ch013

Senthilkumar, T., Manikandan, B., Devi, M. R., & Lokesh, S. (2018). CSEIT1835133 | Technologies Enduring in Internet of Medical Things (IoMT) for Smart Healthcare System. *International Journal of Scientific Research in Computer Science, Engineering and Information Technology, 5*(3), 2456–3307.

Seouser. (2017, October 10). IoT Security: Understanding PKI's Role in Securing Internet of Things. *About SSL Certificates*. https://cheapsslsecurity.com/blog/iot-security-understanding-pki-role-in-securing-internet-of-things/

Shah, S. H., & Yaqoob, I. (2016). A Survey: Internet of Things (IOT) Technologies, Applications and Challenges. In *2016 IEEE Smart Energy Grid Engineering (SEGE)*. Oshawa, Canada: IEEE.

Shaikh, R. A., Lee, S., Khan, M. A. U., & Song, Y. J. (2006). LSec: Lightweight Security Protocol for Distributed Wireless Sensor Network. In *IFIP International Conference on Personal Wireless Communications* (pp. 367–377). 10.1007/11872153_32

Shalev-Shwartz, S., & Ben-David, S. (2014). *Understanding machine learning: From theory to algorithms.* Cambridge university press. intrusion detection. *IEEE Networking Letters, 1*(2), 68–71.

Shanmuganathan & Sallis. (2014). *Data Mining Methods to Generate Severe Wind Gust Models.* Academic Press.

Shaon, M. (2015). *A computationally intelligent approach to the detection of wormhole attacks in wireless sensor networks.* Academic Press.

Sharma, S., & Jena, S. K. (2011). A survey on secure hierarchical routing protocols in wireless sensor networks. *Proceedings of the 2011 international conference on communication, computing & security.* 10.1145/1947940.1947972

Sharma, P. K. (2018). Secure and Soft Handoff Techniques of IoT: A Review. In *Proceedings of the 2nd International Conference on Trends in Electronics and Informatics (ICOEI 2018)* (pp. 271-276). Tirunelveli, India: IEEE. 10.1109/ICOEI.2018.8553740

Sharma, R. R., & Sanganal, A. (2014). Li-Fi Technology: Transmission of data through light. *International Journal of Computer Technology and Applications, 5*(1), 150.

Sharmila, S., & Shanthi, T. (2016). A survey on wireless ad hoc network: Issues and implementation. In *2016 International Conference on Emerging Trends in Engineering, Technology and Science (ICETETS)* (pp. 1-6). IEEE. 10.1109/ICETETS.2016.7603071

Shen, X., Lu, R., Kato, N., Lin, X., & Nemoto, Y. (2009). Sage: A strong privacy-preserving scheme against global eavesdropping for ehealth systems. *IEEE Journal on Selected Areas in Communications, 27*(4), 365–378. doi:10.1109/JSAC.2009.090502

Shen, Z., Arslan Ay, S., Kim, S. H., & Zimmermann, R. (2011). Automatic tag generation and ranking for sensor-rich outdoor videos. In *Proceedings of the 19th ACM international conference on Multimedia* (pp. 93-102). 10.1145/2072298.2072312

Sheth, & Bennett. (Eds.). (2010). Toward a theory of consumer complaining behavior. In Consumer and Industrial Buying Behavior. North-Holland Publishing.

Shi, H., Ushio, T., Endo, M., Yamagami, K., & Horii, N. (2016, December). A multichannel convolutional neural network for cross-language dialog state tracking. In *2016 IEEE Spoken Language Technology Workshop (SLT)* (pp. 559-564). IEEE. 10.1109/SLT.2016.7846318

Shikha. (2016). A Study for Finding Location of Nodes in Wireless Sensor Networks. *International Journal of Computer Science & Engineering Technology, 7*(3).

Shoaib, M., Ishaq, A., Ahmad, M. A., Talib, S., Mustafa, G., & Ahmed, A. (2017). Software Migration Frameworks for Software System Solutions: A Systematic Literature Review. *International Journal of Advanced Computer Science and Applications, 8*(11), 2017. doi:10.14569/IJACSA.2017.081126

Shouling, J., Shukun, Y., Xin, H., Weili, H., Zhigong, L., & Raheem, B. (2017). Zero-Sum Password Cracking Game: A Large-Scale Empirical Study on the Crackability, Correlation, and Security of Passwords. *IEEE Transactions on Dependable and Secure Computing, 14*(5), 550–564. doi:10.1109/TDSC.2015.2481884

Sibi, C. S., Sangeetha, D., & Vaidehi, V. (2019). Intrusion detection system for detecting wireless attacks in IEEE 802.11 networks. *IET Networks, 8*(4), 219–232. doi:10.1049/iet-net.2018.5050

Sicari, S., Rizzardi, A., Grieco, L. A., & Coen-Porisini, A. (2015). Security, privacy and trust in Internet of Things: The road ahead. *Computer Networks, 76*, 146–164. doi:10.1016/j.comnet.2014.11.008

Sidiropoulos, P., Mezaris, V., Kompatsiaris, I., Meinedo, H., Bugalho, M., & Trancoso, I. (2011). Temporal video segmentation to scenes using high-level audiovisual features. *IEEE Transactions on Circuits and Systems for Video Technology, 21*(8), 1163–1177. doi:10.1109/TCSVT.2011.2138830

Siersdorfer, S., San Pedro, J., & Sanderson, M. (2009). Automatic video tagging using content redundancy. In *Proceedings of the 32nd international ACM SIGIR conference on Research and development in information retrieval* (pp. 395-402). ACM.

Singh, J. (1988). Consumer Complaint Intentions and Behavior: A Review and Prospect. *Journal of Marketing. Social Research Methods: Qualitative and Quantitative Approaches.*

Singh, R., & Singh, A. (2016). *A Review : Wireless Body Area Network Performance Dependency.* Academic Press.

Singh, A. V., Juyal, V., & Saggar, R. (2017). Trust based Intelligent Routing Algorithm for Delay Tolerant Network using Artificial Neural Network. *Wireless Networks, 23*(3), 693–702. doi:10.100711276-015-1166-y

Singh, A., & Jain, A. (2018). Study of cyber attacks on cyber-physical system. In *Proceedings of 3rd International Conference on Internet of Things and Connected Technologies (ICIoTCT)* (pp. 26-27). 10.2139srn.3170288

Singh, A., Kumar, D., & Hötzel, J. (2018). IoT Based information and communication system for enhancing underground mines safety and productivity: Genesis, taxonomy and open issues. *Ad Hoc Networks, 78*, 115–129. doi:10.1016/j.adhoc.2018.06.008

Singh, M. D. R. (2015). A Review of Security Issues and Denial of Service Attacks in Wireless Sensor Networks. *International Journal of Computer Science and Information Technology Research, 3*(1).

Singh, R., Singh, J., & Singh, R. (2016). TBSD: A defend against Sybil attack in wireless sensor networks. *International Journal of Computer Science and Network Security, 16*(11), 90–99.

Singh, S., & Majumdar, A. (2017). Deep sparse coding for non-intrusive load monitoring. *IEEE Transactions on Smart Grid.*

Stankovic, D. W. a. J. A. (2002). Denial of Service in Sensor Networks. *IEEE Computer, 35*(10).

Stauss & Schoeler. (2004). Complaint management profitability: what do complaint managers know? Managing Service Quality.

Stavru, S., Krasteva, I., & Ilieva, S. (2012). *Challenges for Migrating to the Service Cloud Paradigm: An Agile Perspective.* Academic Press.

Suh, G. E., & Devadas, S. (2007, June). Physical unclonable functions for device authentication and secret key generation. In *2007 44th ACM/IEEE Design Automation Conference* (pp. 9-14). IEEE.

Suh, C., & Ko, Y. (2008). Design and implementation of intelligent home control systems based on active sensor networks. *IEEE Transactions on Consumer Electronics, 54*(3), 1177–1184. doi:10.1109/TCE.2008.4637604

Sun, B., & Li, D. (2017). A Comprehensive Trust-Aware Routing Protocol with Multi-Attributes for WSNs. *IEEE Access: Practical Innovations, Open Solutions, 6*, 4725–4741. doi:10.1109/ACCESS.2017.2786944

Sun, B., Luh, P. B., Jia, Q. S., O'Neill, Z., & Song, F. (2014). Building energy doctors: An SPC and Kalman filter-based method for systemlevel fault detection in HVAC systems. *IEEE Transactions on Automation Science and Engineering, 11*(1), 215–229. doi:10.1109/TASE.2012.2226155

Sundararajan, R. K., & Arumugam, U. (2015). Intrusion detection algorithm for mitigating sinkhole attack on LEACH protocol in wireless sensor networks. *Journal of Sensors, 2015*, 2015. doi:10.1155/2015/203814

Swietojanski, P., Ghoshal, A., & Renals, S. (2014). Convolutional neural networks for distant speech recognition. *IEEE Signal Processing Letters, 21*(9), 1120–1124. doi:10.1109/LSP.2014.2325781

Szegedy, C., Liu, W., Jia, Y., Sermanet, P., Reed, S., Anguelov, D., . . . Rabinovich, A. (2014). *Going deeper with convolutions.* arXiv:1409.4842

Szegedy, C., Ioffe, S., Vanhoucke, V., & Alemi, A. A. (2017, February). Inception-v4, inception-resnet and the impact of residual connections on learning. *Thirty-first AAAI conference on artificial intelligence.*

Szegedy, C., Vanhoucke, V., Ioffe, S., Shlens, J., & Wojna, Z. (2016). Rethinking the inception architecture for computer vision. In *Proceedings of the IEEE conference on computer vision and pattern recognition* (pp. 2818-2826). 10.1109/CVPR.2016.308

Szilagyi & Wira. (2018). *An intelligent system for smart buildings using machine learning and semantic technologies: A hybrid data-knowledge approach. In IEEE Industrial Cyber-Physical Systems* (pp. 20–25). St. Petersburg: ICPS.

Tabandeh, M., Jahed, M., Ahourai, F., & Moradi, S. (2009). A thermal-aware shortest hop routing algorithm for in vivo biomedical sensor networks. In *ITNG 2009 - 6th International Conference on Information Technology: New Generations* (pp. 1612–1613). 10.1109/ITNG.2009.274

Tajeddine, A., Kayssi, A., Chehab, A., Elhajj, I., & Itani, W. (2015). CENTERA: A centralized trust-based efficient routing protocol with authentication for wireless sensor networks. *Sensors (Switzerland), 15*(2), 3299–3333. doi:10.3390/s150203299 PMID:25648712

413

Takahashi, D., Xiao, Y., & Hu, F. (2007). LTRT: Least total-route temperature routing for embedded biomedical sensor networks. In *GLOBECOM - IEEE Global Telecommunications Conference* (pp. 641–645). IEEE. 10.1109/GLOCOM.2007.125

Talavera, J. M., Tobón, L. E., Gómez, J. A., Culman, M. A., Aranda, J. M., Parra, D. T., ... Garreta, L. E. (2017). Review of IoT Applications in Agro-Industrial and Environmental Fields. *Computers and Electronics in Agriculture, 142*, 283–297. doi:10.1016/j.compag.2017.09.015

Tang, Q., Tummala, N., Gupta, S. K. S., & Schwiebert, L. (2005a). Communication scheduling to minimize thermal effects of implanted biosensor networks in homogeneous tissue. *IEEE Transactions on Biomedical Engineering, 52*(7), 1285–1294. doi:10.1109/TBME.2005.847527 PMID:16041992

Tang, Q., Tummala, N., Gupta, S. K. S., & Schwiebert, L. (2005b). TARA: Thermal-Aware Routing Algorithm for Implanted Sensor Networks. In *Proceedings of 1st IEEE International Conference Distributed Computing in Sensor Systems* (pp. 206–217). 10.1007/11502593_17

Tanin, S., & Khan, A. W. (2019). Choice of Application Layer Protocols for Next Generation Video Surveillance Using Internet of Video Things. *IEEE Access: Practical Innovations, Open Solutions, 7*, 41607–41624. doi:10.1109/ACCESS.2019.2907525

Tardioli, G., Kerrigan, R., Oates, M., O'Donnell, J., & Finn, D. (2015). Data driven approaches for prediction of building energy consumption at urban level. *Published in Energy Procedia, 78*, 3378–3383. doi:10.1016/j.egypro.2015.11.754

Tchakoucht, T. A., Ezziyyani, M., Jbilou, M., & Salaun, M. (2015). Behavioral appraoch for intrusion detection. In *2015 IEEE/ACS 12th International Conference of Computer Systems and Applications (AICCSA)* (pp. 1-5). IEEE. 10.1109/AICCSA.2015.7507118

Team, D. (2018, June 16). *Top 10 Interesting Facts About Future of IoT.* https://data-flair.training/blogs/future-of-IoT

The Importance of UX in IoT I HCL Blogs. (n.d.). *Importance of UC in IOT.* https://www.hcltech.com/blogs/importance-ux-IoT

Thenmozhi, K., & Srinivasulu Reddy, U. (2019). Crop Pest Classification Based on Deep Convolutional Neural Network and Transfer Learning. *Computers and Electronics in Agriculture, 164*, 104906. doi:10.1016/j.compag.2019.104906

Thomson, M., & Turner, S. (2019). Using TLS to Secure QUIC. *Internet Engineering Task Force, Internet-Draft draft-ietf-quic-tls-22.*

Tianfield, H. (2018). Towards Edge-Cloud Computing. In *IEEE International Conference on Big Data (Big Data)* (pp. 4883-4885). IEEE. 10.1109/BigData.2018.8622052

Toderici, G., Aradhye, H., Pasca, M., Sbaiz, L., & Yagnik, J. (2010). Finding meaning on youtube: Tag recommendation and category discovery. In *IEEE Computer Society Conference on Computer Vision and Pattern Recognition* (pp. 3447-3454). 10.1109/CVPR.2010.5539985

Tuen, C. D. (2015). *Security in Internet of Things Systems* (Master's thesis). NTNU.

Tushar, W., Yuen, C., Li, W.-T., Smith, D., Saha, T., & Wood, K. L. (2018). Motivational psychology driven AC management scheme: A responsive design approach. *IEEE Transactions on Computational Social Systems, 5*(1), 289–301. doi:10.1109/TCSS.2017.2788922

Tyagi, A. C. (2016). Towards a Second Green Revolution. *Irrigation and Drainage, 65*(4), 388–389. doi:10.1002/ird.2076

Tyndall, A., Cardell-Oliver, R., & Keating, A. (2016). Occupancy estimation using a low-pixel count thermal imager. *IEEE Sensors Journal*, *16*(10), 3784–3791. doi:10.1109/JSEN.2016.2530824

Uğur, L. O., & Leblebici, N. (2018). An examination of the LEED green building certification system in terms of construction costs. *Renewable & Sustainable Energy Reviews*, *81*(Part 1), 1476–1483. doi:10.1016/j.rser.2017.05.210

Ulges, A., Schulze, C., Keysers, D., & Breuel, T. M. (2008). A system that learns to tag videos by watching youtube. In *International Conference on Computer Vision Systems* (pp. 415-424). Springer. 10.1007/978-3-540-79547-6_40

Ullah, S., Higgins, H., Braem, B., Latre, B., Blondia, C., Moerman, I., ... Kwak, K. S. (2012). A comprehensive survey of wireless body area networks on PHY, MAC, and network layers solutions. *Journal of Medical Systems*, *36*(3), 1065–1094. doi:10.100710916-010-9571-3 PMID:20721685

Uluagac, A. S., Lee, C. P., Beyah, R. A., & Copeland, J. A. (2008). Article. *Designing Secure Protocols for Wireless Sensor Networks*, *6*(5), 503–514. doi:10.1007/978-3-540-88582-5_47

Upasana. (2018, September 20). Real World IoT Applications in Different Domains. *Edureka*. https://internetofthings-agenda.techtarget.com/definition/Internet-of-Things-IoT

Utsav, B., Andrew, W., Chiraag, J., & Madeleine, W. (2019). An Energy-Efficient Reconfigurable DTLS Cryptographic Engine for Securing Internet-of-Things Applications. *IEEE Journal of Solid-State Circuits*, *54*(8), 2339–2352. doi:10.1109/JSSC.2019.2915203

Valarmathi, M. L. (2016). A Survey on Node Discovery in Mobile Internet of Things(IoT) Scenarios. In *International Conference on Advanced Computing and Communication Systems (lCACCS -2016), Jan. 22 & 23, 2016, Coimbatore*. Coimbatore, India: IEEE. 10.1109/ICACCS.2016.7586400

Van Daele, P., Moerman, I., & Demeester, P. (2014). Wireless body area networks: Status and opportunities. *2014 31th URSI General Assembly and Scientific Symposium, URSI GASS 2014*, 2–5. 10.1109/URSIGASS.2014.6929369

Vanjale, S. B., Mane, P. B., & Patil, S. V. (2015). Wireless LAN Intrusion Detection and Prevention system for Malicious Access Point. In *2015 2nd International Conference on Computing for Sustainable Global Development (INDIACom)* (pp. 487-490). IEEE.

Van, N. T., Thinh, T. N., & Sach, L. T. (2017). An anomaly-based network intrusion detection system using deep learning. In *2017 International Conference on System Science and Engineering (ICSSE)* (pp. 210-214). IEEE.

Vathsala, H., & Koolagudi, S. G. (2017). *Prediction model for peninsular Indian summer monsoon rainfall using data mining and statistical approaches. Comput. Geoscience.*

Vazquez-Casielles, R. & Diaz-Martin, A.M. (2009). Satisfaction with service recovery: Perceived justice and emotional responses. *Journal of Business Research.*

Venkataram, P. L. (2000). A Method of Data Transfer Control during Handoffs in Mobile Multimedia Networks. In *IEEE International Conference on Personal Wireless Communications. Conference Proceedings (Cat. No.00TH8488)*. Hyderabad, India: IEEE. 10.1109/ICPWC.2000.905774

Venugopalan, S., Xu, H., Donahue, J., Rohrbach, M., Mooney, R., & Saenko, K. (2014). *Translating videos to natural language using deep recurrent neural networks*. arXiv preprint arXiv:1412.4729

Venugopalan, S., Rohrbach, M., Donahue, J., Mooney, R., Darrell, T., & Saenko, K. (2015). Sequence to sequence-video to text. In *Proceedings of the IEEE international conference on computer vision* (pp. 4534-4542). IEEE.

Veracode white paper. (2019). *The internet of things: a security research study*. Retrieved from https://www.veracode.com/sites/default/files/Resources/Whitepapers/internet-of-things-whitepaper.pdf/

Verma, S., & Gala, R. (2018). An Internet of Things (IoT) Architecture for Smart Agriculture. In *2018 Fourth International Conference on Computing Communication Control and Automation (ICCUBEA)*. Pune, India: IEEE. 10.1109/ICCUBEA.2018.8697707

Vijay, V., Kallol, K., Uday, T., & Michael, H. (2018). A Policy-Based Security Architecture for Software-Defined Networks. *IEEE Transactions on Information Forensics and Security, 14*(4), 897–912.

Vijendran, A. S., & Gripsy, J. V. (2014). *Enhanced secure multipath routing scheme in mobile adhoc and sensor networks*. Paper presented at the Second International Conference on Current Trends In Engineering and Technology-ICCTET 2014. 10.1109/ICCTET.2014.6966289

Vinay, K., Saquib, R., & Nael, B. A. (2014). Interaction Engineering: Achieving Perfect CSMA Handshakes in Wireless Networks. *IEEE Transactions on Mobile Computing, 13*(11), 2552–2565. doi:10.1109/TMC.2014.2314130

Vishwakarma, S. K. (2019). Smart Energy Efficient Home Automation System Using IoT. In *4th International Conference on Internet of Things: Smart Innovation and Usages (IoT-SIU)*. Ghaziabad, India: IEEE. 10.1109/IoT-SIU.2019.8777607

Viswanath, S. K., Yuen, C., Tushar, W., Li, W.-T., Wen, C.-K., Hu, K., ... Liu, X. (2016). System design of the internet of things for residential smart grid. *IEEE Wireless Communications, 23*(5), 90–98. doi:10.1109/MWC.2016.7721747

Vongchumyen, C. T. (2019). Home Appliances-Controlled Platform with HomeKit Application. In *5th International Conference on Engineering, Applied Sciences and Technology (ICEAST)*. Luang Prabang, Laos: IEEE.

Wac, K., Bults, R., Van Beijnum, B., Widya, I., Jones, V. M., & Konstantas, D., ... Hermens, H. (2009). Mobile patient monitoring: The MobiHealth system. In *Proceedings of the 31st Annual International Conference of the IEEE Engineering in Medicine and Biology Society: Engineering the Future of Biomedicine, EMBC 2009* (pp. 1238–1241). 10.1109/IEMBS.2009.5333477

Waluyo, A. B., Pek, I., Chen, X., & Yeoh, W. S. (2009). Design and evaluation of lightweight middleware for personal wireless body area network. In Personal and Ubiquitous Computing (Vol. 13, pp. 509–525). doi:10.100700779-009-0222-y

Wander, A. S., Gura, N., Eberle, H., Gupta, V., & Shantz, S. C. (2005). *Energy analysis of public-key cryptography for wireless sensor networks*. Paper presented at the Third IEEE international conference on pervasive computing and communications. 10.1109/PERCOM.2005.18

Wang, Y., Attebury, G., & Ramamurthy, B. (2006). *A survey of security issues in wireless sensor networks*. Academic Press.

Wang, Z.-Q. (2016). Research on Distributed Intrusion Detection System. Academic Press.

Wang, B., Chen, X., & Chang, W. (2014). A light-weight trust-based QoS routing algorithm for ad hoc networks. *Pervasive and Mobile Computing, 13*, 164–180. doi:10.1016/j.pmcj.2013.06.004

Wang, H., Fang, H., Xing, L., & Chen, M. (2011). An integrated biometric-based security framework using wavelet-domain HMM in wireless body area networks (WBAN). In *IEEE International Conference on Communications*. 10.1109/icc.2011.5962757

Wang, L., Törngren, M., & Onori, M. (2015). Current status and advancement of cyber-physical systems in manufacturing. *Journal of Manufacturing Systems, 37*, 517–527. doi:10.1016/j.jmsy.2015.04.008

Wang, Y., Xia, S. T., Tang, Q., Wu, J., & Zhu, X. (2017). A novel consistent random forest framework: Bernoulli random forests. *IEEE Transactions on Neural Networks and Learning Systems, 29*(8), 3510–3523. PMID:28816676

Wan, J., Wang, D., Hoi, S. C., Wu, P., Zhu, J., Zhang, Y., & Li, J. (2014). Deep learning for content-based image retrieval: A comprehensive study. In *Proceedings of the 22nd ACM international conference on Multimedia*. ACM.

Wei, Tian, Silva, Choudhary, Meng, & Yang. (2015). Comparative Study on Machine Learning for Urban Building Energy Analysis. *Procedia Engineering*, (121), 285-292.

Weirathmueller, M. W. (2007). *Acoustic Positioning and Tracking in Portsmouth Harbor, New Hampshire. In OCEANS*. Vancouver, Canada: IEEE.

Wei, W., Houbing, S., Huihui, W., & Xiumei, F. (2017). Research and Simulation of Queue Management Algorithms in Ad Hoc Networks Under DDoS Attack. *IEEE Access: Practical Innovations, Open Solutions, 5*, 27810–27817. doi:10.1109/ACCESS.2017.2681684

Wei, Z., Jian, C., Yonghong, K., & Yuchen, Z. (2018). Artificial-Noise-Aided Optimal Beamforming in Layered Physical Layer Security. *IEEE Communications Letters, 23*(1), 72–75.

Wei, Z., Jian, C., Yonghong, K., & Yuchen, Z. (2019). Transmit Beamforming for Layered Physical Layer Security. *IEEE Transactions on Vehicular Technology, 68*(10), 9747–9760. doi:10.1109/TVT.2019.2932753

Welsh, M., Moulton, S., Fulford-Jones, T., & Malan, D. J. (2004). CodeBlue : An Ad Hoc Sensor Network Infrastructure for Emergency Medical Care. In *International Workshop on Wearable and Implantable Body Sensor Networks* (p. 5). Retrieved from http://nrs.harvard.edu/urn-3:HUL.InstRepos:3191012

William, S. (2017). Computer and Network Security Concept. In *Cryptography and Network Security: Principle and Practice* (pp. 37–40). Uttar Pradesh, India: Pearson.

Wong, S. P. (2008). Service Continuity for Audio Visual Service. In *IEEE International Symposium on Consumer Electronics*. Vilamoura, Portugal: IEEE.

Wood, A. D., Stankovic, J. A., Virone, G., Selavo, L., He, Z., Cao, Q., … Stoleru, R. (2008). Context-aware wireless sensor networks for assisted living and residential monitoring. *IEEE Network* (Vol. 22). doi:10.1109/MNET.2008.4579768

Wright, O. (1995). Local acoustic probing using mechanical and ultrafast optical techniques. In *IEEE Ultrasonics Symposium. Proceedings. An International Symposium* (pp. 567-575). Seattle, WA: IEEE.

Wu, J., Long, J., & Liu, M. (2015). *Evolving RBF neural networks for rainfall prediction using hybrid particle swarm optimization and genetic algorithm. Neurocomputing.*

Wu, Z., Wang, X., Jiang, Y. G., Ye, H., & Xue, X. (2015). Modeling spatial-temporal clues in a hybrid deep learning framework for video classification. In *Proceedings of the 23rd ACM international conference on Multimedia* (pp. 461-470). 10.1145/2733373.2806222

Xia, H., Zhang, S., Li, B., Li, L., & Cheng, X. (2018). Towards a Novel Trust-Based Multicast Routing for VANETs. *Security and Communication Networks, 2018*, 1–12. doi:10.1155/2018/7608198

Xiao, L., Wan, X., Lu, X., Zhang, Y., & Wu, D. (2018). *IoT security techniques based on machine learning.* arXiv preprint arXiv:1801.06275

Xiao, L., Dusit, N., Nicolas, P., Hai, J., & Ping, W. (2018). Managing Physical Layer Security in Wireless Cellular Networks: A Cyber Insurance Approach. *IEEE Journal on Selected Areas in Communications, 36*(7), 1648–1661. doi:10.1109/JSAC.2018.2825518

Xiao, L., Jing, X., Zhen, F. Z., & Wen, T. Z. (2017). Investigating the Multi-Ciphersuite and Backwards-Compatibility Security of the Upcoming TLS 1.3. *IEEE Transactions on Dependable and Secure Computing, 16*(2), 272–286.

Xiao, Q., Li, G., Xie, L., & Chen, Q. (2018). Real-World Plant Species Identification Based on Deep Convolutional Neural Networks and Visual Attention. *Ecological Informatics*, *48*, 117–124. doi:10.1016/j.ecoinf.2018.09.001

Xing, G., Lu, C., Pless, R., & Huang, Q. (2004). On greedy geographic routing algorithms in sensing-covered networks. *Proceedings of the 5th ACM international symposium on Mobile ad hoc networking and computing*. 10.1145/989459.989465

Xiuhua, L., Wei, Y., Qiaoyan, W., Zhengping, J., & Wenmin, L. (2018). A Lattice-Based Unordered Aggregate Signature Scheme Based on the Intersection Method. *IEEE Access: Practical Innovations, Open Solutions*, *6*, 33986–33994. doi:10.1109/ACCESS.2018.2847411

Xu, Trappe, & Zhang. (2006). Jamming Sensor Networks: Attack and Defense Strategies. *IEEE Network*.

Xu, H., Ye, G., Li, Y., Liu, D., & Chang, S. F. (2015). Large video event ontology browsing, search and tagging (eventnet demo). In *Proceedings of the 23rd ACM international conference on Multimedia* (pp. 803-804). 10.1145/2733373.2807973

Xu, R., Xiong, C., Chen, W., & Corso, J. J. (2015). Jointly modeling deep video and compositional text to bridge vision and language in a unified framework. *Twenty-Ninth AAAI Conference on Artificial Intelligence*.

Xu, W. W. (2017). *Depth Map Super-resolution via Multiclass Dictionary Learning with Geometrical Directions. In IEEE Visual Communications and Image Processing (VCIP)*. St. Petersburg, FL: IEEE.

Yagan, O. (2012). Performance of the Eschenauer–Gligor key distribution scheme under an ON/OFF channel. *IEEE Transactions on Information Theory*, *58*(6), 3821–3835. doi:10.1109/TIT.2012.2189353

Yamashita, R., Nishio, M., Richard, K. G. D., & Togashi, K. (2018). Convolutional Neural Networks: An Overview and Application in Radiology. *Insights Into Imaging*, *9*(4), 611–629. doi:10.100713244-018-0639-9 PMID:29934920

Yampolskiy, M., Horvath, P., Koutsoukos, X. D., Xue, Y., & Sztipanovits, J. (2012). Systematic analysis of cyber-attacks on CPS-evaluating applicability of DFD-based approach. In *2012 5th International Symposium on Resilient Control Systems* (pp. 55-62). IEEE. 10.1109/ISRCS.2012.6309293

Yanai, K. (2014). Automatic extraction of relevant video shots of specific actions exploiting Web data. *Computer Vision and Image Understanding*, *118*, 2–15. doi:10.1016/j.cviu.2013.03.009

Yang, H., Xu, A., Chen, H., & Yuan, C. (2014). A Review: The Effects of Imperfect Data on Incremental Decision Tree. In *2014 Ninth International Conference on P2P, Parallel, Grid, Cloud and Internet Computing* (pp. 34-41). IEEE.

Yang, W., & Toderici, G. (2011). Discriminative tag learning on youtube videos with latent sub-tags. In CVPR 2011 (pp. 3217-3224). doi:10.1109/CVPR.2011.5995402

Yang, Q., Zhang, Y., Dai, W., & Pan, S. J. (2020). *Transfer learning*. Cambridge University Press. doi:10.1017/9781139061773

Yang, T., Xiangyang, X., Peng, L., Tonghui, L., & Leina, P. (2018). A secure routing of wireless sensor networks based on trust evaluation model. *Procedia Computer Science*, *131*, 1156–1163. doi:10.1016/j.procs.2018.04.289

Yanling, Z., Ye, L., Xinchang, Z., Guanggang, G., Wei, Z., & Yanjie, S. (2019). A Survey of Networking Applications Applying the Software Defined Networking Concept Based on Machine Learning. *IEEE Access: Practical Innovations, Open Solutions*, *7*, 95397–95417. doi:10.1109/ACCESS.2019.2928564

Yantao, L., Hailong, H., & Gang, Z. (2018). Using Data Augmentation in Continuous Authentication on Smartphones. *IEEE Internet of Things Journal*, *6*(1), 628–640.

Yaseen, M., Saleem, K., Orgun, M. A., Derhab, A., Abbas, H., Al-Muhtadi, J., ... Rashid, I. (2018). Secure sensors data acquisition and communication protection in eHealthcare: Review on the state of the art. *Telematics and Informatics*, *35*(4), 702–726. doi:10.1016/j.tele.2017.08.005

Yasser, A. B., Vivian, E. S., & Natalia, M. S. (2018). Artificial intelligence techniques for information security risk assessment. *IEEE Latin America Transactions*, *16*(3), 897–901. doi:10.1109/TLA.2018.8358671

Yeo, L. H., Che, X., & Lakkaraju, S. (2017). *Understanding Modern Intrusion Detection Systems: A Survey*. arXiv preprint arXiv:1708.07174

Yeung, M., Yeo, B. L., & Liu, B. (1998). Segmentation of video by clustering and graph analysis. *Computer Vision and Image Understanding*, *71*(1), 94–109. doi:10.1006/cviu.1997.0628

Yick, J., Mukherjee, B., & Ghosal, D. (2008). Wireless sensor network survey. *Computer Networks*, *52*(12), 2292–2330. doi:10.1016/j.comnet.2008.04.002

Yin, J. B. (2012). SNMP-based network topology discovery algorithm and implementation. In *9th International Conference on Fuzzy Systems and Knowledge Discovery (FSKD 2012)* (pp. 2241-2244). IEEE. 10.1109/FSKD.2012.6233879

Yong, F., Cheng, Z., Cheng, H., Liang, L., & Yue, Y. (2019). Phishing Email Detection Using Improved RCNN Model With Multilevel Vectors and Attention Mechanism. *IEEE Access: Practical Innovations, Open Solutions*, *7*, 56329–56340. doi:10.1109/ACCESS.2019.2913705

Yongpeng, W., Ashish, K., Chengshan, X., Giuseppe, C., Kai, K. W., & Xiqi, G. (2018). A Survey of Physical Layer Security Techniques for 5G Wireless Networks and Challenges Ahead. *IEEE Journal on Selected Areas in Communications*, *36*(4), 679–695. doi:10.1109/JSAC.2018.2825560

Yosinski, J., Clune, J., Bengio, Y., & Lipson, H. (2014). How transferable are features in deep neural networks? In Advances in neural information processing systems (pp. 3320-3328). Academic Press.

Yu, L., & Kuo. (2012). *CSI: Compressed Sensing-Based Clone Identification in Sensor Networks*. Paper presented at the 8th IEEE International Workshop on Sensor Networks and Systems for Pervasive Computing. 10.1109/PerComW.2012.6197497

Yu, Y., Govindan, R., & Estrin, D. (2001). *Geographical and energy aware routing: A recursive data dissemination protocol for wireless sensor networks*. Academic Press.

Yuanyuan, K., Bin, L., Feng, C., & Zhen, Y. (2018). The Security Network Coding System With Physical Layer Key Generation in Two-Way Relay Networks. *IEEE Access: Practical Innovations, Open Solutions*, *6*, 40673–40681. doi:10.1109/ACCESS.2018.2858282

Yue-Hei Ng, J., Hausknecht, M., Vijayanarasimhan, S., Vinyals, O., Monga, R., & Toderici, G. (2015). Beyond short snippets: Deep networks for video classification. In *Proceedings of the IEEE conference on computer vision and pattern recognition* (pp. 4694-4702). 10.1109/CVPR.2015.7299101

Yüksek & Karadayi. (2017). Energy-Efficient Building Design in the Context of Building Life Cycle. In Energy Efficient Buildings. IGI.

Yu, X., Yuanyuan, L., Bin, Z., Ruyan, W., & George, N. R. (2018). SDN enabled restoration with triggered precomputation in elastic optical inter-datacenter networks. *Journal of Optical Communications and Networking*, *11*(1), 24–34.

Zahariadis, T., Trakadas, P., Leligou, H. C., Maniatis, S., & Karkazis, P. (2013). A novel trust-aware geographical routing scheme for wireless sensor networks. *Wireless Personal Communications*, *69*(2), 805–826. doi:10.100711277-012-0613-7

Zahoor, A. A., Hasan, T., Malik, H. M., Shahzaib, T., & Klaus, M. (2019). Key-Based Cookie-Less Session Management Framework for Application Layer Security. *IEEE Access: Practical Innovations, Open Solutions*, *7*, 128544–128554. doi:10.1109/ACCESS.2019.2940331

Zainudin, S., Jasim, D. S., & Baker, A. A. (2016). *Comparative Analysis of Data Mining Techniques for Malaysian Rainfall Prediction. Int. J. Adv. Sci. Eng. Inf. Technology, 6*(6), 1148–1153.

Zha, S., Luisier, F., Andrews, W., Srivastava, N., & Salakhutdinov, R. (2015). *Exploiting image-trained CNN architectures for unconstrained video classification.* arXiv preprint arXiv:1503.04144

Zhai, Y., & Shah, M. (2005). A general framework for temporal video scene segmentation. In *Tenth IEEE International Conference on Computer Vision (ICCV'05)* (Vol. 2, pp. 1111-1116). 10.1109/ICCV.2005.6

Zhai, Y., & Shah, M. (2006). Video scene segmentation using Markov chain Monte Carlo. *IEEE Transactions on Multimedia, 8*(4), 686–697. doi:10.1109/TMM.2006.876299

Zhang, M. (2009). Memory Efficient Protocols for Detecting Node Replication Attacks in Wireless Sensor Networks. Academic Press.

Zhang, X., Yang, Y., Han, Z., Wang, H., & Gao, C. (2013). Object class detection: A survey. *ACM Computing Surveys, 46*(1), 10:1–10:53.

Zhang, Z. K., Cho, M. C. Y., Wang, C. W., Hsu, C. W., Chen, C. K., & Shieh, S. (2014, November). IoT security: ongoing challenges and research opportunities. In *2014 IEEE 7th international conference on service-oriented computing and applications* (pp. 230-234). IEEE. 10.1109/SOCA.2014.58

Zhang, D., Li, S., Sun, M., & O'Neill, Z. (2016). An optimal and learning-based demand response and home energy management system. *IEEE Transactions on Smart Grid, 7*(4), 1790–1801. doi:10.1109/TSG.2016.2552169

Zhang, P., & Ma, J. (2018). Channel characteristic aware privacy protection mechanism in WBAN. *Sensors (Switzerland), 18*(8), 2403. doi:10.339018082403 PMID:30042302

Zhang, Q., Yang, L. T., Chen, Z., & Li, P. (2018). A Survey on Deep Learning for Big Data. *Information Fusion, 42*, 146–157. doi:10.1016/j.inffus.2017.10.006

Zhang, Z., Liu, S., Bai, Y., & Zheng, Y. (2018). M optimal routes hops strategy: Detecting sinkhole attacks in wireless sensor networks. *Cluster Computing*, 1–9.

Zhang, Z., Wang, H., Vasilakos, A. V., & Fang, H. (2012). ECG-cryptography and authentication in body area networks. *IEEE Transactions on Information Technology in Biomedicine, 16*(6), 1070–1078. doi:10.1109/TITB.2012.2206115 PMID:22752143

Zhao, K., & Ge, L. (2013, December). A survey on the internet of things security. In *2013 Ninth international conference on computational intelligence and security* (pp. 663-667). IEEE. 10.1109/CIS.2013.145

Zhao, S., Li, W., Zia, T., & Zomaya, A. Y. (2018). A dimension reduction model and classifier for anomaly-based intrusion detection in internet of things. *Proceedings - 2017 IEEE 15th International Conference on Dependable, Autonomic and Secure Computing, 2017 IEEE 15th International Conference on Pervasive Intelligence and Computing, 2017 IEEE 3rd International Conference on Big Data Intelligence and Computing and 2017 IEEE Cyber Science and Technology Congress, DASC-PICom-DataCom-CyberSciTec 2017, 2018-January*, 836–843. 10.1109/DASC-PICom-DataCom-CyberSciTec.2017.141

Zhao, R., Yan, R., Chen, Z., Mao, K., Wang, P., & Gao, R. X. (2019). Deep learning and its applications to machine health monitoring. *Mechanical Systems and Signal Processing, 115*, 213–237. doi:10.1016/j.ymssp.2018.05.050

Zhao, W. L., Wu, X., & Ngo, C. W. (2010). On the annotation of web videos by efficient near-duplicate search. *IEEE Transactions on Multimedia, 12*(5), 448–461. doi:10.1109/TMM.2010.2050651

Zhao, Y., Wang, T., Wang, P., Hu, W., Du, Y., Zhang, Y., & Xu, G. (2007). Scene segmentation and categorization using ncuts. In *IEEE Conference on Computer Vision and Pattern Recognition* (pp. 1-7). IEEE.

Zheng, G., & Hu, Z. (2009). *A Clustering Protocol Based on the Probability Fading Strategy in WSNs*. Paper presented at the 2009 International Conference on Information Engineering and Computer Science. 10.1109/ICIECS.2009.5366020

Zhen, Z., Yuhui, D., Geyong, M., Junjie, X., Laurence, T. Y., & Yongtao, Z. (2019). HSDC: A Highly Scalable Data Center Network Architecture for Greater Incremental Scalability. *IEEE Transactions on Parallel and Distributed Systems*, *30*(5), 1105–1119. doi:10.1109/TPDS.2018.2874659

Zhou, W., Jia, Y., Peng, A., Zhang, Y., & Liu, P. (2018). The effect of IoT new features on security and privacy: New threats, existing solutions, and challenges yet to be solved. *IEEE Internet of Things Journal*, *6*(2), 1606–1616. doi:10.1109/JIOT.2018.2847733

Zhou, Y., Sun, X., Liu, D., Zha, Z., & Zeng, W. (2017). Adaptive pooling in multi-instance learning for web video annotation. In *Proceedings of the IEEE International Conference on Computer Vision Workshops* (pp. 318-327). IEEE.

Zifan, L., Mihail, L. S., & Xuesong, Q. (2018). Fog Radio Access Network: A New Wireless backhaul Architectuer For Small Cell Networks. *IEEE Access: Practical Innovations, Open Solutions*, *7*, 14150–14161.

Zorz, Z. (2015). *USB Killer 2.0: A harmless-looking USB stick that destroys computers*. Retrieved from: https://www.helpnetsecurity.com/2015/10/15/usb-killer-20-a-harmless-looking-usb-stick-that-destroys-computers/

Zorzi, M., & Rao, R. R. (2003). Geographic random forwarding (GeRaF) for ad hoc and sensor networks: Energy and latency performance. *IEEE Transactions on Mobile Computing*, *2*(4), 349–365. doi:10.1109/TMC.2003.1255650

Zulfikar, W. B., Gerhana, Y. A., & Rahmania, A. F. (2018, August). An Approach to Classify Eligibility Blood Donors Using Decision Tree and Naive Bayes Classifier. In *2018 6th International Conference on Cyber and IT Service Management (CITSM)* (pp. 1-5). IEEE. 10.1109/CITSM.2018.8674353

About the Contributors

Pardeep Kumar is currently working as a Professor and Head of the Computer Systems/Software Engineering Department, Quaid-e-Awam University of Engineering, Science & Technology (QUEST) Nawabshah, Pakistan. Additionally, he is also working as Director, Office of Research, Innovation & Commercialization (ORIC), QUEST Nawabshah. Earlier, he had worked as Director Continuing Education QUEST and Coordinator Students' Attendance System at QUEST. He is also working as a member of several academic and administrative committees of HEC Pakistan, PEC Pakistan, QUEST and other universities. Dr. Kumar completed his PhD from Berlin, Germany in 2012. Earlier he did his Bachelor of Engineering in Computer Systems and Master of Engineering in Communication Systems and Networks from Mehran University of Engineering and Technology Jamshoro, Pakistan in 2001 and 2004 respectively. Dr. Kumar joined QUEST in January 2004 and was granted PhD scholarship from HEC Pakistan and DAAD Germany in 2006. His research interests are in the fields of wireless communication, wireless sensor networks, ZigBee, Internet of Things (IoT), next generation networks, communication protocols, etc. Dr. Kumar has authored more than 50 research publications in reputed journals and conferences including several books and book chapters. He has visited different countries including Germany, France, USA, Australia, Italy, Switzerland, Czech Republic, Egypt, Slovenia, etc. to share his research work.is currently working as Professor and Head of the Computer Systems/Software Engineering Department, Quaid-e-Awam University of Engineering, Science & Technology (QUEST) Nawabshah, Pakistan. Additionally, he is also working as Director, Office of Research, Innovation & Commercialization (ORIC), QUEST Nawabshah. Earlier, he had worked as Director Continuing Education QUEST and Coordinator Students' Attendance System at QUEST. He is also working as a member of several academic and administrative committees of HEC Pakistan, PEC Pakistan, QUEST and other universities. He completed his PhD from Berlin, Germany in 2012. Earlier he did his Bachelor of Engineering in Computer Systems and Master of Engineering in Communication Systems and Networks from Mehran University of Engineering and Technology Jamshoro, Pakistan in 2001 and 2004 respectively. Dr. Kumar joined QUEST in January 2004 and was granted PhD scholarship from HEC Pakistan and DAAD Germany in 2006. During his PhD research, he designed and developed a novel MAC protocol for wireless sensor networks and has worked under several European Union projects. His research interests are in the fields of wireless communication, wireless sensor networks, IEEE 802.15.4/ZigBee, Internet of Things (IoT), next generation networks, communication protocols, etc. Dr. Kumar has authored around 50 research publications in reputed journals and conferences around the world including a book and several book chapters. He has visited different countries including Germany, France, USA, Australia, Italy, Switzerland, Czech Republic, Egypt, Slovenia, etc. to share his research work. Recently he has delivered a keynote talk on Internet of Things at the University of Hawaii, USA in January 2019.

Vasaki Ponnusamy is an Assistant Professor at Quest International University Perak, Malaysia. She obtained her Bachelor of Computer Science and MSc (Computer Science) from Science University of Malaysia and her PhD in IT from Universiti Teknologi PETRONAS (UTP), Malaysia (2013). She is currently working on biologically-inspired computing, wireless sensor network and energy harvesting.

Vishal Jain, PhD, is an Associate Professor with Bharati Vidyapeeth's Institute of Computer Applications and Management (BVICAM), New Delhi, India (affiliated with Guru Gobind Singh Indraprastha University, and accredited by the All India Council for Technical Education). He first joined BVICAM as Assistant Professor in year 2010. Before that, he has worked for several years at the Guru Premsukh Memorial College of Engineering, Delhi, India. He has more than 350 research citation indices with Google scholar (h-index score 9 and i-10 index 9). He has authored more than 70 research papers in reputed conferences and journals including Web of Science and Scopus. He has authored and edited more than 10 books with various reputed publishers including Springer, Apple Academic Press, Scrivener, Emerald, CRC, Taylor and Francis publishing and IGI-Global. His research areas include information retrieval, semantic web, ontology engineering, data mining, adhoc networks, and sensor networks.is an Associate Professor with Bharati Vidyapeeth's Institute of Computer Applications and Management (BVICAM), New Delhi, India (affiliated with Guru Gobind Singh Indraprastha University, and accredited by the All India Council for Technical Education). He first joined BVICAM as Assistant Professor. Before that, he has worked for several years at the Guru Presmsukh Memorial College of Engineering, Delhi, India. He has more than 300 research citation indices with Google scholar (h-index score 9 and i-10 index 9). His research areas include information retrieval, semantic web, ontology engineering, data mining, adhoc networks, and sensor networks. He has received a Young Active Member Award for the year 2012–13 from the Computer Society of India.

* * *

Adnan Ahmed is an Associate Professor in the Department of Telecommunication at QUEST, Nawabshah, Pakistan. He completed his Ph.D. in Computer Science from UTM, in 2015. He completed his Master of Engineering in Computer Systems Engineering in February 2012 from QUEST. He is the professional member of Pakistan Engineering Council (PEC) and a regular reviewer of well reputed ISI-indexed journals. His research interest includes routing in Ad-hoc networks, security, trust management in Ad-hoc networks and QoS issues in sensor and Ad-hoc networks.

Shamim Akhtar is an eminent scholar and an active academician. He has done BE and MS in Electrical Engineering in the year 1996 and 2008, respectively. Engr. Akhtar is currently associated with Department of Medical Equipment Technology, College of Applied Medical Sciences Majmaah University, KSA. His main research interest are Biomedical Technology, Machine Learning, and Deep learning. In addition, to the great academic experience, Engr. Akhtar also possessed diversified industrial experience.

Robithoh Annur is currently an Assistant professor in the Department of Computer and Communication Technology (DCCT), Faculty of Information and Communication Technology (FICT), UTAR. She received the B. Eng. and M. Eng. degrees from Gadjah Mada University, Yogyakarta, Indonesia and National University of Singapore, Singapore, respectively. She was a tutor in the Diploma of Electrical engineering in Gadjah Mada University before eventually completing her doctoral degree in

Chulalongkorn University, Thailand. She has already published a series of papers both in international conferences and journals that some of the acknowledged as the best paper award, with a book chapter in a book entitled "Advanced Trends in Wireless Communications, 2011. Currently, she is focusing on the algorithms for tag identification in RFID system, which is simple to implement and performs better than existing known algorithms.

Muhammad Waseem Ashraf received his Master of Science in Physics with Micro Electronics from Government College University, Lahore Pakistan and Master of Science/M.Phil in Micro Electronics Engineering from University of Punjab, Pakistan in the 2008 and 2006 respectively. He received a Doctorate of Engineering (Microelectronics), AIT, Thailand in the year 2011. His areas of interest are Simulation Modeling, MEMS, Nano Technology. Material Processing, Fuzzy Logic, Cloud Computing and Information Security. He is author/co-author above 100 National/International Conferences and Journals.

Said Bakhshad is currently a PhD student at Universiti Tunku Abdul Rahman (UTAR), Malaysia.

Kavita Choudhary received her M.C.A degree in computer science from Modi Institute of technology and Science Lakshmangarh, Sikar. Presently working as Associate Professor at Jyoti Vidyapeeth University Jaipur. She has eleven years of teaching experience in the field of Computer Science and supervising research scholars in the field of E-commerce, Mobile Commerce, Data Mining, Big data and Cloud computing. Dr. Kavita has published several research papers in the reputed 'National and International Journals' as well as National and International Conferences.

Ming-Lee Gan completed his Ph.D. in Computer Science studies at Universiti Tunku Abdul Rahman, Malaysia in 2013. He received his B.Eng. in Electrical & Electronics from Universiti Tenaga Nasional, Malaysia in 2004 and M.Sc. in Systems Engineering & Management from the Malaysia University of Science and Technology in 2006. In March 2012, he joined Universiti Tunku Abdul Rahman, where he is currently a lecturer. His research focus is in network path protection, network routing algorithms and network reliability analysis.

Pooja Gupta is an Assistant Professor at Jamia Hamdard New Delhi.

Manzoor Ahmed Hashmani works as a Assoc. Prof. at Universiti Technology Petronas, Department of Computer & Information Sciences. Dr. Hashmani research interests are in the domain of Artificial Intelligence, Big Data, Communication Networks.

Mamoona Humayun has completed her PhD. in Computer Architecture from Harbin Institute of Technology, China. She has 12 years of teaching and administrative experience internationally. She is an active reviewer for a series of journals. She has supervised various Masters and PhD thesis. Her research interests include global software development, requirement engineering, knowledge management, cyber security, and wireless sensor networks.

Akhtar Jalbani is an Associate Professor at IT Department at Quaid-e-Awam University of Engineering, Science & Technology, Nawabshah, Sindh, Pakistan.

N. Z. Jhanjhi received the Ph.D. degree in ITfromUTP, Malaysia. He has great international exposure in academia, research, administration, and academic quality accreditation. He was with ILMA University, King Faisal University (KFU), Saudi Arabia for a decade, and currently with Taylor's University, Malaysia. He has 19 years of teaching & administrative experience. He has an intensive background of academic quality accreditation in higher education besides scientific research activities, he had worked a decade for academic accreditation and earned ABET accreditation twice for three programs at CCSIT, King Faisal University, Saudi Arabia. Dr. Noor Zaman has awarded as top reviewer 1% globally by WoS/ISI (Publons) recently. He has edited/authored more than 11 research books with international reputed publishers, earned several research grants, and a great number of indexed research articles on his credit. He has supervised several postgraduate students including masters and Ph.D. Dr. Jhanjhi is an Associate Editor of IEEE ACCESS, Guest editor of several reputed journals, member of the editorial board of several research journals, Keynote Speaker for several IEEE international conferences around the globe, and active TPC member of reputed conferences around the globe.

Umair A. Khan received his Master and PhD degrees from Alpen-Adria University, Klagenfurt, Austria in 2010 and 2013, respectively. Since then, he has been working as an associate professor and head of the department of computer systems engineering in Quaid-e-Awam University of Engineering, Science & Technology, Nawabshah, Pakistan. He has also worked in Fraunhofer Institute of Integrated Circuits, Erlangen, Ger- many, and Machine Perception laboratory, Hungarian Academy of Sciences, Budapest, Hungary as a research scientist in 2016-17. His research interests include context based information retrieval from images and videos using deep learning.

Akhil Khare is working as a Professor at CSED MVSR Engineering College, Hyderabad. His areas of interest are Computer Network, Software Engineering and Multimedia System. He has eleven years' experience in teaching and research. He has published more than fifty research papers in journals and conferences. He has also guided twenty postgraduate students and he is recognized Ph.D. Supervisor for various Universities.

Vikram Kulkarni is Assistant Professor at Dept. of Information Technology, MPSTME, NMIMS University, Mumbai. He has completed his Ph.D. in 2019 from VIT University, Vellore, TamilNadu, on Wireless Sensor Networks for Smart Grid Applications. He has completed M. Tech degree in Embedded Systems and B. Tech degree in Electrical and Electronics Engineering, both from JNTU, Hyderabad, India, in the year 2013 and 2007 respectively. He has 11 years experience in Academics. He has published 30 papers in various peer reviewed journals and conferences. He is currently involved in research work on the algorithms on interference avoidance for wireless sensor networks working in 2.4GHz ISM band for smart grid applications. He is also working on improving QoS parameters for WSN. His research interests include Internet of Things, Wireless sensor networks, Smart grid communication Networks.

Rejo Mathew is an Assistant Professor at Dept. of Information Technology, MPSTME, NMIMS University, Mumbai. He acquired his Masters in Technology degree in Information Technology in the year 2011 on the topic low rate Denial of Service attacks from NMIMS and his Bachelors in Engineering degree in Electronics and Telecommunication in 2004 from Rajiv Gandhi Institute of Technology affiliated to University of Mumbai.He has rich industry experience in telecommunications working with

Orange - France Telecom for five years prior to joining NMIMS. He has authored two books and has 40 published papers. He is a reviewer in IEEE Transactions on Information Forensics & Security. His research interest includes Internet of Things, Security and performance issues of communication systems.

Sandeep Mathur, Ph.D. (CSE) degree holder Assistant professor having 12 years of academic and research experience with 25 quality research publications. As a Principle investigator, a research project in Data analytics has been submitted to CSTUP. One Copyright has been granted with registration number SW-9296/2017 for the software & research work completed in the Ph.D. Good Experience of working in the placement, Research, Entrepreneur Cell, Discipline, Cultural and Sports committees. Finalist for the prestigious DST young achievers and thinker's awards conducted by Dept. of science and technology by DST office Govt. of Haryana Panchkula, Chandigarh. Have ample experience in campus recruitment and talent acquisitions. In hand experience of many corporate and consultancy training as a corporate trainer.

Muhammad Memon is Assistant Professor in Department of Information Technology university of Sindh Jamshoro, Sindh, Pakistan. PhD scholar in Department of Computer system Engineering, QUEST, Nawab Shah. He has good experience in Machine learning and Big Data field.

Sindhu P. Menon completed her Ph.D in the area of Machine learning and Big data. She has about fifteen publications in peer reviewed journals and conferences. She has a teaching experience of sixteen years with a citation count of 33. Dr. Menon is presently working as a Faculty in the Department of Computer Science and Engineering at Jain College of Engineering and Technology, Hubli.

Azeem Mirani is a Lecturer in Department of Information Technology, SBBU SBA, Nawabshah, Sindh, Pakistan.

Syed Mehmood Naqvi is a Professor in the School of Applied Computing at Sheridan College, Canada. Formerly, he was Dean of Faculty of Computer Science and Information Technology at Institute of Business and Technology, Pakistan. He received Ph.D. in Computer Application Technology from Beihang University (formerly Beijing University of Aeronautics and Astronautics), Beijing, China in 1999. He did his postdoctoral research in the area of signal processing at the University of Northern British Columbia, Canada. Syed Naqvi has more than twenty years of teaching, research, and administrative experience at various universities, colleges, and institutes in Canada, Pakistan, and the UAE. He has served as an active member of many curricula development and revision committees for undergraduate and graduates computer science and information technology programs. His current areas of research include educational technology, medical image.

Sadia Nazim is an outstanding scholar and currently pursuing her Masters in Computer and Communication Networks. She has done her MSc Computer Science in the year 2003. Her main research areas are Machine Learning, Deep Learning and Cryptography.

Mumtaz Qabulio is a Lecturer in Software Engineering, Institute of Information & Communication Technology, University of Sindh, Jamshoro.

Khalid Rafique is the Director General, Information Technology Board, Azad Jammu & Kashmir, Pakistan since April 2017. He has a lead role in the Digital Transformation campaign for public sector departments in Azad Jammu & Kashmir and unfolding of digital governance vision of the government through technology deployment. He has quite dynamically steered initiatives to materialize vision of public empowerment and facilitation through digitalization of public sector departments. Automation of Judicial system, Computerization of land record, Computerization of driving license, E-facilitation centers, Establishment of Tele-medicine centers, Online complaint addressal mechanism, dynamic interactive web interfaces for public sector departments, telepresence/video conferencing facilities etc. are some of his major achievements in the last two and a half year. Dr. Khalid has also served as Senior Manager Business Development at Pakistan Telecommunication Limited- the largest hybrid (Fixed/ wireless) Telecom operator in Pakistan. He has basic Engineering degrees in Electrical & Telecommunications and a PhD degree in Emerging ICT ecosystem.

Ali Raza Bhangwar received his B.Engr. and M. Engr. degrees in Computer Systems from QUEST, Nawabshah, Pakistan, in 2012. He completed his Ph.D. degree in Computer Systems from QUEST, Nawabshah, Pakistan, in 2019. His research interests are in the field of wireless communication, wireless sensor and wireless body area networks, routing algorithms, network security, etc.

Naveena Regunathan is a final year student, currently pursuing a degree in Communications and Networking in University Tunku Abdul Rahman, Kampar. She shows a high interest in cybersecurity and has planned to get certified as an ethical hacker once she graduates in 2020. Her research is about the attacks and countermeasures in Internet of Things and Cyber Physical Systems. She is determined in doing her masters to produce studies with high quality, in the future. She spends her leisure time playing video games on her computer.

Syed Sajjad Hussain Rizvi is an eminent scholar and an active academician. He is a certified Professional Engineer (PE) of Computer System Engineering (CSE) with Masters Degrees in 'Telecommunication' (MS-TEL) and 'Business Administration' (MBA). He has over 20+ years of experience in Educational Sector. Dr. Rizvi has earned his Ph.D. in the area of 'Image Processing and Information Retrieval'. In addition, he has also been awarded with the status of "Approved Ph.D. Supervisor" by Higher Education Commission, Pakistan. He poses rich teaching experience and used to teach the courses in the domain of 'Computer Sciences', 'Communication' and 'Management' both at Undergraduate and Postgraduate level. Dr. Rizvi is well known in the research and academic community and an active member of various local and international academic bodies like IEEE, PEC, HEC, IEP, IAENG, etc. The research areas of Dr. Rizvi include, but not limited to, EEG signal processing and classification, optimization, image de-noising and image retrieval, and adaptive filtering.

Soobia Saeed is working as an Assistant Professor, Head of publication Department, and Coordinator of Seminars and Training at Institute of Business & Technology-IBT, Karachi, Pakistan. Currently, she is a Ph.D. Scholar in software engineering, from University Teknologi Malaysia-UTM, Malaysia She did MS in Software Engineering from Institute of Business & Technology- IBT, Karachi, Pakistan, and Masters in Computer Science fromInstitute of Business & Technology-IBT, Karachi, Pakistan and Bachelors in Mathematical Science from Federal Urdu University of Art, Science & Technology (FUUAST), and Karachi, Pakistan. She is a farmer research Analytic from University Teknologi Malaysia and supervises ICT & R and D funded Final Year Project (FYP).

Irum Sodhar is a Lecturer in Information Technology, SBBU SBA, Nawabshah, Sindh, Pakistan.

Saima Soomro is working as Assistant professor in IT department at Quaid-awam-university of Science and Technology Nawabshah. she received her BS degree in computer science from QUEST Nawabshah in 2008.MS degree in information technology from QUEST in 2015. Her interest includes Human computer interaction, Software engineering and Artificial intelligence.

Saima Sultana is a prominent academician. She has done BS in Computer Science in the year 2004 and currently pursuing her Masters in Computer and Communication Networks. Ms. Saima is currently associated with PIPFA(Pakistan Institute of Public Finance Accountants), Karachi. Her main research interest are Biomedical Technology, Machine Learning, and Deep learning.

Muhammad Imran Tariq is Lecturer (Computer Science) at the Higher Education Department, Lahore, Pakistan, where he has been since 2006. He received a Bachelor of Computer Science from Allama Iqbal University, Islamabad in 2003, M.Sc Computer Science from Preston Institute of Management Science and Technology in 2008, Master of Science in Computer Science from the University of Lahore in 2013 and finally Ph.D. in Computer Science from Superior College, Lahore in the year 2019. Moreover, he has MCSE, MCP+I, A+ and CCNA certifications. His research interests include Cloud Computing, Information Security standards, Service Level Agreement, Information Security Metrics, Cloud Risks, and its mitigation techniques, Wireless Networks Security, Image processing, Deep Learning, Artificial Intelligence, Sensor Networks, Multi Criteria Decision Making, Fuzzy Logic, and Risk Management. He is author of many impact factor research papers and conferences. He is also the author of 02 books on Cloud Security. He reviewer of International renowned impact factor Journals. Associate Editor of IEEE Access Journal and Member Editorial Board SCIREA Journal of Computer. He is also a member of the research group of Cloud Security Alliance.

Shahzadi Tayyaba received her Bachelor of Science in Computer Engineering and Master in Science from the University of Engineering and Technology, Lahore, Pakistan in 2006 and 2008 respectively. She received a Doctorate of Engineering (Microelectronics and Embedded System), AIT, Thailand in the year 2013. Her areas of interest are Simulation Modeling, MEMS, Nano Technology. Material Processing, Fuzzy Logic, Cloud Computing, and Information Security. She is Author/co-author above 100 National / International Conferences and Journals.

Sanjeev Kumar Yadav is Pursuing Doctor of Philosophy in Computer Application from Jayoti Vidyapeeth Women's University, Jaipur-303122 (Raj.) India. Recognized as a leader with 23 years' qualitative experience in the areas of Delivery Management, Program Management, Client Engagement and People Management in global environment.

Jasmina Khaw Yen Min is an Assistant Professor at Universiti Tunku Abdul Rahman, Malaysia. She obtained her Bachelor of Computer Science, Msc and PhD (Computer Science) from Universiti Sains Malaysia (2017). She is currently working on natural language processing. Her career in academia started in 2017. Her areas of specialization include automatic speech recognition, speech synthesis and machine translation.

Aun Yichiet is an avid researcher working on cognitive and contextual aware system. His prominent works span across intelligent systems, traffic engineering, and mostly revolved on intent based networking. He is also renowned for his passion and unconventional lectures in the domain of modern networking.

Index

A

Activation Function 50, 340, 343-345

Ant Colony Optimization 309, 314, 319

Application Migration 265, 268-271, 273, 280

ASK Belt 277

ASK Confidence Level (ACL) 276

ASK Point 276

Attacks 1-12, 14-16, 18-21, 102-103, 110, 121-123, 125-126, 132, 135-136, 145, 152-154, 156-158, 161-164, 170, 185, 198, 205, 207-209, 212, 231, 239, 241-243, 246-250, 252-253, 257-259, 320

Audit 15, 126-127, 130, 228, 351-354, 359-363, 369, 371-373

Authentication 13, 21, 40-41, 98-101, 109-111, 114, 118, 148, 151, 153, 156-158, 161-162, 165, 170, 203, 215, 217, 219, 223-225, 228-229, 231, 243, 254, 258-259

B

Base Station 83, 146, 153, 161, 163, 227, 241, 243, 254, 309, 311, 314, 316-317

C

Client 11-13, 26, 28, 44, 109, 113-114, 118, 131, 202-203, 212-213, 215-216, 218, 220-222, 227, 230, 351-358, 360-362, 369

Cloud Based 65, 228

Cluster 163, 166, 183, 195, 243, 247, 249, 254, 258, 300, 302, 309-311, 313-315, 317, 319, 358-359, 371

Convolution Neural Network 51, 301, 345

Cryptography 118, 122, 153, 161, 203, 215, 221, 254, 256, 317

D

Data Mining 56, 124-125, 321, 323, 326-328, 330, 332-333, 359

DDoS Attack 109, 113-114

Decision Tree 120, 321, 323-324, 327, 334, 337

Deep Learning 47-50, 52-54, 57, 70, 136, 139-140, 297-303, 339, 341, 345, 347

Device Discovery 76, 84-86, 92, 94

E

Energy Efficiency 3, 61, 63, 161, 179

Energy-Aware 166, 169

Enertiv 71

F

Fog Computing 107-108, 118, 136

G

Green buildings 61-62, 64-65, 69

I

IDS 19, 119-120, 122-128, 131, 135-136, 164, 251, 255, 363

Industry 4.0 1-3, 21

Information Security 8, 38, 110, 198, 202-203, 225, 230-231

Integrity 10, 18, 101, 109, 114, 118, 151, 161, 208-209, 231, 242, 249, 251-252

Internet of Things (IoT) 1-4, 25-30, 32, 34-39, 44, 52, 61-62, 65, 68-71, 76, 98-99, 103, 131-132, 183, 198, 227-229, 231, 240

Ensure Quality Research is Introduced to the Academic Community

Become an IGI Global Reviewer for Authored Book Projects

The overall success of an authored book project is dependent on quality and timely reviews.

In this competitive age of scholarly publishing, constructive and timely feedback significantly expedites the turnaround time of manuscripts from submission to acceptance, allowing the publication and discovery of forward-thinking research at a much more expeditious rate. Several IGI Global authored book projects are currently seeking highly-qualified experts in the field to fill vacancies on their respective editorial review boards:

Applications and Inquiries may be sent to:
development@igi-global.com

Applicants must have a doctorate (or an equivalent degree) as well as publishing and reviewing experience. Reviewers are asked to complete the open-ended evaluation questions with as much detail as possible in a timely, collegial, and constructive manner. All reviewers' tenures run for one-year terms on the editorial review boards and are expected to complete at least three reviews per term. Upon successful completion of this term, reviewers can be considered for an additional term.

If you have a colleague that may be interested in this opportunity, we encourage you to share this information with them.

IGI Global Proudly Partners With eContent Pro International

Receive a 25% Discount on all Editorial Services

Editorial Services

IGI Global expects all final manuscripts submitted for publication to be in their final form. This means they must be reviewed, revised, and professionally copy edited prior to their final submission. Not only does this support with accelerating the publication process, but it also ensures that the highest quality scholarly work can be disseminated.

English Language Copy Editing

Let eContent Pro International's expert copy editors perform edits on your manuscript to resolve spelling, punctuaion, grammar, syntax, flow, formatting issues and more.

Scientific and Scholarly Editing

Allow colleagues in your research area to examine the content of your manuscript and provide you with valuable feedback and suggestions before submission.

Figure, Table, Chart & Equation Conversions

Do you have poor quality figures? Do you need visual elements in your manuscript created or converted? A design expert can help!

Translation

Need your documjent translated into English? eContent Pro International's expert translators are fluent in English and more than 40 different languages.

Email: customerservice@econtentpro.com   **www.igi-global.com/editorial-service-partners**

Printed in the United States
By Bookmasters